THE PSYCHOLOGY OF TEACHING

THE PSYCHOLOGY
OF TEACHING

BY

ASAHEL D. WOODRUFF

Third Edition
Completely Revised and Rewritten

GREENWOOD PRESS, PUBLISHERS
WESTPORT, CONNECTICUT

Library of Congress Cataloging in Publication Data

Woodruff, Asahel Davis, 1904-
   The psychology of teaching.

   Reprint of the ed. published by Longmans, Green,
New York.
   Includes bibliographies.
   1. Educational psychology. I. Title.
[DNLM: 1. Psychology, Educational. 2. Teaching.
LB1051 W893p]
[LB1051.W72 1974]   370.15   73-136091
ISBN 0-8371-5241-0

THIRD EDITION

Originally published in 1951 by Longmans, Green & Co., Inc.,
New York

Reprinted by arrangement with David McKay Company, Inc.

Reprinted in 1974 by Greenwood Press,
a division of Williamhouse-Regency Inc.

Library of Congress Catalog Card Number 73-136091

ISBN 0-8371-5241-0

Printed in the United States of America

TO

ELIAS SMITH AND NELLIE DAVIS WOODRUFF

FOREWORD TO TEACHERS

Close contact and cooperation with experienced teachers in service and prospective teachers in practice has resulted in the conviction that educational psychology the country over is making a very meagre contribution to the work of the average schoolteacher. Especially is this true of the teacher's daily work in the classroom. The consensus among teachers is that the courses they took in college were interesting, but so theoretical and with so little relationship to practical problems that they were of no help. Such a condition may be due to several factors. First, a survey of available texts leaves one with the impression that almost all of them were written for advanced graduates majoring in educational psychology. They are organized logically without regard for teachers' problems, and they assume in the reader a psychological sophistication rarely found even in graduate students. Second, it seems that most courses in educational psychology operate on the assumption that to hear is to be able to do. Applied psychology is a sham unless it leads to the development of functional skills, and functional skills cannot be developed by lecture or discussion. The psychology of teaching must be a laboratory course for the same reason as chemistry, physics, or surgery. Third, although there is a vast and somewhat uncoordinated body of facts in the field of psychology, the teacher actually draws on a fairly small array of psychological facts, but this is not apparent until an effort is made to cut through the maze of theories and schools of thought and pick out the facts upon which good teaching rests. For example, the literature contains endless discussion of the stability of the IQ. Little of this material is functionally useful to a schoolteacher. Furthermore the question of IQ stability is far from settled.

It is hoped that the book is written in such simple terms that any college student can understand it, because one of the greatest faults of texts in general is that they are beyond the understanding of those who should read them. It is further hoped that the discussion leaves few if any fundamental concepts to the previous learning of the student. Experience constantly indicates that such understandings rarely exist in spite of earlier courses.

To recognize the source of all the ideas incorporated in this book is literally impossible by virtue of the nature of learning. Nevertheless, the teachings and encouragement of Professor Guy T. Buswell, formerly of the University of Chicago and now of the University of California at Berkeley, have done much to provide the courage to attempt a task of this sort. Professor Buswell is not, however, responsible for the weaknesses of the book, which is far from being an adequate representation of his teachings. In the revision invaluable help has been received from criticisms and suggestions sent in by Francis J. DiVesta, at The Air University in Alabama, by Robert L. Egbert, at Utah State Agricultural College, by Arthur D. Browne, at Denver University, and by several other users of the text.

Acknowledgment and special thanks are extended to Dr. Dorothy M. Howard for permission to quote in full the unusual "Essay on Teachers" in Chapter XXIII. Appreciation is also extended to the following publishers and journals, for permission to quote from their publications: Appleton-Century-Crofts Inc., Harper & Brothers, Henry Holt & Co., Houghton Mifflin Co., Longmans, Green and Co., McGraw Hill Book Co., The Macmillan Co., W. W. Norton Publishing Co., Prentice-Hall, Inc., Syracuse University Press, John Wiley & Sons, *Educational and Psychological Measurement,* and *The Journal of Psychology.* Dr. Francis J. DiVesta made his cases freely available. Emma Rose Elliott, Ethelwyn Cornelius, and Shirley Smith provided teaching materials that have been used in the projects for students. To these are extended sincere appreciation for their valuable contributions.

SUGGESTION ON THE USE OF THIS BOOK

This book literally grew out of a class in educational psychology for prospective teachers at Cornell University between 1942 and 1949. Consequently, it reflects to some extent the structure of the course in which it was developed. Its use is not confined to such a course by any means, but it is not unlikely that the teacher will realize its greatest contribution to his students, and obtain its maximum helpfulness to himself, through a procedure somewhat as follows.

Students were advised that there would be quizzes on all readings on the date the topic was to be taken up in class, and before there had been any class discussion of the readings or topics. This tended to crowd the text reading into the early part of the term, and to guarantee better class preparation for discussion than had been the case before. Immediately after the quizzes, class discussion of the readings permitted clarification of students' questions, and emphasis on any desired topics in the assignment. Each section of the book was treated as a unit, all the chapters therein being subjected to quizzes one after the other as rapidly as possible. A major block of time was then available for project work, in which the concepts contained in the chapters were carried into practical exercises. The projects at the end of each chapter or section were developed in classes, and came directly from schoolrooms and personnel files. Those now in the text are the ones that survived the exploratory years and proved to have value in helping students acquire a functional understanding of the ideas in the text. Considerably more time was spent on the projects than on the chapters themselves, but the projects served to drive the students constantly into a rereading of the text, and provoked much class discussion of textual content. As the work was concluded on each section of the book, quizzing on the chapters in the succeeding section began immediately, and was followed in turn by attention to the next set of projects.

Subsequent experience has strengthened the belief that the majority of time should be devoted to the projects, and that there are more such materials in the book than can be comfortably accommodated in a typical three-hour course in one quarter.

Students have invariably objected at first to the early load of reading involved in this approach, but have also invariably changed to approval of the system when the returns began to be apparent, and it became obvious that they would not be burdened with assignments toward the end of the course. These suggestions are offered for whatever they may be worth, since in the past teachers have frequently inquired about the instructional scheme envisioned by the author in preparing the text. It is recognized, however, that a truly dynamic teacher is frequently one who has a vision of his own about what should be done in class, and follows his vision with enthusiasm and imagination.

CONTENTS

PART I. INTRODUCTION

PART II. THE NATURE OF HUMAN BEHAVIOR

LIST OF TABLES

LIST OF FIGURES

LIST OF CASES

PART I

INTRODUCTION

CHAPTER I

WHAT EDUCATIONAL PSYCHOLOGY IS

101. *The nature of the subject.* Human psychology is the study of the behavior of human beings. It deals not only with *how* people behave, but also with *why* they behave as they do. Educational psychology is that branch of general psychology which deals primarily with problems of learning, considered from the standpoint of the characteristics of the learner, the nature of what is to be learned, and the process by which learning takes place. Those who plan to become teachers are ordinarily required to have some training in educational psychology, but state certification requirements are often vague about what this training is supposed to contain. It is no more possible to cover educational psychology in one course than it is to cover chemistry or English or business administration in one course. Obviously then, any single course in educational psychology must select from the whole field those materials that are of greatest value to teachers. A course so organized is in reality a course in the psychology of teaching, and not a course in the whole of educational psychology.

Along with a common failure to recognize this limitation, a seemingly endless debate has arisen over whether educational psychology is a science or an art. The answer is simply that, as in all other fields of study, there is a scientific aspect that deals with the discovery and ordering of facts, and there is also an aspect that is essentially artistic or applicatory. In the general field of educational psychology, then, there is a rapidly growing scientific search for facts, the study of which is usually reserved for those who intend to become educational psychologists. There is also an attempt to apply those facts

1

to school problems, and it is within this area that the prospective public schoolteacher should concentrate attention.

The art of effective teaching must necessarily be founded on psychological facts discovered by the scientist. In reality the psychology of teaching should begin with an attack on an organized body of psychological facts selected for their usefulness to the teacher. To avoid an academic sterility, those facts should promptly be fitted into the daily behavior of a student, and there should follow a gradual transition from the learning of facts to the evolution of sound methods of teaching. The point at which the psychology of learning ends and methods of teaching begin defies description by any other than a purely academic method. This is the same as saying that the psychology of teaching bears no fruit without producing the superstructure of sound procedures for teachers, just as a course in methods is as artificial as a paper flower unless it stems from a sound psychological root. This text is built around the position just stated, and while it does not attempt to cover the field of teaching methods, it does not hesitate to carry useful psychological facts over to a speaking acquaintance with school practice. One might venture to hope that a prospective teacher of any merit, who has obtained a vision of the place of psychology in school practice, could thenceforth solve his teaching problems in a sound manner.

102.   *The educative process.* There are three related tasks in every school. First there is the student's task of learning. This is the process of acquiring or making changes in one's knowledge, skills, and preferences. This task is essentially the learner's. It goes on within him and must be carried out by him alone. The teacher is an onlooker, not a coparticipant in this task. Second, there is the task of teaching. This is the art of facilitating desirable learning. It is something that the teacher should do without distracting the learner's attention from his task of learning. It is a behind-the-scenes act whose primary purpose is to set the stage for the learner, but in no way attempt to do his work for him. How it should be done depends on what the learner is trying to do, since its chief purpose is to facilitate desirable learning. Third, there is the task of both pupil and teacher of making a satisfactory

adjustment to the school situation so that their joint presence in school is a source of satisfaction rather than one of annoyance.

103. *What the teacher must know.* The three tasks just enumerated draw upon several areas in the general field of educational psychology. Those that have been selected as the specific burden of this follow:

The nature of human behavior, including the aspects of behavior from which psychological data are derived, and the inferences concerning motivation which are drawn from those data.

The development of behavior patterns, in which biological and social inheritance operate along with several kinds of learning to produce a unique individual who nevertheless fits into a social structure.

The factors that speed up or slow down learning, and that influence its direction toward or away from validity, adjustability, and morality.

The nature of adjustment and maladjustment, and the processes through which one's state of adjustment is attained, together with what is meant by personality and the kinds of experiences that tend to produce motivational health.

The meaning of evaluation as a way of determining progress toward an objective, and the place of various techniques for testing and measuring achievement in the broader concept of evaluation.

Counseling as an aid to development and adjustment, a function shared by numerous people as pertaining to its operation on any one student.

104. *How the book is organized.* Figure 1 is a diagrammatic scheme for showing how the psychology of teaching is viewed in this book. One of the most telling criticisms of educational psychology describes it as a disconnected array of boxes of information that have no relationship to each other, and whose relationship to teaching is so obscure as to be valueless. If the criticism applies to the field, or to any text in the field, it is because someone has succeeded in doing such academic violence to the data of human behavior that in their analysis man has been transformed into an outline

whose head is so much like his feet that it doesn't matter where any particular part is put. Psychology cannot escape the necessity of constructing abstract concepts about behavior, in order to discover the principles operating it. Mastery of such abstractions is not an easy task and is usually marked by a long period of confusion in the student. This is because the student begins on the abstract level and does not have the opportunity to wallow around in the profusion of real human actions while he builds up his own abstractions slowly and fumblingly. Hence the uninitiated who have not emerged from the period of confusion, and who cannot yet see the substantial and rather stable conceptual structure that now exists, are unable to make any applications to the behavior of a student. It is not surprising that they then charge the field with disorganization, lack of utility, and the absence of a fundamental scientific character.

The time at which one becomes clear in his own integration of all the concepts in the field may vary considerably. The kind of integration that enables one to transmit usable ideas to those with no psychological background represents the end of a long and demanding effort. There is nothing to guarantee that it will take place either before or after one is awarded a Ph.D. or any other degree for having completed a prescribed course. It would not be surprising to find that in some cases it never takes place, even in a lifetime of service.

The structure presented in this book may be sufficiently conceptual and abstract to give some difficulty, but there is an organizational scheme that seems to have more justification than a random arrangement of topics would suggest. The foundation of the approach consists of an attempt to send the student back again and again to the observation of human behavior in real people, with some suggestions on what to look for, and how to interpret what is seen. From the behavior thus observed an effort is made to show how explanations of behavior are developed, and how to apply the explanations to further analysis of the observed behavior.

Building on this general description of the nature of behavior, attention turns, then, to observation of the changes which take place in a child as he grows and learns, and to the manner in which those changes are explained. The influences that contribute to the changes are brought into the analysis at that point. Some of them are within the individual himself, both as fundamental characteristics of protoplasm

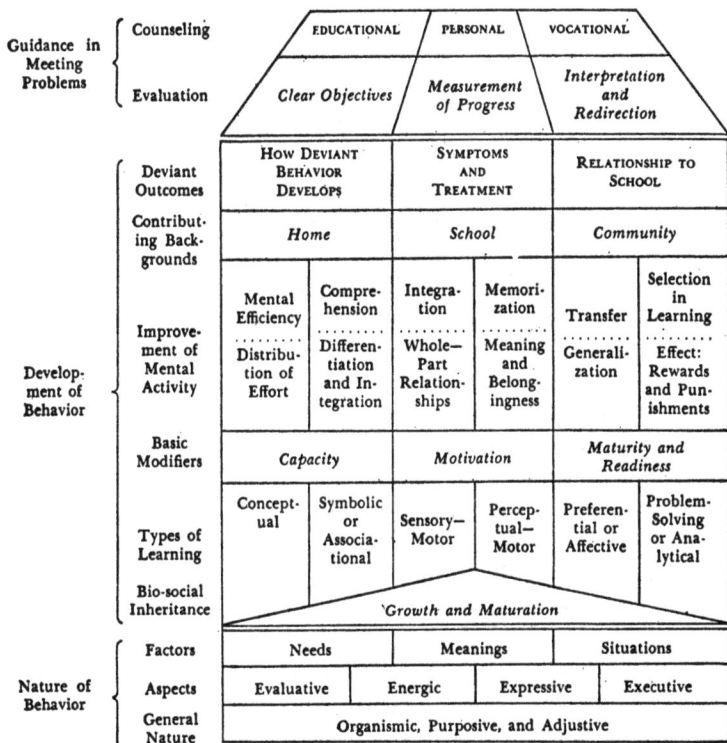

Guidance in Meeting Problems	Counseling	EDUCATIONAL		PERSONAL		VOCATIONAL		
	Evaluation	Clear Objectives		Measurement of Progress		Interpretation and Redirection		
Development of Behavior	Deviant Outcomes	HOW DEVIANT BEHAVIOR DEVELOPS		SYMPTOMS AND TREATMENT		RELATIONSHIP TO SCHOOL		
	Contributing Backgrounds	Home		School		Community		
	Improvement of Mental Activity	Mental Efficiency	Comprehension	Integration	Memorization	Transfer	Selection in Learning	
		Distribution of Effort	Differentiation and Integration	Whole—Part Relationships	Meaning and Belongingness	Generalization	Effect: Rewards and Punishments	
	Basic Modifiers	Capacity		Motivation		Maturity and Readiness		
	Types of Learning	Conceptual	Symbolic or Associational	Sensory—Motor	Perceptual—Motor	Preferential or Affective	Problem-Solving or Analytical	
	Bio-social Inheritance	Growth and Maturation						
Nature of Behavior	Factors	Needs		Meanings		Situations		
	Aspects	Evaluative		Energic		Expressive		Executive
	General Nature	Organismic, Purposive, and Adjustive						

FIG. 1. STRUCTURE OF THE PSYCHOLOGY OF TEACHING

and nervous systems, and as conditions brought about through past experience, which in their turn affect the outcomes of new experiences. Some of them are in the surrounding environment which presses upon the individual, and with which he is in a constant state of interaction.

With all these interwoven lines of influence and growth processes making the individual into something new with each new day, it is shown how some individuals run into difficulties in their strivings and efforts to cope with life, and get into some degree of disorganization and disruption. These experiences are pointed out just as the successful achievements are pointed out. From the unsuccessful experiences are drawn ideas that are used to explain why such disruption occurs, and what might be done to eliminate or correct it.

Thus the role of the counselor is introduced, along with the evaluative devices by which a teacher, parent, or counselor may give assistance when it is needed to the young person who is growing and learning and developing his mature roles.

The book follows this pattern from Chapter II to the end. It constitutes what might be called a psycho-social and developmental approach, with particular attention to the role of personal values in the individual's struggle for adjustment and for the higher goals that stand for ultimate adjustments in whatever future he envisions for himself. The topics of first importance are those that deal with things a real person does at home, in school, and in the community. Theoretical considerations are put into a role subsidiary to actual behavior itself, their only reason for being discussed lying in their contribution to the understanding of the principles that lie beneath the behavior. Theories that seem not to make that kind of contribution to a teacher's problems are not brought into this discussion, but are left for those who devote themselves to such problems.

It should be emphasized here that this book is intended primarily for those people who are about to take up positions in which they will work with growing and learning children and adolescents. It is oriented around such problems as occur daily in that kind of work. If it has value in advanced courses in educational psychology, that is incidental. If it succeeds in helping parents and teachers, however, it is difficult to see how it can fail to help advanced students of educational psychology. There should be no fundamental difference between books used at the two levels. They should be concerned with the same kinds of problems, and the same fields even though they may delve into them at different levels of technicality and theory.

At best one may obtain from a single book or course little

more than a preliminary insight into these fields, and a degree of orientation that should enable one to be judicious in one's reaction to the ideas and practices encountered. One should at least get beyond the illusion that psychology is only common sense, for common sense is sometimes nothing but common nonsense. In addition, it is probable that from such a book as this, one might easily push on in one's own education through suggested readings, even though opportunity to take additional formal courses is not available.

QUESTIONS FOR REVIEW

1. What is the relationship between psychology and methods of teaching?
2. Why does the text differentiate between the three related tasks involved in schoolwork?
3. List the things teachers should know, as outlined in the chapter.
4. Discuss the interrelationships between the various blocks of the structure in Figure 1.

SELECTED REFERENCES

Horace B. English, *A student's dictionary of psychological terms* (4th ed.; New York: Harper and Bros., 1934). Each student should own one and use it regularly.

Arthur I. Gates, Arthur T. Jersild, T. R. McConnell, and Robert C. Challman, *Educational psychology* (New York: The Macmillan Co., 1948), Chapter I.

PART II

THE NATURE OF HUMAN BEHAVIOR

CHAPTER II

OBSERVABLE ASPECTS OF BEHAVIOR—SOURCES OF PSYCHOLOGICAL DATA

A. THE EVALUATIVE ASPECT

201. *An organismic and social approach.* Every teacher is of necessity a psychologist in function, with or without training. A professional psychologist engaged in research addresses himself to the task of discovering what behavior is and what causes it. He uses individuals in order to develop generalizations that apply to all individuals, and in order to discover how individuals differ from each other. The latter facts are also stated in terms of general principles.

The teacher must do over again and again what the research psychologist does, except that he does not develop the generalizations for others to study. He devotes himself to individuals, and to their group memberships and interactions. On an individual basis he must rediscover in every student what the research worker has described in general terms. The rediscoveries however, are highly individualistic, and the teacher uses his discoveries in long continued association with each student for the purpose of helping and guiding the student in his growth and development.

The teacher can be helped greatly by the generalizations of the research worker, for they provide guidance to him in his search for individualistic manifestations of the general laws of life, but they do not automatically give him the unique picture of each boy and girl who comes into his classes or associates with him in his capacity as a guide and friend.

Both the researcher and the teacher are students of the

same thing, one that he may tell others of general laws, the other that he may help the individual he is studying. The same basic data that are of value to the research worker, then, are of value to the teacher. That organization of behavioral phenomena which is of value to one must inevitably be of value to the other. The teacher's task in the field of psychology is to learn to read the living data of each individual person. In order to do that he must have a systematic scheme for studying the behavior of the individual.

There are many possible ways of organizing the data of psychology, for no organization is imposed upon us by nature. Since man creates his own conceptual world by organizing his experiences according to his interests, it follows that those who are primarily interested in the physiological aspects of behavior will organize their findings around the physiological functions they discover in their data. Those who are primarily interested in abnormal behavior will organize their findings around the significant abnormal phenomena. Those whose principal interest lies in basic drives will organize their findings around the identifiable drives and the mechanisms that carry them. The interesting thing about all these approaches to behavior is that each one of them is capable of putting the same broad array of data into its own organizational scheme, using its own language to a greater or lesser extent than others do, and making it appear that its data are not quite interchangeable with those in the schemes built up from other points of view. In this manner the various sciences have subdivided nature artificially, creating hazardous boundaries between chemistry, physics, physiology, botany, psychology, and many other academic fields. All of these fields represent nothing more than different approaches to the fundamental natural laws that govern all kinds of behavior, and one should not be surprised to find that various groups of scientists are struggling with identical conceptual problems, for the solution of which they need the help and points of view of each other.

A person whose task is to understand and influence the behavior of human beings singly or in groups should look for his organizational scheme to the functions that characterize the organism as a unit, and as a member of a social group, in contrast to less organismic functions, which may easily be identified when behavior is subdivided physiologically or otherwise. It is what the organism as a whole is doing that is significant to the educator and counselor. The four aspects of behavior that constitute the organization of this chapter are all of the highest individual and social significance, for they are the four functions that are fundamental to every human act. They offer a natural and orderly means of classifying all other data of a more detailed and minute nature, from the inner neural and physiological components to the overt expressions of the individual and the social interactions that constitute and create social life.

They have the strong advantage over some other organizational schemes of being real and continuous functions rather than isolated events or conditions. Thus they are observable in any organism from the moment it is formed until it expires, and every change brought about through development or learning will show itself in these four aspects.

By way of brief anticipation of the discussion of the four aspects of behavior, it may help to point out what each aspect can tell the teacher after he learns to identify it and read it. It is through the evaluative acts of an individual that we learn what his motives are, what he wants from life, how he thinks he can get what he wants, and how he appraises each object in the world around him. Hence this aspect holds the key to rapport, and points the way to the improvement of most of our educational procedures. The energic aspect of behavior reveals how serious a given situation is to an individual, the extent to which his important values are involved, whether there is threat or promise in the situation as viewed through his eyes. It also tells us how much energy he has for his life tasks, and is the guide to possible deficiencies of that type. The expressive aspect has the power to deceive or to inform the observer about how the individual feels the situation is going for him. The ability to read its messages validly depends on mastery of its many modes and its tricks of camouflage and pose. The executive aspect reveals the more or less fixed modes of response of the individual, which constitute his style of operation, his skills, and the relatively stabilized role he has assumed in his relations with others. Each aspect has its own unique message, and yet each contributes richly to the full understanding of the message of the others. When the unique character of each, and all that it can tell the observer, becomes clear to the teacher or counselor, the basis is established for the development of a penetrating insight into the structure of each personality. Without such insight no one is capable of helping another individual significantly in the solution of his problems or in his continued development.

202. *The evaluative aspect.* From the simplest to the most complex organism, but a function only of a whole organism responding to stimuli, is the evaluative aspect of behavior. Hence, it is both organismically and socially a highly significant function. Although the word evaluation carries an air of complexity, the function can be as simple as the reaction of an amoeba to a mechanical stimulus, or as complex as the reaction of an adult to a social situation. The essence of the function is not altered by the introduction of complicating circumstances. True, the amoeba lacks a central nervous system and therefore lacks some elements in its response mechanisms that are found in higher animals, but that again is a matter of complexity, not one of the nature of the function.

Evaluation consists of all that the organism does in order to obtain the best information about a situation, and make a choice of action that is most satisfying to itself. A number of sub-processes are involved, some of which have been the subject of experimental investigation from the beginning of the science of psychology.

203. *Sub-processes in evaluative reactions.* A stimulus is defined by Boring, Langfeld, and Weld [1] as "any change in the energies external to a receptor which is responsible for so altering the physico-chemical make-up of the receptor that excitation may be said to have been initiated." This would seem to be the first event in all the reactions of an organism. The

---

[1] E. G. Boring, H. S. Langfeld, and H. P. Weld, *Introduction to psychology* (New York: John Wiley and Sons, Inc., 1939), p. 224.

position is held throughout the field of psychology that there is no behavior without a stimulus of some sort, although there are many ways in which stimuli can activate an organism, including a large number of possibilities within the physiological limits of the body.

Among the simplest forms of life, response will take place to such classes of stimuli as *mechanical, thermal, chemical,* and *photic.* These responses are often called *tropismic,* having as their chief characteristic simple movements toward or away from the stimulating objects or forces. Among higher animals *acoustic* stimuli are also effective, and where the response is no longer a simple movement to or from, it is no longer called a tropism.

Stimuli give rise to *sensation,* which is defined by Warren as "an experience aroused from outside the nervous system, which is not further analyzable by introspection; i.e. an element of consciousness," and as "an afferent neural process which commences in a receptor and extends to the cerebrum." [2] Again under this term we may subsume a great deal of specific research and data accumulated over many years. Sensation is conventionally said to have four main attributes, *quality, intensity, extension,* and *duration,* each of which has something to do with the manner in which the organism evaluates his situation. In almost all senses there are a number of primary *qualities,* which in various combinations give rise to even more secondary qualities, as illustrated in color mixtures, sound combinations, mixtures of odors and flavors, and combinations of pressure, pain, warmth, and cold, which make up *somesthetic* or bodily sensation.

Intensity is an attribute having to do with the energy of the stimulus; it produces its increasing effect on the central nervous system by an increase in the frequency of nervous impulses sent along one fiber, and also by bringing additional nerve fibers into action. Hence the intensity of a sensation depends on the amount of neural excitation the stimulus is able to produce. In connection with this phenomenon is a

[2] H. C. Warren, *Dictionary of psychology* (Boston: Houghton Mifflin Co., 1934), p. 245.

host of problems that have been subjected to extensive research and that have much to do with what people see, hear,
and otherwise respond to, whether such sensations are pleasant or unpleasant, and the methods by which the nervous
system tends to screen out or to admit freely various kinds
of stimulation.

Extension is an attribute having to do with size. Some of the
problems involved in the teaching of mathematics depend on
the capacity of the individual to perceive size relationships,
and this capacity varies with individuals, and also with levels
of maturity and intelligence.

Duration is a time attribute concerning which considerable
data have also been gathered. Again, individuals vary in their
ability to perceive time intervals, and this creates critical
problems in teaching subjects such as history and economics.
These topics are mentioned only to indicate that there is
much information available about the manner in which an
individual receives and reacts to stimuli, and that some of the
variations to be found in the behavior of students is not so
mysterious as one might suspect, in the light of information
obtained from research on the processes involved.[3]

Sensation is a more definitive term than stimulus, for it
connotes a function within the nervous system of separating
various stimuli according to their meaning and nature preparatory to a still more central and integrative process called
perception. This is "the awareness of external objects, qualities, or relations, which ensues directly upon sensory processes,
as distinguished from memory or other central processes."[4]
In keeping with the rather minute subdivision of psychological processes that has developed from controlled research, it
should be noted here that perception concerns itself only with
immediately present data, not recollection of past experience
or imagination concerning future experience, both of which

[3] The structure of this brief treatment is taken largely from Boring, Land-
feld, and Weld, *op. cit.,* Chaps. 13 to 19. Another popular source is N. L.
Munn, *Psychology* (Boston: Houghton Mifflin Co., 1946), Part Six. See also
John F. Dashiell, *Fundamentals of general psychology* (Boston: Houghton
Mifflin Co., 1937).

[4] Warren, *op. cit.,* p. 196.

belong to a still more complex mental reaction. Perception is a process by which one gathers in all that can be obtained from the stimulating situation, and makes it available for evaluative purposes. An individual cannot perceive until he is stimulated, or until neural activity takes place and is given its optimum functioning by the motor apparatus of the body which moves the head, eyes, hands, and other parts of the body so that the fullest stimulation and most complete integration of stimuli are possible.

Some of the interesting problems which have been subjected to research and on which there are many significant data include attention or the control of perception, object constancy, which is a compensatory function of perception that makes things seem what they are no matter in what position or situation they are perceived, color constancy, which is a similar function in regard to color, contour perception, which deals with the relationship between a figure and its ground, fluctuation, in which perception changes even when the stimulus does not change, grouping, which refers to the tendency in perception to put together only objects experience tells us should go together, and adaptation, which shows its most familiar effects in contrasts, such as those between sweet and sour tastes which enhance each other.

The next step past perception in this hierarchy of mental functions is *conceptualization,* the process by which more than one object or experience become interrelated and form meaningful concepts varying from class concepts of concrete simple objects to the most abstract ideas. This function is at the heart of the so-called higher mental processes. It is made up of *recollection,* which deals with the real past, and *imagination,* which deals with events not yet experienced but conceived through reorganizations of past experience. It is against the background of concepts that a situation is evaluated, and a *choice reaction* follows the evaluation bringing us to the end of the links in the evaluative aspect of behavior. Choice reactions involve both discrimination between potential stimuli to which to react, and selection of one response from the available responses. Conceptualization has been studied largely through choice reactions, which have been one of the most prolific sources of experimental data, using rats and other laboratory animals.[5]

204. *Inferences that lead to insight for the teacher.* Having now indicated some of the objective studies that can be classified as part of the evaluative aspect of behavior let us see what has happened in the formation of inferences from the data thus collected. Certain observed facts have given rise to hypotheses concerning psychological characteristics that are implied by the facts, but that must always remain in the realm of inferences, as differentiated from the objective facts heretofore described.

Intelligence. Both through controlled studies and through observation of human behavior in schools and elsewhere it has long been apparent that there are significant differences in the quality of evaluation exhibited by various individuals, and from the lower to the higher forms of animals. This observation led naturally to the hypothesis that there were differences in the capacity of individuals, and out of this line of thought emerged finally the concept of *intelligence.* Neurologists long ago established the fact that from the simpler to the more advanced animal forms there is a progressive complication of the brain, with the addition of higher brain centers.

Beginning in 1902, Franz began a series of studies with cats and monkeys on the part played by the brain in learning, and after 1914 he was joined by Lashley with whom he carried on extensive experiments.[6] They studied the restitution of function in damaged brains, the role of the frontal lobes, the brain in brightness discrimination, the brain function in motor habits, the power of uninjured parts of a brain to take over the functions formerly carried in an injured part, and brain waves in relation to various other conditions in the human system.

Between 1890 and 1900, Binet had been experimenting with ways of testing the differences in mental capacity of French school children, and from his work was developed

[5] By far the best application of such experiments to a theory of human behavior has been made by E. C. Tolman in *Purposive behavior in animals and men* (New York: Appleton-Century-Crofts, Inc., 1932).

[6] Henry E. Garrett, *Great experiments in psychology* (New York: D. Appleton-Century Co., Inc., 1941), Chap. VI.

the now famous Binet-Simon scale, together with much of our present knowledge of individual differences in intelligence.[7] Studies of lesser renown but typical of many that have added to the verification of the hypotheses on intelligence as a factor in evaluation are those by Ray[8] and Edmiston.[9] Ray experimented with bright, dull, and medium students in situations calling for generalizing, or learning concepts. He concluded that the frequency of immediate insight into problems is positively related to degree of intelligence, that sudden solutions after a delay occur in all three groups, that trial and error as a method of solution is most common and its frequency is positively related to low Binet scores, and that frequency of partial insight or of a partially correct generalization is related definitely to low intelligence scores.

Edmiston attempted to see whether college students could be improved in their generalizing ability through training, and concluded that it could be done, but that such ability was more dependent on intelligence than on educational factors.

Thought. A very natural inference, growing out of behavior involved in choice reactions, is the so-called thought process by which an individual is popularly supposed to create ideas and produce decisions through no other tools than an undefined "ability to think." The phenomenon is abundantly apparent in behavior in complex situations, where the individual chooses one line of action from many, and in which some individuals are known consistently to choose activities that lead them to what they want by direct and economical paths. Observation soon tells us, also, that those who are thus able to "think" are those who possess generous quantities of what we call intelligence. A stereotyped concept of the thinker as one who ponders a problem, and out of a mental struggle produces a sound solution, has taken hold of us, to the end that we have failed to recognize the real nature of the function. Far from being a process that is "turned on" in

[7] Frank N. Freeman, *Mental tests* (Boston: Houghton Mifflin Co., 1939), Chaps. I and II.

[8] J. J. Ray, *The generalizing ability of dull, bright, and superior children,* Peabody College Contributions to Education, No. 175 (1936).

[9] R. W. Edmiston, "Testing generalizing ability," *Peabody Journal of education,* 12 (1935), 246-51.

critical situations and then set aside, thinking is probably identical with the processes of perception and conception. Unless it is unique among all evaluative functions, it is a constant process that resides in the electrical potentials of the brain. It would seem to be identical with the neural processes by which learning takes place, through the integration of various sensations, and the accumulation of perceptual experiences which make up our concepts. It is to be noted that while good thinking is confined to the intelligent on the whole, not all intelligent people do good thinking, or to be more accurate, intelligent people do good thinking only in situations with which they have had some experience. Hence the process is fully as much a function of conceptual learning, as of intelligence. Good decisions, then, depend on the presence of clear concepts that have direct relationship to the current problem. If the concepts are present, good decisions are made, and if not, the individual must guess, or wait until he can enlarge his experience and develop his concepts.

There is a difference between contiguous thought, which follows the random associational cues based on similarities in form, color, location, time, and so on, and continuous thought, which is held to a purposive line of relationships by continuous reference to a particular situation. In all probability it is the shift from contiguous to continuous recall that has been mistaken for the onset of thinking from a state of no-thinking, and the fact that directed thinking is far less common than random or contiguous thinking that has led us to accept the idea that thinking is something in which we engage only occasionally, and then only under the stress of a state of doubt or perplexity. In this area we are victims of unrestrained inductive inference without the corresponding deductive verification required in objective research, for there is little if any significant research on the vital matter of critical thinking.

Under the position taken here, the quality of a person's thinking is dependent on his intelligence far more than on any training he can be given in ways of analyzing problems, or of gathering or testing data, as already suggested in Edmiston's study. It is treated as a type of learning, however, in

Chapter XVI, where the possibilities of improving it are discussed.

What the research worker has discovered about intelligence and thinking, the teacher will continually rediscover in each individual student. He will use tests, which are nothing more than well-selected and highly controlled evaluative experiences, to see how high is the quality of each student's evaluative reactions in academic matters. He will learn to single out from all other behavioral acts those that indicate capacity in other areas, such as creative ability, constructive imagination, social sensitivity, and so on. To do these things he must learn to use controlled observation, just as he would have to do in research; he will cut out and ignore non-pertinent matters and be sure he is seeing all of the pertinent matters in an objective and realistic manner.

The concept of knowledge. Along another line, studies and observation have made it clear that people with approximately equal capacity react differently to similar situations, and that in general the amount of experience one has had with a given type of phenomenon has much to do with the way one responds to it. From this sort of observation grew naturally the hypothesis that an individual acquires *concepts* through experience, and that these concepts act in the form of inner determinants of behavior. Although concepts, like intelligence, cannot be brought to light and studied, their presence can be demonstrated through studies such as that of Buswell and John [10] who revealed in their subjects not only differences in conceptual content related to various mathematical terms, but also several interesting things about the manner in which such concepts develop in students. From this sort of study has developed evidence upon which we can now build up a respectable description of the pattern of meaning and its role as a causative factor in behavior, as discussed extensively in Chapter IX.

Here again, what the research worker has discovered about

[10] Guy T. Buswell and Lenore John, *The vocabulary of arithmetic,* Supplementary Educational Monographs, No. 38 (Chicago: Department of Education, University of Chicago, 1931).

the directive factors residing within the conceptual patterns of the individual, the teacher must rediscover on a personal basis in each student. He will use tests for the conceptual content of the individual, particularly in the realm of his knowledge of facts and his understandings of subject matter. He will learn what actions are valid signs of the ingrained preferences and prejudices of the individual. Through seeing him make choices in which he consistently rejects some things and accepts and seeks others, he will discover the student's values and preferences, but in order to do this he must be able to sort out those parts of evaluative behavior that reveal mental content from all other behavioral signs, not confusing indicators of content with indicators of capacity, or of need, or of skill, or of traits, or of energy and health, and particularly not being deceived by some of the subtleties of the expressive aspects of behavior.

The concept of need. One other significant inferential development has led to the concept of need, through observation of differences in readiness of both animals and men to respond to various stimuli. People who are tired respond to objects that are associated with rest, and when rested respond more readily to objects that suggest activity. People who are hungry respond readily to food, and those who are sated do not. People who seem to lack affectional relationships are often found seeking such relationships in various ways, to a greater extent than are those who are well supplied. Although these forms of behavior can be observed, needs cannot be observed and exist only in the mind of the observer who creates them hypothetically, so that we have, as one outstanding approach to the problem, the work of Murray at Harvard, and his statement that "A need is a hypothetical process the occurrence of which is imagined in order to account for certain objective and subjective facts." [11] Throughout the first 141 pages of his volume he sets forth the arguments that support the concept of need in human behavior, and follows this with clinically gathered data to illustrate and support his hypo-

[11] Henry A. Murray *et al., Explorations in personality* (New York: Oxford University Press, 1938), p. 54.

thetical structure. Murray's thinking is representative of most current students of human need, at least in its basic formulation.

Physiological needs. Prior to Murray's best-known study, however, there was a great deal of research with animals, especially white rats, on the physiological needs that predisposed the animals toward sex objects, food, water, a litter in a nest, and such stimuli. Illustrative of such studies is one by Warner [12] in which rats were denied food for 0, 2, 3, 4, 6, and 8 days, and then given a small amount of food after crossing a grill from which they received a small electric shock. For the males, the frequency of crossings increased up to four days of deprivation, and then slowly decreased. The females began their decreases earlier, but in all cases it was apparent that hunger furnished a drive to action and predisposed the animals toward food, even when pain was involved in getting the food.

Hundreds of such studies have made possible the formulation of descriptions of physiological needs, their comparative strengths, and their times of greatest strength.[13]

Social needs. The formation of equally precise conclusions on needs of a social nature has been much more difficult. Some animal studies have yielded results of a social nature that have been applied by inference to human beings, but in general there have been few rigorous objective studies of social needs comparable to those of physiological need. This is not surprising, however, when it is realized that conditions involved in social satisfaction are rarely amenable to objective experimentation. As a result, there is less agreement among psychologists on the hypothetical structure of the social needs than on physiological needs, and the studies upon which most conclusions are based are mostly observation studies of human beings in various natural situations. The psychoanalytic view is well presented by Ribble [14] in a dis-

---

[12] L. H. Warner, "A study of hunger behavior in the white rat by means of the obstruction method," *Journal of comparative psychology*, 8 (1928), 273-99.

[13] For a well-organized discussion of the primary drives, see Paul T. Young, *Motivation of behavior* (New York: John Wiley and Sons, Inc., 1936), Chap. 3.

[14] J. McV. Hunt, ed., *Personality and the behavior disorders* (New York: The Ronald Press Co., 1944), Vol. II, Chap. 20.

cussion of infantile experience, which deals especially with the affectional relationships of infant and mother. What has come to be called the dynamic point of view is ably presented by Mowrer and Kluckhohn,[15] who emphasize the learning process in need formation.

Personal needs. What is true of the difficulty of formulating social needs with precision is even more true of needs that have reference to the person's adjustment to himself. Sherif and Cantril [16] have done for ego or personal needs what Murray did for the need concept in general. Their position rejects innate ego tendencies in favor of genetic or developed attitudes toward the self, derived from experience. A similar treatment oriented toward counseling is offered by Snygg and Combs [17] whose thesis is that everything the individual does is directed toward the preservation of his own personal structure. The concept of need will be more fully developed in a later chapter, but it has been introduced here, along with the concepts of capacity and knowledge, to illustrate the manner in which observations of behavior have given rise to inferences concerning the factors that account for what is being observed.

The teacher's observations will tell him the needs of specific individuals if he learns what to look for and how to interpret what he sees. He must remember that attention inevitably turns toward the stimulus that has the most direct relationship to the most driving need of the individual. By watching the trends in attentiveness of his students he will be led to their unsatisfied needs, and will be able to identify ways in which active needs are pulling his students away from their studies. From this sort of insight he can reshape his ways of teaching so that he can make the school serve the needs of the students, and help students find the channels by which they can satisfy their needs in educationally useful ways.

205. *Conclusion.* It can now be re-emphasized that the

---

[15] *Ibid.,* Vol. I, Chap. 3, especially pp. 85-112.

[16] Muzafer Sherif and Hadley Cantril, *The psychology of ego-involvements* (New York: John Wiley and Sons, Inc., 1948). See especially Chap. 5, "The problem and a general characterization of ego-involvements."

[17] Donald Snygg and Arthur W. Combs, *Individual behavior* (New York: Harper and Bros., 1949). See especially Chaps. 4, 5, and 6.

studies and the data classified here under the evaluative function in behavior are all concerned with processes by which the individual receives information about the world around him and arrives at decisions concerning the lines of action he will pursue. Therefore the inferences derived from the data involved will be wholly concerned with problems of motivation, a term that has come to stand for anything that arouses and sustains behavior and directs it to its conclusion. One of the advantages of isolating this aspect of behavior from the others lies in removing many other characteristics of behavior from the observational field temporarily, so that we can concentrate on those characteristics that inform us about a person's motives and not become confused by those characteristics that tell us about his style of operation, or the energy he has available, but are silent on his purposes.

QUESTIONS FOR REVIEW

1. Of what value to a teacher are psychological generalizations?
2. How does research in human behavior help the teacher?
3. What is meant by the term "organism as a whole"?
4. What is the general nature of each of the four aspects of behavior mentioned in this chapter?
5. Make up a definition of evaluative behavior.
6. What are the principal processes involved in evaluative reactions?
7. How might each of the principal subprocesses affect the final evaluative act?
8. Define perception, and show how it is different from conception.
9. Why is intelligence called an "inference from behavioral data"?
10. Describe thought in the popular sense, then in the sense used in this chapter. Show the difference between the two.
11. What is the difference between thinking and problem-solving?
12. In what way is the concept of "knowledge" an inference from behavior?
13. How do we know people have needs?
14. How is it known that people have various kinds of needs?
15. Of what use is the theory of "needs" to teachers?

16. How can you use the theory of "knowledge" in school?
17. What can an observer learn from the evaluative behavior of a student?

SELECTED REFERENCES

Henry E. Garrett, *Great experiments in psychology* (New York: Appleton-Century-Crofts, Inc., 1941), Chapters XIII, XIV, and XV.

Donald Snygg, and Arthur W. Combs, *Individual behavior* (New York: Harper and Bros., 1949), Chapter VII.

CHAPTER III

OBSERVABLE ASPECTS OF BEHAVIOR, Continued

B. THE ENERGIC ASPECT

301. *The energic aspect.* As in the evaluative aspect of behavior, it is only in a whole organism responding to its environment that the complete energic function is present. It is
a highly integrated composite of many sub-processes within
an organism, influenced intimately by the intake of both
physical and psychological materials from the outside. The
energic function is present in a single cell, and is therefore
not bounded even by the limits of the life span of one individual. It consists of the production and discharge of chemical, electrical, or muscular energy, which furnishes the
dynamics or power upon which the organism operates. It is
fundamental to processes of growth and development as so
well described by Carmichael,[1] for it seems that even the development of organic structure and the onset of organic function may be due to conditions produced in the embryo by
the energic functions of the cells in their close formation
within the growing organism. The growth function based on
energic activity lies behind maturation and physiological
readiness to act. This is illustrated by the onset of vision,
which is held up until neural connections are made within
the brain, even after the eyes themselves seem to be ready
to function, and by the onset of complex muscular activities
such as stair-climbing, which must wait until some of the
integrative centers are ready to function, and until some parts
of the muscular system are ready to assume their full function.

The primary data of this aspect of behavior are obtained,

---

[1] Leonard Carmichael, "The onset and early development of behavior," in
L. Carmichael, ed., *Manual of child psychology* (New York: John Wiley and
Sons, Inc., 1946).

as before, from observations of behavior. Thus it is appropriate to make a list of the sorts of things that have been observed, and then to look at the manner in which hypotheses from these observations have led into further observations of objective facts to be found only through laboratory studies, and finally to inferences concerning psychological factors that influence energic activities.

302. *What we see.* Perhaps the first significant fact from observation is the growth process by which two cells unite and develop into a mature organism whose bulk and capacity for action is multiplied way beyond anything contained in the parent cells. Obviously, these acquired characteristics are dependent on the power of the growing organism to bring into itself from its environment the energies which it transforms into tissue and activity. Part of this process is the intake of food and the excretion of waste, which has such a close relationship to the amount of energy and to the growth of the individual. Closely connected with this is the phenomenon of fatigue and its removal by rest, and the opposite manifestation of exuberant activity in a highly'charged youngster. These are such commonplace facts that it is easy to overlook their significance as basic data of research and points of departure for theories and abstract explanations of causation.

Buried under the surface are the visceral organs enumerated later, which operate rhythmically and automatically to circulate blood, control breathing, remind us of the need for food, and in many other ways take care of the production of energy. It is a matter of significance to note that they seem always to operate according to the needs of the organism, except when they are interrupted by outbursts, and the reason for this regularity is a matter for research, as well as the entire system and its functions.

Somewhat more dramatic are those data to be seen in the occasional eruptions of these energy-producing systems, with sudden increases in energy, and a whole host of physical manifestations, not to mention the interferences with normal evaluative reactions. In the other direction, there are reductions of energy below the normal requirements of a healthy person, which accompany states of apathy and are sometimes prolonged and entirely unconnected with such normal reductions as occur in sleep or relaxation.

A further phenomenon of importance is the tendency of human beings to reach a peak of physiological efficiency in the twenties, and then begin a slow decline that eventuates in death. This has given rise to studies of the relationship between physical vigor and the intake of food and drugs, and also the role of the glands and internal organs in the maintenance of health and vitality.

A final item for this list is the frequently observed functional deterioration in cases in which no physical or pathological cause can be found. Searching beyond the physical system for the precipitating factors led finally to the conclusion that psychological factors were responsible, just as they were in emotional disruptions, and opened for research the field of functional disorders including the neuroses and many of the psychoses.

The purpose in listing these obvious and commonplace forms of behavior is to indicate the scope of phenomena that may be usefully classified primarily as energic aspects of behavior, and to point out their common quality of dependence on the energy-producing mechanisms of the organism. Research on these problems has been of major concern to physiologists, neurologists, biochemists, embryologists, psychologists, nutrionists, and others. Physiological facts are fundamental to the full investigation of these matters, and the systems involved have been reasonably well described.

303. *Some physiological bases of energic reactions.* Three systems are involved in the production and release of energy, the neuro-humoral system, the visceral organs, and the somatic muscular system. Within the first category are included the central nervous system, the autonomic nervous system, and the glands of internal secretion. The autonomic system is further divisible into the parasympathetic and the sympathetic systems, which operate in balance to regulate the glands and visceral organs. In general, the sympathetic system is known as the spendthrift system, since when its innervations are dominant the body is thrown into action with

all the energy necessary to meet whatever situation may develop regardless of cost. In contrast, the parasympathetic system is generally conservative, cutting down the expenditure of energy. The effects described are produced by the action of these systems upon the glands and visceral organs that are involved in the energic function. The glands of importance in this capacity are the thyroid, the parathyroid, the pituitary, the ovaries and testes, and the adrenals. The visceral organs are the heart, the lungs, the liver, the kidneys, the gall bladder,, the bladder, the spleen, and the gastrointestinal tract. The third system, the somatic muscles, furnishes the outlet for the energy produced by the visceral organs, through bodily activity of an overt nature as illustrated in running, lifting, or hitting, and in expressions such as are shown through the facial muscles.

All of the parts of these systems and their operations have been studied extensively in laboratory experiments, and a sizable literature is available on the studies. A comprehensive treatment of the neuro-humoral basis of emotions is offered by Bard,[2] who with others has described the reflex mechanisms at the base of the thalamic area of the brain, which control the ordinary operations of the energic system in smooth, rhythmic fashion, through chemical and neural controls. Left to themselves, these controls hold the energic reaction on an even course, and have been shown to do so in the case of animals whose cortex has been removed so that the life of the animal is regulated by the lower brain centers. The fact that people have marked increases in muscular tension, and show many other symptoms of excitement in situations that appear to have special significance to them, however, led long ago to the inference that there was a neural mechanism by which the perception of a situation could affect the energic function. Typical of the research carried out in an effort to understand this problem is that reported by Cannon[3] over a

[2] P. Bard, "The neuro-humoral basis of emotional reactions," in Carl Murchison, ed., *Handbook of general experimental psychology* (Worcester, Mass.: Clark University Press, 1934).

[3] Walter B. Cannon, *Bodily changes in pain, hunger, fear, and rage* (New York: D. Appleton Co., 1929).

period of years at Harvard University, in which he subjected animals to many kinds of perceptual situations and studied their reactions under various kinds of operative alterations in their nervous systems. He and others have established clearly the fact that critical situations provoke us to excessive energic responses, and have revealed much concerning the physiological mechanisms through which such reactions are produced.

304. *Inferences and research lead to perceptual factors.* Through inference, followed up by deductive research, it has been demonstrated that perception of a critical situation, critical from the subjective view of the individual involved, sets up neural excitation from the cortex to the hypothalamus, which sets aside the balance normally maintained, and precipitates a rise in production in anticipation of the needs of the situation. There is a rough relationship between the amount of energy produced and the criticalness of the situation, although there are many complications that sometimes make this relationship appear not to exist.

A significant fact is to be found in the inability of an individual voluntarily to precipitate or to terminate an energic increase, in spite of the fact that the centers of consciousness and thought are able to set off the reaction. This is an important clue concerning the nature of thought, as mentioned earlier, for it suggests that in many ways behavior is regulated by the conceptual content of the brain without, and indeed in spite of, any effort to manipulate it voluntarily and through what might be described as will power. Emotional reactions are completely independent of conscious control. They develop instantaneously whenever the individual perceives a critical situation, and often when his perceptual powers have caught a clue of which he is not consciously aware. They come to an end whenever the critical element in the situation has been removed. This happens asleep or awake, which provides strong evidence that it is an automatic process, even though it depends on perception and conceptual content, and is instigated through the higher centers of the brain.

Of direct interest to the teacher are two enlightening studies of emotional reactions to examination situations. The earlier one, by Brown and Gelder [4] used situations involving critical examinations given to graduate and undergraduate students at the University of Chicago, and provided objective evidence that such situations increase systolic blood pressure, pulse, and respiratory rates, and may increase blood sugar and glycosuria. These effects return to normal after the exams, and tend to return to normal before two-day examinations are ended. Hastings [5] used as his subjects students in the laboratory schools of the University of Chicago, and measured not only the emotions produced by the examinations, but the effects of the emotions on the performance of the students in the examinations. As in most studies of emotional reactions, the effects are unique to the student, some being hindered and some helped by the heightened tensions, and some showing no emotional response to the examinations.

In the field of medical practice, the frequent presence of certain organic disturbances with no apparent physical cause led to the inference that some of these conditions might be produced by excessive energic activity. A compilation of studies directed to that problem has been prepared by Dunbar,[6] showing that many kinds of organic damage and serious illness are traceable to prolonged exposure to critical situations, with consequent breakdown of the physical system.

304. *The problem of emotions seen in perspective.* Because of behavioral difficulties so frequently associated with excessive energic activity, the problem of emotional behavior has been a long-standing focal point for attention, so much so that the basic processes that are always present in behavior have been overlooked by many people interested in the problem. Emotions have been highlighted out of proportion to their importance whereas the conditions that produce them have often been ignored or not understood. Many popular descriptions and explanations of emotions have influenced the thinking of teachers and parents, and a great deal of nonsense about

[4] Charles H. Brown and David V. Gelder, "Emotional reactions before examinations: I. Physiological changes," *Journal of psychology*, 5 (1938), 1-9.

[5] J. Thomas Hastings, "Tensions and school achievement examinations," *Journal of experimental education*, 12, No. 3 (March, 1944), 143-64.

[6] H. F. Dunbar, *Emotions and bodily changes* (New York: Columbia University Press, 1946).

patterns of emotional expression has been passed around in place of facts. A significant advance in the understanding of emotional phenomena is due to studies of the type compiled and reported by Landis.[7] Item by item, he reports that there is no clear pattern of relationship between any kind of emotion and blood volume, blood pressure, chemical changes in the blood, heart reactions, respiratory reaction, metabolic rate, or gastrointestinal activity. This throws us back to the fundamental fact that energic activities exist on a continuum of quantity, but a continuum in which certain qualitative changes take place as various glands and organs are brought into or cut out of activity through increased innervation of either the parasympathetic or the sympathetic tracts. Basically, the position most in keeping with the research is that all energic phenomena are of one kind, any differences being due to the amount of energy produced and the effects exerted on the body by the stress of higher production or the inertia of lower production than normal.

The best application of emotional data to educative problems at the time it was published was that of Prescott[8] in 1938. Following the lead of Dumas, Prescott divided emotional reactions into mild, strong, and disruptive, and related to each level the psychological and physiological symptoms produced by progressively more intense energic activity. In an example of real insight he also suggested that the pleasantness or unpleasantness of an emotion was not determined by the physiological factors, but by the deeper psychological meanings of the situation for the individual. Combining this suggestion with the current emphasis on ego-involvement in all behavior, the conclusion logically follows that there are two distinct factors involved in determining whether an emotional reaction will be pleasant or otherwise. One is the psychological reaction to the situation in which frustrating or ego-defeating experiences will always be unpleasant and their opposites pleasant, and the other is the actual physical pain

[7] Carney Landis, "The expression of emotions," in Carl Murchison, ed., *Handbook of general experimental psychology* (Worcester, Mass.: Clark University Press, 1934).

[8] Daniel Prescott, *Emotion and the educative process* (Washington, D.C.: The American Council on Education, 1938). See particularly Chap. II.

or pleasant sensation produced by the physiological components of the experience.

Another significant idea was advanced by Cannon to the effect that increases in energic production are of an "emergency" nature. That is, they tend to provide the individual with additional amounts of energy appropriate to the activity demands of the critical situation. The principal objection offered to this concept centers around the fact that human beings in modern society do not solve their problems by physical action as animals do, but by symbolic activity in the form of conversation or the exchange of ideas. Hence, it is argued, there is no reason for conceiving the emotional reaction as a survival reaction or as having any relevancy to human life. What is overlooked in this objection is the essential incompleteness of man, when his level of achievement is compared to his potentiality. In a fully mature society it is conceivable that situations that now cause violent emotional outbursts would be almost nonexistent, in which case there would be a greatly reduced incidence of excessive energic reactions, possibly approaching a level consonant with the symbolic methods of meeting personal and social issues. Hence the equipment of man, and his reaction potentials, will be fully in keeping with his manner of living only when he has "grown up" completely and brought all aspects of his life to something resembling maturity.

The key to an understanding of emotional phenomena is to be found in the evaluative aspect of behavior, combined with the facts about the energic continuum presented in this discussion. The amount of energy produced is regulated by the seriousness of the situation, whether it be favorable or unfavorable. The basic determiner of pleasantness or unpleasantness is the psychological interpretation of the meaning of the situation, so that granted the same level of energic production, there is no physiological difference between pleasant and unpleasant emotions. On the other hand, when the energic level reaches proportions characterized by Prescott as disruptive, or even quite strong, there are distinct physical discomforts that can turn into pain, even though a hilarious situation is causing the reaction, and it is quite possible for an unfavorable situation to bring distress to an individual even when the physiological effects of the mild energic level are actually pleasant. A factor that has probably created the illusion that all annoying situations cause unpleasant physical reactions, and all satisfying situations cause pleasant physical reactions, is to be found in the relationship between the annoying-satisfying factor and the level of energic activity each produces. It is suggested as an hypothesis for investigation that favorable situations tend on the whole to produce only mild energic reactions, whereas unfavorable situations tend on the whole to provoke relatively strong energic reactions. Since there is a qualitative difference in the physiological characteristics of mild and strong reactions, it is probable that unfavorable situations have usually been accompanied by pounding of the heart, uncomfortably increased breathing, interferences with digestion and elimination, and often trembling due to the excessive muscular tension. These same symptoms would be present in favorable situations if they were sufficiently critical to stimulate the higher energic response, but ordinarily they do not do so, and are marked by the symptoms of mild emotions, increased efficiency in digestion, better gastric and salivary secretions, slight increases in muscular tension and efficiency and other similar effects that heighten the sense of physical well-being and often produce pleasant sensations in various erogenous zones of the body.

304. *Values determine emotions.* As an integral part of on-going behavior, an emotion gets its name and meaning from the evaluative aspect of behavior. One's values tend to define the areas of emotionality. The stronger emotions are usually experienced in connection with situations that involve the most important values of the individual; those values that are either greatly cherished or seriously avoided. Hence the meaning that the individual finds in the situation through his evaluative reactions determines both the emotion and the attitude. However, once the meaning of the situation has registered its impact on the nervous system and the autonomic nervous system has taken charge, there is no way of exerting conscious control over the physiological reactions that follow. The emotion itself is beyond the control of the cortex and

associated connecting fibers where conscious thought is mediated. Nevertheless the meaning of the situation and a conscious awareness of the sensations coming from the visceral organs are both clearly involved in any intellectual reactions that accompany behavior. From these reactions the individual thinks of himself as being angry, hurt, afraid, excited, or what not. The internal sensations from the viscera tell him only that he is "stirred up." Ordinarily they have no message regarding the specific meaning of the emotion. The meaning comes from the evaluative phase of behavior. The emotional tension does serve, however, to heighten the vividness of the experience so that a strong and enduring impression is made. Some have referred to this as the "stamping in" of whatever is being experienced at the time. Learning may be speeded up when accompanied by emotion, but there is always the serious danger that what is learned may be undesirable.

305. *Forms of emotional expression are learned.* The form of the outward or overt expression of an emotion is learned by the individual. Similarly, the ability to determine an individual's emotional state by looking at his facial and bodily expression or by the sound of his voice is a learned ability, and must be learned for each person so judged, since modes of expression differ with the person. This is the same as saying that there are no universal and instinctive facial expressions to match the common emotional states. Studies of emotional reactions in infants have resulted in the conclusion that there are no identifiable emotional patterns that exist innately in a newborn baby.[9] It appears that every living creature is capable of exhibiting a general state of excitement at birth, but that the expressions, mannerisms, and vocal accompaniments of that state are peculiar to the creature, and the patterns established for them later on are acquired by experience. Thus emotional expression becomes patterned for

[9] K. C. Pratt, A. K. Nelson, and K. H. Sun, *The behavior of the newborn infant* (Columbus: Ohio State University Press, 1930). See also, M. Sherman, "The differentiation of emotional responses in infants," *Journal of comparative psychology,* 7 (1927), 265-84, 335-51; 8 (1928), 385-94. For a general treatment of research, see Arthur T. Jersild, "Emotional development," in L. Carmichael, ed., *Manual of child psychology* (New York: John Wiley and Sons, Inc., 1946).

the individual through the gradual acquistion of learned forms of expression that are unique to the individual. Mothers can recognize the emotional states of their infants by listening to their cries. This ability, also, is learned by repeatedly listening to the infant's cries and gradually finding out what satisfies it in each instance so that the nature of its emotions can be identified.

Emotional climate. Up to this point emotion has been discussed as if it were' wholly determined by the immediate situation. Although the situation is probably the most important factor in emotional experience, it is not the only one. Individuals seem to acquire what may be called an emotional climate, which is a name applied to the level of affective intensity in which they most commonly function. One's emotional climate is in part an outgrowth of one's previous experience. It may also be related to the glandular activities in the body, to the rate of metabolism, and to any other body functions that have to do with energy output. It may also be related to the degree of one's comprehension of and adjustment to one's life-realm. It is undeniably true that some individuals live at a higher normal rate of affective tone than others. Some homes are noticeably charged with an emotional tone that is uncomfortable to those not accustomed to it. Under prolonged conditions of tension, as in combat areas, the emotional climate is warmer than in more peaceful areas.

This emotional climate or temperature may be thought of as a point of departure from which specific emotional experiences take off. Hence it is a factor in specific emotional response. This means that it is impossible to equate the degree of affect of two individuals as shown by photo-polygraph records because each individual has his own unique basic level of affect. Illustrations of this are common. Some people explode into profanity at causes so common that they literally keep the air blue with their sulphuric expressions most of the day, while others going through the same experiences find little to excite them. Many people are seriously annoyed by those whose level of energy and feeling-tone makes them eager to engage in lively discussion or argument or to push themselves more vigorously in various activities than their less "highly-strung" friends. Illustrations in the other direction are those stoical persons who cultivate a low level of feeling or place a high value on the ability to remain calm. Stories of the calm behavior of American Indians under conditions involving pain contain numerous instances of a relatively cool emotional climate.

306.   *Control of emotions.* There is a common misunderstanding about emotional control, which is related to the problem of emotional climate and emotional expression. The physiological phase of an emotion is not subject to a conscious effort to control it. It is entirely futile to ask an angry person to dismiss his emotion by a strong exercise of will power. That he cannot do so is amply illustrated by the common experience of stage fright, which afflicts persons against their wills. Once an emotion is launched it is not possible to control its intensity by any conscious process within the individual.

There are two profitable ways of working to bring emotional behavior under control. The more superficial approach is through self-discipline in the forms of overt expression. Even though the internal intensity of an emotion cannot be cut down, it is possible to learn to control the outer expressions to some extent. An illustration of this is to be found in the case of changes with age. The child screams and kicks, the youth may attack, the adolescent may resort to epithets, the young lady may tone down to the mere use of caustic criticism, and the matron to the use of a lifted eyebrow. A person can modify his actions according to his standards. To do so requires persistent effort.

A more satisfactory approach is to reduce the number of situations that are felt by the individual to be dangerous or harmful to him. There are several ways of doing that:

(1) Goals are important only as they satisfy needs. If the individual is able to substitute other goals for those he cannot attain, he can satisfy his needs even though he cannot reach certain specific goals. If a goal is threatened for such an individual, he is not as apt to respond emotionally as if that goal were his only hope of satisfying the need. Therefore, one way of eliminating potential emotional crises is to make the student acquainted with the healthful ways of getting around

blocked goals and such frustrations, and enlarge his knowledge of life so that he may be able to see many ways of satisfying his needs instead of one or only a few.

(2) People often fear those things that are mysterious or unfamiliar to them. Superstitions are of this sort. Knowledge and understanding remove such fears. When the individual becomes familiar with the limited influence exerted on human beings by black cats, he loses his fear of meeting them. Therefore, another way of eliminating potential emotional crises is to make the student acquainted with the laws of cause and effect throughout life, to broaden his acquaintance with people of all kinds, and with cultural influences other than those of his own environment. In short, he must come to know the nature of the world in which he lives.

(3) A person's feelings are easily upset when he identifies himself and his own survival with things he possesses or has made by his own efforts. Students often become angry when their English themes are criticized severely. They are unable to separate the theme from themselves, and the criticism is looked upon as a threat to their own well-being. If they can be led to see that their own survival is entirely independent of the survival of the theme, the criticism becomes a lift toward better performance rather than a threat of destruction. Students can be helped then, by being led to see things around them objectively and to evaluate their own work dispassionately.

The three lines of attack outlined above have as their common element the broadening of vision and understanding through learning. Most of the causes of unpleasant emotional experience can be reduced in their influence, if not eliminated, for those who become at home in the universe. This fundamental fact is eloquently expressed in one of the handbooks of Buddhism: "Wise people, after they have listened to the law, become serene, like a deep, smooth, and still lake."

From an educational point of view it may be said that while mild emotional experiences may be healthful, all others are harmful and should be avoided for the same reason that the school seeks to avoid harming its students through physical accident or through serving poison in lunches. Lack of understanding of the emotions and their effects on wholesome development has kept educators from making a serious and determined effort to eliminate unpleasant and destructive emotional experiences from the school program. In the light of modern knowledge there is no longer any justification for overlooking this aspect of the school environment.

307. *Conclusion.* In this aspect of behavior, then, we have a guide to the observer toward how critical the situation is to the individual, consisting of the amount of energy produced in response to it. Telltale signs consist of throbbing of the pulses, flushing or paling of the face, dilation of the eyes, changes in perspiration, and evidences of muscular tension. Emotions are only one part of the whole continuum of energic activity, that which is above the normal feeling-tone. Apathy characterizes the range below the normal feeling-tone where the production of energy is reduced through depressing situations. The whole phenomenon is a unified thing, a continuous aspect of behavior inextricably woven into the evaluative aspect and into the other two aspects still to be discussed.

QUESTIONS FOR REVIEW

1. Define the energic aspect of behavior.
2. What energic phenomena can be observed in behavior?
3. What is the general form of the curve of energic efficiency through life?
4. What nerve systems are involved in energic reactions? What is the role of each?
5. What other physiological systems are involved? What are their functions?
6. What is meant by Cannon's "emergency theory" of emotions?
7. To what extent can one consciously control energic reactions?
8. How does the meaning of a situation affect the amount of energy released?
9. Do examinations produce the same effects on all students? Why?
10. Make a technical differentiation between the energic aspect of behavior and the concept of "emotion."
11. What is the continuum of energic reaction? Describe some points on it.
12. How can people go about the job of reducing emotional outbursts?

13. What is a good definition of emotion?
14. What is the difference between feeling and emotion?
15. What effect does a strong emotion have on finger skills? On large leg muscles? On digestion? On ability to run or jump?
16. What effect does a mild emotion have on digestion? On heart action?
17. Values and emotions are related in two ways. State each in a brief sentence.
18. In what ways, physiologically or psychologically, are pleasant and unpleasant emotions alike? In what ways are they different?
19. How and to what extent is the autonomic control of emotions subject to evaluative reactions?
20. Where do we get the forms by which we express emotions? From what original characteristic of the infant do they develop?
21. What is emotional climate? What relation has it to specific emotional experiences?
22. Which part of an emotional reaction can be consciously controlled?
23. Suggest three ways in which an individual can reduce the number of situations that can produce strong emotional reactions. What else can he do to control his emotional behavior?

SELECTED REFERENCES

Walter B. Cannon, *Bodily changes in pain, hunger, fear, and rage* (New York: Appleton-Century-Crofts, Inc., 1929), *passim*.
Henry E. Garrett, *Great experiments in psychology* (New York: Appleton-Century-Crofts, Inc., 1941), Chapter XII.
Daniel A. Prescott, *Emotion and the educative process* (Washington, D.C.: The American Council on Education, 1938), Chapters II, III, and IV.

CHAPTER IV

OBSERVABLE ASPECTS OF BEHAVIOR, Continued

C. THE EXPRESSIVE ASPECT

401. *Nature of the function.* Full and complete expression, as in the case of evaluation and the production and expenditure of energy, is only possible in a whole organism, and has meaning only in a social situation. With the added facts that it, like the other aspects of behavior, is a function that is present from the beginning to the end of life, asleep or awake, and that it is the aspect of behavior of all living things that makes social structure possible, there can be no question of its significance as a basis for observing human behavior, and for organizing a very significant array of psychological and sociological data.

When behavior is viewed from the expressive point of view, it consists of anything the individual does that transmits to others how he feels about things, what his evaluations are, and what ideas he wants to impart. The most significant stimuli to which any of us react are the expressive acts of others. As Park has said, "We live in an atmosphere of suggestion and counter suggestion, the changes and fluctuations of which influence and control us like a social weather." [1]

In this respect, the teacher finds himself in the role of a clinical psychologist, whose most distinctive skills lie in his ability to penetrate the apparently contradictory and confusing mass of behavioral manifestations coming from a subject and to read with accuracy the real messages that are being broadcast in all sorts of coded and devious forms. When this can be done, the clinician can find a valid basis for understanding the individual, and hence for helping him with

[1] Robert E. Park, "Human nature, attitudes, and the mores," in K. Young, ed., *Social attitudes* (New York: Henry Holt and Co., Inc., 1931), p. 33.

39

his problems. Of all people in the world, the teacher finds himself most in need of such skill, for to no other person do so many individuals come so regularly for help. Obviously the teacher cannot spend years in the single-minded pursuit of clinical skill, but he can and must become acquainted to some extent with the fundamentals of expressive behavior and with some of the problems involved in reading it with validity.

402. *The basic data.* For this discussion, expressive acts will be grouped in four categories, language and sound, pictorial and symbolic representations, bodily expressions through position and purposive movement, and reflex signs and involuntary indicators. Only a brief suggestion of what is included in each area will be given here.

Language and sounds. Probably the most commonplace, and at the same time the most amazing thing people do is talk and write. Oral communication has been intimately involved in the behavior of almost all animals as long as life has existed, and it carries a tremendous share of the burden of interaction between human beings. Some of its peculiar characteristics have been observed for centuries, but of all the facets of behavior, the expressive aspect has been the least studied objectively and is subject to the most naïveté on the part of unsophisticated observers. We have had much less trouble interpreting nonverbal sounds than we have had with words. A mother quickly learns how to interpret the various types of cries from her infant, and the infant learns just as quickly how to interpret the mother's mood from the tone of her voice. In the use of words, however, history has been consistent in its revelation of misunderstandings between people, all mixed up with perfectly clear understandings, but with no key to knowing when one is going to be understood and when one is not. There has been abundant evidence of serious discrepancies between what a person says he will do and what he does, and in such deceit the one who speaks is as often deceived himself as is the one who listens.

Wendell Johnson [2] has done some of the clearest thinking on this problem and has put some of the difficulties into lucid form. He has portrayed the process of human verbal com-

[2] Wendell Johnson, *People in quandries* (New York: Harper and Bros., 1946).

1. An event occurs

2. which stimulates Mr. A through eyes, ears, or other sensory organs, and the resulting

3. nervous impulses travel to Mr. A's brain, and from there to his muscles and glands, producing tensions, preverbal "feelings," etc,

4. which Mr. A then begins to translate into words, according to his accustomed verbal patterns, and out of all the words he "thinks of"

5. he "selects," or abstracts, certain ones which he arranges in some fashion, and then

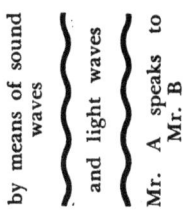

by means of sound waves

and light waves

Mr. A speaks to Mr. B

6. whose ears and eyes are stimulated by the sound waves and light waves, respectively, and the resulting

7. nervous impulses travel to Mr. B's brain, and from there to his muscles and glands, producing tensions, preverbal "feelings," etc.,

8. Which Mr. B then begins to translate into words, according to *his* accustomed verbal patterns, and out of all the words *he* "thinks of"

9. he "selects," or abstracts certain ones, which he arranges in some fashion and then

Etc. Mr. B speaks, or acts, accordingly, thereby stimulating Mr. A—or somebody else—and so the process of communication goes on, and on —with complications, as indicated in the outline in the accompanying text.

FIG. 2. A DIAGRAM OF COMMUNICATION BY VERBAL SYMBOLS.

Schematic stage-by-stage summary of what goes on when Mr. A talks to Mr. B—the process of communication. The functions and possible disorders at each stage of the process are indicated more fully in Wendell Johnson's *People in quandaries,* copyright Harper and Bros., from which this figure is reproduced by permission of the publisher. See footnote.[2]

munication in schematic form, as shown in Figure 2. It becomes obvious in this illustration that communication involves a series of conversions from real things to concepts to words to sound waves to words to concepts to words and so on indefinitely, with a very real probability of distortion at every conversion or transition point. Even if deliberate deceit were controlled the problem of unintentional loss of contact through discrepancies in concepts and in the use of words would be enough to account for serious breakages in communication and consequent misunderstanding and strife. Here, then, are data in prolific quantities, with which we have done little in the way of serious analysis or explanation. The teacher is in a position to be most seriously victimized by difficulties in communication, too, since the educative process today is highly verbalized and tends to become more so as school populations grow.

Pictorial and symbolic representations. We are not so much concerned here with the artistic nature of picturization as with its role as a means of communication, for it is older than written language as we know it today, superseding even the use of cuneiform characters in ancient Assyria, Babylonia, or Persia. It is a potent source of influence in social life today, as illustrated by the use of cartoons, maps, diagrams, signs, and many other nonverbal forms. They have been with us so long we have almost ceased to see them, but they deliver their messages potently in some instances in spite of our lack of consciousness of what we are being told. Some of the most subtle forms of propaganda in the establishment of undemocratic values and concepts are to be found, of all places, in pictures in school readers, where maleness is made to appear better than femaleness, bigness better than smallness, wealth better than lack of wealth, and so on. The same thing is true of the stories told in the readers in many cases, as was so well shown by Geneva Kenway [3] in her value-analysis of the content of readers in use in the schools of Ithaca, New York.

Drawings of abnormal individuals have long been used as diagnostic materials because of the messages they contain for

[3] Geneva Kenway, *A study of the value content of elementary-school readers,* Ph.D. thesis (Ithaca, N. Y.: Cornell University, 1946).

those who are able to read them. Size, line and form, color, and subject or symbol all have significance for diagnosis of various conditions. A brief review of studies in this field is available for those interested in the subject.[4]

Bodily expression. For many years the word "attitude" was used almost exclusively with reference to bodily posture, and although the term has been so cluttered up with other usages that it has lost its meaning, we still learn more from each other about our intentions and feelings in many situations from bodily expressions than we do from language. Gestures are a language in themselves and have often served the purpose of language between individuals whose languages were not alike. Facial expressions are eloquent with communication, particularly between individuals who are familiar with each other, but they may mislead strangers. Feints, and other suggestive movements, are in the nature of incompleted or suspended acts that suggest intent, and they are often used to influence the behavior of others. A boxer tries by a feint to draw his opponent out of position. A bird trails one wing along the ground to draw an intruder away from her nest. Students are full of such expressive devices for suggesting study when they are mentally absent, or for showing distress at the mention of an assignment, when any ground they can gain is more than they know they should have. This, however, is only one aspect of the problem for teachers, for there are countless messages to be read from the postural and gestural language of students to guide a teacher in his work.

Reflex signs and involuntary indicators. In the preceding chapter some of the overt manifestations of emotions were discussed along with their relationship to the strength of the emotion and the relationship of emotional or energic alterations to the mental problems of individuals. These manifestations, which are of energic origin, have their expressive aspects, too, and deliver messages to those ready to read them. Blushing, dilation of the pupils of the eyes, perspiration, changes in breathing, arterial throbbing, involuntary swal-

[4] Robert W. White, "Interpretation of imaginative productions," in J. McV. Hunt, ed., *Personality and the behavior disorders* (New York: The Ronald Press Co., 1944).

lowing, pauses in speech, changes in tone of voice, stammering, gasping and many other similarly difficult-to-control reactions tell the observer that something critical is happening to the individual. These reactions are usually less amenable to deliberate misrepresentation than language or even posture and facial expression. The lie detector is simply a multiple measuring device for recording changes in some of these reactions, and it is a highly reliable instrument in the hands of those who understand the basis of its operation. People sometimes do learn to exhibit some of these behaviors, such as gasping, dramatic pauses in speech, and even changes in tone of voice, in order to produce deliberate effects; hence, they are not entirely without their difficulties in interpretation. In fact, one of our most interesting professions, dramatics, consists essentially of the cultivation of expressive behavior to the point that a completely realistic portrayal of any given role and experience is possible. This is a case in which the expressive aspect of behavior has been lifted out en masse and turned into an executive skill for vocational use, in which case it ceases to be truly expressive of the inner thoughts and feelings of the actor and becomes an expression of the inner life of someone else who is not present in person. This sort of thing is not uncommon among students either, many of whom, to some degree, assume roles and act parts other than their real selves.

403. *Inferences from the basic data.* There is no impressive body of research that has grown out of these basic facts. It is hard indeed to find any research that deals with the problem of expression, and particularly with the verbal modes. Nevertheless, inferences have been made from observations of human behavior, some of which have been sound and helpful, and some of which have been misleading.

The notion of attitudes. As suggested earlier, the word "attitude" at one time was used only with reference to bodily posture. After 1900, however, it came to be used with reference to mental predispositions, which created a serious difficulty. A bodily posture is part of an act *already begun,* even though it may get no farther than a posture. A mental predisposition is an inferred *forerunner* of an act. Note the two differentiating features carefully. The posture is not an inference, it is a fact. The body is actually on the way toward something. It is not a predisposition, it is an act in progression. The choice reaction has already taken place and this overt posture is what it has launched. On the other hand, the so-called mental attitude *is* an inference, not a fact, and it is supposed to be a stable *predisposition* that will make the individual take the same line of action every time he meets the object toward which the attitude is directed. Hence it is not the act itself, but something that *precedes* the act. To call both of these dissimilar things by the same name was indeed an invitation to confusion, and the subsequent literature on attitudes is full of confusion directly related to this point.

What are the observed facts about human expressive behavior? Fundamentally, this is what has been observed through human history. People tend to be consistent in their expressions. Those who express dislike for pickles on Monday, usually do so on other days. Those who are afraid of dogs tend to continue to be afraid of dogs. People who like each other tend to continue to like each other. There is a very apparent stability in the way we react to environmental objects. Hence, it was concluded by many, people must have fixed mental predispositions of a specific type for each and every object with which they have had experience. It was not unnatural, therefore, to extend the concept of attitude back from the actual behavioral posture to the mental operations that determine the overt activities. Such reasoning gave rise to definitions such as this: "An attitude is a mental and neural state of readiness, organized through experience, exerting a directive or dynamic influence upon the individual's response to all objects and situations with which it is related." [5] There are many other definitions, in which attitudes are said to be both dynamic and directive, both specific and general, both mental and muscular, both a degree of affect and an abstract neural response. The contradictions go on ad infinitum, because the basic inference was unsound.

In Chapter II it was pointed out that from the evaluative

[5] Gordon Allport, "Attitudes," in Carl Murchison, ed., *Handbook of social psychology* (Worcester, Mass.: Clark University Press, 1935), p. 798-844.

acts of individuals it was inferred that they had acquired mental content of some sort, which was guiding them in their choice reactions. The nature of those concepts is developed more extensively in Chapter VIII, and particularly in the discussion of the nature of meaning. In anticipation of that discussion it may be said here that what is expressed by an individual is not solely the product of those concepts, but is also determined by the specific situation. The illusion that specific reaction patterns were lodged in the conceptual patterns of the brain grew out of failure to observe everything about human behavior. One of the most significant facts, which has been overlooked in this connection, is that people have a tendency to get into ruts in their lives, so that they continue to face unchanging situations over and over again. Furthermore, their highly stabilized living routines result in stabilization of their concepts, since no new experiences are being encountered to change the concepts. It is inevitable that an organism that faces the same situation repeatedly without changing its conceptual patterns will evaluate that situation the same every time he meets it and will make the same choice reaction every time. This does not imply that his choice-making machinery has become fixed and inflexible at all. Quite the opposite is apparent when such a person is subjected to a significant change in the situation, for his choice reactions will instantly change in harmony with the new meanings to be found in the situation. So, too, will his behavior change even in the same situations, if in some manner his concepts are changed by the impact of some new experience that has implications for those stabilized situations.

The safer concept of expression. The old concept of attitude is misleading. The concept of the evaluative aspect of behavior is much more realistic and useful in diagnosing human behavior. In this case one very notable inference from expressive acts led to serious difficulties and must be abandoned. It is necessary to return to the observable facts and begin again. The fundamental thing to note is that the individual is expressing his feelings in the *specific situation,* not necessarily his feelings in some abstract or generalized version of that situation. Just what he is expressing may not be as easy to determine as it has been supposed. There is abundant evidence that a good deal of what is expressed in situations consists of what the individual feels he must express in order to further his best interests at the time. Schanck [6] demonstrated this rather neatly by measuring what he called the public and private attitudes of Methodists and Baptists toward certain religious beliefs. When studied as members of a group, 90 per cent of the Methodists expressed a belief in baptism by sprinkling only, but when approached on a man-to-man confidential basis, only 16 per cent of the same people expressed such a belief. This is only a sample of the kinds of measurements that were taken, and the discrepancies found between what they expressed in two different situations.

404. *Difficulties in reading expression.* Here, again, it is better to draw on the observed facts than to make hasty inferences. It was once assumed that verbally expressed "attitudes" were valid indicators of what people would actually do in real situations. Experience shows this to be an unsound generalization. A little analysis of expressive behavior compared with the directions actually taken in executive acts will reveal a number of pitfalls for the unobserving person. Here are some possible characteristics of expressive acts, including everything from language to reflex signs. The expression may tell how the person really feels, or it may be deceptive. In either case, it may be what it is through deliberate intent, or without intent on the part of the expresser. Again, in either case, it may deceive the expresser himself, or it may deceive the observer, or both.

It is a commonplace thing for one person to doubt the veracity of a verbal statement of another person, whether the latter is accused of deliberate misrepresentation or not. What has been suggested above is just the natural extension of this fact to all the other forms of expression.

The teacher cannot afford to be unaware of the difficulties involved in reading the expressions of others, for what

[6] R. L. Schanck, *A study of a community and its groups and institutions conceived as behaviors of individuals*, Psychological Monographs, No. 195 (1932).

amounts to clinical ability in this area can only be developed when these difficulties are known and avoided. There is much to be learned about those we teach and guide, which expressive behavior can tell us, when we learn how to penetrate the possible deceptions.

405. *The functions of expressive acts.* Since we are dealing here with both an organismic and a social function, it should be possible to identify the purposes served for the individual and those served in a society. For the individual the purposes are as follows.

Expression aids in perception. Evaluation of a situation depends on getting the best possible information about the situation. Static things are difficult to evaluate, because all true meanings are really functional meanings after all, as discussed more fully in Chapter VIII. Therefore, anything that makes the elements in a situation act makes them easier to perceive and to evaluate. Expression serves this purpose ideally, for our expressive acts serve as the stimuli to which other social objects respond. This is just what is meant by the term "social interaction," which is the continued interstimulation of people in social contact, leading to more complete mutual understanding, and finally to some sort of social structure and function. We make each other act by asking questions, expressing ideas, making gestures, making faces, drawing pictures, and by any or all of the possible forms of expressive behavior. Out of the ensuing reactions we perceive more and more meaning until the situation is clear, and our evaluation of it is complete.

Expression aids in changing a situation. The earlier reference to a statement made by Park [7] suggests the way in which people control each other through expressive acts. We express the intention of acting in the form of both bluffs and reliable indicators, and often these expressions are enough to make others do things that change a situation until it is more to our liking. In various ways we communicate intentions or ideas that break up barriers and dissipate the defenses of others so that we can proceed more easily to a state of adjustment through the attainment of a goal. Sometimes we convey ideas

[7] Park, *op. cit.,*

to others by language and other expressive behavior, as illustrated in discussion of a problem, or in teaching a class, and this changes the situation by changing the concepts of the hearers. In this category may be classified a great many phases of educational programs, which, reduced to fundamental terms, consist of the use of expressive behavior to convey ideas to others and to alter the behavior of those whose ideas are changed.

Expression aids in adjusting oneself to situations. The exclamation "I see!" is an expressive act that tells someone that you have adjusted to the situation by "getting" the idea he is presenting. A public speaker watches the faces of his listeners for signs that they have accepted his point of view and have adjusted to the situation he is presenting. The suitor watches for expressive indications that his lady is adjusting to his suit. The individual frequently stops the insistent pressure of an annoying conversationalist by giving expression, either honestly or deceptively, to the idea that he has accepted the proposed point of view.

Expression aids in the maintenance of mental health. Psychotherapy is described by Maslow and Mittelman [8] as a procedure by which the individual is helped to alter his emotional processes and his ideas of himself, his evaluation of others, and the manner in which he attacks his life problems. This is brought about, they say, through the development of insight produced in a permissive atmosphere when the patient is allowed and encouraged to talk freely. Rogers [9] says the counselor's duty is to provide a setting in which the patient can think through his problems and recognize the relationships in them. He says the "primary technique" is to get the patient to express his feelings freely until he obtains spontaneous insight and understanding. One of the clearest statements of this idea is that of Cameron.

This is the chief aim of therapeutic verbalization: to make social sharing possible under circumstances which permit the pa-

[8] A. H. Maslow and B. Mittelman, *Principles of abnormal psychology* (New York: Harper and Bros., 1941), Chap. XVII.

[9] Carl R. Rogers, *Counseling and psychotherapy* (Boston: Houghton Mifflin Co., 1942), Chap. II.

tient to determine his own attitudes and responses, without interference or direction, and to hear his own self-reactions to what he verbalizes.[10]

Cases are frequently reported similar to one cited by Maslow and Mittelman [11] in which the patient does all the talking, finds his solution, and leaves after expressing thanks to the therapist for helping him solve the problem. In this connection a recent article by Johnson is most pertinent, in which appears this opening statement:

Communication reduces to the event, both commonplace and awesome, of Mr. A. talking to Mr. B. And most commonplace and strange of all—possibly the most distinctively *human* occurrence to be found or imagined—is the case in which Mr. A. and Mr. B. are one and the same person: a man talking to himself.[12]

Tensions are spilled over by singing, dancing, shouting, even fighting, and in many other ways that are fundamentally expressive in nature. One of the best reasons for activity areas and periods in school is the function they serve in the expression of tensions and the promotion of good adjustment.

Expression as a social function. In a particularly clear and sound discussion of social attitudes, Bernard [13] suggests three functions, the last two of which he says are specifically social. The first is to enable the adjusting individual to become aware of his own technique, and therefore to control his later behavior. The second is to enable a competing organism to see what the other will do and thus to take measures to protect itself and further its own designs. The third is to let others know what we want them to think about us, so that they may be stopped in their aggressive acts and brought into cooperation with our own designs. These three functions are in no way different from those enumerated above where expression is viewed as a function of a single organism. The

[10] Norman Cameron, *The psychology of behavior disorders* (Boston: Houghton Mifflin Co., 1947), p. 578. Reprinted by permission.

[11] Maslow and Mittelman, *op. cit.*, p. 288.

[12] Wendell Johnson, "Speech and personality," in Lyman Bryson, ed., *The communication of ideas* (New York: Harper and Bros., 1948), p. 53.

[13] L. L. Bernard, "Attitudes, social," in *Encyclopedia of the social sciences* (New York: The Macmillan Co., 1930), Vol. 2, pp. 305-6.

similarity serves to emphasize an important fact, that no organism can be understood unless the whole social setting is taken into account, along with all the facts about it as an individual. There is no possibility of separating behavior into individual and social categories, or into psychology and sociology, any more than it is possible to separate the four aspects of behavior, but it is possible to observe behavior from various points of view as we are doing here. Unless there are countless ramifications and interrelationships discovered in these various approaches, however, one may suspect that one has fallen into an artificial and unproductive way of thinking.

406. *Conclusion.* Every act has its expressive aspect, as well as its evaluative, energic, and executive aspects. Those who can read these expressions accurately are able to understand the motives and the problems of others. Such a skill is invaluable to a teacher, counselor, or parent, whose roles require a penetrating insight into the mental processes of those with whom they work. The teacher can use the expressive behavior of students in many ways when its functions are known and appreciated. A great many teaching methods take advantage of this function. The teacher often gets the members of a group into a discussion through which each person not only conveys ideas to others and criticizes their ideas, but clarifies his own ideas by attempting to express them to the group. The act of expressing the sorts of ideas involved in education forces a person into a systematic organization of his thoughts and is one of the most profitable and stimulating experiences to be had. It may not be altogether painless while it is going on.

Questions for Review

1. Define the expressive aspect of behavior.
2. What relationship has this aspect to social life?
3. What is its relationship to clinical psychology?
4. Review the four categories of expressive behavior suggested in this chapter.
5. What are some of the causes of failure to communicate clearly in language?
6. What have ordinary sounds to do with the expressive aspect?
7. Give an illustration of a symbolic expressive act.

8. How do drawings help in diagnosing maladjustment? Why is this helpful?
9. Describe some reflex signs that have expressive value.
10. Contrast the term "attitude" with the term "expression" as used here.
11. What are some causes of difficulty with the attitude concept?
12. Why should the teacher learn to read expressions of all sorts?
13. How does expression aid the individual to adjust?
14. What is the role of expression in perception?
15. How does expression produce changes in situations?
16. Explain the use of expression in personal counseling.

SELECTED REFERENCES

Wendell Johnson, *People in quandaries* (New York: Harper and Bros., 1946), *passim*.

Kimball Young, ed., *Social attitudes* (New York: Henry Holt and Co., Inc., 1931), Chapter II.

CHAPTER V

OBSERVABLE ASPECTS OF BEHAVIOR, Concluded

D. THE EXECUTIVE ASPECT

501. *The nature of the executive aspect.* Heretofore we have dealt with evaluation and the making of choices, energy and its fluctuations, and overt expression of feelings and ideas. There remains the fact that when an organism moves to carry out its evaluations and behavior choices, it will do so with some sort of characteristic style or mode of operating, and the possible sorts of mode and style constitute the executive aspect of behavior. More specifically, the executive aspect consists of the skills, styles, and habits that characterize the behavior of an individual. We have here three quite distinct characteristics of behavior, each arising from its own causative factors, each playing its unique role in behavior, and each having its own usefulness to the teacher, parent, or counselor who understands what he is seeing. As in previous chapters, the point of beginning will be the actual facts about what is to be observed in ordinary behavior.

502. *The basic data.* These are commonplace, ordinary facts about the way things act. Everything has its characteristic mode of operating, but in this instance we shall see that some of the executive qualities are present only in human beings, although they are universally present at that level. It is possible to describe at least four kinds of executive characteristics in what we see going on.

Action patterns related to structure. Human beings maintain an erect posture, quadrupeds move on all fours, serpents crawl, and birds fly. These are so obvious as to make it seem ridiculous to mention them here, but they illustrate an important basic datum which reaches much farther than may be apparent at first. Less obvious, but not different in principle, is the fact that animals whose appendages swing from hinges have characteristic motions in water by which they swim, while those without appendages, whose bodies are capable of rhythmic flexible motions, swim by quite different activities. Animals with hands tend to use the hands to put food into the mouth, while those without hands tend to pick up their food with their mouths. Organisms with throats ingest their food through swallowing, which consists of a series of reflex and chainlike muscular reactions, while other organisms absorb their food by physical or chemical processes of a quite different sort.

The previous patterns were discussed on a generalized level, at which they are characteristic of all of the members of various species. There are also ways in which these functions differ within one species and within one variety. Among human beings there are interesting differences in the facial patterns that accompany various evaluative states. Landis [1] demonstrated effectively that there is no single pattern of facial expression that is typical of any emotional state, each person stabilizing on patterns of his own. So it is with the way in which people stand, walk, swim, swallow, laugh, cry, sneeze, snore, and do countless other similar things. So typical of the individual do many of these things become, that any one of them by itself is often enough to identify the person to those who are familiar with his personal characteristics.

As suggested in the title of this section, these patterns are undoubtedly closely related to the physiological structure of the individual and his species, but before attempting to identify the causative factors let us look at some of the other kinds of characteristics for the sake of contrast in both form and significance.

Specific acts that repeat without change. People have many routine, specific action patterns that always go off in the same way, under the same circumstances, with no evidence of thought control. These are acts in themselves, not modes of acting. They usually serve some minor adjustmental purpose for the individual, such as picking the teeth, greeting a friend,

[1] Carney Landis, "Studies of emotional reactions: II. General behavior and facial expression," *Journal of comparative psychology*, 4 (1924), 447-507.

and combing the hair, or draining off excess tension by drumming the fingers, wiping the brow, or wiggling the feet when seated in certain positions. There are hundreds of such acts in the repertoire of almost every person. The term "habit" fits them perfectly, although the term has not been used in connection with the same set of behaviors by all psychologists. There have been several interesting attempts to infer the causes of habits, but here again it may be better to wait until the other kinds of executive characteristics have been identified.

An element of quality. Some people do whatever they do in the most skillful manner, and others are awkward and inefficient. These differences are apparent not only between people, but within one person's behavior as from one time to another, and as between one activity and another. There are the Dempseys and Louis' of boxing, the Carusos and Rembrandts of artistic performance, and their counterparts in all forms of action in which skill can be identified, as well as those who perform at such a low level of quality that they spoil more than they produce. In between these extremes are all of us, at least with reference to something.

It is also a matter of observation that the level of a skill may change, and that continued practice in its use very often puts it on a higher level. This leads naturally to the search for sound inferences about what is responsible for such improvement, and how it may be cultivated deliberately. Methods of teaching such acts, obviously, should be built on the underlying processes, and this is discussed extensively in the chapters on learning. What is more important at this point, however, is that the teacher catch the full implication of the classificatory scheme that is being suggested here, and look beyond the more easily recognized illustrations of acts of skill to see what other acts belong in the same category. If there is a basic underlying explanation for changes in level of skill, which is a different story from that which underlies changes in conceptual knowledge, then it becomes important to identify properly all the objectives of education that are really skills and to avoid confusing them with objectives of a different psychological nature.

An illustration of the foregoing confusion is to be found in the memorization and subsequent repetition of verbal knowledge, such as facts. An experience with a given fact can result in several things, one of which is the memorization of the verbal symbol, and another of quite different nature is the acquisition of a conceptual meaning. The two are not sufficiently interdependent to guarantee that both will happen. It depends on how the stage for the learning experience is set. Memorization of symbols is not a conceptual process, it is a skill closely tied to muscular performance and is far more amenable to skill-producing routines than to concept-producing techniques.

With this excursion into teaching problems, it is suggested the teacher analyze many kinds of human behavior to see how they should be classified and hence what is inferred for methods of teaching in connection with such acts. In the intellectual realm are such things as a store of facts that can be recited. For example, formulas in accounting or in mathematical problems, economic facts related to problems in commerce, political facts involved in group relationships, and the like. (An understanding of the functional interrelationships of the facts is something else.) In the realm of social-emotional skills involved in self-control and in social interaction are manners and customs acquired and brought to various levels of proficiency, systematized and stabilized expressions that have social significance, and personal carriage and grooming. Certain aspects of what is called maturity are nothing more than a given level of skill in the mastery of these activities.

In the area of neuro-muscular skills are many vocational, recreational, and miscellaneous activities, which make up the major portion of what one does. When one makes a thorough inventory of human behavior it becomes obvious that a considerable portion of it is of an executive nature and is amenable to the laws upon which habits and skills rest.

An element of style. There is a little of this in the behavior of the highest animals, but nothing comparable with what is to be found in man. An individual tends to exhibit consistently certain characteristics that pervade all his behavior and color everything he does. We are not concerned here with specific *acts*, as in the case of habits, but with *characteristics* of acts. Furthermore, we are not concerned with the characteristic of *quality*, but with the characteristic of *style*. Careful observation will also reveal another very important fact in understanding this phenomenon. Each kind of style that can be identified is nothing but a reflection of some characteristic of the interpersonal relationships in a society, or the interrelationships between individuals and their environments. This is in part a matter of inference and should be deferred until we have finished listing the observable facts, but on the other hand certain facts about the relationships between people and the objects with which they have interaction must also be observed in this connection, and this is a good time to mention them. The latter may well come first.

Some people are male and some female, some are bosses and some are servants, some are leaders and some are followers, some are mature and some are immature, some dominate and some are dominated, some achieve their ends by dominantly motor acts and some by dominantly mental acts, and so on. These are realities easily identified in social groups. They are fundamental roles present in all societies because they seem to depend on the structure and function of both individuals and societies. These roles have been generalized as characteristics of social organization. Each of them exists on a continuum every part of which can be illustrated by actual people. Extreme maleness to extreme femaleness, extreme infancy to extreme maturity, extreme motorness to extreme mentalness, all of them being easily imaginable in terms of real human beings.

Returning now to individuals as such, a little observation soon shows that every person develops his own characteristic sets of style patterns and soon becomes known by them because of their stability. They are spoken of as his *traits*, and they are given names by psychologists, as, for example, masculinity or femininity, introversion or extroversion, ascendance or submission, and in one case, withdrawal, which seems to have no generally accepted opposite to indicate active contact with reality. It is a little difficult in this discussion to say much about the terminology now in use in the field, because those who have written on these problems have not in general been sufficiently penetrating in their analyses of what they are dealing with to have put their terminology into logical consistency with all the phenomena involved in the problem. At any rate, we have illustrated the underlying facts and indicated something of the ways in which these facts influence and pattern the behavior of individuals, and how it might be possible to develop a consistent list of traits. It is time now to see what inferences have been drawn from the foregoing facts, and what explanations are available upon which to erect useful principles of teaching and counseling.

503. *Inferences from the basic data.* Within this aspect of behavior there is relatively little scientific evidence to support the inferences that have been made. The area has been subjected to considerable speculation, and the hypothetical structures have come and gone freely in the past. Nevertheless, there are some evidences that, together with the support of logical consistency between actual behavior and some cautious generalizations, offer the possibility of setting up analyses of value to the teacher.

Structural determinants of behavior. As suggested earlier, people do many things simply because they are constructed as they are. Snoring is largely due to the structure of the throat. A smile is what it is because of the way the muscles of the face are arranged. We walk upright because we are so constructed that erect posture is almost forced upon us. This principle operates in everything in nature from rocks to geniuses. Many things we do are far more logically explained in this manner than through an esoteric and impenetrable notion like instinct. The principle of parsimony, so important in science, suggests that circumstances be explained first in as simple a way as is consistent with all the facts, before resorting to more complicated or mysterious explanations. This is a point that need not be pursued further here, but which can well be considered seriously by any student of human nature.

Generally speaking, this type of executive behavior is not very much involved in the work of a teacher or counselor, except as an explanatory principle that helps in the understanding of behavior. An important reason for bringing it into this discussion, aside from the value of making the discussion complete, is to show by contrast that some executive behaviors are much more amenable to educative influences than others, and to suggest a principle for determining which is which. Forms of behavior that are dictated by structure are not among the most teachable.

The nature of habits. Since we learned long ago that the structure of every act is determined by some physiological or psychological control within the individual, and that every modification of behavior is a result of experience obtained in adjustive behavior, an explanation of habit should be sought in the same way. To put it simply it is this. Man has a vast and flexible potential in the central nervous system and the reflexes, within which are easily established somewhat automatic pathways between a given type of sensation and an organized and purposive motor response. All motor skills are established on the basis of this system. In the daily pursuit of adjustment, the individual uses countless little acts of a specific type, some of which prove to be more productive than others. The more productive ones tend to be repeated frequently, and under conditions in which they produce satisfaction. This is all that is required for their rather thorough establishment as learned reactions, tied closely to specific cues. Thus they come into play automatically, as it were, whenever the cue upon which they depend is present. Sometimes they persist after their usefulness is ended, but rarely do they persist if circumstances change so that they produce annoying effects instead of satisfying ones.

Since habits are learned through function, rather than through structure, as in the case of characteristics discussed just above, they may be influenced by deliberate effort to change them, and in their initial formation they may often be directed into desired channels. Habits often appear to be hard to change, because they are continually being reinforced by the effects they produce, which keeps the individual from going through the labor of hunting for other actions that produce the same effects. If a specific habit is consistently prevented from occurring, and a substitute activity consistently used with satisfaction, the old habit will disappear and a new one take its place.

Education is sometimes concerned with specific habits, but on the whole they are of minor importance to a teacher. The most significant behavior patterns of an executive type are the skills and traits.

The nature of skills. The same neuro-muscular structure that makes habits possible is also responsible for skills. There are some additional implications however, growing out of the relative *similarity* of habits in individuals, as compared to the relative *dissimilarity* of skills in individuals. A habit seems to serve its purpose regardless of the level of skill involved in its performance, and possibly for that reason skill has never seemed to be a matter of importance in the kinds of acts that are here classified as habits. Now that attention is shifted from an act to its level of quality, however, and it is observed how different individuals are in the quality of their performance, it seems necessary to infer for skills something very much like that we have inferred for differences in the quality of evaluative behavior, namely, a capacity to develop skill. The inference is also that this capacity is different from the capacity to evaluate. The latter is a conceptual activity, and the former is a motor activity. They grow out of different kinds of capacity. The capacity to develop motor skills seems to depend on the facility with which the individual can develop neuro-muscular coordination, and this is certainly a function of the cerebellum and the nerves that regulate motor activity, rather than a function of the cerebrum and the associational areas of the brain. The word aptitude comes nearer to representing a potentiality for skill than does the word intelligence, although aptitude is generally used to include also the readiness of an individual to develop an interest in an ability along with the readiness to develop proficiency. The differences in skill between individuals also suggests that people differ in the *capacities* to develop skills, and that some will develop them much more easily than others. The relative levels of skill in different kinds of acts within the same individual also suggest that one does not have a uniform level of capacity for all *kinds* of performance, and that there will be some kinds of things he can learn to do better than others. These inferences have given rise to the development of a wide variety of tests designed to measure special abilities, the best and most modern treatment of which is Cronbach's.[2] His treatment is divided into spatial and perceptual abilities, psychomotor abilities, mechanical knowledge, artistic abilities, and sensory abilities. Except for the inclusion of something on comprehension and reasoning under the discussion of mechanical knowledge, his classifications are in agreement with the thesis that skills are based on capacities different from those on which conceptual and analytical abilities rest. The inclusion of analytical items in these aptitude tests does not necessarily contradict the thesis, for the tests are constructed with the practical objective of helping the counselor and are not limited to non-analytical activities.

Observation that individuals frequently raise their levels of skill led long ago to the recognition of a learning function related to practice. Practice indiscriminately applied to almost everything in the curriculum and, without control of other vital elements involved in learning, may have been due to premature formulation of laws of learning in which the important differences between various types of learning were not recognized. Buswell[3] seems to be one of the few contemporary psychologists to have recognized the significance of these differences in teaching and learning, and his outline is still the most complete and constructive formulation from the educator's point of view. A more recent text by Kingsley[4] contains approximately 220 pages devoted to discussion of learning in seven forms, including motor skills. Some of the early experiments in motor learning were compiled by Pyle[5] in a text now almost forgotten, but still useful from this point of view. One of the best applications of research to the class-

[2] Lee J. Cronbach, *Essentials of psychological testing* (New York: Harper and Bros., 1949), Chap. 10.

[3] Guy T. Buswell, *Outline of educational psychology*, Students Outline Series (New York: Longmans, Green and Co., Inc., 1939).

[4] Howard L. Kingsley, *The nature and conditions of learning* (New York: Prentice-Hall, Inc., 1946), Part IV.

[5] William H. Pyle, *The psychology of learning* (Rev. ed.; Baltimore: Warwick and York, Inc., 1928).

room, however, is Reed's,[6] in which specific recognition of the types of learning is given by treating learning in relation to the individual subjects in the curriculum. In the area of skills he has applications to language and typewriting, for the secondary schools.

The learning of motor skills is reserved for treatment later, the purpose of this section having been accomplished if motor acts have been given their proper relationship to the rest of behavior.

The nature and origin of traits. In enumerating the observable facts of behavior in the nature of style, it was pointed out that each of the several patterns of style is the counterpart of some natural feature of human beings or of their interaction with each other and with the objects of reality around them. In other words, they are directly related to relative roles in interrelationships. When one organism is a male, the other must be a female for certain functions. When one is a leader there must be another who is a follower. If one is aggressive there must be one who is submissive. None of these patterns has any meaning by itself. Each is relative to some other degree of intensity of the characteristics in another individual. In other words, they are comparative differences on one continuum. The comparisons are always interpersonal.

In looking for the origin and meaning of such traits it must be remembered that the relativity of these patterns in individuals is observable by others only because the individuals themselves have come to possess such traits and to show them consistently in their behavior. Therefore it is inferred that something of an evaluative nature has gone on within each individual concerning himself, and his comparability to others. This implies a consciousness of self, and a tendency to examine the self in terms of the roles one perceives in other individuals, and in one's relationships with the real world around him. It is assumed, then, that the traits which finally emerge in an individual, do so because the individual discovers that he is able to function most effectively in his

[6] Homer B. Reed, *Psychology and teaching of secondary-school subjects* (New York: Prentice-Hall, Inc., 1939).

relationships with other people and things by doing so in such a manner.

There is widespread acceptance of this position today. In modern times it has had its most vigorous early exposition in the ego concept of Freud [7] from whom it has been taken over in various versions by psychiatry, clinical psychology, and social psychology, among other disciplines. Current versions of it are to be found in books by Sherif and Cantril,[8] Snygg and Combs,[9] and Murphy.[10] In the last are two significant statements, which suggest the essence of this self-evaluation. "No one can enhance or defend himself without encroaching upon the self-enhancement and self-defense of others." "In our culture, the concept of competitive self-enhancement is clear in almost all normal children by the age of three or four." This recognizes clearly the relativity of the roles upon which traits are based.

In later chapters on motivation and on learning the process of formation of the concepts involved in this development are discussed. We have gone far enough at this point to show the significance of traits in the executive aspect of behavior, and to indicate what information about the individual can be obtained from observing them. These are the fundamental points. Traits do not reveal the motives of an individual. They tell the observer the manner in which a person will do whatever he sets out to do, but not what he will set out to do. Their message is confined to the style of operation of the individual. On the other hand, they are the only characteristics of behavior that give a clear picture of the way in which the individual has evaluated himself in comparison with others. They are not subject to efforts to deceive to any extent. They show with reality what relative position on the various scales of interpersonal relationships the individual has had to take

[7] For the clearest statement of Freud's conceptual scheme, see A. A. Brill, *The basic writings of Sigmund Freud* (New York: Random House, Inc., 1938), pp. 3-32.

[8] Muzafer Sherif and Hadley Cantril, *The psychology of ego-involvement* (New York: John Wiley and Sons, Inc., 1947).

[9] Donald Snygg and Arthur W. Combs, *Individual behavior* (New York: Harper and Bros., 1949).

[10] Gardner Murphy, *Personality* (New York: Harper and Bros., 1947). See especially Chap. 22.

in order to make the best adjustments and to satisfy his needs optimally. This does not mean that a naïve person can make a valid diagnosis of one's self-evaluations from watching one's style of operation. Aggression does not mean that the aggressor feels himself to be a superior person at all. It is frequently, if not usually, a style adopted to compensate for the opposite feeling. With a little training in the fundamentals of ego-centered problems, however, one can begin to understand what is being manifested in the behavior of students and children by their traits. Note in the following brief case how the beginning of a trait and a struggle to overcome it are illustrated.

Case 1

Beginning of a Trait

Until I was twelve I lived in New York City. We necessarily lived in rather a poor district since my father was a social worker in the settlement house in which we lived. I was not allowed to play in the streets with the neighborhood "street kids" and because of that my only playmates were those I met in school. My school was not very near my home and most of the children did not live very near either, so I did not have a very good opportunity to meet other children and play with them. When we moved to a small city, I was quite shy and unsure. I felt ill at ease and did not mix in readily with the other children. This made me feel very unhappy as I felt the need of having friends very much. I was even so shy as to be afraid to say "hello" to some acquaintances whom I met in school and in the street. I realized what was wrong and that there was no reason for my feeling this way and I resolved to "snap out of it." I put forth a very conscious and direct effort to overcome the barrier. I forced myself to say "hello" to all my acquaintances when I met them, even if they were not the first to speak. I made a very conscious effort to put myself into groups in school. I forced myself to volunteer in class, and I joined various organizations in school. All of this required a great deal of effort at first and a strong drive. But as time went on I found it getting much easier. I did not have to drive myself quite so hard and I was getting more response and recognition from the other children. From then on I became more sure of myself through experience.

504. *Conclusion.* Executive aspects of behavior are those characteristics of style or mode of operation that stabilize through sensory-motor learning or through self-appraisal and adjustment to roles in interpersonal relationships. Habits tell us nothing about the motives of people. They tell us only that whenever the individual does something that has come to be a habit to him, he will do it automatically, in the same way, without giving it thought. In these acts he will probably not change much. Skills tell us nothing about the motives of people. They tell us how *well* the individual is able to do whatever he does, and this is extremely important in many kinds of jobs and many activities. For the teacher, the measurement of skill is an important part of the whole evaluation process in the encouragement of learning. Traits tell nothing about *what* an individual will try to do, but they tell us much about the *manner* in which he will try to do it. He may do things in a feminine, aggressive, extravertive, childish manner, or in a masculine, submissive, introvertive, and mature manner, or in any one of numerous other possible combinations of traits. Whatever his traits, it is also possible to work back from them to his self-evaluation, a very important part of the work of a counselor and parent, and an avenue to understanding of the inner feelings of an individual about himself, which the teacher should use in guiding his experiences and helping him make a good adjustment in school.

QUESTIONS FOR REVIEW

1. Behavior is said to have four aspects. What is the principle characteristic of each?
2. In which of the four aspects of behavior would you include such characteristics as habits and traits? Why?
3. Define habit.
4. What is the relationship between habits and evaluative action in determining ways of acting?
5. Define the executive aspect of behavior.
6. What are the four fundamental kinds of executive characteristics mentioned in this chapter?
7. What has structure to do with executive skills and characteristics?

8. In what ways are structure and instinct confused?
9. What uses of the term habit create confusion with such acts as thinking, perception, and conception?
10. What is the basic nature of skill?
11. Why is skill listed as an executive characteristic?
12. What can be learned about a person's motives from observing his executive acts?
13. What is the difference between executive and evaluative reactions?
14. What is to be learned from observation of executive characteristics?
15. Is the term "intelligence," or the term "aptitude," more nearly related to executive actions? Why?
16. What is a trait? How does it form?
17. In what way are all traits related to each other?
18. What does extraversion indicate about an individual's past experience? Try the same exercise with masculinity, aggression, and babyish acts.

Selected Reference

Harold E. Jones, *Development in adolescence* (New York: Appleton-Century-Crofts, Inc., 1943), Chapter X.

Class Exercises on the Four Aspects of Behavior

Things To Do in Class

1. Read aloud some selections from *Psychology through Literature,* An Anthology, Oxford University Press, 1943. Have the class members identify examples of each of the aspects of behavior as they appear in the reading.

Things To Do outside Class

1. Select a novel or biography in which a character is described skillfully and thoroughly. Become well acquainted with the character and then pick out selections as follows:

   A. One or more incidents in which the evaluative aspect of behavior is clearly illustrated.
   B. One or more incidents in which the expressive aspect of behavior is clearly illustrated.
   C. One or more incidents in which the energic aspect of behavior is clearly illustrated.

D. One or more incidents in which the executive aspect of
behavior is clearly illustrated.

Copy these excerpts in typewritten form, underlining or otherwise indicating the parts you think most pointedly illustrate the
aspect of behavior involved. Give a full bibliographical listing
for the book you select, including author, title, publisher, length,
copyright date, etc. You need not read the whole book, only
enough to be sure you are clear in your understanding of the way
the character fits into this problem. The reports may be brought
to class on an agreed date, for open discussion, or may be exchanged between students, for criticism. In the latter case it is
best to omit the name of the student who wrote the report, using
an identifying number instead.

CHAPTER VI

PURPOSIVE TRENDS IN OBSERVABLE BEHAVIOR

601. *Behavior is adjustive.* When Caesar said "Veni, vidi, vici," he was using a formula which, with variations, describes all human behavior. "I came" says he met a situation. "I saw" says he examined the situation and found its meaning and its possibilities. "I conquered" announces his satisfactory mastery of the situation. Everyone is continually "coming" to situations. Almost every human act is performed as a reaction to some situation. A person meets a situation when he glances out of the window and sees rain falling. His response may be no more than a grunt. A man meets a situation when he is ordered by a bandit to throw up his hands. The possible kinds of situations are limitless.

Throughout the preceding chapters there are hints and allusions to the purposive nature of behavior. The two concepts belong together, as we shall see. To say that behavior is *adjustive* is to say that it serves the purpose of bringing the individual to a state of adjustment. This is done by removing a disturbing stimulus, by altering the self so that the stimulus is no longer disturbing, or by draining off the muscular tensions produced through an unadjusted situation. The last is not a satisfactory solution, but it often brings something approaching adjustment temporarily. To say that behavior is *purposive* means that the choice reactions of the individual go as they do because the individual has "learned" through experience that adjustment may be had by so acting.

This dual concept is so important in understanding both adjustment and its by-product learning that it has come to occupy the central place in explanations of behavior. Learning has sometimes been treated as the explanation of all kinds of behavior. It has so dominated the attention of parents and teachers in general that they have been largely unaware of the problem of adjustment. Even when personnel problems have been brought to the fore, they have frequently been regarded as having no special relationship to the learning process. The facts are somewhat to the contrary. For our primary data we refer again to the actual behavior of individuals.

602. *The way people act.* Four kinds of significant things may be seen taking place in the behavior of any organism, but they are seen in their most complete form in people.

An individual acts only when he is disturbed. The intimate relationship between each disturbing stimulus and the way the individual meets that disturbance is lost in the complexity of human behavior, although it operates there as a basic principle. It is more apparent in its simple forms in lower animals, and it is apparent in human beings in some simple situations. A tropismic reaction is a response to a single disturbing stimulus, and the reaction always ends when the stimulus has been removed. A drowsy dog stirs when the fine hairs within his paws are moved, and settles down when the irritation is removed. A person becomes restless when he is hungry, and his restlessness ends when he is fed. Many stimuli are not as simple as these, and their disturbing effects are not as easily removed, but they cease to be effective when they have been cared for. In the meantime many other stimuli have disturbed an individual, so that he is in a constant state of activity, but the continuity is maintained by a changing array of disturbances, not by any inner will to be active. The most satisfied people in the world are the idlers who are content to lie in the shade in a state of near-perfect adjustment. The producers are unadjusted. These are two of the significant facts, then. *The individual acts only when he is disturbed,* and *he ceases acting when he has overcome the disturbance.*

The third significant fact to be observed is that *sometimes—not always—the individual is changed while he is overcoming the disturbance.* He may discover a new way of meeting the problem. His preferences may change. He may become somewhat more skillful in doing the thing required to restore adjustment. When this happens the fourth fact becomes apparent. *Thereafter, he may not be disturbed by things that formerly disturbed him, or he may be disturbed by things that*

*did not formerly disturb him, or he may handle his disturb-
ances in new ways,* or all of these interesting possibilities may
show up together. So far nothing has been explained. Reference has only been made to the actual facts available to anyone who will take the trouble to watch the behavior of others.
This sort of observation should be one of the most absorbing
occupations of a teacher or parent. One conclusion is inescapable, however, that learning is not the primary concern of any
organism. Adjustment is the primary business, and sometimes
learning takes place while adjustment is being sought.

603. *The purposive-adjustmental point of view.* To get
to the point as briefly as possible, and to acknowledge those
who have done more than any others to establish the basic
concepts, reference will be made primarily to the contributions of two men, Tolman in the case of purposive behavior,
and Cannon in the case of the adjustive or homeostatic
concept.

Purposive behaviorism. Committed to the use of objective
observation and working largely with rats, Tolman has
thrown more light on human behavior than many of those
who have worked solely with human beings. His text on
purposive behavior is one of the landmarks in the field, which
was too far ahead of its time for ready acceptance. Within
the first chapter he sketches the essentials of his point of view,
which are represented here only by his statement concerning
the element of purpose, and the summary:

Behavior as behavior, that is, as molar, *is* purposive and *is*
cognitive. These purposes and cognitions are of its immediate
descriptive warp and woof. It, no doubt, is strictly and completely
dependent upon an underlying manifold of physics and chemistry,
but initially and as a matter of first identification, behavior as behavior reeks of purpose and of cognition. And such purposes and
such cognitions are just as evident, as we shall see later, if this
behavior be that of a rat as if it be that of a human being.[1]

· · · · ·

Behavior, as such, is a molar phenomenon as contrasted with
the molecular phenomena which constitute its underlying physi-

[1] Edward C. Tolman, *Purposive behavior in animals and men* (New York:
Appleton-Century-Crofts, Inc., 1932), p. 12.

ology. And, as a molar phenomenon, behavior's immediate descriptive properties appear to be those of: getting to or from goal-objects by selecting certain means-object-routes as against others and by exhibiting specific patterns of commerces with these selected means-objects. But these descriptions in terms of gettings to or from, selections of routes and patterns of commerces-with imply and define immediate, immanent purpose and cognition aspects in the behavior. These two aspects of behavior are, however, but objectively and functionally defined entities. They are implicit in the facts of behavior docility. They are defined neither in the last analysis, nor in the first instance, by introspection. They are envisaged as readily in the behavior-acts of the cat and of the rat as in the more refined speech reactions of man. Such purposes and cognitions, such docility, are, obviously, functions of the organism as a whole. Lastly, it has also been pointed out that there are two other classes of behavior-determinants in addition to the immanent determinants, viz., capacities and behavior-adjustments. These also intervene in the equation between stimuli and initiating physiological states on the one side and behavior on the other.[2]

His points, then, are eight. Behavior is a *molar* phenomenon, the whole organism is doing it and it can only be understood when all that the whole organism is doing is taken into account. Behavior is *purposive*. Behavior is *cognitive,* the organism perceiving what is going on and the perception registering. Behavior involves getting to and from certain preferred *things,* by certain preferred *paths,* and using those things in certain defined *ways.* Behavior reveals *capacities* that make the acquisition of these characteristics possible, and it reveals *docility,* or the power to change the patterns of reaction.

The point of view is documented with laboratory experiments that give it full support. Tolman, unfortunately, coined new terms for almost all of his excellent concepts, and thereby increased greatly the difficulty of reading his material by those with other backgrounds. Two of his terms might be discussed briefly here. The preferred *things* or *goal-objects* should be conceived not merely as actual objects, such as the rat seems to look for when he is hungry, but also as states or conditions equivalent to goals of all kinds. People move toward the acquisition of kind words, or the satisfaction involved in a feeling of achievement, just as a laboratory animal moves toward a pellet of food. Also his *means-object-routes* are not confined to actual paths in a maze, but must be made to include any process or experience through which a person obtains his goal. In Chapter VIII is a discussion of the nature of meaning, which will help to clarify this matter; therefore, at this point, it is merely suggested that everything we contact is really a process that does something to us, not just a static object in the environment. A book is a process made up of light waves in such patterns that they deliver messages to us from the pages and take us through various kinds of experiences. From a functional point of view the book is equivalent to those experiences, it is whatever it does to us. Hence it qualifies as a means-object-route or path, which leads to whatever the experience produces for us. Relieved of some of the austerity of its terms, Tolman's point of view is ideally suited to the work of a teacher, for it fits smoothly as an interpretation of what is happening in human adjustment and learning. With the addition of the concepts of adjustment and homeostasis we will have a relatively practical and sound conceptual framework.

Adjustment and homeostasis. Fundamentally a physiologist, Walter Cannon made a major contribution to the understanding of the relationship between activity and disturbances which upset the equilibrium of an animal. In his very significant *Wisdom of the Body* he develops the concept of homeostasis to deal more adequately with behavior at the organismic level which resembles very closely the bodily tendency to achieve equilibria. He credits Richet in Paris with an early recognition of the stability of the body.

The living being is stable. It must be so in order not to be destroyed, dissolved or disintegrated by the colossal forces, often adverse, which surround it. By an apparent contradiction it maintains its stability only if it is excitable and capable of modifying itself according to external stimuli and adjusting its responses to the stimulation. In a sense it is stable because it is modifiable—

the slight instability is the necessary condition for the true stability of the organism.[3]

In his own introduction he explains the concept of homeostasis as follows:

The constant conditions which are maintained in the body might be termed *equilibria*. That word, however, has come to have fairly exact meaning as applied to relatively simple physiochemical states, in closed systems, where known forces are balanced. The coordinated physiological processes which maintain most of the steady states in the organism are so complex and so peculiar to living beings—involving, as they may, the brain and nerves, the heart, lungs, kidneys and spleen, all working cooperatively—that I have suggested a special designation for the states, *homeostasis*. The word does not imply something set and immobile, a stagnation. It means a condition—a condition which may vary, but which is relatively constant.

It seems not impossible that the means employed by the more highly evolved animals for preserving uniform and stable their internal economy (i.e., for preserving homeostasis) may present some general principles for the establishment, regulation and control of steady states, that would be suggestive for other kinds of organization—even social and industrial—which suffer from distressing perturbations. Perhaps a comparative study would show that every complex organization must have more or less effective self-righting adjustments in order to prevent a check on its functions or a rapid disintegration of its parts when it is subjected to stress.[4]

Cannon's work is documented fully with research conducted at Harvard. In various chapters he applies the concept to blood sugar, blood proteins, blood fat, blood calcium, neutrality in the blood, salt content of the blood, water content of the blood, and body temperature. It is inevitable that it will be applied to the psychological behavior of an organism, since it offers the best explanation of what seems to be happening.

[3] Charles Richet, *Dictionnaire de physiologie* (Paris, 1900), Vol. IV, p. 72.
[4] Walter B. Cannon, *The wisdom of the body* (New York: W. W. Norton and Co., Inc., 1932, 1939), pp. 24-25. Reproduced by permission of the publishers.

An individual is in reality the nucleus of a closed system, the boundaries of which extend out as far as the physical and social forces upon which his conceptual world depends. The system exists in his conceptual structure, and the forces and stresses in it are as real and as definitely interrelated in his struggle for stability as if the boundaries of his universe could be objectively described. Lewin has developed this concept better than anyone else in his discussion of life-space.[5] The system is subject to change through conceptual learning, particularly in the light of any experience that alters the individual's concepts of himself, or his social relationships, but within that changing system he exemplifies perfectly the concept of homeostasis in his constant movement toward goals that are attractive because they represent fulfillment of conditions that satisfy needs.

604. *Adjustment and its changing basis.* The application of the concept of homeostasis to all forms of behavior is inevitable and necessary, in spite of some cautions to the contrary.[6] In the application, however, it is necessary to show why it appears that human beings may not be moving toward a state of equilibrium in some of the things they do, as illustrated by their strivings for ideals and their seeming willingness to seek conditions of unadjustment.

Symonds[7] has recently given emphasis to the idea that adjustment is really equal to survival on the biological level, and that when this concept is raised to the psychological level it may be spoken of as need-fulfillment. By his logic, any action that fulfills a need is thus an act of survival or adjustment, even with reference to the personal needs that give rise to ideals and ambitions projected into the future.

Survival as a concept is not limited to a constant or single level of operation. In its simplest form it may be used to refer to the provision of essentials for life. When it is so used it is

[5] Kurt Lewin, *Principles of topological psychology* (New York: McGraw-Hill Book Co., Inc., 1936).
[6] John M. Fletcher, "Homeostasis as an explanatory principle in psychology," *Psychological review*, 49 (January, 1942), 80-87.
[7] P. M. Symonds, *The dynamics of human adjustment* (New York: D. Appleton-Century Co., Inc., 1946), Chap. 2.

based on a definition of life as the maintenance of metabolic processes. In this case survival requires the constant furnishing of food and water, with appropriate amounts of rest and the elimination of wastes. The life spoken of here is a vegetative thing in which the human being seems to differ in no important respect from any other animal or plant. Insofar as there is consciousness associated with this type of life it is primarily concerned with immediately disturbing stimuli from the visceral region or from the muscles. In an embryo there is surely no consciousness at all. There is little if any meaning or knowledge involved in such survival. The plant sucks in its food from the environment. The animal usually prowls around until it finds food or water, or until it reaches a spot appropriate for elimination or rest. The human being does the same thing if he has no higher mental life. When these irritations are quieted there is no more activity until the same needs are again active.

With his superior brain and his conceptual abilities, however, man develops more than a one-dimensional life. He therefore has more than one kind of survival to be concerned with. In addition to physical survival of an immediate nature, he is concerned with social survival, and with ego or self survival. The minimal essentials for survival in these areas may not be so neatly described as for the physical area. They depend on what this new life has come to be for the individual. Each person conceives of his social life in a manner that is unique to himself. What he needs to survive depends on what he is trying to preserve. Hence it follows that an effort to maintain a certain level of prestige in a club is just as literally adjustment for survival as is any act of eating.

This sort of life elaborates in terms of what is presently needed to survive, and it also takes on a time extension and begins to project itself into the future. It is often true that a different social life is envisioned for the future, one that requires the addition of something to what is now possessed. In that case the individual makes adjustmental moves that have a futuristic aim, that will bring about a certain state of affairs later on. If this state of affairs is considered by the individual to be critical to his survival at that later time, and this is surely the case in spite of the fact that his aims may go beyond minimal requirements for bare survival just as they do in the matter of eating, then this type of seeking for self-development, or self-fulfillment, or realization, or whatever it may be called, is at heart an adjustmental move and has a strong survival value, but it is not simple biological survival any longer. Following this line of thought it may be argued that all ambitions and ideals represent levels or qualities of life according to the conceptual patterns of the individuals who hold them, and therefore survival in any adequate sense depends on the achievement of what is desired.

Now it must be noted that those ideals and future ambitions that are able to arouse an individual and make him work for a future adjustment are not ordinarily apparent to an observer, and it is easy to overlook their presence in the acting individual. Their effect on him is to make him do things that would seem, on the basis of purely objective observation, to lead him into unadjustment rather than adjustment. For example, he might leave a comfortable parental home and go away to school where he will be insecure, will have to work hard, will sacrifice many comforts, and face numerous trying experiences. On the surface it appears that he is contradicting the thesis that all behavior leads toward adjustment. Actually, he is moving toward an adjustment that is conceived by him in the future, and he is really disturbed by a need that is in no way connected with his present situation, but is wholly couched in his conceptualized future. He is able to accept a present state of disturbance because the futuristic need is more powerful and more disturbing than the need for immediate adjustment.

All such self-developing behavior is thus a response to important needs. If those needs were ever satisfied, regardless of the level of the life conceived by the individual, the behavior would cease and the person would be quiet and content. The fact that few if any persons ever become quiet and content does not contradict this thought, but it does furnish an illustration or evidence of the fact that the patterns of need in social and ego levels of living become comprehensive and complex to the point where it is almost literally impossible that all of them could be satisfied at any given time.

Animals versus men. One of the striking differences between animals and men is in the nature of the cycle of adjustment. It begins with a disturbance, continues with a search for what is needed, and ends with acquisition of the need and satisfaction of the drive. The animal is then ready for another disturbing stimulus, having returned to the same base from which he was disturbed earlier. An animal changes very little indeed from early life until death.

With men the cycle rarely returns to the base from which the individual was disturbed earlier. It is more like a spiral. There is the disturbance, which precipitates the search for satisfaction. It is followed by a search in which cognitive factors are always gathering up new conceptual content and changing the organism so that the base upon which adjustment was had earlier is no longer adequate for adjustment. Through the formation of ideals, broader concepts of value, newer ideas of what is good enough and not good enough, the old basis of adjustment may be forever rendered ineffective. Adjustment is attained, but not at the same level as before. A new base is established, and the movement has been like the first loop in a spiral, which can go on as long as man continues to change through experience. It is primarily the nervous centers, which make abstraction and generalization possible, that are responsible for this phenomenon. It is almost exclusively, but not wholly within the areas of social and ego needs that these endless spiral changes occur and man builds up conceptual worlds which, as Whitman says in his "Song of Myself," make him dissatisfied, demented with the mania of owning things, responsible, industrious, and reverent, and embroiled in sweating and whining, while the animals are placid and peaceful.

605. *Summary.* People act only when they are disturbed, and they act to seek adjustment as directly as possible. Through such activities they are often changed, and deliberately cultivated learning must be sought within this framework. When an equilibrium is attained, the individual will become quiescent. This pattern of action for restoration of

adjustment is a survival or need-fulfillment activity, but needs change with experience, and so do one's ways of fulfilling needs. Out of this process come ideals and ambitions, which are conceptually imagined needs for a future, anticipated state, but which disturb us now. Hence man's constant striving for equilibrium that is never reached because it is always being moved farther out in front. This is the basis of social evolution and individual improvement, for which only man has the mental capacity.

In all efforts to influence the development of people, the teacher must utilize the adjustive tendencies in behavior. The individual must be disturbed, and for the fulfillment of his needs and a return toward equilibrium he must be provided with new experiences that will change him in desirable directions. He must be disturbed again and again, every time he shows signs of approaching equilibrium and coming to rest. The most effective learning is produced by basing the new experience on real needs and the serious preoccupations of students.

Questions for Review

1. What is meant by the statement, "Behavior is adjustive"?
2. What is a drive to self-realization?
3. What is purposive behavior? Is it the same as conscious behavior? Why?
4. What four kinds of phenomena are listed in this chapter, in discussing the way people act?
5. What makes people act?
6. What has Tolman contributed to this discussion?
7. What is Cannon's principal contribution to this discussion?
8. What does homeostasis mean? How does it apply to social and personal needs?
9. What happens to the base of adjustment, while adjustment is being sought?
10. What is the homeostatic and purposive way of explaining man's continued growth in ideals and ambitions?
11. In what way is survival involved in a time extension in human life? Why is this found only in human beings?
12. Explain: Progress is possible only because man deals with things that do not exist in nature.

SELECTED REFERENCES

Walter B. Cannon, *The wisdom of the body* (New York: W. W. Norton and Co., Inc., 1939), Chapter I and others by selection.

Percival M. Symonds, *Dynamics of human adjustment* (New York: Appleton-Century-Crofts, Inc., 1946), Chapter II.

Edward C. Tolman, *Purposive behavior in animals and men* (New York: Appleton-Century-Crofts, Inc., 1932), Chapter I.

CHAPTER VII

NEEDS AS A FACTOR IN MOTIVATION

701. *What motivation includes.* Teachers often say, "I must motivate my students." What they really mean is, "I must stimulate my students." That which is applied to an individual from without to make him act is a stimulus. The teacher may stimulate by offering an incentive, but the motivation that determines how the student will respond is entirely within the student. This book is constructed around the position that there are three basic elements in all motivational phenomena. One is a pattern of needs within the individual, any of which are capable of making him restless and ready to act if they are in a state of short supply. Another is a pattern of meaning within the individual, which consists of his concepts and preferences, and which determines how he will perceive any new experience and react to it. The third is the situation in which he finds himself. Objectively, the situation is defined by whatever is actually stimulating him. Subjectively and functionally, it is whatever he perceives it to be. The situation or stimulus is something outside of his nervous system. It is the factor within which the teacher and counselor work. Teaching is the setting up of situations that will stimulate the individual and cause him to have developmental experiences. All of these things together make up the generic concept of motivation.

702. *The nature of needs.* Anything that is requisite to the maintenance of a state of affairs is a need. In describing human needs it is necessary to be precise about what the state of affairs is, and about what is requisite to its maintenance. Since the state of affairs is not static in a growing organism, the pattern of needs will not be static. As the life of the organism changes new needs will come into existence, and some old needs will disappear. In the physiological realm these changes

will come about largely through physiological development. In the social and personal realms, which are conceptual in nature, the changes will occur through conceptual learning. Therefore, the development of needs and the development of conceptual meanings will take place together.

There can be no fixed and final list of human needs. Some generalizations can be drawn about human needs in general, but if one person's inner life differs from another's, there will be some difference in their specific needs, and of course this is also true for different stages in the development of one person. The safest process for discovering the needs of an organism is to look at each developmental stage and describe the kind of life that exists there, from which it may be possible to infer and later to verify what is needed to maintain that life.

There is some confusion between the words "need" and "ought." When someone says an individual *needs* to grow, or *needs* to have experiences that will make him develop, he is misusing the term "need." What he means is, the individual *ought* to be given experiences that will make him develop, in the sense that it would be a good thing for him. He does not *need* such experience. He could get along quite well without it and adjust comfortably at that level. If we are to understand the operation of needs in human behavior, we should avoid this confusion in ideas, and use some other term for things we think are good for a person. Teachers *ought* to be concerned with what is good for the future well-being of an individual, but they do not *need* to be so concerned, unless they have come to regard their own lives as depending on the extent to which they make others better. Then what they *ought* to do, they also *need* to do.

If, then, attention is given briefly to some of the developmental stages of an individual, it may be possible to see how needs develop at the same time.

703.   *Physiological needs.* The egg cell is a simple organism. Its needs are wholly chemical, and they are supplied by osmosis. It maintains its chemical life by absorbing food and eliminating waste. Since it has no muscles, it does not get tired and need sleep. A foetus has a much more complicated

life. It needs oxygen but it does not need hydrogen dioxide, since its lungs are not yet functioning. It needs nutrients but it does not need food of the kind an adult eats, because its stomach is not yet functioning. Its needs are determined by the kind of life it is carrying on. After it is born that life will change. It will need food, water, and elimination of wastes, none of which were needs before. Needs for rest and activity, which were present before birth to some extent, will now be much more in evidence, since the life of the infant includes greater freedom of movement and a greatly increased production and expenditure of energy. By this time the essential qualities of physiological life are fully present and the pattern of physiological needs is relatively complete. It will change little, if any, throughout life. As its tastes develop and change it will use various things to satisfy its need for food and water, but they should not be confused with its basic needs, since they are among the many substances in the world from which all of us may select the ones we prefer to use in the service of the basic needs. Food, water, air, rest, activity, elimination, and the relief of distensions in glands such as the gonads and testes are the basic physiological needs.

An important part of the definition of a need is its power to disturb the individual and put him into a state of restlessness when the need is active. This is, in fact, one of the most important tests of a need, and the technique most commonly employed in studying needs is to measure the amount of drive an organism has as a consequence of a given amount of deprivation of a basic need. An excellent discussion of some of this literature was published in 1936 by Young.[1]

In Chapter VI it was said that an individual acts only when it is disturbed by a stimulus. We now add to that the fact that a state of need is a more fundamental source of disturbance than any stimulus as such. The effectiveness of most stimuli that disturb an organism is due to the fact that the organism is receptive to stimulation because it is in a state of disequilibrium due to an unsatisfied need. Otherwise the stimulus would be ignored, and the organism would not be

[1] Paul T. Young, *Motivation of behavior* (New York: John Wiley and Sons, Inc., 1936), Chaps. 2 and 3.

stimulated. It is possible to create a state of need for an individual by saying or doing something to him, and when this is done he is being stimulated by the same set of circumstances that put him into disequilibrium. Technically, the two processes are not the same, although at times they occur together and appear to be the same to a casual observer.

704. *Social needs.* It is an easy matter to describe such a substantial form of life as a physiological body and say what it needs to maintain its physiological life. The body is there where it can be seen, and the substances and functions that are necessary to it can be examined objectively, both before and while they are being used by the organism. When attention is shifted from the physiological to the social aspect of life the problem is not as easily handled. This is not because there is any significant doubt about what is going on, but because both the social life and all of its needs exist only in the conceptual patterns of people and are much more difficult to point out and to observe.

Social life comes into existence for an individual when he becomes conscious of the existence of other people around him. His concepts of social life will always be made up of the conceptual residues of his social experiences. The mother is dominant for most infants in their first social life. Most of her contacts with the infant coincide with his physiological care. Her presence is temporally tied to the satisfaction of his physiological needs. She bathes and feeds him, changes his wet clothes, removes irritations, fondles him, and in many ways acts as the source of his earliest basic satisfactions. Other members of the family come gradually into his world in a similar way. The people with whom he has his early experiences have various effects on his physiological comfort. Some are sources of discomfort, among whom, unfortunately, are many mothers who do not love their babies and resent having to care for them.

Two types of meaning are emerging constantly from these experiences. One is the conceptual understanding of mother and others in their roles related to his bodily needs. It includes also his understanding of food and any other object of his environment that plays a part in satisfying or disturbing him. This slowly forming conceptual world is the nucleus of all of his intellectual life, and anything that may become incorporated in it in the future will be to a large extent influenced by this early nucleus. The other type of meaning is preferential. It consists of the formation of likes and dislikes for all the things with which he has experience, depending on how they affect his need satisfactions or his physical comfort. Those that produce satisfying results will become liked, and those that produce annoying results will become disliked. Here, too, is the beginning of his lifelong pattern of preferences, which will always show the effects of its fundamental structure laid down in early years.

His social life has now taken its place in his total consciousness, as a composite of people with whom he has relationships. The most significant facts about these relationships are that it is through them that his physiological needs are met and that he is dependent upon them for his basic satisfactions. This will always be true, even in adulthood, because of the social structure in which we live. Therefore, it is inevitable that he will discover that the amount and kind of satisfaction he can attain for his basic needs depends on how he is regarded by those who are in a position to control his satisfactions. For two reasons he now has clear and definite social needs. First, because he is dependent on his social world as cognitively known through his experience, and second, because he has formed some preferences for people who have brought him satisfactions and to whom he is now attracted.

Elements of social life. The exact nature of his social needs can be described only on the basis of an accurate description of what the social life consists of. There are four elements in all social experience, on the basis of which rewards are given generously or grudgingly by those in control to those who are dependent. Each one constitutes something of a continuum ranging from a maximum amount of the element in positive form, through a neutral position, to a maximum amount in negative form. Society generally gives its greatest rewards to those who occupy certain positions on these continua, and deals harshly with those who occupy certain other positions thereon. A description of those elements will reveal the grounds upon which one is rewarded or not, and will therefore reveal the basis of the most fundamental social needs of an individual. Since there is no way of arranging them in any logical order, they are taken up in random order.

Belongingness. The first is an element of person-to-person and group-to-person ownership or belongingness. The family is one of the most stable groups in a society, and it takes a possessive attitude toward its members. Other social groups do the same thing to their members. Members are conceived as "ours" or part of "us." Identifications are formed, and extended to new members. This is probably stronger in parents than in the controllers of other groups, and the feeling of belongingness is transmitted to the baby who is usually the focal point for its strongest display within the family. The baby belongs to the family, and soon comes to share that feeling.

The converse of this element is also apparent in social groups, including the family. Individuals are sometimes rejected as not-belonging, not wanted, and pushed to the outside of the group. These are the two extremes of the continuum. At the center is the neutral area, marked by expressions neither of belongingness nor rejection.

Here are three brief cases in which the intense feeling of need for social belongingness is apparent.

Case 2

Illustration of a Social Need

I was a sophomore in high school. I was sixteen at that time and much to my consternation the only girl in our small high school with long hair, as at that time short hair was very much in fashion. I had not had my hair cut for about seven years and it was quite long. My mother who has never had her hair cut would not let me cut it, and it was an annoyance. The only way I could care for it was to wear it in pigtails, which caused my fellow students to nickname me "Pigtails" which I deeply resented. I was continually conscious of my hair and it made me feel different from the rest so that I sought to withdraw from social contacts with other students. Finally, after suffering about half the year, I couldn't stand it any longer and implored my mother to let me get my hair cut. She wouldn't give her consent. In desperation, I sought my father's help. He finally said that I could get it cut, which I did against my mother's disapproval.

Case 3

A Threat to a Social Need

Having to go to a party with a present which was all right, but which I felt was unsuitable (i.e., a tie instead of a game) embarrassed me no end. Then when a child pushed it under the sofa pillow I was practically sick for the afternoon and couldn't wait to get home. I wouldn't tell mother because she felt, I knew, that we were being foolish. A few months later one of brother's friends gave a party, but told him he wasn't invited because he'd probably only bring a tie for a present. I hoped mother would then see how we felt. She didn't, so I refused to have her give me a party so that I'd never be invited to any more. I wasn't, and the hardest thing for me to do today is go to a party. Especially a mixed group or one that I don't know extremely well.

Case 4

Need To Be Like Others

I was the first of my family to start going to school as my two younger brothers started after me. I rode to school by bus to the nearest town, four miles away. I was the only child, I think, without older brothers and sisters, so I felt alone even though I knew some of the children.

I wore homemade clothes very often and was not conscious of them. However, one winter my aunt made me a black velvet hat with red plaid trimming on it. It was too large and just kept falling over my eyes. I wore it anyway because it was "something nice from Aunt Clara." As it slipped down I would lean my head back and drag it above my forehead by pushing up my head against the seat. Two older boys, who meant no harm, made remarks about the hat, and I detested it immediately. I didn't want to wear it. I cried one night in bed thinking about how awful it was to have to wear it, how I disliked it, and how probably all the kids would dislike me because I wore such a hat.

The next morning I put on a light tam. It was cold and my mother asked where the heavy winter hat was. I said, "Do I have to wear it? I don't know where it is and this is warm enough."

From my voice my mother gathered that there was trouble and said no more. If she had pressed the issue I'm sure I would always have felt conspicuous in all the homemade things I frequently had in school.

The rewards that groups give are given to those who belong. They are denied to those who do not belong. Everyone makes this empirical discovery quite early in life (even though he may not be consciously aware of it or able to discuss it), and on the basis of it finds that the satisfaction of his needs depends on whether he belongs or not. Hence one basic part of the framework of social life is the kind of belongingness he enjoys in one or more groups, and belongingness becomes thereby a fundamental social need.

Affection. The second is an element of person-to-person attraction that varies from the warmest and most intimate regard to the coldest and most complete disregard. It is independent of the element of belongingness, which is a matter of allocation and membership. This is warmth and intimacy, or love. It may be given to one who belongs, and to one who does not belong, just as it may be withheld from one who belongs and from one who does not belong. The neutral area of this continuum is indifference. Here, again, the richest rewards within the control of an individual or group tend to be given to those who are loved, and denied those who are despised. This empirical discovery also creates a social need that has as its root another fundamental part of the framework of social life, and we have a social need for affection.

Social approval. The third is an element of evaluation, expressed toward an individual by other individuals and groups. It expresses itself in approval and disapproval at the two extremes, with a neutral quality again resembling indifference. Approval judgments are based on the standards of the group or of the judging individual. Those who are at or above the acceptable level in any important characteristic are approved, and those who fall below acceptability are disapproved. Once again the rewards of society are given to those who are approved, and the punishments of society inflicted upon those who are disapproved, while those who are lost in the middle ground are let alone to take what satisfactions they can obtain for themselves. In this manner society puts a premium on approval, particularly with reference to the characteristics and values that are dominant in the social pattern, and thus creates for its members another social need.

Freedom or constraint. The fourth is an element of control. It is a composite of several dimensions of control such as intensity, directness, consistency, pervasiveness, and others. An unusually stimulating discussion of this problem was presented by Anderson[2] in 1944. All of these dimensions run along a line or continuum from dominance to submissiveness, with independence in the neutral position. Someone is in a relatively controlling position in almost all social interactions. At one extreme an individual is the completely dominating party, and at the other position he is completely dominated. This pattern soon takes shape in the family in its general organization, although the various members of the family often move around in their relative roles, depending on what is going on.

In this instance the rewards are not as neatly correlated with any particular direction on the continuum. Among some people dominance is rewarded, while submissiveness is rewarded among others. Examples of whole cultural groups illustrative of these variations are to be found in Mead's[3] writings. Within any one cultural group, and even within one small social group, an individual may find dominance more rewarding than submissiveness, or vice versa, depending on the nature of those with whom he has personal relationships. Individual experience is the key to this need, and the individual will have to discover empirically from his own explorations which role is most rewarding to him. It seems that experiences very early in infancy have much to do with the establishment of trends in an individual's life in this as in so many other lines of his development. At any rate, social relationships always produce fairly well-stabilized roles of dominance and submission, and thus social life reveals an-

[2] John E. Anderson, "Freedom and constraint, or potentiality and environment," *Psychological bulletin*, 41 (January, 1944), 1-29.

[3] Margaret Mead, *Cooperation and competition among primitive peoples* (New York: McGraw-Hill Book Co., Inc., 1937).

other of its fundamental elements and its accompanying social need.

Summary of social needs. In the last few pages have been sketched the ways in which social contact and social experience regulate the attainment of satisfactions by individuals within the social structure. It has been shown that social life consists fundamentally of at least these four kinds of relationships, and that those who occupy the right positions in these relationships find it easiest to fulfill their fundamental desires. Hence they need to have the right relationships, and it is upon this dependence that all social needs develop. The cognitive awareness of these needs (not to be confused with the conscious awareness of them) is only possible when the individual has acquired the conceptual understanding of his social life. In fact, as far as his own motives are concerned, he has no social needs in the psychological sense, until he is aware of his social world and the manner in which it affects him. The emergence of social needs is, then, contingent upon the development of a social life, and the nature of those needs depends on what that life is and what the individual is trying to maintain in it.

705. *Personal needs.* One of the most fascinating phenomena in human psychology is the fact that an individual can have conscious cognitive experiences without being aware of the self that is having the experiences. Cognitive processes constitute one of the wonders of the world. An infant's attention goes freely to any stimulus that his sensory organs are capable of picking up, but he never discovers his own mental processes. He has a physiological life, and the beginnings of a social life, but no personal life. Just when this discovery of the self is made cannot be stated with any certainty. Unquestionably it is a highly individualistic matter. There are evidences in the behavior of three- or four-year-old children that they are conscious of their own selves as entities, but there are also cases of children as old as twelve who have gone through something of a shock in the sudden realization that they were independent entities not attached to anyone else and in full control of their own powers and determinations.

Social pressures for conformity, as discussed in the preceding section, seem to force upon the individual a consciousness of the fact that he has or has not acceptance, affection, approval, or working relationships with those around him. They do not, however, require that he discover his own causative role in the establishment of these statuses. One of the significant facts about infantile and childish thought is the assignment of blame for difficulties to other people and to objects in the environment. It is characteristic of little children that they do not comprehend their own roles as causative factors in the attitudes of others toward them. This is because they have not yet discovered themselves in the sense that they are thinking, knowing, determining agents. This discovery is a slow process, but unless it is made there is no basis for a personal life, or for the existence of personal needs.

One of the most constant elements present in the experience of infants and children is the comparison of the child with others by those around him. The contrasts are expressed in many ways, both orally and in actions involving reward and punishment. "He is too small" means someone else is a better size. "His grades are poor" means others have set a standard above his performance. "Why aren't you more like your sister?" means she is better than he is. "Her hair is *so* straight," (with proper inflections) means someone else has prettier and better hair. "Isn't he cute" means he compares favorably with others who are not cute. Non-vocally we imply relative judgments by giving food, attentiveness, manifestations of love, corporal punishment, privileges, and such things, in greater or lesser quantity than we give to those who are higher or lower on the scale of approval.

There are at least three important results of this barrage of judgments. One is adoption by the child of what is expressed as his standards of judgment. They are usually accepted uncritically, because of the great social pressure behind them. A second is a more or less forced turning of attention to himself, and the application to himself on his own initiative of the standards that are being pressed upon him. This must have much to do with his eventual discovery of himself as a psychological entity and furnishes the concepts of himself that constitute the general picture of the self he finds.

A third result seems to be the discovery of the relationship between the judgments of others about him as an individual and their treatment of him within the social world. When he realizes that he is a center of attention for others, just as others have been for him all the time, and that it is what others see in him that determines how they react to him in social relationships, it becomes apparent that his social status depends on the extent to which he possesses within himself the qualities that are rewarded in his society.

Out of this sort of experience, then, is born a personal life, and the awareness of its critical role in his social survival. His self consists of an amalgamation of qualities that the evaluative expressions of others have led him to feel that he possesses.[4] Having discovered his self he will probably also do some comparing of his own between his self and those around him, and between his self and the standards he has adopted from his society. His one great need will be to find himself at or above the level of quality that is acceptable in his circles. Since the standards are now lodged within his conceptual pattern, his need is for self-approval. If he finds himself below his standards in matters of right and wrong, he will have a feeling of guilt. If he finds himself below his standards in non-moral comparative qualities, he will have a feeling of inferiority. Both are threats of impending loss through the alienation of those in society who mediate the rewards and punishments.

In this discussion it has been stated that a need is something requisite to the maintenance of a life. It has also been stated that man lives a threefold life consisting of physiological, social, and personal realms. The first is based on structural and functional characteristics of the body, but the other two exist only in the conceptual patterns of the individual, and their needs are defined in terms of what those conceptual patterns contain.

Each of these three systems of need is capable of exerting a dynamic effect on the individual quite independently of the other two. A lack of any essential element places the indi-

[4] See a theoretical discussion by Peter A. Bertocci, "The psychological self, the ego, and personality," *Psychological review*, 52 (March, 1945), 91-99.

vidual in disequilibrium, and looses within him a restless drive that sends him into a search for adjustment.

One simple example is in order. Mr. X is attending a lawn party, at which some of the men have been jumping backwards from a mark, in friendly competition. He is lying on the grass in a relaxed state while others are jumping. Suddenly, he jumps to his feet and goes to the mark, where he makes a strenuous effort to jump again. He does so, and resumes his relaxed position on the grass. Why? He was secure in his social and personal needs until someone else changed the basis of comparison by making his former mark inferior. This created a gap between what he knew he had done and what he felt he must do, and he was in a state of personal need. The need aroused him, and he used the energy thus liberated in bringing himself back into adjustment by raising the level of his performance, and closing the gap between his standard of superiority for himself and his actual attainment.

Whenever a person's concept of his social or personal "life" changes, his needs will be changed thereby, since they are composed of whatever he needs, to keep the life in balance. Needs are very pressing in highly competitive societies, and very placid in noncompetitive societies, giving rise in the former to increasing tensions and increasing mental difficulties, primarily due to social and personal problems.

QUESTIONS FOR REVIEW

1. Compare "motivate" and "stimulate" as terms applied to getting students to act. Which is the better term, and why ?
2. Define need, in human psychology.
3. Outline the three principal types of need, and the main characteristics of each.
4. Differentiate between "need" and "ought" from a psychological point of view.
5. What characteristics of social life give rise to needs?
6. What is the fundamental characteristic of personal or ego life? How does it create a need?
7. Under what conditions will needs change? Be quite specific.

SELECTED REFERENCES

Walter C. Langer, *Psychology and human living* (New York: Appleton-Century-Crofts, Inc., 1943), Chapters 3, 4, 5, and 6.

Daniel A. Prescott, *Emotion and the educative process* (Washington, D.C.: The American Council on Education, 1938), Chapter VI.

Muzafer Sherif and Hadley Cantril, *The psychology of ego-involvements* (New York: John Wiley and Sons, Inc., 1947), Chapters 5, 7, and 8.

Donald Snygg and Arthur W. Combs, *Individual behavior* (New York: Harper and Bros., 1949), Chapter IV.

Henry A. Murray, *Explorations in personality* (New York: Oxford University Press, 1938), Chapter II.

Paul T. Young, *Motivation of behavior* (New York: John Wiley and Sons, Inc., 1936), Chapters II, III, and p. 67.

CHAPTER VIII

THE PATTERN OF MEANING AS A FACTOR IN MOTIVATION

801. *The nature of the pattern of meaning.* Every evaluative experience [1] through which the individual goes adds something to his knowledge. The acts of perceiving what is involved in a situation and of making a choice reaction based on interpretations that are provided by past experience are the only kinds of experience a person can have with the objects that make up his environment. As suggested earlier, perception is the process of getting meaning from immediately present circumstances, and conceptualization is the process of combining present experience with past experience through recollection and imagination. Through this process each perceptual experience leaves some residue of meaning, which takes its place in the person's whole conceptual pattern. Little by little what we call knowledge is accumulated and integrated in this manner. When we say a person interprets a situation in terms of his background, we mean that his past experience has provided him with concepts that enable him to understand what is involved in the situation, and to predict what will happen to himself if he proceeds in certain ways.

There are two broad types of residues from experience that play fundamental roles in determining what one will do in a situation. One of them is meaning, by which we refer to the person's understanding of things. The other is preference, by which we refer to a non-intellective discrimination which has nothing to do with the meaning of a thing. Preferences are commonly called likes and dislikes, and it is sometimes said they lead to choices made on the basis of feelings, as contrasted with choices made on the basis of thought or understanding. The discussion in this chapter begins with the element of

[1] See section 202, page 11.

meaning and the forms it takes, deals briefly with the way preferences are acquired, and ends with a description of how meaning and preference influence the behavior of the individual.

802. *The nature of meaning.* As far as human behavior is concerned, one might as well dismiss from one's vocabulary such a word as knowledge, when it is defined as "clear perception of truth." [2] It is a pure illusion to believe that children who have been exposed to a given set of experiences in school and in play have somehow acquired a "clear perception of truth" about their world and about each other. If one is to understand the role of cognitive mental processes in behavior, the first and great fact to be accepted is that all meaning is functional, empirical, subjective, and biased. In many instances it is seriously incomplete if not downright invalid. Nevertheless, behavior will rest upon these subjective meanings, not upon objective facts.

From infancy through old age conceptual meanings are operational. Things mean to us what they do to us. They exist for us in moving pictures that we see in "the mind's eye." This is inevitable in view of the fact that behavior is an adjustive reaction through which the individual engages in commerce with his surrounding objects and with people in order to get into a state of adjustment. His basic interest in things lies in what they do to him, how they affect him, their roles as disturbers or satisfiers in his search for adjustment.

To illustrate: Milk gives the infant some kind of taste experience, it makes him swallow, it stops the uncomfortable feeling in his stomach. Therefore he will retain from his experience with milk only the empirical findings, and they are essentially processes. Light makes him blink, hot water makes him warm, cold water makes him cold. Fur gives him an experience with softness. These are all processes. It is the effect of the process that remains with him in residual form as his concepts.

The example of milk may be carried further. Milk means whatever its relationship to the stomach and mouth demonstrate at first. Later it derives some meaning from its relation-

2 *Webster's collegiate dictionary.*

ship to cows, bottles, dairies, glasses, and so on. Relationships are all functions or interwoven operations of two or more things. In this illustration the glass is a function of holding or containing, the cow is a function of giving the milk, the dairy is a function of preparing the milk, the bottle is a function of containing and conveying the milk to the home. In later years the individual may discover other functions of milk, which will enlarge his concept. For example, he will learn that it does certain kinds of things to the body, because it introduces bacteria and minerals into the system and causes the system to create some important vitamins. When he speaks of the calcium content of milk he is referring to this process. In time he will pull together a great many processes by which outside elements are introduced into the stomach and assist the body in making energy, and these he will combine into the abstract concept of "food," after which he will attach that symbol to milk along with all the other things that produce the food-effect on the body. As far as one cares to go with the development of a concept and its integration with other concepts, the meaning is always a functional or operational one. The fact that children are taught to define things in abstract terms does not change the nature of meaning, but it tends to obscure from our recognition the operational nature of concepts and turn the verbal version of the environment into a world of "things" instead of processes.

In the Binet intelligence test a child of two is shown a cup and asked what it is. To obtain credit for passing that test he can reply, "You drink out of it." When shown a stove, he can answer, "We cook on it." He never replies that a cup is "a small open bowl-shaped vessel," or that a stove is "a furnace . . . or a kiln." His answer reveals what is in his conceptual pattern, and it is a function that he remembers as the result of an actual experience with the cup or the stove.

This is one of the points that Johnson [3] emphasizes repeatedly in trying to bring language into agreement with the nature of reality. "What is essential is a sure 'feel' for process in whatever one has to deal with and in oneself."

[3] Wendell Johnson, *People in quandaries* (New York: Harper and Bros., 1946), pp. 32 ff., 75, and *passim*.

It has already been stated a number of times that concepts consist of many elements of past experience brought into some form of functional relationship. This implies that the individual is constantly engaged in an inner process of integration. It is the normal and natural tendency to organize one's world into a whole, which is consistent and meaningful, so that an adjustment can be made within it. This tendency is recognized in Gestalt psychology as the principle of closure. It is an adjustive act of mental behavior. Were it not for this tendency it is difficult to see how the vast and miscellaneous array of past experience could ever become sorted out and systematized into the logical structures of knowledge in our social heritage.

Nothing that has been said so far is meant to imply that the cognitive experiences of an individual are necessarily conscious experiences of which he is aware. Many of them are, but probably more of them are not. This introduces the concept of subconscious mental processes, which owes its place in modern thinking to Freud [4] and his followers. Their position may seem extreme and untenable to those not familiar with its rationale, but there can be no question about the basic fact that mental processes seem perfectly capable of capturing the functional meaning of experience even when the individual does not realize what is going on. It is further evident from observation of behavior and through the use of indirect tests that motives of which the individual may not be aware are capable of directing his behavior even when he talks about motives of quite another nature.

Here, then, are certain characteristics of meaning that contribute to our understanding of motivation. It is functional in that it consists of processes, or effects produced upon the observer. It is subjective in that the individual has only his own empirical findings from which to make up his concepts, so that his meanings can only be those that have come to him, not those that have come to others in their experiences. It is

---

[4] A. A. Brill, *The basic writings of Sigmund Freud* (New York: Random House, Inc., 1938), Book II, Chap. VII, particularly pp. 540-44. A more modern account is given by W. C. Langer, *Psychology and human living* (New York: D. Appleton-Century Co., Inc., 1943), pp. 107-16.

an integrated pattern insofar as the individual can find any interrelationships between the referents of his experiences, even when he is required to rationalize his own explanations of relationship in order to obtain the integration. Finally, it is not necessarily consciously known by the individual, either in its acquisition or in its control of behavior, and in his verbal expressions he may and often does say things that are not in harmony with his deep-seated concepts or with his overt purposive acts.

All the characteristics of concepts herein described must now be carried forward into the following discussion, for regardless of the type of concept under consideration, it will possess the foregoing characteristics.

803. *Types of concepts.* From the operational point of view there are three types of concepts within the pattern of meaning. Some objects and conditions are conceived as goals to be attained. Some are conceived as means for obtaining goals. These two types are not objectively separable, for whether any particular object is seen as a goal or a means depends entirely on the point of view of the individual at the time. Its function in behavior depends on which it is at the time. The third type is the concept of self as the acting party, the party that is unadjusted and seeking adjustment.

804. *Relativity of means and ends.* Two of the ideas presented previously are important in understanding this phenomenon. The one is the fact that every act of behavior is an adjustive act, directed toward the resolution of a conflict, or state of doubt, or the fulfillment in various ways of the needs of the individual. The other is the fact that all of reality is a process-reality, which consists of things acting upon other things and producing an ever-changing world. Putting these two ideas together results in the proposition that there is only one real end or goal, and that is adjustment. Everything else the individual may seek has its value to him because it helps him achieve adjustment, or move nearer to the point at which he believes he can reach adjustment. Since adjustment in the social and personal realms is entirely a state of mind—these forms of life have their existence only in the *mental* life of the individual—the one significant goal or end

that is really entitled to that designation is not a real object in the world at all, and the real objects and objectively describable conditions in life are all actually means employed by people to reach their conceptualized ends.

In addition to this proposition, it is essential to recognize that everyone gets his ends and his processes mixed up. This is probably a matter of inability to see across horizons, with resultant lack of penetrating analysis into what it is that constitutes the value of things to us. It is no doubt due, also, to the manner in which we talk to each other about the things we are seeking, and the prices we are willing to pay to get them. These revelations of our evaluation of things infer to others that the things we seek have value in themselves, an illusion into which we easily fall in our own thinking. Let an example illustrate this. Robert is trying to get a newspaper route. If he could get it he would then be all right. (It looms up as a goal.) When he is pressed for his reason, he says he wants to save money to go to college. (Is this really a goal?) Beyond that he hasn't thought much. The thing to do is to go to college. Everyone does. He is still too far from it to be able to see over the horizon and follow through it to wherever it leads. When he approaches college he is beginning to think beyond it. He begins to see college as a process that leads to something else. It is no longer his goal, because it is shifting into the role of a means. His goal now is a job with the General Chemical Laboratories. (Is this one really a goal?) When one has a job he has arrived. However, when he gets into the job he discovers that it, too, is only a process, and that adjustment is still farther out in front. In his college days he probably talked about the job in completely goal-oriented terms, and along with everyone else helped to preserve the illusions we all hold that the attainments just up the road will have value in themselves.

John Dewey has put this characteristic of human thought into a concise statement.

An end is merely a series of acts viewed at a remote stage; and a means is merely the series viewed at an earlier one. The distinction of means and ends arises in surveying the *course* of a proposed line of action, a connected series in time. The "end" is the last act thought of; the means are the acts to be performed prior to it in time. Means and ends are two names for the same reality. The terms denote not a division in reality but a distinction in judgment.[5]

The distinction in judgment is psychologically real. It is an important distinction in the study of motivation. It doesn't matter how much a given concept moves back and forth from end to means or means to end, whichever it is at any given time will determine how it operates in the determination of behavior at that time. The idea of "value" belongs to concepts when they are operating as *ends*. They are sought to the extent that they have come to be valued by the individual. When a particular *goal* is at the center of attention, it determines what *means* will be attempted in order to reach it. These determinations are drawn from past experience with such goals, since our concepts consist of the process-nature of all things within our experience. Our goals determine the kinds of barriers we face in behavior, too, since the goal determines the path we must take, and the barriers are inherent in the paths. The feelings and expressions that mark the goal-seeking behavior of a person are expressed toward the *means* that lie between him and the goal. If the means are congenial the feelings and expressions are pleasant, and if the means are uncongenial and frustrating the feelings and expressions are unpleasant.

805.   *The hierarchy of ends.* In studying the behavior of a student, or oneself, some way of handling the relativity of goals is useful. Since any concept is subject to the means-end transition, the method of organizing one's goals should be a relative rather than a fixed scheme. Here is one that is fairly simple, and quite helpful.

The goals of an individual may be classified as immediate, intermediate, and ultimate or near-ultimate. There are many, many immediate goals, consisting of such things as the attainment of physiological requirements of food, rest, elimination, and the like, or social and personal goals such as a quiz to

[5] John Dewey, *Human nature and conduct* (New York: Henry Holt and Co., Inc., 1930), pp. 34 f. Reprinted by permission.

pass, a lesson to complete, a date to be arranged, a letter to write, a conference to be held, and so on. They are more easily seen as processes and means than the more distant goals, but even so they partake generously of the nature of goals when we are actively engaged in seeking them. They are fairly concrete, have little lasting value, and any one of them is relatively insignificant in the whole life of the individual. Since they are small and numerous, they are easily subject to substitution in case any one of them proves too difficult, or unobtainable. If one can't get meat, one can have eggs, cheese, fish, or vegetable, and still take care of the need. In fact the meal can be prepared at home by cooking, or by opening cans, or it can be had at a restaurant, cafeteria, or night club. It might even be missed without too much strain. The scope of one's repertoire of available short-term ends is a fairly good index of one's ability to adjust to difficulties and barriers.

The intermediate ends consist of somewhat more generalized concepts. A college degree, a promotion, a new house, a better job, a family of four, a contribution in research, and so on. There is a certain amount of concreteness in all of these, but they represent the culmination of hundreds of immediate goal-achievements, which lead up to these intermediate goals. They are still far from being the ultimate goals, but in various combinations they offer the making of the ultimate goals. The promotion, the new house, the better job, and the family of four contribute, together, many of the elements that will make up the "home life," which is a much larger generalization and a more ultimate goal. The college degree, the better job, the contribution in research and other such achievements build toward a generalized value of "social service," which is more like an .timate goal. In contrast to the more immediate goals, these intermediate goals are fairly significant individually, since they are harder to reach, are much more directly related to the ultimate goals, and are fewer in number. Substitutions are not so easy to make, both because of the smaller number, and because the paths leading into them are numerous and extensive and have been built up over a considerable period of time and experience. Changes or substitutions are serious because they require the uprooting and rearranging of a large amount of effort and of a well-established integration of process concepts.

The ultimate goals are highly generalized conditions of living that the individual has built up in his imagination out of the best things he has discovered in his past experiences. They are often called values and ideals. The values are so important in behavior that they justify separate treatment, which is provided in Chapter X. There are not many of these ultimate goal concepts. Those that can be described are fairly stable throughout a culture, if not throughout the human universe, as far as their generalized characteristics are concerned. This does not mean that every individual sees them in the same detailed pattern. Substitutions are almost impossible, for the reasons stated in the preceding paragraph, which are even more highly magnified here. Value concepts acquire their positive or negative strength over a lifetime and are extremely resistant to change. They are the points of reference around which one evaluates all other situational elements. When high positive values are not achieved the individual is genuinely frustrated.

At a still higher level of complexity and abstraction are the ideals of the individual. These consist of mental constructs, built of the most desirable conditions of which the individual can think. The mind projects these perfect pictures onto the horizon, so to speak, and the individual then sets his course toward his ideal. When the ideal has to do with personality, the individual is quite apt to run across some person who seems to incorporate the admired qualities to a high degree, and the mental construct fastens itself to that person for the time. The person then becomes the ideal. When the ideal has to do with a condition of living, it is likely to take shape in some verbalized description of a place like heaven or the promised land. This verbalization then becomes the focal point for the wishes and strivings of the individual. The fact that the mind tends to build up these ideal concepts is independent of the question whether such conditions actually exist in reality, and cannot be used as evidence either for or against the existence of such concepts *as* realities. The supreme example of this interesting process is to be found in human thinking about God. Whether there really is such an independent fact in the universe is not important to the question. In either event the mind works out its own vision of what God is, putting into it all the attributes of personality that he feels to be highly desirable and keeping out of it all undesirable attributes. To this ideal he gives his devotion and allegiance and it operates as effectively in his life as if it were a fact in the universe, as far as his own conduct is concerned.

Ideals have two interesting characteristics. They are far enough off so that they cannot conceivably be reached in the visible future, but they are not so far off that they appear to be impossible of attainment. Thus they challenge because they seem possible of attainment, and they retain their challenge indefinitely because they are never quite reached. They are never reached because the individual is constantly reconstructing them and setting them farther up and ahead. When any new concept of perfection is acquired it is added to the ideal, and when any previous concept of perfection is discarded through progress it is dropped from the ideal. Thus ideals are differentiated from goals, which are set up, achieved, and passed. Goals are the mileposts to which the individual pays temporary attention in his march toward his ideal.

The final point in this hierarchy is the concept of adjustment, or equilibrium, which lies at the apex of the scheme. It is the only true end, but every concept in the hierarchy can look like an end from some position, and like a means from some other position. The ideals and values look like ends almost all the time to almost all people, because their attainment is never complete, and they are always being reconstructed upward by the individual.

806. *The nature of preferences.* It is essential in dealing with motivational problems to keep every descriptive and explanatory idea thoroughly anchored to established psychological functions. Preferences and tastes are no exception. They are not free-floating entities that intrude into the mental processes to exert their influences on behavior. They are lodged in the conceptual structure and are based on concepts,

for which they constitute what amounts to a fourth dimension. They owe their existence to the following psychological facts.

First, it must be kept in mind that meaning is the primary residuum of experience, resulting in the formation of a conceptual pattern. The meanings are functional, inasmuch as they consist of the manner in which things have affected us. That means that a concept consists of an understanding of processes that will move us toward this or that goal and processes that will keep us from reaching this or that goal. In other words, a concept consists of the utility value, or the productivity of the referent for which it stands, with special reference to the individual's own values and goals. Therefore, there is an intellective or cognitive basis for preferring one thing more than another, based strictly on utility, even without the formation of emotional preferences.

The energic aspect of behavior, however, provides a feeling accompaniment for all experience. The feeling-tone is accelerated in critical experiences, in harmony with the seriousness of the experience to the individual. Those experiences in which goals are being attained are satisfying and are accompanied by pleasant energic reactions or emotions. Those in which goals are being blocked are annoying and are accompanied by energic tensions and unpleasant feelings. These are emotional reactions that take place as a direct result of the on-going experience. Through the process of conditioning, a tie is formed between the referent involved in the experience and the effect it produces, both cognitively and emotionally. The feelings thus become attached to the concepts, and a preference or an antipathy is formed for the concept. This is going on all the time. The attachments of feeling may be positive, or negative, depending on how the object is being interpreted in its relationship to the satisfaction or frustration of the individual. If the object seems to have no connection, the feeling will be neutral. Every part of the cognitive pattern is subject to this accompanying feeling-tone. Since one is rarely conscious of the neutral feelings, however, the effect of a continuum of affect for all concepts is not sensed and understood. Awareness extends usually just to those for which pronounced likes and dislikes have formed, since they turn out to be the critical elements in one's life. See in this brief case how one dramatic episode with a strong annoying feeling resulted in a dislike for a teacher.

Case 5

Formation of a Dislike

The schoolteacher I had in fifth grade turned me against her by her constant scoldings. I annoyed her more than I did any other teacher, I think. If I whispered to the person across the aisle, she said she would spank me. Finally, one day she set me up in the corner and told me that if I didn't behave she'd have me sent to a school where I'd have to mind. I had never been threatened before, and I had always gotten along fine with my other teachers. I went to a one-room country school where threats to one pupil are outstanding and make him the special object of ridicule.

That night I went home crying and told my story to my mother. I was terribly frightened for fear she'd have me sent away from my home and loved ones. As I look back on it now, that fear seems very real. My parents had never threatened me and it was something new and frightening.

My mother was wise about it. She explained to me that I would have to obey, but that the teacher could never have me sent away. Her soothing talk made me feel better, but I never liked that particular teacher. Fate was kind, for she left for another school the next year, and I never saw her again.

Feelings of a strong type exert a powerful effect on behavior, probably because they involve both energic reinforcement and strong cognitive value judgments. Reactions to them are rather easily stabilized as long as they continue to appear in the roles in which they have been experienced in the past.

807. *The concept of self.* The basis and nature of this concept was discussed in Chapter VII and will not be repeated here. There remains the need for describing its relationship to the total pattern of meaning, and its effect on behavior.

When the individual has discovered his self and caught something of its role as a causative agent in what he does and how others react to him, he is drawn irresistibly into a life-long process of self-rating. The burden of praise or blame for his status must inevitably fall upon the self, although this is not clearly recognized at first. The amount of self-rating is undoubtedly closely related to the extent to which the individual accepts within himself the responsibility for his acts and his well-being.

The fundamental question in the rating is, "How adequately am I meeting this situation?" It has to be answered in part on a comparative basis with other people as the standard of comparison, and in part on an absolute basis in terms of how successful the individual is in getting over his obstacles and in achieving his goals. In the absence of other people the individual has available the already formulated standards of quality that he has acquired from his social experiences, but these, also, are established comparatively with other people as the pace setters. Hence, his concept of his self becomes a composite of the judgments of the past, and he thinks of his self as having various high and low points in keeping with the way he has seen himself from a causative point of view.

The self is also the center and intentional beneficiary of every act of adjustment. Logically this is so because all the needs discussed in Chapter VII have their roots within the individual. They grow out of *his* bodily satisfaction, or *his* social acceptance, or *his* approval of himself. Whenever he acts to achieve adjustment he is acting to fulfill *his* needs. Hence it is true that all behavior is egocentric or self-centered Such a position is inescapable. A person can never get away from his own needs or out of his own body. He may learn imaginatively to "put himself into" another person's place for a short time, but there is nothing permanent about the move and he always comes home.

Self-centered behavior is not the same as selfish behavior. Whereas all behavior is self-centered, only that behavior is selfish which consists of attaining personal satisfactions at the expense of others. There is a process—identification—by which people learn to obtain their personal satisfactions without damaging others, and even to the benefit of others.

Since this is a fundamental problem in motivation, it is appropriate to examine that process here.

Identification is defined by Warren [6] as "an unconscious mental process which expresses itself in the form of an emotional tie with other persons or situations in which the subject behaves as if he were the person with whom he has this tie." Some of the standard texts in general psychology describe it as the process by which a person frustrated in some desire obtains his satisfaction vicariously by identifying with the hero of a movie or some successful performer.[7] As a principle it is not limited to such cases. It can and does occur whenever the individual finds in another person some quality or activity that has developed value in his own life, whether he is attaining that value himself or not. Such identification is seen more commonly in the mother's attachment to the baby than in any other relationship, but it is the basic process upon which love depends. Of course it must be understood that love is not synonymous with sexual attraction or gratification, or with any other gratification that one person supplies to another. Those things can take place without any identification, and often do, when the parties to such gratifications see each other only as means processes, and not as persons with the qualities of persons.

Identification depends, then, on the discovery of the personal element in other people. As long as they are just objects there will be no development of close personal relationships. Here, again, the self is the determining factor. Until the individual discovers his self, and becomes familiar with its inner nature and localizes in it the seat of his basic satisfactions and desires, he has no conceptual basis for finding the personal element in others. He cannot move on to identification and is unable to form intimate attachments to other people. This failure to mature in the realm of the self is not an uncommon cause of difficulty in social life, let alone in its more intimate forms such as marriage.

[6] H. C. Warren, *Dictionary of psychology* (Boston: Houghton Mifflin Co., 1934), p. 130.

[7] Norman L. Munn, *Psychology* (Boston: Houghton Mifflin Co., 1946), p. 248; E. G. Boring, H. S. Langfeld, and H. P. Weld, *Introduction to psychology* (New York: John Wiley and Sons, Inc., 1939), p. 180.

Through identification the individual draws into his concept of himself those others in whom he finds lovable or admirable qualities. It is natural that these discoveries are made in those with whom there is intimate association, such as the members of the family and close friends. It is natural that they are not made in strangers, and people far removed from us, as evidenced in the lack of warmth between the citizens of different countries or even of different towns and states. Since there is no other process by which love can develop between people, and therefore there is no other process by which a person can enlarge his private world and bring in others, it follows that selfish behavior is to be expected to dominate the relationships of people generally. There is no question about the support for this proposition that is provided by actual human behavior.

Self-centered behavior seeks the well-being of all those who are brought into the personal realm, just as if they were the person himself. To ask people to forget themselves in the service of others is not psychologically sound. To ask them to love others *as* they love themselves is quite reasonable, but the accomplishment of this request depends on the very interesting steps presented in this discussion. To summarize briefly, they include discovery of the self, exploration of the feelings and qualities of the self, discovery of admired and cherished characteristics in the personal lives of others through discovery in them of the symptoms and indicators by which the feelings of the self are expressed, and identification with others in whom those qualities are found, making them a part of the world of the self. Behavior moves from selfishness to unselfishness as this takes place, and with reference to those for whom it takes place. It does not become less selfish toward those who are not so drawn in and loved. The safest indicator of whether a given person is included in the self-concept of any individual is his behavior toward or affecting that person.

> Love and I had the wit to win.
> We drew a circle that took him in.

808. *Operationally conceived pattern of meaning.* Throughout the chapter in many ways the role of concepts in behavior has been discussed. In conclusion a systematic statement of the operational scheme may help in bringing the whole idea into an orderly picture.

The pattern of meaning consists of the concepts developed from experience, plus the preferences attached to them by emotional conditioning. Each concept from the most concrete to the most abstract and highly generalized, and any possible configuration of concepts, is responsive to definite cues or stimuli that were present when the concept was being developed. They will always respond to those stimuli.

Every situation has its own configuration of stimuli and sets up thereby its own frame of reference within the pattern of meaning of the individual. The situational stimuli are not unlike the keys of an organ drawing upon a vast repertoire of meanings held there in reserve. When the cues are present in the situation whatever familiarity the individual has with that particular situation is brought into activity either consciously or subconsciously to take its part in the determination of his behavior. Every situation may then be conceived as a point from which various paths of action depart, some to move toward the ends that will satisfy active needs, and some to move away from them. The paths will always differ in the obstacles they incorporate or in the ease with which they produce satisfaction.

Evaluation is the selection of paths to follow. It is based in part on the pressure of the immediate need that has made the individual restless. The immediate goals are surveyed first of all for their ability to meet the immediate needs. At the same time the emotional preferences of the individual exert their influence for and against various paths that have become infected with emotional residues from past experience. In the larger sense the person's major values exert a strong influence to lead him to choose those productive immediate paths that are also in harmony with his major values, in preference to those that are not. All the behavior will be centered around the needs of the acting individual, but the breadth of his concept of himself will exert its influence by directing him into paths that promote the well-being of all those whom he has brought into his inner world while it is promoting his own more narrowly defined and immediate satisfactions. It is a complicated picture, but it need not be a mysterious one.

QUESTIONS FOR REVIEW

1. What is the source of the pattern of meaning?
2. What is a pattern of meaning?
3. What are some of the forms in which directive dispositions exist in the individual?
4. Define meaning. Differentiate between meaning and truth.
5. What is an operational definition? What has it to do with the pattern of meaning?
6. Explain the term "process concepts." What other kinds of concepts are there?
7. What does consciousness have to do with concept formation? Is it necessary?
8. What is the relationship between means and ends? Is it constant? Explain.
9. In the means-end relationship between values and attitudes, which term is related to means and which to ends?
10. What is a value pattern and where does it come from?
11. What is an ideal? How is it formed?
12. What differences between values and goals are significant to behavior?
13. What is a value?
14. What is a preference? How is it formed? How is energic behavior related to it?
15. Explain the concept of self. What is its role in directing behavior?
16. What is the nature of self-evaluation?
17. What determines when the discovery of self will take place?
18. What is the relationship between the concept of self and the development of love?
19. What are some of the common ways in which people have visualized self-realization?
20. What is the important difference between self-realization and selfishness?
21. Can the behavior of a delinquent be characterized as self-realization? Why?

SELECTED REFERENCES

Harold E. Jones, *Development in adolescence* (New York: Appleton-Century-Crofts, Inc., 1943), Chapter IX.

Walter C. Langer, *Psychology and human living* (New York: Appleton-Century-Crofts, Inc., 1943), Chapters 7 and 8.

Daniel A. Prescott, *Emotion and the educative process* (Washington, D.C.: The American Council on Education, 1938), Chapter VII.

Muzafer Sherif, *The psychology of social norms* (New York: Harper and Bros., 1936), Chapter IX.

Donald Snygg and Arthur W. Combs, *Individual behavior* (New York: Harper and Bros., 1949), Chapters 5 and 6.

THE SITUATION AS A FACTOR IN MOTIVATION

901. *Stimulus versus situation.* It is an accepted axiom in psychology that behavior begins with a stimulus. As Dashiell says,

There can be no expression without impression, no response without stimulation. A man does nothing, is not active, in any manner involving the effectors ... unless in some way he is being influenced by energy-changes occurring inside or outside of him which play upon his receptors—provided we except a few cases of smooth muscle and gland excitation by hormones.[1]

This is true at all levels of life, from the simpler multicelled structures to the most complex. The amount of complexity involved in the stimulus-response mechanism varies considerably, however, from one level of life to another. The sponge and the sea anemone have rather limited sensory capacities, and react to most of the energy-changes playing upon them with little or no variety of response. The earthworm is a more complicated animal. He can be stimulated in a wider variety of ways than the sponge, and he has a larger repertoire of responses to make in connection with his various types of stimulation. It is a long jump from the earthworm to man. It is even a long jump from the higher apes to man. In fact, Fiske long ago said that "the difference between man and the highest of apes immeasurably transcends in value the difference between an ape and a blade of grass." [2] Nowhere is this statement so true as in the case of the complexity introduced into behavior by the highest brain centers, which man shares with no other animal.

[1] John F. Dashiell, *Fundamentals of general psychology* (Boston: Houghton Mifflin Co., 1937), p. 223. Used by permission.

[2] John Fiske, *The meaning of infancy* (Boston: Houghton Mifflin Co., 1883), p. 2.

The term "stimulus" seems an adequate term for the sponge, or even for the earthworm, but it implies too much simplicity and discreteness in the effect produced by a stimulus upon a complex organism. In the case of man this inadequacy is most significant. The typical introductory text in psychology unfortunately gives the student the impression that one stimulus impinges upon one sensory ending, and starts man acting. Obviously no author intends to do this, but the atomistic fashion in which behavior is discussed in most psychology textbooks tends to obviate the development of an adequate concept of the wide variety of stimuli that constantly assail man, and the configurational characteristics of his perceptions and reactions. Stimulus is too simple a term for man with his many sense modalities and his intricate conceptual world.

It is more realistic to recognize that stimuli come in combinations or patterns. A combination of stimuli have in them the making of a *configuration* or *situation*. Webster offers three or four definitions of situation that seem much more adequate for man's behavior than the simple stimulus concept. The definition allocated to the field of drama is most appropriate, "A particular complex of affairs at a given moment in the action." [3] To the sensory psychologist this suggests at once a bombardment of stimuli of all kinds, playing upon many receptors at the same time, and giving rise to sensations and perceptions of a complex sort. To the social psychologist this definition might well suggest an interaction both personally and socially significant to the individuals involved, and partaking of meanings related to the past, the present, and the future, and to all phases of one's life. In either case it is realistic, and the implication of *situation* is much more typical of life than is the implication of stimulus.

The significant levels of human behavior are those that involve one's conceptual responses to situations that bring individuals into contact with each other and that launch each individual on a search or that add fresh stimulation to a search for need-fulfillers of several kinds at once. It is

[3] *Webster's collegiate dictionary* (1936).

to the complexities of the situation that one must look for an answer to behavior, and for that reason it is proposed that all stimuli be put together in language as they are in reality and spoken of as the situation.

902. *The nature of the situation.* In setting up a meaningful and realistic description of the situation and its role in behavior, the problem is not so much to create something new as to bring existing ideas to a state of completeness and organization. Some very good things have been written about the situation. They have not always been thought of as going together by the writers who have proposed one or another of them. In spite of this some of them do fit well together, and with some rounding out add up to a fairly clear and useful concept. In this chapter an effort is made to provide a central point of view about the situation, and to build around that point of view all the usable material now available, and to suggest other thoughts looking toward completion of the construct. Three of the significant ideas advanced in the past are cited here. The first is fundamental in general psychology and is partially represented by the statement quoted from Dashiell at the beginning of the chapter. Without forgetting the limitations of the term "stimulus," it is important to keep the concept in mind throughout any discussion of the situation. Perception operates according to some fairly well-known principles, and these must be part of a construct that is intended to help explain behavior.

Boring, Langfeld, and Weld [4] point out three requisites to perception. The object or event must produce some effect on the sense organs, there must be neural activity including the cooperation of the several senses, and there must be motor activity to facilitate sensory cooperation and stimulation. They also point out the importance of stimulus level, and priming, as factors that help determine what a situation will do to an individual. Stimuli may not induce perception unless there is some priming, and an appropriate level of stimulation.

[4] E. G. Boring, H. S. Langfeld, and H. P. Weld, *Introduction to psychology* (New York: John Wiley and Sons, Inc., 1939), pp. 411-20.

The following quotation extends this idea somewhat.

A stimulus is any event that activates a sense organ and its receptors. It is a stimulus only when it stimulates. Light is not a stimulus to a totally blind person, nor are the radio waves that fill the air a direct stimulus to any organism. Many phenomena of nature, because they affect no sense organs in any organism, come to our attention only indirectly by their effects or by the elaborate inferences of science.

The simplest forms of animals respond to all these classes of stimuli (mechanical, thermal, acoustic, chemical, and photic) except the acoustic. Their responses, which occur automatically with very little variation, are called tropisms, and the list of tropisms is a catalogue of the kinds of stimulation that are effective. In higher vertebrates and man, whose responses to stimulation are ever so much more varied, we do not call the behavior tropistic. The higher animal forms have much greater sensory capacity than the lower. Not only do they perceive sound and all the classes of stimuli that the lower forms perceive; they are also sensitive to much smaller differences in excitation.[5]

The second significant idea may be represented by a quotation from Frank.

If it were not liable to gross misunderstanding, the personality process might be regarded as a sort of rubber stamp which the individual imposes upon every situation by which he gives it the configuration that he, as an individual, requires; in so doing he necessarily ignores or subordinates many aspects of the situation that for him are irrelevant and meaningless and selectively reacts to those aspects that are personally significant. In other words, the personality process may be viewed as a highly individualized practice of the general operation of all organisms that selectively respond to a figure on a ground, by reacting to the configurations in an environmental context that are relevant to their life careers.

... the personality may be viewed as a dynamic process of organizing experience, of "structuralizing the life space" (Lewin) according to the unique individual's *private world.* This conception may be made precise and operational by seeing the individual and his changing environment as a series of fields which arise through the interaction of the individual personality with his selective awareness, patterned responses, and idiomatic feelings, with the environmental situations of objects, events, and

[5] *Ibid.,* pp. 496-97. Reprinted by permission.

other persons. A field organization or configuration arises out of this interaction wherein, as suggested, the personality distorts the situation, so far as it is amenable, into the configurations of its *private world,* but has to adjust to the situation in so far as it resists such distortion and imposes its necessities upon the personality.

What is highly important to note is that every observation made must be ordered—given its quantitative and qualitative interpretation—to the field in which it occurs, so that the idea of pure objectivity becomes meaningless and sterile if it implies data not biased, influenced, relative to the field in which it is observed. Likewise the conception of a stimulus that may be described and measured apart from the field and the organism in that field is untenable. The "same" stimulus will differ in every field, and for every field and for every organism which selectively creates its own stimuli in each situation. Indeed, this dynamic conception of the personality as a process implies that there are no stimuli to conduct (as distinct from physical and physiological impacts) except in so far as the individual personality selectively constitutes them and responds to them in its idiosyncratic patterns. In other words, the stimuli are functions of the field created by the individual interacting with the situation.[6]

The third idea has been expressed by Lewin in connection with his concept of life space, which he says must be seen to include "the totality of possible events." According to this view, a change in the situation means "certain events are now 'possible' (or 'impossible') which were previously 'impossible' (or 'possible')." Thus the most logical way of describing a person and his state is in terms of "possible and not-possible ways of behaving."[7] Lewin emphasized that this recognition of possible and not-possible ways of behaving has nothing to do with science or objectivity. Possibility is not determined so much by reality as it is by point of view.

This view of the situation as ways of acting is in accord with the point of view presented earlier that a situation must

[6] Lawrence K. Frank, "Projective methods for the study of personality," *Journal of psychology,* 8 (October, 1939), 389-413.

[7] Kurt Lewin, *Principles of topological psychology* (New York: McGraw-Hill Book Co., Inc., 1936), pp. 14-15. Quotations by the courtesy of the publisher.

be viewed as function or process rather than as an array of static entities, and that one's concepts are in a very real sense process concepts. Lewin's agreement with this is shown when he says,

> The center of interest shifts from *objects to processes*, from states to changes of state. If the life space is a totality of possible events, then "things" that enter the situation, especially the person himself and psychological "objects," have to be characterized by their relationship to possible events.[8]

Those three ideas offer a substantial amount of what is needed to construct a realistic and functional theory of the situation. Each situation consists of a variety of possible ways of acting, which owe their form to the selective perceptual powers of the individual, and which come into existence for the individual when he is in a state of need and is acted upon by some external events that activate his sense organs. In essence, these stimulating externalities are, to the individual, processes or ways of acting resulting from his past experience. The individual views them as being more or less possible, the "possible" having reference to his constant objective of finding satisfaction for whatever needs are active at the time. Now it becomes our problem to utilize these ideas and others that will make them a more complete formulation, to show by what process and through what factors the situation is interpreted by the individual, and also how response is affected by the various characteristics of situations.

903. *Interpreting the situation.* Attention will be given to two aspects of this problem, the factors that determine interpretation, and the tendency of the individual to distort or change the situation rather than to adjust himself to it.

Factors that determine interpretation. In considering the factors that influence the person's interpretation of the situation, one may easily get lost in a philosophical puzzle. Should one be an idealist or a realist? Or is there some other position that is more in keeping with the facts of human behavior? This is a matter beyond the scope of the current discussion,

[8] *Ibid.*, p. 16. Reprinted by the courtesy of The McGraw-Hill Book Co.

and its conclusion is not imperative in this treatment. It would certainly seem, however, that there is something real out in the situation that is sending various kinds of sound or light waves or other stimuli toward the individual. It also seems obvious that whatever is out there is probably never seen as it really is, for the individual sees whatever he sees by permission and through the operation of his existing pattern of meaning. Hence it becomes a matter of interest to inquire into the factors that influence this process of interpreting the situation.

Some of the factors are extrinsic to the individual. They belong to the reality outside. Technically, they may be called the classes of stimuli (mechanical, chemical, auditory, photic, thermal), with their attributes of quality, intensity, extension, duration, and so on. As the individual becomes accustomed to certain configurations of stimuli with fairly stable class and quality characteristics, he begins to react to situations on the basis of reduced cues, depending on his pattern of meaning to complete the picture of the situation. Therefore, he may easily misinterpret a situation if it contains certain cues that have come to stand for another sort of situation in his experience. An example may be found in the polite and casual conversation that is part of the concluding minutes of a reception. As long as a guest's tone of voice is right, and his expression right, he may use almost any combination of words including some very uncomplimentary ones, and his hostess is apt to "hear" him say that he had a good time. Therefore, whenever situations become fairly stable for an individual, and he begins to reduce the cues (this is never done deliberately or consciously) to which he responds, the situations begin to lose their ability to evoke valid perception. On the other hand, when a combination of stimuli becomes so demanding, through significant alterations in the customary levels of quality, intensity, extension, duration, or particularly configuration, the tendency to respond to reduced cues is sometimes rudely interrupted and the individual finds himself facing a new and forceful experience. Having found that his first reactions were not adequate, and that he must "come again," as it were, to understand the situation, he is in a state where new meaning may be added to his pattern of meaning. Therefore, some of the responsibility for an individual's interpretation of a situation lies in the forcefulness of the experience, and its ability to demand and obtain a fuller measure of perception from him.

Teachers know that there are many ways of providing this kind of shock treatment to students. They are accustomed to using movement, color, human examples, contrast, and other techniques in order to "catch the attention" of those to whom new ideas are being presented.

It is apparently true that the intrinsic factors are more numerous and ordinarily more powerful in directing interpretation than the extrinsic. These include the pattern of meaning, and the needs that are dominant at a given time, as two of the most important items. Others are fatigue, toxic conditions, any form of temporary disability, current interests, ongoing mental reactions such as memory, thinking, or preoccupation with some external process, various kinds of mental devices and mechanisms in use by the individual, and his absolute and differential thresholds. This is intended to be a suggestive list, not a complete and systematic coverage.[9]

The figure-ground idea is a convenient way of representing the relationship between elements of central as against peripheral importance to the individual in a situation. The complexity of a set of stimuli arising out of a typical social situation is so great that it is quite possible to imagine it being interpreted in a large number of ways by the individual. We say it would depend on his set and mental state. Perhaps what this really means is that the individual is likely to see as the figure something that has significant relationship (from his point of view) to his current needs, especially those current needs that are dominant. Other elements in the situation may be viewed as part of the ground against which

[9] More complete and technical discussions of the factors in attending and perceiving are available in such books as N. L. Munn, *Psychology* (Boston: Houghton Mifflin Co., 1946), Chaps. 17 and 18; Boring, Langfeld, and Weld, *op. cit.*, Chaps. 13 to 19, where the several modalities are discussed in detail; and Dashiell, *op. cit.*

this figure is perceived. A hungry person will perceive food in preference to some other thing, whereas an ego-disturbed individual will perceive those elements in a situation that may yield him recognition and approval. In each case that part of the situation which holds the key to the satisfaction of the dominant need will appear in "figure" prominence with the rest of the environment as a backdrop or ground. In the ensuing reaction the individual will respond to the whole situation so as to obtain his immediate needs in the manner that seems most productive in the light of the ground elements present, and so as to promote his ultimate values.

For example, this is what might take place in a class in cooking. Suppose the teacher were to say, "We will try an experiment on the effect of baking powder on the flavor of pancakes after the holidays." This presents a situation to the students. What will they perceive?

Student number 1: The girl is hungry. She will hear something about "the flavor of pancakes," and the rest of the situation will drop into the background. She may later have to ask what the teacher said about the time when the pancakes were to be prepared.

Student number 2: This girl is enthusiastic about learning to cook. She will hear something about "an experiment on the effect of baking powder on" some sort of food. She may later have to ask the teacher when it is to done, and with what article of food.

Student number 3: This girl is tired of school and eager to get away. She will hear "after the holidays" and be delighted to learn that the holidays will precede any further work. It will be time enough for her, after the holidays are over, to inquire about what it is that was to be done.

In this situation three different figures have emerged for three different individuals, against three somewhat different grounds.

It is not possible to state with any specificity how all of these intrinsic factors put their effects together in the final perceptual product; we can only indicate general possibilities. The pattern of meaning has been discussed in earlier chapters. Its influence is largely cognitive. It supplies the concepts that constitute the private world of the individual, and extrapolates itself out into the external world whenever the extrinsic factors do not prevent it. The needs of the individual may be the key that determines which of two or more meanings will be applied to a given object. An object of food that is small and round and relatively firm can also be used as a weapon of attack. Eggs have been eaten, used as decorations, and thrown. Green tomatoes have been cooked and they have been thrown. Bananas have been eaten, and they have been used to grease the skids under new ships. In each case the needs were different. When hunger was satisfied, or when other needs were dominant, objects of food were perceived as something else, and used accordingly.

Under conditions of fatigue tasks take on forbidding proportions, and an individual who is discouraged in addition tends to perceive many not-possible and destructive paths to the exclusion of the possible paths in a situation. DiVesta's research [10] revealed a distinct difference between well-adjusted and poorly-adjusted adolescents in this matter. The adjusted individuals talked much of possible paths, while the unadjusted talked largely of not-possible paths. This was in response to an inquiry about ways in which they attempted to obtain certain kinds of satisfactions. Thus the apparent chances of success or failure in a given situation seem to be subjectively determined, and to be at least partly due to the state of adjustment of the individual.

Previous achievement also has the power to raise or lower the perceived possibilities in a situation, as shown in many studies of the relationship between level of achievement and level of aspiration.[11]

[10] Francis J. DiVesta, *The role of personal values and process concepts in the personal and social adjustment of adolescents*, Ph.D. thesis (Ithaca, N. Y.: Cornell University, 1948).

[11] Three illustrative studies are suggested: R. Gould and H. B. Lewis, "An experimental investigation of changes in the meaning of level of aspiration," *Journal of experimental psychology*, 27 (1940), 422-38; M. Hertzman and L. Festinger, "Shifts in explicit goals in a level of aspiration experiment," *Journal of experimental psychology*, 27 (1940), 439-52; and E. R. Hilgard, E. M. Sait, and G. A. Margaret, "Level of aspiration as affected by relative standing in an experimental social group," *Journal of experimental psychology*, 27 (1940), 411-21.

The effects of drugs on perception have been reported by many. Alcoholic toxicity is famous for its effects on perception as well as its effects on motor control. Preoccupations such as revery have a screening effect on perception, making it necessary at times to increase the strength of stimuli way beyond normally effective levels before attention can be secured. The tendency to adjust to the level of stimulation also affects perception. One not accustomed to the roar of a newspaper press can hear almost nothing else in a pressroom, but the pressman can carry on a conversation with someone else in the room, or on the telephone, and can hear many little variations in the sounds related to the operation of certain parts of the press. Furthermore, he could sleep beside his press while it is running if he were not on duty, but he would wake up suddenly if the press should stop.

From this brief suggestive reminder of facts treated at length in the literature on physiological psychology or on personal adjustment, it must be apparent that the situation can be made into almost anything the individual is prepared to perceive. The final result will be something that comes as close to his expectations as the forcefulness of the external realities permits.

Distortion of the situation. If the external world were completely idealistic so that it offered no resistance to the interpretative activities of the individual, most adjustments other than the physiological could be made entirely within the conceptual processes by perceiving whatever was wanted. Because of the compulsory nature of some situations that do not permit the individual to distort them successfully or to achieve an adjustment without some change, he is put in a position where he must decide whether to become more wishful in his thinking or to begin to cope with the obstinate realities around him. Obviously one cannot be dogmatic at this point, about what the tendencies will be but observation of human behavior leads to the conclusion that the first attempt of the individual will be to change the situation, when he is satisfied that he cannot distort it perceptually into what he expected to find.

Failing in that, he will turn as a last resort to the unpleasant task of changing himself. Here, then, is a suggested sequence. In every situation the individual will tend first to perceive the situation as he wants it to be. If he strikes a barrier to distortion, he will probably try to change the situation enough so that it can be interpreted in a comfortable and adjustive manner. If the situation proves to be so resistant and forceful that it cannot be altered adequately, and the individual cannot leave it and make his adjustment elsewhere, he will begin to change himself until he has reached a state at which adequate adjustment can be made.

This is not, on first acquaintance, a complimentary picture. It suggests that we learn only as a last resort. Nevertheless, there are some interesting substantiations to be found in a re-examination of much common behavior. On the other hand, it has certain admirable characteristics connected with the unwillingness of the personality to be pushed around if it can prevent it. All learning is not good and desirable. Sometimes an individual has something in his conceptual makeup that should not be cut to fit the pattern of mediocrity of his social world. Prophets and statesmen are, in this language, individuals who find their situations out of harmony with their private worlds, but who are so powerful and are so broadly oriented in their total look-at-the-world that they reach out to the realities around them and make them into something different and better. This unwillingness to change in the masses gives stability to society and to the individual, so that it takes a powerful individual to bring about social change. There are times when stability gets in the way of progress, but it is a fair assumption that without stability progress would mean nothing but aimless wandering in no particular direction. Nevertheless, those whose task it is to bring about certain changes in the social world will do well to pay attention to this problem.

What are the substantiating characteristics in behavior that support the proposition just stated? One of them is the typical use of language. It is at once apparent that scarcely anyone talks for the purpose of changing himself. He talks in order to change his conversational partner. He gives forth ideas, scarcely listening to those offered by the other part, or he listens so as to alter his line of presentation to make it more convincing. When there is conflict between two social groups, as in the case of the color line in America, the superordinate group magnanimously moves to resolve the conflict by making the subordinate group like itself. It does not try to make itself like the subordinate group. It does not even consider the possibility that the subordinate group might want to be different from the superordinate group. It just assumes that the thing to do is to make the rest of the world over to its own pattern so that an adjustment can be made with the least amount of disturbance of the *status quo*. It usually succeeds unless the subordinate group becomes strong enough to resist and force some of the required change back onto the superordinate group.

Sometimes through experience individuals discover the fact that it is often more advantageous to change themselves than to continue arbitrarily trying to change reality according to their wishes. Under the influence of this discovery steps and safeguards can be set up that enable the individual to evaluate both himself and his situation in terms of his major goals, so that he will know whether he should try to change the situation or change himself. This requires the formulation of objectives to be used for judging the desirability of a given state of affairs and the development of an evaluational program to determine what states of affairs are most productive of desired ends. When this happens the situation is apt to be perceived with more objectivity and less distortion.

One of the outgrowths of this sort of controlled observation and evaluation is the idea acquired by adults that it is a good thing for new members of the race to curb their tendency to distort situations or to change the situation to their liking and concentrate deliberately on the process of changing themselves. These changes are to be made efficiently and systematically, accepting the wisdom of the elders in place of critical evaluation on the part of young people. A school system is therefore set up, and over a period of time those who attend acquire the point of view that it is improper to try to change the situations that are presented to them. A contradiction is born. They are not to distort the situation, but are to learn to see it as it really is. On the other hand, they are to adapt themselves to the situation as it is presented, without having an opportunity to discover whether that which has been presented to them is distorted from reality by those who present it. The net result is a loss of confidence in their own perceptual powers and the development of an overwhelming confidence in the veracity of all authors and adults in official positions. They learn to come to an authority for all their answers.

One of the wholesome tendencies of young children is to ask "why?" of every instruction presented to them. This tendency is discouraged during the educational years because of the difficulty involved in answering the questions, but when the young person reaches the advanced years of college education no one seems to know why he has lost interest in verifying what he is told and in doing some original thinking on his own initiative. There can be little doubt that one's sensitivity to the real meaning of situations can be badly dulled by being told constantly what to see. This is the process by which society preserves its conceptual patterns, often at the expense of needed change, and with a loss in the ability of the individual to think for himself.

904. *The effect of the situation on response.* If the situation presents the individual with an open path to adjustment, and requires the acquisition of no additional knowledge or skill, his behavior will constitute a simple adjustive response. There will be no more than the minimal amount of tension required to move his physical mass over whatever distance is involved in the operation. There will be no learning, no change in the individual. Some forms of daily behavior have these characteristics. A worker becomes hungry at noon, and eats the sandwich he brought with him from home. If the throat becomes dry, a drink is secured from the fountain just outside the door. At night one falls into bed in a routine fashion to meet the need for rest. Aside from the fact that some individuals permit their lives to degenerate into a set of such cut-and-dried patterns, and perhaps most people live in this manner more than they realize,

there are countless situations in which no path is completely open and well-established, so that reaching adjustment involves certain problems.

When a path is not-possible, to use Lewin's term, it is because there is a barrier there for the individual. The barrier will be determined by the individual's concepts most of the time, and it will have certain important effects on the behavior of the individual, and on his pattern of meaning from that time on, depending on how he reacts to it. As the effect produced will depend on the nature of the barrier, it is important to see what kinds of barriers may exist. Since this problem is common to both normal and abnormal behavior, the treatment in Chapter XXI is sufficient for the purpose of this section also.

905. *Conclusion.* The significant stimuli in human life are too complex to be adequately illustrated by the simple stimulus-response pattern of a lower animal. They arise in "situations" that incorporate several kinds of needs at once, present many possible kinds of response-possibilities, and are perceived by the individual according to the demands of his own private world. People thus tend to become insensitive to many of the meanings inherent in situations, their perception being influenced by a multitude of extrinsic and intrinsic factors. There is a tendency to perceive what one wants to perceive if possible. When the forces in the situation are too strong to permit that kind of distortion, the individual tends next to try to change the situation into something with which he can make an adjustment. Failing in that possibility he will change himself to adjust to the situation. Sometimes a person learns that it is good for him to make many adjustments, and subdues the first two tendencies for a time while he cultivates changes within himself. This can lead to too much acceptance of external authority unless the natural tendency to question things is kept alive and encouraged. Some situations present no problem beyond the existing powers of the individual, in which case no change occurs in him through his response. It is only when barriers to immediate adjustment are present that the individual is required to change, and that is when learning takes place.

1. Contrast the terms "stimulus" and "situation" for use with human beings.
2. What is meant by configuration? How is it related to situation?
3. What are the three psychological requisites to perception? Are they always involved in human behavior? Explain.
4. Explain Frank's use of the term "private world." What does it have to do with perception?
5. What does Lewin mean by "life space"?
6. Differentiate psychologically between possible and not-possible paths.
7. What makes a path not possible?
8. What are the intrinsic factors in interpretation of a situation?
9. What extrinsic factors operate to influence perception?
10. Describe the three stages in reaction to a situation, beginning with the effort to distort the situation. Why do they occur as they do?
11. What is it in a situation that determines whether the individual will learn something or not?
12. How does preoccupation influence perception in a particular situation?

SELECTED REFERENCES

Lawrence K. Frank, "Projective methods for the study of personality," *Journal of psychology*, 8 (October, 1939), 389-413.
Kurt Lewin, *Principles of topological psychology* (New York: McGraw-Hill Book Co., Inc., 1936), Chapter I.
Donald Snygg and Arthur W. Combs, *Individual psychology* (New York: Harper and Bros., 1949), Chapter 2.

CLASS EXERCISES ON THE SITUATION

Things To Do outside Class

1. Write out in some detail a recent incident in your life, showing these things:
   a) The situation as you saw it.
   b) The possible effects (upon yourself) of which you were aware at the time.
   c) The relationship between these effects and your important values in life.

    d) Your emotional and attitudinal reactions in the situation, and the line of action you followed.

Check these against the outline of behavior in Chapters 2 to 9 to see how many points in it you have illustrated.

CHAPTER X

THE CONCEPT OF VALUES

1001. *Values and value patterns.* Whether a person is satisfied with "a loaf of bread, a jug of wine and thou" or a "castle in Spain" depends primarily on his pattern of values. Values may be thought of as the criteria of success for an individual. Life is a success when it incorporates those conditions cherished by the individual. It is a failure when the cherished conditions are impossible of attainment. The feeling that all is well with the world is described by as many synonymous words and phrases as is any other common experience of men. For one group it is expressed in the words "Peace! It's wonderful!" There is the idiomatic "All this and heaven too!" It is the theme of the following paragraph by O. O. McIntyre: "There's the blank, placid peace on the face of a Salvation Army lassie. There's the appealing serenity of a congregation moving out of a Christian Science church. There's the exalted vision of a Negro at a revival. Illumined. But if you wish to see a bit of heaven on earth, watch a small boy who's just found a nickel in the gutter. I beheld the miracle this evening near Bryant Park." It adds up to a sense of well-being. It means that one's important values are being achieved.

A nickel in the gutter would not produce heaven on earth for everyone; a nickel and what it can buy are not the chief values of many people. No doubt there are some conditions of life that appeal to many people, but certainly not with the same degree of appeal for all. There are many ways of describing all the possible conditions of life that can be made up from the myriad elements that contribute to life. The possibilities are so great that it is doubtful whether any two people have exactly the same concept of what constitutes a good life. In other words, patterns of value differ greatly among people. What each person sees to be of value is determined by his own personal experiences, and the individuality of personal experience guarantees that unique points of view will develop.

1002. *The value concept.* The word "value" has been used in the past largely with a philosophical orientation. From this usage it has acquired a degree of absolutism that has no place in psychology. Consequently, the use that was characteristic of Spranger's types of men [1] and the several derivative applications as illustrated in the Allport-Vernon *Study of Values,*[2] and the much more subjective and relativistic use proposed here, will give the reader difficulty unless he succeeds in differentiating that which the individual believes has value for him from that which the history of the race has set up as the ultimate values in life. For a philospher to say that excitement is not a value is simply to admit that he speaks from a highly generalized social point of view, and not with understanding of individual psychology.

In psychology, value must be determined with reference to the subjective experiences of the individual.[3] That is of value which produces what he wants.[4] In this sense value can come to be attached by the individual to objects and conditions at all levels of concreteness or generality, and at all points in the nearness-remoteness continuum. Each goal has value because it furthers the attainment of another goal, which furthers attainment of a still more distant or general type of goal, and so on until the chain of progressive achievements leads to a truly ultimate goal or final end. That end has already been identified as equilibrium, adjustment, a sense of well-being, self-realization, or whatever state one

[1] E. Spranger, *Types of men,* tr. Paul J-W. Pigors (5th ed.; Halle [Saale]: Max Niemeyer Verlag, 1928).

[2] G. W. Allport and P. E. Vernon, *A study of values* (test) (Boston: Houghton Mifflin Co., 1931). See also the authors' description of the test, "A test for personal values," *Journal of abnormal (soc). psychology,* 26 (1931), 230-46.

[3] James M. Reinhardt, *Social psychology* (Chicago: J. B. Lippincott Co., 1938), Chap. 9.

[4] Daniel A. Prescott, *Emotion and the educative process* (Washington, D. C.: The American Council on Education, 1938), pp. 104-7.

seeks that has these essential characteristics. The closer we approach the ultimate, or in other words, the more generalized the goals become, the more stable they also become, and the fewer there will be of them. The farther we get away from the ultimate, or the closer we get to the immediate present and each specific situation with its related acts of behavior, the more there are of objects and conditions that have value of varying degrees, and the less stable they will be.

To attempt to describe an individual's pattern of meaning in terms of these near or immediate values is a hopeless task, because they are subject to relatively easy change, and because there are so many of them which can be made to serve a given goal. The individual can pick from among endless immediate processes in his daily efforts to reach his most immediate goals. That is the basis of the inability to find consistency in attitude studies. Such studies have attempted to find which process concepts the individual consistently values or devalues on the assumption that he will react to each of them in the same way all the time. That has proven to be a frustrating expectation. Attitudes toward specific things change as the particular thing changes its position in the frame of reference of the individual, and its utility to the immediate goal.

Consistency in the individual's evaluation of these process concepts will increase as one approaches the larger generalizations and thus gets nearer to the more potent sources of equilibrium and satisfaction.[5] Such generalized concepts are no longer specific, nor do they have the character of objects any more. They consist of clusters of the more immediate and concrete concepts of the individual, sorted out into families corresponding to the large ideational subdivisions of the society. Home life is such a family of processes. It

[5] Constructive discussion of these ideas may be found in William R. Inge, *Faith and its psychology* (New York: Charles Scribner's Sons, 1910), Chap. 3; Floyd H. Allport, "Teleonomic description in the study of personality," *Character and personality*, 5 (1937), 202-14; and R. E. Park, "Human nature, attitudes, and the mores," in K. Young, ed., *Social attitudes* (New York: Henry Holt and Co., Inc., 1931), Chap. II.

is a generalized concept which stands for a whole cluster of life processes that go on around the family and home. In this concept is lodged the final balance of all the emotional attachments that have formed around the elements that make up the concept. This is a fairly stable and rigid formulation, resistant to change because its roots extend into all the experience of the individual, and its unique and long-established form has been the basis on which all new experience has been interpreted for quite a while. Thus it has fortified itself through the operation of selective perception, and will continue to do so in the future except as new experience is forceful enough to break up this perceptual set and demand recognition of something different.

When these value concepts are properly measured, there will be a high degree of stability in the pattern thus obtained. Because they are *cognitive* concepts, their *content* can be measured when adequate concept tests are developed. Because they have a very definite *value* quality, one's *preference* for them can be measured if a sufficiently sensitive and manipulable value test is used. Because of this value attachment, and its stability, the individual will hold these concepts in a rank order of preference that will not change easily in time and that will be constant in all his behavior, for their effect on behavior will be constant regardless of the situation, and regardless of the specific means elements that seem to be available in the current situation. These are the points of reference that will determine the individual's so-called specific attitude toward any given thing when he meets it, because each object in experience will be judged on its power to contribute to those conditions that are highly valued by the individual. To these highly generalized conditions of living the term, *values,* as a definite psychological construct, is logically applied.

In the discussion of conceptual hierarchies, in Chapter VIII, these value concepts were said to consist of the higher abstractions, which are drawn out into a fourth dimension by the pressure of the hedonic or feeling association attached to them.

A pioneer study in the formation of value patterns in preschool children has just reached completion as this manuscript is going to the printer. Braithwaite [6] spent many hours in intimate observation and participation with children at the ages of 3, 4, and 5, obtaining records of their relationships with people and objects around them, and what those relationships meant to the children. He has supplied a rich picture of the manner in which value gradually becomes attached to objects and individuals by the child, as these things play satisfying, annoying, or neutral roles in his own inner feelings. At first the value is very immediate and concrete in its nature, as compared with the highly generalized and abstract value concepts to be found in the motives of adults. Braithwaite's case reports will have great utility in further studies of the formation of value patterns.

Farther up the age scale, Hawkes [7] has studied the values of elementary school pupils, and Egbert [8] has studied the effects of certain experiences on the value patterns of students, tested in late adolescence and early adulthood.

Research has thus far shown a number of facts about values and their role in behavior. Values related to the principal function of a stable group of people have been shown to be highly consistent among the members of such groups. Values related to certain types of activity, such as attendance at church, consistently differentiate groups who behave differently in those matters. Value patterns have been shown to be significantly related to economic status, social status, level of education and intellectual aspirations, size of home town and accompanying variations in experience, sex (in the case of such values as social service, wealth, and home life), and social mobility. [9]

[6] Royden C. Braithwaite, *A study of the values of preschool children*, Ph.D. thesis (Ithaca, N. Y.: Cornell University, 1950).

[7] Glenn Hawkes, *A study of the values of elementary-school children*, Ph.D. thesis (Ithaca, N. Y.: Cornell University, 1950).

[8] Robert L. Egbert, *The effect of some childhood and adolescent experiences on the emergence of values*, Ph.D. thesis (Ithaca, N. Y.: Cornell University, 1949).

[9] Asahel D. Woodruff, *A study of the directive factors in individual behavior*, Ph.D. dissertation (Chicago: The University of Chicago, 1941). A library edition was published and distributed, containing the essential portions.

When groups in two different locations are found to be doing the same things in the same ways, as in the case of students in theological colleges for example, their value patterns have been shown to be alike.[10]

Values have been shown to vary with professional attainment and level of security among college students and staff,[11] and with religious backgrounds.[12]

Studies by the Bureau of Educational Research and Service, and the Colleges of Home Economics and of Agriculture at Cornell University, extending over a period of several years, have shown that values may yet solve the riddle of prediction of vocational adjustment.[13]

DiVesta[14] has shown that values and social concepts, as measured by his instruments, clearly differentiate between five types of adjustment and maladjustment in adolescence, and throw considerable light on the mental processes that produce such behavior as aggressive delinquency and withdrawal.

Cutler[15] has shown that values play a powerful role in determining one's satisfaction with one's house, because the house has a decided influence on the possibility of engaging in certain general conditions of living.

Eshleman[16] has made an enlightening value analysis of the United Brethren cultural group in Pennsylvania and

[10] *Ibid.*

[11] Asahel D. Woodruff, "The relationship between functional and verbalized motives," *Journal of educational psychology*, 35 (February, 1944), 101-7.

[12] Asahel D. Woodruff, "Personal values and religious backgrounds," *Journal of social psychology*, 22 (1945), 141-47.

[13] Asahel D. Woodruff and Francis J. DiVesta, "The role of values and interests in the vocational satisfaction of extension workers," unpublished MS., Cornell University, Extension Office of New York State College of Agriculture, 1949; and unpublished data on graduates of the College of Home Economics.

[14] Francis J. DiVesta, *The role of personal values and process concepts in the personal and social adjustment of adolescents*, Ph.D. thesis (Ithaca, N. Y.: Cornell University, 1948). Published as Memoir 287 by Cornell University Agricultural Experiment Station.

[15] Virginia Cutler, *The development of an educational instrument to reveal personal and family values in the choice of a home*, Ph.D. thesis (Ithaca, N. Y.: Cornell University, 1946).

[16] Robert F. Eshleman, *A study of changes in the value patterns of the Church of the Brethren*, Ph.D. thesis (Ithaca, N. Y.: Cornell University, 1948).

has shown that significant deviates can be clearly identified by their value patterns.

All of the foregoing studies are based on *A Study of Choices*,[17] a test of values that has been revised into several forms for the specific purposes of the studies mentioned above.

Numerous studies have been reported on the use and analysis of the Allport-Vernon *Study of Values*, and some other value tests.[18] These studies offer evidence of the effect of values on behavior. In general, results obtained from the Allport-Vernon test suffer from the fact that the test includes too few values and is too rigidly set up to allow the individual to express himself in his own subjective style. When that handicap is corrected, as in *A study of Choices*, prediction jumps considerably.

Ralph White [19] has pioneered another approach to the analysis of values. He made a thorough survey of the printed material that represents expressions of our culture and identified in that material all concepts that have value connotations. From these bulky materials he worked out a systematic list of value concepts which, if not completely exhaustive, at least includes the great majority of possible value concepts at various levels of generality. When these are raised to the level of generality typical of the *Study of Choices*, it appears

---

17 Asahel D. Woodruff, *A study of choices* (test) (Provo, Utah: Science Building, Brigham Young University).

18 The Allport-Vernon test analyses have been summarized from time to time. One such summary is by E. Duffy, "A critical review of investigations employing the Allport-Vernon Study of Values and other tests of evaluative attitude," *Psychological bulletin,* 37 (1940), 597-612. The following articles each present data on another such test: E. M. Glaser and J. B. Maller, "The measurement of interest values," *Character and personality,* 9 (September, 1940), 67-81; George W. Jacobs, "Investigating the student's system of values," *California journal of secondary education,* 14 (October, 1939), 339-41; Louis Raths, "Approaches to the measurement of values," *Educational research bulletin,* 19 (May 8, 1940), 275-82; A. C. Van Dusen, S. Wimberly, and C. I. Mosier, "Standardization of a values inventory," *Journal of educational psychology,* 30 (January, 1939), 53-62; F. Wickert, "A test for personal goal-values," *Journal of social psychology,* 11 (1940), 259-74.

19 Ralph White, "Black boy: a value-analysis," *Journal of abnormal and social psychology,* 42 (October, 1947), 440-61.

that the twelve basic values in that test are among his values, and that he has a few additional values not included in the original test, such as freedom, health, and beauty.

Applying his techniques to individual cases, White has shown how powerful values are in their effect on behavior, and how consistently certain values may be found to be expressed in the behavior of an individual. Using White's value-analysis technique, Kenway [20] has shown to what a large extent grade-school readers are impregnated with American value stereotypes that are contrary to the verbalized ideals of democracy.

The value concept is proving to be the key to personality integration and to the prediction of behavior. It is safe to forecast a rising effort among psychologists and sociologists to submit this concept to analysis from many approaches, and this will be particularly true for those interested in education, guidance, and clinical and social psychology. However, the value concept alone will not yield a complete picture of the controls of behavior. It must be supplemented by some means of measuring the process concepts of the individual. DiVesta's work started with that as its major goal and in spite of some rather phenomenal results, which tended to distract him from that aim, he refined to an important extent a technique developed earlier at Cornell on an exploratory basis. [21] The measurement of social process concepts is almost a virgin field, but ranks second to none in its importance for understanding individual behavior.

1003. *Some value patterns.* A few illustrations will show both the uniqueness of personal values and the relationship between the values and the major goals of the person. In each case the most cherished values are at the top of the list and the least cherished or most antagonistic at the bottom.

[20] Geneva Kenway, *A study of the value content of elementary-school readers*, Ph.D. thesis (Ithaca, N. Y.: Cornell University, 1946).

[21] Asahel D. Woodruff and Francis J. DiVesta, "The relationship between values, concepts, and attitudes, " *Educational and psychological measurement*, 8 (Winter, 1948), 645-59.

Case 6

Fred's Value Pattern and His School Problem

Social service
Political power
Personal improvement
Intellectual activity
Friends
Social ease and poise
Security
Home life
Society
Comfort
Excitement
Religion
Wealth

Fred is a college freshman. He has been very active in boys' organizations as a leader and organizer. He intends to specialize in international relations and go into the foreign service of the United States. His reason for this is that it seems to offer the greatest opportunity to get at social problems in a big way. There is close agreement between his value pattern and his choice of lifework.

Case 7

Ralph's Value Pattern and His Proposed Career

Political power
Excitement or thrill, incident to forward-moving activity
Wealth
Intellectual activity for its own sake
Society
Dynamic religion in daily life
Personal improvement
Friends
Security for self
Intellectual activity on a job
Social service
Home life
Comfort
Security for all
Excitement for its own sake
Formal religion

Ralph is also a college freshman. His father wants him to become a chemical engineer and go into laboratory research. Ralph says he couldn't stand such a career, but doesn't know how to present his case to his father. He wants to have a political career built on a sound training in political science. In addition he believes he could combine journalism with his career and make more money. In fact he thinks he would enjoy being a foreign correspondent.

In both of these cases home life is very low in the pattern, and their vocational choices will make intensive home life impossible. Fred's vocational ideas differ from Ralph's with regard to the elements of excitement. Ralph is sure he wants a life of variety and glamour. Fred isn't concerned with excitement, but wants to improve the world. These differences are in close agreement with their evaluations of excitement and social service.

Case 8

Helen's Value Pattern and a Change in Objectives

Personal improvement
Relaxation and recreation
Intellectual activity for its own sake
Excitement
Friendship within one's field of activity
Home life
Formal society
Wide friendships
Physical comfort
Wealth
Social service
Political power
Security
Intellectual activity related to one's work
Religion

Helen is a junior in college. She was in the teacher-training program, just beginning her practice-teaching, when she discovered she did not want to teach. In fact, teaching became almost a nightmare to her until she developed the courage to face her advisor with the problem and attempt to change her program. Subsequently she was "persuaded" by friends to go on with her preparation for teaching, but became so irregular and irresponsible in the course that her presence became a source of difficulty to others involved in it. Teachers generally have a high evaluation of social service and intellectual activity on the job, and a low evaluation of excitement.

Case 9

Alice's Value Pattern and a Teaching Objective

Home life
Social service
Physical comfort
Intellectual activity for its own sake
Personal improvement
Security for the masses
Religion
Relaxation and recreation
Friendship
Personal security
Intellectual activity on the job
Society
Political power
Excitement
Wealth

Alice presents an interesting contrast to Helen. She intends to become a home economics teacher and is enjoying her preparatory work. She is less interested in wealth, excitement, and leisurely living than Helen, and is more interested than Helen in social service, home life, and intellectual work.

Case 10

Professor Young's Value Pattern and His Way of Living

Intellectual activity
Home life
Relaxation and recreation
Social service
Security
Friendship
Social ease and poise
Dynamic religion in daily life
Political power

Physical comfort
Wealth
Institutional religion
Society
Excitement
Personal development through one's work

A somewhat different picture is to be found among those who engage in research and similar activities. Professor Young does some teaching and considerable technical research. He is not by any means a laboratory recluse, however, for he maintains a good deal of home and family activity. His classes deal in a technical aspect of nutrition. He is concerned not only with subject matter, but also with finding ways of making the work clearer for the students. His values are much like those of other college professors on his campus.

1004. *Values may change.* Those who are living in conditions they feel to be important have a sense of well-being that puts them at ease. That sense of well-being is missing when the conditions of life are contrary to one's values. In such cases the individual is usually ill at ease and anxious to make a change. Because values change to some extent as the individual matures, it is not possible to make highly accurate predictions about adult activities from any information obtained during the childhood or adolescent years. Because of this tendency for values to shift with experience, most vocational choices of young people in secondary schools or earlier are extremely unrealistic. Such unrealism is so prevalent in choices made even at the college level as to cause considerable discontent and vocational maladjustment among college graduates. For that reason secondary-school teachers should be cautious in their discussions of vocational selection with their students. Although it is motivationally profitable to use the current interests of students as points of departure for work in various fields, it is dangerous to plan a student's whole program around his adolescent interests in the expectation that he will make a career along these lines. The temptation to do so is great because it takes advantage of current enthusiasms. The real difficulties will not show up for years in many cases, but when they do show up they may be serious. If the values of the person have changed materially in the meantime, without a corresponding change having been made in his academic program, the sense of well-being that accompanies his first efforts in that direction may eventually be replaced with conflict and frustration.

1005. *Values and maladjustment.* Behavior under conditions of frustration may run the whole range from mild annoyance and cross words to attempted suicide. There are even illustrations of mass suicide under completely intolerable conditions, such as the case of Japanese soldiers threatened with capture in the South Pacific and the Aleutians. The strain that accompanies frustration is presumably directly related to the degree of frustration and the seriousness of the conflict to the person involved. Students working in programs adverse to their values have been known to be sullen, unhappy, tearful, and in constant scholastic difficulties. In numerous specific instances such students have become radiant, confident, and successful when a satisfactory adjustment in program was arranged. The strain that accompanies frustration in achievement of one's values, aside from being relative to the seriousness of the frustration, is also directly related to the degree of disorganization produced in the individual by such frustration. Excessive emotional tone set up through such experience operates as a saboteur to impair and, in extreme cases, to destroy the normal adjustmental skills of the individual. It is clear, then, that the usual accompaniment of serious frustration is a tendency toward maladjustment.

From a practical point of view, it may be said that teachers who understand the relationship between values and well-being or frustration can see in the behavior of the individual clear indications of how he regards the situation in which he finds himself. Troublemakers are trying in the only way they know to say that conditions are very unpleasant for them. It is absurd for teachers to expect such students to make accurate and complete analyses of their own problems and to solve them without help. "Getting after" such students merely increases the unpleasantness of the situation for them without removing any of its undesirable or frustrating elements. Any form of deviant behavior on the part of a student is a clear indication that something is wrong for that student. A diagnosis is in order, however simple or complex it may be. To ignore such signs is dangerous.

1006.   *Functional values and verbalized values.* In studying cases of discontented students it is well to remember that one's real and effective values are not always clearly recognized by the individual. When asked for a list of the things they value, people are able to name only those they have verbalized, or consciously thought out. Many of their values have not been subjected to such a conscious analysis. In most cases it is necessary to resort to indirect means of discovery to get at the functional values. Where fairly complete observational records are available it is often possible to see clearly what values are dominant in the individual's behavior. To base one's analysis of deviant behavior on the wrong values will only confuse the problem. It is an absolute necessity to get at those that really direct behavior, and then find what is thwarting the individual in his efforts to satisfy those values. It seems logical that insofar as the school can help the student become aware of his functional values, and make an intelligent analysis of them, it will have aided the development of good motivational health. This is certainly true in the sense that it will put into the hands of the student the means of clarifying his own thinking with regard to his ambitions and goals. It is true also because such clarity in thinking would enable the student to choose his activities more purposefully.

QUESTIONS FOR REVIEW

1. Under what condition does a person have a sense of well-being?
2. What sort of relationship exists between values and vocational adjustment?
3. Why do values have an important role in determining vocational satisfaction?
4. In terms of values and interests, what support can be given to the extension of general education into the college years?
5. How are values related to maladjustment?
6. What is a verbalized value pattern? How would *you* rank the values discussed in the chapter?
7. What kind of value pattern does a person have other than his

verbalized pattern? Is this more or less important than the verbalized pattern? Why?

8. In what significant ways does the curricular atmosphere of the school affect the sense of well-being of the students?

9. Make a list of a few important characteristics that should be cultivated in the school program to˙further the wholesome adjustment of students.

SELECTED REFERENCES

William H. Cowley, "The educated man concept in the twentieth century," School and society, 52 (October 19, 1940), 345-50.

James M. Reinhardt, Social psychology (Chicago: J. B. Lippincott Co., 1938), Chapter IX.

Ralph White, "Black boy: a value-analysis," Journal of abnormal and social psychology, 42 (October, 1947), 440-61.

Asahel D. Woodruff, "Personal values and the direction of behavior," School review, 50 (January, 1942), 32-42.

————, "Personal values and religious backgrounds," Journal of social psychology, 22 (1945), 141-47.

————, "The relationship between functional and verbalized motives," Journal of educational psychology, 35 (February, 1944), 101-7.

————, "Students' verbalized values," Religious education, 38 (September-October, 1943), 321-24.

————, "An approach to the cultural personality type," The journal of educational sociology, 18 (September, 1944), 45-50.

————, "The concept-value theory of human behavior," Journal of general psychology, 40 (1949), 141-54.

————, and Francis J. DiVesta, "The relationship between values, concepts, and attitudes," Educational and psychological measurement, 8 (Winter, 1948), 645-60.

————, and ————, "The role of values and interests in the vocational satisfaction of extension workers," mimeographed bulletin, Ithaca, N. Y., Extension Office of the New York State College of Agriculture, 1949.

CLASS EXERCISES ON THE NATURE OF HUMAN BEHAVIOR

Things To Do in Class

1. When eleven college professors were asked to rank the following twelve values by inspection, putting them into the rank order of importance to them, the pattern for the group came out as shown in list I A. When the same professors were

given a somewhat indirect value test, the group pattern emerged as shown in list I B. A similar comparison for one college student is shown in lists II A and II B. What are the possible reasons for such differences, and how will the differences show up in behavior?

I A	I B
Social service	Home life
Intellectual activity	Intellectual activity
Home life	Friendship
Friendship	Social service
Comfort	Personal improvement
Security	Security
Personal improvement	Religion
Political power	Comfort
Religion	Society
Wealth	Wealth
Society	Political power
Excitement	Excitement

Rank order correlation = .85

II A	II B
Security	Personal improvement
Friendship	Social service
Religion	Home life
Comfort	Friendship
Intellectual activity	Comfort
Home life	Religion
Society	Intellectual activity
Excitement	Society
Personal improvement	Wealth ⎱ Tied
Social service	Security ⎰
Wealth	Excitement
Political power	Political power

Rank order correlation = .20

2. Read aloud one of O'Henry's stories, such as "Squaring the Circle," in which the concepts and desires of a character are thoroughly described. For this character discuss the following items:

a) His chief values.

b) His concepts of the various ways of achieving those values, and the moral and social acceptability of each from his point of view.

c) His interpretation of one or more significant situations in which he finds himself, emphasizing the outcomes he thinks are possible.

d) The four aspects of his behavior in each such situation.

3. Select a case from Davis and Dollard, *Children of Bondage*, Washington, D. C.: The American Council on Education, 1940, and discuss it as outlined in the preceding exercise.

4. Show one of the following films, or others of the many available, and discuss the pattern of meaning and the aspects of behavior of one or more characters as outlined above:

a) "Captains Courageous" comes in two sound reels, the school sequence and the fishing sequence. Both are desirable, but either one can be used alone. They are available for a small rental fee from the Film Library of New York University, Press Annex Bldg., 26 Washington Place, New York 3, or from film centers which carry films prepared by Teaching Films Custodians.

b) "Boss Didn't Say Good Morning," and "The Happiest Man on Earth," both sound films, available from the Bureau of Visual Instruction, 404 Administration Building, University of Minnesota, Minneapolis. Each deals with a case of adjustive behavior in which the motives are clear to the audience and in which the aspects of behavior can be studied.

Things To Do outside Class

1. Using the same book as in exercise 1, *Things To Do Outside of Class,* Chapter V, pick out selections as follows:

a) One or more incidents in which the person's values, process concepts, and tastes and preferences are clearly revealed.

b) One or more incidents in which the person's most pressing needs are clearly revealed.

c) One or more incidents in which the person's subjective interpretation of the situation is clearly revealed.

Prepare these excerpts in the same manner as before, and be prepared to engage in the same analysis.

2. Begin in the preparation of a lesson plan that is to be progressively developed as you go through the text in ensuing weeks.

The form in which the plan is set up is of relatively little importance in this course. Emphasis is to be given to the psychological aspects of what you propose to do, in order to illustrate the manner in which psychological principles should be extended into teaching. At this point go only as far as indicated in the following directions.

a) Select a topic in the field of your subject-matter specialization, which can be handled adequately in a period of from four to ten days of class work.

b) Describe briefly the group of students you visualize as the class in which this unit will be used.

c) State your objective in conducting the unit. Be sure you state it in the form of an objective, not as a group of activities.

d) State your scheme for launching the unit and getting the class interested in it. Do not deal with actual learning activities at this point, just the task of obtaining enthusiastic acceptance of the unit.

e.g.   What motivational characteristics of the group can you count on to make them interested in the unit? How does the unit fit those characteristics? How do you anticipate producing a change in the interests of the students as you go through the unit? In what manner will you present the unit to the class?

e) Be prepared to discuss the lesson plan in class as follows:
   (1) Put essentials on the blackboard and describe briefly what you plan to do.
   (2) Obtain group discussion of the objective with reference to its value to students, clarity to them, and attractiveness to them.
   (3) Discuss with the class the soundness of the introductory scheme.

Some suggested topics:
1. Folding as a technique in cooking.
2. Sawing along a line, or decorating a cake.
3. Learning a mathematical process: finding square root, multiplying fractions.
4. Differentiating between muslin and linen, or the meaning of catalysis.
5. Item 3, with special emphasis on how to get students to like it.
6. Item 4, with special emphasis on the development of the ability to think.

PART III

THE DEVELOPMENT OF HUMAN BEHAVIOR

CHAPTER XI

BIOLOGICAL AND SOCIAL INFLUENCES IN DEVELOPMENT

1101. *The bio-social partnership.* The purpose of this chapter is to point out two important things about the development of behavior patterns. The first is that behavior, in almost all of its forms and manifestations, is amenable to change through environmental influences. The changes that are possible are not unlimited as would be the case if the organism were completely detached from a genetic background, but they can be significant. It makes little difference that there may be several factors contributing to the total personality structure, as long as it is clear that factors of an environmental nature can produce important changes in that total structure, and in almost every individual phase of that structure.

The other important objective is the indication of some of the ways in which environmental forces make their contributions to the behavioral patterns of the individual. For too many teachers and parents there is lack of understanding of the wide variety of ways in which genetic inheritance is guided and modified in its ontogenetic manifestations by influences that operate upon the biologically transmitted possibilities from without. Being unaware of many of these types of influence, one is an easy victim of the urge for closure and integration. Through rationalization every personal characteristic that does not respond quickly to spontaneous efforts to change it is assigned to the limbo of "inherited traits." It matters not that the efforts to change it may have violated every principle of learning, or that they were instituted somewhat too late, or maintained for too short a time. An unwholesome fatalism prevails among surprisingly large numbers of teachers and parents concerning what can be done in the improvement of human behavior. The fact is that a great deal can be done—a great deal more than is generally believed possible. Like any other project, however, the amount and quality of what is produced depends on the method of procedure. There is no less need for accurate information and rigorously correct procedures in education than there is in the manufacture of automobile engines, or angel food cakes, or atomic bombs. Behavior just *does not respond* to injunctions and ultimatums based on nothing more constructive or psychologically lawful than outraged dignity and titanic will power. Men do not "gather grapes from thorns or figs from thistles." Psychoculture, if you will, is based on grounds no less precise than horticulture, and tomatoes do not grow up on stakes just because they are told to do so. Furthermore, it is ridiculous to say that nature intended tomatoes to sprawl out on the ground, and there is nothing that can be done about it.

The means by which biological inheritance is achieved are fascinating to study, and a knowledge of them is vital to those who are engaged in the controlled alteration of biological form. The teacher's work is somewhat different, however, for it consists almost entirely of efforts to bring environmental influences to bear on development. Hence this chapter makes no pretense of dealing with genetic principles.

Inheritance is a function that is carried out in various ways. It means to come into possession of something. In human behavior inheritance can be biological or social, and probably of other kinds too. Often one is asked, "Is this behavior inherited?" Such a question cannot be answered until the asker and the answerer are in harmony in their use of the word inherit. There are many channels of social inheritance by which an individual comes into possession of certain ways of acting that he might never acquire if he were not in a particular social setting. The idiomatic factors in learning do not by themselves select all the patterns of activity that are learned. They have to make many of their selections from among the patterns to which the individual is exposed, and the particular variety is very often determined by the cultural forces into which the infant is born. Hence it is proper to speak of inherited patterns of behavior, provided it is understood that much of such inheritance is social, and might easily have been of a different nature had the social structure been otherwise, or the educational guidance of the individual been otherwise or better planned, or more soundly carried out.

Neither individuals nor social groups must necessarily be victims of the past, unless they allow the past to control in an unrestricted manner the experiences in which those in formative years are acquiring their patterns of conduct. Deliberate education is an absurdity for a fatalist. It is an almost unlimited possibility for those who accept and understand the facts about human learning and development.

1102. *An undefined partnership.* Nothing is so apparent in the effort to explain the interrelationships of nature and nurture today as the near impossibility of arriving at precise descriptions of the role played by each. That is, nothing is so apparent except perhaps the fact that the roles are intimately intertwined and practically inseparable. What have been thought by many to be strictly biological transmissions in plants and animals, such as color, height, or even the specific function of tissue in certain critical spots in an organism, can be shown to be responsive in surprising ways to environmental forces. What have been supposed by many to be factors entirely determined by individual experience, such as ideas and preferences, can be shown to have an underlying foundation of biologically inherited factors. This interrelationship has been discussed in various ways, two of the most informative approaches being those of Jennings [1] and Murphy.[2] The details of the problem will be left to such discussions and attention will here be turned to a brief sketch of

---

[1] H. F. Jennings, *The biological basis of human nature* (New York: W. W. Norton and Co., 1930).

[2] Gardner Murphy, *Personality* (New York: Harper and Bros., 1947), Chap. 3.

what is going on in the research on the problem and to some
suggestions on a way of looking at the matter for teachers
and counselors.

Research is incomplete. One of the factors that has shown
up consistently in studies of delinquency, crime, and vice is
what is called the ecological influence in social behavior. An
excellent summary of work in this field is that of Faris.[3] These
forms of antisocial behavior occur most frequently in slum
areas, and most infrequently in outlying residential areas.
Faris says the underlying factor seems to be disorganization
in the area. Close integration of families with neighborhood
communities provides informal social control, which maintains obedience to customs and mores. There are, of course,
some positive forces that promote delinquency, such as traditional ways of inducting new members into neighborhood
gangs, and the like. For social workers a careful study of these
factors is mandatory, and it is highly valuable to teachers, all
of whom should maintain close contact with the homes of
students.

Research in other factors has thus far been relatively unproductive as far as its contribution to the work of parents
and teachers is concerned. See, for example, a discussion of
heredity by Penrose [4] and a discussion of the relationship
between physique and personality by Sheldon.[5]

Of more potential value to teachers, probably, would be
an attempt to formulate a scheme for estimating the possibility of doing productive work in an attempt to influence
various aspects of an individual's personality and development, and an indication of some of the ways in which environmental forces produce their effects. The rest of this section, and of the chapter, will be devoted to such an attempt.

A time relationship. A simple but meaningful fact sometimes overlooked has to do with the periods of time within
which genetics and experience can make their respective con-

[3] Robert E. L. Faris, "Ecological factors in human behavior," in J. McV.
Hunt, ed., *Personality and the behavior disorders* (New York: The Ronald
Press Co., 1944), Chap. 24.

[4] L. S. Penrose, "Heredity," in Hunt, ed., *op. cit.,* Vol. I, Chap. 16.

[5] W. H. Sheldon, "Constitutional factors in personality," in Hunt, ed., *op.
cit.,* Vol. I, Chap. 17.

tributions. It is meaningful primarily because it helps one to understand the comprehensive nature of environmental factors, and the far-reaching effects of genetically inherited possibilities.

The genes in a particular egg cell and a particular sperm cell are fully determined by the time the cell is formed, as a result of a selective process by which one of an almost infinite number of gene combinations is made up. Within the ovaries there is probably one egg cell at a time in most instances, so that, if that cell is fertilized, part of the genetic inheritance of the child is determined by the time the egg cell is formed. Every egg cell is not fertilized, however, so that the genetic pattern of the "next" child to be born to any woman is never really determined at that point. Within the testes of the male there are many sperm cells, each of which has its unique genetic pattern, and any one of which could fertilize the egg. Obviously, nothing about a child as yet unconceived is determined prior to fertilization. Nevertheless, each parent has something of a defined set of possibilities, however broad they may be, regarding the patterns that may be produced in an egg or sperm cell.

At the moment a sperm cell fertilizes an egg cell, however, the genetic possibilities of the new organism are determined, and there is no known way of altering them. From that time on biological inheritance will produce its effects through a progressive series of developments and emergents as the child matures. Within the ebb and flow of environmental influences the potentialities will unfold as they can, subject to environmental inhibition or stimulation. Biological processes have no way of introducing new genetic influences beyond the point of fertilization.

On the other hand, environmental forces seem to have no way of influencing the organism prior to fertilization. The genes seem not to respond to the experiences of the carrier. They are protected from environmental factors. Whatever an individual acquires from experience, which is not biologically inherited, cannot work its way into the genetic structure and be passed on to offspring, so far as present knowledge is concerned. Hence each individual begins life all over again as far as learned behavior is concerned, facing the necessity of picking up for himself, if he does pick them up, any experiential acquisitions of his parents. They will not descend upon him biologically.

The immediate implication of this fact lies in its suggestion that all the things that can and do happen to an organism from the time it is no more than a fertilized cell are environmental forces and events. They are subject to deliberate influence. They are not inevitable. It is possible to learn how to do something about them and to produce in that manner great and powerful influences on the development of the child.

What are the varieties of environmental influences? It is not important here to list them all or to discuss them in detail, but some suggestions about their general nature may be worth offering. The food of the embryo is furnished through the mother's body and carried to the placenta in the mother's blood stream. From there it is picked up by the embryo through its own system. This is an important environmental factor. The growth of the embryo depends on the kind of food furnished to it. It is subject to poisons, diseases, shocks transmitted mechanically to it through the mother's body, and to damage inflicted particularly at the time of birth.[6] The viability of the mother constitutes an important environmental influence which is thought by some to be responsible for the failure of some foetuses to develop properly before birth.

Postnatal influences include food, personal relationships, physical experiences, such as accidents and shocks, diseases, stimulation and challenge provided by the environment, early experiences in success and failure, and many others. The course of prenatal development is treated by Carmichael,[7] and postnatal forces through infancy, childhood, and adolescence are treated by Ribble, Murphy, and Blanchard.[8]

[6] Two informative chapters on this and related problems are written by Karl C. Pratt and Edgar Doll, in L. Carmichael, ed., *Manual of child psychology* (New York: John Wiley and Sons, Inc., 1946), Chaps. 4 and 17.

[7] Carmichael, *op. cit.*, Chap. 2.

[8] Hunt, ed., *op. cit.*, Chaps. 20, 21, 22.

Aspects of personality vary in responsiveness. Some aspects of personality are unquestionably more amenable to educational efforts than are others. As indicated earlier no precise formulations can be made here, but some general suggestions may be offered.

The clearest evidenct for direct carry-over between parental stock and offspring is in the field of physical characteristics, such as body shape, size, color, and similar items. The evidence becomes progressively less clear, and the possibility of doing any well-controlled research grows progressively remote as one moves over toward such characteristics as personal tastes and preferences, aims, ideals, and the like. This suggests a rough continuum, beginning with physical structure and moving on toward personal characteristics, which are progressively less dependent on physical structure, and more obviously unique to the offspring. In the realm of structure, however, are the brain and central nervous system, the glands, the sensory endings, the visceral organs, and the skeletal and muscular structures. The brain and nervous system play the dominant role, apparently, in the determination of intelligence. The glands play a vital role in the determination of the energic production of the system, and hence in the temperament and drive of the individual. The nerves and muscles play an important role in determining the potential limits of skills of several kinds that are based on neuro-muscular coordination. Hence the structural bases of intelligence, skills, and temperament are probably less amenable to environmental influences than are the intelligence, skills, and temperament themselves. These in turn are probably less amenable to environmental forces than are such behaviors as mannerisms, modes of expression, traits, preferences, aims, and ideals. In the case of these characteristics, so much depends on the concepts of the individual, and so little on the physical structure, that environment must play the dominant role in their development. Here is a rough continuum. All of the elements which a full analysis would place along it are produced by both genetic and social factors. Those toward the conceptual end of the continuum, however, are more subject to the influence of the person's cognitive experiences than are those at the structural end. Given intelligence anywhere within a very wide range, an individual is able to acquire meaning from experience, and the meaning he acquires will be unique to his experience. None of it is born in him. None of it can be poured into him in the thought patterns of someone else. Whatever he acquires must be screened through his own evaluative processes. His ideas, and all of his adjustments based on them, are so thoroughly a product of environmental and educational forces as to be practically unaffected by biological heredity.

A fact of tremendous significance can now be pointed out and given the prominence demanded by reality. Almost all of the significant personal and social behavior of modern man lies at the conceptual end of this continuum, not at the structural end. It lies in the realm of characteristics that are subject almost entirely to environmental influences. The implications of this fact are powerful and far-reaching. They lead to the conclusion that we are responsible, by the manner in which we control ourselves and each other, for the behavior that produces crime, delinquency, vice, ignorance, corruption, greediness, bestiality, and all of the other symptoms of social disorganization. They lead also to the conclusion that we are similarly responsible for all of the progress, individual achievement, beauty, and idealism that have marked the highest levels of human life. The forces that have produced these extremes in the past will continue to produce them now and in the future as long as they are permitted to operate. We can be realistic in our understanding of the processes by which the heights and depths of human behavior are produced, and move toward the heights, or we can blame the depths on human nature and the genes and shrug off the peaks as genius, over none of which the gods have given us any influence.

1103. *Modes of social transmission.* Learning is the process by which all acquired behavior takes shape. Learning is variable, however, taking place in several ways, and as a result of several kinds of effect. Allport,[9] in his discussion of

[9] Gordon Allport, "Attitudes," in Carl Murchison, ed., *A handbook of social psychology* (Worcester, Mass.: Clark University Press, 1935), pp. 798-844.

attitudes, included some of the ways in which an individual takes on patterns of behavior from his environment. He mentioned first the accretions of experience, which result in a "residuum of many repeated processes of sensation, perception, and feeling." This is the integration of numerous specific responses. Next he suggested individuation, differentiation, or segregation, which suggests that patterns grow out of coarse, undifferentiated matrixes into increasingly specific form. This is no doubt part of the learning process, but does not explain how social patterns are acquired by the individual. His next two suggestions are more helpful. Dramatic or traumatic experiences drive into the individual the necessity of behaving in certain ways to avoid frustration and obtain satisfaction. These experiences can only arise over critical social values, and they always involve social behavior patterns into which the individual fits himself to avoid further discomfort. The fourth process is called imitation. It consists of the adoption of patterns in ready-made form from parents, teachers, or playmates, often before there is any appropriate experimental background for such actions. Racial, religious, and marital concepts are illustrations. Young people take on the ideas to which they are exposed, on the strength of their dependence on the adults who express them, and this is done uncritically. The motives behind these adoptions are conformity and belongingness. The adopted patterns may be contradicted by later cognitive experience with the subjects of such concepts, but the early adoptions tend to set the trends in the person's behavior.

The home usually occupies the position of first influence in setting the trends of thought in an individual. One way of regarding a family is to see it as a system of cognitive concepts, or points of view about the world in which it is couched. The expressions of the adult members and older children will keep that look-at-the-world constantly before the new members through verbal statements, insinuations, innuendoes, expressions of optimism or pessimism concerning particular aspects of that world, and numerous gestures and other bodily indicators of ideas. It is to this family, and within this expressed framework, that the new child must fit himself and satisfy his physiological needs through getting and keeping a secure social adjustment. Since the degree of his acceptance is contingent to a large extent on conformity, the pressure to accept the family's conceptual framework is powerful. If the new child develops strong affectional relationships to the parents and siblings, this too provides a powerful push toward conformity.

One of the types of outlook that is passed along in this manner consists of *explanations* of the events and forces that constitute life. Some of the points of view will have to do with things that happen or are supposed to happen to individuals or to the family. Often the explanations take on a note of mystery, or of inevitability, and give rise to superstitions or fatalistic points of view. They reach into all the phases of life and give rise to political stereotypes and prejudices, to racial concepts, to notions about education and vocational matters. They frequently pass on concepts about religion and established positions concerning the spiritual life of man. All of these socially transmitted explanations give rise to a cognitive pattern, which may consist of highly stereotyped concepts, or of tentatively structured concepts that are kept alive and growing; of unreal and highly rationalized concepts, or of valid, empirically sound ideas; of antisocial and immoral concepts, or of ideas in harmony with the best that men have found in life.

Another type of outlook transmitted in this manner is a *generalized set,* which predisposes the individual to see and to expect things of a particular sort in preference to something else. This grows quite naturally out of the specifics that make up the *explanations* just described. The explanations may take a generally pessimistic or optimistic turn and give rise to such mental sets. It is not necessary for the family to be specific about the nature of the dire expectations, or even to be conscious of the general point of view. Such an orientation is usually marked by tensions that reveal themselves in worry and anxiety. These tensions are frequently passed on from one generation to another through the simple mechanism of the transmitted point of view upon which they feed. This can happen when such a point of view is held by only one parent. A daughter who has such a mother may pattern her life after the mother's orientation and perpetuate all the characteristics that make up the total personality of the mother. This sort of thing can go on indefinitely, especially in families who tend to maintain some solidarity.

A third type of outlook that is handed down from the family to its children is the *evaluation of the child*. Originally formulated by others in the family, it is frequently taken over by the child himself and forms the foundation of his concept of himself with which he goes on into his own adulthood. It therefore determines many of his traits, and thus affects in a serious way his relationships with others throughout his life. Out of this may develop a characteristic way of regarding all the members of the family, and such a self-evaluation can be passed on from one generation to another. It is especially obvious in tightly structured societies where a family is rigidly kept in a certain class or confined to a given family trade or position. The attitude of a ruling class, or a servant class, is transmitted in this manner. A child has often incorporated within himself a role imposed in this manner long before he has an opportunity to make a legitimate evaluation of himself to see what he can really do, and what he might become.

As long as the child remains within the family the pattern of the family is in a powerful position to entrench itself. The first significant modifications of these inherited dispositions are likely to occur when the child starts exploring the world outside the home. Pressure for acceptance by playmates and the families of playmates will force some modifications. How much of this will take place depends on the extent to which the child clings to the home and its security pattern, or takes to the secondary groups and finds his security in them. In early years this sort of conflict does not involve any particular cognitive burden, because the child is far more conscious of the problem of relationships with others than he is of the need for validating his concepts against reality. These first ventures out of the home mark the point at which the larger society begins to get its chance at him, to shape him into a less provincial and more broadly social individual.

The world of peers beyond the home and the neighborhood will be filled with contradictions and variations in the patterns carried into it by the young person. There will be the pressure of social acceptance to force the issue, and also the pressure of empirical findings from personal experience and from the experiences of others in whom he finds confidence. If the individual is to develop within himself any degree of independence and confidence, he must ultimately give preference in his cognitive judgments to the evidences that come to him from actual experience, and preferably from verified and objectively controlled experience. Only in this manner will he make a satisfactory adjustment to the world of reality. To a large extent, even among adults, the social pressures for acceptance tend to prevent us from acknowledging the empirical meanings of experience and from moving along toward a real maturity.

In considering how we may move toward the improvement of environmental forces that operate on each new generation, this should be the ideal: To have early social imitation begin in a pattern that will be in harmony with later empirical findings from experience, so that it is valid from the beginning, even though it will always require many years to become mature.

QUESTIONS FOR REVIEW

1. What is the meaning of inheritance? Is there more than one meaning?
2. Why is it impossible to separate biological and social factors in inheritance?
3. In what ways is research incomplete on this problem?
4. How far back in one's life can the operation of environmental factors be traced?
5. What are some of the environmental influences that operate before birth?
6. List as many postnatal environmental influences on development as you can.
7. What aspects of personality are most amenable to experience?
8. What principle lies in the continuum of amenability in the chapter?
9. Where on the continuum are the personal and social worlds of the individual?

10. Can you name some directive dispositions that are biologically inherited?
11. If biological inheritance is responsible for behavior patterns, what is the implication for education?
12. In what ways are dispositions handed on environmentally?
13. How is a person's concept of himself and his traits affected by inheritance?
14. How can some forms of nervous behavior be transmitted through several generations without involving biological inheritance?

SELECTED REFERENCE

Arthur I. Gates, Arthur T. Jersild, T. R. McConnell, and Robert C. Challman, *Educational psychology* (New York: The Macmillan Co., 1948), Chapters II and III.

CHAPTER XII

THE MEANING OF MATURITY

1201. *The concept of maturity.* The word "maturity" has very little meaning from a scientific point of view. Maturity is not something that can be measured precisely, subjected to experiment, described in exact quantitative terms, or produced regularly by following a formula. Furthermore, there is no way of knowing exactly whether any person is fully mature, or what the criteria for full maturity should be. In the face of all this lack of precision and objectivity, the concept of maturity nevertheless comes nearer to representing the supreme objective of all educational and advisory programs than does any other goal. It is one of the most significant focal points of attention in all the strivings of man. It has a great deal of meaning from a humanitarian point of view.

Maturity is basically a property of living things. In education, where human living is the subject matter, the maturation of people is the main issue. Since maturation has its most significant aspect in the psychological life of man, it is a problem that justifies a position of central importance in the psychology of teaching, even though it is marked by all the scientific difficulties mentioned above. It can be nicely skirted in a text on experimental psychology, but not here. Even though it may not be possible to talk about what has been discovered experimentally, or even by controlled observation, we are obliged to suggest an approach to the task of helping students move toward maturity.

The concept of maturity suggests that an individual has arrived at something like completeness, by a process that has taken him through stages from a beginning marked by immaturity. Reference was made earlier to Fiske's treatment of the relationship between infancy and modern man's great achievements. In contrast to lower animals, man is

born with the germs of many complex capacities which were reserved to be unfolded and enhanced or checked and stifled by
the incidents of personal experience in each individual. In this
simple yet wonderful way there has been provided for man a long
period during which his mind is plastic and malleable, and the
length of this period has increased with civilization until it now
covers nearly one third of our lives. It is not that our inherited
tendencies and aptitudes are not still the main thing. It is only
that we have at last acquired great power to modify them by
training, so that progress may go on with ever-increasing sureness
and rapidity.[1]

Fiske suggests that the type of maturity that may be
achieved seems to be dependent on the type of immaturity
available within which to work on the attainment of maturity. Creatures whose maturity is born with them have a
very limited type of maturity indeed, as illustrated by the cod-
fish. It is significant that man has an infancy approached by
no other creature, either in length or the initial helplessness
and plasticity of the neonate. Out of this contrast may be
drawn, by those who do not mind indulging in ideals now
and then, the implication that the maturity men attain on the
average today may be only a poor imitation of what is possible were they to take the fullest advantage of the opportunities provided by nature. A description of what might be obtained is available only through imagination, but part of the
composite of a fully mature man may be found in individuals
here and there in history, as illustrated by Gandhi, Tolstoi,
Lincoln, and many others.

The concept of completeness is always an *ideal* concept,
and it must be described in segments corresponding to the
segments of life with which one is familiar. In that case, it
may have a close relationship to the process of development,
which takes place in such a way that it can be studied in
the same segments. A generalized composite description of
maturity can give little guidance to those concerned with
growth and development.

If a generally acceptable statement of what constitutes ma-

[1] John Fiske, *The meaning of infancy* (Boston: Houghton Mifflin Co., 1883,
1899, 1909), p. 12. Reprinted by permission.

ture behavior in social relationships, or in intellectual activity, or in economic life can be developed, there is thus created an objective toward which effort can be expended. It is also possible to describe stages in the movement toward that objective and to provide ourselves with rough milestones to indicate progress. The diagnosis of delayed development is also made easier, for it helps to localize the type of growth that is not taking place, and to focus attention on possible reasons for the delay. Maturity is assuredly an organismic concept, but here, as in the discussion of the nature of behavior, analysis of any organismic phenomenon is helped by some kind of analytical method.

For example, here is a case of difficulty presented by Horrocks and Troyer[2] in one of their very helpful case-study instruments.

Case 11

Connie Casey, a Girl with a Social Problem

Connie is 17, of Irish-Italian ancestry, attending high school. She has been absent for two days. The excuse she brought was forged, and she admitted this under pressure, bursting into tears. The first day she attended a movie, and the second went to the park and read. She didn't know why she had stayed out. In her junior high school years she had earned a grade average of 96, but was absent excessively. The principal said she was well liked, quiet, reserved, and not too friendly. Her Binet I.Q. was 142. At high school she is taking a college entrance course. Her averages so far are: Sophomore, 94; Junior, 95; Mid-Senior year, English 97, Latin 91, American History 97, Chemistry 90, French 95, and Physical Education, F. The principal has talked to her about absences from gym, but Connie just bursts into tears, says she forgot.

What is the cause of her trouble? Here is a composite picture of a girl who is not abnormal in any way, but who is having difficulty. Is she as mature as she should be at her age? Is her trouble due to immaturity in some aspect of her

---

[2] John E. Horrocks and Maurice E. Troyer, *A study of Connie Casey* (Syracuse, N. Y.: Syracuse University Press, 1936). Sketches included here by permission. The instruments provide experience in analyzing the causes and remedies for the problems.

development? If so, what is it? The answers to these questions cannot be found by just watching the composite actions. They are down in the details of the various segments of her life, where a little analytical observation will turn them up. A good beginning toward isolating them could be made by determining in what strands of her development she is immature, if any, so that the possible causes of delay could be found.

In adult life almost everyone is an example of some lack of adjustment due to relative immaturity in some aspect of development. Mr. W is a businessman, unmarried, living at a club. He is uneasy around women, fearing they are "after him." He always wears the same kind of suit, a pattern that was approved by his mother before her death. He is successful in business, agreeable with other men, neat and clean in person, but unable to escape from the routines set up for him by his mother, or to go through a normal courtship and get married. There is one basic immaturity in his total make-up. He is still a child with respect to his domination by his parents. Had he continued to mature in this respect he would now be free to develop normal heterosexual relations, and to govern his personal life on the basis of current considerations. As it is, he is tied to the past because he is tied to an individual who is forever locked up with the past. He is still obeying his mother, not in a generalized adherence to her ideals, but in the details of daily activity connected with clothes, food, and the like, just as is normal for a child. It is not normal for a man.

1202. *An ideal concept of maturity.* In physical life the terminal or ideal concepts are established partly by the genetic inheritance of the individual, and partly by the stimulation or interferences introduced into the growth process by environment. Through biological observation and research, we are aware that there are both maximal and minimal possibilities in physical maturation. Biological research has contributed greatly to the movement toward the maximal possibilities and has so stimulated the imagination that ideal concepts of physical maturity are commonplace. They include taller and better-formed people, disease-resistant structures, better brain formations, greater length of life through increased ability to throw off poisons and maintain vital processes. Life expectancy has risen from approximately thirty-three to near seventy within the memory of some still living.

As yet the attack on maximal possibilities has not become as well organized or as fruitful in the psychological aspects of life. There the terminal concepts have no absolute limits. What is desired is the best of possible conditions of adjustment, made possible by the best world we can create. It is both an individual and a social problem, for an individual makes his adjustment in a social world, but since the social world is made up of the individuals who are trying to make their adjustment, each depends on the other and both must move upward together. Only an occasional person will exceed the typical level of maturity, for most people are overcome by the pressure of conformity. Before a tendency to exceed it can be developed, it will be necessary for teachers and parents to learn how to show individuals convincingly that their own well-being is much more likely to be achieved in a world marked by behavior of the ideal-concept type than in the world as it is now. In fact their own well-being can be shown to be helped greatly by their own attainment of such a level, whether others succeed in making it with them or not. Although it is an ideal concept, it has its most appealing roots in what it has to offer to the most basic motives of every individual.

Left to itself, life reveals some stages of development as the individual grows. It also reveals a norm of maturity consisting of whatever kind of behavior patterns are present in the majority of people who have quit growing. The kind of progress through the stages apparent in life reveals what happens under laissez-faire, or natural survival conditions. Some men are not content, however, to be pieces of driftwood on any tide. They try to visualize their possibilities, and then move toward them, using the forces in the universe to help them along as fast as they can master them. Whatever a man visualizes as his best possibilities become his ideal concept of mature living. That is what he believes it is possible for him to attain, and what it is desirable to attain.

A group of advanced students at Cornell University in the summer of 1948 became interested in the nature of maturity and the stages of growth and development leading to it. Dividing into groups, they combed the literature for descriptions of various strands of human behavior at several levels of development.[3] Their reports furnished the basic materials from which the Grograph in Figure 3 was subsequently developed. Across the top are a series of descriptions indicative of some of the characteristics that might constitute ideal maturity. They are grouped under eight strands of human development. The rows in the figure represent five very general levels of development, and the content of each section of the figure is a rough indication of the behavior typical at each level of development under each strand of growth. Nothing about the Grograph is finished. It is a project, the completion of which will probably be different in every group that works on it. Its value lies in its suggestiveness about what constitutes maturity, how it might be studied, and how to provide experiences that will lead to the ideal concepts.

On an individual basis such a graph can be used to make a profile of the level of development of the individual. He can be "located" on each column, by seeing where in the column his behavior seems to be most nearly described. Thus an eight-point profile can be drawn through the levels of development that seem best to characterize his behavior.

1203. *Levels of maturity and cultural pressures.* Adolescence has long been recognized as a culturally induced re-

[3] Some of the sources used are: Nancy Bayley, "Mental and emotional growth," in P. Witty and C. E. Skinner, eds., *Mental hygiene in modern education* (New York: Farrar and Rinehart, 1939); Fowler D. Brooks, *Child psychology* (Boston: Houghton Mifflin Co., 1937); Charlotte Bühler, *The first year of life* (New York: John Day Co., Inc., 1930); Luella Cole, *Psychology of adolescence* (Rev. ed.; New York: Farrar and Rinehart, 1942); Margaret Curti, *Child psychology* (New York: Longmans, Green and Co., Inc., 1930); A. O. Gesell and H. Thompson, *Infant behavior* (New York: McGraw-Hill Book Co., Inc., 1934); Arthur T. Jersild, *Child psychology* (New York: Prentice-Hall, Inc., 1946); Mary M. Shirley, *The first two years*, Institute of Child Welfare Monographs (Minneapolis: University of Minnesota Press, 1933); C. E. Skinner and P. L. Harriman, *Child psychology* (New York: The Macmillan Co., 1941).

GROGRAPH

A SCALE OF PERSONAL MATURITY

STRANDS OF DEVELOPMENT

LEVEL OF MATURITY	1. SELF-DIRECTIONAL
INFANCY	Full and complete dependence on parents in all matters.
CHILDHOOD	Complete dependence on others for basic needs. Situations are largely defined by parents. Periods of negativism show first clumsy efforts to exert self-determination. School child begins to assume some responsibility for own behavior. Still blames much on others. Some expressions of independence in taste for clothes, friends, etc. Complete acceptance of authority in parents, teachers, policemen, religious leaders.
ADOLESCENCE	Outside contacts begin to supersede family as source of approval and security. Conflict between desire for independence and for protection. Conflict between need for guidance and for independence. Loss of protected status as environment expands. Growing awareness that price of independence is responsibility. Recognizes limitations without admitting them or seeking relevant advice directly. Venturesome behavior to demonstrate worth to self and group. Search for an independent frame of reference on philosophical-intellectual matters. Strong conformity to peer standards. Conflict between communal life and home code. Doubt of validity of ideas of parents, teachers, religious leaders.

YOUNG ADULTHOOD	Most decisions are own, some determined by parents, employers, etc. Puts great weight on ideas of important people in making own decisions. Some actions are shaped by direction of others without recognition of influence. Impressed by people of superior status, defer to their judgment. Hesitant about acting contrary to pronounced views of important groups or individuals. Has not clearly distinguished between friendship and obedience. Will control others without realizing their need for freedom. Not keenly aware of values of self-determination.
IDEAL CONCEPT OF MATURITY	Values self-determination above all other things. Makes all own decisions. Seeks information and ideas from others, but weighs them objectively. Able to take stand contrary to persons or groups. None of behavior is a reaction shaped by dislike or dominance in others. Self-management is calm, objective, free from signs of rebellion or escape. Accepts responsibility for welfare of dependents. Tries to help others become independent without being rebellious. Parents and former guides are warm and respected friends. Can differ in decisions without disturbing friendly relations.

167

GROGRAPH

A Scale of Personal Maturity

LEVEL OF MATURITY	STRANDS OF DEVELOPMENT 2. Intellectual
INFANCY	Recognizes objects, sounds, smells, but does not reason about them. Sensory curiosity, explores all available objects. Gradual awareness of simple meanings precedes ability to express them. No integration of experiences, everything concrete, specific, immediate.
CHILDHOOD	Has made transition from mere perception to conception and integration. Has basic vocabulary as foundation for thinking, reading, writing. Begins to distinguish between real and make-believe. Shows growing ability to memorize. Applies simple thought to increasing variety of subjects. Can recognize a problem and is capable of brief thinking about it. Capable of thinking socially and exercising self-correction. Accepts values of adults, and adult authority without question.
ADOLESCENCE	Exploratory interest in various intellectual disciplines. Has mastered first problems in abstract reasoning, as in geometry. Shows evidence of some abstract thought in other areas, e.g., humor. Vocabulary and other symbolic skills expanding rapidly in abstract fields.

Attention span increasing, near half hour.
Challenges values and ideas previously accepted from authority.
Readily separates fantasy from reality in own thinking.
Imaginative composition shows signs of discipline and organization.
Aware of many social problems, interested in discussing them.
Interested in causal relationships.

YOUNG ADULTHOOD

Thinks independently, draws own conclusions without dependence on others.
Has learned to generalize validly, using scientific criteria of proof.
Is aware of, attempts to eliminate, irrelevant facts, superstition, and subjective considerations in making judgments and in generalizing.
Has developed some special intellectual interests.
Selects plays, music, books, partly for thought-provoking qualities.
Can concentrate on intellectual problem for at least an hour.
Can employ complex symbols in thinking.
Has code of right and wrong, based on own background.

IDEAL CONCEPT OF MATURITY

Clear ideas of cause and effect relationships based on natural law.
Decisions based on fact, not prejudice.
Tests authority before accepting it.
Purpose is superior to knowledge and directs search for and use of knowledge.
Tests purposes in light of experience of race.
A few highly developed interests occupy major attention, conversant in many.
Sees true place of own special interests in whole of life.
Fully aware of other points of view and systems of thought, can weigh them and his own without prejudice.
Able to adjust own position in light of valid information.

GROGRAPH

A Scale of Personal Maturity

LEVEL OF MATURITY	STRANDS OF DEVELOPMENT
	3. Philosophical
INFANCY	Universe consists of bodily sensations and nearby sensory objects. No integration and no evident concern.
CHILDHOOD	Causation is all personal, some animistic, no concept of natural law. Law is all statutory, no concept of nature as a system of relationships between facts. Need for consistency not felt, all problems purely momentary, solutions based on want. Curiosity about life limited to immediately present phenomena. Explanations of very shallow form satisfying. No awareness yet of integrated nature of universe. Right and wrong based on authority, usually in parent, but also in teacher or officer. Unprejudiced toward other groups; cultural stereotypes not yet felt; all seen as alike or equal, judged by personality.
ADOLESCENCE	Deeply concerned about right and wrong, but not yet clear of authoritarian sources. Distrustful of persons as authorities, especially those near at hand. Intensely curious about God and spiritual problems. Critical of childhood teachings. Developing sense of justice, fairness, regard for others, but prejudiced toward certain groups; holds cultural stereotype. Operates on parental codes of conduct, but questions them verbally. Groping for basis of honesty, morality, etc. Confused about relativity of standards.

YOUNG ADULTHOOD	Sees men in terms of stereotypes of youth. No adequate sense of brotherhood. Has only partially complete notion of his world. Lots of contradictions and mysteries. Confused on concept of natural law and its bearing on human life. Unable to see long-range view of human experience to understand social and psychological laws. Rigid on values, or completely fluid, not sensing basis of determination. Acts on the "principle" of things. Often unrealistic about his own place in life and what he can expect to achieve. Resentful of situations that reveal his limitations and block his desires. Conducts life on a day-to-day basis, or accepts what circumstances bring, infrequently sets out on self-chosen paths. Values not detached from inadequate notions of universe and life. Often antisocial in a large sense.
IDEAL CONCEPT OF MATURITY	Has achieved an integrated view of his universe so that everything in it has at least a potential explanation, and fits. Accepts natural law as fundamental, with intelligence using it to attain purpose. Has clear concepts of good in an ultimate sense, has organized his life around it. Has clearly differentiated between stable and relative or fluctuating values, knows which may be set aside and which may not. Does not confuse values with symbols, or with means of attainment. Keeps concepts consistent with total point of view, can suspend integration at times pending further experience. Has a considered view of own place in world, what is possible for him, what are his chances of doing it. Has a realistic plan of life for himself on the basis of his view of life as a whole. Puts all human values first, without favoritism toward any persons or groups.

GROGRAPH

A Scale of Personal Maturity

LEVEL OF MATURITY	STRANDS OF DEVELOPMENT
	4. Social.
INFANCY	Gradual dawning of relationships with persons in home. Sensitive to signs of approval and disapproval, but not yet fully controlled by them. Not aware of own role in relationships. Recognizes people, but not ideas that differentiate them.
CHILDHOOD	Unaware of social groups outside the home atmosphere. Acts solely on basis of personal wishes and needs. Dawning interest in cooperative group play, as long as it fulfills personal objectives. Becoming aware of social groups at the perimeter of his social environment. Tolerant of ignorance and insensitivity to social stimuli. No systematic approach to leadership, haphazard, but authoritarian.
ADOLESCENCE	Increasingly aware of social groups in his environment; constantly attempts to become participating member in one or more significant groups. Has become increasingly aware of social values, but still acts on personal values. Eager to be identified with a social group irrespective of purpose, action, or nature of administration. Increasingly aware of caste and class organization of society. Bossy in leadership roles, more systematic and thorough than before.

YOUNG ADULTHOOD	Finds social security through belonging to social, economic, political or religious groups. Overt behavior is in conformity with group pressures. Can work with others and understand their point of view. Can submerge his identity in achievement of a group objective. Lacks sufficient experience to accept all groups. Somewhat autocratic in leadership.
IDEAL CONCEPT OF MATURITY	Can feel secure within himself; get along with or without social groups. Has ability to understand other group and family goals and values. Can adjust to normal working relations with maximum personal and group satisfaction. Can retain individuality when subject to influence of group action and ideology. Can understand and identify himself with other nationalities, races, and social groups. Can lead without being domineering or autocratic. Can hold to his own stable values without infringing on others or making them feel uneasy.

173

GROGRAPH

A Scale of Personal Maturity

LEVEL OF MATURITY	STRANDS OF DEVELOPMENT
	5. EMOTIONAL
INFANCY	All impulses are carried out without inhibition. Unrestricted use of voice, arms, and legs to spend energy. Diffuse explosive pattern, not well differentiated. Afraid of loud sounds, being dropped, resists being confined. Uses voice vigorously to express feeling of well-being. Sleeps whenever tired, regardless of who is present. Gives immediate vent to physiological needs without regard to those near.
CHILDHOOD	**EARLY CHILDHOOD** Few inhibitions; gives full expression to all feelings, especially vocally. Bites, scratches, screams, fights to escape or attack annoyers. Free with affection to any accepted person. Tries to get wants by making others act for him through expressive actions. Temper tantrums and negativism show up frequently. **LATER CHILDHOOD** Mixture of full expression by noise, and symbolic means; calls names, expresses dire thoughts. Swings from abuse to affection easily and quickly. No sense of inconsistency. Little capacity to conceal disappointments or pleasures. Still frequent muscular attacks when angered. Expresses dislikes and likes with little hesitation.

ADOLESCENCE	Expressions mostly symbolic and verbal. Says cutting things to those not liked. Overcoming childish fears and restraints on activity. Tries to cover emotional reactions to appear sophisticated. Denounces people and ideas verbally and vigorously when he disapproves. Has self tied up in his productions, easily hurt by criticism. Extremely sensitive to criticisms and judgments of peers, easily elated or depressed. Easily embarrassed by parents who too obviously take care of him. Sensitive to evidences he is not a man.
YOUNG ADULTHOOD	Freer in expressions of amusement than adolescent. Better able to take criticism, but not entirely detached in personal feelings. More conservative in expression of dislike, fear, annoyance, anger, etc. Worries about coming difficulties while trying to anticipate them. Afraid to give voice to cheerful feelings out of self-consciousness.
IDEAL CONCEPT OF MATURITY	Detached from his work, can take criticism constructively. Limits expressions to constructive ideas rather than retaliatory moves. Can conceal feelings of either kind; able to keep exciting secrets to himself. Can face unpleasant situations and analyze them calmly. Is rarely excited because he sees the issues instead of the feelings of others, and analyzes the issues. Avoids worrying over troubles not yet present, but seeks to prevent them. Is free to express wholesome feelings without inhibition or embarrassment.

175

GROGRAPH

A Scale of Personal Maturity

STRANDS OF DEVELOPMENT

6. Heterosexual

LEVEL OF MATURITY	
INFANCY	No knowledge or consciousness of sex.
CHILDHOOD	**EARLY CHILDHOOD** Girls prefer some feminine, boys some masculine, play materials, much play with same materials. Differentiate in clothing and personal grooming. Clear self-identification concerning sex. Curiosity about physical features, some manual exploration. Play together indiscriminately. **LATE CHILDHOOD** Curiosity about functions of sex organs and secondary characteristics. Tendency toward mild sex play. Boys and girls play together, same activities, but aware of sex differences, and note them occasionally. Clubs in each sex group.
ADOLESCENCE	**PREADOLESCENCE** Gangs of one sex, especially with boys. Outward antagonisms between sexes. Boys tease and annoy girls regularly. Girls show great resentment, which hides basic sense of delight. Each sex groups by itself at social functions but is furtively aware of other. Loyalty to own sex as superior, overt disapproval of interest in opposite sex, especially among boys. Considerable interest in and discussion of sex matters within own sex group.

MIDDLE ADOLESCENCE

Much mixing and exchange of partners.
Crowd of mixed membership replaces gang.
Consciousness of appearance.
Effort for much contact with opposite sex.
Many informal parties at homes and school.
Self-consciousness in social situations.
Some tendency toward steady dating, but not for long at a time.

LATE ADOLESCENCE

Reduction in widespread shopping around—much steady dating.
Crowd parties plus individual dates.
Parties more formalized—less at home.
Confidence in social relationships.
Personality factors become more important than before; sex more familiar and less disturbing.
Crowd less dominating in dating.
Engagements and talk of marriage and its obligations.
Love-making activities, not always confined to the steady partner.

YOUNG ADULTHOOD

Selection of mate, often marriage.
Love-making centered on one person.
No crowd membership; preference for a few couples.
Less dancing, more varied type of social activity.
Easy relationships with all members of opposite sex.
Discussion of sexual matters without personal involvement or embarrassment.

IDEAL CONCEPT OF MATURITY

One partner for life; no romantic interest in others.
Lively state of romance and love with own partner.
Wide friendships with members of both sexes.
Interest in personality rather than sex, particularly the romantic aspects of sex.

GROGRAPH

A SCALE OF PERSONAL MATURITY

STRANDS OF DEVELOPMENT

LEVEL OF MATURITY	7. ECONOMIC
INFANCY	Completely dependent on adults. No sense of values. Wasteful, destructive.
CHILDHOOD	No adequate concept of budget. Spends on impulse. Unaware of earning problem and the limits it imposes on spending. Not worried when money is gone, expects more on request. Very limited sense of obligation. Easily forgets. No interest in a vocation. Flighty attention to romantic aspects of jobs. Unaware of own personal resources or of their role in his adult economic life. Moderately careful, but still frequently destructive and careless of economic goods.
ADOLESCENCE	Explores various vocational fields. Takes some jobs primarily to see if he can get or hold a job. Trying out various capacities and potentialities in different lines of work. Partially aware of some varieties of vocational activity. Partially independent only, major support from home. Earnings used mostly for short-range satisfactions.

	Uses money not altogether skillfully, needs experience in budgeting. Spends lavishly at times, then runs short. Concerned over ability to support a family.
YOUNG ADULTHOOD	Able to give up present economic advantages for program of betterment. Committed to one line of vocational activity in which success is possible. Self-supporting and responsible for own dependents. Knows own resources and makes effort to bring best skills to their optimal form. Understands need for work and something of its creative possibilities. Lives near limit of an increasing income, but invests in long-range satisfactions.
IDEAL CONCEPT OF MATURITY	Valid understanding of own capacities and resources, and full utilization of highest. Adjustment to level of economic life appropriate to earning capacity. Recognition of balance between psychic income and material income in a good life. Realistic attitude toward necessity and use of money. Full appreciation of worth of all constructive work. Knowledge of the world's work in all its varieties. Shares in production of complete family life with all members of family on division of labor basis; budgeting, decisions on responsibilities, etc. Willingness to share with others the "costs" of civilized life. High sense of obligations incurred.

GROGRAPH

A SCALE OF PERSONAL MATURITY

LEVEL OF MATURITY	STRANDS OF DEVELOPMENT
	8. RECREATIONAL
INFANCY	No distinction between leisure time and any other time. No serious preoccupations. Almost constant physical activity, between rest periods. Readiness to enjoy anything that is marked by variety.
CHILDHOOD	Play is major activity, serious responsibilities few and not demanding. School is regarded more as recreation than as serious study. Some beginnings in hobbies, interest usually transitory. Rarely carries a hobby through to real completion. Dabbles in all sorts of activities, but always as participant. Very little spectator capacity. Dominant interests in overt physical forms of recreation. Beginning of interest in mental pursuits, such as reading or writing, music, and others. Shifting from individual play to group play and cooperative activities. Much playing of roles, imitating adults and spectacular characters.
ADOLESCENCE	Higher skill in fewer activities. Shifting toward boy-girl activities to some extent, but increased interest in highly taxing competitive activities. Noticeable increase in spectator role at major sports events.

	Enjoyment through identification in movies, radio, books, etc.
	Pleasure in reading about people, romance, complex plots, social problems.
	Activities suited mostly for groups, not one or two people.
	Spends less time in play than a child, but much more than an adult.
	Crowd associations absorbing—no activity, just visiting.
YOUNG ADULTHOOD	Preoccupied with work, very little time for recreation.
	Few if any hobbies.
	Usually no activities fitted for one person, or not requiring much equipment.
	Very limited reading activity or interest.
	Rare participation in dances or active social events.
	Almost always in spectator role at games, shows, etc., which are infrequently attended.
IDEAL CONCEPT OF MATURITY	One or more hobbies that do not require heavy vitality.
	A few games that can be played alone or with only a few, without much equipment.
	Fluency in reading, and a regular reading program.
	Membership in a few clubs or groups that furnish close, friendly relationships.
	Responsiveness to the qualities of many different kinds of things, which show their intriguing natures, and offer entertainment.
	A few lines of thought that are developed extensively and provide challenge.
	Contact with sources of some vital and lively materials for small talk.
	Ability to meet people easily and find topics of mutual interest.

action.[4] The particular behavior patterns, and the years over which they are customarily exhibited, are determined by the demands of the society, not by the physiological changes involved in pubescence. Although it has not been as widely acknowledged or discussed, the same thing is true of the behavioral patterns of childhood and adulthood. They are determined by social pressure or social custom, and that which is the norm tends to reproduce itself in each succeeding generation. The newly maturing must achieve their acceptance by the adults who are in control, and who preserve the patterns under which they have made their own adjustments, tending to reject those who do not conform. The newly arrived generations are similarly controlled by parents largely according to patterns that were inherited from their childhood homes. Thus the characteristic behavior patterns at any stage of development are produced by cultural forces rather than physical growth tendencies.

Cultural forces have definite channels through which they are brought to bear on children, those channels being the parents, the teachers, the community leaders, and others who have dominating relationships with children. A cultural norm viewed in general is a fairly stable pattern and can be found in its typical form all through a culture. The individuals who transmit to children, however, are not all alike in their interpretations of the cultural pattern, or in their unique ways of influencing the behavior of their charges. Therefore, some significant variations always exist from family to family, parent to parent, or teacher to teacher, in the manner in which the child's development is influenced.

Delays in maturation. By exactly the same kinds of pressures that bring about cultural similarities in behavior patterns, significant individual differences are also produced in children. Some of them take the form of delays in development, when the methods of control of adults are such as to inhibit activities that produce certain kinds of development. For example, a child who is not permitted to express himself

---

[4] E. DeAlton Partridge, *Social psychology of adolescence* (New York: Prentice-Hall, Inc., 1939), Chap. II; Luella Cole, *Psychology of adolescence* (New York: Farrar and Rinehart, 1936; 3rd ed., 1948), Chap. I.

in the home may fail to develop the ability to think for himself and to present his views to others as an adult. Here, then, is a culturally imposed immaturity. That is, it was imposed by one small segment of the social group, and it produced behavior that was not typical of the group as a whole. It is probably better to speak of such deviations not as cultural, since they are atypical, but as the product of local environmental forces in the home or the neighborhood. The principle is the same, however.

These inhibiting influences, or atypical stimulating influences, may succeed in blocking a strand of development, delaying it seriously, or accelerating it prematurely. Particularly in the cases of delayed development of some functions such as expressive ability, techniques for adjusting to secondary groups, or facility in making his own decisions, the individual is thus kept unprepared for a later stage of development, and even though he is not at the later time held back by environmental forces, he may be unable to go on into the new stage because of his own lack of readiness.

1204.   *The principle of readiness.* The term *readiness* has been used for a long time in connection with reading, where tests of reading readiness have been developed and used with considerable success. Reading readiness is only a special case of the general problem involved in every strand, and at every stage, of growth and development. The basic principle may be summed up as follows: *An individual is ready to start on any new and more complex function when he has brought to a usable stage the various individual sub-processes that are required in the new function.* Since this principle is absolutely fundamental to all forms of maturity, its importance cannot be overemphasized. Illustrations exist in every area of learning. In typing, a person is ready to copy from a page only when (a) he has usable finger dexterity sufficient to enable him to get the right finger on the right key without looking at it, (b) he can read the material he is to copy. This is obvious, but it is a good illustration of the principle. One is ready to read when (a) he can distinguish one written symbol from another, (b) he knows the oral symbols that stand for the concepts he will read about, and (c) he is aware of the fact that the printed symbols have a relationship to his oral words and his concepts. One is ready to go to a dance when (a) he is interested in getting closer to the opposite sex, (b) he can control his feet and body sufficiently to avoid being any more awkward than the others around him, and (c) he has enough other social skills to be able to engage in social relations without undue embarrassment. In all sorts of situations, individuals have been inhibited and unable to participate because some of the required sub-processes were missing and they were afraid or incapable of taking on the next higher complication in that area. Since the principle has been stated here, further elaboration may appropriately be left to the next two chapters, in which its operation should be apparent.

1205. *Loss of potentiality.* Another principle of importance in the attainment of maturity has to do with changes in the rate of growth that take place over a period of time. The principle is well-established in physical growth, where growth rates or gradients move in at least three known directions. Proximo-distal trends mean that growth rates are higher first in the central portions of the body, and become higher later in the distal or outer portions. Anterior-posterior trends mean that growth rates are higher first in the anterior sections, and become higher later in the posterior sections. Cephalo-caudal trends mean the same thing in a direction from the head toward the tail.[5] The principle is also apparent in a contrast between the rates of growth for lymphoid tissue, nerve tissue, general bodily structure, and genitals. Each has a unique sequence of changes in rate, so that some of them are growing rapidly while others have ended their growth or have not yet begun it.[6]

The application of this principle to the development of behavioral patterns is not yet generally recognized, but its effects can be seen in certain delays in maturation and must

[5] Norman L. Munn, *Psychological development* (Boston: Houghton Mifflin Co., 1938), pp. 60, 324-25; Florence L. Goodenough, *Developmental psychology* (New York: Appleton-Century-Crofts, Inc., 1934, 1945), pp. 105-8.

[6] Goodenough, *op. cit.*, pp. 232-33.

operate far more widely than is yet apparent. It appears that a principle somewhat of the following sort is operating: *There are some kinds of behavioral development that normally take place at certain levels of maturity, and if they do not take place at such a time, either do not take place later, or take place only under conditions of serious difficulty for the individual involved.*

An example may be taken from the tool subjects of the elementary school. Children who do not learn to read well early in their school experience tend not to overcome this failure later in life. Cases of this type are so well known to school people at the secondary and higher level as to need no citations. The reason for the almost universal failure to achieve later what is ordinarily done earlier is probably not a physical or mental one. It is more likely a social circumstance inherent in the roles that are pressed upon the members of a society. The curriculum of the primary grades and earlier is so arranged that a great deal of time and effort is spent on all the lines of development that feed into the more complex act of reading. This is especially true of preschool experience. For several years the very young child is engaged almost exclusively in the exploration of the common objects that make up the majority of his surroundings. He is also learning the words that stand for these objects and functions, and particularly he is delving into all the implications, ramifications, and refinements of the conceptual pictures of the world that he and his associates share. It takes much time and attention to accomplish this task in a manner adequate to later adult communication and operation. If it is not accomplished during early childhood, or at any rate by the end of the primary grades, there is a drastically reduced chance that it can be accomplished after that. From that time on the individual is expected to use these early acquired insights to enable him to turn his attention to printed materials, and use them from that time on to a large extent as the means of further enlarging his understandings and knowledge. He is so hemmed in by the new schedules that he cannot go back and do what he should have done as a child. The result is often a lifelong failure to overcome the effects of an unused growth period. All sorts of later growth are prevented or handicapped by this earlier failure.

Another example is found in the behavior of unemancipated adolescents who are still dependent on parents or their counterparts for direction in all their decisions. These individuals have passed up the period in which they were normally ready to take over their own control, and have had pressed upon them rather forcibly by their parents a pattern of submission and dependence that has become stabilized by usage and by lack of training in the making of decisions. The time is past during which the issues upon which they could practice were relatively insignificant and therefore harmless, which further drives them to avoid the gamble entailed in deciding bigger issues without experience, and they turn to adults for instruction. Adults find themselves sufficiently busy to tend to avoid taking the time necessary to lead such individuals gradually through the experiences required to make them self-determining, and thus choose to instruct them rather than emancipate them. Here again, the individual is the victim of lost opportunities, and in many cases the failure to switch to self-control in late childhood and early adolescence remains to block various kinds of development in adult years. Two examples of this behavior are cited by Cole [7] in a discussion of the problem.

Although, as stated earlier, it is a little premature to be dogmatic, what evidence there is and the logic of the problem seem to suggest the following points as tentative guides in working with growing people.

1. Growth proceeds in a definite pattern, both physically and mentally, with certain natural sequences occurring in every phase of development.

2. Each part of a sequence seems to depend on a preceding phase of growth and development.

3. The better the preceding growth, the better the current phase can be. Failure in a preceding phase may prevent a current phase from taking place.

4. The development of any function depends first on the

[7] Cole, *op. cit.*, pp. 302-6.

development of the neuro-muscular apparatus that carries it, and after that on the development of the several more specific functions that go together to make it up.

5. A growth gradient is a period of high rate of growth, during which a given part of the body or behavioral function seems to need to be encouraged for its maximal development. When the gradient is passed it may be difficult or even impossible to obtain the growth, regardless of stimulation.

1206. *Conclusion.* The teacher, parent, and counselor are in highly responsible roles. They can foster the maturation of the child, or block it. If in any way they prevent him from using his normal opportunities to launch out on the development of new functions, they will inhibit his development. They can help most significantly by looking ahead of the child's present status to the new demands that will be made of him in the future, and particularly to the ideal concepts of maturity and the functions they require. These new functions must be anticipated and the necessary preparatory experiences provided for growing boys and girls so that they will not taper off at the mediocre levels of function that constitute the norms of society, but by the momentum of better and earlier beginning continue to mature toward higher and better levels of activity. The demands of this sort of guidance are beyond a disinterested teacher, but they are challenging to one who teaches because he wants a better life for his students.

QUESTIONS FOR REVIEW

1. Can you define maturity scientifically? How?
2. What is the basis for defining maturity?
3. What is Fiske's idea of the relationship between infancy and maturity?
4. Why is it possible to speak of an ideal concept of maturity?
5. Review the concepts of maturity in the Grograph.
6. Describe each of the eight strands of development in the Grograph.
7. What might cause delays in maturation in independence? In each of the other strands of development?
8. Define readiness. How is it related to maturation?
9. Apply the principle of readiness to marriage, obtaining a job, making a religious adjustment.

10. What is meant by "loss of potentiality" in the chapter?
11. State some tentative principles of maturation as suggested in the chapter.
12. How can the Grograph be used to rate a person's maturity?

SELECTED REFERENCES

Luella Cole, *Psychology of adolescence* (3rd ed.; New York: Rinehart and Co., 1948), Chapters I and XVIII.
Harold E. Jones, *Development in adolescence* (New York: Appleton-Century-Crofts, Inc., 1943), Chapter VII.
Daniel A. Prescott, *Emotion and the educative process* (Washington, D.C.: The American Council on Education, 1938), Chapter V.

CLASS EXERCISES IN THE NATURE OF MATURITY

Things To Do in Class

1. Using the Grograph in Figure 3, the framework of which might be placed on the blackboard, have the class members examine cases 12, 13, 20, or 21. The individual being studied should be placed on the Grograph with a mark, at the position which best seems to match his behavior in each strand of development. When all eight strands have been rated, a profile may be drawn through the marks.
2. Ratings may be made, in the manner described above, of any well-known individual who is not likely to be embarrassed by actual contact with members of the class. The one selected should be a person concerning whom a great deal is known. It might be a character in a moving picture, a novel, or a biography.

Things To Do outside Class

1. Each student can rate himself on the Grograph, and prepare an analysis of his own maturity and whatever factors he can identify which have had a bearing on his maturity. This might form the basis for interviews between the instructor and individual students, in the case of any who desire such interviews.

CHAPTER XIII

FOUNDATIONS OF MATURITY IN CHILDHOOD

1301. *Products of normal growth processes.* There is a decided and important difference between changes produced in an organism by natural physical growth processes and changes produced by psychological striving on the part of the individual. What the individual and society may become depend on the latter almost entirely, although the former must take place to furnish the foundation on which the latter builds. Natural growth is not easily discouraged. Its principal requirements are a moderate amount of food, rest, and activity. The dynamics behind it are provided by the cells and organs of the body, and the innate blueprints transmitted through the genes. Under even scanty conditions, barring serious injury through accidents or poisons, natural growth will take care of the enlargement and specialization of tissues until the body has attained its adult stature, the nervous system is complete and sound, and all the organs are functioning properly. This sort of thing happens to the individual whether he tries to help it or not. The results do not constitute an achievement on his part, for he has inherited them from his ancestors. Under optimal conditions of food and activity he may contribute somewhat to the maximal development of these physical characteristics, but even in that case such stimulation is ordinarily provided by others and does not depend on the effort of the individual himself.

Goals of growth of this type are vitally important to the welfare of the individual and his ultimate maturity, and they should not be discounted in that regard. In this discussion, however, the problem is to determine what can be done by a teacher to facilitate the development of students toward maturity and good adjustment. That which is well done by nature need have only passing attention here, where major attention should be given to what man must do for himself, or do without.

Normal growth will take care of three important goals, physiological and sexual maturity, motor skills adequate to complete function, and mental growth to full capacity for learning.

Body height, weight, and shape are largely inherited, but are subject to the influence of food and exercise. Bone and muscle structure follow genetic patterns in a similar manner. The rates of growth for these various structural characteristics follow sequences that are fairly standard for the race, although some individuals come into their high growth gradients at an earlier age than others. Primary and secondary sex characteristics develop in natural sequences and in periods of fairly uniform nature for all individuals. Physiological growth processes themselves are responsible only for the physical characteristics of sex, however, not for the roles the sexes play in the social structure. Cultural forces are largely responsible for all the roles except childbearing and nursing. Ideas of a weaker and stronger sex, a mothering function in women, a fighting function in men, mannerisms and clothes, and all the so-called masculine or feminine modes of acting are imposed on what nature builds by the pressure of custom. Where custom permits, women make just as good soldiers, laborers, and executives as men, and men do as well as women in cooking, sewing, and other so-called feminine pursuits.

Motor skills reach their functional levels largely through maturation, after the nerves and muscles are individually ready for the development of integration. The acquisition of high levels of skill depends on practice, but the normal activities of life are sufficient to produce ordinary motor efficiency.

The brain and central nervous system reach their maturity without any conscious effort on the part of the individual. By living in an environment of even low-average stimulation, intelligence seems to mature so that the individual has at his command whatever capacity he inherited. His IQ is relatively independent of any effort on his part to exercise it. What he does with it, however, is another matter.

1302. *The tasks of childhood.* Growth does little more than provide one with equipment. From that point on the individual is the arbiter of his own development, as long as it is understood that what he becomes is determined by his own strivings and the forces brought to bear upon him by his social setting. Achievements that depend on the striving of the individual toward a goal are like tasks that one may assume or reject. They are not accomplished by nature as the result of the passage of time. Age does not produce them. In the Dhammapada is a passage that reads, "A man is not an elder because his head is gray; his age may be ripe, but he is called 'Old-in-vain.' "

There are some types of development, which we shall discuss presently, that should take place during childhood, but that will take place only to the extent that the child assumes responsibility and directs his energies to their accomplishment. These are true tasks, and significant accomplishments in them represent real achievements on the part of the child. His own motivation is primarily responsible for what he accomplishes, but his motivation can be significantly influenced by those around him through guiding him into challenging situations and helping him acquire visions of what he might be. The tasks discussed here are fundamental to later maturity. Unless they are carried to a significant degree of success, the individual will lack the tools with which to accomplish the tasks that face him in adolescence and adulthood. The ideal levels of maturity indicated in Figure 3 are possible only to those who have carried their childhood tasks to outstanding heights. Nothing is more important than these achievements in childhood, and nothing should be permitted to take precedence over them in the home, the neighborhood, or the school. This is the real general education for productive citizenship, good adjustment, continued growth, and peaceful relationships. The sanity and quality of the adult world is determined by the degree to which children achieve their possibilities in these tasks.

Development of speech and communication.[1] A review of sections 402 and 405 would be appropriate here, particularly on the functions of expression in human life. Speech and thought are closely tied up with each other, to the extent that no one seems to be capable of deep or comprehensive thought who does not have the companion ability of expressing what he sees and thinks. There is nothing in life that mandates the development of high communicative skill. People have struggled along in the past with grunts, or signs, or basic vocabularies, but they have never developed great patterns of living along with such limited communication. The great contributors to human thought have been people of high communicative skill, and the complexity of language goes hand in hand with the level of civilization.

Growth of language proceeds in an orderly manner. Familiarity with objects is its starting point, for language is only a symbolic tool for referring to the real world. The little child seems to identify objects rather early, and to learn the words for those objects while the concepts are developing. For this reason nouns tend to appear first in his vocabulary, since they are the names of objects. He becomes acquainted with actions a little less easily, because they are not as real and concrete as objects, but in their turn verbs come into his vocabulary since they describe actions. Still more difficult for the child to discover are differences between objects, so that the appearance of adjectives in his vocabulary is somewhat later than that of nouns and verbs, but adjectives denote differences, and they appear when the differences are discovered. In this manner all the other parts of speech make their appearance, depending on the child's discovery of his world, of the real things that constitute the referents of these parts of speech, and on his learning the names of those things. Thus it may be seen that language is only a reflection of personal experience, just as thought is only a reliving

[1] Arthur T. Jersild, *Child psychology* (New York: Prentice-Hall, Inc., 1940), Chap. V; Carl Murchison, ed., *A handbook of child psychology* (Worcester, Mass.: Clark University Press, 1933), Chap. 8; Charles E. Skinner and Philip L. Harriman, eds., *Child psychology* (New York: The Macmillan Co., 1941), Chap. 6; L. Carmichael, ed., *Manual of child psychology* (New York: John Wiley and Sons, Inc., 1946), Chap. 10.

of personal experience. Both are necessarily limited by the individual's contact with his world, and for that reason they are always in close relationship in his inner mental life and in his symbolic dealings with others.

Childhood is the ideal time for basic exploration of the world. There is no other pressing business to distract from it. Through several years the individual should be permitted, and stimulated, to peer into every corner, examine every form of life, inquire into every feeling and thought, until he becomes at home in his universe as only a thorough explorer is able to do. Since the demands of later years will preclude such uninhibited investigation, this is essentially a task of childhood.

Time is a significant element in this form of learning, as illustrated by the appearance of vocabulary. The infant tends on the average to be able to speak two meaningful words by the time he is one year of age. Studies have shown, however, that he has a listening vocabulary many times larger than two. This is easily tested with any baby by asking him to put his hand on such objects as his eye, nose, mouth, head, a cup, spoon, or bottle. Words are known by their sounds long before they are spoken, and their relationship to objects is also known before they are used in expression. At the age of two, a spoken vocabulary of 150 words is normal. This tremendous increase in rate for the second year is possible only because of the very great accumulation of experience during the first year, which only begins to make its contribution obvious when the child learns to speak the words that have been familiar to him for some time. At the end of the third year the vocabulary is normally around 900 words. Many of these, also, have their foundation back in the first year when the child was beginning to comprehend some of the complex phenomena around him and to sort out the symbols that were used in connection with them by his associates. The two words that appear at the end of the first year are nothing more than the tiniest eruption of a great store of meaning that is taking shape in his mental processes. The breadth of that first year's experience has almost unlimited significance for his later maturity, but it does not begin to reveal its influence until later. So it is with each succeeding year's experience. When poverty of early experience is finally manifest in the later years of childhood, or in adolescence or even adulthood, it is too late to go back and remedy the defect. Other demands will be in the way. The child whose early years were crammed with exploration will reap dividends throughout his life in the ability to deal with subsequent experience in a wider, deeper, and more complex manner than those with narrow backgrounds.

Vocabulary in itself is not a primary objective. Large vocabularies cannot be developed and kept by those who do not have broad understandings to support them, but vocabularies can be quickly expanded through direct attack on words, by those whose experiences have already given them the background for using words in a meaningful way. Jersild points out that children typically have vocabularies of about 2500 words when they enter school, are likely to have as many as 7500 different words in the middle elementary grades, and the average high-school senior has been estimated to have a vocabulary of about 15,000 words. There will always be wide differences between individual children at any age, both in the number of words used, and in the particular words included in the total.

It should be emphasized again that this kind of development does not reach its best forms without significant effort on the part of the child. Effort does not mean unpleasantness or unwillingness. Ordinarily it is quite the opposite. The explorations that lead to skill in language usage are exciting and attractive, especially when children are egged on in such a task, but they can be seriously hampered or inhibited by barriers placed in the way on the part of irritated adults or those who feel the child should keep quiet and stay in the background. The will to perform this task with vigor can be turned into a dispirited submission to control. Even though the child is not to blame for his lassitude, he is the one who will suffer the penalties of immaturity the rest of his life, and he will inflict his narrowness on others to follow, as it was inflicted on him by his parents or teachers.

Socialization.[2] The ability to live with other people is one of the most significant aspects of modern life and constitutes an important facet of maturity. Whatever the adult is able to accomplish in this respect depends on how the task was carried out in childhood, where social skills and preferences are established and rather thoroughly set.

It is suggested by many psychoanalysts that the first relationships between mother and infant set the stage for the later social life of the infant. It is at this time, when the world of reality is an undifferentiated and unfamiliar mass of sensations, that the infant can be turned back within himself to get away from shocks and rebuffs, or coaxed out into reality by warm and satisfying reactions. The mother is the one most strategically situated to determine which kind of experience the infant will have at first. To the extent that this is a sound hypothesis, it appears that the first tendencies are established at the discretion of others, and not by the infant's own will or striving, although it is by no means unlikely that some infants strive more vigorously to contact reality than do others, and that some may give up rather easily. Such striving is not a cognitive intellectual thing, but if it does occur it is the infant who makes it occur.

The external world of the child includes everything around him, people and objects all mixed together and undistinguished. Early in his life he will separate people from objects, and objects and people from himself, and begin to work out his approaches to each of them, and his ways of using each in the satisfaction of his needs. This begins when the adults start to take care of the child and thus provide him with his first social experiences. The first year is full of tentative responses and explorations. People around him are appraised and tried out in many ways. Their reactions, the ways in which they treat him, the effects they produce on his own feelings, the richness or poverty of their contributions to his various needs, register on his conceptual processes to give him the beginnings of social concepts. From these foundations he will be primed to find in others what

[2] Jersild, *op. cit.*, Chaps. VI and VII; Skinner and Harriman, *op. cit.*, Chaps. 10 and 14.

he has found in his first acquaintances and will perceive all subsequent experiences in a manner substantially determined by his first experiences.

At first and all the time his interactions will revolve around his own needs and feelings. People will be means through which his needs are affected. The way he treats them will be a function of this interaction, determined at first by what his parents and others let him do to them. He will learn to do to them whatever makes them do to him what he wants them to do. This early shaping of his behavior will have a profound effect on his later social techniques.

The child tends to hold his interactions within his own family, but if he is to accomplish his task of socialization significantly he must soon get out beyond the limits of the family, in a journey that will eventually take him clear out into the whole world. Neighborhood play groups serve a wholesome purpose in this connection. Children should be encouraged to take their feelings of belongingness out into such groups, beginning the break with the home in a gradual but very purposeful manner. Adult maturity requires complete emancipation from parental control, and the beginning of that break is in the early years of childhood. The child who succeeds in adjusting to the neighborhood group has already won an advantage in his transition to the school group, and success at that stage lends him confidence and ability for the succeeding moves out into broader segments of society. When he becomes an adolescent he will be faced with tasks that are all but impossible unless he, by that time, possesses skill in living with his peers. At that stage he will have neither the opportunity nor the time to go back and work gently through all the little ventures into the outside world, with his doting family standing behind him ready to support him and provide him with complete security.

Late adolescence will take him afield into strange and alien social relationships that will repel him if he has not by that time achieved a mastery over the techniques of social intercourse and a feeling of security in the large and rather complex world. This task will never come to completion without genuine striving by the individual. In spite of mixed successes and failures he must continue to explore himself as a social being, until he finds his own capacities and learns how to use them in cooperative activity with others. In this manner he will lose his fear of strangers, and face the heterogeneous society of a world with confidence in his own abilities and appreciative interest in the lives of others.

Cultural orientation. This is the task of mastering one's own culture first, and then learning step by step how to live peacefully and considerately with the rest of the world and its wide variety of cultural patterns. A person does not need to abandon his own cultural pattern to become mature, although there are many would-be sophisticates whose claim to sophistication consists of a demonstration of their ability to turn their backs on the customs of their childhood cultures. It is quite true that a person may find it highly desirable to evaluate his own youthful culture, and perhaps to modify in some ways some immature and unsound beliefs and practices in it, but evaluation does not inevitably lead to the discovery of immaturities. It may lead to demonstration of the soundness of cultural patterns whose value was taken for granted in early years purely on the strength of the influence of admired adults. It is a distinct mark of maturity to be able to make such evaluations objectively and to arrive at conclusions uninfluenced by a feeling of need to demonstrate either one's independence or one's docility.

A fully mature individual must be able to participate with others in his world in a gracious, considerate, skillful and understandable, and morally acceptable manner. There is more to it than even these adjectives indicate. It is a complex achievement, realized by far too few people. Its relative rareness is probably due to the general absence of attention in educational programs to basic manners and customs. The task is a little too complicated to be left to the ingenuity of the average individual. A partial listing of the problems involved in it may indicate why that is so. Even a simple culture has many, many elements in its *pattern of rights and wrongs.* No one learns all of them well enough to sense all their interrelationships, particularly in any culture as complex as the modern civilized world. The *religious systems* of the world are also highly complex and divergent, and very much interwoven with the systems of right and wrong. The *accepted forms of behavior and manners* are almost unlimited in their ramifications, as suggested by the wide variety of table manners to be found within the families of one neighborhood almost anywhere in America. The *high and low forms of language,* including alterations related to conversation with children, familiar adults, superiors, technicians, scholars, religious leaders, and many other kinds of people, are almost a lifetime study in themselves. The system of what is approved or disapproved in the way of *goals and ambitions* for young people has its complications and peculiarities within each culture. The *caste and class relationships* and all the privileges and prohibitions entailed in them is a scientific study in itself. The vast array of *school materials and subjects,* including the language, the number systems, the historical and political points of view that prevail in a culture, and many other such kinds of orientation, are forbidding in their scope. The *esthetic heritage* from the past is mastered by very few, and only slightly understood by not many more.

Social, intellectual, and philosophical maturity are impossible without adequate cultural orientation. Furthermore, the person who is involved in social relations outside of his own primary group faces the task of acquiring at least the essential rudiments of orientation in several other cultures than his own. The extension of familiarity into distant cultural groups is not ordinarily possible in childhood, but a tendency to adjust easily to other patterns is certainly encouraged by wide participation in groups of all kinds. The childhood years mark the formation of mental sets toward his own groups and members of different groups, making it easy or difficult for him later to participate with such people. During childhood also there are many opportunities to discuss the customs of the group and to evaluate their effectiveness and desirability. In contrast to this is the practice of having children accept them without question. The results of the two approaches are distinctly different. Children who have learned how to examine their own cultural patterns critically are able to continue understandingly in the observance of what is good in them, whereas blind acceptance tends to set the stage for later wholesale discard of the entire system when any part of it is found to conflict with compelling realities turned up through study or social readjustments. Children who have learned how to analyze their own cultural patterns are also inquisitively ready to explore the patterns of other cultures with a similar frankness and open-mindedness. This readiness is essential to the kind of maturity that makes for good-neighbor relations between nations and countries. It is the rigidly indoctrinated individual within his own culture who ridicules all other cultural systems and refers to them with such names as wops, foreign scum, and dirty immigrants.

Cultural orientation is a difficult task for it depends on the initiative and striving of the individual, whether he inquires deeply and evaluatively into his own cultural pattern or takes it uncritically by adoption. It also depends on the accessibility of personal experiences and materials by which he can explore fully the very broad scope of beliefs and practices that make up even one cultural pattern, let alone the other significant patterns to be found elsewhere in his world. The elementary school occupies a very important place in the child's struggle with his tasks, as a brief comparison of its curriculum with these tasks will show.

1303. *The elementary curriculum and the tasks of childhood.* In this discussion three major tasks of childhood have been identified, and it has been suggested that all of childhood is devoted to their accomplishment. If they are as important as has been indicated here, it may be expected that the program of the elementary school will be set up around the tasks in an effort to facilitate their achievement.

Socialization and the early school years. Children now enter some schools as young as two. These are nursery schools in which a child may obtain as much as three years of experience before entering the kindergarten. Nursery-school programs are not in any sense subject-matter programs. They are devoted to helping the child make an adjustment to the social world and develop independence in caring for himself. The activities consist of dressing and undressing themselves at the appropriate times, finding and maintaining their own lockers and pallets for the care of clothes and for naps. They learn to lie down in rooms occupied by others and take a quiet rest even though they may not be sleepy, to avoid disturbing those around them. They play a great deal with shared toys, exchanging both toys and roles, helping each other and being helped in turn. The teachers rarely direct activities or solve social problems. They help the children understand that problems exist, and lead them into experiences in solving their own problems. They watch for opportunities to help each child discover how others feel, and learn to think of others in social situations. The children wait on themselves as early as their motor control permits, and learn to eat with others. They are coached toward the point at which they can visit and eat at the same time, getting both done reasonably well.

They find and develop new interests, both individually and in cooperation with others. The interesting activities of one become a center of observation and inquiry for the others, with increasing exchange of ideas and participation. They sing together when they want to express feelings in song, they have stories together, and they take back and forth from school to home the interesting events in each place to pass on to the family or their schoolmates. In this rich social experience, children from various kinds of homes mingle and learn to play together harmoniously.

Everything about this program is intensively pointed at the child's task of becoming a socialized being. He is drawn easily out of his home, and launched not only into neighborhood groups, but into city-wide groups. Not infrequently he is thus exposed to world-wide contacts through the children in attendance with him. Little children frequently cry when first separated from their parents at the beginning of the experience, but because they find so much security and interest in this outside group, they soon begin to let go of the home and develop confidence in their ability to adjust to others. The unhurried pace of the nursery-school day allows the child to adjust at his own pace, so that when he does move fully into the group it is done at his own motivation and tends to develop in him the practice of making his own decisions.

In a similar manner, though with somewhat less concentration, the program is significant in its stimulation to his exploration of the world around him and to his formation of meanings upon which he can develop communicative skills of a high level of quality.

It makes a significant contribution, also, to cultural orientation in at least two ways. The child learns what one does or does not do in many situations through the patient guidance of the teachers and the mutual correction of the students by each other. He also engages often in talk about why it is done or not done in this way or that. He is thus encouraged to think about his manners and modes of living, with reference to their effect on the happiness of the people involved.

When these objectives of the nursery school have been recognized, there is not much left that has not been recognized. The program would seem to be formulated almost entirely around the tasks of childhood, and particularly around the socialization process.

The work of the kindergarten is largely an extension of the later years of the nursery school. There is an increase in cooperative play and projects and in sharing in the exploration of the world around the neighborhood and school. Reading is done by the teacher, who exposes the children to books filled with interesting stories and pictures. Some children are learning to read for themselves at this time and have access to simple reading materials. None of them are pushed into reading, however. The principal functions are related to continued socialization and more rapid increase in the conceptual backgrounds of language and communication.

Through the next three or more grades there is a continuation of the social function, while other educational activities are gradually introduced. Until the child leaves the elementary school entirely he is never free from consciously planned experiences in learning to live with others comfortably and considerately.

Speech and communication in the early school years. As already shown, experiences fundamental to concept formation are prominent in the nursery school, and increasingly prominent in the kindergarten. With the advent of the child in the first grade reading begins to receive some systematic attention. Readiness tests are used, and there are many procedures by which teachers lead students to the ability to distinguish printed symbols from each other, and to associate them with words and objects. For many children, this has been going on at home and in school for some time. For others it is just beginning. There is no regimentation. The natural rhythms of development of the children are now given free play, for reading must not be allowed to bear the burden of distaste that would come from its being forced upon children who are not ready for it. While this conceptual and symbolic development is taking place, the child learns to draw, to cut, and to build things with his hands. He continues his social education through much group participation in activities designed to introduce him to the esthetic side of life, and little by little he begins exploring his own culture and the cultures of other people.

Through the second and third grades reading ordinarily develops rapidly and is fed by rich supplies of interesting books, plus a number of workbooks in which the pupil can show the teacher how well he understands what he is doing and in what ways he needs help. By the time he reaches the fifth grade he is using his reading skill as a tool for exploring many areas of knowledge about his nearby world and his distant neighbors. The social sciences take a prominent place in his readings, and he begins in earnest the regular mastery of knowledge in a systematic way.

Cultural orientation and the early school years. In this gradual overlapping manner the three large tasks of childhood are brought into the school program. With the development of communication to a usable stage the attack turns with increasing emphasis to mastery of the many things that make up one's cultural setting. The number system was introduced early in the grades through simple experiences with quantities and their symbols. In the third and fourth grades simple calculations are instituted. Within two years more complex calculations in multiplication and long division are mastered, and fractions are explored. From then on the higher functions appear regularly, and the problems are such as to take the functions of mathematics out into the everyday world. Throughout the rest of the elementary school, and well into the secondary-school program, serious attention is given to the mastery of the subject matter that represents the world in which we live. The high-school program will show a shift in another direction, but until the child is moving into his preadolescent years, the school concentrates its attention on the three major tasks outlined in the first part of this chapter.

1304. *Conclusion.* Childhood is a period in this culture within which the individual carries no other serious responsibilities than those involved in the tasks of getting himself well founded in his exploration of the world, substantially prepared to communicate with others, understandingly oriented in his own culture, and securely launched into ever-broadening social relationships. For approximately twelve years these are his preoccupations, and the extent to which he masters them will have much to do with his success in meeting the challenges of the next phase of his development. The whole elementary-school curriculum is devoted to their facilitation. With the end of this period of his life, however, demands will be made on him by society and by his own preoccupation with other things that will make further development along these lines an incidental rather than a major activity. To all practical purposes the tasks of childhood must be carried to substantial completion by the end of childhood, or they may never be advanced much beyond that point. If they are completed, the individual is ready for his next tasks, which are defined by his immanent transition to the status of an adult. Whether he can become mature in any real sense depends on how ready he is for his adolescent tasks, for the achievements of childhood furnish him the foundation from which he will build poorly or well into his adulthood.

QUESTIONS FOR REVIEW

1. What is the difference between "goals of growth" and "tasks of development"?
2. What aspects of maturity will normal growth take care of?
3. What aspects of maturity will not be cared for by ordinary growth?
4. What are some of the things that might hinder development of speech and communicative maturity? What will help it?
5. What are some of the stages in attainment of socialization during childhood?
6. What does the need for belongingness have to do with social development?
7. Name several aspects of cultural orientation.
8. What are some of the complicated problems of right-wrong orientation?
9. Show how the elementary-school curriculum is built around the tasks of childhood. How does the nursery school help?

SELECTED REFERENCES

Arthur I. Gates, Arthur T. Jersild, T. R. McConnell, and Robert C. Challman, *Educational psychology* (New York: The Macmillan Co., 1948), Chapters IV, V, and VI.

Walter C. Langer, *Psychology and human living* (New York: Appleton-Century-Crofts, Inc., 1943), Chapter 9.

E. D. Partridge, *Social psychology of adolescence* (New York: Prentice-Hall, Inc., 1939), Chapter I.

CLASS EXERCISES ON THE TASKS OF CHILDHOOD

Things To Do outside Class

1. Where feasible, assign students to visit classes throughout the elementary school and to prepare detailed descriptions of the ways in which the pupils are being helped with their developmental tasks, as discussed in this chapter. Students should be assigned to specific grade levels, so that the reports will include observations from all the grades, the nursery school, and the kindergarten. The reports should be discussed in class.

CHAPTER XIV

MOVING INTO ADULTHOOD THROUGH ADOLESCENCE

1401. *The nature of adolescence.* The position was taken in Chapter II on the analysis of human behavior that anything so complex was inevitably baffling without an analytical scheme that identified basic functions and revealed cause-and-effect relationships. The same position is taken here. Adolescence in modern society is the result of several forces operating on the growing person. The nature of those forces, and the status and plight of the individual when they begin to strike him, are keys to an understanding of what is going on. No one is capable of understanding or helping an adolescent, or of giving sound counsel to one who is approaching adolescence, who does not understand the whole phenomenon.

Part of the picture is revealed best through an examination of primitive cultures, with attention to the changes that take place as the culture becomes progressively more complex. Another significant insight is obtained from observing the contrast between the roles of children and adults. A third enlightening analysis has to do with the manner in which children are introduced to the transition, and the effects produced in them by various modes of introduction. Each of these approaches will be treated briefly in this section, after which the most potent preoccupations and tasks of adolescent people will be discussed, with particular reference to the problem of attaining a high level of maturity.

Childhood and adulthood in simple cultures. Margaret Mead has given us helpful accounts of the way children grow up under various cultural conditions.[1] In the simplest cul-

[1] Margaret Mead, *Coming of age in Samoa* (New York: Blue Ribbon Books, Inc., 1936).

tures children and adults do much the same kinds of things. All the males may fish a good deal. The child does it for fun, the adult to get food. There is little real difference in what they do. When the child reaches an age that is significant to the group, he is initiated into adulthood with some form of ritual. After that he goes with the men rather than with the boys. What he does is not altered to any significant degree. He knew how to do it before he was initiated, and he fits smoothly into the adult world. Since the roles are alike, he requires no training, and there is no period between childhood and adulthood in which he undergoes a transition. Under simple, natural conditions, then, there are only two periods in life, adulthood and childhood. One turns smoothly into the other whenever the group takes steps to recognize the new adult.

This two-period system can only exist when the two roles are enough alike to need no intervening period of training or preparation. When the adult role begins to include functions that have not been practiced by the child and that the child is not allowed to practice, the two periods are pushed apart by the necessary insertion of a training or transition period, during which the child gets ready for the adult role. In this manner a cultural artifact is injected into what is otherwise a smooth process of growth and maturation. A new period is created by the cultural demands, not by the physiological growth processes.

As the two basic roles become more and more dissimilar, the intervening period becomes longer and more difficult, because of the difficulty involved in dropping the role of the child and assuming the role of the adult. This tendency is further aggravated when some of the roles of the adult are artificially held in reserve and denied to the transitional individual, not because he is not ready to assume them, but because the adults will not allow him to practice them for various reasons. Along the way from the simple life of the Samoan culture to the complicated life of an industrialized and urban American city it is possible to find many stages of this transitional alteration and many differences in the intervening periods through which the children must pass into adulthood. The period is known quite generally now as adolescence.

Many degrees of difference from simplicity to complexity have been known in American history, and the adolescent adjustment has varied in difficulty accordingly. Among the frontier families of early America, life was quite simple. The principal occupation of all males was clearing ground, farming, fishing, and hunting, with an occasional house-building. Boys took their places in this serious business as soon as they could handle the tools. When they were physiologically ready to marry they did so, without preliminaries or delay, and moved along to some free ground where they merely resumed for themselves the activities they had been engaged in for their parental families. The girls were in a similar situation. Adolescence had very little meaning to them, and indeed they were seemingly almost unaware of it. As the settlements grew into communities, and the occupations began to change through the addition of new and specialized skills and practices, and increasing division of labor, adolescence became a period of real adjustment and change. Not only were the adult roles becoming more complex and difficult, but the childhood roles were also becoming simpler and easier, because, through the division of labor, the provision of fuel and food by the old methods became obsolete, and children turned from labor to play for their major preoccupation.

In very few places today is adolescence a simple period of change. The adult and child roles are so different, and the adult role so complex, that adolescence is fraught with many shocks and surprises, and marked by tension over long periods of time. In fact it is no longer just one period of induction. It has evolved into a series of periods known as preadolescence, early, middle, and late adolescence, and young adulthood, a set of progressive apprenticeships, which are truly impressive to the observer.

Contrast between childhood and adulthood today. If the two periods were essentially alike at one time, what can be said about them now. The contrast is striking. In Table 1 are two lists of characteristics, one for children and one for adults, leaving adolescence out for the present.

TABLE 1. CONTRASTS IN ROLES OF CHILD AND ADULT

The Child Is:	*The Adult Is:*
small	large
protected	protector
confined in action	unlimited in action
weak	strong

The Child Does These Things:	*The Adult Does These Things:*
plays	works
studies	teaches
obeys	instructs
asks questions	gives the answers
belongs to family	"owns" or has the family
seeks authority	constitutes authority
asks for money	gives money
watches privileged be-	engages in privileged be-
havior enviously	havior he denies child

The list is suggestive only, for it could be expanded greatly. The significant thing about it is not the particular items that are included, but the rather complete contrast in the two lists. It is not easy for an adult to step out of his role and recall the outlook of a child. It may be made a little easier by remembering, from one's own childhood, experiences suggested by each item in the list, and recalling how the child regarded the adults in the experiences. The world as it appears to an adult is something that the child has never imagined or experienced in any way whatever.

As an illustration, take the matter of going to work. All the child sees of it is what can be observed at home. The parent gets up in the morning, has the right of way in the bathroom, gets preferred treatment in the kitchen, and the household is organized to some extent around the business of getting him off to work. He goes off in the car, or on the bus, and is gone all day, somewhere in that mysterious void which lies beyond the home and the neighborhood. What he does is left to the imagination of the child. He comes home in the evening, dripping fragmentary and mysterious allusions to unknown and rather awesome goings-on out in the world that the child has never explored. The child has no way of sensing the meaning of long hours of work, of continuous responsibility, of complex decisions upon which hang worry and risk, of occasional conquest and frequent disappointment and annoyance. Going to work is a game to be played, an exciting adventure akin to saving ladies from dragons, or at the very least an excursion into the world that is open only to the parent and therefore inviting and romantic.

It has been said that a university exists when Mark Hopkins sits on one end of a log and a student on the other end. What that university is like, however, depends upon whose end of the log you are sitting on, Mark Hopkins' or the student's. So it is with the child and the adult. The world is one thing to a child, and quite a different thing to the adult. The adult has some recollection of the child's world, for he was a child once even if he has lost most of his childhood feelings and interpretations. The child has no idea what the adult world is like, because he has never been an adult, and has no experience on which his imagination can play.

Observation of the actions and remarks of children lead to the belief that when they talk about "getting to be a big man" or "when I am a daddy" or "when I get married and have babies" they have a status in mind that has little in common with reality. The role of "daddy" consists of all the privileges and marks of status they have observed, without any of the burdens and difficulties that have not yet been revealed to them. A "daddy" is one who is the boss, who tells the children what they can and cannot do, who sits in the favorite chair, who gets the paper first, who has the respectful obedience of everyone in the family, who keeps the money in his pocket, who comes and goes when he pleases, and who does a great many things he will not allow his children to do. The child is in no position to know that a daddy is also one who gets very tired every day on a job that may be quite difficult, who is worried about the budget, who spends some sleepless nights for his family's sake, who sacrifices many of his own comforts and pleasures for his children, or who subjects himself to the will of others in order to obtain the things his family needs.

How children are introduced to adulthood. It is a mistake to assume that children know about adulthood through living with adults. Their concepts are unrealistic, imaginative, and romantic. On the whole, the child is in for something of a shock, although he is given a long period of time to make the transition, and most of the disillusionments come gradually throughout that period. At the same time the child is picking up more constructive points of view and gathering in the skills required in the adult world.

No small part of the difficulty of the transition lies in the length of childhood during which this irresponsible role is carried on. From infancy until a child is anywhere from six to twelve years of age he is allowed the unhampered life of a playboy. There is little change in what is expected of him during those years. The role becomes highly stabilized and well established. The child makes a very firm adjustment to life within the patterns of the role. Six to twelve years of practice are sufficient to make it extremely difficult to abandon the role, particularly when the abandonment is somewhat precipitously pushed onto the child by surprise, as it quite often the case.

Theoretically, there are two ways of approaching adulthood, which are suggested in Figure 4. One is the typical long childhood of the laissez-faire variety, marked by no serious attempts to assume responsibilities, or to develop social and intellectual capacities. For several years parents make no marked effort to direct the child progressively into more mature experiences and roles. This type of growth always has a period of eruption when the adult world suddenly interrupts the child's pleasant fairyland, requires him to discontinue his customary activities, and makes him begin to be an adult. The ensuing struggle for readjustment is described subsequently as preadolescence, and illustrated in the upper part of Figure 4.

The other is a no-less-ample childhood marked by play and exploration, but one in which the level of the play and exploration are constantly raised as the increasing capacity of the child permits, so that by the time he has reached the usual preadolescent years he has already anticipated the

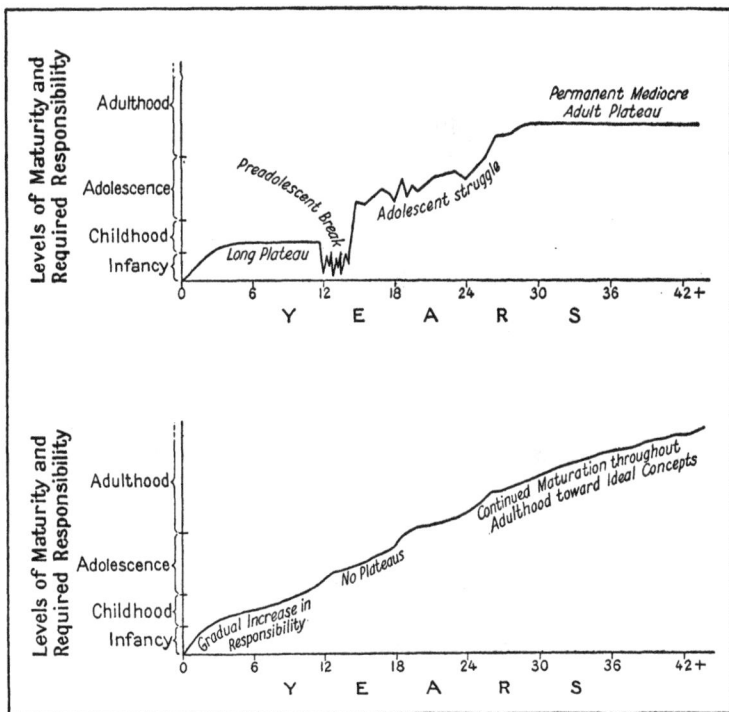

FIG. 4. TWO THEORETICAL CURVES FOR MATURATION OF PERSONALITY

nature of the more mature roles and is well on his way into them. There is no eruption because there is no sudden demand, no disintegration of a highly stabilized irresponsibility, and no sense of insecurity as a result of such disorganization. Progress through the mastery of adult points of view and functions is equally smooth because of the same gradual attack and anticipation. Adulthood is not then viewed as a pinnacle that marks a final adjustment and a stopping place, but as a role of responsibility within which one continues in the rewarding exploration of new worlds.

Both of these types of development are illustrated in actual children in every community. The irregular pattern is far more common that the other, largely because parents and teachers do not give enough time and thought to the planning of experiences that will produce the curve of constant growth. The constant rate of increase is the objective behind many programs for children and youth, such as Scouting, 4-H Clubs, and the numerous semi-educational and activity programs of churches and other agencies. This kind of growth can be accomplished without interrupting the great values to be obtained from play and affectionate dependence in childhood. They do not constitute an attempt to make little children into miniature adults. They involve only the increasing use of the higher levels of capacity that normally appear as the child grows, rather than the practice of allowing capacity to increase without use for several years, after which a frantic effort is made to overcome lost time all at once.

1402. *Preadolescence.*[2] If the child is allowed to run without progressive upgrading in personal maturity, he faces almost inescapably a certain amount of shock when he is finally required to move into the adolescent transition. Since this is a very widespread condition, its genesis and nature should be understood by parents and teachers, so that they will know how to deal with it.

The cause. Security is a state that is characterized by good adjustment. It is possible because the individual has patterns of behavior that successfully resolve the problems he faces and bring him regularly back to a state of relatively adequate satisfaction of his needs. As long as his behavior patterns are adequate to meet his situations he will feel secure even though he is constantly moving into and out of states of need with their temporary unadjustment.

Individuals who are gradually exposed to new situations

2 Acknowledgment is made to Dr. Fritz Redl for the realistic and enlightening ideas delivered in lectures at the University of Chicago in the summer of 1940. Those ideas are the foundation of this section, and are also represented to some extent in an excellent book by Peter Blos, *The adolescent personality* (New York: Appleton-Century-Crofts, Inc., 1941), Part 3, Chaps. 2, 3, 4.

will gradually readjust their process concepts through the experiences involved in seeking new ways of satisfying their needs. There are minor tensions involved in such readjustments, because they consist of minor crises or frustrations, and a certain amount of exploration is required to develop the new response patterns before satisfactory adjustments are possible. Over a long period of time large changes in behavior can be brought about through this steady process.

When a person's situation is changed so much that he finds no help in his old patterns of behavior, he has only one possibility, which is a regression to previously held patterns that have long since been left behind. The fact that they are usually patterns of a more immature period accounts for the use of the term regression. In such drastic situations one cannot take the time required to work out totally new ways of behaving, because the pressure for adjustment is too great. Typically, people exposed to such situations make an initial cursory search for appropriate lines of action, then show the usual frustration symptoms and turn to some degree toward infantile reactions.

Tensions accumulating under failure to adjust, show themselves in certain ways that are fairly uniform for certain levels of tension. As shown in Chapter XXII, many typical expressions of tension may be grouped as casual overt behavior. These are usually present in mild degrees of maladjustment. Taken in concentrated form they make up a large part of the so-called mechanisms that accompany mildly neurotic states. In what Horney [3] calls a *character* neurosis, they are more or less *permanently* adopted into the reactions of the individual, as channels for the spending of tension. In her *situational* neuroses they show up *temporarily*, until the individual resolves his conflicts, after which they disappear. The intensive or explosive reactions illustrated by sudden frights, apprehension, loss of contact with reality, or violence in arguments, indicate on the whole more serious frustrations, and probably a longer period of maladjustment, than the casual overt symptoms. There are other

[3] Karen Horney, *The neurotic personality of our time* (New York: W. W. Norton and Co., 1937).

kinds of symptoms that indicate unsolved problems listed in Table 6, page 446, some of which have a bearing on preadolescence.

Preadolescence has all the characteristics of a situational neurosis for a great many young people. It develops when the adults in control of the young person begin by various means to deny him the use of his childhood patterns and start to force him into more mature behavior. If this is a relatively sudden change for him, he does not have enough time to explore casually for new patterns that have the approval of his elders. The result is a startled attempt to cope with the situation, followed by a typical frustration reaction, and a regression to less mature patterns. Since he has not progressed much beyond babyhood as yet, the infantile patterns tend to be the next lower level to which he can drop. He begins then to show a combination of infantile reactions, plus many of the casual overt symptoms of maladjustment.

It is surprising to what extent this change in parental attitude is a relatively sudden thing. It is often precipitated by the realization on the part of parents that Jack and Alice are "getting to be pretty big for such childish irresponsible behavior—it's time they were showing a little responsibility and acting like adults." This is often coincidental with arrival at the limit of toleration for the irresponsible behavior and with a resolution to put a stop to it. In various ways it is possible for somewhat rude interruptions to be thrown into the life of a child, when he has been allowed to remain at a low level of maturity longer than necessary.

The typical behavior of a preadolescent is marked by what appears to be an abandonment of all the standards of conduct that may have marked his childhood up to that time. He becomes slovenly, will not wash or comb his hair, or keep his clothing tidy, or in any way groom himself. He throws his things around, neglects his daily duties in the home, drops all pretense of responsibility, is late for his meals and unsystematic in everything. He becomes fretful and testy, quarrels a great deal, fights with his friends, seems to take delight in deliberately hurting those he loves, but does all of this without any deep-seated animosities, and feels sorry immediately after. He daydreams a great deal, pays no attention to teacher or parent, and may have some-what fantastic dreams and fantasies. In his imagination he compensates for his frustrations by becoming a knight, a pilot of a fighter plane, a notorious bandit, a superhuman crime buster, or a powerful person who grants the humble request of his former schoolteacher in paternal mercy. He is as unpredictable as he is irresponsible. He may look a teacher in the eye and hear nothing of what is being said, or be called upon for gazing out of the window and respond with a perfect answer to the question. He compulsively kills time, even when being urged to hurry, but may move back and forth between periods of impenetrable lassitude and periods of violent activity.

His regressive reactions often reinstate thumbsucking, enuresis, and whining, along with other devices for getting attention or other indications of loss of coordination. On the whole the behavior is bewildering to those who are not prepared for it, and who have to live with it for the year or two it may take the child to regain his bearing and drop his symptoms of frustration.

By suggesting that this situation is equivalent to a situational neurosis, it was intended to point out that the maladjustment is in almost all cases temporary rather than permanent. It is a product of loss of security through denial of the use of customary reaction patterns. It will last only as long as the individual requires to reconstruct his orientation to life and to begin the formation of new approaches to the satisfaction of his needs. Hence the kind of help he needs is indicated by the course of development of his mental state.

Course of development. One of the reasons for contrasting the roles of children and adults in the first part of this chapter was to indicate the magnitude of the problem facing the preadolescent. The complete reconstruction of a childhood pattern into an adult pattern is more complicated and difficult than the slow and steady infiltration of new ideas into a changing pattern. Dr. Redl suggests that perhaps only the disintegration of the old pattern, under the stress of its seemingly complete inadequacy, will permit the radically new adult pattern to take shape. There is an apparent difficulty here that must be explained. In reality the adult pattern contains many elements carried right over from the childhood pattern. These would include such things as standards of right and wrong, cleanliness, morality, manners, consideration for others, and so on. To the preadolescent, however, there is no way of knowing that some elements of his former behavior are still acceptable and that he is being curbed primarily because of the objectionable nature of other elements. This is probably because the objectionable elements are distributed through almost everything he does, and he is therefore called to task in almost all areas of his daily behavior. He is being corrected because, as a child, he does not think for himself about what he is doing, he has not learned the need for sharing with others the privileges of the living room, the radio, the newspapers, and other common properties of the family. As a child he has been allowed to be unaware of the feelings of others, to be the center of attention too much of the time, to show his disappointments too forcefully, and so on. These behaviors are mixed with his standards of cleanliness and the like, and those who criticize him are far more likely to do so with general demands to behave himself than with specific instructions on what it is that he is doing that he should not do, and what he is not doing that he should do, and what he is doing that he should keep right on doing. In the absence of specific help in redirecting his behavior, he does not discriminate between acceptable and unacceptable parts of his activity and concludes that none of it is satisfactory.

For that reason, in all probability, he drops his standards of goodness along with everything else, and appears to have disintegrated morally and in every other way. It is a common part of the reaction to begin to swear, to resort to slang, and to engage in a variety of activities that have been taboo in the past.

The disintegration of behavior patterns leaves him without systematic methods of meeting daily situations. This

seems to be the best explanation of his inconsistency, change-
ability, indifference to time or schedules, and frequent
escapes through daydreaming and fantasy. This sort of reaction seems to last for a year to two in most cases. The
length of time suggests that following the breakdown of
the childhood patterns something very much like the long
slow period of concept formation in infancy is taking place.
The individual is actually starting over in the accumulation
of new concepts from experience. With his attention forced
toward "acting like an adult," he is experimenting with all
the behaviors that seem from his point of view to be significantly adult. Very often the ones of which he is most
conscious are the ones which have been made prominent
through much repeated prohibition. He has been told
he cannot smoke because it is only allowed to adults, which
makes it decidedly an adult behavior. Therefore it offers a
way of acting like an adult. Similarly reserved for adults
are the privileges of swearing, dominating others, regulating
their own schedules, staying out late at night, and so on.
The groping individual may very well try each of these in
his search for adult reaction patterns. Any attempt to engage in them will, of course, only confuse him further, because in most cases he will be punished for such behavior
even more vigorously than for his childish actions. On the
other hand, when parents permit him to engage in such
activities they tend to become fixed quickly, because it then
appears to him that he is making an adjustment to the new
demands.

Throughout the period of this exploration the greatest
needs are for time to explore, freedom from pressure that ag-
gravates the maladjustment, opportunity to drain off tensions
without being squelched (which would almost inevitably
tend to destroy initiative and reduce the child to an insipid
submissiveness), and as much guidance toward what the
child is seeking as his associates can give him without taking
the initiative from him.

The outcome. Where the deviant behavior is due only to
the preadolescent disturbance, with no complicating personality difficulties underlying it, the normal course of events

will lead to a readjustment on a desirable plane in time. There would seem to be two things that help it along significantly.

One is a dawning interest in the opposite sex, which ordinarily begins to manifest itself near this period. The effect of this new interest will be to turn attention to personal appearance and manners and to reinstate the standards of propriety that were temporarily dropped. The effect of this factor is often seen suddenly, following the discovery by the individual that another particular person is somehow surrounded with a halo of attractiveness. There are excellent accounts of this sudden appearance in some of the cases presented by Blos.

The other apparent factor is the gradual formation of concepts about what adulthood is, so that the child begins to see, faintly at first, what he is expected to become. Such an insight, however incomplete at first, would constitute a new frame of reference that would begin to provide him with confidence in meeting new situations, and would reinstate a feeling of security that has been missing throughout the preadolescent period. With this substantial gain, the young person is able to learn much more rapidly how to go forward with the further development of his adult roles, and he is well launched into the transition period during which he will gradually become an adult. In other words, he has become a true adolescent. He has emerged from the newest of the artificial, culturally-created periods forced in between childhood and adulthood. He has succeeded in dropping childhood and is now ready to become an adult.

1403. *Adolescence.* The period of adolescence has lengthened out in modern life until it claims some individuals in one way or another from the age of about twelve to as much as twenty-five or more. Those who are preparing for some of the most highly specialized roles in society find themselves involved in the longer reaches of the adolescent transition. Again it is apparent here that the phenomenon is not produced by any weakness of the organism, for it manifests its most persistent tendencies in the lives of some of the most capable and potentially mature young people.

Their lengthy involvement grows out of their decision to try for the more cherished and highly guarded roles in the society. It is obviously a socially inflicted state.

There are two ways in which society extends the period beyond what would normally be required to turn a youth into an adult. One is through premature demands, extended downward into the late years of childhood, for manifestation of certain adult characteristics. In many instances there is an early push for some aspects of adult self-direction, for mature forms of analysis of certain problems, for adult social skills, and for control of emotional expressions beyond the level normally expected in late childhood. These demands throw the individual somewhat out of equilibrium and precipitate his entrance into adolescent readjustments sooner than it might otherwise occur.

At the other end of the period, the maturing individual is denied the privilege of taking on certain adult functions after he is ready for them. He is not given full self-direction because adults want for various reasons to continue controlling his actions. He is not allowed complete intellectual freedom by adults who do not want to risk disruption in systems within which they have become securely adjusted. He may not be allowed to marry because he is required to go without income for a long time, in extensive training, in internships, or in unprofitable apprenticeships. Sometimes these requirements are in the interest of improving his competence, but often they are intended to keep him from competing with older people for available income. For similar reasons he is kept from certain economic privileges.

All of these prohibitions not only delay his full emergence from the adolescent role, but subject him to conflicts and tensions that sometimes result in violations of the moral codes, a surreptitious marriage, or the necessity of seeking subsidies and sacrificing personal freedoms in order to fulfill the natural urges to take on the full role of the adult. The resolution of these problems is in the hands of society, rather than of young people, but the problems should be recognized by parents and counselors.

The Tasks. Following the formulations of Cole,[4] eight tasks are discussed in the rest of this chapter. They correspond to the eight columns in Figure 3, the Grograph for measuring personal maturity. Attainment of full self-direction and emancipation from adult control, development of integrated cognitive concepts of the world and his place in it, establishment of objective intellectual methods of dealing with life, attainment of satisfying adjustment to all kinds of social situations, mastery of satisfying and socially acceptable patterns of emotional expression, productive and wholesome adjustment to the opposite sex, development of his best economic possibilities and adjustment to them, and the development of some healthful recreational interests are the achievements that lie between the early adolescent and a state of full maturity. Any one individual will be much more conscious of some of these tasks than he will of others. Some will be almost totally unaware of any of them. Some will be vitally concerned about all of them. If those who are lacking in awareness are to move ahead without danger of losing their opportunities for maturity, they will have to be aroused by a counselor or parent who is in a position to see their needs and help them discover them.

The attainment of maturity in these aspects of life is up to the individual, as was stated in the case of the tasks of childhood. Maturity will not come about merely through continued living, or through being exposed to the demands of society. The growing individual will stop growing and level off at any point where his own motives are satisfied. Unless he feels pressed to strive for a higher level of life, he will remain immature to some degree. Hence they are tasks in every sense of the word, but unfortunately they do not become in reality the tasks of every young person. At least not all of them do, and some of the most vital to a mature society tend to escape the attention of altogether too many young people. Some of the tasks do claim the vigorous attention of nearly all young people. In those cases there is need for impressing them with the highest concepts of ma-

[4] Luella Cole, *Psychology of adolescence* (3rd ed., New York: Rinehart and Co., 1948).

turity, and in other cases there is dire need for ways of making young people aware of a keen sense of loss that can only be overcome by a struggle for maturity. One cannot aim for something one does not see. Herein lies one of the greatest functions of either teaching or counseling, at home, in the school, or anywhere else.

1404. *Achievement of full self-direction.* Children like to make their own decisions, but there are reasons why they do not do so. Parents step in when economic assets are involved or whenever the child's decisions may lead to personal harm, social disturbance, or loss of opportunities for development. Children have such limited concepts of either means or ends that they frequently find themselves lacking in insight and ask for help. They are particularly prone to ask for help when parents take over their direction unnecessarily and do not take counter measures to see that the children exercise their own power to make choices as much as possible. Dependence can be cultivated through the granting of security to those who give up their freedom.

The cultivation of independence is usually accomplished at the cost of some kinds of security and safety. That security which is founded in protection afforded by others is crippling to mental growth. It is a dubious form of security in the long run and has serious weaknesses even while the supporting adults are present. It assumes that the adults are capable of knowing and doing what is best for the child all the time. That is impossible, because many of the determinations of what is good for any individual are to be found within his own feelings and inner thoughts. In the long run parental domination is dangerous because the parents will eventually be gone, and the dependent young adult must then turn to someone else for his decisions. If all children were raised in this manner, and many are, to whom would they all turn for decisions when all their elders were gone? It is a dangerous situation for society to breed automatons when our need is for thinkers.

The more stable form of security is that which is discovered in one's own ability to meet and to handle new situations. The first ventures in independence require a certain amount of courage, and willingness to take the consequences. Such courage is likely to be developed if young people feel that they have backing in the home when they need it, along with freedom to develop themselves. With parental coopera-tion, most young people will accept the challenge of self-direction and struggle for its fullest and best manifestations.

Adolescents have many opportunities for the development of self-direction. The use of money, the selection of friends, vocational choice, the solution of their own difficulties, the making of dates, and many other daily problems offer them significant practice in independence at a time when they can easily obtain advice if they need it. Parents who stand by for consultation, and who help their children discover good ideas in connection with their problems, become dear friends and highly respected confidants as time goes on. Thus they may secure for themselves a continuing place in the affection and the companionship of their children far more satisfactorily than by attempting to maintain control of their behavior. Children who do not become submissive under excessive parental control reveal their resentment by trying to get completely away from dominating parents when cir-cumstances permit. The one most important characteristic of a home for adolescents is a graded program of cultivated emancipation, encouraged by the parents and striven for by the adolescent.

1405. *Establishment of objective intellectual analysis.* Some of the essentials in this development are a general ques-tioning of personal authority, a reliance on evidence and a tendency to test it for validity, a lively sense of doubt con-cerning ideas that have no evident support, the wide birth of interest in many aspects of life with intensive curiosity in a few that can be carried on with deep satisfaction, a growing awareness of the existence of other points of view and other systems of thought than those that were inherited in the home culture, and the ability to step aside, as it were, and look at one's own position or one's own productions without feeling that there is personal threat or insecurity in doing so.

Glenn Frank, as president of the University of Wisconsin, was frequently the recipient of letters from parents deploring the doubts their children had acquired in school. In a general reply he said, among other things,

> We need, I think, to remember that the will to doubt and the will to believe are companion habits of the mind and that neither is essentially more religious or less religious than the other.... All of modern science has its origin in the will to doubt. And yet the doubt of the scientist is in itself a superior kind of faith and it combines an unwillingness to accept the unproved with a willingness to adventure into the unknown. The will to doubt is the God-given faculty by which we protect ourselves against spiritual fraud. It is only when it is perverted that it leads to spiritual famine.

Final answers issued in dogmatic form are the most damaging influences on intellectual development. There is a natural inquisitiveness in human beings, which shows repeatedly in the child's free use of why and what questions. In the busy day of a parent it is far easier to turn them aside with the assumption of infallibility within the parent then to cultivate the desire for explanations and the tendency to investigate. Since intellectual maturity is the kind of achievement that can only occur where initiative and striving are present within the individual, any influence that discourages the quest for facts and evidences runs the risk of closing the door to maturity. In this task the young person must bear the burden of the adventure, but he needs all the encouragement and stimulation that can be given him.

Evidence of the hunger with which some people pursue this type of growth is to be found in the thousands of research-minded adults and young people all over the country, in laboratories, offices, and fields of mental investigation of all kinds. These are the minds that are providing civilization with the tools for its accelerating movement toward a heaven or a hell. Which it is to be will be decided partly by intellectual analysis and partly by an integrated philosophy of life.

1406. *Development of an integrated philosophy of life.* Blos' cases [5] and those of Cole [6] reveal some of the philosoph-

---

[5] Blos, *op. cit.*, pp. 129-40, 290-98. These cases offer concern with religion and related matters of universal orientation.

[6] Cole, *op. cit.*, pp. 367-68, 384-90, 407.

ical questions that absorb a great deal of attention from adolescents. The escape from childhood with its authoritative ceiling in parents and other adults seems to open up the universe and to expose the adolescent to the need for finding some other and higher source of integration and authority. He turns easily to questions about God, the nature of the universe, his place in the world, what it is possible for him to do and what he must do in this larger universe that is just a little appalling. If he is making an intellectual struggle for facts at the same time, he is faced with the problem of explaining the meaning of the facts he finds, but since his facts come from all over the universe, and do not come in pre-integrated form, he is deeply stirred to locate some focal point that will give him a sense of wholeness and closure. The universe without this can be a frightening place. Hence his lively interest in the development of a pattern of meaning that will give direction and unity to life. He is genuinely concerned with the question of values. He is optimistic and idealistic as a natural result of his discovery of unlimited horizons of knowledge and freedom.

In his initial search for a point of integration it is conceivable that he may be persuaded by various trends around him to settle on any of a number of possible positions. He may construct his world around a supernatural first cause, a concept of natural law, a pessimistic acceptance of chaos, a world subject to the whim of an almighty being, or a concept of intelligence achieving its will through a universe that can be conquered because it is lawful. In some such orientation he will find what he thinks matters most in the world and then in his own life and will set up his ultimate values and ideals accordingly.

The safety of himself and others, and the opportunity of every person in the crowded modern world, all depend on the philosophical maturity of those who rise to leadership, but it is also true that what the world's leaders can do depends, far more than is widely accepted by the people of the world, on the philosophical maturity of the masses. The solution of problems of conflict, both local and international, will follow the lines laid down by the value patterns of those who make and support the decisions and will follow them only as effectively as their intellectual maturity makes them capable of realistically coping with aggression and hostility wherever they are found.

Here is a task, along with some others, that is so important to the race as well as to the individual that nothing should be spared to stimulate its attainment by every young person. The adult world of today, taken as a whole, is not very mature either intellectually or philosophically. What the next generation will contribute to the situation depends on the striving of each young person as he comes along through his transitional years.

1407. *Ability to meet social situations.* Because of the close-knit nature of society no one lives alone. Everyone is a member or a participant in one or more social groups, usually several. The development of social needs (Chapter VII) arises from the individual's almost complete dependence on the social structure and the judgments of members of his society for the satisfaction of his basic physiological needs and all their derivatives. To the immature person who has only a vague understanding of social relationships and social psychology the power that society wields over his survival is complete, and he has no basis for knowing that within himself he can control to a large extent how society reacts to him. Therefore he is docile, uncertain of his safety, patronizing, and dependent. Society enslaves immature people through its pressure for approval. It makes "joiners" of them, people who seek diligently for ways of improving their belongingness. They have no core of security within themselves and are equally immature in intellectual and philosophical ways.

Young people have their first insight into what makes social maturity possible, when they begin to develop their own concepts of themselves and to realize the critical role of the self in determining what their social relationships will be. Conformity to social pressures in the abject sense is no longer necessary for social adjustment. The individual now has in his own hands a way of influencing his own social acceptance and can find out what obtains for him the sort of social acceptance he needs. He can become selective in his conformity. Furthermore, he can analyze the patterns of his group and study their effects on the group's welfare and growth, and its relationships with other groups. Through a certain amount of social experimentation he can find out what is important to social groups other than his own, and analyze intergroup relationships as he does his own relationship to his group. All of these discoveries and insights are highly suggestive to an active and growing person who is already engrossed in intellectual and philosophical analyses of life. They offer not only a path to better satisfaction of his own personal and social needs, but a path to a possible contribution to his world, which has a strong appeal to an idealist like the typical adolescent.

If he becomes excited by this problem and accepts its investigation as one of his tasks of development, he may achieve a high level of social maturity. He will discover that the world is a hodge-podge of social systems, often antagonistic in their relationships, but also usually alike in their basic values and ideals. He will find that these systems differ in their ways of reaching their goals, and clash over these process concepts. He will discover that someone must learn to live above their quarrels and find a way of bringing them into peaceful relationships. Here is a vision of great challenge to a healthy adolescent, or to any adult who has not settled down into the ruts of present social muddling.

Social maturity requires the development of ways of participating with various groups so as to influence them without antagonizing them. That means one must know their values, their customs, particularly their considered and highly important mores and values. This sort of growth must begin early in childhood, as sketched in Chapter XIII, in the child's task of socialization. It requires cultivation of all sorts of social skills, such as courtesy, manners, basic respect and regard for others (which depends on intellectual and philosophical maturity), conversational ability, the essentials of good appearance appropriate to various occasions. It means skill in leading without dominating, and often in leading without a knowledge on the part of the other that he is being led.

The ideal maturity in social matters means such insight into group problems that one is a master of his own social acceptance and carries his own security within himself. He can lift himself above fear of group pressure when occasion demands, but has basic group loyalties that he does not violate needlessly or just to reveal his independence.

It is obvious that this sort of achievement can never be wrought by the mere growth processes of the body and the passage of time. It is an achievement of a very high intellectual order, growing out of a very lively sense of motivation. Without a great struggle kept in line with a clear goal it cannot be won. There are few individuals who have attained it with any completeness in the world's history. Circumstances sometimes force people into roles that push them along such lines, but to wait for such events to bring about widespread social maturity would be ridiculous. Adolescents do not all have the capacity or the drive to rise to the highest attainment in this area, but they can achieve much more than they have done in the past if teachers, parents, and counselors will help them obtain the insights that bring the challenges and stimulate them to vital attacks on these goals. This should be first-order business in the school, with right of way over almost anything else.

1408. *Wholesome adjustment to emotional situations.* The emotional explosiveness of an infant grows out of his inability to tolerate frustration, his ignorance of the factors that operate around him, and his lack of self-control in expression. The course of development of emotional maturity follows those three lines for the most part. The foundations of it are laid in childhood if the tasks of childhood are achieved. If they are not, the adolescent has little chance of moving on to maturity.

Intellectual expansion occupies a very important role in emotional maturity. Most fears, worries, uncertainties, mysteries, and disappointments arise because the individual does not know the world around him and cannot tell how it is going to affect him. He is in the dark, with unseen forces moving around him. He is at their mercy and apprehensive of what they may do. Vision into these circumstances destroys fear and its allied states. To see the world clearly is to be able to make a satisfactory adjustment in it most of the time. This in itself prevents emotional disturbances from arising.

The development of self-direction also provides a means of avoiding emotional crises by putting the control of sequences into the hands of the one whose needs are involved. Thus, self-directive maturity is an essential prerequisite to emotional maturity. Economic maturity will prevent many frustrations from developing by having the individual prepared to attain his security through the best use of his resources and to adjust to the conditions of living that are possible to him because of his economic assets. Intellectual and philosophical maturity help the individual to accept conditions that he can do nothing about and to choose with some wisdom the lines of attack he will make on conditions that can be changed. Hence his achievements will be greater and his frustrations fewer.

Emotional maturity does not all consist of reducing the conflicts between him and his world, however. Part of it is the schooling he must have in living with the conflicts that will inevitably arise. Under conditions of stress there is no way of preventing the energic reactions that fill us with smoldering or explosive tensions. There are ways in which the expression of these tensions can be controlled so that they go out in harmless channels and avoid upsetting others. The infant's absence of control is the antithesis of the mature man's perfection of control.

Smothering of the emotional feelings is not mature control. It often indicates immaturity. There are times when anger should be expressed in unmistakable terms, when to submerge it is a sign of weakness and immaturity. There are times when one should sing, or shout, or laugh, or dance, or fight. To know when to do so and when not to do so is part of emotional maturity. To be able to do what the situation requires is also part of emotional maturity. These powers are acquired by practice and by philosophical development of values and standards of right and wrong. They are not easily attained, any more than is the vision or intellectual growth that dispels fears through knowledge and vision. Their attainment represents a long struggle within oneself for mastery of one's own behavior. It is motivated by a vision of the freedom and peace that are possible when one is above subservience to the actions by which others annoy us, and by a concept of the power a person acquires over the forces around him when his own inner life is at his command, rather than in command of him.

This is a task, the significance of which may never occur to many young people. The discovery of its importance can easily come too late to permit much of an achievement. Because of that, a heavy responsibility for its revelation rests upon parents and teachers, and particularly upon counselors whose task is to help those who are already victims of emotional immaturity.

1409. *Mature adjustment of the sexes.* This is one of the most demanding of the tasks of adolescence. A young person never needs help in discovering his urges in this area, for their appearance in due time is guaranteed by physiological maturation. The task lies in the matter of adjusting to the demands of the physiological system in such a way that the moral and spiritual values of the society are preserved and cultivated at the same time.

The course of development in this line of growth involves several kinds of shift, both in the persons with whom the relationships exist, and in the nature of the relationships. Beginning in infancy and childhood, the affectional relationships are between the baby and the parents as a natural result of the intimacy of their association. Older people continue to draw the closest affectional ties clear up into early adolescence, at which time it is not uncommon to find young people with crushes on older friends of the opposite sex, or even of the same sex. During adolescence the affinity normally shifts to one's age mates of the opposite sex, and the ties with older people remain on the basis of friendship but not romantic infatuation.

Throughout most of the early adolescent range the sex

attraction is so new and strange that it tends to obscure the importance of personality factors in the making of close friends. As familiarity with the opposite sex develops, the sex attraction is less likely to absorb all the attention, and qualities of personality begin to emerge into prominence. It is largely on the basis of personality factors that the field of possible partners is narrowed down, until under ideal conditions it centers on one person to whom is given a lifetime of undivided affection, intimacy, and fidelity. Coincidental with the selection of a life-mate is a shift in the nature of relationships with other members of the other sex. The personality factor comes more and more prominently into focus, and the sex factor less and less. The mature individual has many warm friends of the other sex, just as he has many warm friends of his own.

The attainment of maturity in this line of growth is not particularly difficult if the individual is permitted to have the experiences appropriate to each stage of development. There is no possible substitute in childhood and adolescence for lots of contact between the sexes. The overwhelming fascination of the newly blossomed sexual attraction can never quiet down to permit personality mating without close contact, and mating that is not very soundly based on personality matching, is an open invitation to a struggle in the building of a happy marriage, if not to complete failure.

The marriage pattern is a cultural matter. The sexual urge is a physiological matter. Marital compatibility is a personal matter. Maturity includes adherence to the cultural pattern, and through that, preservation of the solidarity and values of the culture. To violate it is to challenge it, weaken it, and open it up for further violations by others. Maturity also includes legitimate satisfaction of the sexual urge. To smother it usually results in conflict and difficulty in adjustment, unless it is done at the price of rigid self-control and adequate compensation in other lines that prove satisfactory sublimations. Maturity includes cultivation of the self-control and consideration for the partner that are necessary to make any close relationship succeed. No marriage has its success predestined by any universal power. Every happy marriage represents an achievement in which both partners have cooperated and sacrificed for the common goal.

Heterosexual immaturity is prominent. It is apparent in the vast need for marriage counselors, and in the widespread failure to progress beyond childhood or adolescence. Fixations at these levels can never be accompanied by genuine· satisfaction. Adolescent shopping around, accompanied by disregard for the mores of the society, is marked with conflicts and troubles for those so engaged, and it seems to be difficult for such people to move on into mature relationships unless they do so at the usual time of life.

This is truly a task that requires striving and purpose within the individual. There are several values to be preserved throughout the period of growth and courtship. There is the delightful but not easy matter of developing the necessary social graces and approaches that make courtship smooth and easy. There is the perplexing problem of selecting a mate with whom it is possible to live a rich and mutually satisfying life.

This task holds the intense interest of almost all young people, and those who are not absorbed by it should be helped to become so. Parents and teachers should foster circumstances that encourage its achievement, and avoid any unnatural segregations or barriers that interfere with its fullest achievement.

1410. *Adjustment to economic realities.* The adolescent is at the point where he must begin to select his career. This requires the exploration of a number of lines. One important problem is the appraisal of his abilities and resources. This cannot be done without trying himself out in various directions. Some of this exploration is provided by the school, where he can discover something about his intellectual possibilities, his interests in various fields of study, and a little about his manual skills. Other aspects of his potentialities will require actual excursions into the economic life of the community. One of his concerns is whether he can get a job on his own initiative. He can find this out only by trying. In so doing he may obtain employment in a number of different small jobs, each of which gives him some insight into economic activities. Even though the kind of job he eventually prepares for is not like those in which his first efforts were spent, they help him build his confidence and understand to some extent how well he can get along.

Along with his appraisal of his own powers, he must learn the value of money, for he lives in a money economy. He must also learn how to balance the two factors against each other, for he can only spend what his powers enable him to earn. It takes a long time to come to realism in these matters, and the explorations that lead to it are often begun in childhood. No little help is provided by Scouting and similar programs, because they lead young people into various activities that have economic potentialities in the future.

Economic maturity requires the discovery that work is necessary, that it is constructive and useful for other things than earning money, and that the world's work includes all kinds of tasks varying in skills, cleanliness, laboriousness, mentality, and reward. Real maturity includes the discovery that every constructive task is dignified and valuable to society.

Maturity involves completion of enough training to make entrance into the proper field possible, and it also involves the concept that skills sufficient to start one on a career can be continuously improved from then on to the mutual benefit of everyone in the society. It is a part of economic maturity to realize that the wealth of a people is in its labor no less than in its natural resources, and that the standard of living can be as high as people want it to be when they solve the problems of distribution and cooperation.

The final and satisfactory selection of a field of work is not the principal part of the struggle for economic maturity as so many young people seem to think. It is almost the last step in a long drive for the ideas and capacities that make a good adjustment possible. In this task there is room for considerable counseling, for the purpose of helping young people make their appraisals validly and showing them where the economic opportunities exist. The individual who is intellectually and philosophically mature is much better able to make a good economic adjustment than one who is not, because he has a sense of reality about the world and has been able to visualize a place in it for himself in which he can realize his values and be happy. There is a lot of vocational maladjustment because people drift into employment without planning or vision of where they are going. A person's work determines many things about the rest of life, such as where he can live, what kind of home he can have, with whom he must associate most of the day, and the kinds of activities in which he must engage. It may determine whether he can attend or participate in church, and even regulate many of his personal habits. Anything so far-reaching in its effects should have the most serious attention at an early stage in its evolution. This is a task that will have every chance of turning out badly unless it is given a central place in the education of young people.

1411. *Maturity and recreation.* Play is the business of the child, but it is the medicine of the adult. The balance of life activity shifts gradually from all play and no work to enough of the right kind of play to keep one able to work effectively, as one moves from early childhood into maturity. As indicated in the Grograph, what the adult needs is an activity program, or hobbies or other diversions, which he can enjoy alone or in company, without much special equipment, and without elaborate preparation. The need is not for any particular kind of activity, but for a change of activity that permits recouping of freshness and vitality. The recreation of a mature person must match his responsibilities in order to give him a rest and a distraction. Recreation helps one keep alive during the years of productivity, and a properly developed leisure-time program can be expanded into a stimulating occupation for the years of retirement.

Games, reading, social activities, club memberships, studies of special interests, and many other things have the potentialities of good recreation. They are rarely employed by chance, however, for studies have shown repeatedly how inadequate are the recreational plans of people at any age.[7]

Normally, during adolescence, recreational activities taper

[7] F. T. Spaulding, *High school and life* (New York: McGraw-Hill Book Co., 1938); Cole, *op. cit.*, pp. 401-10.

off rapidly to make way for serious vocational purposes. Maturity could be greatly stimulated if schools were to use their recreational programs to teach the sort of activities that could be turned directly into recreational programs for busy adults who do not have high-school or college equipment at their disposal. This task must be shared by the individual and the educational institutions, but the individual who senses the need for regular recreation can work out his own channels for achieving it, even if the schools do nothing about it.

1412. *Conclusion.* Among these tasks are the real preoccupations of adolescents and young adults. How real they are in the thinking of youth is apparent in the cases presented by Blos, cited earlier. The elementary school is well planned to facilitate the achievement of the tasks of childhood. The secondary school has not yet been able to adapt itself as nicely to the tasks of adolescence. The adolescent presents a much more complicated problem than the child. His tasks are more diverse, involve widely scattered types of experience, and the best ways of providing these experiences are not easily determined. The struggle to meet this challenge is still marked by plans of various kinds for the structure of the secondary-school curriculum. Whether the approach should be called progressive education, life-adjustment, or traditional subject-matter organization makes very little difference. Of much more importance is the need for stimulating adolescents through individual contact and guidance, to help them to discover ways of fulfilling their tasks and to realize the significance of tasks that are not yet clearly in their thinking. In some manner the ideal concepts of maturity must be brought into the spotlight, to show what can be done with oneself through an effort to adjust at the highest possible level. This should be contrasted vividly with what is ordinarily accomplished by those who do not press for a better adjustment. It is a dual problem of providing vision and stimulation, with whatever experiences the school and home can furnish to foster development toward these higher goals.

QUESTIONS FOR REVIEW

1. What gives rise to a problem of adolescence?
2. How are complexity of culture and the problems of adolescence related?
3. Review some of the contrasts between children and adults today.
4. Describe the child's view of adulthood.
5. In what way does the long period of childhood increase the difficulty of the adolescent adjustment?
6. How can the preadolescent disruption be prevented?
7. Describe the nature of the preadolescent conflict.
8. What symptoms usually appear in preadolescence? What do they mean?
9. Differentiate between situational and character neuroses. Which is most like preadolescence?
10. What is the prognosis of preadolescent disturbance?
11. What has caused the adolescent period to become so subdivided into different periods?
12. Name the tasks of adolescence.
13. Make a brief explanation of each one, and why the individual is likely to be intensely interested in it.

SELECTED REFERENCES

Peter Blos, *The adolescent personality* (New York: Appleton-Century-Crofts, Inc., 1941), Part 3, Chapters 2, 3, and 4.

Luella Cole, *Psychology of adolescence* (3rd ed.; New York: Rinehart and Co., 1948), Chapters I, II, III, IV, VII, IX, XIII, XIV, XVI.

E. D. Partridge, *Social psychology of adolescence* (New York: Prentice-Hall, Inc., 1939), Chapters V, VI, VII, VIII, IX, X, XI, XII.

Muzafer Sherif and Hadley Cantril, *The psychology of ego-involvements* (New York: John Wiley and Sons, Inc., 1947), Chapter 12.

CLASS EXERCISES ON THE TASKS OF ADOLESCENCE

Things To Do in Class

1. Each student is to think carefully of his own recent experiences in attempting to arrive at a satisfying state in one of the eight tasks discussed in the chapter. A report on his experiences

should be prepared, either in outline form or written in full. Students who are willing to volunteer might present their cases to the class. If anonymity is desired, the teacher can read the reports of those who indicate a willingness for theirs to be so used. Factors that hindered or helped in achieving a satisfying adjustment toward maturity should be especially emphasized.

CHAPTER XV

THE LEARNING PROCESS

1501. *The process distinguished from influencing factors.* The process of learning is the vehicle by which the individual is changed from a bundle of potentialities to an acting organism with ideas, habits, skills, preferences, and other distinguishing personality characteristics. Learning is something that happens within the organism as a result of responding to situations. Some kind of change takes place in the nervous system, particularly the central nervous system, which manifests itself subsequently in changed behavior. There are many unsolved problems that confront the research worker interested in the neurological and physiological bases of learning. Therefore it is impossible to take a positive position on the exact nature of what goes on within the organism when learning is taking place. Nevertheless, it is generally agreed that whatever the minutiae of the internal process are it is an organismic process and it is always involved whenever any behavioral alterations take place.

In this treatment no attempt will be made to deal with the theoretical aspects of learning. The teacher is faced with a person who is doing things, which are holistic reactions to situations, and which move in certain interesting sequences toward outcomes in the nature of changed behavior. Learning may be discussed in terms of those overt or observable holistic reactions. In such an approach one is dealing with the raw data of learning, not with the theoretical explanations of the data. It is impossible to avoid some reference to theory, because explanations of some sort, either simple or complex, always serve to clarify the understanding of what is being observed. The simpler explanations are to be preferred in every practical teaching situation, as long as they provide insight of the kind required in teaching. Explanations need become complex only to the point required to make insight possible in cases of larger and larger blocks of raw data or to promote understanding of the major abstractions and generalizations that give meaning to some phases of human behavior.

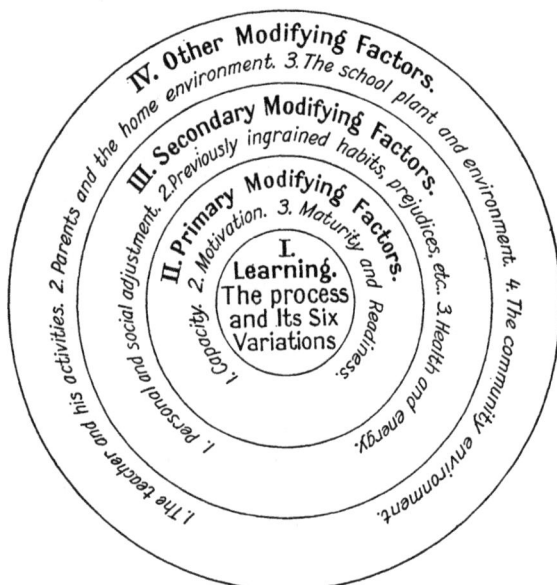

FIG. 5. FACTORS THAT INFLUENCE THE LEARNING PROCESS

The process of learning as such is modified and influenced by many factors that determine the *direction* in which learning goes, how *fast* or how *slow* it moves along, what is *included* or *excluded,* and how *far* it goes. Some of the factors wield much influence, some little, but they only modify the learning process; they do not take its place. Figure 5 illustrates one way of visualizing this idea, by giving the learning process itself a central position and showing the various modifying factors around it in concentric positions of relative importance. Basic intelligence, motives, and the level of maturity of the individual are powerful modifying factors. Others seem to be less powerful, but still influential.

This chapter and the two following deal essentially with

the learning process itself. The modifying factors are treated in later chapters. This may seem to be an unnatural and confusing way of dealing with processes and factors that are never really apart in real life. But, as suggested in previous sections of the book, observation of any phenomenon yields little significant insight until the observer has an analytical system of observing and narrows his examination to one specific thing after another. No one lives or learns in a vacuum. Therefore learning never takes place apart from the many modifying factors that determine its direction. As a means of becoming familiar with any phenomenon, however, it is helpful to lift it out of its natural setting and to examine it as if it were in a vacuum. When this is done, there is always the obligation of putting it back into its natural setting after such familiarity is developed, and there continuing the examination until it is possible under natural conditions to recognize the phenomenon itself, as well as the ways in which it is changed or modified by each of its important modifying factors. It has been popular among educational psychologists of the past to say "other things being equal" certain things would happen in certain well-defined ways. This phrase is in disrepute now because it always preceded the description of factors that were never put back into their natural settings where other things are seldom if ever equal. With this caution, the learning process will be treated first as if it were in a vacuum, after which an attempt will be made to immerse it gradually in the veritable sea of modifying factors that seem always to surround it.

1502. *The steps in learning.* When all theories and schools of thought are peeled aside, and the bare facts about learning are exposed, it becomes clear that regardless of theoretical points of view the learning process contains certain common sequential steps. These steps seem invariably to be present when learning occurs. Let us see how they are derived.

In 1935, Dashiell [1] published the results of a careful analysis of theories of learning. He approached the analysis by recognizing three general types of learning theories. One

[1] J. F. Dashiell, "A survey and synthesis of learning theories," *Psychological bulletin*, 32 (1935), 261-75.

is the English "trial-and-error" concept, which has had wide backing in America. Another is the Russian "conditioned-response," introduced by Pavlov and Bekhterev, and pursued in America by Watson and many others. The third is the German "gestalt" concept, introduced through Wertheimer and Köhler. The latter was said to include "dynamic" ideas, "sudden insight," and "purposive" characteristics. Dashiell collected research reported from all three of these major theoretical points of view and examined it carefully to see what common principles might be rooted in all three. He reported the following eleven.

1. The subject must be motivated. 2. A field or complication of motives exists. 3. Obstruction is offered to the principal motive. 4. Hyperactivity (or hypertonicity) is aroused. 5. Response is multiple and varied. 6. The response is to relations of stimuli. 7. The most important relation is between means and objective. 8. Selection or least action appears. 9. The selected responses originally occur fortuitously. 10. The effects of responses are crucial. 11. The rate of learning varies in degrees from gradual to abrupt.

The first eight of the common principles may be observed to be in parallel with the sequences involved in the behavior of an individual. The ninth reveals a characteristic of the manner in which selection and response takes place. The tenth suggests the explanation for establishment of a trend in responses to repeated situations. The eleventh refers to the time-element involved in learning, and indirectly to other factors that determine the time-element.

Here, then, are three somewhat antagonistic theoretical points of view, which agree implicitly as to the major significant steps involved in learning. Since teachers have no particular need for theoretical analysis and would certainly not be helped by such analysis in its present state of confusion, the obvious value, for teachers, of Dashiell's excellent survey and synthesis lies in the unquestioned soundness of the pragmatic and empirical picture of what an individual actually does when he is exposed to a learning situation. From this highly suggestive beginning, the following organization of the sequential steps in learning was developed. A condensed

TABLE 2. SEQUENTIAL STEPS IN LEARNING

1	2	3	4	5	6
Motivation within the learner makes him receptive to stimulation.	A goal becomes related to the motivation. A. The goal is not at once attainable. B. A barrier exists.	Tension arises. A. Energy is released within the learner; he is ready to act. B. The barrier prevents an appropriate discharge of the energy and creates tension.	Learner seeks an appropriate line of action to reach goal. A. In every situation there are a number of possible ways of acting. B. The selection of one of those ways of acting will involve elements of chance and/or analysis. C. When the selection is made action toward the goal is attempted. D. If the selected line of action is inappropriate steps A, B, and C will be repeated until an appropriate action occurs. E. When an appropriate action occurs it will involve: 1. Some degree of success in terms of the goal. 2. A sense of satisfaction and a reduction of tension to the extent that the motive is satisfied.	Learner fixes the appropriate line of action. A. Skills are acquired by drill or practice. B. Concepts are developed by becoming familiar with the referent. C. Memorization is accomplished through meaningful repetition. D. Tastes and preferences are established by the satisfyingness or annoyingness of the experience. E. Ability to solve problems is a product of A and B above. Speed of Learning Varies A. May be relatively sudden. B. May be very slow. C. Depends on: 1. Nature of the problem. 2. Degree of motivation. 3. Capacity of the learner.	Inappropriate behaviors are dropped. A. Yielding no satisfaction, they lose attractiveness.

version of the steps is presented in Table 2. Each step will be discussed separately, although it must be remembered that any attempt to separate them into discrete parts of the learning process is wholly artificial and academic and is to be justified only in terms of its ability to help the student become familiar with the process in its entirety. At times the learner seems to rush through the steps in a manner that suggests they are all parts of one movement or that some of them are missing. At other times learning seems to bog down on one step or another for varying lengths of time and for various reasons. In still other cases it seems as if the learner shifts back and forth over a few of the steps until some condition is satisfied before the process moves on to completion. In other words, there is no apparent uniformity of movement from one step to another during learning, and yet in spite of the many different ways in which a learner may run through these steps, there is uniformity in the fact that the steps are always there and can be identified by a trained observer.

A case to give reality to the steps. Even though the sequential steps consist of what people actually do, they can become detached from a real person and lose some of their naturalness. As a method of preventing this, a case of actual behavior in school is presented first. Here is a girl involved in a problem that developed within one of her classes. Marginal notes indicate which of the sequential steps are being illustrated throughout the behavior. Read the case carefully before reading the steps. Then read the steps through, thinking of the girl's behavior. Then return to the case, rereading it bit by bit, referring back to the steps until they take on life in connection with every incident in the case report.

Step Number

1   In junior high school, I presume I was an average student. In seventh grade I was exposed to a variety of unrelated subjects, including music and art. 1 was very enthusiastic about art despite one or two discouraging, humiliating (they were at the time) episodes in which the teacher bluntly proclaimed that my art work was poor and clumsy. I felt that having reached the age of twelve and the sev-

1

enth grade, I was ready to begin to accomplish wonders and make up for previous discouragements. The regular teacher was on leave for the first two weeks of school and an older woman who had retired several years before substituted. The first day consisted of the preliminary work of getting supplies and looking over work done by previous classes, during which I hoped, wished, and daydreamed. When the actual work began, it was quickly proven that I was "all hope and no technique"! I am awkward in some eye-hand coordination which may or may not be due to left-handedness. My work was clumsy, sloppy, and uneven in composition. For several days the substitute teacher nagged me about how clumsy I was and that my work was comparable to that of a fourth-grader —which was probably true. For some reason, I felt that somewhere along the line I had missed some work in composition and the handling of various types of pens and brushes. I began to create violent illnesses on days of the art class because I felt ignorant and stupid to see the others several projects ahead of me and I was tired of being laughed at. I played ill for two days and I was tired of staying in bed, so on Friday, the last day that the substitute was to be there, I went to art class. Things went from bad to worse. I managed to drop and spoil about everything I touched. The teacher went around the class, holding up each student's project and commenting upon it. When she came to mine she held it up and began to laugh and said, "I guess you will have to go back to grammar school three hours a week to learn how to paint!" My seventh-grade pride dissolved into tears and I ran from the room. It was the most terrible disgrace I had experienced. Although it was the middle of the afternoon, I went to my locker, got my wraps and left, still crying. I went to the movies with the money I had been given for bus fare. I couldn't bear to go home and tell my mother that I, a seventh-grader, had to go back to grammar school for artwork! I sat in the movie until nearly 8 o'clock when my uncle finally found me and took me home. Relations were

1

2 & 3

Speed C 3

4 D

4 D

strained all the way home. I was crying because he was my favorite uncle and I didn't want to tell of my disgrace and he couldn't decide whether to scold me or comfort me!

I told my mother the whole story and, instead of scolding me, she assured me that the next day would be a better one and that with the return of the regular teacher, who was well-liked and very talented, I might get along better.

On Monday I entered class and was met by the teacher who had heard of the episode. She asked me to see her after class which I did. We talked for a few minutes and she suggested that I remain after school to help her do background work for a large poster that was being made by this teacher and some students. I was flabbergasted, but I appeared after school. She was working on one part of the poster and she very carefully explained what she wanted me to do, which was to draw a castle for background. She showed me pictures and then went to great lengths in explaining how to do this. The first day I made sketches of castles. As I came back day after day, I unconsciously found myself actually doing neat and somewhat imaginative work. Each new step that I tackled was explained and then I practiced painting, inking, and shadowing on scrap paper. I soon found myself catching up with the class. No one knew of these sessions after school which made me feel better. I still had to go over and repeat some things several times until I accomplished them.

Step Number
4 D

4 E and
5 A

Speed
C 1, 2, 3.

5

Interwoven through this experience is a clear illustration of ways in which the teacher affects the student's movement through the steps. Note this, but set it aside for the present and concentrate on the girl's delayed and difficult progress through the steps.

1503. *Step 1—Motivation within the learner makes him receptive to stimulation.* There are four facts about motivation that are of importance here: (1) A motive is any condition within the learner that arouses and sustains activity. (2) It is always within the learner and never exists apart from his own mental processes. (3) It is not put there by the teacher, but grows within the person as a direct result of his experiences throughout life. (4) All purposive behavior (goal-seeking activity) begins with a motive; there is no such behavior without motivation.

A person's motives tell why he does what he does. He eats (action) *because* he needs food (motive). He laughs (action) *because* an event occurs that he feels is satisfying to him in some way (motive). He studies (action) *because* he believes he needs information to become successful (motive). The most basic motives are needs, often being divided into the categories of physiological, ego or personal, and social (see Chapter VII). Conditions under which these needs are best fulfilled come to be valued by the individual. When such conditions are described in generalized form they may be called values (see Chapter X).

It is incorrect to say that a teacher motivates his students. When a teacher presents the work of a course in such a manner and form that the student sees a relationship between the work and his needs and values, he is *stimulated* to do that work because he believes his motives (needs and values) can be satisfied by doing the work of the course. Unless the student has within him some urge to act, however obscure, there will be no purposive behavior. Random or vegetative behavior may occur, but nothing useful to the educative process. A student without motives or with sickly motives can scarcely be helped by the best teacher, while one with highly developed motives will learn much in spite of the worst teacher. *What* the student learns will depend to some extent on what the teacher does; *how much* he learns depends on his own motivation. Since one's own inner motivation is the absolute prerequisite to learning, good teaching methods start with an attempt to understand the motives of the students.

1504. *Step 2—A goal becomes related to the motivation.* Often the urge to act is something as indefinable as a general physiological restlessness. At such times the individual seems to be actively seeking some kind of a goal that will satisfy his restlessness. When a goal is selected, such as a beefsteak or a glass of water, action toward that goal can begin. Motives of value in schoolwork are more often in the social and personal realms. Examples are the desire to be a success in life or in some particular area, the desire to be recognized or approved, the urge to make some change in one's knowledge or skills to meet a particular need, or the desire to pursue some special interest that has developed over a period of time. When the learner is led to see and desire to reach an attainable goal that is obviously contributory to his strong motives, the second condition or step in learning has been satisfied, and action can then proceed toward the goal. For the learner, nothing will become a goal that does not in some way satisfy a motive. Those things that satisfy the strongest motives become the most attractive goals. On the other hand, many tasks arbitrarily set up by teachers have no apparent relationship to the important motives of students and therefore fail to enlist spontaneous effort to reach such goals. Schoolwork of that type is drudgery because it drags the student away from his natural interests and requires him to expend his energies in a direction that to him is not only useless, but often distasteful. Effective learning of the sort desired by such a teacher is practically impossible without the use of threatening incentives of such hideous proportions as to scare the student into action. Along with whatever learning is achieved under such conditions, there comes also a learned dislike if not open hatred of one or more aspects of the school situation.

(a) The goal is not at once attainable. (b) A barrier exists. When the student is able at once to behave in the manner described by the goal, he does not need to learn. For example, two boys have decided to become engineers. As a goal along that path, ability to use algebra is important and interesting to both boys. One of them can use algebra, and one cannot. If an assignment is given in which a principle of algebra must be mastered, one of them faces the barrier of inability to perform the function and must learn it. The other is able to perform the function at once and faces no barrier in that particular situation; therefore it is not a learning situation of any significance for him.

There are many kinds of barriers that interfere with the immediate mastery of a goal or with adjustment through the satisfaction of needs. An analysis of the principal kinds of barriers that confront an individual in various situations is presented in Chapter XXI. Of the four types discussed there, the one consisting of difficulty, or absence in the individual of the necessary skills and knowledge to perform the actions involved in reaching the goal, is the only one that has a place in school. The others may be thought of as psychiatric barriers, and they are always potentially dangerous to good adjustment. They should be eliminated entirely from the school if possible. The educative process, however, consists of a graded and systematic attack on such educational barriers as knowledge, skill, and preference.

There are several kinds of psychiatric barriers that intrude into learning situations in spite of our efforts to keep them out. Some of them consist of an inadequacy on the part of the learner, such as low intelligence, lack of fine neuromuscular coordination, specific inaptitude, prejudice, or faulty concepts. These barriers may not always be fully overcome and may succeed in permanently thwarting one's mastery of a given goal to some extent. Other barriers grow out of a disturbed condition of the learner, such as emotional blocking, fears, or other conditions of maladjustment. The teacher's personality may be a barrier for some students. Poor teaching techniques constitute barriers to learning. They may be due to ignorance of the effective motives of pupils, disregard of a student's level of attainment in a subject, or lack of effective ways of organizing and presenting the materials of learning, including the use of poor textual materials.

When the barrier consists only of a lack of the particular knowledge or skill involved, learning usually proceeds normally to the point where the goal is attained and the motivation satisfied. When the barrier is of the other kinds described here, unpleasant tension usually arises and something other than the usual techniques of study is required before a wholesome adjustment can be achieved. Such problems are discussed in later chapters.

1505. *Step 3—Tension arises.* (a) Energy is released within the learner; he is ready to act. When a hungry dog sees meat he salivates and tries to reach the meat. He is ready to act and his behavior shows that physical energy is ready to move him toward his goal. There is considerable evidence for the statement that it is satisfying to act when one is ready to act, and annoying to be prevented from acting.

(b) The barrier prevents an appropriate discharge of the energy and creates tension. Regardless of its nature, a barrier that prevents the student from moving toward his goal operates as a dam behind which the energy that would normally be used in making an adjustment is allowed to build up under pressure. It must be remembered that a true motive is a condition that will not stop agitating until it is satisfied or otherwise removed. If the boy who has to learn algebra to become an engineer cannot easily give up his goal, and if he cannot master the algebraic process needed in his work he will feel a growing tension whose intensity will be determined by the strength of the motivation and the resistance of the barrier. If he can easily give up his dream of becoming an engineer, he can substitute another goal for the unattainable one, and the tension will be released.

Mild tension may be an aid in learning. It tends to organize one's energies and facilities into an efficient and vigorous attack on the problem. Strong tension is often disruptive in its influence on the learner. At times deaths that occurred under conditions of extreme tension without actual physical violence have been ascribed to a disorganization of normal life processes through excessive emotional disturbance. Most of the tensions that accompany barriers not directly due to the mere absence of the knowledges and skills sought are undesirable. Even in the case of those barriers inherent in the challenge of a difficult assignment it is not healthful to create great tension through excessive challenge. The difficulty of any school task should be held within a safe range determined by the capabilities of the learner. Skill in so doing is difficult to acquire but is an essential part of good teaching.

1506. *Step 4—The learner seeks an appropriate line of action to reach his goal.* (a) In every situation there are a number of possible ways of acting. For example, if one has to find the meaning of a new word, he can use the dictionary, ask someone, see how the word is used in a sentence, guess at its meaning, or try something else. The cat in the cage can scratch the wall, push at the door, bite the pole in the cage, or in some other manner seek to escape. It is theoretically possible for the individual to try any one or more of the possible courses of action in any given situation.

(b) The selection of one of those ways of acting will involve elements of chance or analysis or both. Chance implies random selection without the aid of logical indicators of what it may be appropriate to do. It may show up in behavior in two ways. (1) Mental exploration is often the random sampling of various possible lines of action. Asked what two plus nine equals, the child may begin by saying "one" and proceed on up the scale until he hits the right number. (2) Random physical activity often involves many kinds of movement, which may have little or no real relationship to the problem. The cat trying to escape from the cage may, for example, claw the pole in the center of the floor, or bite it, or scratch the wall or the floor, or rub his back against some part of the cage, or stand still and meow.

Analysis implies a more or less organized examination of the known parts of a problem to see what they have to offer as leads toward the solution. For example, one may look up the meanings of words involved, or lift and feel the cloth being studied, or recall similar experiences and try to apply them to the problem, or look for apparent relationships among the various parts of the problem. The amount of random activity of the purely chance variety will probably diminish as the learner's familiarity with his problem increases. Conversely, logical analysis will probably tend to become an increasingly prominent part of the learning process as familiarity increases.

(c) When the selection is made, action toward the goal is attempted. The fact that the student has decided on a line of action does not necessarily mean he has selected the appropriate or best action. Nevertheless, having decided to try a certain approach, he will begin what he thinks to be a movement toward his goal. If he has selected a sound approach, he will probably get through to his goal in time, but if he has selected an unsound approach, he will find himself blocked by some barrier.

(d) If the selected line of action is inappropriate, Steps 4A, 4B, and 4C will be repeated until an appropriate action occurs. These steps are often called the trial-and-error process because so often the learner decides to try something only to discover he has tried the wrong thing and must try something else. Trial-error-trial-error-trial-success would be a more accurate and enlightening term. If, however, one speaks of maturation and the development of insight, one is talking about the same basic facts as is the trial-and-error disciple. They differ only in their ways of describing the facts. To pursue such academic differences in this presentation would serve no useful end, but it is helpful to know that much of the apparent confusion in the field of psychology is due to a lack of universally accepted terminology rather than to conflicting facts. The student should keep this in mind in reading psychological literature.

Regardless of how this process is designated, then, any line of action that does not offer satisfaction to the motive or any useful solution to the problem or lead to the goal is discarded and another line of action is sought in the same general manner as that used to find the first one. This will ordinarily continue until a useful line of activity is found. In cases where the barrier is too great, learning may break down or move in an unexpected direction at this point. Such problems are discussed in Chapter XXI.

(e) When an appropriate action occurs, it will involve some degree of success in terms of the goal, and a sense of satisfaction with reduction of tension to the extent that the motive is satisfied.

(1) Any act that moves the learner toward his goal may be regarded as successful to some degree. That is, it brings about a condition that is satisfying to the organism because it tends to fill the need that is motivating the behavior. It is the nature of most goals in the learning process that they do not recur once they have been achieved, dismissing for the

present the tendency to forget. For example, one may learn to read the daily newspaper. This learning need not be repeated. When once fully achieved such a goal (*ability* to read) ceases to be a motivating force in behavior and may become a tool for the achievement of another goal. On the other hand, it is the nature of many goals set up in an effort to maintain a state of equilibrium in life that they recur with varying degrees of regularity and frequency and need new satisfaction each time they recur. For example, one needs to eat each time hunger recurs. The fundamental difference between these two types of goals is that one requires the mastery of a new *way* of doing something, while the other merely requires the repeated use of some process already learned. The first is a goal in the learning process. The second is a goal in the continuous process of maintaining a state of adjustment. Problems (other than learning) in continuously adjusting to life conditions are considered in Chapter XXI. Any motivating drive is ended when the sought-for condition is fully or adequately produced.

(2) Tension is relieved in proportion to the satisfaction of the motive. Most goals in learning are won by degrees rather than all at once. Each degree of success seems to have the power to bring some degree of satisfaction to the learner and therefore to temper the agitation produced by the motive. Since tension is directly related to inability to satisfy a motive, release of tension is directly related to satisfaction of a motive. When a motive is fully satisfied, the tension related to it is fully released, and the effort to learn stops. If the motive is *not fully* satisfied, the student will continue his efforts to master the problem, but only up to the point where his motivating need is satisfied, regardless of whether that point is short of or beyond the goal set by the teacher. This is not to say that any other tensions due to still unsatisfied motives will disappear. (Persistent tensions due to unsatisfied motives of long standing are discussed in Chapters XXI and XXII.)

There are several important implications for teachers in this fact. First, it probably explains why many students do a little of their required work with interest, and then turn their attention to something else, while others occasionally go way beyond the requirements of a course. There is a discrepancy in each case between the teacher's goal and the student's goal. Second, it explains why some students have a glassy-eyed indifference to anything proposed by the teacher. For such students the teacher's objectives have never become functional goals at all. To make matters worse for the teacher, every normal healthy student has plenty of other interesting goals that will arouse and direct his behavior unless they are superseded by a more dynamic goal within the work of the course. Therefore, the teacher's failure to set up an attractive goal in learning does more than leave the student unmoved, it literally opens the way for him to direct his energies toward his other personal goals. This often results in a breakdown in planned learning activities. Third, it offers an explanation of many of those cases of disturbance that are continuous and chronic. A student trying to satisfy a personality need such as status in his group is able to obtain only partial satisfaction of his need through the disturbing acts he performs. He cannot stop because his need is not satisfied, nor can he change his attack because he may know no other and the learning process is seeing to it that those acts which obtain partial satisfaction are becoming established on an increasingly permanent basis. Effective methods of dealing with such cases must of necessity be based on the psychological facts involved in this discussion, namely, provision by the teacher of a more attractive goal than the student is then pursuing, or of a more satisfying and socially acceptable technique for attaining his present goal. Traditional disciplinary measures are not so based.

1507. *Step 5—The learner fixes the appropriate line of action.* The processes by which students fix learning vary with the type of goal sought. (See Chapter XVI.) Five common types of goals are motor skills, concepts, memory, tastes and preferences, and problem-solving ability.

(a) Skills are acquired by drill or practice. Fingers learn to coordinate in the act of writing through actually performing the act over and over until it becomes established in a certain pattern. Most skills require some degree of neuromuscular coordination, which means that the various separate

muscles involved in a given act have to be brought into unified action. One muscle must contract while another relaxes
in order to get a certain movement. Each muscle is capable
of acting alone without practice, but when cooperation is required there must be rehearsal. The higher the skill sought,
the more drill or practice is required, because higher skill
usually means that a more complex or exacting type of muscular cooperation is required.

(b) Concepts are developed by becoming familiar with the
referent. This puts a premium on personal experience with
the thing to be known. A student handling a book is having
a personal experience with that book. From the acts of opening it, turning pages, feeling it, smelling it, hefting it,
examining the printing in it, and so on, he will develop
an understanding of what a book is. This understanding is
a concept. The real book is the referent. The word "book"
is the symbol by which the concept is known.

(c) Memorization is accomplished through meaningful
repetition. Memory is the product of associational learning.
That means that two or more things have been associated together in the experience of the learner until he always thinks
of those things as belonging together. A word is associated
with an object and becomes known as the name of the object.
The words of a poem become associated together and the
poem becomes memorized. A list of ingredients become associated together and a recipe is memorized. The presence of
meaning and belongingness aids this process greatly, but repeated experience with the associated items is necessary in
most cases before memory is established.

(d) Tastes and preferences are established by the satisfyingness or annoyingness of the experience. Most tastes and
preferences are by-products of an experience that had as its
goal another end product such as knowledge or skill. If the
search for the end product was satisfying, the learner is apt
to come to like the circumstances under which that search was
carried on. Thus students develop likes and dislikes for various subjects and other things.

(e) Problem-solving is in essence not different from any
evaluative reaction to a situation, except in one respect.

An individual perceives a situation. The cues in the situation, acting upon his pattern of meaning, evoke a conceptual frame of reference. From the residues of experience in that pattern of meaning which *are there at that moment* he makes a choice reaction and moves ahead on it. Obviously, there are some situations in which the conceptual meanings available at that moment are inadequate to permit a very good choice to be made. The so-called problem-solving technique is not a way of "thinking" so to speak, or a technique by which thinking is brought into the situation. Thinking was defined earlier as the mental processes by which perceptual experiences are differentiated, integrated, drawn out into abstractions, and woven into generalizations. Choices have to be made on the basis of the meanings currently available. The problem-solving technique is simply a way of holding up an immediate choice in the situation, while the individual exposes himself to additional learning. The technique consists of the ways of deciding what sort of learning should be sought, of evaluating what is experienced during the learning period, and of deciding when one has learned enough to permit one to make the choice reaction safely. Since it is primarily a *technique* for use in improving the quality of decisions, it involves both a direct and an indirect approach. The indirect approach consists of continually learning more about one's world, so that the conceptual pattern becomes more and more adequate to the making of sound choices in the future. The direct approach involves becoming aware of and familiar with the techniques for holding up a decision and directing the search for more insight. These techniques include holding a decision in abeyance without becoming tense or frustrated, examining the problem carefully to see what kind of information is required to arrive at an answer, locating that information and obtaining possession of it through whatever experiences are required to let the new concepts take shape, and deciding when enough new knowledge is present to permit a sound choice reaction to be made. Some other concepts, too, must be known so that they can be used as guides in the search for information. They include evidence, propaganda, induction, the hypothesis, and others. Each serves a purpose in the promotion of validity or in the directing of the search for more information. These concepts are not easily acquired by an unguided individual, for they represent rather high-level abstractions and generalizations. They will be learned much more quickly and easily if someone points them out and helps the individual explore them. Then there is the matter of skill in the use of these techniques, and skill requires practice, which can be provided in almost any part of the school program if the methods of teaching are purposefully arranged to make such provision.

1508. *Step 6—Inappropriate behaviors are dropped.* Yielding no satisfaction, they lose attractiveness. This is in a sense a form of forgetting, but it differs from the usual problem in that the items forgotten were not learned to any significant degree. Even granting the hypothesis that everything one does leaves some trace in his biological make-up, the trace left by a trial-and-error exploration into an unsuccessful line of action is very slight indeed. It requires no measurable amount of forgetting to render it unlikely to produce such behavior again. Therefore, the fact of interest here is that behaviors that yield no progress and no satisfaction to the motive seem to be dropped almost as if they had never been tried. Whether the learner avoids them in the future because he knows they won't work or because he becomes unaware of them after he finds a successful line of action is not clear. Even so, it is a problem of interest primarily to research psychologists at this time.

1509. *The speed of learning varies.* If, as previously stated, some goals in learning are won by degrees, it follows that learning may proceed at various speeds from very slow to very rapid, if not abrupt. For example, much time and intensive drill are required to master the harp, but it is a common experience to find oneself suddenly in possession of a new idea or point of view that has apparently emerged all at once. The ejaculation "I see!" often follows such discoveries. The speed of learning depends on several factors: (1) Learning proceeds more rapidly when the learner's intelligence is high than when it is low. (2) Learning proceeds more rapidly when motivation is intense than when it is mild or weak. (3) The speed of learning is related to the nature of the problem and the material being learned. For example, most motor skills require some drill scattered over a period of time, whereas many simple associational or conceptual learnings are complete with one brief experience. A finger applied to a hot stove tells its owner all at once and in a very final manner that stoves are hot.

It is no longer considered possible to lay down with exactness a set of laws that govern learning, but some practically useful facts are available on the relationship between some of the conditions that may be present when learning occurs and the efficiency of the learning that takes place at those times. Those factors are discussed in Chapters XVII, XIX, and XX.

The sequential steps offer a way of studying students and of determining where they are stopped in their efforts to learn or to adjust. If the teacher can find where in this sequence the student is stopped, he can help remove the obstacle to progress, whether it be motivational, a barrier, poor selection of a path to follow, or faulty methods of fixing learning. Before the formulation can have that kind of utility for the teacher, however, he will have to become so familiar with it, and learn to see it in real human behavior so well, that it becomes his natural way of regarding behavior. In addition to the case presented earlier, which should be reviewed now to tie the steps to the actual behavior, another case is presented here. In this case there is an excellent illustration of movement back and forth over Step 4, in the struggle to find a path through to the goal. Again the steps are indicated in the margin.

Sequential
steps

1 is implied.   As a freshman at ———, I had included in my registration a course in college algebra. At about the time five weeks' marks were due a prelim was

2   given to the class. As I proceeded with the exam, I found that the algebraic part of my mind was blank or nearly so as far as solving the problems was con-

cerned. When I handed the paper in I knew I had failed miserably.

I was a freshman at ——— and had failed miserably in one of my first exams! The feeling began to weigh on my mind more and more. I began to think about failing and being forced to leave school. In my family it would not be acceptable behavior, for scholastic failures were rare.

Later on in the day I met several of my classmates who reported to me that they had done poorly on the examination. As we talked over the exam we began to bolster up our courage by deciding we would get some credit for using the right method. This was a temporary relief from the tension I had built up about failing.

In the very next class our prelims were handed back. My mark was 25. I noticed others in the class ranged down to 0 with several above my 25. The professor then broke the silence by telling us we had no business being in college. He advised us all to leave and added that there was not a person in the class who had the intelligence to get through college. He became bitterly sarcastic in his remarks and walked out of the room at the conclusion of his speech, leaving us no chance for rebuttal.

The bottom fell out of my world for me. I saw myself getting notice to leave school. I knew my father would be wild. I just did not know what to do. Everyone else in the class was so affected personally that he or she didn't consider it from a class viewpoint. Each one was too concerned with his own situation.

I cut my other two classes that day and went back to my room. What could I do? I couldn't go to work. I wasn't equipped for any job. The problem weighed on my mind with no solution in sight until one o'clock in the afternoon when the urge to eat asserted itself. I ran into a member of this class who told me he was going to drop the class. I was astounded and asked him how he could stay in school. He told me that he would pass his other four courses and that would give him enough credits.

Margin annotations (left column):

3
4 A

4 A, B, C,
through
rationali-
zation
4 E
Small degree

2, 3
added
barrier
4 A through
suggestion
from others

Incomplete
perception
due to
mental set

4 A

4 A

4 B

4 C
and
6

Suddenly my whole problem was solved. At least it was solved as far as my not having to leave school. This chap pointed out to me that I didn't have to pass mathematics to stay in school. I would have enough credits if I passed the other courses.

4 E
4 A, B
supple-
mentarily

The tension being relieved, I went back to my room to work on my other courses. Then I began to think of algebra again and this time I thought of how I could pass it—how high my marks in my remaining exams would have to be to make this possible. After thinking the matter through, I de-

4 C

cided to let the next exam tell the story. I still wasn't really convinced that I could pass the course but now that I knew I could remain in school re-

4 E

gardless, the problem lost its gigantic proportions.

4 E
Psychiatric
barrier
removed by
another
individual

Two days later I went to this class. The professor apologized to us all. He told us that since everyone had failed it must have been his fault. He had there-fore raised all the marks 50 points for our five weeks' mark. He announced that he would start the course all over.

5 B

He proceeded to teach at a slower pace and ques-tioned us to see if we understood. Previously, he had assumed we understood. He made up problems from everyday life and forgot the textbook. He gave

5 B
and
4 E 1 and 2

homework on what he had taught us instead of on new material which we would have to work out our-selves. At the end of the term I found that not only had I passed the course but that I had enjoyed the work.

The student will want to see if he agrees with the marginal notes that indicate the steps in the behavior in each case. In later parts of the book there are other analyses of certain forms of behavior and other cases in which the same steps are identified. See Chapter XXI for applications to maladjust-ment.

1510. *Retention and forgetting.* Learning and forgetting are parts of the same process. The learner continually adapts his behavior to his situation and this adaptation involves pick-ing up new modes of behavior and dropping old modes as the life situation changes. Activities designed to further learning and activities designed to apply the products of learning to practical problems both have the effect of improving and maintaining what is learned. When neither learning activities nor using activities are going on, forgetting is likely to show up most clearly because the three factors that produce it are not being counteracted. In other words, forgetting is going on theoretically all the time, but it is not apparent when practice is occurring. Thus, logically, practice is never as profitable as it could be if the factors in forgetting were completely eliminated. These factors always function to keep learning back to some extent.

Forgetting is the result of the operation of definite factors, and not merely the result of disuse or the passage of time.[2] Three factors have been identified which seem to be universally present. The first is called retroactive inhibition. This means that any activity, which is engaged in between the time something is learned and the time it is tested for recall, tends to erase some of what was originally learned. The most common form of interfering activity is the learning of something else. For example, if a student studies American history for a while, then studies the plot and story of *Macbeth,* and then takes a test on American history, he will not do as well on the test as he would have done had he not studied *Macbeth* in the meantime.

Retroactive inhibition does not always affect all learning to the same extent. Its effect is greater when the *materials studied* in the original and the interfering activity are alike than when they are different. Its effect is greater when the *type of activity* in the two periods is the same than when it is different. Its effect is smaller when original learning is relatively complete than when it is relatively incomplete. Its effect is greater when the material lacks meaning and integration than when it is meaningful and integrated. There are obvious implications in these facts for teaching procedures. The teacher, however, must be prepared to compromise in his efforts to set up conditions that take complete advantage

[2] John A. McGeogh, *The psychology of human learning* (New York: Longmans, Green and Co., 1942), Chaps. VIII and IX. This is an outstanding summary of research, dealing with all aspects of retention and forgetting.

of these facts. A practical goal would be to set up conditions in school that involve as little concession to the factors in forgetting as possible.

From a practical point of view it is not always possible to do everything that would cut down the factors in forgetting. For example, although retroactive inhibition will operate to interfere with what is learned in a French class and an English class, where one follows immediately after the other, scheduling considerations may not always permit separation of such courses. The same thing is true of such subjects as history and civic problems, which are so much alike in the nature of content that they might well interfere with each other. The same problem will arise in study periods, where the student finds it necessary to study two similar subjects, both within a given period of time. Some penalties in forgetting are inevitable when these situations cannot be changed.

With regard to the effect on forgetting of incomplete learning there are again practical difficulties that cannot always be overcome. Some school tasks require more time in which to complete original learning than the schedule allows. The introduction of a new concept in mathematics is an illustration. If it cannot be completed within the period, and the students cannot be given time to bring the ideas to some sort of mastery, there will be more forgetting between then and the next class meeting than would otherwise occur. This cannot be helped without upsetting the schedule of the school, although it can be reduced greatly by planning the attack on new materials so as to allow for completion of whatever is involved in the concept or the learning exercise before the class ends.

The effect on forgetting of lack of meaning cannot be prevented at times. As an example see what happens in social studies. The term "democracy" is used constantly in readings and discussions of American history and life. The concept of democracy, however, is somewhat more complex and inclusive than the subjective version of it that is possessed by most high-school students. For many of them its meaning is not very clear. Nevertheless, it has to be used in the pursuit of further learning, and the partial nature of its content for students will cause them to forget the additional ideas they acquire through its use. Nothing would be gained by waiting until the concept is more fully matured in their thinking, for that will take many years. In the meantime they must go on with their studies. This cause of forgetting can only be offset by taking every possible precaution in teaching to see that basic concepts used repeatedly in a course are as clear as they can be made. This might profitably be given attention rather frequently throughout the year.

The second factor in forgetting is the alteration of the stimulating conditions so that the products of learning are measured under different conditions from those under which they were learned. This is inevitable in all cases except those where measurement is an integral part of the teaching process. Inasmuch as all learned behavior occurs as a response to stimulation, there is a tendency for the behavior to change as the stimulation changes. When one's setting changes, the stimuli used in learning are not all present any longer, and some stimuli are present that were not there during learning. Hence, some forms of behavior will be called forth by the new stimuli present, and some of the old behavior that was tied to stimuli now missing will not be so likely to occur. Such changes in stimulating conditions cannot be wholly avoided under any circumstances because life is a process and not a static condition.

Loss of learning that shows up in a test in school may be due to the fact that the student does his intensive study in his room at home where he is surrounded by a particular set of stimuli. These may include his photographs, the clock on his table, the pictures hanging in the room, a little constant attention to his dog, and a background of radio sound effects. What he learns in that setting becomes associated to some extent with some of those stimuli. When he takes the test in school none of those stimuli are present, and they have some effect on his ability to recall what he learned the night before in his room. Forgetting that is caused by a similar circumstance but that is not seen by the teacher is that which is due to the shift from the school in which learning occurs, to out-of-school situations in which it is supposed to function. Some loss is due to this shift in stimulating circumstances, just as to those in the shift from home to the schoolroom.

The third factor in forgetting is the set of the student. He will probably recall his original learning better when he is expecting to be measured for it than when he is not. This infers that announced quizzes will tend to have better scores than unannounced quizzes.

The speed of forgetting can be shown graphically by means of retention curves, which show how much of an original learning is retained at various periods of time after practice ended.

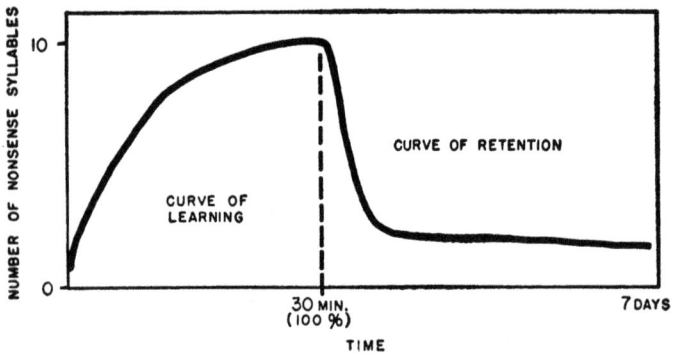

FIG. 6. SCHEMATIC ILLUSTRATION OF THE CONTINUITY OF CURVES
OF LEARNING AND RETENTION

Reprinted by permission of John A. McGeogh, *op. cit.*, p. 316.

Figure 6 shows the theoretical structure of a curve of both learning and retention. Its form is representative of memorized material without meaning. It does not represent with exactness the progress of learning and retention for other kinds of material, but its general form will be found to occur in most kinds of learning. This figure will serve to illustrate a sound principle of study. Suppose a student has prepared a lesson in history that involves some new concepts and some memorized dates and sequences of events. During the time immediately after he has completed his study up to a satisfactory point he will forget more rapidly than he would do later. Within twenty-four hours he will have forgotten a significant amount of what he learned. At that time he reviews the lesson until he has brought his grasp of it back to the point of his original learning. During the next twenty-four hours the rate of forgetting will be lower than during the previous twenty-four hours, and he will have been able to bring his grasp of the lesson up to the original learning in much less time than was required the first time. Twenty-four hours later he reviews again, and returns to original mastery in much shorter time again. As before, the subsequent forgetting is much less in amount than during the preceding intervals. Each succeeding review requires a very small amount of effort to restore what has been lost. After a short series of such reviews the curve of retention remains at a high level, and forgetting has been checked.

Theoretically, the foregoing practice has the effect of cutting up the curve of retention into segments representing the amount that is forgotten during each of the twenty-four-hour periods. Each review brings the curve back to its highest position, but after that the steepest part of the curve is no longer present, because it was removed by the preceding review. Hence, with each review the curve becomes flatter as later and later portions of it are brought up to the point of mastery of the material.

Contrast this study procedure with one that is exceedingly common in high-school and college. Initial learning takes place at the time an assignment is made. There is no review after that until immediately before the final examination. In the meantime many succeeding lessons have been studied in the same manner, each interfering to some extent with the ones before it. A very great amount of effort and time are required prior to the final examination to bring the overwhelming contents of the whole course up to the point of recall. It is such a prodigious feat that it is usually not accomplished. After the examination, the curve of forgetting is just about as steep as it was after the initial learning, and most of what has been learned is lost permanently, because there are no reviews after the examination.

The first procedure divides the study time over many days, and cuts it up into small amounts. The second procedure crams the study time into one concentrated period of very strenuous effort. It is doubtful if the first approach requires much more total time than the second, but in the second instance there is little or no final retention, whereas in the first there is relatively permanent retention.

Several conditions have been identified as having an effect on the curve of retention. One of them is the material or activity learned. Nonsense material is forgotten quickly, and meaningful material more slowly. Any material is nonsense material if it does not have meaning to the student. Trying to memorize rules of grammer that have no meaning to him is the same from a psychological point of view as trying to memorize nonsense syllables of the type used by Ebbinghaus.[3] Memory work should never be required in the absence of clear conceptual understanding of the material.

Conditioned responses and motor skills seem to be held more easily than verbal material. Why this is so cannot be said with any certainty. The nature of such acts involves several parts of the neural and muscular structure, more so than verbal learning, and it may be that there is greater reinforcement of the learning through this great involvement.

. Another factor in retention is the degree of learning. Material or activity that is learned well deteriorates less rapidly than poorly learned material. Krueger [4] states as a result of experiments with the learning of nouns, and in the learning of finger mazes, that 150 per cent overlearning (studying 50 per cent longer than is required to obtain one perfect response) results in a very significant improvement in recall and retention. Overlearning beyond 150 per cent does not yield as much return for the time spent as does that between 100 per cent and 150 per cent. Even though one may not go beyond the point of one perfect performance, re-

[3] Henry E. Garrett, *Great experiments in psychology* (New York: Appleton-Century-Crofts, Inc., 1941), Chap. X. This is the work of Ebbinghaus and illustrates some of the best experimental work in learning.

[4] W. C. F. Krueger, "The effect of overlearning on retention," *Journal of experimental psychology*, 12 (1929), 71-78; ———, "Further studies in overlearning," *op. cit.*, 13 (1930), 152-63.

tention will be much greater than for lessons dropped before that time.

One other factor in recall or ability to repeat what has been learned is the method of measurement used in testing. The ability to recall material falls away much faster than the ability to recognize it. Recall tests include free-response answer questions in which only a question is given the student and he must supply the whole response, questions which require writing lists or series of things, problems to be solved in which the method of solution is not mentioned, and any other form in which no suggestion of the answer is given.

Recognition tests include multiple-choice, true-false, matching and other types of tests in which the right answer is included with some wrong answers, the student being required only to recognize the right answer. Learning up to the point of recognition is therefore easier than learning for recall, and it is suggested from that, that such learning is less complete and less likely to remain.

One outstandingly important generalization from this discussion is that those study methods which produce the best learning are generally the best for retention also. Although they vary somewhat for different types of material, the better methods include striving for meaning first and letting it support memory work, learning to a high level of mastery or even to overlearning before stopping, and periodic reviewing to bring learning back to the required level. These methods in place of sporadic study, and last-minute cramming, will vastly improve the scope of learning, and its retention.

There is a curious phenomenon known as reminiscence, which enters into the problem of retention. It seems that in certain cases the amount of learning actually increases after practice ceases. Following a period of such increase or reminiscence, forgetting begins to show up and retention drops in the usual manner. Reminiscence is not typical of all kinds of learning. It appears to be limited largely to cases involving two conditions: the learning must be incomplete when practice ends, and it must be pretty generally associative in character. Thus one may work on the memorization of a poem, stopping before the poem is completely memorized, and then find that the poem can be recited throughout without error after a period of rest. Reminiscence is not likely to occur in the case of abstract material, of which the most common example is the development of concepts. There seems to be no substitute for a continued experience with the referent in that case.

Questions for Review

1. What is the relationship of the learning process to the psychology of teaching?
2. What are the primary modifying factors in learning?
3. What are some of the secondary modifying factors in learning?
4. Can you justify the manner in which certain factors are allocated to the primary position and others to the secondary position?
5. Why are the factors in the outer ring of Figure 1 so placed?
6. Give the sequence of steps in learning.
7. Write a thorough but brief description of the fundamental facts about motivation.
8. Which of the following depends most on a student's motivation? Why?
   A. What he learns.
   B. How much he learns.
9. What is the one condition needed before a teacher's objective becomes the goal of a student?
10. What are four different kinds of barriers that may need to be considered in school?
11. What is the chief difference between random trial and error, and activity designed to develop insight?
12. What is tension?
13. What are the four or five most distinctly different types of goals in learning?
14. What factors determine the speed of learning? Why is each one important?
15. What are the circumstances that account for forgetting?
16. What is reminiscence, and in what situations may it *not* be expected to occur?
17. What is the major generalization on study methods in the discussion of forgetting?

18. In terms of the sequential steps, what is the difference between learning and adjusting?

SELECTED REFERENCES

Peter Blos, *The adolescent personality* (New York: Appleton-Century-Crofts, Inc., 1941), Part 3, Chapters 1 to 5.

John F. Dashiell, "A survey and synthesis of learning theories," *Psychological bulletin*, 32 (1935), 261-75.

Henry E. Garrett, *Great experiments in psychology* (New York: Appleton-Century-Crofts, Inc., 1941), Chapter X.

Arthur I. Gates, Arthur T. Jersild, T. R. McConnell, and Robert C. Challman, *Educational psychology* (New York: The Macmillan Co., 1948), Chapters IX and X.

Howard L. Kingsley, *The nature and conditions of learning* (New York: Prentice-Hall, Inc., 1946), pp. 494-511.

John A. McGeogh, *The psychology of human learning* (New York: Longmans, Green and Co., Inc., 1942), Chapters VIII and IX.

Donald Snygg and Arthur W. Combs, *Individual psychology* (New York: Harper and Bros., 1949), Chapter III.

CLASS EXERCISES ON THE NATURE OF LEARNING

Things To Do in Class

1. Identify the sequential step most closely related to each of the following items, and discuss the reason for that selection.
   A. The physics teacher said the class could study how to make bombsights if it wished.
   B. A pupil stammered when reading for the class, and then cried.
   C. The teacher thought of giving a quiz but decided to use a home assignment instead.
   D. It is hard to develop speed on the typing sequence H U M.
   E. Some people never develop speed on H U M.
   F. The janitor tried several keys before he found the right one.
   G. No one is ever late to Miss B's class.
   H. Some people do not know why they stay in college.
   I. Some stay because they like the crowd.
   J. His first good sleep in weeks came after he passed the final exam.

    K. Learning sometimes proceeds by trial-and-error.

    L. Movies speed learning.

2. Spend a few minutes learning one or more of the items listed under *A*, to have an experience with the sequential steps in learning. Immediately at the conclusion of each learning task, describe your reactions according to the outline under *B*. Be careful to avoid trying any of the tasks until you are ready to do so experimentally.

A

    1. Learn to pat your head and rub your stomach at the same time, or to wiggle your ears.

    2. Write your name in mirror form until it is easy, or write your name with the hand not ordinarily used, or toss a coin into a jar until you reach some level of skill.

    3. Learn the names and faces to match for 10 or more members of the class. Select those you do not already know. Any other type of memorization can be substituted.

    4. Through any available means, develop familiarity with one of these concepts: malingering, organismic age, plateau, complex, amentia, etc.

B

    1. What was your goal?

    2. What was your motivation? (Be honest and accurate.)

    3. What was the nature of the educational barrier?

    4. Were there any psychological barriers? If so what were they?

    5. What evidences of tension did you feel during the early part of the learning process?

    6. What possible ways of doing the task occurred to you?

    7. What were the relative amounts of chance and analysis involved in your search for the appropriate action?

    8. Was the first selected line of action appropriate? If not, describe further efforts to find the appropriate activity.

    9. What were the first indications that success was coming?

    10. Describe your first awareness of satisfaction and reduction of tension.

    11. Which subdivision of the fifth step was involved in your task? Check on the appropriate steps on pages 252-255 to see if you recognize them in your experience.

    12. Account for the speed of your learning.

  A. What was the relative difficulty of the assignment?
  B. How strong was your motivation?
  C. What was your capacity for this problem?
3. Illustrate in the following manner how experience leads to the formation of definitions (descriptions of concepts):
  A. Through free class discussion, develop on the board a comprehensive list of ideas about learning which have been part of the classwork in the last few meetings.
  B. Select from the list the most significant items for use as major subdivisions under which to list all the others.
  C. When all the statements are sorted into related groups, put them together into a lengthy statement or definition.
  D. Condense this statement into a manageable definition.
  E. Point out the fact that the definition represents a great deal of experience with the referent under various conditions, and that the formation of a definition corresponds to the process of generalization by which concepts are brought to a state of clarity and sharpness.

CHAPTER XVI

TYPES OF END PRODUCTS OF LEARNING

1601. *The types.* Having examined the learning process as if it were something apart from all other aspects of living, it is now necessary to begin putting it back into its natural setting. As a first step in that orientation process, it may be said that an important modification in the actual act of learning is directly due to the nature of what is to be learned, the end product. The student acquires thousands of knowledges, skills, and preferences during his life and it is convenient to classify these end products of learning into six categories whose characteristics differ in educationally significant ways. Table 3 contains the six types, each of which is discussed in this chapter.[1]

It is apparent upon examination of these types that they differ primarily in Steps 4 and 5 of the learning process described in Chapter XV. The five parts of Step 4 and one part of Step 5 are present in each type of learning, but are carried out in different ways. A knowledge of these varied ways of finding how to do something will help the teacher discover the best way of helping the learner.

The six types of end products presented here are based on the fact that there are six distinct types of behavior that can be identified and differentiated in the total repertoire of an organism. One is automatic motor behavior, such as walking. Another is motor behavior that is guided by perceptual cues, such as playing a piano. A third is repetition of symbolic material that has been committed to memory, no matter whether it is memorized completely or in the most frag-

[1] Guy T. Buswell in his *Outline of educational psychology*, Students Outline Series (New York: Longmans, Green and Co., Inc., 1939), presents several types of learning in a way that is helpful to teachers. The structure of this chapter represents an adaptation from his material.

mentary form. A fourth is cognitive interaction with the meaningful elements in a situation, recognition of meaning, and choice of paths on the basis of meaning. A fifth is biased reaction based on feeling rather than on meaning or opinion, essentially non-cognitive in nature. The sixth is the deliberate postponement of a choice reaction, probably what is usually referred to as a delayed response, while the individual acquires additional information that will enable him to make a decision of the kind mentioned as type four above. This sort of reaction is also referred to as problem-solving.

Nothing in the whole literature on learning gives us any reason for thinking that behavior is acquired through any other process than engaging in it. Therefore, it must be assumed that one learns to do each of these unique things by doing it, that is, by going through the processes involved in that kind of behavior. Since each is unique, it presumably has its unique form of learning. What the teacher needs is not a theory that reduces all forms of learning to one or two generalizations, but a realistic picture of what goes on when an individual learns something. It is what the organism as a whole does that matters in teaching and counseling. Hence, it is necessary to see just what happens in the acquisition of each type of behavior, and what has to be done by a teacher to help along the learning process in each type. In the following sections the six types are presented as types, and then discussed from the point of view of how they are learned. Suggestions follow in each case on the relative functions of the teacher and the learner.

1602. *Sensory-motor skills.*[2] Many motor acts that involve considerable balance and rhythmic performance become established fairly early in life and thenceforth are automatic. That is, they function without conscious mental control. The cortex and the association fibers of the brain, within which associational and thinking processes are mediated,

---

[2] John A. McGeogh, *The psychology of human learning* (New York: Longmans, Green and Co., Inc., 1942), pp. 11-13 and parts of Chap. V. McGeogh recognized the types involved in this discussion, but seemingly assumed the sensory-motor patterns and did not discuss them apart from perceptual-motor acts.

apparently do not have the principal control of such behavior. For example, one may engage in a complicated conversation while walking along a straight path, and do both well. The walking is automatic and does not interfere with the conversation. It would be more difficult to carry on such a conversation while walking along the top of a fence because conscious perceptual-motor processes would be called into action in the placing of the feet and the maintenance of balance in this unusual situation. Such walking would no longer be automatic since something out of the ordinary has been added which requires conscious attention. Hence, the complicated conversation would meet with interference. Whenever a motor act remains on the purely automatic level it is properly classified as a sensory-motor performance. This means that it is able to function independently of any stimulus except that which it creates by its own activity. Walking creates its own stimuli through the pressures on the foot, joints, and muscles, which send neural sensations to some nerve center where they are transmitted into appropriate motor impulses without the need of any outside stimulation such as printed instructions, or other patterns to be followed or the conscious thought required to follow them. As a matter of fact, highly automatic motor skills can often be upset by giving conscious attention to them after they are established. For many people dancing is an illustration of this phenomenon. Having learned to manage themselves, one's feet seem to object to being watched as they go through a dancing routine.

1603. *Learning sensory-motor skills.* Although sensory-motor skills function automatically they require conscious attention in the early stages of learning. The child's first efforts to get on its feet are accompanied by close attention to what it is doing. As soon as a few steps have been taken, the attention is directed toward some goal, such as a parent's outstretched hand or the chair a few feet away. The feet are then left to function independently of conscious direction. If, however, at any later time the individual wants to learn how to walk with more grace, conscious attention must again be given to the parts of the body concerned until the desired

TABLE 3. TYPES OF END PRODUCTS OF LEARNING

Type	Definition	Example
Sensory-motor skill	Independent motor skill that functions automatically and without conscious control.	Walking, running, riding a bicycle, standing upright, etc.
Perceptual-motor skill	A motor skill that can be instantly put to the service of an incoming perceptual pattern.	Drawing, typewriting, playing a piano, tracing a pattern, etc.
Mental association	Knowledge, such as facts, names, relationships, laws, perceptual differentiations, etc.	Ability to identify colors, sounds, smells, tastes, or tactile sensations; possession of specific facts, such as number combinations, names of objects or people, poems, grammatical forms, etc.
Concept	An idea or mental image of an action, thing, quality, condition, etc. It often takes the form of a definition or generalization.	The meanings of words, especially abstract ones, such as busy, plutocrat, etc.; differentiation between fine distinctions, differences such as warm and hot; varying degrees of greenness, or various meanings of green.
Tastes and preferences	Discrimination based on liking rather than on analytical evaluation.	Preference for a particular color, type of music, style of home, article of food, personality characteristic, etc.
Skill in problem-solving	The ability to hold decisions in abeyance while additional objective information is secured and brought to bear on the problem.	Ability to identify basic issues, to set up problems for solution, to apply principles of logic, to gather and classify evidence, to make sound deductions from data, etc.

form of movement is established after which automaticity replaces conscious direction again. Obviously, then, the greatest value of learning sensory-motor acts under skilled direction lies in the attainment of good form more than in the simple learning of the act. Since most sensory-motor acts have value in proportion to their skill, good form is important.

The beginner has no choice but to engage in random overt movement until he chances upon a successful performance. In order to repeat this successful performance, he must identify and reinstate the sensations that accompanied his first successful act. The golfer recalls that his first good drive occurred when his left arm was held relatively still and there was a characteristic muscular pull, which will help him capture and reinstate that position another time. During this process he pays much attention to the position of his arms and feet, the action of his wrists, the focus of his eyes, and so on. He swings his club slowly, feeling consciously for those telltale sensations that indicate proper form. When he begins to find himself taking the proper stance and following through in approved style without realizing that he has been doing it, the period of profitable conscious direction of movement is coming to an end and further conscious attention to form will tend to retard the development of efficiency except for those periodic checkup or drill periods when he engages in slow-motion practice to re-emphasize certain aspects of form. Henceforth the golfer is told to keep his eye on the ball and his mind on the fairway out there where the ball is supposed to land. He lives with the ball instead of with the stroke. In other words, he fits his new act into its larger setting so that it becomes attached to the whole process and carries itself out as a smooth part of that process rather than as an isolated unit of behavior. Practice is now the answer to improvement in efficiency.

The teacher's greatest contribution to this process lies in is ability to demonstrate good form to the learner, to anticipate early developments of bad form and to keep them from materializing, and to furnish a critical analysis of the learner's performance, which the learner himself is in no position to do. This contribution seems to be divisible into the following specific steps: (1) Analyze the movement in terms of sequence and form. This may be done by slow-motion film or some other means of catching each phase of the movement so that it can be studied by itself. (2) Watch the learner's performance to identify those parts of sequence and form that are correct and those that need improvement. Those needing improvement should be tackled one at a time, and those already correctly installed need not be discussed when the learner is still in the confusion of first efforts to perform. (3) Illustrate or describe the correct performance and (4) tell the learner how to know whether he is doing it right or not. Such cues often consist of the position of the back of the hand, a muscular pull, a sound, a sense of balance, or an awareness of smoothness in place of awkwardness. (5) Watch for early indications of common difficulties and eliminate them before they have become established as parts of the process. The teacher is in a much better position to recognize these incipient dangers than the student because he is an onlooker and because he has made an analysis of such difficulties and the ways in which they develop. (6) Drill or practice periods should be regulated in length and frequency to obtain the most efficient learning. The teacher should know what these lengths and frequencies are for his subject.[3] (7) Knowing how important the early stages of learning are, the teacher should be particularly watchful at first, and may check the learner's performance at increasingly longer intervals as the act takes on correct form and begins to drop into the area of automatic control. The typing teacher needs to watch the students' hands and fingers very closely during the early parts of the beginning course, and less closely later on. The dancing instructor gives a great deal of attention to the position of feet at first and not so much later.

Sensory-motor skills are involved in a number of school subjects. They include penmanship, some phases of sewing and other activities in home arts, dancing, swimming and other physical education, typing (developing form), and others. Most of these subjects also include other types of

[3] See Chapter XVII.

learning, and the teacher must be able to analyze all of his work in terms of the types of learning involved in it.

STUDENT AND TEACHER ACTIVITIES SELECTED
TO FIT SENSORY-MOTOR LEARNING

The Learner	*The Teacher*
1. Making of random overt movements, seeking the successful movement.	1. Analyze the movement in terms of sequence and form.
2. Accidentally making successful movement.	2. Offer needed directions as need arises.
3. Identifying and reinstating the sensations that accompanied the successful movement.	3. Provide ideas on correct performance by verbal or illustrative techniques.
4. Give attention to parts of body and how they move in very early stage of learning until correct acts have been identified.	4. Give cues for identifying correct form (feelings, observation, sounds, etc.).
5. Shift attention to objective results of movement after correct acts have been identified.	5. Watch for common difficulties and warn students when they first begin to show up (e.g., over-attention to organs, poor position, etc.).
6. Practice activity until mastered.	6. Establish best sequence of drill and rest.
	7. Check very closely at first and with less frequency later.

1604. *Perceptual-motor skill.*[4] When a motor skill is attached to a perceptual pattern something has been added to the simple sensory-motor function. In this case a motor function must have reached a stage of development where its form is independent of conscious control, but where its direction can be dictated by a momentary perceptual experience. For example, a typist learns to strike the keys in a form that does not change from one job to another, and that is therefore automatic. She must, however, be able to direct her fingers to certain keys in exact harmony with the printed pattern she is following. Therefore, the fingers are performing according

4 See footnote 2.

to a perceptual pattern that involves uniqueness rather than simple repetition. The perceptual pattern may be a fresh one never before experienced, such as a news article being copied, or it may be one previously experienced and lodged in the memory, such as the typing of a memorized poem. Typing from copy, whether by sight or by memory, is perceptual-motor activity, whereas drilling on a typewriter by merely striking the F and J alternately is sensory-motor activity. Referring to an earlier paragraph again, mere walking is sensory-motor activity, but walking along the top of a fence is perceptual-motor activity because the feet are being placed according to an incoming perceptual pattern and not by an automatic control.

1605. *Learning perceptual-motor skills.* Since perceptual-motor skills have two distinct aspects, form and response to pattern, they involve three learning problems: (1) form, (2) understanding the pattern, and (3) making the pattern function through the motor act. Correct form is established according to the steps involved in sensory-motor learning. Developing an understanding of the pattern is a problem in conceptual and associational learning, and is discussed later. Suffice it to say here that it is conceptual because it requires a comprehension of the nature of the function represented by the perceptual pattern. It is associational because the learner must memorize the relationship between notes and keys, or any other paired items in the pattern and the physical performance that follows it.

Making the pattern functional is the unique part of perceptual-motor learning. For the learner it involves these steps. (1) Each item in the pattern must be associated with some specific part of the motor act. The typing student learns that the letter "a" calls for action by the fourth finger of the left hand, and that the finger strikes in its "home" position. Remember that the form of the stroke, either for home position or any other part of the keyboard, is presumably already established. The finger is able to carry through as soon as the visual stimulus from the letter "a" is able to get over into the correct motor channel. This is a conscious process for most stenographers, although it may approach automaticity in the case of those who engage in contest work or develop unusual speed and efficiency.

(2) When the student first sits before a machine and reads an "a" from copy, the left little finger is likely to falter considerably in its task of striking the key because the learner is trying to do at once two things that heretofore have not been done at once. This breakdown in motor performance is not serious and will probably disappear as that single unit of action is learned. The same thing will repeat for each symbol on the keyboard. The first evidence of perceptual-motor coordination will be in the establishment of these single units of action. The beginning learner goes from letter to letter, rather than from word to word.

(3) When smoothness in the unit responses begins to appear, there will be a gradual enlargement of the size of the unit to which a response is made. Single-letter responses in typing may give way to two-letter responses such as i-t, u-p, o-n, followed by longer and longer combinations, until whole words of all lengths become the units of reaction. The word "can" is no longer composed of three separate actions, c-a-n, but is only one somewhat more complex action in which the three strokes come along in the same effort. The reaction is to a word, not to three letters.

(4) Drill is again the prerequisite to increasingly smooth and rapid performance, with occasional attention to form lest gradually it change in the direction of undesirable characteristics.

The teacher facilitates this process best when he follows these guides: (1) He aids the development of the motor acts in accordance with sensory-motor analysis. (2) He aids the development of understanding of the pattern by the correct use of associational procedures. (3) He brings to the learning situation a complete understanding of the process of attaching motor acts to perceptual cues, and regulates the first efforts of the learner so that good form and rhythm are not lost in confusion. Slowness is often the best approach to speed because it allows the learner to act calmly and without unnecessary interference with form. (4) He sets up drills so as to develop the small unit acts from which more complex acts can be devoloped, and keeps the drill material coordinated with the learner's state of perceptual-motor coordination. He never jumps from single-letter typing exercises to those which involve complex scientific terminology, nor does he keep the class on single-letter drills when it is ready for longer combinations. (5) He matches the drill material to the situations in which the learner will perform when he is ready to go to work. Much drill material for typing classes is actually selected from books or letters in the special fields for which students are preparing. (6) He regulates practice and rest periods in accordance with the facts about economical learning as they fit his particular subject.

Perceptual-motor learning forms an important part of the work in such subjects as typing (copying), machine sewing, instrumental music, drawing, and others.

STUDENT AND TEACHER ACTIVITIES SELECTED
TO FIT PERCEPTUAL-MOTOR LEARNING

The Learner	*The Teacher*
1. Establish correct form. (See sensory-motor process.)	1. Follow sensory-motor process in getting motor acts established.
2. Develop understanding of the perceptual pattern. (See conceptual and associational processes.)	2. Follow conceptual process in developing meaning of perceptual pattern.
3. Attach motor act to the perceptual pattern by following steps:	3. Follow associational process in tying pattern to specific motor responses or key positions, etc.
3a. Associate parts of pattern with specific parts of motor act.	
3b. Random efforts to make correct motor performance while giving major attention to perceptual pattern, characterized by some breakdown or interference in smooth motor performance.	4. Guide learner in developing neuro-muscular coordinations, by: 4a. Providing correct information on position or other way of getting motor act in its correct setting.
3c. Gradual establishment of small unit responses to pattern.	4b. Have same analyses made as for sensory-motor process,

The Learner	*The Teacher*
3d. Gradual enlargement of size of unit responded to.	and watch performance accordingly.
3e. Major attention on form at first and on speed and form later.	4c. Set up drills so as to insure good form in early stages (slow, rhythmic, etc.) and development of efficiency later.
	4d. Provide specific drills matched to state of learner's coordination (e.g., common groups of letters in typing, or commonly associated words, etc.).
	4e. Grade drill materials to match coordination and span of recognition of students.
	4f. Regulate practice and rest periods.

1606. *Established mental associations.*[5] Much of what is learned consists of various ideas committed to *memory* in such ways that they have established relationships for the individual. Two or more ideas or objects are experienced together in such a way that when one of them is encountered it will tend to remind the person of the other one. A meaningful vocabulary is probably the best evidence of such associations. Illustrations may be found in the naming of objects such as cat, stove, and hat, or in learning names for variations of one kind of object such as Holstein, Jersey, and Guernsey, or in learning symbols for abstract concepts such as H_2SO_4, P. M., tertiary, and subliminal, or in learning systems or orders of things such as 1, 2, 3, 4, and A, B, C, D, and $4 + 9 = 13$, or in picking out and remembering certain items in reading matter such as the *types* of sentences that may be used, or the *ways* in which a given function may be carried on. The outstanding characteristic of such forms of knowledge is that two or more things, which have been associated together in

[5] McGeogh, *op. cit.*, pp. 6-11 and Chap. V.

experience, become so interrelated for the learner that one of them has the power to recall the others. To the spoken word "cow" a person may respond mentally with "Jersey," if the words cow and Jersey have become associated for him.

1607. *Establishing mental associations.* Regardless of the process by which such associations are established within the nervous system, it may safely be said that those items of experience which occur together will tend to recur together. Numerous conditions may justify modification of this statement, but it is a useful generalization. The child sees a cup, and hears the word "cup" at the same time, and those two items of experience are likely to recur together if either the cup or the word is encountered. The one encountered will tend to suggest the other one. Repeatedly encountering these two items of experience together will reinforce this linkage until the child has learned the name of the receptacle from which he drinks his milk. Since associational learning seems to hinge around encountering two items together, good teaching probably depends on a knowledge of what is important in that associational relationship.

The idea of experiencing together those things one wishes to tie together in learning applies alike to single items and to whole categories of information. That is, the principle is present in learning the essential facts about the gestation period and also how it fits into the larger area of biological reproduction. For that reason one of the first things the learner should do in this sort of problem is survey the material to be learned, and see what it covers in general, then recall what he already knows of it and try to see how this new material fits into the whole scheme. Failure to do this may not affect his ability to learn the specific facts in the daily lesson, but it is likely to result in the learning of a lot of unrelated blocks of specific facts rather than a well-coordinated body of knowledge. Along with this attack, the learner should also pick out of his reading material or lecture notes or other source of information the items to be learned. These items should be arranged in some system of relationship. The most useful system is usually indicated by the material itself and the purposes for which it is being studied. This system of relationships offers the most efficient basis for associating items together. For example, if a student of animal husbandry is trying to learn the identifying characteristics of a good milk cow, he finds himself dealing with such characteristics as the size of the barrel, the shape and size of the udder and teats, the bony structure, especially of those parts of the cow concerned with delivery, and others. These facts must be grouped together and around the idea of how they affect milk production or any other related problem and when so grouped and studied will become learned as parts of a whole picture. Well-spaced teats then become related in his mind to good milk production, and when they are mentioned the learner tends to think of their effect on production.

Most school subjects require that the learner organize many such groups of material and eventually acquire familiarity in a fairly large and complex area. For this reason the learner must move on from one grouping to the others that need study. He should not, however, rush from one group to another until he has gone over the desired associations and impressions for a long enough time to make them begin to hang together. In the course of an hour's study on a given subject, learning can be greatly facilitated by coming back to such blocks of material from time to time and renewing the process of experiencing them together. This combination of working systematically through several blocks of organized material and then coming back to repeat the process is the heart of the so-called part-whole method of learning. The parts may be well learned without developing any interrelationship, and on the other hand one may learn the major categories of a given area without knowing anything definite about what is contained in each category. For example, it is possible to learn that the five major divisions of the animal kingdom are fish, amphibian, reptile, bird, and mammal, and yet be unable to tell fish from fowl. Hence, the desirability of keeping the parts related to each other while learning the content of all the parts. Poems offer excellent illustrations of this problem. When attention is given to one verse until it is completely learned before learning another verse, the learner often has difficulty saying the whole poem or getting the verses into their proper order. These facts about associational learning offer the basis for the development of good teaching methods in this area.

A student facing new material to be learned is often unable to find its meaning or how it is related to his previous experience, simply because it is new to him. The teacher must then use all appropriate means to see that the learner finds the meaning. He may try to do this in at least three ways. First, show how it is related to the work that has immediately preceded it and how it will lead into work to follow. This gives it belongingness in a large and important scheme. Second, offer the learner some keys to an understanding of the important meanings of the material in and of itself, some of its points of interest or challenge or peculiarity. Third, lead the learner to understand how this material, as also the whole scheme of the course, will fit into his life problems and needs.

To take advantage of certain known factors of importance in efficient learning, the teacher should arrange the material to be learned in such an order that the most important ideas are seen first and lead naturally into the lesser ideas, or the ideas that are formed primarily of the subdivisions of the main issues. The teacher should also arrange the material so that each successive block logically and systematically follows and is related to the previously learned material. It is also helpful to introduce items to be learned as close to the time they are to be used as possible. Because students may drop into faulty study habits, it is also helpful to examine their study methods at intervals, and show how they may be improved. There is a noticeable disregard of this important function of teaching in high schools and colleges, and probably not enough of it at any level. In conducting supervised study, the teacher has the obligation of making the provision for the essential steps in study and seeing that they are carried out. Supervised study implies that the teacher is very actively engaged in the study work, not idly resting at a desk or engaged in some task of his own that keeps him from participating with the students.

Although this discussion is concerned principally with

verbal material and memory, it is obvious that meaning is involved in it. Much of what has been said deals with the matter of finding meaningful relationships in the material to be committed to memory. This is because memorization is faster and more permanent with meaningful materials than with nonsense materials. However, once the meaning is present, high-level memorization depends on repetition, for which there is no substitute.

Student and Teacher Activities Selected To Fit Associational Learning

The Learner	*The Teacher*
1. Survey material to see what it covers.	1. Use all appropriate means to see that learner gets the meaning in the material to be learned.

2. Note familiar parts of it, and try to see how it is related to anything you already know about it.	a. Relate it to previous or following work.
	    b. Make its own inherent message clear.
	    c. Orient it in the learner's own world.

3. Impress in mind the items to be learned. Go over them several times.	
4. Look for natural forms of order and relatedness in the material, especially those to be remembered.	2. Present in first positions those items most important in the material.
5. Run over these asociations and impressions for a time before going on to next part.	3. Arrange material so that each successive block logically and systematically follows and is related to the previously learned material. (Offset retroactive inhibition.)
6. At end of a short study period, recall in a systematic way what has been learned. Do this at several points in long assignments.	
	4. Introduce items as close to the time they are to be used as possible. (recency)
7. If reading for knowledge, make a synopsis or *brief* outline of material covered.	5. Examine learner's study methods and suggest improvements as needed.
8. Concentrate while studying, allowing no mind-wandering.	6. In supervised study make

The Learner	*The Teacher*
a. Read textual material as rapidly as possible.	provision for steps in learner's list.
b. Remove from environment anything likely to threaten concentration.	

1608. *Concepts.* Concepts differ from ordinary mental associations primarily in depth. The concept deals with the *meaning* an individual attaches to a word or other symbol, rather than with the mere fact that any given symbol is associated with any given object. The concept of a cat would include what a cat consists of, what it looks like, the noises it makes, the way it acts, and so on. To be valid, this meaning must fit into a wider context of meanings or related concepts in peculiar ways that show that it agrees with the common experiences all other people have with cats.

In section 802 the nature of meaning was discussed. Since concepts are meanings, the content of that discussion should be kept in mind at this point. Reference back to it is advisable before going on.

There are several kinds of concepts. Concrete concepts consist of one's understanding of the *specific* objects one has encountered. A concept may consist of a unique, individual object, not yet related to a class, or related to a class but still seen as a unique member of that class. When objects are put into classes they are referred to by nouns. Individual objects are usually referred to by their unique names, if names have been assigned them by those who associate with them. Nouns, however, represent only classes of objects taken altogether, so that these concepts are not as specific or as concrete as are the first.

The grouping of objects as indicated above is an almost limitless possibility. The larger the grouping, the more general will be its characteristics. Through increasingly general classification a hierarchy of concepts is built up. For example, an individual begins by having experience with a juicy object that he eats. Then several others are encountered. He identifies a class of objects, which he names oranges. Later he has similar experiences with other objects of a somewhat similar nature, which he calls apples. These two class concepts, along with others, he finally combines into what he calls fruit. Still later he identifies in several such general conceptual classes certain common elements, by reason of which he calls them all food. Beyond this he identifies, among all the food objects and some other objects, certain still more general characteristics, which lead him to refer to all of them collectively as life necessities. In each case of moving up to a higher class-concept, the characteristics become more general, less specific, and somewhat farther removed from objective realities that can be contacted by the sense organs.

Another direction in which conceptual hierarchies proceed involves *abstraction*. This is a process of identifying the characteristics of objects or actions, and turning attention from the object or action to its characteristics. Thus the characteristic is "taken away" from the object and handled conceptually and symbolically (through words) as if it were a "real" in itself. For example, several objects are so constituted that they yield to the touch, and change shape as outside pressures are applied to them. This characteristic comes to be known as softness. By the same process objects or activities are said to be friendly, eager, helpful, blue, cold, quiet, and so on. These qualities exist primarily through the activities and nature of the sense organs and the sensations they convey to the central nervous system. Such abstractions may be drawn from very concrete concepts, or from highly generalized concepts. Thus we have characteristics of large groups. Society is a large group concept. One of the qualities that has been identified in certain societies is democracy, which is a characteristic of the behavior within the group. Both generalizations and abstractions may go on to exceedingly complex forms.

Another form of conceptual structuring involves causes and effects. Out of observation, principles or laws are derived, in which the form is, essentially, where A is present, B will follow.

An ideal is a concept created in the mind by putting together the most admired concepts possessed by the individual. When an abstract concept is thought of as being a real entity in itself, it becomes a reified concept. For example, Uncle Sam is a mental construct. Insofar as he is felt to be a reality he is a reification of the spirit of the United States. Gravity is a *reified concept* for the average layman who visualizes it as a constant downward pull. The student of physics is more likely to think of it as a statement of the way matter behaves, which would make it a generalization.

Since concepts are not born full grown, their ultimate maturity depends on keeping them in a state of flexibility so that they can develop enlarged meanings with every opportunity. To the extent that the early parts of the concept are well learned growth will be cumulative and gradual. Concepts are not born in children as part of their native endowment but develop in a form peculiar to the child's environment. They begin to form when the child receives his first usable impressions of anything whatever to which a symbol may be applied. In fact, it is conceivable that highly unique individual experiences may result in concepts for a given individual for which no general symbol exists—some forms of religious or esthetic experience, for example. The symbols, most of which are words, by which conceptual meanings come to be known are the tools that make education possible, and in turn, education is concerned with the acquisition of other concepts and their symbols not yet possessed by the student.

From an extensive survey of the literature on concepts [6] the following conclusions have been drawn:

[6] Asahel D. Woodruff, "Implications for teachers in recent studies of the development of concepts," unpublished MS, 1940. Since the MS is not available for distribution, it is not feasible to list the 51 carefully selected titles included in the survey. A few that may serve to illustrate what is available are listed here:

William H. Burton, *The nature and amount of civic information possessed by Chicago children of sixth-grade level*, Ph.D. thesis (Chicago: The University of Chicago, 1924).

Guy T. Buswell and Lenore John, *The vocabulary of arithmetic*, Supplementary Educational Monographs, No. 38 (Chicago: Department of Education, The University of Chicago, 1931).

W. S. Gray and Eleanor Holmes, *The development of meaning vocabularies in reading* (Chicago: University of Chicago Press, 1938).

1. Mere ability to read is no guarantee of comprehension. Many children can read material without grasping its meaning.

2. Poorly formed concepts or the lack of important concepts in certain subject areas prevent children from understanding the material presented to them.

3. Textbook vocabularies are often too difficult for intended readers, since they contain key words for which the children have inadequate concepts or none at all. This is especially true for technical or other special vocabularies.

4. There are many more concepts that subject-matter experts consider it necessary for children to learn than the present rate of learning will allow them to learn in some subjects during the total school years.

5. Most children are unable to make free use of date concepts in the solution of problems in history.

Since concepts are the basic meanings that enable people to think and work together with mutual understanding, and since the literature reveals some disturbing facts about the state of development of the concepts of young people, there are several serious problems to be solved in this phase of schoolwork. The very interesting semantic problem of the meaning of words is concerned with the inability of people to understand each other through the use of verbal symbols. Granted that every person had the same concept for the words used in a paragraph, every one of them would obtain the same meaning from reading the paragraph. As the factors of incompleteness and confusion in those conceptual meanings are introduced, the difficulty, if not the impossibility, of having all the readers obtain the same idea from the paragraph arises. Some of the most commonly used words in the average American vocabulary, words such as liberty and democracy, are subject to this difficulty. They may mean a condition of lack of responsibility for one, and a condition of heavy responsibility for another. It is unquestionably true that much of

---

Eugenia Hanfmann and Jacob A. Kasanin, "A method for the study of concept formation," *Journal of psychology*, 3 (1937), 521-40.

Lloyd L. Ramseyer, "Measuring 'intangible' effects of motion pictures," *Educational screen*, 18 (September, 1939), 237 ff.

the inability of teachers to reach and to influence students is due to the lack of mutual understanding between them that results from the teacher's unfamiliarity with the state of the students' concepts.

1609. *Developing concepts.* The literature dealing with the development of concepts contains several important studies whose major findings are worthy of attention. Here is a list of such findings:

1. Personal experience seems to be the most powerful known factor in concept development. This is evident in such facts as these: (a) Concepts are made up of meanings peculiar to the culture of the child and his experience. (b) The ease with which concepts form is closely related to the intimacy of the child's experience with the referent and the clarity of the situation in which it occurs. (c) Boys tend to develop more concepts than girls and wider experience is suggested as the probable factor. (d) Amount of reading and size of vocabulary are related, but it is not known which, if either, is the causal factor. Reading is, of course, a major way of having experience. (e) The symbol that usually accompanies a common experience becomes established as the symbol for that concept. Thus language obtains meaning.

2. Concepts tend to consist of general impressions first, while refinement of the specific features develops more slowly. (a) In early years many concepts exist before the child is able to express them. (b) Concepts often begin with specific part meanings, to which are added other parts of the whole meaning by means of later experiences. (c) When a symbol has acquired one meaning for a child it is harder to add another concept to the same symbol than it was to connect the first concept. (d) In young children there is a tendency to make compromises between childhood theories and opposing scientific theories presented in school. (e) As concepts develop many erroneous as well as correct meanings are adopted, and refinement takes place with added experience. (f) Students tend to guess at meanings of words with which they are unfamiliar, taking cues from such things as the appearance or sound of the word.

3. Intelligence or mental age is an important factor in the ability to formulate new concepts correctly. (a) Ability to define concepts in generalized terms tends to develop as the child progresses through the grades. (b) Only superior people tend to be able to recognize their own vocabulary troubles. (c) Some factor related to economic status seems to accompany the development of large vocabularies.

4. Some concepts are more difficult to develop than others. (a) Technical and abstract concepts are more difficult to learn than number and other specific and concrete concepts. (b) Children are less likely to recognize their limitations on abstract or general concepts than on specific meanings. (c) Events closely related in time present greater difficulty for concept formation than those widely separated. (d) Concepts related to speed are difficult to learn when objects move in circles instead of straight lines.

5. The nature of instruction and the manner of presenting concepts seem to have an important effect on the development of meaning for a concept. (a) The regular order of learning is concept first, then symbol, then definition, with other sub-steps no doubt. (b) Social science pamphlets and such materials aid more in the development of social science concepts than do ordinary text materials. (c) Concepts presented in pictures, especially moving pictures, are more easily learned than those presented otherwise. (d) Dotted and shaded maps are very difficult for lower-grade students to understand, and hence do not aid concept development in geography. (e) Line and bar graphs are less helpful in the development of concepts of quantity than circular graphs, and relative-size pictograms are better than many other types of size comparisons. (f) Vital and humanized material tends to aid the development of concepts more than material that is remote from the child's interests and activities. (g) Concepts presented by episodes are learned better than those presented by mere descriptions. (h) Special vocabularies can best be developed by direct instruction, as contrasted with indirect learning. (i) Time and place relationships can be mastered better through direct instruction than through incidental instruction. (j) Context or footnote explanations of

new words tend to aid somewhat the development of the concept for which the new word stands. (k) It appears that many concepts are not reduced to exact definitions until a formal school situation demands it and that many of the most common concepts are erroneously assumed by teachers to be well defined and thus are never tested (l) Books only mildly interesting provide greater concept development than those intensely interesting or uninteresting.

From the studies summarized above, it seems the learner's part in developing new concepts should involve the following general steps: (1) Have as much and as varied personal experience with the referent as possible. For example, in trying to learn about seed germination the student should see several illustrations of the process of germinating for as many different kinds of seed as possible. When the problem of understanding negative numbers is presented, the students should be taken through a variety of experiences with negative numbers so that the peculiarities of their ways of being related to other numbers may be amply illustrated. (2) Hear the term that applies to the concept and associate it with the recognized parts of the experience. The word "germination" should be used frequently and always in the right way while such exploratory experiences are going on. There should be several explanatory amplifications of what is meant when the term is used to be sure the learner sees the particular phase of germination that is being illustrated at the moment. (3) Have repeated experience with the referent to fill in heretofore missing parts of one's understanding of it and to add clarity to the whole picture. This involves two processes: (a) Cutting out those peripheral and non-related parts of the experience that have no meaningful relation to the essential characteristics of the referent. For example, a seed may germinate in a cup, but the cup has no real connection with the process. Unfortunately, whenever a common human experience is lifted out of its natural setting and brought into the school for study, it runs the risk of having the students attach to it those circumstances in the schoolroom under which it is experienced when these may have no real connection with it at all. (b) Adding in constantly those parts of experience that are belatedly recognized by the learner but that are essential to the completeness of the concept. The child may not notice for some time that there is a distinctive difference in the structure of the tails of horses and cows, but eventually this difference should be added to his concepts of horse and cow and will be so added if he continues to see more and more of the animals. (4) After much experience the learner must begin the task of drawing out of all his experiences the common elements in them that make up some of our more complex concepts. For example, he draws on his experiences with human beings to note that in many cases the relationships between them were marked by a warmth and mutual regard and solicitude. He notices also that when this type of relationship is referred to it is often called by the name "love." He will also conclude in his generalizing that love is not an invariable condition in human relationships, and out of this process of adding and delineating, he will arrive at the abstract concept of love. Eventually, his experiences with relationships marked by the presence of love will enable him to differentiate kinds of love, and degrees of love, and his concepts will become clearer and more complex with such development. (5) The process of becoming definite leads finally to the formulation of definitions which perform the function of stating in precise form what a concept contains and eliminating thereby what it does not contain. Only after the concept has acquired its proper symbol or label and its rigorous definition can it be skillfully used by the individual, but these steps cannot be taken until experience with the referent provides the materials to which the symbol can be attached and from which the definition is developed.

The teacher's contribution to this type of learning is indicated by what the student must do. The teacher must: (1) provide experiences with each new referent introduced in a course. The experience must be realistic and natural, not theoretical and abstract. Many times the best that can be done is to provide such experiences vicariously, but this does not sanction overlooking the need for reality and vividness. Some of the concepts dealt with in a course may already be partially developed in the students so that only supplementary experiences are needed. (2) Introduce the term by which the concept is to be known and handled as soon as there is any meaning to which it can be attached. These terms should be so well couched in a meaningful context at first that there can be little chance of their being misunderstood, and they should be used frequently and repeatedly while the concept is developing. (3) Strike a balance between the amount of experience that could be introduced to the learner and the amount needed to make the concept clear. Enough such experience is needed to provide clarity for the learner, but unnecessary repetition of those aspects of the concept that are already clear results in wasting time and often in boring students. The teacher must be sure that clarity has been achieved, however, and not be content to take it for granted. (4) Speed up the learner's attempt to pull out of experience the important generalizations, by pointing out the key facts as experience progresses, so that they can receive pointed and purposeful attention by the learner. This will hasten the development of clarity in all concepts, concrete as well as abstract. (5) Give the learner many chances to use his new terminology in such ways that he will show whether the concept is correctly formed and fully developed. This often requires presenting words in tests in ways that require their use for all their important meanings, not just for one meaning. (6) As a result of such evaluation, the teacher may find it necessary to provide more experiences with the concept, particularly experiences designed to supply the parts of the concept that seem to be hazy or missing.

Looking across the imaginary line between educational psychology and methods of teaching, one sees several important implications for sound procedure. It is apparent, for example, that the common practice of introducing a new idea by giving it a name and a definition, is completely contrary to the process by which concepts develop. It means exactly nothing to the average college student to tell him that a neurosis is a highly systematized mechanism of behavior originating in conflict which becomes buried by repression. A string of nonsense syllables would be almost as meaningful. After the student has seen systematized mechanisms at work, has examined people squirming under conflicts, and has observed how repression pushes things out of the conscious level of thought, such a definition may have life, but not before. Those teachers who have new concepts to give their students must set up their methods in harmony with the facts about concept development, or fail in their tasks.

Student and Teacher Activities Selected To Fit Conceptual Learning

The Learner	*The Teacher*
1. Encounter the referent. Experience it as fully as possible.	1. Provide or recall to learner experience with referent.
2. Hear the terms involved and associate them with the recognized parts of the experience.	a. Keep experiences realistic and natural, not theoretical or abstract.
3. Repeat experiences with referent, adding to clearness as understanding develops.	2. Introduce the terms as soon as they can be associated with some meaning.
a. Progressively cut out those parts of experience that are not related to the concept.	3. Amplify experience economically.
b. Progressively add to concept those parts of experience related to its meaning.	a. Enough facts to give clarity. b. Avoid multiplication of more than needed facts.
4. Draw on many concrete situations for elements common to them, and thus build up abstract concepts.	4. Emphasize the key facts to speed up learner's generalizing process.
a. Refinement comes as in Steps 2 and 3.	5. Provide a variety of opportunities for use of new terms to see how clear the concept is.
5. Make description (definition) of concept precise by gathering all essential elements together and eliminating all unessential elements.	6. Augment learner's experience as needed in light of use of terms.

1610. *Tastes and preferences.* One's preferences are usually fairly definite concerning those things that are commonly experienced. Concerning the things seldom or never encountered, tastes and preferences are yet to be formed. They develop as part of one's experience with the subject. In most cases, the person is unable to give a valid explanation of his tastes, a fact that suggests that most of one's tastes and preferences arrive via the underground. Some, however, are apparently based on deliberate mental action, or are at least developed while such action is going on. Because of this apparent relationship between analysis and enjoyment in such subjects as art, a common confusion has developed about what is included in the meaning of the word appreciation. It may mean to some that one is impressed by the skill of the artist as evidenced by certain criteria of a good painting, and it may mean to others that one is simply enjoying the painting. For that reason this discussion avoids the use of the word appreciation and deals with tastes and preferences as distinguished from the ability to analyze.

The analysis of an object of art is based primarily on the possession of certain concepts and perceptual skills, not on an inner feeling of exhilaration, whereas most tastes are based on how the object makes one feel. The first is primarily mental, and the latter primarily a matter of feelings and emotions. Herein lies the answer to the perplexing problem of developing a love of good music or any other form of beauty. The most common approach is to engage the student in a dry analysis of the subject, instead of in a thrilling experience with it. That some students learn to love good music while analyzing it is not to be credited to the analytical methods, but to incidental learnings due to certain concomitant experiences not necessarily provided purposefully by the instructor. Developing a love of art is more the job of a good salesman than of a professional artist, but developing artistic skill is another matter.

1611. *Acquiring tastes and preferences.* It seems we learn to like those things with which we have pleasant or satisfying experiences. In all probability the process by which a taste or preference develops is conditioning. This involves encountering the new experience in a setting that is already satisfying or pleasing to the individual. The new experience tends to take on and attach to itself the feeling tone that characterizes the learner at the time he encounters the experience. If a given experience is encountered several times under the same circumstances, that continued and uniform association of new experience and affective condition will strengthen and eventually establish a preference or taste that will stand on its own feet. This process is amply demonstrated by experimentally induced fear of various objects in babies, and the later experimental removal of those fears. If some frightening sound is made each time a child touches a rabbit, the fear of the sound will eventually attach itself to the rabbit, and the child will fear the rabbit. Such fear can be removed by having the child encounter the rabbit under very pleasant circumstances, with no exceptions, until the fear gives way to enjoyment. Any teacher can obtain for the asking evidence that students develop dislikes and even open hatred of certain subjects which for them were constantly accompanied by unpleasantness and frustration. Dismal rooms, unpleasant teachers, social embarrassment, and continued adverse comparisons have done their part to create aversions to various school subjects. On the other hand, subjects in which students excel are usually those in which they have the most satisfying and enjoyable experiences, and consequently are those ordinarily preferred when choices are allowed. Children's attitudes toward home owe their form to the affective experiences in the home. Musical selections take on the coloring of the setting in which they are heard, some of them becoming loved because they have been part of a happy circumstance and some of them disliked because they were heard only under unpleasant conditions. All in all people come to like those things that have brought them happiness and satisfaction. When this thought is applied to the tastes and preferences of the American public, it suggests that American life is so arranged that we rarely meet the literary classics, symphonic music, or superb examples of sculpture or painting under circumstances that are noticeably and consistently pleasant and satisfying.

The teacher's task in fostering the development of tastes and preferences is clearly indicated by what the learner must do. The setting in which the learner meets what he is supposed to learn to like must be so arranged that it is pleasant and enjoyable in itself. The new experience must be so introduced into this setting that it is an important and prominent part of it, not to be escaped unnoticed. The new experience must not be repeated under any circumstance that is not enjoyable during the learning period. Each repeated participation in the new experience should be brought to an end while the enjoyment is at its height. This prevents boredom from counteracting the effects of enjoyment as the learner reaches the end of his effective interest span.

There are numerous implications for methods of teaching in these important guides. In a literature class, for example, the teacher may have read a classic in such a way that it was thoroughly enjoyed. This might be followed by an assignment to read some additional selections at home. The home conditions under which such study is done vary considerably among students. In some homes the good start obtained in class will be furthered by a pleasant evening with the material, but in other homes it will be offset by a disagreeable home experience—an exception to the rules has been allowed to occur too soon. Many a high school's efforts to develop a love for good music has been wrecked by failure to set the stage for enjoyment. Rooms that have long since become associated in the students' minds with hilarity, scuffling, or scoldings, have too often been designated for use during experimental music hours. The students have been allowed to rush noisily into the rooms and continue talking until silence was enforced by the faculty, after which the music was presented. The typical reproducing equipment is far from perfect and music is thereby distorted. Under such conditions the musical selection faces too much competition and too much antagonistic feeling-tone in the students. On the other hand, college football players have been seen to walk for the first time into a room of such breath-taking beauty that to a man they involuntarily turned back to the door to wipe their feet and remove their hats. In that room students who had never been able to listen through a symphony before were seen to recline in attractive and comfortable chairs, or stretch at full length on a soft pale blue rug for an hour at a time listening to classical music reproduced on a faultless sound system. That dream room was the answer to the problem of learning to like classical music for many a student, but its effect could have been reduced or even canceled by any number of disharmonies, such as too much glaring light in the wrong places, frequent disturbances in the room, a scratchy record or needle, or the requirement that each person was to sit up straight "like a little lady or gentleman."

> Earth's crammed with Beauty
> And every common bush afire with God,
> But only he who sees takes off his shoes.
> —Browning

Beauty is where you find it all right, but the eye can see only what it has the power to see and the power to see is "caught" from experience as far as likes and dislikes are concerned.

Student and Teacher Activities Selected
To Fit the Acquisition of Tastes
and Preferences

The Learner	*The Teacher*
1. Encounter the experience in a given setting characterized by some feeling-tone or state of affect that is pleasant.	1. Present the experience in a setting that is enjoyable in itself.
2. The new experience tends to take on the feeling-tone of its setting and is associated with it.	2. Make the new experience an important and prominent part of the total setting.
3. Continued association will strengthen the relationship if it is consistent.	3. Avoid any repetition of the new experience in settings not enjoyable in themselves.
	4. Stop each experience when the enjoyment is at its height.

1612. *Ability to solve problems.* The popular idea that
thinking is a tricky and indefinable mental act that is turned
on in special situations for the purpose of making solutions
out of pure intellectual power leads to nothing but confusion
and frustration. The so-called method of critical thinking,
or the scientific method, is not a method of thinking out a
solution. That sort of thing is done by the brain all the time,
providing it has a conceptual repertoire available from past
experience, which fits the situation. It goes on whether the
individual is aware of what he is doing or not. Behavior
always "keeps its bargain with experience," as Cowley has
so well said.[7]

The scientific method, or problem-solving, is essentially
a technique for postponing the making of choices in situations in which there is not enough meaning present to permit
a good choice to be made. The system also includes a set
of steps that are somewhat formalized so that they will not
be overlooked or sidetracked. The steps are calculated to
produce additional learning pertinent to the problem, which
is valid, and which is systematically organized so that it
provides the individual with the kind of meaning he needs
to make the choice. In other words, it is not a method of
thinking out solutions, but a method of instituting and directing learning in the middle of a choice-situation.

One of the chief obstacles to the solving of problems is
the absence or inadequate state in the learner of the important concepts involved. There are, first, the concepts in
the problem itself. Logical thinking proceeds with difficulty,
to say the least, when the specific concepts that enter into
the making of a sound solution to a given problem are fuzzy
or incomplete. In the second place, the concept of what is
involved in the process of problem-solving is often so unclear
that the individual does not know what steps to take to solve
any problem.

There are at least these essential steps in problem-solving:
recognizing the problem, looking through what is known
about it for the most intelligent guess about how it may be

[7] William H. Cowley, "The educated man concept in the twentieth century," *School and society*, 52 (October 19, 1940), 345-50.

solved, deciding what else it is necessary to know before the solution can be completed, gathering and organizing this new knowledge, and applying it to the question at hand. A student wonders whether he should attend college A or college B. He *knows* he wants to become an architect and that there is an art department in both colleges. He *needs to know* whether architecture is taught in those art departments, or if not whether it is offered anywhere in the colleges, which college has the program most useful to him, what the relative costs and living conditions are, and any other factors that are important to him. When he gets this information from college bulletins or other sources, he can solve his problem.

Rarely, however, are the facts sufficient to indicate a clearly unequivocal answer, and upon the thinker descends the awful burden of making a decision on the basis of indications rather than complete evidence. Technically, such a problem is still in the data-gathering stage, but practically, it is often necessary to reach conclusions on the basis of good indications. Probably the two most useful assets in such situations are high intelligence and broad experience.

Incidental to the solution of a problem are a number of side issues which, on first inspection, seem to add considerable complexity to the underlying technique of problem-solving. For example, there is the evaluation of evidence in its various forms, and the examination of assumptions upon the basis of which the problem is attacked. In reality, each of these is a problem in itself and is handled by the same techniques used for the central problem to which it belongs. That is, evidence is evaluated by the problem-solving method. The process may be compared to the building of a structure that requires parts not already in existence. Those parts must also be built before they are put into the structure, and they are built by the same tools that eventually assemble the structure and bring it to completion.

It seems, then, that the important ingredients in problem-solving ability are enough intelligence to handle abstract ideas, a functional concept of what is involved in setting up a problem and carrying it through, and clarity in one's concepts about what the problem is and what is involved in it.

1613. *Developing problem-solving ability.* Since this technique represents a concept in its most abstract and complicated form, and since it is necessary in the development of even simple concepts to follow the steps indicated in the discussion of concept development, it is all the more important to see that the learner has a very complete and adequately long experience with this concept if he is to master it. Therefore, attention may profitably be given to the teacher's task before considering the student's task. This is necessary because the problem-solving procedure is not something to be found lying around in nature waiting to be experienced in the same manner as a meadow, a sandwich, or a color. It exists at the difficult end of the range of understandableness among all the concepts with which the human mind deals. It is seldom discovered by the average person, and rarely discovered by anyone who is not shown its secrets by someone else who has himself been led to them. Hence the necessity of beginning with the teacher's task.

Incidentally, those who do not know thoroughly what is involved in true problem-solving *cannot* teach it to others. Since it shows up in its best form among only a portion of the world's thinkers, it is not to be expected that problem-solving will be effectively taught by the typical educator until he himself has been taught its full meaning and nature. Furthermore, in the face of what is known about the relative absence of transfer of training in most school subjects, it is the height of folly to expect students to devolop problem-solving skill as an incidental learning unless considerable time and attention is devoted directly to it, in which case it ceases to be incidental. It is far more likely that something about civic affairs will be learned in a unit on problem-solving, than that problem-solving skill will be devoloped in the typical unit on civic affairs.

Nowhere in schoolwork is demonstration more useful and necessary. The teacher must lay a problem before the class and take it through to a solution with the class participating and identifying each step as it is carried out. This requires, first, identifying the concepts involved in the problem and developing them to a state of usefulness, if necessary. In the case mentioned earlier—of a prospective architectural student faced with the choice of a college—the concepts include what a college is, what a college course of study or curriculum is, a college library and its connection with study, the many ways in which a staff is important, dormitories and various kinds of living costs both by items and in the aggregate, degrees, availability and types of jobs in architectural activities, and so on. Before these ideas can enter into a solution, they must have form and meaning.

Second, each of these ideas must have a name by which it can be handled, and it is likely that there are some considerations involved in this problem for which the average student has no adequate name. Therefore, the necessary terminology must be selected and established if it is not already present. Abstract thought processes break down when concepts have no handles by which they can be manipulated.

Third, the problem must be stated in such a way that the important issue is clearly defined. In the case under discussion it must be determined whether the problem is where to find a good course in architecture, or how to decide which of two given schools has the best course, or whether to choose between architecture and another subject, or what not. The teacher and the class must settle the matter of just what it is they want to find out, and what are the contingencies upon which the answer rests.

Fourth, the available facts must be assembled and examined to see what they indicate in the way of a tentative answer to the problem. There is usually considerable mental trial and error involved in this process, and it should be demonstrated and identified.

The question is, are the necessary process-concepts present yet? If not, the individual may need to continue his learning until they are.

The facts available in the illustration are as follows: The student knows he wants to study architecture. He knows there is an art department in each college. He knows he wants to attend one of the two colleges. Up to this point the balance is apparently perfect for the two colleges. There is no indication of which is the better for him. He can say to himself that he could attend either one so far as he knows now. Suppose that in addition to these facts he also knows that a dear friend of his will attend college A, his father attended college B, there is a successful commercial artist in his town who attended college B, and there is no participation in competitive football at college B. Each of these facts offers a chance for a mental excursion, and he must get some more information about them. College A looks good because he would be with his friend, but that would mean he would not be in his father's fraternity. However, he would like to play football so A looks good again, but on the other hand B has already turned out one very successful artist to his knowledge, whereas he knows of none from A. At this point he might make a tentative guess that college B seems to have an edge, although that edge is based on very incomplete evidence. He has tried out each college with each fact in mind, and rather than having arrived at a clear-cut decision, he has arrived only at the conclusion that he is not at all sure what to do and that he needs more facts about the other aspects of the two colleges not revealed by the facts now available. For example, he wants to know if the known commercial artist is typical of all graduates of college B, whether he also represents the type of product usually turned out in architecture at that college, what kind of boys attend college B, whether his father's fraternity still exists on the campus, what are the relative facilities at each college for good architectural training, and so on.

Fifth, it is important to obtain facts that are complete and representative enough to avoid giving false impressions. The student can examine the colleges' catalogues, but each college will be telling its story as favorably to itself as possible. He can inquire of graduates of both colleges, but they may be biased in their opinions or may know nothing of the courses in architecture. He can look in some impartial rating book for comparative facts about the two colleges. Each of these sources of evidence may be discussed and demonstrated in terms of their relative completeness, pertinence, and accuracy. The teacher may at this point have the students go into the criteria of good evidence in exactly the same manner in which they are tackling the original problem. Here it should be clearly indicated that the main issue has been sidetracked temporarily while one of the blocks needed in construction is conceived and manufactured. When it is ready the original task can proceed again.

Sixth, the data must be organized and interpreted when they are finally secured. The teacher may lay the new facts before the class, examine each one to see how it contributes to the problem, decide how much weight each fact is entitled to in terms of its accuracy, completeness, and pertinence, and what each fact tells about the relative desirability of each college. Since obvious and unquestionable solutions are seldom if ever offered by facts alone, it may be expected in this problem that the findings will go something like this: College A offers certain excellent advantages and has certain shortcomings; college B may be similarly characterized. The conclusion could be that the issues of greatest importance to the student are best provided for in one college even though it does not offer everything he wants, or that there is still no important difference between the schools as far as he can see. In other words, he can make a decision by weighing relative values if he wants to, or he can decide to extend his search to include other colleges or he can renew his search for facts about colleges A and B in the hope of finding something more significant than he now knows.

It is assumed that throughout such a demonstration the teacher will constantly point out to the students what is being done, why it is being done, what it is called, what it involves, and how to do it. All of these steps must be shown to have an important relationship to the whole process.

Having watched such a process, the learner must at once have a firsthand experience with it. The demonstration is to some extent a vicarious experience for the students. The personal experience comes when the learner faces a problem and begins to work on it himself. The teacher's task now is to check the learner's efforts at each step to see that the steps

are properly arranged and that each step is adequately understood.

Every useful skill in the world is based on a systematic
scheme or plan of action. In their developmental stages most
of them are crude and inefficient. Problem-solving skill is no
exception to this generalization. If anything, it is likely to
have a longer period of youth and maturation than most of
the world's skills, for the same reason that the human being
has the longest period of helplessness and development in all
the animal kingdom. It is complex and represents the characteristic of man that most clearly differentiates him from
the animal kingdom. It is the highest known function of the
human brain.

The foregoing discussion has dealt with the necessity and
the way of establishing the *concepts* involved in critical
thinking. Up to this point the task is one of concept development and requires a *direct* approach by teacher and student.
Such concepts must be set up as the principal objectives or
end products of the lessons or class periods in which they are
studied. When the concepts have been developed, however,
the techniques must shift, for the acquisition of skill in
critical thinking requires practice from this point on. Such
practice should be available in every class in school as an
incidental aspect of study. Hence, the development of skill
in critical thinking becomes a by-product rather than the
chief end product once the concepts involved in the process
have been acquired.

A fact of great importance to lesson planning is revealed
in this matter. Tastes and preferences, and problem-solving
ability are potential *by-products* of every school situation,
whereas memorization, concepts, perceptual-motor skills and
some sensory-motor skills are the principal *end products* in
the various subject-matter courses. Therefore, three goals are
involved in the preparation of every lesson: (1) the facts,
concepts, or skills involved in the subject matter to be mastered, (2) the feeling of enjoyment the students should develop for the subject, school, and teacher, and (3) the ability
to think critically in the area being studied. Unless the
teacher is aware of the psychological processes involved in

each of these types of learning, and unless he makes specific provision for the kinds of experiences that lead to achievement in *each* of the three directions, one or more of them will fail to devolop or will even move into the realm of negative results such as mental laziness or a dislike of the subject.

1614. *Summary.* Although the learning process can be described by a generalization, it is profitable to look into the various ways in which the learner may seek and find an appropriate line of action to reach his goal. These ways depend to some extent on what his goal is. Therefore, the teacher can be most helpful to the learner when he is able to recognize the type of learning product involved in a given goal and provide a setting for the student in which the most appropriate and profitable activities may be had. One single form of lesson plan does not make provision for these different sorts of learnings. The lesson plan must take its form from what is known about the way in which learning occurs and the modifications introduced into that process by such variables as the type of end product sought.

STUDENT AND TEACHER ACTIVITIES SELECTED TO FIT DEVELOPMENT OF PROBLEM-SOLVING ABILITY

The Learner	*The Teacher*
1. Identify the concepts involved in the problem.	1. Identify the concepts involved in the problem and develop them if necessary.
2. Check for clarity in the terminology involved.	2. Select and establish the necessary terminology.
3. Experience the processes demonstrated by the teacher until they become fully developed concepts with functional understanding.	3. Explain and illustrate how the problem is defined in its setting.
4. Try to identify these concepts in a problem whose solution can be observed.	4. Illustrate how preliminary exploration leads to the selection of a line of attack on the problem.
5. Attempt the solution of a problem under supervision.	5. Demonstrate how the line

The Learner	*The Teacher*
6. Practice setting up problems of several kinds.	of attack directs the search for data.
7. Practice the use of problem-solving techniques in various problems.	6. Point out the need for and ways of assuring pertinence and validity in data.

7. Give a technique for analyzing data:
    a. Breaking it up.
    b. Analyzing it.
    c. Seeing relationships.

8. Demonstrate the drawing of conclusions that are related to the problem.
    a. Proportion of solution reached.
    b. Part of problem still unsolved.
    c. Formulation of new direction for further search.

9. Show how this process (Steps 4 to 8) is repeated until the problem can be solved.

10. Set up a demonstration and have class identify processes in operation.

11. Set up a problem for class to solve. Check progress at every stage to see what help is needed in each step.

12. Demonstrate the application of this approach to a variety of different *kinds* of problems.
    a. Determining a cause.
    b. Finding a method.
    c. Discovering a fact.
    d. Determining an appropriate course of action.

QUESTIONS FOR REVIEW

1. Define a sensory-motor skill.
2. Define a perceptual-motor skill.
3. With what part of a motor skill must the teacher be most concerned?
4. What is the significant difference between a sensory-motor skill and a perceptual-motor skill?
5. What is the unique problem in perceptual-motor learning?
6. What is the most useful learning activity in the acquisition of a motor skill?
7. Upon what basic principle is memorization dependent?
8. Why is clarity of meaning so important in memorization?
9. Define a concept.
10. What is the most powerful factor in the development of a concept?
11. What is the most powerful factor in the development of tastes and preferences?
12. What are some of the possible conditions that might result in a disliking for arithmetic?
13. What common form of learning is fundamental to the conscious use of a problem-solving procedure?
14. Name the three factors said to be essential in problem-solving. Can you defend each?
15. For what sorts of learning-objectives would you use the following procedures:
    A. Repetitious practice.
    B. Exploratory experience.
    C. Meaningful repetition.
    D. Satisfying experience.
16. How do concepts differ from ordinary memory materia¹?
17. What is the basic principle of associative learning?
18. What is the relationship between conceptual learning and associative learning?
19. What are the two constant by-products of academic learning? Why are they always present?

SELECTED REFERENCES

Henry E. Garrett, *Great experiments in psychology* (New York: Appleton-Century-Crofts, Inc., 1941), Chapters V, VI, VIII, and X.
Arthur I. Gates, Arthur T. Jersild, T. R. McConnell, and Robert

C. Challman, *Educational psychology* (New York: The Macmillan Co., 1948), Chapters XI, XII, XIII, and XIV.

Howard L. Kingsley, *The nature and conditions of learning* (New York: Prentice-Hall, Inc., 1946), Chapters XI, XII, XIII, XIV, and XV.

Homer B. Reed, *Psychology and teaching of secondary-school subjects* (New York: Prentice-Hall, Inc., 1939), *passim.*

————, *Psychology of elementary-school subjects* (Boston: Ginn and Co., 1938), *passim.*

CLASS EXERCISES ON THE TYPES OF LEARNING

Things To Do in Class

1. Assign a student to occupy ten minutes in class teaching a subject selected from the public-school program, for the purpose of demonstrating how to promote differentiation. Make a similar assignment for demonstration of integration, abstraction, and generalization.

Things To Do outside Class

1. Resume work on the lesson plan started earlier in the course.
   A. Prepare a statement of the common barriers that often retard learning in the general area of your objective. Show how you would anticipate those barriers and minimize their effect on student progress.
   B. Identify the type (or types) of learning involved in the objective, and describe sound procedures appropriate to your objective. Make provision for all phases of learning from the first exploratory efforts to the final stage.
   C. What provisions could be made to promote thinking on the part of the students?
   D. How would you guard against the development of a distaste for the subject? How would you work for development of a liking for it?

In each of these subdivisions begin with a statement of the psychological facts involved, and show how they lead to a specific plan of action.

CHAPTER XVII

LEARNING AND THE NATURE OF MENTAL ACTIVITY

1701. *Introduction.* There are many facets to a study of learning. The general nature of the process itself was discussed in Chapter XV. At that point it was stated that any general description of learning could not escape being somewhat unreal and academic, since it could not possibly take into account the unlimited variety of conditions under which individual students tackle specific lessons. The first attempt to put flesh on the general description constituted an examination of certain types of human behavior, and the kinds of actions people go through in acquiring each of those types of behavior. As soon as one specifies a particular thing to be learned, he thereby departs from any general concept of learning into one of the more specific types. Although they share the common sequential steps, each of the different types has its own characteristic expression of those steps. Each type is therefore a closer approximation to what happens when a real person learns something, than is the general description of learning.

A further step in the direction of classroom reality is attempted in this chapter by introducing into the learning process some additional facts about mental activity that have an important bearing on the efficiency of learning and the direction it may take. If these facts are understood by the teacher, he is in a position to plan his classwork and assignments so as to improve the efficiency of his students' efforts, and make his own work more enjoyable and rewarding.

Briefly, these facts have to do with keeping mental reactions at a high level, hastening the development of understanding and enlarging comprehension, improving the integration of what is learned, speeding up memorization and making it more lasting, spreading the effects of learning to other subjects and activities, and spurring effort and influencing the direction in which learning moves.

1702. *Keeping mental efficiency at a high level.* There are some fairly consistent limits to the length of time an individual can concentrate on a given task to good advantage. Beyond those limits his learning proceeds on the basis of diminishing returns. When a student has reached that point he faces two alternatives. One is to keep on studying on that subject, getting progressively less and less for the time spent, but getting something as long as he stays with it. He may have to do this if he has only so many hours in which to learn his lesson before having to use it. The other alternative is to leave the task for a while, resting or turning his attention to some other kind of effort, while his mental efficiency comes back to normal. At that time he can return to his task with the original rate of efficiency and make his time count at the highest level of return. If he has enough calendar time in which to do this, he will always be able to work at his highest level of efficiency, once he learns appoximately what his periods of best concentration are.

Students will not, as a rule, recognize this characteristic of mental activity sufficiently to govern themselves to best advantage. The teacher is in a better position to know the peculiarities of his subjects in this regard, and the variations related to the age of his students, and to regulate the work in his classroom accordingly, at the same time recommending the best study procedures to his students for work done outside of class.[1] In many cases the teacher will have to determine for himself the length of the optimal periods. For this purpose the teacher should experiment with his classes, using different distributions of time to see which periods seem most effective in each specific situation he faces.

How short should a period of effort be? One fairly well-established fact seems to be that intervals as short as one-half

---

[1] Two good books for this purpose, one for the secondary level and one for the elementary level, are Homer B. Reed's, *Psychology of elementary-school subjects* (Boston: Ginn and Co., 1938), and his *Psychology and teaching of secondary-school subjects* (New York: Prentice-Hall, Inc., 1939).

minute, or one minute, or two minutes, are probably too short for optimal learning in many subjects. On the other hand, almost any form of learning is likely to proceed better if learning periods are kept down under an hour in length. There are, of course, exceptions to both these statements. The final decision should rest on what seems best in the given situation. As a tentative guide to practice one might use the following suggestions:

1. The *minimum* length of a period should be determined in part by (a) the time required to get materials out and ready to use, and (b) the time required to perform the function being learned. Some cases of learning deal with materials that cannot be put into action in less than a given period of time. Obviously, to restrict practice to a period no longer than that length of time would result in little or no advancement. It is also apparent that it would be difficult to learn the nature of an operation that requires ten minutes to carry through if the practice period is less than ten minutes in length. It may be advisable to go through a given function two or three times or more within one period.

2. The *maximum* length of the period should be determined by (a) the point at which fatigue begins to interfere with function, (b) the amount of time during which the learner remains well motivated, (c) the total calendar time available between the starting point and the point at which the function must be mastered, and (d) the number of other functions or activities that must be accommodated within a given class period. The length of time one may practice or study before fatigue begins to interfere with progress varies with the individual and with the nature of the task. Young children have less sustained energy for difficult tasks than older people, and dull children seem to have less than bright children of the same age. Motivation varies in a similar manner. The interest span of a young child is quite short. Older individuals are able to concentrate over longer periods of time than children. From a practical point of view, it is not always possible to space practice periods in the most desirable manner because there is often a limited amount of over-all time allowed for the job. Therefore, some concentra-

tion of effort is required as a practical necessity. Through concentration the *total elapsed calendar* time required to learn a function may be cut down, although the *rate of learning per minute of time spent in practice* will not yield as high a return as if the periods were spaced. Another practical problem faces the teacher who has to deal with more than one matter during the period or day. If the whole period is available for one subject, then practice can be distributed in almost any manner desired. If other functions must also be carried out within the period, they will have a practical limiting effect on the amount of time that can be spent on any single part of the total task.

These suggestions offer almost unlimited flexibility in the setting up of learning periods, but they also suggest a method by which the teacher may discover the optimal length of time to be spent in any concentrated attack on a problem. In this case, as in so many others in teaching, common sense must take the lead, obtaining its cues from a few known indicators of psychological soundness.[2]

1703.   *Hastening understanding and broadening comprehension.* The mental processes by which understanding is developed have already been treated with reasonable adequacy in Chapter XVI. The purpose in mentioning them here is twofold, to direct the teacher's attention specifically to the processes as such, and to suggest ways of taking advantage of what is known about them, in teaching.

Differentiation. This is the process of becoming aware of detail in what was up to then an undifferentiated general experience. For example, sisters of almost the same age, dressed alike, are often thought by those who see them on the street to be twins. The differences between them are not apparent at first glance, but with a little additional observation they become apparent. When first learning to recognize animals by name, children often confuse horses and cows. They see no differences between them. With continued observation, they will discover the details that differentiate

[2] An extended discussion of this problem is available in John A. McGeogh, *The psychology of human learning* (New York: Longmans, Green and Co., Inc., 1942).

them. Differentiation is probably more rapid for highly intelligent people than for those of low intelligence. It is more rapid for those who have learned how to observe than for those who look much and see little. It is probably modified in its speed of development by other such factors, but it depends primarily on continued experience. It is the result of familiarity. Teachers can count on the fact that children will not recognize the differentiating characteristics of lesson materials or experiences at first glance.

The most profitable thing the teacher can do is know in advance what points of differentiation are most important in the concepts being presented. These points of difference should then be given special deliberate attention in discussing the material and in directing the observations of the students. Where this direction is not given, students may gradually make the discoveries for themselves, or they may miss them altogether. A student may not know just what he is supposed to look for in an assignment or other experience and may spend his time and attention on something that is not significant in the course. The teacher has not done a good job if this happens with any regularity among his students.

Integration. This is the process of putting together, systematically, parts of earlier experiences that have become sufficiently differentiated to stand out, and that can be seen to be related to each other in various ways. Integration usually takes place around function. Here are two examples of how it may take place. Pulling is a *function.* When the child discovers the function, he begins to classify objects according to whether they pull or not. He will find out in time that horses, oxen, mules, dogs, engines, cars, and several other things are used for pulling purposes. Thus they have a functional relationship as "pullers." This provides the basis for integration of all these things with reference to one function. They may be completely rearranged and integrated in various patterns with other objects, where different functions are concerned.

In a second example, integration is based on a *cooperatively shared* function. A cow, a barn, a pail, a bottle, and a milking machine are just so many isolated objects in nature until one discovers that they all belong in one operation, the production of milk and its delivery to the consumer. When this integration is made, the learner can talk about a "dairy" and be dealing with all of the individual concepts at the same time. There are other ways in which integration takes place. In teaching, one should know one's field well enough to identify all the significant integrative ideas and be prepared to point out the basis of such relationships to one's students. Again, they might be discovered in time without direction from the teacher, but that is a wasteful procedure.

Abstraction. This is the process by which such concepts as soft or hard are finally separated from specific objects and recognized as qualitative aspects of many different situations. For example, the child learns that the blanket is soft. At that stage softness is probably thought to be a property only of blankets. After a while the child learns that a pillow is soft, a kitten is soft, and the furry toy is soft. Softness finally begins to stand out as an independent quality of each of these things until it becomes a concept by itself and can be applied to any new situation as appropriate. This, too, is a process that depends fundamentally on time and breadth of experience, but it is also modified by intelligence, instruction, and other factors.

Abstraction is rather fully discussed in Chapter XVI. For those who want additional treatment, reference is made to Stoddard's discussion of abstractness as a basic element of intelligence.[3]

Generalization. This process is discussed in section 1608. At this point only a brief reminder of its characteristics will be given. It involves picking out of a large number of experiences the significant common meanings that persist and seem not to be changed by additional experience. It is the basic process in the establishment of scientific facts. Whether it occurs depends on the extent to which the individual is aware of the meaning of his ongoing experience,

[3] George D. Stoddard, *The meaning of intelligence* (New York: The Macmillan Co., 1943) , pp. 15-21.

and the extent to which he is looking for such generalizations. It is certain that the process is materially helped when teachers direct the attention of their students to the significant meanings of experience. Without direction, many students fail to make such sumaries. It, too, seems to be a function of time and the accumulation of experience, but it proceeds more rapidly and more accurately among the intelligent than among the dull.

1704. *Improving the integration of what is learned.* The day is all but gone in American education when children are required to learn things just for the sake of knowing them. Knowledge for knowledge's sake is a bad investment. Education is concerned with the problems of living. The aim is to have students learn how to live more effectively, how to solve their problems, how to get along with their neighbors, how to produce what they need for good living, how to keep well and happy, and so on. Subject matter is important only to the extent that it contributes to these major accomplishments.

A curriculum that has been made up of materials that are known by adults to have practical utility in problems of living does not always reveal its functional foundations to students. Sometimes they fail completely to see the usefulness of assignments. When that is the case, they are working under the handicap of a sense of studying just for the sake of studying. What they study consists of isolated blocks of material. Even though they learn them well, they may never get them all put together into the functional relationships that led the curriculum planners to include them.

What is needed is closer alignment of the specific item being studied with the broader setting in which it is supposed to function. If things are studied in this close alignment, there is some chance that they will function in that relationship in the student's life. This is a broad principle, and it applies to the whole curriculum. The research carried out on it, however, has been largely confined to such problems as the memorization of verbal materials, or the acquisition of motor skills.[4] There are no exact answers to

4 McGeogh, *op. cit.,* pp. 188-96.

the question of whether materials should be learned as wholes or divided up into parts, but the research gives rise to some helpful suggestions with which teachers might well experiment in their classes.

The value of keeping a thing whole lies in the more complete meaning, relationship of parts, and purpose and function of each part which any overview provides. A comprehensive view automatically sets up a goal, not only for the whole thing, but also to guide the learning of the various parts. This has been demonstrated in industry where a person works on one small part of an airplane. His work is performed more efficiently and with greater interest when he knows how that part is going to be fitted into the finished product, and what function it performs within the final product.

The value of dividing a job into parts lies in the fact that some wholes are too large for the learner to handle at one time without losing sight of one or another part all the time. The smaller units can be grasped and learned with greater speed. Learning is made more interesting because the rewards of accomplishment are enjoyed more frequently, and the suspense and tension that accompany the learner's early random attempts to familiarize himself with any new material are reduced both in time and in intensity. It amounts to saying that learning is more fun when the goals are spaced so that a new one can be reached easily and frequently, rather than once in a long time.

When a unit of material is short enough to be learned easily as a whole, it should be kept intact. This is determined not only by the material, but also by the age, capacity, and interest of the learner. Children of four who listen to *The Night before Christmas* a few days before Christmas Eve have such a keen interest in the story that they cannot tolerate any attempt to break it up into sections. They demand a relatively rapid run through the whole story. Furthermore, they will memorize the whole thing by hearing it read only a few times. This is not because they have a higher memorizing ability than adults, but because they have a terrifically intense motivation at the moment. Note, for example, how hard it is to get a child to remember to hang up his clothes. No motivation.

When the material is too long to be learned easily as a whole, it should be overviewed before it is subdivided. The overview should be thorough enough to give the learner a good general idea of what the matter contains and how the parts are related. Then it may profitably be broken up into parts that have in themselves some characteristic of completeness. When the parts are learned, the attention should go back to the whole thing so that the parts may become integrated and lose their independence. A very common difficulty at this point grows out of having practiced a given part over and over again without also practicing at the same time coming into it from the preceding part, and going from it into the following part. This is easily illustrated with poetry. Most people can recite the first stanza of a number of poems, but are unable to go beyond that point. The reason may very well be that the associations set up in the learning have operated to make the last word of the stanza lead directly back into the first word of the same stanza instead of to the first word of the next stanza. This is almost sure to happen when the first stanza is repeated over and over again by itself. Obviously, in the repetitions, the last word has been followed by the first word of the first line over and over again. Thus the two words become associated, and this association prevents the individual from going from the first stanza to the beginning of the second.

In arithmetic, drill tends to center on specific operations, such as addition or multiplication. Some students who have not practiced using these operations as subdivisions of a larger problem are unable to perform the larger task even though they can do any single part of it correctly. In testing, there is a way of getting at this problem. Instead of asking students to give the answers to problems, the test can require them to show by what *process* they would seek the answer, and the answer itself is not required.

In general, then, every specific process, fact, or other item to be learned should be studied at least part of the time in its context within the area to which it belongs functionally. Then, if specific drill on a portion of that whole area is required, it is possible to improve mastery of a part in that manner.

1705. *Improving memorization.* Memorization was described in sections 1606 and 1607 as the process of fixing symbolic or verbal materials so that they can be repeated at will. This is an associational process, in which two or more symbols become tied together so that one of them brings the others back to recollection. Some of the earliest experiments in psychology had to do with memorizing nonsense syllables, such as sok, bim, nux, zef, arb, hif, and so on.[5] The evidence very clearly shows that this kind of learning is much faster and more permanent when meaning is present than when it is absent.[6] From a practical point of view, this means that it is a waste of time and effort to have students attempt to learn lists, or words, or combinations of anything, until they understand them well enough to see some meaning in them.

Meaning helps, apparently, because it provides an integration of the materials into a configuration, something whole that can be "seen" all over again whenever the person recalls his experience. This configurational view of things constitutes a stable framework to which can be attached names or other verbal elements. When such verbal materials are learned in connection with such a clear picture of past experience, they are not only learned much more easily than they would be without that meaningful picture, but they are also retained much better and longer.

It is when a person tries to memorize verbal material without that meaningful frame of reference that he is said to be learning nonsense materials. Such learning is slow and hard, and is easily and quickly forgotten.

For example, consider the matter of direct vocabulary

---

[5] The classical research was reported by Ebbinghaus. For a convenient account see Henry E. Garrett, *Great experiments in psychology* (New York: Appleton-Century-Crofts, Inc., 1941), Chap. IX.

[6] McGeogh, *op. cit.,* Chap. V.

study. It has little value unless the student already possesses the concepts for which the new words stand. If he has the concepts, direct attack on vocabulary through word lists and definitions is profitable. Note, however, that in school where learning is reduced to a logical and systematic order very little like the random exploration that characterizes most human reaction to environment, there is a very real temptation to proceed in reverse. How easy it is to say to a class, "Today we are going to study respiration in plants. It is an osmotic and chemical process by which a plant absorbs oxygen and gives off the products formed by the oxidation in the tissues." For most of the students in a first course in biology, the bulk of these two sentences is composed of nonsense syllables. That is, the student has not yet had enough experience with the phenomenon involved to know what the instructor is talking about. He has little chance of remembering the definition, then, because he has no meaning to tie it to. After the experience has been provided and familiarity with the process is developed, the definition will almost formulate itself, and will probably never be forgotten. Definitions do not provide students with meaning They only represent meaning. Experience provides the meaning. This is much more fully discussed in sections 1608 and 1609.

For a quick experience with the matter under discussion, read the following two rows of words:

> the little red hen laid two brown eggs in a yellow nest
>
> two the in red little laid hen yellow a brown nest eggs

Which is easier to read? Both sentences contain exactly the same words. Now memorize both of them. Which takes the longer? After completing the memorizing wait about fifteen minutes and try to repeat both of them without looking at the page. The results will demonstrate the effectiveness of belongingness and meaning on symbolic learning. The words in the first sentence "belong" together because each one carries meaning in relation to the ones before and after it. Those in the second row do not.

Which of the following word combinations belong together?

young child
white thorough
table ocean
blue sky
Lincoln Sampson
Julius Caesar

Those that serve to complete the meaning in the one before or after have an integral relationship that exists within the conceptual structure of the person, and are therefore easier to read, easier to remember, easier to use.

A general rule that might be said to represent this phenomenon is: When it is desired to have a student associate two or more things together, so that experiencing one of them tends to recall the others, it is advisable to help the student discover the manner in which the items are related, so that the natural belongingness among them supplies a basis for the association.

This principle applies to all kinds of verbal learning: numbering systems, names of objects, lists of characteristics, steps in processes, dates and other items in history, rules of grammar, recipes, diagrams or plans, formulas, and many other symbolic representations of conceptual ideas.

1706. *Transfer of training.*[7] If a student's progress in English is better because he has studied Latin than it would be if he had not studied Latin, he has benefited by transfer of training. How much can a teacher depend on this indirect form of learning when it is left to chance? Very little. Beliefs among teachers in service run all the way from a complete denial of any transfer to the naïve assumption that "exercising" the brain (as if that were possible) on any tough problem makes it more efficient in any other line of activity. The truth is that, while the effects of learning in one area probably do spread out into one's behavior in other areas, such gains are usually so small that they may not be depended on to take the place of direct attack on any desired goal. In other words, unless Latin is wanted for its own sake, it is a poor detour by which to approach a study of English. The safest assumption for teachers to make is that each important goal must be

7 *Ibid.,* Chap. X.

approached in its own peculiar way. Otherwise, it is not likely to be achieved by any kind of teaching thus far known to educators.

This does not mean that one may turn his back completely on the question of transfer. That it does actually occur is not open to question. Even though the amount to be gained by it is not as great as once thought, it is still of sufficient importance to justify cultivation.

The secret of transfer seems to lie in the process of generalization. This is a process of identifying the common elements in a number of situations so that their points of similarity and difference become clear. For example, there are certain steps involved in driving any kind of automobile. The process of discovering and identifying those common steps is the process of generalization. To use this in teaching it would be necessary for the teacher to be sure the student became aware of those common steps. If the student were learning to drive by using only a jeep he might at first confuse those general steps with the specific arrangement of the controls in the jeep. However, jeep controls are not identical with the controls in some other cars. Whether the student can drive another car only by virtue of his training in a jeep depends on whether he has sorted out the general steps clearly enough to be able to apply them to a car with somewhat different controls. In early American schools arithmetic was always studied as a pure process, not related to any practical problem. It is commonplace now to find arithmetic texts in which the processes are developed within practical situations so that students can see the relationship between the arithmetical processes and the quantitative aspects of daily life. Coming close to home, it must be clearly understood that educational psychology as a subject will very soon be forgotten except for those parts of it that manage to become related to the practical work of the teacher. To every fact or principle encountered in the subject the prospective teacher should say, "Where do you fit into the teacher's job?" Unless an answer is found, there will be little profit in the study.

In all probability, further study of the transfer problem will establish the fact that transfer of training is merely a case of learning which involves a special application of the associational type of procedure. If this is true, such learning will involve identifying on the one hand the generalized aspects of what is being studied, and on the other hand a generalized description of the kind of situations in which that generalized knowledge properly fits, and then tying those two or more generalized items together by associational learning. For example: (1) Reduce the method of driving the jeep to a series of general steps that are typical of all cars. (2) Put before the learner the fact that all cars are operated by those generalized steps with slight variations in the manner of carrying them out. (3) When the steps are learned, see that the learner associates together the two ideas: (a) the steps, and (b) the idea that other cars are driven by those steps. If he can then have an experience in applying his generalized knowledge to one or two new situations, he will probably be able to apply it to all new situations after that without difficulty.

1707. *Influencing effort and direction in learning.* Without doubt the most persistent question among teachers is how to get students to study. Implicit in the question is a little deeper meaning. It is not just how to get students to study, but how to get them to study a particular thing. That is, how does one go about setting up a lesson in such a way that the student's attention is drawn to it, and particularly to those parts of it that are most important for him to learn. There is a direct relationship between the satisfyingness of an activity and the amount and kind of learning that occurs in it. This relationship has been studied rather vigorously, and has come to be spoken of as the *law of effect*.[8] Whether the present amount of knowledge about it justifies the use of the word "law" may be questioned, but there is no question about the proposition that *effects* are critical in determining learning. That is, those activities that give relief to an active motive seem to do two things—they become learned and they give satisfaction to the learner. Hence, it is of practical value to know that satisfyingness or reward aids learning. It is important to note, however, that "reward"

[8] *Ibid.*, Chap XIV.

as used here refers only to the relief of a motivating tension. Therefore, it has to be a direct result of the act that obtains it, not an artificial form of bribe handed out by an outside party, and having no relation to the process that has been going on. Of course, there is an important difference between solving a problem for the sake of getting a deeper understanding of a principle and solving a problem for the sake of the teacher's approval. A gold star would be an artificial reward for solving a problem, but it would be closely related to the teacher's approval. The truth of the matter is, however, that in the second instance the student is learning how to win approval, not how to become a good problem-solver. A gold star is of little satisfaction to a child who can't build a bomber wing to suit himself even though he does the best job in his class. Teachers who use rewards in such ways that their students' motives become a desire for approval or recognition are quite likely to have sidetracked the student in his basic motivational development. This is not to say that a student learns no algebra when he studies to win a high mark; only that such rewards do not elicit the wholehearted effort that a natural interest in algebra could produce. They lead also to the idea that external rewards are more to be cherished than self-improvement or the satisfaction of intellectual curiosity.

It is not at all clear how learning is affected by annoyingness or punishment.[9] In all probability, punishment has no direct effect on learning. It has nothing to do with the relief of the motivating tension. It is a pure distraction in an already difficult situation. On the other hand, anything that helps the learner discover how near to the goal is his response is an aid to learning. It gives him direction and a basis for evaluating his effort. From a practical point of view the teacher can count on these facts:

(1) When an action occurs which satisfies a basic motive, the act will bring satisfaction, and it will be learned as a response to that condition which it satisfied.

(2) Artificial incentives tend to take the child's attention away from the problem the teacher hopes he will solve and

9 *Ibid.*, pp. 580-84.

divide it between that problem and the new problem of status created by the offer of the incentive.

(3) When artificial incentives are used the following conditions should be met: (a) They should be used only when the students have no initial interest in an activity in which they must engage. (b) The activity should be conducted in such a way that it contributes on its own merits sufficient enjoyment and satisfaction to make the artificial incentive become progressively less prominent and less important when compared to the normal enjoyment involved in the activity. (c) As soon as possible the artificial incentive should be dropped and the natural motivation of the situation used in its place.

QUESTIONS FOR REVIEW

1. What are the six major problems discussed in this chapter?
2. Under what general condition is massed practice more effective than distributed practice?
3. What determines the minimum length of a practice period?
4. What determines the maximum length of a practice period?
5. If a long list of items is broken up into parts to be learned, what steps would you follow to insure best learning?
6. What are the psychological reasons for saying that belongingness aids learning?
7. Under what conditions can a learning exercise in one subject be made to help a person in another subject?
8. Write out a short, psychologically sound definition of reward that will hold true in all cases.
9. When is an incentive artificial?
10. How can you use artificial incentives so as to keep the work as motivationally healthful as possible?
11. What has differentiation to do with concept development?
12. What is the relationship between differentiation as a mental process and class discussion as a teaching process?
13. When would you use "part" learning?
14. Why does "part" learning often provide better stimulation than learning by wholes?

SELECTED REFERENCES

Henry E. Garrett, *Great experiments in psychology* (New York: Appleton-Century-Crofts, Inc., 1941), Chapter IX.
Arthur I. Gates, Arthur T. Jersild, T. R. McConnell, and Robert

C. Challman, *Educational psychology* (New York: The Macmillan Co., 1948), Chapter XV.

Howard L. Kingsley, *The nature and conditions of learning* (New York: Prentice-Hall, Inc., 1946), Chapter XIX.

John A. McGeogh, *The psychology of human learning* (New York: Longmans, Green and Co., Inc., 1942), Chapters V, X, XIV, and pp. 580-84.

Homer B. Reed, *Psychology and teaching of secondary-school subjects* (New York: Prentice-Hall, Inc., 1939), *passim.*

———, *Psychology of elementary-school subjects* (Boston: Ginn and Co., 1938), *passim.*

CLASS EXERCISES ON THE NATURE OF MENTAL ACTIVITY

Things To Do in Class

1. To illustrate the process of differentiation, draw an irregular unfamiliar design on the board and cover it before it has been observed. A sheet of paper or cardboard makes a useful cover. Tell the class to look at it when it is uncovered, and give them three seconds to view it. Cover it again, and ask the class to draw it. Repeat this several times, or until most drawings are reasonably accurate. Have the students describe the gradual emergence of the details of the design through repeated experiences with it.

2. To demonstrate the function of belongingness in memorizing, prepare four lists of ten short words each as follows: Two lists in each of which the words are closely related, and two lists in each of which the words are not related at all.

   A. Give half the class copies of one of the related lists and the other half copies of one of the unrelated lists, taking care that they do not look at the words until told to do so.

   B. On signal, have them spend fifteen seconds trying to memorize the lists.

   C. At the end of fifteen seconds collect the lists and ask the students to write them out in correct order. When written, give credit either for each word in the correct position or for each word remembered, regardless of position. Record the scores for each side.

   D. As a control on individual differences in ability, reverse the groups and use the other two lists of words, repeating the procedure.

   E. Put the scores on the board showing the difference in achievement between related and unrelated word lists.

PART IV

FACTORS THAT MODIFY LEARNING

CHAPTER XVIII

PRIMARY MODIFYING FACTORS IN LEARNING

1801. *Introduction.* Previous discussions of learning have not dealt with any of the differences introduced into the process by individual students. They have stayed in the realm of learning as it occurs in all people, by dealing only with learning itself. Now it is time to talk about the individual who learns. He brings some unique factors into a learning situation with him, and they have much to do with his learning. In the next few sections of the book discussion will turn to some of the important characteristics of individuals, and to the differences that exist between individuals in those characteristics.

1802. *The significance of individual differences.* Group instruction is based on the assumption that pupils are enough alike so that what is done for the group as a whole will be adequate for each child in the group. On the other hand, those who urge teachers to give more attention to the individual child do so on the assumption that children are sufficiently different to need individual attention.

The educative process is most successful when it involves the right combination of group and individual instruction. This requires a knowledge of the nature of the similarities and differences among school children.

Similarities. Such statements as "people are the same wherever you find them" refer to generalities rather than to specific characteristics. Whether individuals are alike or different in any characteristic depends on the perspective of the observer. From a distance, restricting observation to gross features, many similarities exist. Physically, people are alike in that they walk on two legs, have arms and hands, their faces are at the front of their heads and contain the same general array of features, and they tend to cluster around an average height of about five and a half feet. Intellectually, people are alike in that they all have a brain and central nervous system that are different from those of other animals, they all tend to learn by the same general sequential steps, and personal experience is the most important factor in learning. Socially, people are alike in that they tend to seek security in groups, they gravitate toward those who have the same interests and preferences, and they tend to set up cultural systems and conform to them in behavior. Emotionally, people are alike in that they have the same general neuro-glandular equipment, their physiological reactions follow a common pattern, and they all experience recognizable emotional reactions now and then. These few general comparisons touch on a small part of the total list of similarities among human beings.

Differences. Many of the characteristics listed above are related to the educative process. It is a serious error to assume, however, that because all individuals go through approximately the same steps in learning they all go through those steps in the same way, at the same speed, for the same reasons, with the same inner emotional reactions, or with the same net result. When the observer moves up close to the living child, intimate characteristics of the utmost individuality begin to come into view. Furthermore, if one watches the child go through a typical day, it becomes obvious that those characteristics in which he is a unique person have a great deal to do with his behavior. It is only when such characteristics are known by the observer that the child's behavior is fully comprehensible. It follows logically, then, that a teacher cannot deal appropriately with a student unless the student's unique characteristics are known. Hence, a knowledge of the ways in which students differ significantly is of vital importance in the psychology of teaching.

Within this chapter the three factors felt by the writer to be most important in modifying learning will be discussed. They are *capacity, motivation,* and *maturity and readiness.*

FACTORS IN LEARNING

1803. *Capacity.* Within a relatively brief space, and in view of the needs of prospective teachers, it would not be appropriate to attempt a detailed treatment of capacity. Rather it seems best to indicate a way of conceiving it, and some of its effects on learning in school. In a very broad sense, capacity is that which an individual has potentially within him, on the basis of which he can learn to meet his situations. This is a very comprehensive definition, but it is necessary if one keeps the whole person in mind. No single or specific portion of capacity is an adequate substitute for the organismic picture that should be seen at the beginning of this discussion. Each individual possesses a rich and varied array of potentialities, which may show their effects in quite different kinds of behavior. All of them together constitute his total capacity, even though there is no way at present of measuring the whole complex thing.

Stoddard has offered the most comprehensive definition of capacity thus far, but his is limited to what he calls intelligence, and does not explicitly include such things as psychomotor potentials. He says:

Intelligence is the ability to undertake activities that are characterized by (1) difficulty, (2) complexity, (3) abstractness, (4) economy, (5) adaptiveness to a goal, (6) social value, and (7) the emergence of originals, and to maintain such activities under conditions that demand a concentration of energy and a resistance to emotional forces.[1]

Each of the terms in the definition is suggestive much beyond the typical definition of intelligence. The first three should be clear enough. Economy implies the best use of energy to arrive at solutions without wasting time or energy. Adaptiveness to a goal implies the power to reorganize one's techniques, perceptions, and directions, in order to move toward whatever goal one seeks. Social value implies an understanding of what one's behavior means to one's associates, and the ability to plan action so that it preserves social values. The emergence of originals implies that the

[1] George D. Stoddard, *The meaning of intelligence* (New York: The Macmillan Co., 1943), p. 4. Used by permission.

individual can do some creative reorganizing of his experience when the occasion demands, and produce something that is his own creation. The latter part of the definition says that intelligence is more than intellective power, it also includes the ability to mobilize one's resources in the face of difficult barriers, and to keep working in an integrated and purposive manner even when conflicts and tensions are present.

This is an organismic picture, and a very good one to keep in mind in working with the whole personality, but it is a concept of capacity too broad and inclusive to be measured all at once. Then, too, there are specific times when a comprehensive score on this broad capacity would not be as helpful to a counselor or a teacher as a specific score on some particular attribute of capacity. For these two reasons some narrower concepts of intelligence and its attributes have come into existence, along with the development of tests to measure those attributes.

The first quantitative measurement of intelligence was made by Binet in France in 1910. He was working on general intelligence, as it was recognized in French schools in what was called brightness and dullness. His work was particularly slanted to the kind of work done in school. It leaves out such things as motor potentialities, for example. Following his work, the principal developments have led to a number of intelligence tests, a few diagnostic tests of patterns of mental functions, some rather elaborate experimental work in the measurement and identification of special mental abilities, and a large number of tests of aptitudes. Those of greatest interest to teachers are the intelligence tests of a general nature. The others will be discussed very briefly.

General intelligence. Underlying the whole structure of mental capacity is a factor which, because it shows itself in many different kinds of mental activity, has been called the general factor, and is sometimes referred to in factor analysis as G. Like many other characteristics of the individual, it matures with age, coming to its full maturity somewhere around the age of seventeen. Tests devised for measuring it record it in units known as mental age, which correspond to months. The tests are so arranged as to difficulty that they can be equated to the chronological age scale. The theory is relatively simple. Any test item that is consistently passed by half of the children of a given age who try it is put into the scale at that age level. Thus an item that is successfully passed by half of those who are twelve years and six months, would be put at the 12-6 point in the test. Those younger than that who passed it would be said to be brighter than average, and those older than that who failed it would be said to be duller than average. From this kind of scaling each item in the test can be given a value in months of mental age. Thus a person taking the test is scored in such units.

About 1914, Stern proposed the use of a quotient for making comparisons between children, especially those of different chronological ages (CA). He proposed that their mental age (MA) score be divided by the CA score and the result multiplied by 100 to put it at or near 100, and thus make 100 the average quotient. He called this quotient the intelligence quotient, or IQ. Since the tests that measure MA are arbitrarily controlled so that all they yield is an MA (with no indication of whether each one in the scale is the same amount harder than the one before it), this process results in stabilizing the IQ throughout the life of an individual. Thus a child of ten can be compared as to relative brightness with a child of four by using the IQ. Obviously, IQ represents a rate of maturation or mental growth. An IQ of 110 means the individual is growing in intelligence at a rate that is ten points faster than the average.

This score is useful in school, provided it is used with discretion. It helps understand the educational resources of a student, so that he can receive the kind of help, and the kind of work, that is best for him. It also permits studies to determine how high a person's IQ needs to be to enable him to engage successfully in various levels of mental work. As a result of such studies various kinds of frequency tables have been published, concerning both the relationship between the IQ and the school and that between IQ and certain general designations of performance. In Table 4 are some typical data.

TABLE 4. CLASSIFICATION OF INTELLIGENCE

IQ	Class Names	Per cent in Total Population by Binet Test [2]	Per cent in High Schools of St. Louis, Mo., by a group test, 1936.[3]
140 +	Genius	1.3	1
120-139	Very superior	11.3	16
110-119	Superior	18.1	24
90-109	Normal	46.5	51
80-89	Dull	14.5	7
70-79	Borderline	5.6	
Below 70	Feeble-minded		
50-69	Moron	2.5	Below 80 1
25-49	Imbecile	.2	
Below 24	Idiot		

These high-school figures do not represent a guide to what will be found in all high schools, since selective factors vary with schools. They do show a tendency for high-school students to be selected from among the brighter young people to some extent, which is typical throughout the country. This trend is much more noticeable in college, where Traxler [4] reports, for example, from a study of 323 colleges, the following median IQ's. For the highest colleges, the freshman median was 123. For all colleges it was 109. For the four-year colleges it was 109. For junior colleges it was 105. For teachers colleges, 105. For the lowest colleges, 94.

Reports on college seniors indicate still greater selection, with the median in the neighborhood of 130.

[2] Maud A. Merrill, "Significance of IQ's on the revised Stanford-Binet Scales," *Journal of educational psychology,* 29 (1938), 641-51.

[3] George R. Johnson, "High school survey," *Public school messenger,* 35 No. 4, (1937), 1-34.

[4] Arthur Traxler, "What is a satisfactory IQ for admission to college?" *School and society,* 51 (1940), 462-64.

Keys,[5] in a study of California students, attempted to find out to what extent group test IQ's could be used to predict success in college. His study was based on all pupils leaving Oakland, California, High School from midwinter 1928-29 to midwinter 1933-34. The IQ's were taken on the Terman Group Test of Mental Ability, between grades seven and ten, and before the fifteenth birthday in every case.

For 290 who entered the University of California, the IQ's averaged 115.5 ± 0.44. For the 154 who succeeded in graduating from the University of California, the average IQ was 118.3 as compared with 112.4 for those who withdrew before graduating. Of the 154, only two had IQ's below 95. Both of them were from homes in which two languages were spoken, and this may have depressed their test scores. Of the 135 who graduated without honors, only one had an IQ as high as 140, and she was only .02 short of the necessary average of 2.00 for honors. Of the nineteen graduates with honors, only one had an IQ below 106. This one registered an IQ of 99 in junior high school after only eighteen months in America. He had a straight "A" record in high school.

Keys calculated the academic prospects for various IQ levels, and gave these results. For those with IQ's between 70 and 84, the chances are sixty-eight in a hundred that no more schooling will be attempted beyond high school, while the probability of going to a degree-granting institution is nil. For IQ's around 100 (95-104), forty in a hundred stop at the end of high school, while less than one in four are likely to gain admission to a degree-granting institution. For the group between 105 and 119, which includes the average college entrant, three out of ten will not go beyond high school, and scarcely one in three of the Oakland group will enter the University of California. For those with IQ's between 120 and 139, only about one in five stops with high school. Nearly half of the group observed actually enrolled at the University of California alone. For those with IQ's above 140, 100 per cent applied for admis-

[5] Noel Keys, "Value of group test IQ's for prediction of progress beyond high school," *Journal of educational psychology*, 31 (February, 1940), 81-93.

sion to degree-granting institutions, and 44 per cent graduated from the University of California alone with honors. Of the 4 or 5 per cent of junior-high-school pupils with IQ's between 85 and 94, who later entered the University of California, only one in three succeeded in graduating. With an IQ between 120 and 130, there are roughly three and a half times as good chances of entering the University of California, and seven times as good chances of graduating there, as for those with IQ's of 100. For those at IQ 140 +, the chances of graduating from the University with honors are a hundred times as great as for the group between 95 and 104, and eleven times as great as the group from 120 to 139.

These data apply specifically to Oakland High School and the University of California. They may not apply in other situations. They do, however, offer one illustration of the manner in which capacity affects success in school and indicate something of the extent of individual differences in general intelligence among high-school and college students.

Some differences associated with intelligence. Stout [6] investigated the extent to which ten-year-old children of normal intelligence differ among and within themselves in such characteristics as physical health, social status, economic status, mechanical ability, musical ability, school achievement, and behavior tendencies. The IQ's were measured by the Haggerty Intelligence Examination. Of all those measured, fifty-eight children ten years of age with IQ's between 90 and 110 were obtained. Health was measured by the records in the school, socioeconomic status by the Sims Score Card, general mechanical ability by the Stenquist Assembling Tests, musical ability by the Kwalwasser-Dykema Music Tests, achievement in the common branches by the New Stanford Achievement Test, and behavior tendencies by the Haggerty-Olson-Wickman Rating Schedules. In all of these items the variations between students were very great, and all the intercorrelations low. Stout concluded that "Not one has all of his achievement scores within the scope of one school grade; not one even approximates an average score

[6] H. G. Stout, "Variations of normal children," *Journal of experimental education,* 6 (September, 1937), 84-100.

in all the music tests; and only one comes within twenty per cent of a uniform normal rating in behavior." There is "no evidence that there is an 'average' child."

One of the most serious and important differences between children with equivalent general intelligence is found in their abstract ability. Until quite recently the extent to which this characteristic is independent of that which is measured by the Binet test has not been clearly recognized or demonstrated. Nor has the relationship between abstract mental ability and one's capacity to adjust easily to new experience been as clear as it might have been. Halpin [7] recently carried out a well-controlled and very enlightening study of this problem. He worked with children around the six-year period. His data show a striking relationship between abstract ability and the adjustment of the child, and practically no relationship to intelligence as measured by the IQ, for the children in his study. He was able also to show for the first time some stages by which abstract ability seems to emerge from complete concrete types of reaction, although it is not apparent whether a given child is moving along the path from one stage to another. There are some important implications within his data, which suggest the home environment may have much to do with the presence or abšence of abstract ability in the child, and which offer leads for studies in that area. A non-abstract child seems to have difficulty and to feel insecure in dealing with any of the complex relationships that are so much a part of education and adult social life.

Uses of the IQ. There are a number of cautions connected with the use of scores from intelligence tests, and particularly the I.Q. In the first place, it is not an appropriate way of measuring the intelligence of anyone beyond the age of about sixteen. Since mental growth is approximately complete at that time, there cannot be further units of mental age against which to compare chronological age, which continues to increase. Therefore, the quotient cannot be calculated with

[7] Andrew W. Halpin, *Sorting test performance of six-year old children—a study of abstract concrete behavior,* Ph.D. thesis (Ithaca, N. Y.: Cornell University, 1949).

validity. Unless one is tested prior to that age, the IQ should be replaced with some other score. One in very common use is the percentile score, which indicates relative position on a scale of 100 percentiles. A score of 50 means that one's performance is superior to 50 per cent of the cases on which the test norms were established. Since such a score has meaning only in terms of the group from which the norms were derived, that information must be given along with the score. Norm groups frequently used are college freshmen, college seniors, high-school seniors, or any other group against which comparisons may be desired.

The IQ from the Binet test, which is always given individually to one child at a time, probably varies less from one testing to another than most tests allow. Generally, an allowance of plus or minus five points is made on a Binet IQ, which means that if the individual were tested again several times, the scores would stay within five points of the first score half of the time. This indicates that no such thing as a pin-point measurement of intelligence is possible, even with the Binet test. On group tests, those given to a group of children all at once, the variation for individual children is usually greater. Because of the time required to give the Binet, however, most of the tests used in schools are group tests, among which are the American Council, Henmon-Nelson, Kuhlmann-Anderson, Ohio State University Psychological Examination, Otis, California Test of Mental Maturity, Wonderlic, and many others.[8]

Group test scores are better than the best guess an instructor can make about a student's intelligence. So many interferences can keep true capacity from showing up in a pupil's work that it is dangerous to guess at intelligence. It is equally true that strong motivation often takes a person with a mediocre capacity considerably farther than some

8 Asahel D. Woodruff, and Maralyn W. Pritchard, "Some trends in the development of psychological tests," *Educational and psychological measurement,* 9 (Spring, 1949), 105-8. In this article reference is made to the *Cornell University Test List,* prepared by the staff of the University Testing Service, Cornell University, Ithaca, N. Y. It was last revised in 1949, and is available for 50 cents. It contains well over 1000 tests of all kinds, and lists their publishers.

much brighter individuals who do not utilize their capacities. It is for reasons of this kind that Stoddard's definition has great merit for those in teaching, who often see resistance to difficulty, and persistence, doing what higher intelligence sometimes fails to do for those without such qualities.

Where further reading is desired on the validity of psychological tests, the best source is Buros.[9] For an excellent discussion of psychological testing in more technical detail and broader coverage than here, the reader is referred to Cronbach.[10]

Mental diagnosis. The diagnosis of patterns of mental activity in individuals requires specialized tests, which are sometimes helpful in counseling. Since the general intelligence tests fulfill most of the needs of teachers in general, the reader is referred to Cronbach again for treatment of that subject.

Special mental abilities. In addition to the general factor in intelligence, there are certain special abilities that have been the subject of research by Thurstone and others. Some of those identified through factor analysis, and known now as primary mental abilities, are number facility, memory, visual facility, word fluency, perceptual speed, verbal ability, and inductive ability. The study of these factors is currently under way; it is too early now to see what the best uses of these findings will be in teaching. At the moment they indicate two things that are important for teachers: the fact that each individual is more than a unitary function which can be neatly allocated to one spot on a scale of ability, and a suggestion of what will be at least the general nature of some of his special capacities. The relationship between these capacities and various parts of the curriculum is plain, although for most students scores on tests of primary mental abilities will not be available.

Aptitudes. The standard work on aptitudes, by Bingham,[11]

[9] Oscar Buros, *Mental measurements yearbook* (New Brunswick, N. J.: Rutgers University Press, 1949).

[10] Lee J. Cronbach, *Essentials of psychological testing* (New York: Harper and Bros., 1949).

[11] Walter V. Bingham, *Aptitudes and aptitude testing* (New York: Harper and Bros., 1937).

is now getting a little old in view of the vigorous developments in vocational counseling and testing in recent years. Nevertheless, it is a good discussion of the general problem of predicting one's success in a particular line of development. Bingham defines an aptitude as the capacity to learn to do a particular thing well, *and* to develop an interest in it and stay with it. He takes this double approach because he is trying to find a way of predicting more than the power to do a job. He wants to know who will stay in a vocational field and be contented and well-adjusted there. This is essentially the counselor's point of view. The answer to such questions requires several kinds of tests. Among them are tests of special abilities, which Cronbach classifies as spatial and perceptual, psychomotor, mechanical knowledge, artistic abilities, and sensory abilities. A very large number of tests in these areas are listed in the *Cornell University Test List* cited above. Since individuals differ widely in their capacities for these types of learning, it is wise to find out all that can be learned about one's aptitudes before entering a particular line of vocational training. Each individual will also be found to have a varied array of potentialities within himself. Some are high on all counts, or low on all counts, but most have their high and their low points. It is quite common to find a person who is very apt in functions requiring finger dexterity, and rather slow in abstract performance, or who has other variable highs and lows, and who would have difficulty in one line of work where his aptitudes are low, but would succeed comfortably in an area in which his aptitudes are somewhat higher.

What is true of special abilities is also true of general intelligence. Two individuals with an IQ of 115 can be almost completely unlike each other in the details of their capacities. Tests on which IQ's are calculated are all tests of general intelligence, and the scores are earned through a variety of types of mental tasks. The IQ is a composite score in which some parts of the test may have higher scores than others. Similarity in IQ's carries no necessary implication of similarity in profiles, or of equality of accomplishment in similar tasks.

Throughout this section it has been emphasized that, with regard to basic capacity to learn, people differ greatly from each other, and differ within themselves on particular types of learning. Whatever each one possesses in the way of potentiality for development, tends to define an approximate ceiling toward which he can move *if* he has motivation, and takes advantage of his opportunities. Capacity is only one of the variables that determines what he an accomplish, but it is a very fundamental one.

1804. *Motivation.* One of the most puzzling problems in school is created by the student who does not fit into the regular work and take advantage of the school program. So-called discipline cases, which are really motivation cases, are the first to be brought up by teachers-in-service when they have an opportunity to obtain help in their work. In this section the fundamental principles that lie behind a student's application to his work, or his efforts to escape from it, are discussed. The fundamental concepts for this discussion have already been laid down in Chapter II on evaluation in behavior, Chapter VI on purposive trends in behavior, Chapters VII, VIII, and IX on needs, and Chapter X on values. At this point there will be no attempt to repeat what is discussed in those chapters, but their specific relationship to the motivation involved in school attendance and learning will be made quite explicit and illustrated with live cases.

Three elements in the motivational structure of the student are particularly involved. One element consists of what he wants. This is based on his values, and the particular goals of which he is conscious and toward which he is trying to move. One consists of how he thinks he can get what he wants. His ideas in this area are based on his process concepts, which consist of his repertoire of paths, empirically derived ideas of how things affect him and how he must conduct himself in order to promote the effects he wants. Again it should be reiterated that a person's concepts are not necessarily consciously recognized by him. The last is what he likes to do. This consists of his pattern of interests, his preferences for activities, those that he likes, quite independent of any cognitive involvement such as is to be found in values and process concepts.

Values and process concepts. In a study of the relationship between values, process concepts, and expressed attitudes, the hypothesis that was amply supported by the experimental data was stated as follows:

An individual's attitude toward any object, proposition, or circumstance will be *favorable* if, *according to his concepts,* that object seems to favor the achievement of his strong positive values. His attitude will become *unfavorable* if any change in the situation, or in his concept of the object, makes it seem to him that the object endangers his strong positive values. Conversely, one's attitude toward any object, proposition, or circumstance will be *unfavorable,* if, *according to his concepts,* the object seems to threaten his strong positive values. His attitude will become *favorable* if any change in the situation or in his concept of the object makes it seem to favor his strong positive values. The strength of the attitudinal expression will be a function of the importance of the values to which the object or condition has any relationship and the extent to which the person feels the object or condition will affect his values.[12]

Applying this directly to a student in school, it may be said that whenever a student has process concepts that show the school to be destructive of his strong positive values, he will attempt to avoid the school, or whatever part of its program is involved in the detrimental process concepts. He will conversely seek out activities that consist of productive processes within his conceptual structure for the attainment of his values. On the other hand, if, according to his concepts, he can best attain his values through the school program, he will be a cooperative and willing student.

The testing of this proposition requires measurement of the student's value pattern, measurement of his process concepts, and a valid record of how he conducts himself so that his behavior can be checked against his motives. Francis

12 Asahel D. Woodruff, and Francis J. DiVesta, "The relationship between values, concepts, and attitudes," *Educational and psychological measurement,* 8 (Winter, 1948), 645-60.

DiVesta [13] made intensive studies of a number of adolescents to do just this thing. Two of his cases are reproduced here. One portrays an antisocial aggressive individual, the other a well-adjusted and excellent student.

Case 12

An Antisocial Aggressive Boy

This boy was suggested to the investigator for study on the grounds that he was one of the most serious disturbers in the school and in the community. The suggestion came from the Principal of his school, after conference with some of the teachers, as to which students might present some of the contrasting behavioral patterns desired by the investigator. The boy is very popular among many of his peers, but has considerable difficulty adjusting to the large school population. In his neighborhood, and by the city authorities, he is considered a problem child. He participated freely in several non-directive interviews with the investigator away from the school buildings. A transcript of some of the significant parts of those interviews is reproduced here verbatim, omitting only the interviewers' minor comments here and there.

"I don't like attending school. I don't like to sit around and do nothing. I don't like to take orders from my teachers, only from my mother and father. It's a lot of fun to get fooling around in class. Somebody gets starting it off and everybody gets into it. It's a lot of fun instead of sitting around all day unless the teacher says you can talk. School was all right when I was in the seventh grade, but now—we met more guys then and had a lot of fun.

"The kids I don't like are the ones who don't fool around and who just do everything everyone says. They just hang around the teachers so they can get good marks. I don't like the kind of kids who don't play sports.

"I smoke and swear lots. There ain't no crime in it. Some of the kids are just plain sissies. Some of them you ask a question of and you get a foolish answer.

"We shoot pool most of the time. I like it because it shows that you are better than someone else when you play. I don't go make

[13] Francis J. DiVesta, *The role of personal values and process concepts in the personal and social adjustment of adolescents,* PH.D. thesis (Ithaca, N. Y.: Cornell University, 1948).

friends at the pool room. Our gang stays mostly by ourselves. I don't like the country. There aren't so many people around. You have to go to the city to make your friends, to meet them and to mess around. You have to go so far and if you don't have a car you have to take a bus or hitchhike.

"We get out to raise cain at night. Sometimes I stay out 'til two or three o'clock in the morning and sometimes until morning. I like to play tricks on people. I went around with a guy who used to race a lot with his car and I think that is a lot of fun. If someone else asks for a fight we don't mind fighting otherwise we don't go out looking for a fight. We roam the streets at night, go up to the diner, mess around, then roam the streets some more until we get tired. We get some real excitement out of that. It is especially fun when we get the cops chasing us. They chased us until three o'clock one morning. We had turned off the lights in back of the school. Some cops we like and some we don't. The ones we like are those who will help you and the others we don't like are the ones who just yank you in. The cops will tell us to go home but we don't. We just walk around the block and come back. The cops we like will come up to you and talk right to you, and the ones we don't like will holler at you.

"I like my English teacher better than others. My home room teacher is crabby. You say something, just fooling around, and she will grab at you. She hollers at you. Last year I was absent from school a lot and she read my excuses to the class. I didn't like that and I don't think it was right.

"Most of the time when I was absent from school, I stayed out because I stayed in bed too late. I wouldn't come to school because if you were late you had to stay in detention and I don't like detention.

"If I was out of school I could have a car. A car saves you a lot of walking. You can go out of town dancing instead of taking a bus or hitchhiking. I don't like it around home. It's the same old talk, I mean, it's the same people you talk to all the time. I'd rather be down playing pool with the kids I know.

"I never did want to be a leader. I'd rather do it and have the fun of doing it rather than to tell somebody to do it. I don't like to give orders. I'd rather do it myself."

Value Pattern of Case 12

Non-conformist friends
Excitement (pure and work)
Freedom (physical and intellectual)

Privacy (solitude and group)
Power (leadership and control)
Informal social activity
Prestige (recognition and acclaim)
Conformist friends
Religious activity (living and organization)
Formal social activity
Home life (family and home setting)

These values correspond fairly well to those discussed in Chapter X. They are modified in DiVesta's revision of the test to conform more closely to the adolescent's point of view. In this test as in the original, each value can be split into two aspects if the individual is sufficiently sensitive to the two meanings to make such a split. Friendship can be split into conformist or non-conformist friends. Excitement into pure excitement or exciting work, freedom into physical or intellectual, privacy into personal or group, power into leadership or control, social activity into formal or informal relationships, prestige into recognition or acclaim, religion into religious living or participation in religious organizations, and home life into family life or the physical aspects of a home. In the pattern above, those that were not split are indicated by parenthetical indication that both qualities of the value are kept together.

This pattern is typical of the antisocial individuals in DiVesta's study, of which there were many. Non-conformist friends is always high and is almost always separated widely from conformist friends. Freedom and excitement are always high. Home life, formal social activity, and religion are usually quite low. An examination of the interview record will show that there is a marked tendency to express liked or disliked activities in terms of the dominant values of the individual. For example, he talks of school in terms of "sitting around," "authority," "detentions," "few friends." School, therefore, interferes with the attainment of his dominant values.

Privacy is rated rather high. This should not be confused with the uniform tendency of withdrawn individuals to rate privacy even higher. In this case it is placed below non-conformist friends, excitement, and freedom. It is frequently in first place for a withdrawn individual, who also tends to put these three highest values in rather low positions. A withdrawn boy also puts friendship very high, but seems unable to see any difference between conformists and non-conformists. He just wants friends, but he wants privacy more.

The nature of Case 12's concept of non-conformist friends is revealed in some parts of the interview. He likes those who fool around, play pool, annoy policemen, disobey authority, and are not sissies.

Process Concept Pattern of Case 12

Processes	Excitement	Freedom	Friends	Prestige	Religion	Privacy	Power	Social activity	Family	Attitude Score
Belonging to a club	4	1	5	5	5	5	5	5	3	3
Playing sports	1	1	1	1	1	1	1	1	1	1
Attending school	5	4	1	3	3	5	4	2	1	
Going to western and crime movies	1		1	1	1	1	1	1	3	1
Going to parties	4		3	2	2	2	3	3	2	3
Living in the city	1	1	1	1	1	1	1	2	1	1
Skipping school	2	1	1	1	1	1	1	1	3	1
Playing pool	1		1	1	1	1	1	1	2	1
Belonging to the boy scouts	4	5	5	4	4	4	4	4	3	4
Hitchhiking	3	2	2	2	3	3	3		3	3
Raising cain in school	2		2	2	3		3	3	3	4
Being able to win a fight	1		1	1	1	1		2		1
Obeying the policeman	5	5	5	4	5	4	4	4	1	4
Getting away with something	1	1	1	1	1		1		1	1
Being a class officer	4	4	3	5	4	3	2	3	3	4
Staying at home	2	3	2		2	1	2	1	2	4
Doing something daring	2		4	2	4		3	3	3	3
Living in the country	1	1	4		1	1	2	1	1	1
Smoking and swearing		1	1	1	1	1		2		1
Making others do what you want		3	3	3	5	4	4	4	3	3
Obeying the teacher		4	3	3	4	5	4		3	5
Being tough		1	2	1	1	1	1	1	3	1

Aggression score = 26
Average score = 2

This pattern was determined by asking the boy to rate each of the processes for each of the values. That is, if belonging to a club is highly productive of excitement, then rate it 1. If it is moderately productive, rate it 2. If neutral, rate it 3. If mildly detrimental to excitement, rate it 4. If highly detrimental, rate it 5. The ratings were taken on forms not shown here. They were set up for the purpose of keeping his attention on one process at a time, so that the process could be described and the individual could get himself oriented in it before making his ratings. The picture in this pattern, his recorded interview comments, and his actual behavior, have a very high agreement. This was found to be uniformly true in all cases studied, which leads to the conclusion that concepts may be validly studied in this manner. The technique and its validation data are available in the thesis, but are too lengthy to introduce here.

The last column in the pattern shows how the individual rated each process on a purely general basis, independent of any values, the criterion being solely his own feelings about the process. Thirteen processes, including eleven of those shown here and two other ratings that did not belong in this set of scores, were interpreted by the investigator to be aggressive processes. By adding the subject's general rating of all of these thirteen processes, an aggression score was developed. The lower it is the more aggressive the individual is said to be. If the aggression score is divided by thirteen the result is the average rating given each of the aggressive processes. For Case 12 the aggression score is 26, with an average of 2, which puts the aggressive processes decidedly above neutral. This might be compared with his ratings on belonging to the scouts, obeying the teacher, staying at home, or being a class officer.

These scores reveal the preferred processes for attaining his values. His concept of the results to be achieved by following each process may be seen by reading across each row. Thus belonging to a club is fine for making friends, but quite undesirable for all the other values. The various processes that would help or hinder the attainment of each value may be seen by reading down each column. Playing pool helps him achieve excitement and friendship. Obeying the teacher destroys freedom and privacy. Being tough helps make friends and win freedom and privacy. Obeying the policeman destroys excitement, freedom, and friendship. Skipping school is productive for his highest values.

Here is a straightforward picture of what is going on in the motivational pattern of the boy. It is obvious why he is a trouble-maker in school and in the community. How he acquired these concepts is another matter. At this point he has them, and they are directing his behavior. How he managed to acquire this particular pattern of values is another matter also. Now he has his values in this formation, and the pattern is just about the same one that is found in all the cases of antisocial aggressives in the study. With this inside or subjective view of the world, he can scarcely be expected to do anything much different from what he is doing. He is bound to resist efforts to change his activities, because any significant change would threaten his adjustment. On the other hand, his behavior will change without pressure if his values and process concepts can be changed.

For contrast, so that the same principles can be seen operating in the production of behavior that is socially approved and personally developmental, another case is presented.

Case 13

A Well-adjusted Successful Student

This boy was recommended for investigation because he represented the type of student who is believed by his teachers to be making the most of his opportunities. The materials are presented in the same sequence as was used in Case 12, but without the explanatory comments on technique. Here is part of the interview record. The investigator reported being impressed with neatness, calmness, an easy, mature, and pleasant attitude. The boy belongs to several activities in school, and at least one outside of school.

"In school I have a chance to meet a lot of peole. I am interested in my courses especially science and math. I don't care for English and German. In science you can prove things. In English you have set ways of doing things. That's the way it was in junior high too. In grade school it seemed more like work. Here (in high school) you meet a lot of new people and make many friends.

"I belong to the glee club and band. You get to know a lot of people in these activities. They are also recreation. It is something you can do to pass the time and enjoy doing.

"I am on the club committee for club nights in the high school. It gives me a chance to offer my views. The club committee gives you experience in group leading.

"I am vice-president of my fellowship at the church. I like to help the other people and have everybody doing things along the same lines. I wanted to be leader and vice-president of the fellowship before I was elected. It builds up your friends.

"The fellowship is with the church. We have a chance for evening service. It gives you another chance to talk in front of people.

"I used to be a scout but am one no longer. I liked it because we went on hikes and helped each other out. Our troop disintegrated and when it started up again I had so many new things I didn't feel I ought to join again since it would hurt my grades.

"My best friends are with the fellowship. I don't like the bunch that is always smoking, drinking, and showing off. I am in with a bunch from near where I live that is pretty nice. They have the same interests that I do. One of the kids in school I don't like especially. He is one that is always looking for a fight. I think they feel left out. I don't like the bunch that sits out in front of the school smoking and swearing. If you are with people who smoke and swear others that you want to like you will dislike you. These kids also get into trouble with the police. They are reckless. I still think they realize they can't be a member of the regular bunch and do reckless things to make friends and of course when they do it they just keep from making friends.

"I like home. I live with my brother-in-law and sister. We have a little trio since each of us plays an instrument. We are building an addition on to the house and I like that. I can hardly wait to get home at night to help. We are coming to the most interesting part of the wiring now.

"I have never skipped school. On nice days like today I wish I was out but if I skipped school I wouldn't be able to explain it. I haven't felt like skipping lately anyway since I have been having so much fun in school. I think skipping school is wrong too, because you are supposed to be in school. If you skip once or twice it doesn't make much difference as far as friends are concerned but if you skip a lot like a kid I knew last year you will lose the friends you had.

"I think people my age are mainly concerned with having other people like you. It gives you a better feeling.

"Last year I was lieutenant in the traffic squad, stage crew, and head electrician in the stage crew. I was free when in the traffic squad to walk around the halls and we also had something to say about making out the rules. I knew the chief advisor of the traffic squad very well that way too. I liked the operator's club. I couldn't go out for sports because of rheumatic so I had to make up for it through other ways."

Value Pattern of Case 13

Formal social activity
Friends (conformist and non-conformist)
Religious activity (living and organization)
Home life (family and home setting)
Leadership
Informal social activity
Freedom (physical and intellectual)
Excitement (pure and work)
Prestige (recognition and acclaim)
Privacy (group and solitude)
Control

There is a striking contrast in the value patterns of the two cases. Here formal social activity is first; in Case 12 it was next to the bottom. Friendship is not split here, probably because the awareness of non-conformists as a class has never entered the thoughts of Case 13. Religion is high here, and low for 12. Home life is relatively high here, and last for 12. Excitement and freedom are low here, whereas they are very high in 12. Case 13 has divided power into leadership, which is relatively high, and control, which is very low. This is in conformity with his generally democratic and cooperative manner, for control is an aggressive non-democratic value, whereas leadership involves more recognition of the worth of others.

This pattern is typical of the well-adjusted adolescents included in the study. There is nothing particularly unique about it when compared to those who are behaving as this boy behaves.

Process Concept Pattern of Case 13

Processes	Excitement	Freedom	Friends	Prestige	Religion	Privacy	Power	Social activity	Home life	Attitude Score
Belonging to a club	1		1	3	1	4	1	1	1	1
Playing sports	1	1	1	2	1	4	1	1	1	1
Attending school	2	1	1	1	1	4	1	1	1	
Going to western and crime movies	2		5		1	5	4	4	2	1
Going to parties	1		1	3	1	5	3	1	1	1
Living in the city	1	1	1		1	4	2	1	1	2
Skipping school	5	1	5	5	5	3	4	5	5	5
Playing pool	2		3	4	4	3	4	3	4	3
Belonging to the boy scouts	2	2	2	2	1	4	1	1	1	1
Hitchhiking	5	2	3	3	2	5	3		3	1
Raising cain in school	5		5	5	5		5	5	5	5
Being able to win a fight	3		5	5	5	2	5		5	5
Obeying the policeman	5	1	3	3	1	4	1	2	2	1
Getting away with something	3	5	5	5	4		1		4	5
Being a class officer	3	3	3	3	2	5	1	1	1	2
Staying at home	4	2	3		3	2	3	3	1	2
Doing something daring	3		5	5	4		4	4	3	4
Living in the country	3	1	3		1	4	3	2	1	1
Smoking and swearing	5	4	5	5	1	5			5	4
Obeying the teacher	1	3	2	1	4	4			1	2
Making others do what you want	5	5	5	5	1	5	5	5	5	5
Being tough	5	4	5	5	1	5	5	5	5	5

Aggression score = 49
Average score = 3.8

Here, too, the scores reveal the preferred processes for getting to each value. The aggressive processes as a whole are somewhat on the detrimental side.

It appears from other aspects of DiVesta's study that most well-adjusted adolescents are relatively unaware of aggressive possibilities or processes, because they are positively oriented to, and absorbed in, the socially approved processes. In this case school activities provide him with friends, the church fellowship provides him with religious satisfactions and leadership opportunities. His music and family activities together satisfy his high evaluation of home life. His ratings indicate quite general rejection of the aggressive and antisocial processes of skipping school, being able to win a fight, raising cain in school, getting away with something, smoking and swearing, making others do what you want, and being tough. He expresses here his conviction that they destroy almost all of the values in the test, not only those he cherishes most highly. On the other hand see his equivocal ratings of western and crime movies. Here is a passive entertainment, to watch which can scarcely be called antisocial. It has its points, which would seem to be related to the family associations in attending, to its exciting nature, and presumably to its moral inferences. Nevertheless, excitement is not one of his major values, and he seems to spend little time in such shows, but much time with his family in other pursuits. Attending school is highly productive for everything but promoting privacy, in which he is not interested at all.

The daily behavior, both in school and at home, of Case 13 validates all of these patterns.

Interests. Although there are several good interest tests, it is not always necessary to use them to obtain relative and valid pictures of what a student likes to do. Some of the interests of Cases 12 and 13 are evident. Case 12 is relatively impoverished in interests. He depends on excitement for enjoyment to a large extent. Nevertheless, he likes to play pool, he enjoys some sports activities mildly. He has practically no interest in any intellectual pursuits. Case 13 enjoys music, some scientific and mechanical activities such as wiring his home, intellectual activity, and social activities. These interests are based on enjoyment, which is of course a product of successful resolution of conflicts and satisfaction of needs. Hence they tend to develop in activities that are also regarded as profitable processes for the attainment of goals and values. They have no necessary relationship to capacity or aptitude, as has been shown repeatedly in counseling test records.

Interests pertain to specific activities. They may change with experience,. and very often do. Unless students have strong antipathies to certain activities, such as a violent dislike for mathematics or chemistry or some other type of school activity, they can be brought into participation without much difficulty when their values and goals and process concepts are so aligned as to make the activity seem profitable. In those cases of strong dislike, the usual cause was a frustrating experience with the subject at an earlier date, so that the subject represents a negative process concept as well as a strong affective dislike. To remove such a blocking requires helping the individual discover that he can do well in such activities, and they will bring him satisfying results. This requires remedial teaching, and counseling.

Summary. Motivation consists essentially of one's subjective pattern of values, process concepts, and interests, operating on an underlying dynamic drive furnished by the needs of the individual. Students have to go toward the things which experience has shown to be satisfying in the resolution of their needs. Their values grow out of their experiences in meeting needs under various conditions. Then they become powerful directive factors in subsequent behavior. Everyone is doing what he thinks will promote his values. If the school and its program does not fit into his pattern of meaning as a productive process, he has no choice but to try to get out of it. Before he can profit from an academic educative program, he *must* have a re-education in his motives. To avoid starting on it only fortifies the trouble, even though such re-education is difficult.

1805. *Maturity and readiness.* In the life cycle of a physical organism it is possible to identify a period within which the organism may be said to be physiologically mature. In that sense maturity partakes somewhat of an absolute nature. Even there, however, there is an element of relativity, when the stage called maturity is compared to the immature stages. The relativity of the term becomes even more dominant when the complex functions of a full human life-scheme take the center of attention. The question then becomes not whether the organism has developed to any set point, but whether it is ready to undertake a particular activity or phase of development. That is, at any given time, and for a given task, does the individual have ready, in usable form, what he needs to engage in that task? If so he is *ready*, psychologically speaking. Hence the problem of first importance, the reason for being interested at all in the maturity of the individual, is to know whether he is ready for whatever he has to do. In general, readiness depends on sufficient development in the physiological mechanisms to permit neural connections and proper muscular function, and sufficient conceptual development to provide comprehension for the new experience. If these elements are present at least in minimal degree, then the individual is more or less ready. In other words, he has matured to the point where he can take the next step, develop the new insights or acquire the new skills. He may not be mature in an absolute sense, but that is not important for learning.

Reading readiness. Of all the subjects in the curriculum, this is the one that is mostly developed within the years of school attendance. Perhaps it is for this reason that in this subject alone an awareness of the full meaning of readiness exists, and a number of tests of readiness have been developed. Speech, numbers, motor activities, and other functions have their beginnings before school years. The school picks up a going process and carries it along. In reading, almost the whole burden falls on the school.

Readiness to read is based on possession of a few fundamental processes used in reading, which have not yet been integrated. The child must have the concepts about which he will read, or the words will mean nothing to him even if he learns to recognize them. He must know the words he is going to read and have them related to the concepts orally. He must be able to differentiate one printed symbol from another when he sees them, or he cannot learn to recognize printed words. If all these skills and concepts are present, then he must also make the discovery that it is possible to get meaning from the symbols on a page, after which he becomes absorbed in the puzzle, hunting for ways of getting the meanings. Under these favorable conditions he will probably learn rapidly. Otherwise he will show little progress and little interest.

In the *Cornell University Test List,*[14] there are twenty-

[14] University Testing Service, Cornell University, Ithaca, N. Y.: Mimeographed edition, 1949.

three preschool readiness tests, including such familiar names as the *Betts Ready to Read Tests, Gates Reading Readiness Test,* and the *Metropolitan Readiness Test.* Most of these are specifically directed toward reading, but some of them are broader in scope. There are also some visual tests that may be used to check on the readiness of the visual apparatus.

Olsen [15] suggests that reading is a function of the growth of the whole organism, and in some of his unpublished materials has abundant evidence for the effect of maturation on progress in reading.

Arithmetic. There are no tests available for testing readiness in arithmetic, but several tests for use in the first grade and higher, in connection with achievement. In a sense, every test constitutes a check on readiness for the next higher level of function. What is needed in arithmetic is a familiarity with the abstract idea of quantity, and the realization that there is a system of quantitative relationships. Before the child is aware of number as such, he deals with real objects, such as two balls, or three blocks. When he recognizes two-ness by itself, just as two, not as two balls, he is ready for the symbol that stands for the abstract two. After that he can begin to sense the possibilities of dealing with numbers in the absence of real objects. Therefore, he is ready for arithmetic.

Speech. Since this is largely matured by the time the child comes to school, it is not a problem for the teacher to any degree, but it is nevertheless a function that depends upon readiness. Control of the vocal organs, and an awareness of variations in sounds, and the relationship between those variations and specific elements in experience constitute the chief needs for speech readiness. In most infants, at approximately one year, there appears rather suddenly an outbreak of voluble babbling in which all kinds of sounds come in rich abundance and confusion. It sounds exactly like human language except that it consists mostly of unfamiliar syllables. This is preceded for a long time by vocalization of single

[15] Williard C. Olsen, and Sarita I. Davis, "The adaptation of instruction in reading to the growth of children." *Educational method,* 20 (1941), 71-79.

sounds, not altered or varied noticeably. Quite smoothly, the voluble babbling slips into words, and speech is well under way. The varied babbling seems to be providing the last maturation that will yield readiness to talk. It brings control of the vocal organs to a functional level, while the infant imitates all the speech sounds that seem at last to have caught his ear. Words are just stabilized sound patterns with conceptual attachments. Therefore, when the infant has mastered the ability to make the sounds, he can begin to formulate the words and bring his sounds into stabilized patterns.

The school becomes involved in speech readiness when foreign languages are included in the curriculum, and also when an effort is made to improve elocution and clarity of speech. It is a factor in singing, too.

Walking. Muscle strength, bone structure, and maturity in the reflex neural system are required before the child is ready to walk. This usually takes place during the first year. The more complex activity of stair climbing needs a little longer for its readiness, and roller skating still longer. Some of the studies on the relationship between maturation and motor learning indicate that it is relatively useless to attempt to teach a child to perform a motor act for which he is not physiologically ready.[16]

Readiness for a course or lesson. This is a more complex problem than readiness for the functions cited heretofore, because it involves additional psychological factors. A student is ready for a course or lesson when he senses a need for it and has a place for it in his scheme of living, and when he has the previous concepts and processes required to make it go along smoothly. In the absence of these conditions, serious difficulty is encountered. A course for which he has no use is something to avoid if possible because it is a barrier to other things he wants. The absence of fundamental concepts blocks his efforts to comprehend higher processes. One who has not mastered at least the fundamental arithmetical and

[16] Norman L. Munn, *Psychological development* (Boston: Houghton Mifflin Co., 1938), pp. 219-24.

algebraic processes is in no position to attempt calculus or trigonometry.

In *previous academic achievement* the students of any grade level always show a large spread. Since it is customary to promote pupils through the elementary years by whole grades, rather than by subjects, one may expect to find in the eighth grade, for example, pupils with fourth-grade reading skill and others with reading skill adequate for college work. The same variations may be shown in most other subjects, and at almost any level in the educational ladder. Aside from the fact that pupils with low achievement are being turned out as educated individuals, the real problem for the teacher is to find a way to help such students fit into the work of a given course. There are good diagnostic techniques for almost every subject. Few of them may be found in the form of printed tests, and many printed tests are of poor quality. The techniques are not used with any satisfactory universality; if they were, academic failure could be materially cut down. The common complaint that time does not permit such diagnostic work with an individual pupil is not sensible. Failure to do such work inevitably involves the teacher in many wasted minutes and hours working with a "stupid" pupil, when a little corrective work could often set the pupil on his own feet and enable him to go ahead with the group. The most common factor in academic difficulty is a missing or inadequate concept. For that reason teachers should give special attention to the whole process of conceptual development. Another common difficulty is failure to read properly. It may be correct to guess that by far the largest part of the difficulties teachers have with failing students grows out of one or both of these two inadequacies.

Developmental status. In place of chronological age, which measures only time elapsed since birth, a new measure of development known as organismic age is coming into use. It is called organismic because it attempts to incorporate in one figure all aspects of growth and development that can be measured. In other words, it represents the whole organism. Some of the strands of growth and development commonly included in organismic age are mental age, height age, weight age, grip age, dental age, carpal (bone ossification) age, and educational age. Each of these developmental ages is determined by comparing the individual's measurement at a given chronological age with the statistical norm for all other known cases at the same age. If, for example, the average twelve-year-old boy is fifty-seven inches tall, then every boy who is fifty-seven inches tall is said to have a height age of twelve years. That means that a boy who is eleven years old chronologically, but is fifty-seven inches tall, is approximately one year advanced in height. There is a noticeable tendency for individuals so measured to be consistent within themselves. That is, the various lines of growth go along fairly close together. They also tend to follow a fairly constant rate of growth, when all the strands are considered in one complete measure. Although any single strand of growth may change its rate throughout the years, the average figure, organismic age, usually maintains a constant rate.[17]

The usual method of assigning an individual to a grade is on the basis of chronological age. Consequently, there are significant differences between individuals in the same grade in the matter of developmental status. The more rapid growers will soon draw ahead of the others in most ways. The slower growers will fall behind. Most of the students will be in the average group. Developmental status affects learning in a number of ways. Greatly accelerated or retarded individuals may become upset about the changes that are taking place or failing to take place in themselves in contrast to the average individual. Spurts in height in early adolescence, the onset of puberty, changes in body proportion, and other similar adolescent problems are often accompanied by uneasiness in students who do not know what is happening to them, or who come to worry over whether they are normal. Also, such developmental differences may create social problems among the students, because social standing

[17] See the Case of Dan, Case 21 in Chapter XXII. The developmental ages are shown in his growth data, for mental age, educational age, reading age, arithmetic age, weight age, height age, neuromuscular coordination age as revealed through hand squeeze, and dental age.

is not infrequently tied up with one's state of development.

Here is an interesting case which illustrates the impact of a developmental problem on a student, and the manner in which the problem was met by the parents of the student.

Case 14

Developmental Status and Adjustmental Difficulties

My tiny stature was continually a source of grief to me. This trouble started in the sixth grade when other children kept growing up and expanding, but I stopped. People began making their outstanding observations regarding my build and, still, today, for want of conversation, remark about it; however, their comments no longer bother me as much.

The first day that I entered high school, a teacher looked at me and made the comical remark that she thought children began their schooling careers in the kindergarten. To my embarrassment the whole class laughed as I blushed frantically. I felt like going back to kindergarten with people who looked my age. Every other class that I attended that day holds a similar unhappy memory. The teachers kept remarking that the classes were getting younger and that a certain student made them think they were in grammar school, as they stared directly at me. I went home in tears, thinking that something was radically wrong with me.

Whenever I met new people I went through the same process of hearing them say, "Why, you certainly don't look your age." I got so that I didn't want to meet new people and preferred to become a social hermit. The fact that my friends started to shop in the "Junior Miss Department" for their clothes which were becoming more and more sophisticated looking while I was left behind in the "Children's Shop" with infantile styles bothered me tremendously. I became super-sensitive and developed a complex in which I thought that people were continually noticing my size and commenting about it. I was so worried because I didn't mature any physically, that I started reading all magazine ads, etc., to discover how I could make myself grow. I performed stretching exercises and similar things daily, but to no avail. It was at this point that my parents noticed how bothered I was and they came to my rescue.

Mother and daddy tried to point out to me the merits of being "petite" as they called it. They took me to see Helen Hayes, a tiny, famous actress in "Twelfth Night." They explained that a woman who had poise and a pleasant personality was much more attractive than a beautiful woman who lacked these qualities. They tried to help me to discover and develop my hidden talents and to impress upon me how desirable it was to be tiny.

As my parents were trying to rid me of my inferiority complex, the high-school dramatic club decided to put on a production. The leading character called for a person who was small and dark to enact the part of a French girl. Because of my appearance, I won the part. The play was a success and as a result I received many compliments. This part led to many more parts, each more exciting than the previous one. My morale was lifted as I realized that I wasn't a total failure.

I started heeding my parents' advice and tried to think that I heard an envious tone in people's voices as they told me I was of a small stature. This, plus my newly found acting talent, helped me to become readjusted and happy again.

Another aspect of developmental status is illustrated in the question of readjustment of grade assignments. Special promotions or retardations in school should be decided on the basis of total developmental status rather than on the single basis of academic achievement. Learning will be facilitated by seeing that all adjustments made in school are based on the whole organism and not on one or two aspects.

In Chapter XII the concept of maturity is discussed at length. The ideal concepts of maturity presented in the Grograph illustrate readiness for certain forms of adult behavior that are not possible at lower levels of maturity. An adolescent is not *ready* for many adult roles, because he hasn't the necessary insights and skills to understand or to execute them. Therefore he can't be taught them, but he will grow into them when he matures. This is illustrated vividly in the discussions of the tasks of childhood and adolescence, and their places in preparation for adult living, throughout Chapters XIII and XIV.

1806. *Summary.* In the first discussion of learning in Chapter XV, it was said that learning is a process that can be examined in its theoretically pure form, but that after such an examination it has to be put back into its natural setting. Figure 4 suggests that the most important modifying factors in the natural setting are capacity, motivation, and maturity or readiness. Each of them makes some important determinations concerning the nature of learning. Capacity determines to a large extent *how much* a person can learn. Motivation determines largely *when* he will learn, and *how much,* for he will not respond to any stimulus unless he is in a state of need and feels that he can help himself by responding. Readiness determines the *relative difficulty or ease* with which he will move into a new experience, assuming that he has the basic capacity potentially within him. These are powerful modifiers. Those to be discussed in the next chapter are influential, too, but they are much more easily influenced, and can themselves be fairly easily changed by learning under the right conditions.

QUESTIONS FOR REVIEW

1. What is the right combination of group and individual teaching?
2. What does capacity include?
3. Differentiate between general intelligence and special abilities.
4. How is the IQ derived? What is the IQ of a person seven years old with an MA of 92 months?
5. What are some of the uses of the IQ?
6. What are some important cautions in its use?
7. What per cent of the population falls in the range of normal intelligence?
8. What are some important aspects of capacity other than scholastic ability?
9. What seem to be the primary elements of scholastic ability?
10. What differences can exist between people with the same IQ?
11. Review the general expectation for college success at some different IQ levels.
12. Differentiate between intelligence and aptitude.
13. How does motivation affect the success of a lesson presentation?
14. What is an interest? What do interests deal with?
15. What sort of differences exist in value patterns, and how do they affect school activities?
16. What are some useful ways of grouping people to bring out differences in their interests?

17. Why do needs vary for different persons?
18. What is reading readiness? Can it be cultivated? How?
19. What constitutes readiness for arithmetic?
20. What determines readiness for a course?
21. Describe the organismic age concept.
22. What is a developmental age unit? What are some of the commonly used units?
23. Describe a psychologically sound basis for making grade assignments.
24. Why do people of the same chronological age differ in developmental status?
25. Name some personal assets of value in achieving social adjustment.
26. Why is the school interested in individual differences?

SELECTED REFERENCES

Theodora M. Abel and Elaine F. Kinder, *The subnormal adolescent girl* (New York: Columbia University Press, 1942), Chapters I to V.

Luella Cole, *Psychology of adolescence* (3rd ed.; New York: Rinehart and Co., 1948), Chapter XV.

Henry E. Garrett, *Great experiments in psychology* (New York: Appleton-Century-Crofts, Inc., 1941), Chapters I, II, and III.

Arthur I. Gates, Arthur T. Jersild, T. R. McConnell, and Robert C. Challman, *Educational psychology* (New York: The Macmillan Co., 1942), Chapters VII and VIII.

Harold E. Jones, *Development in adolescence* (New York: Appleton-Century-Crofts, Inc., 1943), *passim*.

George D. Stoddard, *The meaning of intelligence* (New York: The Macmillan Co., 1949), Chapter I.

Asahel D. Woodruff and Francis J. DiVesta, "The relationship between values, concepts, and attitudes," *Educational and psychological measurement*, 8 (Winter, 1948), 645-60.

CLASS EXERCISES ON FACTORS THAT MODIFY LEARNING

Things To Do in Class

1. Have each student mark out on scratch paper two rough squares approximately two inches square. At a signal students are to begin tapping in the first square with a pencil as fast as they can. When the first signs of fatigue begin to appear, the teacher will give a signal and the students will shift to

the second square. After ten seconds in the second square the teacher will give a signal to stop tapping. Students will count the marks in the second square. The scores obtained may be listed on the board and will demonstrate individual differences in tapping speed and resistance to muscular fatigue.

2. Administer to the members of the class one or more tests such as the Stenquist or Bennett Mechanical Aptitude, or selected sections of a group mental test. Collect scores anonymously and show the distribution. A short five minute test of reading speed is excellent for this purpose. Surprising individual differences will be found in any college class.

3. Administer a test of personal values, or obtain brief written statements from members of the class on what they consider the most desirable goal in life. Without identifying members of the class, show wide differences in the motivation of class members.

4. Read to the class a list of words that have unfamiliar plurals, asking students to supply the plural form. Check results for differences in vocabulary achievement. A variation is to read the vocabulary of words from the Binet test and ask for a quick check on meanings.

5. Here are two short stories by high-school freshmen. After reading them discuss all the individual differences you can identify in the two authors.

"The New Foreman of the Flying Bar"

Most of the boy of the Flying Bar were working on the Flying Bar rang. When a lone rider was seen in the distance the rider was rapidly becoming larger showing that he was coming towards them. "I wonder who that can be?", exclamied the foreman. Who was a big thickly musled man with a black beard and dark eyes that resembled the eyes of a hawk. His face was scared showing that he had been in many fights. His features resembled a hawk's so much that the cowboys had nicknamed him Hawk. The lone rider was pulling up in front of Hawk now. He was a tall man about six foot two. He was dressed in an old pair of chap, faded blue shirt and an old battered setson was sit cookledy on his head. Are you the foreman of this outfit? He asked Hawk." "I am the foreman here" replied Hawk,". What about it? Do you need another good cowhand here? asked the cowboy. My name is John La Barr. No I don't need any more help replied Hawk. Just then the boss of the Flying Bar rode up and said. "Who is this Hawk?" "Just a cowboy looking for a job" said Hawk. But we got enough as it is. The boss turned to John La Barr, "and asked," "How well can you ride a wild horse". Get me one and I'll show you said John. "Allright" said the boss I will. "Hawk"! said the boss get a couple of the boys and come on. We will let La Barr ride Black Storm. "But Boss"! said Hawk, You know I can't ride ride Black Storm, and I am the best rider around here. "We'll see about that," said the boss. At the ranch they roped Black Storm and "Hawk said" "I will get the saddle." He got the saddle and cut the cinch almost into. He put it on Black Storm and the John La Barr got on; and the horse was let loose but the cinch broke and he was thrown. John got up and looked at the saddle, "and said "this cinch has been cut." "A good excuse" said Hawk. "I'll ride him bare back" said John. And he got on him and rode him. The boss turned to Hawk and said. Get your things packed Hawk I've just Haired a new foreman.

"When Nero Killed His First Roe-Deer"

It was in the late summer months when Nero killed the deer.

Made bold by the truce that reigned in the woods, she was seeking a fragment of fresh vegetation that might not be completely covered by snow.

The hackles on Nero's neck rose when he saw her. The growl died in his throat. He stalked her mercilessly, in perfect silence.

After the kill, the howl that grew and swelled in his great throat filled the forest with the threat of doom.

Every living creature that heard it trembled.

Nero attacked the dead doe savagely. Then, satisfied, he lay panting in the snow to rest.

The twilight deepened.

Suddenly a quiver ran from the great dog's nose to the last hair of his pluming tail. He began to hear now the call of home. Before him lay the mangled body of his prey. The shudder shook him again. Remorse flattened his ears. His tail sank between his legs.

Silently, secretly, oppressed by a sure sense of guilt, he slunk from the shadow of the trees.

6. The following two reports were written by seventh-grade social-studies students. What can you tell about the differences in their achievement?

"Why Am I Interested in My Latin American Neighbors?"

I would like to know if the Latin American countries does much trading? I want to study Mexico very much but I know that Mexico is like our own country in the cities. But in the country of Mexico the people live more sanitary in the city than the people that live outside the city. I know that the coast line is very regular. They have good harbors, a few bays. South America is like North America in one way which is South America is divided into countries. Even though South America is like North America I would like to know the ways that South America is not like North America.

End

(A map of South America appears on the other side of the report.)

"Latin America Country"

It's one of our close neighbor. The catital is Rio de Janeiro. Racial are 50% white, 22% mulatto 14% negro, 13% mestizo. They dress like the U.S.. The country was discovered in 1500 by its own Portuguese Columbus by named. Pedro Alvares, Cabral. They grow: sugar, tea, tobacco, cotton & U.S. don't grow they export most of their crop. Befor the ware we got ton and Ton of sugar. Brazil got their named from one of the trees of the Tropical forest. They have lot of fishing.

7. Have each student bring to class a digest of an article that discusses the educational or vocational possibilities of people at various levels of intelligence.

8. Here are two short case reports taken directly from materials in the student's folder in the high-school office. Each report was compiled in approximately thirty minutes, including brief discussion with one or more teachers. In each case the report is sufficient to indicate the answer to the problem, as subsequent developments clearly proved. What is the cause of the trouble, and what would you suggest as a method of overcoming it in each case?

Case 15

Ralph Richards, a Boy without an Objective

TEACHER'S COMPLAINT:

Not interested in any schoolwork. Stays out of school a great deal and usually very much behind in work. Fights with his older sister in the same school. Dislikes school and wants to quit. Absent 37 times during the year up to February.

Teachers say he comes from a "poor" home. There are many children, with small means to provide for them. Both parents drive taxis, and the home is nothing more than a house where members of the family come and go.

Name: Ralph Richards.
Father and mother, taxi drivers of American extraction.
English is spoken in home.
Parents maintain a home for the whole family, and have a large number of children very nearly the same age. Ralph is one of the older ones. Parents expect him to take care of self so they can care for younger ones.
Age at present, 16-9 (middle of 12th grade).
Intelligence test: Terman, 8th grade, CA 13-2. MA 15-1. Fifth decile.
Achievement tests: Public School Achievement test, at CA 13-2.

Reading, 5th decile. Algebra, 6th decile. English, 2nd decile. Av., 5th D.
No elementary school or junior high school records. Attended parochial school prior to senor high school.

Senior high school marks:

Eng. 1 = 2 *	Gen. Biol. = 2, 1	Sales = 2
Eng. 2 = 3	Gen. Sci. = 3	Retail = 2
Eng. 3 = 3	Civics = 1	Design = 3
Eng. 4 = 3	Soc. Studies = 3	Machine Shop = 3
	History A = 3	Health = F
	Intro. to business = 1	Health = F
	Com. Arith. = 4	Mech. Drawing = Inc.
	Econ. Geog. = 4	
	Typing 1 = F	

Analysis of folder in office. Absences distribute as follows:
Absence for illness (usually earache or toothache) 15.
Absence to accommodate mother (to tend a sick child, etc.) 11.
Truancy through lack of interest, 8.
Disturbance complaints causing him to be sent out of class, 2.
Out of town for test, 1.

* 1 = high, 4 = low.

Note added one year after above data were assembled:
Withdrew from school in May of senior year and went into Navy.
Has written and reported to school since, and reports have come
in from his bases. He is doing good work, is interested in what
he is doing, and making a good record. Has approached the
high school with the request to be told how he can complete his
work and graduate while he is in the Navy.

Case 16

Marion Jay, a Frustrated Student

TEACHER'S COMPLAINT:

Reported by sewing teacher. Will not complete a project.
Begins one and then gets discouraged, saying she can't do it.
Cries a lot in class, especially if any work goes wrong. Asks the
teacher to do her work for her, saying that if she does it herself
it will have to be undone anyway. Losing interest in class work.
Indifferent to any sort of incentives applied by teacher. Likes to
wear nice clothes, and can't afford to buy them, but will not use
her opportunity in school to learn to make them.

Name: Marion Jay.
Living with parents, father works in a hotel as porter.
Age at present, 18-7.
Entered school at age 5-5. Entered Sr. H.S. at age 16-5, (10th
grade).
Now in 12th grade.

Home: Syrian and English languages spoken; nationality Syrian.
Parents both living, they own their home, girl and family have
good health.

Elementary school record:

1932 — 1A, 7Bs, kindergarten.
1933 — 2As, 3Bs, 2Cs, 3Ds, 1F, first grade.
1934 — 3Bs, 9Cs, 1D, first grade repeated.
1935 — 4Bs, 1C, 3Ds, second grade.
1936 — All S marks, third grade. Other marks discontinued at
school.
1937 — All S marks, fourth grade.
1938 — 8Ss, 2S–, fifth grade.
1939 — All S marks, sixth grade.

Junior high school records:

7th grade — 7Bs, 5Cs.
8th grade — 3Bs, 7Cs, 1D.
9th grade — 5Cs, 1D.

Senior high school records:

	1 (high)	2	3	4	5 (low)	F
1942			3	2	1	
1943		1	2	2		3
1944				2		

Other marks on current term's report (1944-45)
   Bookkeeping 4U, Health 5, Elementary Algebra 3, American History 3, English IV 3.

Standard tests recorded

	Reading	Arithmetic	Nat. Int. Test	Henmon-Nelson
Grade	6	6	6	9.9
CA	12-10	12-10	12-10	15-0
Score	59	72	72	37
Decile	10	8	10	9
			MA 10-3	MA 14-4

Note: The family is pushing the girl to take a six unit program this year (senior) and try to graduate.

CHAPTER XIX

SECONDARY MODIFYING FACTORS IN LEARNING

1901. *Adjustment and learning.* Personal and social adjustment frequently determines the extent to which a student is free to use his resources in a wholehearted and unbiased reaction with his environment. Because of that, it is a significant modifying factor in learning. In keeping with the systematic development of the factors sketched in Figure 5, this would be an appropriate time to discuss the ways in which adjustment affects the learning process. To do so now, however, would create unnecessary duplication, since Part V of the book is devoted to adjustment and maladjustment on a larger scale. For that reason this discussion will be limited to a few ideas that are directly related to the modification of learning and will depend on the later chapters to carry the burden of the matter.

Social adjustment. Students differ widely in the extent to which they are accepted by the class or group. A feeling of security depends on adequate acceptance, and without security learning is likely to suffer. Acceptance or rejection may hinge around two fundamental considerations. The typicality or normality of the individual, and his social techniques. Those unfortunate individuals who are different from others in important ways, and who have poor techniques for making and keeping friends, present perplexing problems to the teacher. It is also necessary to know who is unusually well adjusted in the group, or where the lines of natural leadership run in order to take advantage of such individuals in maintaining a high group morale.

Personal adjustment. Unresolved personal problems almost always interfere with schoolwork. They may originate at home, in the school, or in social contacts outside the school. There are a number of ways of studying personal adjustment. Several tests are available. Most of them are subject to serious criticism on validity, but they have practical value if they are understood and used intelligently. Teachers can become aware of common symptoms of personal maladjustment, and simplified check lists may be used to lend objectivity to the observation of students. It is unwise to overlook cases of poor personal adjustment for two reasons, for such a condition interferes with the work of the student and of the class, and unless corrected tends to keep the individual from developing optimally and from enjoying life as he might.

Maladjustment always implies an unresolved conflict. Hence, a maladjusted person is always intensely occupied with at least one problem that does not leave him alone at any time. It may be so severe that it occupies the center of his attention and tends to exclude other things. Any competing stimulus would have to be quite significant to such an individual to take precedence over the conflict. In less severe form a conflict may operate as a constant bias in his perception of other things, so that he has a tendency to interpret everything around him in terms of his conflict. This is especially noticeable in a paranoid, who makes persecution out of everything, even out of actual efforts to help him. A conflict may be relatively mild, and operate primarily as a distraction that breaks irregularly into situations, and makes attention a fleeting or unstable thing. It is very difficult to react in a wholehearted fashion to anything when one is involved in an unresolved problem.

On the other hand an adjusted individual is free. He can perceive broadly, because he is not so compulsorily preoccupied. He is usually more sensitive to the possible meanings of a situation, because he does not bring a constant mental set with him. He can stay with a task longer and enjoy it more than one whose attention is constantly being demanded by worries.

The successful mastery of school lessons, and the ability to profit from extra-classroom activities depends on freedom to immerse oneself in them and make the interaction as full and exploratory as possible. This is seriously limited by maladjustment.

1902. *Predisposing habits, traits, and prejudices.* It was just stated that the adjusted individual is free to perceive broadly and accurately. This is only partly true, because adjustment is just one of the factors of its kind that can interfere with learning, through upsetting perception. Various kinds of prejudices operate also as selective factors in perception, and while they do not exclude possible perceptual experiences as the severe preoccupations with conflict do, they manhandle them rather badly so that at times they scarcely resemble reality at all, as they finally register. Three such factors are prejudices, habits, and traits. They will serve the purposes of this section, and illustrate how learning may be modified by the set of the individual.

Selective perception. The principal structure of the psychology of perceptual distortion was outlined in Chapter IX. In brief, the individual may be said to perceive what he is prepared to perceive in a situation. This has been shown to be related to personal values, to amount of familiarity and consequent reduction of cues, and some other things. It is also true that a person tends to have some trouble perceiving things he is not prepared to see. For example, in the development of concepts and learning names to go with them, it is true that having learned to conceive a thing in a certain way makes it relatively more difficult to conceive that same thing in a second and different way. If a word is used in connection with one conceptual meaning, it is harder to develop another conceptual meaning for that word than it was to develop the first meaning.[1] Meltzer says concepts serve as a footing for perception and reasoning, as guides to action. Therefore, incorrectly formed concepts give rise to distortion of further processes of perception, and result in the formulation of false new concepts.[2]

---

[1] J. A. Gengerelli, "Mutual interference in the evolution of concepts," *American Journal of psychology*, 38 (1927), 639-46.

[2] Hyman Meltzer, *Children's social concepts*, Contributions to Education, No. 192 (New York: Teachers College, Columbia University, 1925).

For some people, notably optimists, desire has an influence on what is believed. Cronbach reports correlations ranging from 0.74 to -0.27 between belief and desire.[3] Obviously, within his group there is considerable variation from person to person. Ambiguity, familiarity, plausibility, importance, and a desire to acquiesce seem to be factors in determining belief also.

Some people are more logical and scientific in their reactions to situations than others. Students who go to technical colleges have that characteristic more markedly than those who attend non-technical colleges, but even in their behavior Sinclair and Tolman [4] see no evidence that logicality or reasonableness transfer from scientific fields to social or ethical considerations.

It is difficult to change the naïve beliefs that children bring to school with them. Superstitions from early childhood tend to hold on through school. Education neither removes nor prevents them, as indicated in a number of studies summarized by Lichtenstein.[5]

These are indications of the kinds of findings that have been reported in the last twenty years, from studies of prejudice, concept formation, and attitude. They warn every teacher that in going before a class to make an assignment, discuss an idea, ask a question, give an instruction, or attempt any form of communication, he faces the selective processes that distort perception and make it fit what the individual is ready to see, or wants to see. The significance of this factor in modifying learning can hardly be overrated. The only safeguard against it is the practice of having assignments and new ideas discussed back and forth, so that distortions that are present can be detected and corrected. If the teacher cares to examine his ways of presenting ideas, in the light of the amount of selective perception he finds

[3] Lee J. Cronbach, and Betty Mae Davis, "Belief and desire in wartime," *Journal of abnormal and social psychology*, 39, No. 4 (October, 1944), 446-58.

[4] J. H. Sinclair, and Ruth S. Tolman, "An attempt to study the effect of scientific training upon prejudice and illogicality of thought," *Journal of educational psychology*, 24 (May, 1933), 362-70.

[5] Arthur Lichtenstein, *Can attitudes be taught?* Johns Hopkins University Studies in Education, No. 21 (Baltimore: Johns Hopkins Press, 1934).

operating in his classes, he should be able to improve his presentations. New experiences that must compete with existing points of view will need to have all the vigor and clarity it is possible to put into them.

Habits. This aspect of one's executive behavior gets its resistance to change from the satisfaction it continues to provide to the individual and the fact that it happens without conscious direction, and often without awareness. For the second reason, it is difficult to break up a habit because it starts before the individual realizes it and can't be easily repressed. For the first reason, every repetition furnishes a significant strengthening of the old patterns and keeps them in force. New and more desired habits can't get established because the old ones take such good care of the little needs they serve. If a new act can't get itself practiced when the need is present, obviously it can't become established. Of course, if the individual can devote himself to a round-the-clock watch for a week or two, he can probably break up an old habit and get a new one started, but most people will not pay such a price. Hence habits tend to remain.

In a similar manner skills tend to level off at the point where they serve the individual adequately. It is difficult to bring them up to higher levels, although it can be done by practice. Handwriting can be greatly improved through practice, but it degenerates rapidly to a serviceable level unless the individual gives it constant attention. When psychomotor patterns become set, it is difficult to introduce new patterns without disrupting others and meeting resistance. Left or right handedness furnishes a good illustration. It is possible to change, or to become bi-manual, but the established order does not break over easily. Early attempts to learn typing or any other similar skill in which poor form was present make doubly hard the acquisition of good form later.

Traits. Here is another executive aspect of behavior that was discussed in Chapter V. It is an outgrowth of self-appraisal, in which the individual has worked out various roles for himself in relation to other people, because those roles work out best for him. Again because of the continual reinforcement derived from their practice, the roles keep themselves in force and prevent new ventures in behavior which could upset or change them. When the student participates in school he does so in harmony with the roles he has adopted. Those roles will determine a number of things about his further learning. For example, if he has become a dominant individual, he will tend to take a leading role in class and school activities. He will therefore have many opportunities for development and will grow accordingly. If he were a submissive individual, he would tend to avoid such opportunities and forego the development they offer. Furthermore, the dominant individual will inject many of his own ideas into his interactions, and wield influence on the thinking of others, bringing them somewhat to his own points of view. The submissive individual will receive, and shape himself by incoming percepts. The atmosphere in a classroom is often as much determined by the traits of one or two students, as by the teacher's presence.

A confident individual will have higher levels of aspiration than a fearful one. He will look farther into his subjects, welcome more extensive responsibilities, and work with less concern for the outcome. The timid individual works hesitantly, avoids new ventures, courts security by being more agreeable than critical, and therefore misses educational opportunities that sometimes make the difference between good achievement and great achievement.

These traits determine the social atmosphere in a class, making it smooth and harmonious, warm and comfortable, cold and forbidding, or unstable and unpredictable. Under the conditions that prevail for the group as a whole, each individual adjusts to his educational activities as best he can. Regardless of capacity, motivation, readiness, good adjustment or any other factors, this one too affects learning through determining the manner in which the individual will participate with his social and physical environment.

1903. *Health and energy.* In the past there has been a tendency to conceive the health of the child much too narrowly, and to fail to catch the full significance of even physical illness. Even now, in many instances, the physical examination is a protective device for the other students to a far greater extent than it is a diagnostic device for regulating the experiences of the individual. It is a splendid thing to have all school children subjected to some sort of physical inspection to prevent the spread of disease. It should be carried much farther than it has gone. In spite of it the school is one of the most potent trading centers for colds and the common childhood diseases.

In addition to the prevention of further infection, the health program should be turned toward the adjustmental and developmental problems of the individual child. It takes energy to grow, to overcome sickness or strain, to work, to study, and to play. Everything the child does makes its claim on his available energy. Whatever he has to draw upon can be divided out only as far as it will go, after which he begins to work at a decreased rate of efficiency. Health is a state in which *all* the resources of the individual are in good condition, and he is able to function well all over. He is far more than a physical organism. He is a social being, and he has an intensive personal world, in both of which realms he has demanding needs that are not satisfied without a price in energy. Each of these realms takes out something from his total inventory of energy, and each puts in something that helps to determine what his total inventory is. When one aspect of his make-up is not contributing, his total drive will not be up to par. But it is even worse than that. The part that is not contributing will probably be draining off more than its share of energy, so that his total output is not available for distribution over the normal demands of a healthy child. It matters little which part of him is preempting more than its normal energy, he will be below par for some of his normal activities.

Olsen [6] has established quite firmly the child-as-a-whole way of looking at health. In twenty years of making longitudinal studies of growth and development he has accumulated growth records and charts in which the organismic

6 Willard C. Olsen, and Byron O. Hughes, "Growth of the child as a whole," In *Child Behavior and Development*, Barker, Kounin and Wright, eds. New York: McGraw-Hill, Inc., 1943. Chap. XII.

integrity of the child is clearly apparent. Chronological age norms for development in height, weight, grip, dentition, bone ossification, educational achievement, and several other lines of growth have been used to derive developmental age scores similar in nature to the mental age score in intelligence testing. When the developmental age scores for all measured aspects of growth are averaged, as of any given date in the child's life, an organismic age score is obtained which is the composite of his total growth at that time. This score may be higher or lower than chronological age and has a high degree of stability throughout the growing years of the individual's life. Curves plotted from successively derived organismic ages are almost straight lines, with practically no deviations from one point to another in the trend. Because of this tendency for the organismic age to show steady growth, in spite of rather wide possible variations in the single strands of growth mentioned above, it has been regarded as a center of gravity for the individual, and indicates that he has a fairly constant amount of total energy available for everything he does. When one aspect of his structure is using more than it previously used, some other aspect is found to be using less.

If this concept is valid, and it seems now to be quite well established, it also applies to health, for health is just a way of describing the condition of the organism with reference to its readiness for action. A full health examination would have to include physical, social, and personal checkup. A physical examination is not enough to determine whether a child is ready to take on a full day's educational struggle. There is not the slightest doubt that one can be quite ill within his personal needs, and thereby be so badly incapacitated that he is incapable of functioning adequately in school.

A still further fallacy in physical examinations lies in their reliance upon the presence or absence of symptoms of disease for deciding whether the child is fit to attend school. When this superficial type of examination is made, and it is ordinarily found primarily where large numbers of children are being hurried through by one overworked nurse or doctor, children who are physically tired, or poorly fed, may be passed by and declared ready for school. Tired children not infrequently sleep in school, and they can scarcely help themselves. Underfed or improperly fed children lack normal vitality, which reduces their ability to concentrate on study, and participate in physical activities.

The case of Marion Jay [7] illustrates the interference of badly upset personal needs. Through excessive failure Marion had reached a point where she couldn't make herself try persistently. She turned away from unrewarding effort toward compensatory behavior. When her illness was diagnosed and cured, she became well to the point of resuming her normal attack on schoolwork.

Students who cannot see or hear well enough to keep up with what is going on in the classroom should be moved into positions in which they can see and hear. If such readjustments do not prove enough, they should be referred for examinations. Teachers should be aware of health records in the school office, and be particularly on the alert for special disabilities, such as heart ailments, or other conditions that justify special regulation of activity.

Here is a case in which poor vision was responsible for a general breakdown in function.

Case 17

Vision and School Achievement

My eyes have always been very poor. Glasses were fitted to me when I was in the first grade. They were shell-rimmed affairs, quite dark and reddish in appearance. I felt very conspicuous for my presence. In the later part of the fifth grade I discontinued wearing them entirely.

The last half of my sixth year I was again fitted to glasses. This time, silver-colored rims, but the lenses were bi-focals, and I felt like a grandmother to my peers. I wore these constantly for a year, after the first few weeks, the oddity of a child's wearing bi-focals was no longer a novelty to my teachers or classmates.

In the latter half of the seventh grade, we moved to New York State, from our western home. This was the first time I had ever

[7] See page 365.

changed schools and in that year, many new things came about. In my new school I got along just fine in everything except geography. The study of the geography of New York State was entirely new to me.

At this time my glasses caused particular embarrassment. Even with their aid I could not see the blackboard. The teacher had me in the last seat in the last row. Many times I was asked to recite from the board, I read jerkily, a matter which provoked the teacher. One day she demanded that I smooth out my reading. I tried to do better, but could not see, tears came to my eyes, and the situation grew worse. Finally, I told her I would read smoothly if I could see it in the first place. Of course, such impudence wasn't accepted. She told me I had glasses and should be able to see. All this time I was standing at my seat in the back of the room and all eyes were turned upon me.

The teacher probably thought I was using my eyes as an excuse for my poor reading. No matter what she thought she should have tried some subtle ways of finding out if my eyes were really poor.

Her general attitude made me feel guilty that I had poor eyes. Classroom tensions began to pervade my play, the children quizzed me, and I began to feel very inferior. I began to develop a negativistic attitude toward her, and became obstinate.

Later, she removed the pressure and did not require me to read from the board. I became better adjusted in the other (class) rooms and was doing well. Apparently my situation was discussed among the teachers, for I began to feel that she respected my abilities.

In this broad concept, health is a very significant factor in modifying learning. The current trend is to shift health over more and more into what has been long called personality adjustment, that is, a condition in which everything about the organism is in sound condition. It is a good trend. Application of its basic concepts to education can improve the quality of learning.

QUESTIONS FOR REVIEW

1. Why is adjustment a factor in learning?
2. What causes preoccupation of such intense nature as to prevent learning?
3. In what way does a habit prevent learning in school?

4. What effect can traits have on a student's reactions in school?
5. How do childhood views interfere with study in science?
6. Name several aspects of total health.
7. In what ways are school practices violating the organismic idea of health?
8. What significant reason is there for talking of the child-as-a-whole?

SELECTED REFERENCES

Roger G. Barker, Jacob S. Kounin, and Herbert F. Wright, *Child behavior and development* (New York: McGraw-Hill Book Co., 1943), Chapter XII.

Harold E. Jones, *Development in adolescence* (New York: Appleton-Century-Crofts, Inc., 1943), Chapters V and VI.

CHAPTER XX

OTHER MODIFYING FACTORS IN LEARNING—
SCHOOL, HOME, NEIGHBORHOOD

2001. *Introduction.* In previous chapters the discussion has followed a pattern that began with the nature of human behavior, its observable aspects and what can be learned from watching them, and the causative factors that control behavior. From there attention was narrowed to learning, which is the process by which behavior is developed and changed. Learning was isolated as a pure process first, then broadened into its component types, and pursued further into some of the mental processes that determine its outcomes. Attention was then turned from the process itself to the individual student and the effect produced on his learning by his own capacity, motives, maturity, adjustment, perceptual sets, and health. It is time now to go out beyond the individual student to the setting in which he works and to complete the process of putting together all of the things that cooperate in determining what a person will become. If this sequence from an academic concept of learning, to an individual student developing in his home, school, and neighborhood is not clearly visualized, there should be enough rapid review of the outline of the book to make it clear. Otherwise it is quite possible that what precedes this chapter will be regarded as having no unity with this discussion, and the full appreciation of what learning involves will be missed.

2002. *Learning differentiated from going to school.* There are many educated people in the world who acquired their education outside of schools. Learning is not confined to the schoolroom. It is one of nature's constant processes. It has been going on as long as there has been a nervous system in a living organism. Men learned before schools were formed. Men learn today while they work, play, eat, and even while they sleep. A school is just a place in which people pay deliberate attention to learning, and try to guide it toward selected goals. Sometimes learning takes place in schools, too, but sometimes it does not. Going to school should help very much and usually does. So the school should be seen for what it is, and not confused with the process it was built to cultivate. In the same sense, the home and the community are educational agencies, sharing with the school in the task of teaching young people how to live more satisfactorily. For the present, then, instead of seeing education from inside a school, and regarding the child, the home, and the neighborhood as external parties that come to the school and fit into its program, let us shift the center of orientation to the child. From that point of observation, let us see how the home, the school, and the neighborhood loom up as three parts of his environment. It is himself and his life that is central, that gives cohesion to his experiences in these three institutions. For him, there is no school program, there is just a way in which the school fits into his program. There is no community program, but just a way in which the community fits into his program. With the home it is different. He is part of his home and it is part of him. He belongs there, and it is his base of operations.

This proposal would move the school out of the center of any orbit, and make it just one element in a structure built around something else—a growing child. Almost every new educational idea that has gained acceptance in recent years is implicitly based on this point of view. There is still a tendency, however, for the school to regard itself as an institution with a special dispensation of wisdom and competency, and to be annoyed when the home and the community attempt to reach into its program and alter it. With greater clarity in our views of the whole educative process, however, that will break down into a genuine sharing, both in the activities around the lives of people, and in the mutual interchange of suggestions for the improvement of all three, the home, the school, and the community.

Since education is the child's function, then, and he

participates in three institutions intimately in his educational activities, each one deserves some scrutiny to see how it affects learning and how it could work best with the other two.

2003. *The school and the teacher.* The school is an institution, not a process. It is an organized group of teachers with materials prepared and set aside for the use of students. Its effect on learning depends on what it contains, how it is organized, and how it operates.

Schools exist because it is assumed they can speed learning, can see that every pupil has an opportunity to learn, and can

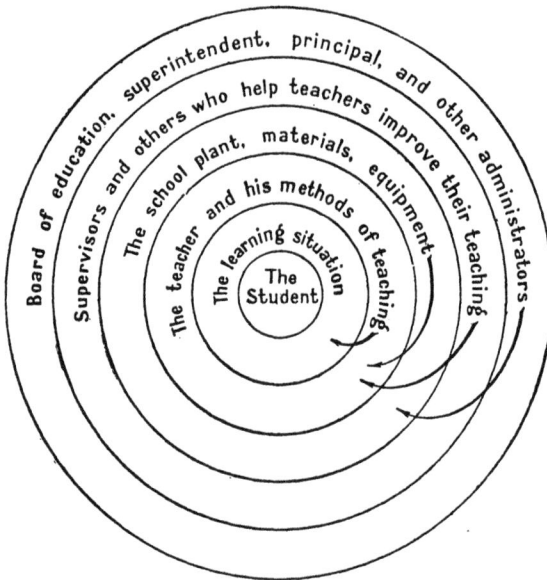

FIG. 7.   FUNCTIONAL RELATIONSHIPS WITHIN THE SCHOOL

do all this more efficiently than can be done without organization. These assumptions have some implications for the form of organization and the administration of schools: (1) The student must be the central figure in the school both in terms of action, and in terms of priority of needs. (2) Other elements of the school must function primarily for the good of the pupil. (3) Efficiency in learning is more important than efficiency in non-learning matters in the management of the school, but both are desirable.

Figure 7 illustrates one way of conceiving the proper relationship of the various components of a modern school. The student occupies the central position. The most important part of the school system to the student is the setting in which he will learn, the actual on-going learning experience within the classroom. Therefore it stands next to the student in the diagram. The teacher who manipulates the learning situation is the next most important part of the school. Probably the most significant aid to the teacher is the school plant, which includes the building and all the equipment and materials available to the student and teacher. Looking in upon all this is the supervisor, who works with the teacher much as the teacher works with the student. Preparing the physical stage for the supervisor and teachers is the administrative staff, including the board of education and all its subsidiary officers down to the staff of the individual school. Each of the concentric rings of the figure represents a part of the school organization that should perform its function in such a way that it contributes to the effectiveness of those parts that are more centrally located. As long as this relationship is maintained, the school is likely to be moving toward its major objectives. Progress will be hindered to the extent that this relationship is forgotten or changed.

Student-teacher teamwork. As suggested earlier, the educative process involves three tasks, which are so interrelated that they go on at the same time, but which can profitably be separated for analysis: (1) The student does the learning. (2) The teacher does the teaching. (3) Both of them must make a satisfactory adjustment to the school situation. The teacher cannot reach into the student's learning process, but he can do things as an onlooker that may influence the learning behavior of the student. The student's work is quite different from the teacher's. The student pays attention to what he is learning. The teacher pays attention to the student. They watch each other with regard to personal adjustment and social satisfaction during the process.

The psychological aspects of the teacher's influence on the

student are extremely significant with reference to how the teacher should do his work. Figure 8 illustrates how inaccessible the mental processes of the student are to the teacher. It is as if the teacher were trying to control the behavior of a child within a box, when the only means of communication consist of a porthole for passing in food, a window through which the child may look out, a sound system for sending in sounds, and a ventilator for sending in air. The only other means of influencing the student within would be to whack the box or shake it, a practice of little if any educational worth. As implied in this illustration, the brain of the

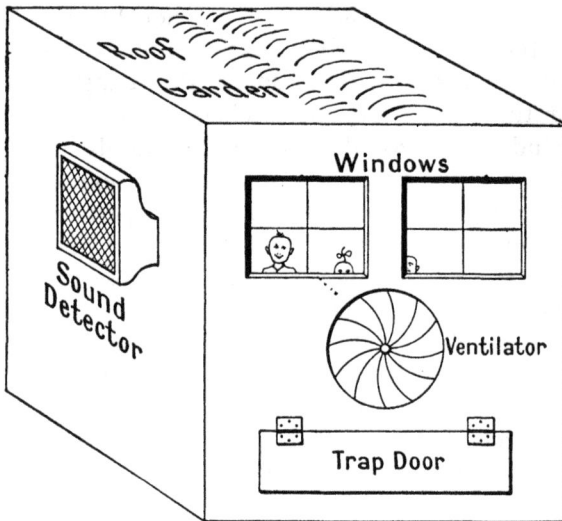

Fig. 8. The Difficulty of Getting Through to the Student

student is beyond the teacher's reach. What goes on in the student's mental processes cannot be controlled directly by the teacher. Those mental processes respond to stimuli from the outside such as light waves, sound waves, tastes, smells, and temperature changes, as in the customary processes of making assignments, having discussions, using visual aids, and the like. They also respond when a student is slapped or ridiculed or punished in any manner. The response, however, is never completely determined by what the teacher does on the outside. It depends to a large degree on the student's pattern of meaning and values. Obviously, it is an art of the highest sort to so stimulate students as to get them to act in desired ways. Under the conditions thus pictured, it is clear that good relations between the teacher and the student are the best answer to the question of influence. The teacher must understand the student, and the student must understand, respect, and trust the teacher. Developing an understanding of the child is a form of evaluation, and is discussed in Chapters XXV to XXVII.

The teacher's personality is a major factor in determining the kind of teamwork between teacher and student. Another important factor is the type of social relationship in the school, including teachers and students as a single population. All of these matters enter into the school environment. They make up the conditions under which the student works. The teacher's task is to manipulate these conditions in such a way that the student learns efficiently those things which contribute toward the major objectives of education.

Manipulating conditions—the teacher's task. The teacher has the responsibility of seeing that the students are able to satisfy their important needs. This requires a general knowledge of the common needs and interests of all children, and the ability to recognize the specific needs and to interpret the behavior of each student. This can be done when the teacher is familiar with the facts about motivation and mental health, and is sensitive to indications of how things are going for the individual student.

Part of the task of manipulating the conditions of the school is the cultivation of a state of good personal relations between all the members of the school community. This requires that teachers keep themselves in a state of mental health and cultivate desirable personality characteristics, as well as that they keep before them the objective of wholesome personality development for each student in the school. This can be done when the teacher knows the facts about the development of personality and about social relationships and their part in living.

A third part of the teacher's task is the maintenance of conditions in which the fullest self-realization is possible for everyone in the school. This involves the use of democratic procedures, realistic experiences, challenging situations, and opportunities for exploring the world and becoming acquainted with it on a wide basis. Such conditions are most likely to be maintained when the teacher believes in the integrity of the individual student and in the right of each person to live a satisfying, upward-looking life. It also requires a knowledge of the principles of human growth and development and of the factors that promote the kind of living that fits into the philosophy of democracy.

The fourth aspect of the teacher's task in manipulating conditions in the school is that of using proper methods of conducting the course of study. This involves knowing the learning process so well that a student's position in any given stage of learning can easily be diagnosed. It also involves an easy familiarity with the psychological nature of subject matter and the ability to adapt teaching methods to the particular objective of the moment, whether it be a motor skill, a concept, a taste, a degree of analytical ability, or a fact lodged in the memory.

Providing for motivation at three levels. It is typical of educators in general that they confine their discussions of motivation to ways of making the student carry out a specific unit of work. It is implicitly assumed that whether the student enjoys his lesson depends on how well the teacher succeeds in making the lesson attractive. As a matter of fact, such a point of view amounts to putting the cart before the horse. It is an attempt to deny the old proverb that "You can lead a horse to water but you can't make him drink." If the horse has been led to water when he doesn't need a drink, why should he drink? If the student has been led to the wrong lesson, or to a lesson he does not need and has no reason for wanting, why should he like it or want to participate in it?

In the interests of sound motivation it is suggested that there are three levels at which motivation must be considered. When it is not considered at the highest level, the burden is increased at the next two levels. When it is not considered at either of the two higher levels, as is often the case, the burden is so great at the lower level that it is impossible to carry it successfully.

(1) The first level is that of the curriculum. The student has the right to be placed in a curriculum that runs in the direction he wants and needs to go. There are two fundamental questions to be asked of any curriculum before a student is committed to it. Does it lead where he wants to go? Does the student *see* that it leads where he wants to go? There is no excuse for having to shove a student through a curriculum that leads in a direction he will finally approve, even when it is known that he will eventually appreciate it. The most important opportunity to stir up his motives and make him work independently and vigorously is lost when the school fails to take the time and trouble to sell its wares to the student. This task belongs jointly to the counseling program and the classroom teacher.

(2) The next level at which motivation should be considered is that of the course or subject. The same questions are in order. Does it make an important contribution to the student's major goals? Does he *see* that it does? Granted that the student has been enrolled in the proper curriculum for him, it is possible to show that almost any course in the curriculum has value for him. Because that value is apparent to the teacher or the administrator is no proof that it is apparent to the student. Time taken at the beginning of a course to show students how the course will be of value to them in a realistic way pays rich dividends in highly motivated effort throughout the course. This task, too, should be shared by the counseling program and the classroom teacher.

(3) The third level is that of the lesson or daily unit of work. Is the unit vital to the student? Does it fit into the objective of the course? Is it launched in such a way that its value is clear? Does the student know what is expected of him in the lesson? Is the unit handled in such a way that it is as enjoyable as possible? This task is the teacher's.

The difference between counseling or guidance activities and teaching is more imaginary than real. The major purpose of each is to find out what the student needs and wants, and to provide for it as efficiently as possible. Teaching is not to be confined to the mastery of subject matter. It has a prior task, a very important task, of teaching the child the *importance* of the curriculum, the subject, and the lesson. If this were done well, considerably less high-pressure teaching of subject matter would be needed, because the student would learn gladly and energetically.

The school plant. There is an important relationship between the materials of the school and the learning process: (1) Sensory aids are a valuable means of enriching experience so that concepts develop rapidly and accurately. (2) Reading materials also enrich experience and enlarge its boundaries if they are selected to match the needs and developmental level of the students. (3) Architectural arrangements affect learning in two ways. They influence the physical comfort and efficiency of the students and teachers, and they contribute to the pleasantness or unpleasantness of the educative process. Conditions of light, heat, ventilation, sound control, and physical comfort may add to or detract from the student's progress in learning. The beauty of the room, the balance in its design, and other forms of esthetic enrichment become effective by the process of conditioning in helping the student form likes and dislikes within his various experiences.

Other parts of the school. The contribution of supervisors, superintendents, principals, and other administrative and supervisory staff members is made in their service to the teacher. The supervisor watches the teacher and student in their interaction while the teacher watches the student who watches the experience within which he is learning. The administrator has the task of providing as efficiently as possible whatever the teacher and supervisor require for their work. All of them work to the same end, the achievement of the objectives of education. The result of their coordinated efforts is the educative process—organized and directed learning.

Characteristics of a good school. There are still heated discussions going on in schools of education over which of the cults should rule the school. Progressivism seems currently to be opposed to the Life-Adjustment program. The content people argue with the methods people. In the meantime school goes on and thousands of individual teachers go into their classrooms and use their unique individual ways of stimulating young people. If all the outstanding teachers were identified and observed, some of the steam would disappear from the academic arguments. Among these best teachers would be many so-called progressives and many so-called subject-centered traditionalists. If all the progressives were compared, there would be more differences than similarities in their methods of teaching. The same is true for the traditionalists. A good school is not made by mental commitment to a particular school of thought. It is made by good individual teachers doing their work in good individual ways and maintaining an atmosphere in which development is encouraged.

Such an atmosphere can best be depicted through certain basic characteristics of its over-all program, and by describing the kind of person who teaches in that program.

In its over-all aspects a number of criteria of quality can be mentioned. Any list of criteria is necessarily only suggestive, for it is unlikely that two individuals would produce the same list, although many of the ideas contained in the suggestions of serious observers would be alike. The faculty is the most important element of a school. Teachers should be employed who *know students, understand their problems, and work comfortably with them.* This would take care of the vital matter of personal relationships, making them enjoyable for both students and teachers. It would also tend to guarantee sound guidance to the students, which is not possible when teachers do not know their students. Of equal importance, the *teachers should be healthy and well-adjusted themselves.* There is an amazing tendency for maladjusted people to want to become counselors. They seem to feel they can solve all the problems in the world but their own. They often show a morbid interest in the details of other people's conflicts. Were it not for the careful selection practices in colleges, such people would overrun the programs in clinical psychology. No one who is embroiled in personal conflicts is in a position to give balanced guidance to someone else.

Within the program of the whole school there should be *the utmost effort to avoid arousing unpleasant emotions in the students.* Much of the tension that exists is unnecessary. It frequently grows out of the making of rules and their rigid enforcement on everyone uniformly. Rules help systematize things, but individual differences in growing children do not fit well into systematization, especially where personality problems exist and need attention. Administrative officers. cannot avoid making serious mistakes in regulating students. if they do not keep in very close touch with the students.

Since some emotional tensions will always be aroused in groups, the school should *make provision for adequate release of emotional pressure.* The means of doing so will differ with age level, and will need variety at each level to meet the needs. Activities used for this purpose should be chosen in the light of student needs and capacities. Sometimes they are rendered unfit for this purpose by turning them into highly controlled learning situations, whereby they often begin to engender more pressures, instead of relieving those that already exist.

The instructional program of the school should be arranged solely on the basis of *sound objectives.* Since the school is a service institution set up by the community for its own children, the obligation exists to discuss objectives with parents and other adults in the community. Although this is not often done, it would obviate difficulty in the end, and result in communitywide betterment through broad mutual education of the adults on the needs of children.

In the light of the sound objectives, the *methods of conducting classes and actvities should be based first and foremost on the psychological facts about growth, development, and learning.* A great many teachers are using classroom procedures they inherited from their own childhood and high-school teachers, and even worse, their college teachers. They do not know whether the methods are psychologically sound, because they have had no help from psychology in learning how to make such an analysis. Much of what they do.

is psychologically right, but some of it is not, and they should be able to tell which is which so that they can improve what they are doing. Education in service is almost inescapable for this sort of improvement.

As the final criterion in this list, *the school should maintain very close contact with its community,* in several ways. Conferences on its program and objectives should include parents and business people, community leaders, and specialists in community life. People trained only in education do not have sufficient background to do this vital job alone. Their training is a specialization within the larger community life program, but what the school should be *attempting* to do is a community responsibility fundamentally. Teachers should be brought into a community only when they are prepared to *conduct themselves in harmony with the community's mores and cultural pattern.* People who are fundamentally individualists talk a great deal about their personal rights, and overlook the collective rights of a community to protect the patterns of life it feels are valuable. If an individual feels his own values are threatened by a particular code of behavior, let him get out of that threatening situation into one in which he feels a greater sense of self-fulfillment, and at the same time avoid becoming a threat to the former situation. The curriculum of the school should include a number of ways of *getting students out into the community on educational missions,* both for their own development and for the information of the community. Such moves promote solidarity through all of the agencies that serve child development, and provide good stimulation for the adults.

Characteristics of a good teacher. In addition to the two characteristics mentioned above, *teachers should continue to grow as they teach.* All adults should do this, but with teachers it is mandatory for the sake of their work. Otherwise they become obsolete, and serve as examples of what the school is attempting to overcome. The teacher should continue to *examine his efforts until he feels that he is doing a satisfying job,* so that he can maintain the right kind of personal influence in all his relationships. A constant feeling of failure creates a bad environment for children. He should *maintain a satisfying private life,* with whatever he needs in the way of recreation to keep himself fit. This is more important to his students than a continual load of work after hours, which drains his good will and turns him into a martyr.

Within his own field of specialization the teacher must be a master. It makes no difference that he may be teaching the subject at an elementary level. Unless he is thoroughly at home in it himself, he cannot possibly give it the real attractiveness and value that is inherent in all of the subjects taken from our cultural heritage. One of his most important responsibilities is to reveal that value to his students. In addition to this he must be *broadly educated so that he can see his own field in true perspective,* as *one* of the elements that make up the whole culture, and only as one. Education does not consist just of English, or history, or home arts, but of whatever is required to make human living. This point of view *he must demonstrate personally.* Otherwise it is just a cliché which everyone speaks, but which no one comprehends. Finally, there must be a *genuine love of young people, and contentment to spend one's life working with them.* Such a commitment has its gains and its losses. The teacher must be contented with them, or he should not stay in the business.

These are rather demanding criteria. They would have little value if they were not. The schools will be of little value, too, unless they aspire to maintain standards equivalent to these criteria. The basic consideration is what is required to educate children in the best way, not what is an easy and comfortable situation for the school staff.

2004. *The home and parents.* Strategically, the home and parents occupy the most important position in the child's educational environment. They might well have been discussed before the school and the teachers, except for the fact that this whole book is devoted to preparation for teaching, and the school is the principal agency in which teaching is formalized and recognized as the major occupation.

There are two ways in which the home influences the child's learning. One is the direct influence, amounting almost to control, throughout the preschool years. The child's fundamental concepts of life, his values, most of his habits, and his basic adjustments are established during these years. As shown earlier, they reach over into the school years and exert a selective influence on what is learned then. The predominant influence in these early years is the parents, and their points of view.

There is in addition to this, however, an influence that is being exerted on the child during all the school years, which supports or undermines the efforts of the school and community. The case of Connie Casey was mentioned in Chapter XII. Upon investigation, it was learned that her father had no use for education for girls. Her work in the college-entrance curriculum was in direct opposition to his wishes, and created tension at home, which certainly had its ramifications in school. Even more noticeable, however, is the effect produced on Connie's school behavior by two other home factors, seriously deficient diet, and inadequate provision of a setting in which Connie could meet her would-be friends.

The influence of the home is very pervasive. It precedes the child to school, and marks him before he can speak for himself. He is not just Johnny in school, he is that Hammond boy. Whatever his family is known for follows him and determines attitudes toward him, which in turn beget reciprocal attitudes from him.

Ralph Richard's problem is presented in Chapter XVIII. Note that eleven times during the year his mother kept him out of school to tend the baby, and his parents did nothing to correct earache and toothache, which kept him out an additional fifteen times. Beyond this, much of his lack of interest in school could be traced to the fact that no one had ever talked with him about what he was going to become, or how schooling could help him, or any of the values to be found through self-development. The parents were busy, as most parents are, but therein they undermined the educational program of the school, for Ralph could find no value in attending. He became a very industrious student later when he discovered a goal toward which he wanted to move.

In the same chapter the case of Marion Jay illustrates another kind of home influence. Here is a girl with low capacity, but with a family who want her to make an achievement in school by graduating with her class. That it is a physical impossibility is probably not known to them, but they are urging her to take a six-point program during her senior year. There is certain frustration and failure awaiting the girl, if the influence of the home prevails.

Here is another case in which the cooperation of the home resulted in removal of a difficulty for a student.

Case 18

How a Home Helped a Student's Adjustment in School

When I was in the lower classes of grade school, my voice was harsh and nasal, due to a condition of my tonsils and adenoids. Whenever I was asked to read in class, I was extremely embarrassed and made many unnecessary blunders. As soon as I heard my name called I became very nervous before I started to read a word. I believe my teacher realized that something was bothering me, and she tried to help by calling on me as little as possible. I also believe during Parent-Teacher week she spoke to my mother about my condition. Since I hadn't acted that way at home, mother was surprised. The result was I had my tonsils and adenoids removed a short time later and gradually gained more confidence in myself until I no longer dreaded the reading situations.

In the following case the manner in which pressures at home can result in the development of conflicts and maladjustment, is well illustrated.

Case 19

How a Home Hindered a Student's School Adjustment

It happened in grammar school. I was in the third grade at the time and just learning to use pen and ink. Every day after class, I'd come home with ink spots on my dress much to the disapproval of my guardian. One day she put a new dress on me and warned me not to dare to come home with ink marks on it. That morning our task was to fill the ink bottles and as luck would have it, my bottle fell upon the desk, sending the ink in all directions. My dress was a thorough ruin, no amount of wiping would remove the stains. I was terribly afraid to go home and lingered around the school long after class was out. Finally, I knew I could stall no longer and decided to face the music. My guardian was in a rage of temper at the sight of the damage and demanded to know what had happened. I was afraid to tell her the truth and so tried lying my way out. I told her the janitor had been filling the ink bottles and had accidentally dropped one my way. She said nothing as I told my story and when I had finished went over to the telephone to call the school. I ran to my room and burst into tears. I knew she'd find out the truth. That evening nothing happened.

The next morning, the teacher asked to see me during recess. She wanted to know why I had blamed the accident on the janitor. I told her that my guardian had warned me specifically against getting ink on the dress and when I had I didn't know what to do. After recess, she read the story about George Washington and the Cherry Tree to the class. From that time on, the teacher never referred to the incident again and, much to my amazement, neither did my guardian.

My lying was the first step to maladjustment in this situation. Apparently the teacher and my guardian had enough foresight to see the cause and effect relationship; because I was afraid of the consequences, I lied. Had they lingered on the incident much longer, they might have caused serious maladjustment in me. As it was, no one was hurt (except the poor janitor and he never knew about it anyway) and it taught me a lesson to tell the truth always.

There is a persistent myth abroad to the effect that there is something that can be defined as "home environment" that is good for people. It rests on the assumption that just being in a home automatically provides a child with some wholesome influences that cannot be found anywhere else. A prominent mayor of a large eastern city once stated in public address that a child was better off to be with the worst mother in the city than to be in the best institution. A "home" is not of itself good for anyone or bad for anyone. The pattern of living that is there is the important element, and it varies widely in many ways from home to home.

A good home. Here are some widely accepted criteria of

a good home for children. Provision of the *essential food, clothing, shelter, and protection.* Impersonal items to be sure, but very necessary. Regular daily *instruction* by the parents, under all conditions and in many ways, *in socially approved and personally satisfying ways of living.* Instruction is not to be confused with control or restriction of freedom, for it can go on in the freest and most permissive environment. *Consistency* in the manner in which the child's life is supervised and influenced. The most disturbing situation imaginable is a world without system or dependability. Consistency is far more important to mental health than the type of control that is used. *Affection and love felt and expressed freely* between members of the family. When other influences are in balance in the home, there is no such thing as too much love. No one need fear that love will make a child dependent as long as the next criterion is met. A scaled program of *increasing self-direction and cooperation by the children,* beginning in infancy and continuing steadily through adolescence. It should be pushed as fast as the child can safely take over his own control. There is scarcely a week or month in his developmental years when he cannot take over some new form of independence. The parents in the home, who are the principal ingredient in home environment, should live such personal lives that they illustrate the qualities of a good home and personality. For example, they should *live rich personal lives,* even though they must sometimes and in some ways bow temporarily to the need for sacrifices to their children. They should *keep their own romance alive* and delightful, for there is no other good way for children to learn about the happiness of marriage and no better way to make parents charming people. They should *get all the joy possible out of parenthood,* rather than regard it as a chore. In their efforts to do good to their children they should not confuse servitude with service. *Help should be matched to real needs,* not to little barriers which provide opportunity for learning. In the latter case learning is prevented, and children made dependent on parents who become slaves. They should have some *active participation in community life,* because of its effect on the home, their effect on the community, and the bridge it creates for the child who needs to move out into the community.

Under home conditions described above, so much vital education goes on that a rather insignificant margin is left for the school to handle. Even so, the home and school should maintain a rather close relationship, with parents visiting school, and teachers visiting the home. There are frequently times when the child and teacher would welcome a three-way conference with parents in planning the child's educational activity. There are also many occasions when the teacher would be glad to contribute her understanding of the child to the solution of a problem in the home. Then there is the more formal activity in the Parent-Teacher Association, which should be much more than a casual club that is attended as a duty. P. T. A. programs vary as much from one community to another as it is possible to imagine. Where fathers hold vital offices, along with mothers and teachers, the association is frequently a powerful force in the determination of school programs. It should be such a force. Administrators should be kept conscious of parental thinking, and should have the benefit of the critical suggestions of competent adults in the community. There should be no question about domain or rights. No one need defend prerogatives. Education is a joint adventure by all agencies, and should be kept integrated through fluid contacts.

2005. *The neighborhood.* Nothing can so easily undermine the ethical teachings of the school as ruthless business practices, or corrupt city government. The business policies in force, the nature of civic pride and practice, and the personal lives of the adults in the neighborhood are the courts of last resort when young people evaluate the ideals offered them in the church, the school, and the home. When deceit and crime pay well in money and prestige, the verbal instructions in idealism can scarcely be heard. When the admired and "successful" adults exemplify consideration for others, the satisfaction that comes from broad education and larger outlooks, the continuation of education and development beyond the years of schooling, and the happiness that comes from greater maturity and spiritual depth, there is no need for admonition. The lessons are far more eloquently taught than can be done by any tongue.

What makes it good. Exemplification of cultural ideals, so that what is being taught is also being practiced. Provision of *educational opportunities for people of all ages,* adapted to their needs and interests. Thus adults may be kept alive and growing, and the civic life kept vibrant and constructive. Ample *facilities for families to play together,* and for young people to play together without their families at times. Good *church programs,* and inspiring *illustrations of the arts* and the beautiful things in life. *Good government supported by the people,* with control of those who profit from crime and vice. In this kind of community adults should be *community-minded,* doing what is required to keep things going smoothly, *sharing in the responsibilities,* using the facilities for *leisure-time activities,* and *exerting influence on the schools and homes.*

The neighborhood should gather in the school building frequently, and for various purposes, so that it may be a familiar place to them, and the school staff should be part of all community activities. Where school buildings are used by scouts, brownies, local civic organizations, election officials, and various miscellaneous neighborhood groups, there is better integration in the educational environment of all the children. The curriculum also reaches out into the neighborhood, which is used as a laboratory for study in various subjects. The results are unification in the lives of the young people of their homes, schools, and communities, so that education can be effective in the highest degree.

2006. *All of this is education.* Education is living under guidance, in anticipation of later living without the guidance. It is an internship in community life. The real setting is not just the school, it is the whole life realm of the child. It is impossible for the work of the school to be unaffected by the rest of the circle. See Figure 9, in which this circle is illustrated. Each part makes its own contribution, but within the child the individual contributions are given integration of some kind. If the individual contributions are contradictory and discrete the child's task is confusing and

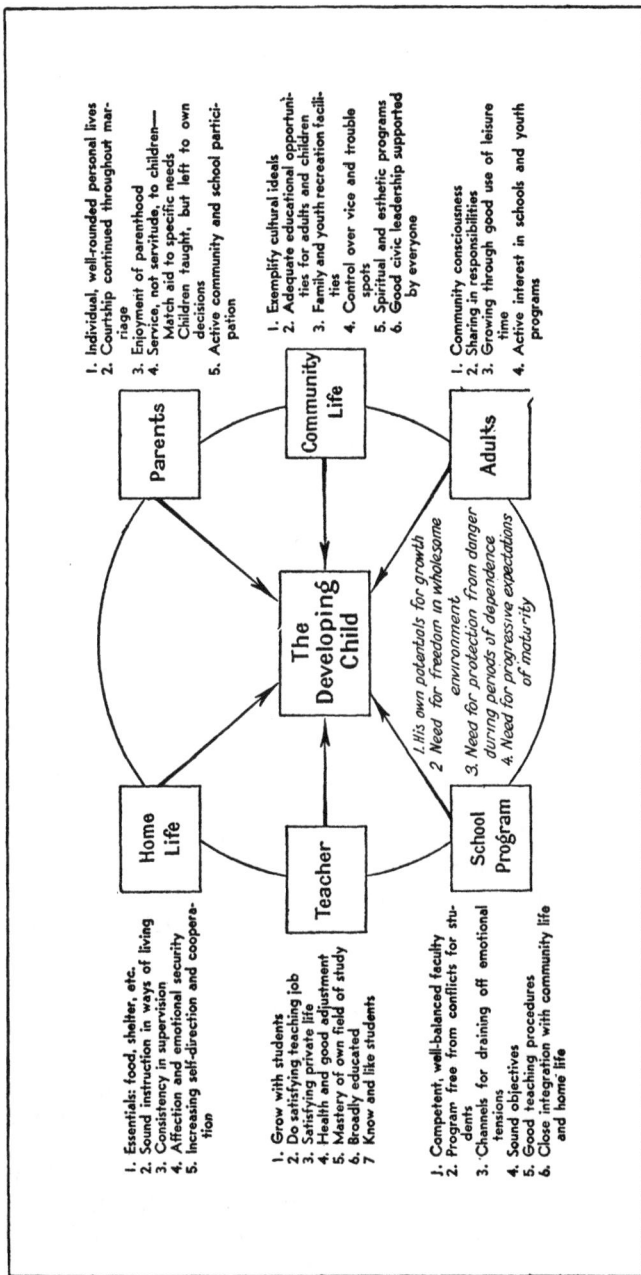

The developing child diagram with surrounding factors:

Parents
1. Individual, well-rounded personal lives
2. Courtship continued throughout marriage
3. Enjoyment of parenthood
4. Service, not servitude, to children—Match aid to specific needs Children taught, but left to own decisions
5. Active community and school participation

Community Life
1. Exemplify cultural ideals
2. Adequate educational opportunities for adults and children
3. Family and youth recreation facilities
4. Control over vice and trouble spots
5. Spiritual and esthetic programs
6. Good civic leadership supported by everyone

Adults
1. Community consciousness
2. Sharing in responsibilities
3. Growing through good use of leisure time
4. Active interest in schools and youth programs

The Developing Child
1. His own potentials for growth
2. Need for freedom in wholesome environment
3. Need for protection from danger during periods of dependence
4. Need for progressive expectations of maturity

Home Life
1. Essentials: food, shelter, etc.
2. Sound instruction in ways of living
3. Consistency in supervision
4. Affection and emotional security
5. Increasing self-direction and cooperation

Teacher
1. Grow with students
2. Do satisfying teaching job
3. Satisfying private life
4. Health and good adjustment
5. Mastery of own field of study
6. Broadly educated
7 Know and like students

School Program
1. Competent, well-balanced faculty
2. Program free from conflicts for students
3. Channels for draining off emotional tensions
4. Sound objectives
5. Good teaching procedures
6. Close integration with community life and home life

FIG. 9. THE CHILD AND HIS EDUCATIONAL ENVIRONMENT

sometimes unsuccessful. It is better for the environmental forces to do some integrating before the child appears for his education.

1. What is the difference between schooling and learning?
2. Where does the school fit, in a child's concept of his world?
3. How many educational institutions are at work on the child? What are they?
4. Explain the interrelationships in the figure on the school.
5. What is the difference between the student's task and the teacher's task?
6. What is the meaning of Figure 7?
7. What is included in the teacher's task of manipulating conditions?
8. What circumstances are necessary to do a good job in this regard?
9. What are three levels at which motivation must be provided? How do you do it at each level?
10. Explain why failure at the first two causes trouble at the third.
11. Name and explain the characteristics of a good school.
12. Do the same for a good teacher.
13. How does school architecture influence learning?
14. How does the home influence pervade other areas of life?
15. How can a home influence cause frustration in school?
16. How can home influence cause a child to loaf at school?
17. What are the criteria of good homes, and good parents?
18. Who are the chief influences in a neighborhood?
19. What makes a good neighborhood?
20. How can the school develop the best relationships with other educational agencies?

SELECTED REFERENCES

John E. Anderson, "Freedom and constraint or potentiality and environment," *Psychological bulletin,* 41 (January, 1944), 1-29.
Peter Blos, *The adolescent personality* (New York: Appleton-Century-Crofts, Inc., 1941), Part 5, Chapters 1 and 2.
Luella Cole, *Psychology of adolescence* (3rd ed.; New York: Rinehart and Co., 1948), Chapters VIII, XII, and XVII.
Harold E. Jones, *Development in adolescence* (New York: Appleton-Century-Crofts, Inc., 1943), Chapters I to IV.

James L. Mursell, *Successful teaching* (New York: McGraw-Hill Book Co., 1946), Chapters I, II, III, and IV.

W. Carson Ryan, *Mental health through education* (New York: The Commonwealth Fund, 1938), Chapters I, II, and III.

Raleigh Schorling, *Student teaching* (New York: McGraw-Hill Book Co., 1940), Chapters I and VI.

Donald Snygg and Arthur W. Combs, *Individual psychology* (New York: Harper and Bros., 1949), Chapters X and XI.

CLASS EXERCISES ON THE PSYCHOLOGY OF LESSON PLANNING

Things To Do in Class

1. A film of classwork in progress can be shown and discussed with relation to the psychological strengths and weaknesses of the procedures illustrated. A suggested film is "School," two reels with sound, which shows a day with fifth graders in the Hessian Hills School, Croton, New York. The dialogue is natural and several phases of the educative process are shown. It is available from New York University Film Library, 20 Washington Place, New York 3. McGraw-Hill Book Company has a set of text-films, available for rental from most film libraries, or for purchase from McGraw-Hill. The films deal with several phases of the teacher's work, including working with an individual student, the problem of discipline, and the matter of method in teaching. The films provide excellent opportunity for class discussion of the psychological principles involved in such matters.

2. The following lesson plans were prepared by teachers for use in junior and senior high-school classes. Make the suggested analysis of each one:

   A. Is the objective clearly stated? Is it really an objective? Is it of value to the students? Is it attractive to them?

   B. Is the introductory scheme well suited to the age level and motivation of the students? What effect will it have on their subsequent work in the lesson? Can you suggest a better way of winning student support for the lesson?

   C. With what types of learning is this lesson concerned? Are the proposed activities appropriate to the types of learning involved? Could the psychological soundness of the procedures be improved by any rearrangement or alteration? What effect will this lesson have on the students' ability to think, or on their tastes and preferences for the subject?

INTRODUCING THE STUDY OF PERSONAL ECONOMICS[1]

Ninth-grade Social Studies Class

EMMA ROSE ELLIOTT

An Introductory Explanation by the Teacher

Situation:

Three comparatively small groups of pupils enter this high school each year at the ninth-grade level, although most ninth-graders attend the nearby junior high school. These three groups which come directly to the high school from small elementary schools form a rather heterogeneous group. Their home backgrounds are quite different. One group comes from the local parochial school. These pupils tend to be from the lower-income group of families, and many of them come from homes where some language other than English is spoken most of the time. A second group comes from certain rural areas. These tend to be the poorer farming communities, as the better ones provide facilities for their pupils to attend the junior high school. The third group of pupils are those from the wealthiest residential section in this vicinity, and its children have had the advantages usual to professional groups.

This high school's ninth-graders vary in age from twelve to sixteen years, with most pupils thirteen or fourteen years old. All of them take Social Studies. They come to the Homemaking Department, where they take one term of their year's work in Social Studies. About one-half of this term's work—that is, eight or nine weeks, is in the area of personal economics.

Objectives:

The one main object of study in the area of personal economics is to help these boys and girls to learn to handle their money more wisely. The work, then, is to be pupil-centered rather than centered upon the subject matter of consumer education.

A means of introducing the study is needed which will help pupils approach the question of money as a problem of their own everyday living. They need to see as clearly as is possible the process they are going through in adjusting to a large city high school, and the process of growing up that they will experience during the years they attend high school. If they can

[1] Reproduced by permission of the author.

gain insight regarding this process of adjusting and growing up, they can better understand their true needs, and learn to use whatever money they have to best satisfy those needs. They can better evaluate their other resources and develop them to add to their satisfaction in living.

This study-aid for introducing personal economics:

With former ninth-grade classes, I have tried a variety of ways of introducing study in the area of personal economics. With several class groups, I tried using stories. A story was read to the class which we then discussed. Three different stories were used. Success seemed to depend upon the degree to which pupils identified themselves with characters in the stories. It was, however, difficult to gauge success, for some pupils said little in the succeeding discussions, and it was difficult to tell just what they were thinking.

This story technique seemed to me to have more possibilities than other methods I tried. A story was needed which would present an opportunity to each of these ninth-grade pupils for self-identification, and a means was needed for pinning down the responses so that the teacher could better gauge the reaction of each individual pupil. I have, therefore, written this story about Frank, a boy whom I happen to know well—organizing it so that succeeding study questions bring out many problems in the area of personal economics. I have tried to design it so that it will:

1) help the boys and girls see money management as involving real problems of everday living;

2) provide the boys and girls an opportunity to identify themselves with Frank so that, as we pull out and summarize his true needs, they will recognize them as their own needs—for they are the needs common to all young people;

3) provide me as their teacher with an opportunity to see their relative concern with various problems and recognize a suitable area for continuing our study—whether it be getting money, making friends and enjoying leisure time, buying clothing, or whatever.

I have tried to design the story to provide each of these pupils with an opportunity for self-identification. Like these pupils, Frank is a ninth-grader entering a large city high school from a small school. His immediate background includes a foreign language as does that of some of these pupils. He does not have as much money as he would like, but he understands his family is doing its best for him. Most pupils from low income groups feel this way about their families. He strives toward the group of high-school pupils who are among the more sophisticated—this group of "they that have" is brought in to make identification easier for our ninth-graders from the higher income homes—Frank's desires being similar to theirs in the social and scholastic areas.

I have tried to design the study-guide questions which follow the story in such a way that they will help the pupils. The first ones keep directing them back to the story for the reading comprehension of these ninth-graders often leaves something to be desired. The story and its succeeding study questions follow.

First Day:

Pupils distributed a copy of the study to each class member at the beginning of the class. Pupils numbered their copies and reported the numbers to the class librarian. They decided they wanted the teacher to read aloud the first time we read it, so I did. When I finished, one boy said, "I don't see what this has got to do with money management!" I didn't say anything, and he didn't insist on a response. They were full of questions about Frank—did I know him? What was he doing now? How did he get along in high school? I told them I knew him, but that it would spoil the fun of the questions that were being distributed now if I told them any more about him. They figured out how old he would be now and decided he was probably in the Army or Navy. I had to promise I would some day tell them how he did make out. Then we read pages 5, 6 and 7 of the questions, and they began work. They were quieter and more attentive to their re-reading and writing than usual. One boy stopped to talk with me. He said he had earned all the money for his own clothes since he was ten years old. We talked about the kind of clothes he wears. He had a mackinaw and would like to save for a leather jacket. He went on to speak confidently about the family earnings and their struggles to get along. His father sometimes comes to him for money.

Second Day:

We discussed their answers, summarizing those for page 5 on the blackboard. This required the whole period, for the pupils would get into quite heated arguments. One group felt Frank was pretty "bad off," that he couldn't possibly learn to feel comfortable or have a good time without more money. Another group thought he could make out perfectly all right. (It is interesting to notice that although they were very decided in their views, none of them yet knew what amount of money Frank did have each month.) In general, their comprehension of the story had to be clarified a good deal. Some pupils said the story stated that Frank could not speak English. Others thought the story said he was never invited to join the fraternity. We had to go back to the story many times in getting the one page of answers summarized on the board.

Third Day:

We started to summarize the answers to page 6 on the board, but one boy pointed out that each succeeding sentence or two in Part II of the story gave one point. He finally read Part II a sentence or so at a time, and listed the points as he went along. The rest of us got them down, and then the pupils worked at solving the points (page 7 of the questions). While the class was writing, one boy came to ask me to help him get a part-time job.

Fourth Day:

We started with their answers from page 7, but we didn't get very far. First we had quite a long discussion of ways of getting acquainted with teachers and finding out what teachers expect from pupils. I would not intentionally have begun such a discussion for fear pupils would call teachers by name and air their opinions in non-constructive ways. This did not happen, however, and the discussion was worth while, I think. We went on to consider Frank's poor writing. Pupils compared their pens and costs, and we decided we'd better do a little research on that. Some pupils thought Frank ought to investigate typewriters and learn to type. Others were sure he couldn't afford it. In our next class meeting, we planned to come back to the consideration of his arrangements for study outside of school. One pupil said, "Gosh, he can't study at home, he's got to get a job." But others thought he should worry about his schoolwork first of all.

At the rate we are progressing, I would judge it would take us at least three weeks to complete the study guide questions. I believe the pupils are identifying themselves with the story. Some of them seem almost too disturbed about it. I am eager to see whether their interest in it will be sustained until the questions are finished.

The Lesson

WHAT ARE THE THINGS FOR WHICH A HIGH SCHOOL
PERSON NEEDS TO SPEND MONEY

A Story About

FRANK

a Ninth-Grade Boy

PART I

(pages 1 to 4)

Frank was thirteen years old when he entered high school in Rochester in 1935. That year of 1935 was quite a jump for him. He had always gone to one-room rural schools of some twelve to fifteen pupils. During the fifth, sixth, seventh, and eighth grades his mother had been the teacher. It was snowy in Northern New York, and he and his mother went to school on snow shoes during the winter months. Most of the families in that community were Polish, and they worked hard to get a living from their farms. This meant the children had little time for play and so Frank would go skiing or skating alone when he had some spare time. During the evenings, he would usually read while his mother did her schoolwork. Frank knew there were certain ways he had to behave in school because he was the teacher's son. For instance, he had to take a good share of the blame whenever anything went wrong on the playground—otherwise some of the children might think he was being favored. Sometimes this was pretty hard to take in school, but afterwards he and his mother would talk it over. They would plan how they would use her pay check, so Frank knew all about the money matters his mother had to attend to. This really gave him some practice in making monthly plans for the use of money. While he was in the eighth grade, they saved to buy him the new clothes he would need when he went to a city high school. They bought an overcoat; Frank had never had that sort of coat before. During that year they planned how much money his mother could spare for him each month when he went to high school.

PART II

Can you imagine how he felt when he first entered high school in Rochester? Hundreds of boys and girls went to this school.

The corridors were busy and noisy. He had a different teacher for each class, and they were all strangers to him. He noticed that his handwriting was poor, and that the pupils and teachers did not approve of certain words and expressions he had learned to use among the Polish families.

In his ninth-grade Social Studies class he was asked to plan his four-year high-school program. His older brothers and sisters had gone to college, and Frank had sort of taken it for granted that he was going to go to college. However, his guidance counselor noticed his low grades in English and wondered whether he should plan a college entrance course. He was allowed to plan that sort of course, but Frank knew his school grades would be watched to see whether he could continue it. He thought he would like to be a Farm Bureau Agent or an optometrist when he got through college. His older brother was a Farm Bureau Agent, and his brother-in-law was an optometrist.

PART III

Outside of school hours, boys and girls his age seemed to have lots of time for recreation. But they did things he did not know how to do—the boys played ping-pong and basketball at the Y, went to various homes and played card games, or went to the movies. This school had fraternities and sororities, and the group of pupils which belonged to any one club would spend lots of time together. The older boys in one fraternity seemed to Frank to be topnotchers, and he hoped they would ask him to join when he was a tenth-grader. That fraternity, however, had quite high dues because its members did things like having formal dances, and inviting friends for week-end parties at the summer cottages of the pupils' families. Frank was half inclined to feel guilty for wanting to join a fraternity when his mother worked hard to send him money each month.

PART IV

Frank was now living with his older sister and her husband. He was fond of this sister, but he really had not seen a great deal of her except for short vacations. She was already in college when he was born. He and his mother had discussed the fact that he would be a boy in a home where there had been no other children. His sister was able to help him in lots of ways. She worked for the Board of Education, and so she knew quite a little about the high school he attended. When he realized he wanted to improve the way he talked, she and he made a bargain. Every time he made a mistake she would cough, and he would grin and try to say it right. Frank thought his mother must be lonely without him, so he tried to write and tell her all he was doing. She would send him the money as they had planned, and he had to decide how much of it he should pay his sister for his board and how he would use the rest. He had plenty of problems there. His appetite was enormous and, among other things, he was growing so fast he kept growing out of his clothes. He would have to take trousers to the tailor to be lengthened every month or two.

His sister and brother-in-law bought a small cottage on Canandaigua Lake that first year he was in Rochester. The cottage hadn't been used much for several years, and it was in need of lots of cleaning, painting and fixing up.

(page 5)
Now, let's go back and see how this little story about Frank has been told.

Part I tells you a little about *Frank's life before he entered high school in Rochester.*

Part II tells you about *his school life when he first entered high school.*

What does Part III tell you?

What does Part IV tell you?

From Part I, let's see how many things you can say Frank knew when he entered high school. For instance, you might say: *he knew how to play alone and have a good time.* Make just as long a list as you can.

(page 6)
Read Part II over again. What are the things Frank has to do or to learn while he is in high school? You might start your list like this:

1. *He has to get used to having lots of people around.*

(page 7)
Think about Frank as he is at 13 years of age—the things you've said he knows. He has his own good, healthy body, 24 hours a day like the rest of us, and some money. Try to make the best suggestions you can about how he can do each thing you've listed across the page. For the first one, you might think this won't bother him very long if he doesn't get tired, or nervous or discouraged. If so, you might write down:

1. *Get enough sleep.*
   Try not to do more things than he can do well.

(page 8)
Read Part III over again. What are the things Frank needs to learn or to do during his high-school years?

1.

(page 9)
Make the best suggestions you can about how he can do each thing you've listed across the page.

(page 10)
Read Part IV again. What are the things Frank needs to do or to learn during his high-school years?

(page 11)
Make the best suggestions you can about how he can do each thing you've listed across the page.

1.

(page 12)
Now let's look back over the suggestions you have made for Frank that have any bearing on how he should use his money. Read over your suggestions for Parts II, III, and IV. Every time you come to anything you have said he should do that would cost him any money, underline that suggestion. It might stand out more clearly if you used a colored pencil.

When everyone in your class has done this underlining, you might like to make a list on the board of all the things you have said Frank should do with his money.

(page 13)
Frank's mother sent him $30 each month, and he knew that was all she could afford—in fact, he hated to accept that much from her. His sister lived about twenty blocks from the high school he attended. The shopping district of the city was even farther from their home. The city bus fare was $.05. Prices in the cafeteria of his high school were much like those of other schools—a good lunch cost $.20 or $.25. The dues for the fraternity Frank hoped to join were $5 a month. Books were furnished for pupils in his high school, though he sometimes thought he would like to own some of them, especially since they were often written by the teachers of his classes.

How do you think he should figure it out? Do you think he needed a plan for the use of his money? Try to make a good one for him to follow during the ninth grade. Then suggest any changes that you can see are necessary for the tenth grade.

(page 14)

Frank is *one* boy in this country of ours. He is a little bit different from anyone else. His experience has been a little different from anyone else's. On the other hand, he is much like others his age. The things he needs to learn or to do are in many respects like those of other high-school people. Like most people, he has some money but probably not enough for all the things he wants to do.

Let's see if we can make a summary of the things we have said Frank should do with his money, and say it in such a way that it would apply not just to Frank but to *any* high-school person.

(page 15)

As you have worked on this summary, it probably has become apparent to you that you can't separate money from other things in living. Try to answer this question as well as you can, giving some illustrations:

How do the things you know and the way you use your time influence the way you need to use your money?

GETTING MONEY FOR THE THINGS I NEED[2]

Ethelwyn Cornelius

One week's class plans as worked out from an 8th-grade source unit.

Problems of this class (used during this week):

How can I earn money?

What can I learn well enough to be paid for doing?

Could I prepare food to sell?

Could I help someone in their home?

When they are entertaining?

With their regular housework?

What other resources do I have besides money for getting the things I want?

Values or goals:

To help the girls see and evaluate the things they could do to earn more money in order to get some of the things they need and want.

To help the girls realize their need for reasonably good man-

[2] Reproduced by permission of the author.

agement of their resources, their money, their time, as a means of gaining more freedom for themselves.

To help them understand that to gain more freedom they must show their adults that they are able to take responsibility, and are capable of managing such freedom.

Opportunity to practice actual techniques that can represent earning power. Each girl will have a chance to exercise judgment in using these techniques. Concepts of various jobs and their possibilities will be given, rather than acquiring of real skill in each one.

To maintain high standards, which can be done more easily through the desire to earn, that may prove a real impetus.

To help the girls understand that the development of these and other personal resources will bring them many of the things they want; that money is just one of the resources we have; and that we need more abilities as well as more money.

Brief summary of what went before this week's work:

Introduction to the unit was carried out by arranging the room as a placement office. Each pupil was interviewed by the teacher concerning her abilities and experience. This was recorded by a "secretary."

Girls listed possible ways of earning money: the reasons why they want more money, people who might hire them, problems they had found or problems they now had concerning money, earning it and spending it.

Discussion was carried on as to how we might tackle these problems; the particular needs of these girls; the necessity of good techniques; management; how we could prove to parents and others that we can do these things; the need for "practicing" in order to do jobs well; how we could judge and evaluate the things we do; the resources we have to work with. Plans were worked out with the girls as to how we could really attack some of these problems here in the class.

Two 9th grade girls who have done a good job of working in the cafeteria and other people's homes came into the class and discussed their experiences and their work.

Several lessons on appearance, manners, courtesy, and grooming with each girl trying to improve her appearance, see her own good points and poor ones, etc.

Then the following, which is one week of the classwork at this point.

First Day:

Each girl had selected a job in which she felt she needed more help or practice. Reference material was provided for each of these jobs, and previous lessons on how to use it had been given. The jobs were to be done on a rotation basis, with each girl having a chance to do each one. Those who were unsuccessful in doing their work were given another chance to practice it. Some of the jobs they listed as a possibility for earning money were:

Baking cookies	Polishing furniture
Washing towels	Cleaning house
Helping get supper	Cleaning pots and pans
Pressing clothes	Darning socks
Hanging skirts	Cleaning sinks, washing dishes, etc.

Teacher demonstrated on one of the pupils how to hang a skirt. Half of this was done by the teacher, and then left to be finished by the girl who had that as her job for that day.

After the demonstration each girl was given a card on which was written her "job" for the day in the form of a problem. For example:

Alice Merrill:

You are working for Mrs. Brown from 5:00 until 7:00 every night. Tonight, she would like to have you make some creamed peas on toast for supper. She would like to have it ready, and the kitchen cleaned up by 5:45.

Each girl then went ahead, looked up her own recipe, equipment materials, etc., and did the job.

This did not work out well as these girls became confused and wasted much time trying to find recipes, directions and equipment. Also, they were often unable to understand the recipes and directions in the reference material. They wasted much time asking questions, etc. They often considered a job well done when it was very poorly done.

Second Day:

A homemaker with a small child, who often hired girls to help her at home, came and talked to the girls. She discussed with them what she expected of girls she hired and what the girls could expect.

After the homemaker left, two of the girls finished their job of the day before, which was the making of oatmeal cookies, as a demonstration. The class looked on and evaluated their work. The points brought out were: needed better recipes, needed more demonstrations and quicker ones, needed clearer directions, girls needed to read carefully and think before they started their job.

Third Day:

Teacher did a series of quick demonstrations, making them simple and in steps which were printed on cardboard or on the board. The demonstrations were set up ahead around the room, the class following the teacher around as she gave each one. About 5 minutes was spent on each one, which meant that the demonstration was not always finished, and this was left for a pupil to come back and finish. The demonstrations given were:

> Method of mixing cookies
> Washing out a towel
> Pressing a towel
> Polishing furniture
> Cleaning a teakettle

After the demonstrations, each girl was given her card with her job for the day and she set to work.

After each girl finished her job, she called the teacher, who together with her judged her job and discussed how it could be improved. Where it seemed important the whole class sometimes came over to help judge the job or the products.

The following score card was one of the means of evaluation used by those who were preparing foods.

How can we tell whether our food is good?

	Good	Fair	Poor
How does it look?			
Is the shape even?			
Is the color good?			
Is the size right for its use?			
How does it taste?			
Was the texture fine, smooth, well-grained?			

Fourth Day:

The cookies made yesterday were shown, tasted, judged by the score card and discussed. Girls were given a chance to bring up any problems they had and these were discussed. As the quick, short demonstrations seemed to prove of real value to this class, it was decided to continue them. The teacher gave the following short demonstrations after the discussions.

> Making a white sauce
> Cleaning a sink
> Cleaning a refrigerator
> Cleaning out a kitchen cupboard

The girls were then given out their jobs for the day, which they did. Class was brought together at the end of class to look over the jobs which had been done and to evaluate them.

Fifth Day:

Teacher gave the following demonstrations:

> How to darn a sock
> How to hem a skirt (the one which had been hung before)
> How to wash dishes

Girls then went ahead with their jobs as before. Individual evaluation was done at the end of each job. This was kept track of on a large chart, so that each girl could see her development.

Sixth Day:

In order to help these girls to judge and evaluate more carefully, a different type of demonstration was done today. At this time, the teacher who had kept track of the various mistakes and poor methods the girls had used, demonstrated some of the same things over. This time she did the things incorrectly, using the same mistakes that she had previously seen the girls use. Each girl was given a piece of paper and a pencil, and asked to write down all the mistakes she saw. The teacher demonstrated those jobs which seemed to be causing the most problems, such as

> Making cookies
> Washing out towels
> Cleaning sinks

In the time left the girls went ahead on their individual jobs as before, with the evaluation at the end.

Last Day of Class:

Part of the period was given over to those who still had jobs needing finishing, while those who were through were given some reference material to read on the ways we had been learning in order to earn money.

The whole class then took part in a general discussion and evaluation of the things we had learned, what we still needed to learn, what they could do at home in order to obtain skill in these things, other abilities they could develop, and those they could strengthen, what they might do with the money they earned, and how they could make adults see that they could do these things. The chart, on which they had kept the evaluation of their jobs, was used at this point and proved very helpful.

Things To Do outside Class

1. The following lesson outline was prepared for use in a home-making class. It is reproduced here in unfinished form to provide an exercise in analyzing types of learning involved in an objective. Read the introductory material and make an analysis along the suggested lines:

A. For each section of the outline indicate the major type of learning involved.

B. For each section with its type of learning, tell briefly what sort of experience or activity the teacher should arrange to secure the type of learning desired. Be specific to the objective.

C. Consider the interrelationships between the various parts of the outline, and discuss whether it is possible to arrange any of the learning experiences so as to serve more than one part of the outline at the same time. Be cautious about suggesting any learning activity which is not realistic, or which disregards limitations in the ability and background of the students. E.g., it is not feasible to send a committee out to look over articles in a shop until they know what to look for and how to evaluate what they see. Keep in mind what you know about concept formation. Try to arrange the learning activities in good psychological sequence so that later activities will profit by what is learned in earlier activities.

D. Be prepared to discuss these questions in class:
  1. Is motivation adequately taken care of in the unit? What are the strong points in this regard? What weak points can you find?
  2. How can the class be given a broad experience with the factors to consider in selecting a gift, without slowing up the early work to the point of annoyance and loss of interest? Note that this experience must include type of article, pattern, material, and processes needed to complete the gift. What implication does this question have for the arrangement of certain sub-goals in the whole lesson?
  3. What is an economical and psychologically effective way of getting the class through Part II without spoiling their materials and without requiring the teacher to supervise each act on each article?

A UNIT PLAN[3]

SHIRLEY JANE SMITH

The Situation:

This is a ninth-grade class of 12 girls in homemaking which meets five 55-minute periods per week for 38 weeks. The pupils have had two years of work in homemaking. In their seventh- and eighth-grade sewing units the pupils have gained some degree of coordination and ability to manipulate in hand sewing and have learned to use the sewing machines. However, they have made articles which involved considerable initial preparation of the materials on the part of the teacher, the use of very simple patterns, and more machine-sewing than hand-sewing. These units have been brief, one 9-week period each year, and have not developed the degree of skill in hand sewing which the pupils will need before they can easily be taught garment construction.

Group-preplanning:

In the Fall, the teacher and pupils together made a general plan for the units they would like to have during the year and the group decided to have a 14-week period of sewing. The teacher suggested at the time that it would be nice to have their

[3] Reproduced by permission of the author.

sewing unit around Christmastime so that they could make Christmas gifts and the pupils agreed to this suggestion. The pupils also expressed interest in making clothing and it was agreed that some clothing construction would be included in the unit.

The first meeting for this unit has been scheduled for six weeks before Christmas holidays and it was planned to spend these first six weeks of the unit in the making of gifts.

No further plans for the unit were made at that time and no replanning has been done which affects the choice of time or the length of the unit.

Teacher preplanning:

Note: Up to this point the word "unit" has been used in reference to the entire 14-week sewing period. Throughout the remainder of this plan, the word "unit" refers to the first six weeks of the total period, and it is for these six weeks that this plan is being made.

The teacher's objective for this unit is to have the pupils experience and understand the complete process involved in a simple construction problem in sewing; to develop some degree of skill in the performance of the various parts of the process; and particularly to improve their skill in hand sewing. It is intended that the experiences planned for this unit will help prepare the group for the more complex processes involved in garment construction. The degree to which this objective will be realized for each pupil will depend upon the way in which the unit is conducted and the ability of the child.

The process will involve three major parts. The activities included in each part of the process will involve various types of learning. If it is to be most successful the method used in teaching each part of the process will need to be consistent with the kinds of learning involved.

Outline	Kinds of Learning	Possible Learning Activities
Part 1. Selection and planning A. Article to be made 1. Factors to consider in selecting a gift		
2. Choosing a particular article		
a. Ability of pupil to perform process involved		
b. Suitability to purpose		
B. Pattern or general design of article		

1. Color
  2. Decoration
  3. Suitability to purpose		

C. Choice of materials		

1. Fabric
  2. Materials used in making decoration
  3. Threads		

D. Selection and knowledge of use of necessary sewing equipment and materials		
Part II. Preparation of material for sewing A. Shrinkage and pressing		

OUTLINE	KINDS OF LEARNING	POSSIBLE LEARNING ACTIVITIES
B. Straightening		
C. Measuring D. Cutting		
E. Measuring, pinning and basting hems, mitering corners, and pressing		
Part III. Simple hand-sewing and the use of simple decoration		
A. Hemming		
B. Stitches used in decoration		
1. Decoration may be a part of construction of the article—such as hemstitching 2. Decoration may be applied to the article as in appliqué		

2. Each student should observe a teacher at work for one or more hours, after which a report should be written in this form:
   A. Tell what the teacher was trying to accomplish.
   B. Describe in some detail what the teacher actually did.
   C. Discuss the teacher's performance in the light of the four aspects of the teacher's task described in section 2003 of the text, under the topic "Manipulating Conditions."
3. Find a table or graph in a psychological journal which illustrates the distribution of one or more psychological characteristics of human beings, and discuss the influence of such differences on the work of the teacher.

PART V

ADJUSTMENT AND MALADJUSTMENT

CHAPTER XXI

THE LEARNING PROCESS AND MALADJUSTMENT

2101. *Deviant behavior is learned.* Learning is often defined as a process by which the behavior of the organism becomes changed through experience. Unless the definition is faulty, learning also accounts for maladjustment, since that, too, is a change in behavior due to experience. That it is not so obviously a matter of learning is probably due to the fact that parents and teachers are apt to watch intently for the emergence of desirable outcomes and to remain unaware of the gradual development of deviant behavior until it reaches a point where it can no longer be ignored. Not having watched its development, they are surprised to find it there in full bloom. Consequently, the process by which it developed escapes their notice.

It is psychologically sound to assume that each student will do his work unless there is something wrong with him that needs attention. However, this excellent point of view will cause trouble if the teacher allows himself to forget the latter part of it, or if he is unable to recognize the early signs of trouble and know how to deal with it when it is present. Ideally, the teacher should manage the educational process so soundly that each child should learn only the desirable forms of behavior. Practically, that is not possible yet, because most teachers cannot maintain educational processes at such a high level and because the beginnings of undesirable learning for many students lie outside the realm of the educational system. The best approach, however, is to find out where in the learning process undesirable trends are born, what causes them, how to prevent them, how to recognize them once they

418

are started and what to do about those that are already under way.

When learning takes place without difficulties, the normal process involves a motivating drive to attain some objective, meeting the barriers that prevent immediately reaching the objective, and overcoming the barriers by means of acquiring some skill, knowledge, or needed substance. When the barrier is unduly resistant, however, and the motivation is too insistent to be denied, frustration is experienced by the individual. He is then apt to turn to anything that offers help, even though that may involve him in socially or psychologically undesirable forms of behavior. Hence, it is at the third of the sequential steps, the barrier, that incipient maladjustment first begins to come into the picture.

The field of abnormal psychology sometimes appears to the layman to defy psychological law and become mystical. This may be an illusion produced by unfamiliarity with some of the characteristics of the learning process, and it may also be due to the nature of some of the explanations offered in the literature. The learning process is not necessarily fully exhibited by what goes on when a person learns to multiply, or to write a sentence in French, or to ride a bicycle. These are just a few of the most obvious products of the process. There are many others which occur within us all the time, but of which we are usually unaware. One may be further misled by reading about an ego, or super-ego or id, which are characterized as active forces. To most people this connotes an independent element within, which acts as it pleases with responsibility to no one, and produces queer and unlawful changes in one's "mind."

Deviant behavior is not fundamentally difficult to understand. There are some kinds of abnormality that are produced by organic damage or deterioration, and they will not be discussed in this book. They are medical problems for the most part. But most of the abnormal behavior found so plentifully in the whole population is the product of ordinary learning, and follows the laws that govern learning just as faithfully as the subjects learned in school.

Heretofore the discussion has proceeded on the assumption that it was within the power of an individual to get to his goals and satisfy his needs if he really tried. The barriers discussed in the chapters on behavior and learning were largely discussed as if they were just missing ideas, or missing abilities, which could be acquired by the individual through regular study or practice. In Lewin's language, he could move through the possible paths with a little effort, and get to his objectives, satisfying his needs and coming to adjustment. When he couldn't make an adjustment with his existing patterns of action, he could acquire whatever new behavior he needed (that is, turn some not-possible paths into possible paths) and then reach an adjustment. That is the usual concept of learning.

These assumptions are based on a further assumption, which was not indicated, that the only thing that keeps persons from adjusting is their own lack of skill or knowledge, that when this lack is corrected by the individual a reasonably complete adjustment can be attained, and that anyone can make such a correction by trying. It is necessary now to recognize two other possibilities, which are present whenever a person faces a situation under the pressure of unfulfilled needs. One is that even if he tries, he may not succeed, and it is necessary to see what would then happen. The other is that even if he can succeed in getting to the objective that will satisfy his driving need, he may upset other needs in so doing, and get himself unadjusted in other ways. That is, the path he finds possible may get him where he is trying to go, but in so doing may destroy something else that is also essential to his continued adjustment. From these two possibilities we can move systematically into a reasonably straightforward explanation of the manner in which deviant behavior is learned. No matter which of the two takes place, the individual will have made a bad adjustment, and that predicament is what is referred to by the term *maladjustment*. All it means is that, because the course taken by the individual does not satisfy his needs, his drives continue to push him for relief, and in the manner of grasping at straws he uses any form of behavior he can find that tends to cut down the conflict and reduce the tension.

2102. *Maladjustment and the sequential steps in learning.* The point at which maladjustment arises in learning is shown in Figure 10. The numbers refer to the sequential steps discussed in Chapter XV. The barrier may consist of any kind of constraint, within the individual's conceptual pattern or imposed from without. At the point where these constraints keep one from moving to adjustment by existing patterns, three general possibilities seem to exist.

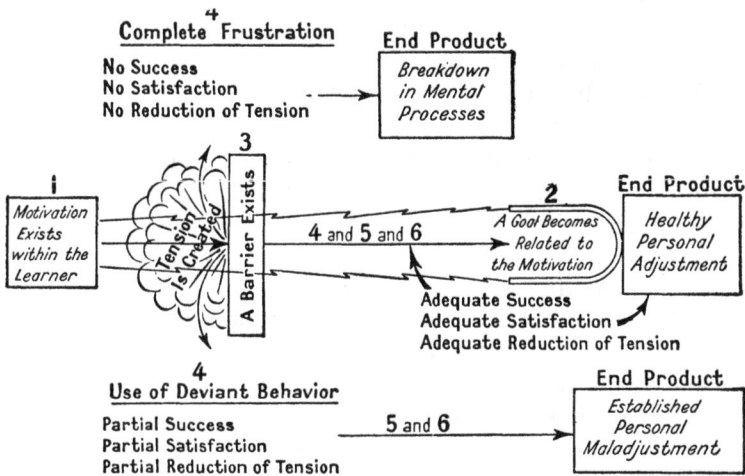

FIG. 10. RELATIONSHIP BETWEEN PERSONAL MALADJUSTMENT AND THE LEARNING PROCESS
(Numbers refer to sequential steps)

When through study, analysis, obtaining help, or some other process one is able to overcome a barrier and reach a goal that is closely related to the basic motivation, the success is adequate because it satisfies the motive. Therefore, the tension is dissipated and the organism becomes quiet. It is in a state of relative adjustment as far as that particular goal is concerned. At the other end of the scale of possibilities, the barrier cannot be overcome at all, and the motivation will not subside. The tension created when important motives are completely blocked is often sufficient to cause a severe breakdown in mental processes. In the first instance, the fact, skill, preference, or act that produced the satisfaction becomes learned in harmony with steps 4, 5, and 6. In the second instance, nothing is learned because the process was interrupted by the breakdown of normal mental activity before any solution was found. In effect, the problem and the person's problem-solving behavior up to the moment of breakdown are held in an incompleted and interrupted state from which the individual can be rescued only by psychiatric help, unless a fortuitous change in circumstances should remove the barrier or end the motivating drive. Even so, recovery of normal function is difficult.

Most deviant behavior, or behavior that departs sufficiently from the accepted norm to be objectionable for one reason or another arises when the clash between motives and barriers is at neither extreme, but somewhere between the two situations just described, that is, not resolvable by typical learning procedures, nor so impossible as to cause an outright escape through mental breakdown. When the individual cannot attain an important objective by any acceptable means, he may break through the bounds of reality and select a type of behavior that has only an indirect relationship to the original goal and that will therefore yield only partial success. If the motive is not adequately taken care of, however, the tension will not be completely or permanently removed, and the individual will find it necessary to repeat his performance again and again as the renewed tension drives him to act. The fact that some satisfaction was derived from his act, whereas other acts had yielded no adequate satisfaction up to that time, means that the act will become related to the goal. Hence it becomes a learned form of behavior. More than that, however, it becomes a form of behavior that must repeat itself as often as the tension demands. Since the motivation is never fully satisfied by the act, the demands are likely to be continually recurrent. Hence a form of compulsive behavior may be developed from a frustration or conflict that has never been completely settled. In time, the conflict may become buried in the subliminal mental processes through repression. When that occurs the individual is beyond helping himself, and beyond the help of the layman who lacks the techniques necessary to uncover the unsettled problem and find a way of settling it satisfactorily. Many forms of compensatory reactions become established in this manner, such as daydreaming, malingering, and dangerous rationalization. Apparently, also, such extreme forms of maladjustment as psychoneuroses may have such origins.

There is one exception to the general description just given. Sometimes the individual chooses an antisocial act, the constraints against which are not his own but those of society. If he violates a social norm that does not happen to have any importance to him individually, he may thereby satisfy his driving need and reach a perfectly satisfying adjustment. In such a case, the act need not occur again for any compulsive reason, because there is no residual tension left over from the drive that made him act. He is, of course, learning to perform this sort of act, but in no sense is this learning different from any other kind that may take place in school, as far as his psychological state of mind is concerned. If he escapes any clash with society, there is nothing to make him feel maladjusted. He will probably tend to turn to that behavior more easily the next time he is faced with a similar situation, but in the meantime it may disappear from his actions. To repeat, however, this well-adjusted outcome is only possible when the person's internalized standards of personal conduct do not include the social taboo that is violated by his act. If he has made this constraint part of his own personal standards, then he is violating more than a social taboo, and the outcome does not constitute an exception to the condition stated first.

If we are to understand fully the nature of these constraints, and how their violation affects behavior, it will be necessary to draw some parallels with earlier discussions.

2103. *Four dangerous paths and their consequences.* Lodged within the pattern of needs and its closely integrated pattern of meaning are four allied but somewhat distinct kinds of goals that are constantly sought by the individual.

They are to be found in the discussions in Chapters VII and VIII, but not in quite the formulation suggested here. To avoid confusion, they will be quite explicitly listed from the standpoint of the dangers they involve.

1. *Excessive difficulty in meeting regular needs.* The first type consists of all small immediate goals, the pursuit of which constitutes most of the daily behavior of the person. Almost all the acts that satisfy physiological needs are of this kind, easily aroused, and quickly concluded. Many other small goals that yield satisfying effects on the concept of self, or on one's social status are of this short and immediate nature. Ordinarily, there are many ways of meeting these small recurrent needs, a wide variety of possible paths, so that substitution is not particularly difficult. Because of the relative ease of substitution, one rarely becomes upset over finding one such path blocked.

Along with these immediate goals, and frequently built upon them in pyramidal form, are some rather important and less numerous intermediate goals, toward which the behavior of many days, or even years, makes a steady contribution. Due to the length of time required to build up toward these goals, they cannot be easily set aside or altered by substitution. Therefore, they become much more crucial to the individual and are marked by much greater emotional attachments than the little daily goals. Also, because we tend to have difficulty seeing much beyond these intermediate goals, in our deeply intrenched patterns of meaning, we often attach much greater importance to them than they really carry, because they are, after all, not the big ultimate goals in life and do not constitute the only paths to those ultimate goals. Since this is customarily not apparent to people, it is a fact in which they can find no comfort, and it does not prevent them from consciously attaching undue importance to the goals they can visualize.

By far the most significant constraint that keeps one from achieving these goals easily is the difficulty of acquiring the knowledge or skill needed to move on to them. A person's path or process concepts exist in his pattern of meaning, to be sure, and are of his own making as a result of past experience, but they also move through realities and have to contend with facts and laws of nature. Hence, he often faces resistances set up in nature that may vary from the zero level clear up to 100 per cent impossibility. It may be that he can learn easily what he needs to be able to do, or that it is absolutely beyond his power to learn it.

As long as the difficulty is within a reasonable range, his experience will probably be developmental, although what he learns will depend on the circumstances. He will learn something undesirable just as easily as something desirable if his experiences endow the undesirable formation with power to satisfy his needs and bring him to adjustment. As the difficulty involved in a path increases, frustration becomes more and more possible. It may range from minor annoyance to major disappointment and a sense of complete failure. These experiences provide the individual with opportunity to devaluate himself, just as his successes provide him with opportunity to improve his self-rating. A significant part of his concept of himself is determined by the balance between the two aspects of this type of experience. If the balance is on the negative side, he may develop a feeling of inferiority, and if on the positive side, a feeling of confidence and self-approval. This type of constraint is potentially present in every form of human behavior, whether it is directed toward the satisfaction of physiological, social, or personal needs.

The extent to which the individual will strive against the difficulty of a path depends on the stress of his driving needs, and the pressure to get to a solution. Under stress a person may try harder than he would ordinarily do, and succeed in reaching an adjustment. Sometimes tremendous development takes place under these conditions, but not without its price in wear and tear. On the other hand, he can become frustrated through persistent failure and begin to revise his estimate of himself downward, as has been experimentally shown in studies of level of aspiration.[1] The extent to which he will continue to hunt for possible paths, or persist in trying to get through one path, has also been

[1] See footnote 11, in Chapter IX.

shown to depend on what seem to him to be the chances for success, and the number of alternative paths he sees in the situation.[2]

In cases in which stress is great and failure is the result, the setting is appropriate for important changes in the personality structure, particularly in such traits as submission, introversion, and withdrawal. The outgoing dynamic traits may suffer, and the individual may turn toward acquiescent and conformative types of behavior.

There is still another possibility, which is even more fraught with potential trouble than either of the first two. When there are no possible paths through which the individual's capacities will move him in conformity with social standards, his own ideas of right and wrong, and his constant search for his major values, he may be forced by pressure of needs to step over into paths that involve violation of these kinds of constraints. That is when he moves to the satisfaction of a driving need, at the cost of destroying his equilibrium in some other way, as suggested in section 2102. When that happens, his act automatically puts him into one of the other three dangerous paths mentioned in the introduction to this section, and starts him on the pursuit of a reconciliation with the kind of need he has disrupted. This is an almost certain path to some form of psychiatric disturbance. In order to see what the nature of the disturbance will be, and what possible forms it may take, it is necessary to examine each of the other three kinds of goals, the constraints that are built up around them, and the effects of violating them.

2. *Threats to social status in seeking ordinary needs.* It was pointed out in Chapter VII that belongingness in a group was essential to the steady flow of the commodities with which a person satisfies his basic needs, and that such belongingness is contingent on the approval and affection in which the individual is held by the group. Since this is contingent on the maintenance of reasonable conformity

[2] E. E. Robinson, "An experimental investigation of two factors which produce stereotyped behavior in problem situations," *Journal of experimental psychology*, 27 (1940), 394-410.

to the group in the matters that are considered important in the group, this gives rise to a potential constraint on some lines of action tabooed by the society in spite of their other productive qualities. Those who violate these written or unwritten constraints find themselves in social difficulties if their actions are discovered. Social acceptance depends on others, not on a person's own judgment of his actions. As long as society continues to reward an individual there is no pressure that will make him become upset over his flaunting of social mores. Therefore, his only concern is to avoid getting caught at his antisocial behavior. If he can do that he can maintain a comfortable adjustment.

This possibility, as stated before, depends on whether the individual has incorporated the social norm into his own personal standards for himself. For example, he may have developed a personal acceptance of the practice of drinking, but refrain from it in order to hold the respect of the group which does not approve of it. This sort of barrier puts no strain on the inner life of the individual. He can violate it with no compunction as long as his group does not learn of his behavior. Therefore, it produces no personal maladjustment, but may produce social maladjustment if it is discovered. In that event, the individual may try to cover his actions and may even develop a sense of alienation from his group in anticipation of its judgment of him.

The delinquent is a case in point. He is ordinarily a well-adjusted individual, personally, but poorly adjusted to the larger social group. Delinquency is not meanness or deliberate antipathy toward society. It is the logical and natural way of satisfying needs according to the process concepts of the particular individual. The origin of the difficulty lies in the circumstances within which the individual acquired his process concepts. At some time in the past he was seeking satisfaction for needs, and found it in a manner which, he finds later, is not approved by others. Or he finds out later that he has come to want the respect of others to whom it matters, although at the time he acquired these ways of acting he was not interested in the social approval of those who disliked the acts he was learning to perform.

It is a characteristic of first offenders that they are surprised to find themselves in trouble, and, because of the social disapproval involved, the experience often results in a relatively traumatic change in the moral tone theretofore ascribed to the disapproved actions. Unfortunately, this wholesome tendency is often upset by the harsh manner in which the offender is handled, and the names which are applied to him. When society becomes the aggressor (as it seems to do to such a person) the individual is easily convinced that society is his enemy, and that he must protect himself against it. Society, being the dominant force, calls the individual an enemy of society, whereas the individual usually thinks of society as an enemy to him.

Not infrequently a person who has acquired anti-social patterns of conduct without awareness of the social disapproval attached to them may, through the social pressure later brought to bear on him, absorb these standards into his own personal standards of right and wrong. If this happens when he is apprehended for his behavior, he may become involved in the type of trouble that constitutes the third dangerous path, and is subsequently discussed. Whether the latter occurs depends on whether his process concepts are changed by his experience, for it is often the case that the individual is not convinced that society is right. His previous experience may have been atypical and socially wrong, but if it has been consistently rewarding for him in the past, it will yield only with the greatest difficulty. This sort of problem is very common in delinquency areas where a sub-group has set up an antisocial environment within which the younger children become "good" members before they make effective contacts with the larger group mores.

3. *Threats to self-approval in some productive paths.* Another of the demanding needs mentioned in Chapter VII is the need for self-approval, through measuring up to the standards a person has accepted for himself. Since these standards exist solely in his own mental life, his status depends entirely on his own judgment of himself. Some paths have a degree of impossibility because they are not in har-

mony with his accepted standards of performance. These standards can be ethical, moral, spiritual, or social. The problem is
intensely personal in nature. It has nothing to do with what
others think about an action, for a path that would be approved by others may be disapproved by the individual. The
standards that determine self-approval are those that the
individual has built up within himself on the basis of his
own impressions of what is right and wrong, good and bad,
proper and improper, admirable or detestable, good enough
or not good enough. There may be paths within his pattern of
meaning that are within his ability, that would obtain for him
his cherished values, and that would be approved by his
society, but that he cannot take because he feels they are not
up to his standards. He cannot follow that line of action
without developing a feeling of guilt, unworthiness, or bad
conscience. Unless he can maintain his behavior at the level
of his own personal standards, he finds himself an uncomfortable person to live with. This is the basic ingredient in
the production of personal maladjustment and the formation
of psychologically deviant behavior.

The degree of guilt reaction depends on the wrongness
of his behavior. Any standard that has been pressed into him
under stress by concepts of serious and dreadful outcomes for
its violation may be capable of throwing him into various
neurotic symptoms if he flaunts the constraint.

4. *Threats to dominant values in some productive paths.*
Values were described earlier as generalized conditions of living that have come to be very important to the well-being of
the individual. They can be measured quite accurately when
the test sets up such highly generalized value concepts.
People are not generally fully aware of their big values, but
the values nevertheless operate to guide their behavior
whether they know it or not. Such values are as near to
ultimate goals as one can have, for they really represent composite conditions under which adjustment seems most possible. In reacting to a current need, the individual looks for
paths that lead to the circumstances that will satisfy the
needs, but tends to choose from all the available paths those

that promote his big and important values and avoid his negative values. Case 12 furnishes a good illustration, in Chapter XVIII.

Under conditions of stress, when there is no productive path that does not involve destruction of personal values, the individual is forced into a sense of terrible loss and consequent self-destruction. When major values are very seriously threatened, the individual faces the most powerful constraint on his behavior, for his own well-being is at stake. Actions or circumstances that destroy his major values are more likely to be brought upon him against his will, either by error on his part, or by the actions of others. A person may no doubt override constraints where relatively little threat to personal values is involved, but not without some feeling of loss no matter what else the action may gain for him.

Since values are also mental constructs, the judgments that set up their constraints are within the individual, just as are his standards of goodness. So this type of violation of constraint brings his own judgment upon him. There is no way of escaping it, any more than one may escape his own conscience. The disturbance is within the personal life of the individual, and expresses itself in psychiatric disturbances in behavior.

For example, the father in the play *All My Sons* destroyed his home life by his disregard for the safety of the men who were to fly the planes he helped build. When he discovered that he had lost the love of his own son because of this, he killed himself. In destroying his home life he had destroyed the principal condition of living under which self-realization and well-being were possible for him. His only escape from the awful loss was through suicide.

2104. *The structure of psychiatric problems.* In the preceding section, four dangerous paths of action were sketched, and the natural effects on the individual who violates the constraints were indicated. It was pointed out that these paths all take their departure from the barrier that prevents ready adjustment, just as all forms of learning do. Learning may operate to establish many combinations of deviant behavioral

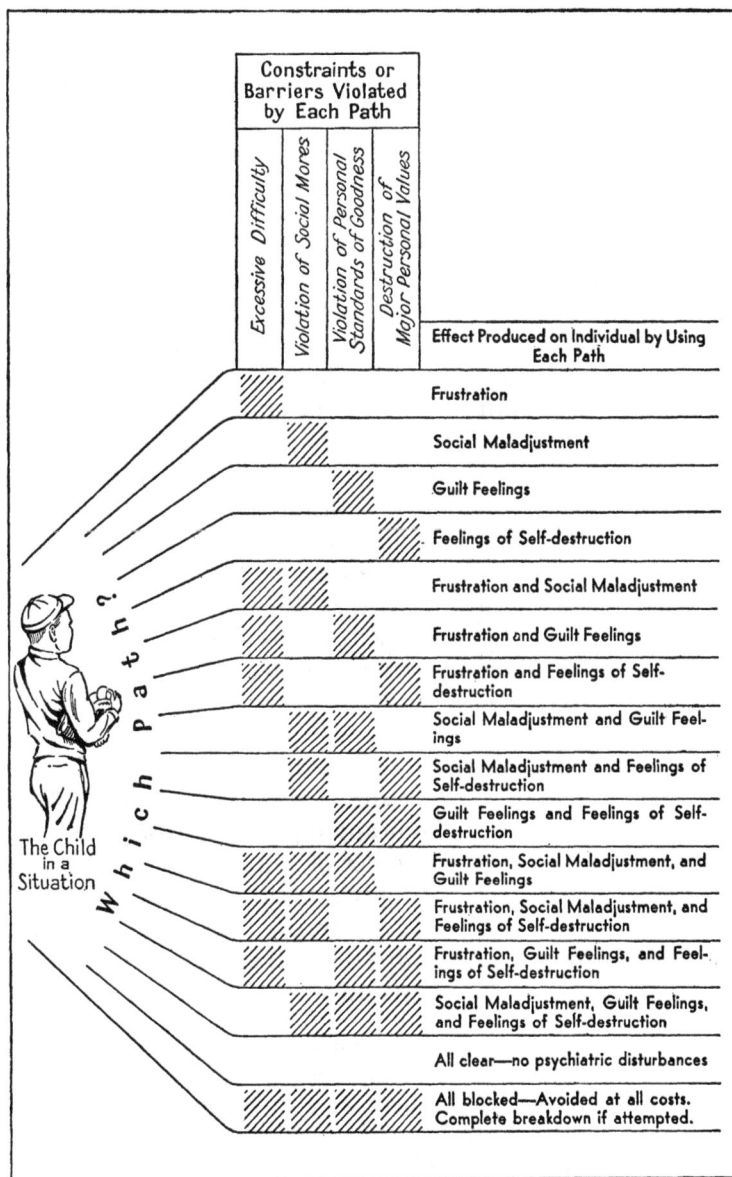

FIG. 11. SCHEMATIC REPRESENTATION OF THE SITUATION WITH ITS POSSIBLE PATHS

symptoms, all of which are made up of one or more of these four general forms of reaction, in combination. Figure 11 is offered as an aid in visualizing the possibilities. It is suggestive of some of the complications that may develop from violation of constraints or barriers, but the full possibilities constitute a field of such proportions that adequate treatment requires a large volume devoted to nothing else. Within the scope of this treatment it is possible only to point out the basic processes by which deviant behavior develops and indicate some of the ways in which teachers may try to prevent it.

In the first place, all four of the types of constraint described here can be quite dangerous. The last three are *always* dangerous, and always result in undesirable additional conflicts and tension. The first barrier, difficulty, is only dangerous when it is too powerful. As long as it is within the possibilities of the individual to overcome his difficulties and get through to his goals, that kind of barrier is developmental in its effect, and not dangerous. It might be referred to as an educational barrier. The other three, and the first when it is too severe, might be called psychological or psychiatric barriers. Examples of them include personal defects, such as low intelligence, maladjustment, and physical disability; undesirable teacher characteristics, such as poor personality, faulty methods of teaching, ignorance of students' problems, and lack of interest in students; conflicting cultural demands, conflicts in one's goals or values, handicapping social status, inability to analyze problems, and a number of similar things. Such barriers may exist singly or in any sort of combination. It is a characteristic of much maladjustment that as it progresses the barriers to wholesome adjustment become more and more complex, interwoven, and inclusive.

TABLE 5. TYPES OF DISTURBING FACTORS IN SCHOOL

Forty-six prospective teachers were asked to describe briefly incidents from their own experiences that illustrated four types of disturbing factors in their school experiences. The following list was tabulated from their replies, with the number of people who mentioned each factor. What does it indicate about fruitful ways of improving the atmosphere of a classroom?

Teacher's personality	22
Extraneous pressure to do well	16
Unjust punishments and rewards	14
Using student as an example	13
Failure to provide for individual differences	13
Too high scholastic standards	13
Deliberate embarrassment of student	12
Discontinuity in learning experiences	11
Undiagnosed physical disabilities	10
Arbitrary requirements	9
Awkward or inefficient social techniques	8
Too much competition	5
Too slow or too rapid physical development	5
Poor physical status	5
Not recognizing student's effort	4
Too much time pressure	3
Favoritism	3
Heterosexual adjustment problems	3
Objectives not clear or realistic	2
Making pupils stand out too much	2
Pupil's preconceived prejudice against teacher	2
Family's social status	2
Cliques among pupils	2
Teacher threatens pupil's social status	1
Fear of reciting	1
No goal in student's mind	1
Too much help with home work	1

27 items
183 tabulations

According to the data in Table 5 the three dangerous kinds of constraints and pressures are present in school to such an extent that twenty-two of forty-six students had at one time or another been badly upset through personality clashes with a teacher; sixteen of the forty-six had been badly upset by pressures brought to bear on them for social approval in connection with marks, and so on. This is suggestive of the problem faced by school people in cleaning the dangerous barriers out of the school. It should be said about these forty-six people, that they are all well-adjusted adults, who have by now successfully completed their college programs and graduated to responsible positions in society. They are the survivors, so to speak, who have come to the top in their struggle to become something. They should represent that part of their high-school contemporaries who came out least damaged by frustrating and upsetting experiences. It is quite possible that the incidence of disturbing conflicts would be much higher among those who didn't get through, for it is well known that many students drop out of both high-school and college because of the disappointments and conflicts they meet.

What has just been said adds up to this—there is only one kind of barrier that can stand between a student and his adjustment without causing trouble for him. That barrier is the lack of knowledge or skill he needs to reach his goal and adjust. Without such a barrier there would be no learning. So while some sort of barrier is required to force people to make changes in themselves, all of the barriers described here except one are to be avoided in the school, and everywhere if possible. The remaining one must be kept under control and regulated so that it does not exceed the point at which the individual will give up or fail.

QUESTIONS FOR REVIEW

1. Where in the sequential steps does maladjustment develop? Why?
2. What is meant by deviant behavior?
3. Name two reasons why a person becomes involved in dangerous paths.
4. Differentiate between delinquency and personal maladjustment.
5. Why can a delinquent be well adjusted personally?
6. What is the essence of each of the four dangerous paths described?
7. What is the psychological result of excessive failure?
8. What reactions follow violation of a personal standard? Why?
9. When a person violates a social standard what are the possible results?
10. How can a clash in cultural patterns create difficulty for an individual?
11. Why is violation of values called self-destruction?

12. Describe some of the combinations of maladjustment suggested in Figure 10.
13. What kinds of barriers are safe in school? What kinds should be eliminated?
14. What are the essential elements of the process by which deviant behavior comes into existence?
15. Make a list of barriers we meet continually that are not dangerous to mental health.
16. What are the important differentiating characteristics between educational, or routine, adjustmental barriers and psychiatric barriers?
17. What is the relationship between success in an effort and the tensions that accompany the effort?
18. At what stage in the development of deviant behavior can you be sure psychiatric help is needed?
19. Why does deviant behavior occur?
20. From what you know of the psychology of delinquency, what general approach to its prevention seems most promising?
21. Describe the essential elements in an adequate educational program for the prevention of maladjustment.

SELECTED REFERENCES

Luella Cole, *Psychology of adolescence* (3rd ed.; New York: Rinehart and Co., 1948), Chapters IX and X.
Arthur I. Gates, Arthur T. Jersild, T. R. McConnell, and Robert C. Challman, *Educational psychology* (New York: The Macmillan Co., 1948), Chapters XVIII and XIX.
Walter C. Langer, *Psychology and human living* (New York: Appleton-Century-Crofts, Inc., 1943), Chapters X and XI.
E. D. Partridge, *Social psychology of adolescence* (New York: Prentice-Hall, Inc., 1939), Chapters XIII and XIV.
Donald Snygg and Arthur W. Combs, *Individual psychology* (New York: Harper and Bros., 1949), Chapter VIII.

CLASS EXERCISES ON THE DEVELOPMENT OF MALADJUSTMENT

Things To Do in Class

1. Discuss the behavior involved in a case, by using the scheme in Figure 11. Show what barrier was involved, and what psychological reactions were produced. If more than one barrier was involved, see if the effects of each can be identified in the person's behavior. For this purpose use some of the cases

in this text, or cases from Allison Davis and John Dollard, *Children of bondage* (Washington D. C.: The American Council on Education, 1940) or from *Psychology through literature: An Anthology* (New York: Oxford University Press, 1943) or obtain the Horrocks case studies from the Syracuse University Press.

Things To Do outside Class

1. Each member of the class should prepare a description of an incident in his own school experience that illustrates the most serious difficulty he can recall. In the description, he should tell the setting, what happened, how it affected him, and how it turned out. Some of these should be discussed in class. When they are all turned in, the instructor should read each one, decide the type of frustrating or disturbing factor involved, and make a tabulation similar to the one in Table 5. The results should be checked against the data in Table 5.

CHAPTER XXII

THE RECOGNITION AND CORRECTION OF MALADJUSTMENT

2201. *The meaning of normal.* Normal behavior is that behavior which is within the range of tolerated differences. There is no absolute line between normal and abnormal. Individuals who are somewhat different from the crowd are looked at with suspicion—not because their characteristics are intrinsically good or bad, but because they are different. If their behavior is sufficiently different from that which is customary in the group, it is called deviant behavior. Such a designation may be applied to delinquency, neurotic actions, or any other undesirable form of behavior. It is not customarily applied to unusually brilliant performance. Abnormal means anything that is not normal, whether it is considered to be desirable or undesirable, but only those who depart from the norm in undesirable directions are popularly called deviates. The most useful way of thinking about normality is in terms of the normal curve. That area of approximately two-thirds of the curve's enclosed space represents normality. It is possible for the amount to vary with the sample, and it is also possible for a single item to be a significant distance from the exact center and still be within the range of normality. So it is with human behavior.

However, there is also something more to serious maladjustment than just being different. The difference moves in directions that are not all apparent on the surface. In serious cases, there is a great deal more tension than usual, somewhat more than the person can handle and still continue to carry on his regular activities. This excess tension then begins to constitute an interference with normal adjustmental resources. In addition to this, there is excessive preoccupation with a very limited segment of one's total environment or perceptual field. Everyone tends to concentrate on pressing issues until they are resolved and toned down. Under severe conflict, however, this preoccupation becomes so demanding that it tends to incapacitate the individual for normal perception. Therefore, while both of these conditions may be described as differences from others, it is what the differences do to the behavior of the individual that matters more than just the fact that he is different. When teachers and parents are familiar with the signs by which such dangerous differences are indicated, then the symptoms serve a useful purpose in pointing out those who need help.

Everyone is maladjusted to some extent. It is the lack of adjustment that keeps us from folding up and going to sleep, so to speak. The unfulfilled needs that are always present in changing patterns drive us as long as we are alive. The tensions that mark a normal individual, his characteristic bodily tonus, his ever-present feeling tone, his susceptibility to stimuli, these are all produced by his lack of adjustment. Most people have something approaching the "normal" amount of tension, some more, and some less. Each individual seems to have a range of toleration for unsettled tensions, such that as long as he remains within it there is no undue strain he cannot handle and still keep going in a normal manner. It is when our tensions get beyond our point of toleration that we begin to lose ground and become involved in disorganization of our adjustmental skills, and exhibit psychiatric symptoms and mechanisms of behavior.

2202. *Diagnosis of maladjustment not simple.* Behavior that is indicative of maladjustment takes many forms. The form, however, is not necessarily related to the cause of the maladjustment. In diagnosing physical disease, the physician is usually able to discover from the symptoms both the specific disease and the specific cause of it. His treatment is then indicated and he works directly on the cause. In cases of maladjustment, the relationship between symptoms, type of maladjustment, and cause is never uniform. Any serious conflict of whatever nature can give rise to almost any form of maladjustment, and any form of maladjustment can probably be shown to have originated at one time or another from almost every possible sort of serious conflict. A disease is the progressive logical outgrowth of the operation within the body of a specific virus, fungus, or malignant process. In maladjustment, there is no continuous unbroken line of controlled cause and effect relationships. The individual is not invaded by a pathogenic organism which lives according to law. He is upset by a psychological problem. What he does in his efforts to get away from the torment depends on what seems feasible under the circumstances. This behavior may vary tremendously from one individual to another. When indications of maladjustment are discovered, it is clear that something is wrong but the symptoms never reveal the source of the difficulty.

A general approach. Merely as an indication, and not in any sense as a complete description, some of the essentials in diagnosing and helping maladjustment will be sketched. Many problems that are of fairly recent origin, or that have not been so overwhelming as to be buried through repression, are known to the person who is upset. He may even bring his problems out for a discussion. When the problem is consciously known there is no reason why any mature adult who respects the integrity of the individual cannot help him. The first step is to become acquainted with the problem, and with the resources of the individual for dealing with it. This may require some observation of his behavior, some conferences, and whatever information can be had in other ways. The elements that are causing the difficulty must be located, whether they are in the home, the school, or the neighborhood. When all of this is apparent, the individual can be helped to plan a line of action that will overcome the constraints and barriers between him and adjustment. Mutual confidence is quite important in the relationships between the counselor and the counselee.

Sometimes a problem is pushed out of the conscious realm and forgotten. This creates a difficulty for the counselor for several reasons, which are touched on here. In the first place, the counselor usually has to find the cause of the difficulty without the help of the individual. This requires a high degree of familiarity with the ways in which conflicts develop, and the indicators they create in the behavior of the person. Sometimes his behavioral symptoms furnish some clues to the nature of the problem, as indicated in Figure 11, but the actual conflict is not revealed in that manner.

In the second place, a repressed conflict cannot be removed until it is brought back to conscious recognition and solved properly, as it should have been in the first place. It is not always difficult to bring a conflict back into recognition, although sometimes it is hard to get the individual to accept again a realistic picture of himself. He can't just be told what has upset him. He has built up a resistance to its discovery. The real problem is to bring it up for analysis without destroying the rapport between the counselor and the individual, and to keep the path open for solution.

This leads to the third difficulty, the emotional disturbance that will be reactivated when the conflict begins to come to the surface. Sometimes this involves a period of real stress, and the individual needs careful direction under such conditions to avoid being further hurt. Hence, the fourth problem is to help him find a solution that removes the conflict and restores equilibrium. In conflicts of sufficient seriousness to become repressed it is not easy to guide the individual back to a realistic use of his own resources. If the guidance is poorly done here, the person may be injured even more than he was before he came to the counselor.

A fairly safe guide for the classroom teacher who is not also a well-trained counselor is to work with problems that are not repressed, but refer the others to someone who has been properly trained for such a task. Caution is the better part of wisdom. Haste is usually not helpful. Let the teacher provide friendly contact for all who need help and learn to observe wisely before jumping to conclusions in the matter of treatment.

2203. *Common forms of maladjustment.* Maladjustment means bad adjustment. In other words, the individual is under tension because his life situation is awry in some way. As a factor in learning, maladjustment is so important that every teacher must be able to recognize it easily, regardless of the form in which it appears. When normal mastery of

CORRECTION OF MALADJUSTMENT

a barrier is thwarted, the individual may adopt any of a number of sorts of behavior. There is no end to the behavioral forms maladjustment may take to find release for the individual. A complete catalog of them might occupy a whole volume on clinical symptoms and their meaning. A convenient guide for quick reference is to be found in Drake's *Outline of Abnormal Psychology*.[1] No effort is made to list all the be-

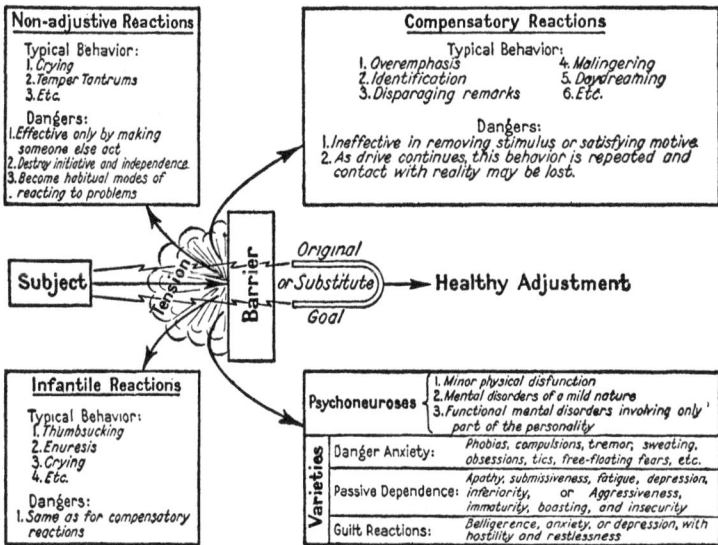

FIG. 12. POSSIBLE FORMS OF DEVIANT BEHAVIOR

havioral forms here, or to show all the symptoms. Instead, attention is given to some of the most common general forms of reaction. Anyone who works regularly with young people should become familiar with these general forms and learn gradually to recognize the kinds of specific reactions that could be classified under each of the more general headings. The four general types of reaction discussed here are illustrated in Figure 12, which is set up along the lines of the sequential steps, as a continuation of the scheme started in Figure 10.

[1] Raleigh Drake, *Outline of abnormal psychology*, Students Outline Series (New York: Longmans, Green and Co., Inc., 1936).

442 THE PSYCHOLOGY OF TEACHING

1. Sometimes under tension an individual's organized effort to solve a problem will disintegrate into some form of *non-adjustive reaction*. The reaction is usually one that has no possible value in terms of solving the problem, but that enables the individual to give vent to pent-up emotions. Temper tantrums of all sorts are the most common or noticeable non-adjustive reactions. The hammer that hits the thumb is thrown away. The golf club that will not get the ball out of the sand trap is broken. The chair that is in the way in the dark is given a vicious kick. The person who is baffled by some form of resistance may resort to tears of exasperation. Any act that releases pressure without contributing anything to the problem situation is of this type.

There are three dangerous characteristics of non-adjustive reactions: First, they do not remove the conflict because they neither overcome the barrier nor put an end to the motivation. Hence, they are valueless unless they induce someone else to act. Second, in such a case they tend to lead in the direction of surrendering the initiative to someone else whenever the going is rough. Such behavior will ultimately destroy individual initiative and originality. Third, because it is easier and more satisfying to get someone else to act than to act one's self, behavior is likely to follow the line of least resistance and the non-adjustive reaction may become established habitually.

The only successful prevention of cure for non-adjustive reactions is to ignore them, so that they will not produce a result that is satisfying to the individual. Any form of attention brought to the child by such behavior may provide sufficient reward to set it up as a preferred type of response. As paradoxical as it may sound, a spanking given to a screaming child to stop his screaming may result in strengthening the screaming reaction, because it brings the mother's attention with it. Attention is one of the most frequent goals of children, and if it can't be had pleasantly it will be sought unpleasantly.

2. Another form of reaction to tension is found in *compensatory behavior*. Any sort of behavior can be compensatory if it involves an effort to overcome or to redeem one's

self from a sense of defeat or inferiority. Sometimes this can be done by constructive effort in a direction other than that in which the inferiority developed. In some cases it is accomplished by applying one's self to the original task with such concentration that a triumph is finally achieved in spite of the original difficulties. This type of reaction is not undesirable unless it results in so much overemphasis on the compensating activity that it warps the individual's life. Even so, there is little doubt that some great contributions to social advancement have come from persons whose abilities could be traced to compensatory adjustments. Often compensation is found in wholly undesirable ways such as excessive daydreaming and withdrawal from reality, malingering, rationalization, and other psychological evasions.

Compensation involves a side-stepping of the original conflict, which usually means that the original conflict is never solved. At least it is not solved by the compensatory behavior. The usual history is somewhat like this: The individual is frustrated in some manner that is serious to him, through social embarrassment or continued defeat in his efforts to find satisfying status and adjustment. Through these defeats he develops a strong feeling of inferiority that disturbs his adjustment with himself, and he tends to believe that others regard him in the same way. This feeling becomes quite absorbing in its own right, apart from the conflicts that produced it, and the individual turns his attention to finding ways of assuring himself and others that he is not inferior. No matter what he does, he cannot solve his original problem in this manner; therefore, the compensatory behavior tends to continue indefinitely.

Compensatory reactions can be dangerous as well as useful. When they result in a socially valuable achievement, they are useful. If they operate within an individual to drive him to a socially useful achievement, but do so at the expense of his well-being in another direction, they may be both useful and harmful at the same time. When they are used primarily to restore self-respect through such escapes as rationalization, daydreaming, and the use of disparaging remarks, they involve two distinct dangers to mental health: First, they are ineffective in completely resolving the conflict between the person's motives and inabilities, so that the urge to act is never quite stilled. Second, because they provide some satisfaction and relief from feelings of defeat and inferiority, they may be resorted to so much that contact with reality is lost. The individual may retreat into an imaginary world and cut off thoughtful contact with the real world around him. When that happens it is literally impossible to reach him with any form of outside stimulation. Such people become immune to suggestion, innuendo, or logical analysis and discussion. When the isolation becomes well established, the individual does not possess the power to break it. If he re-establishes contact with the real world, it will probably be through the efforts of a psychiatrist or psychologist who is able to diagnose the original cause of the difficulty and correct it.

3. *Infantile reactions* are sometimes resorted to in conflict. The characteristic of an infantile reaction is a return to a form of behavior that is typical of an earlier stage of life than the present. Such reversions may happen when the person's usual ways of behaving turn out to be inadequate for a situation. In such a case, the alternatives are to find a new, appropriate way of acting or to withdraw from the battle and engage in some activity that was useful earlier in life in getting attention or relieving tension. Thumbsucking is a means of relieving tension and seems to be satisfying to those who engage in it. Enuresis gets attention, is a way of striking at those who take care of the individual, and involves sensations that may in themselves be satisfying to some degree. Having a good cry is for many people an excellent way of dispelling tension.

Preadolescence is a period marked by confusion about one's role in human culture and by ignorance of what actions are appropriate to the situation. Reversions to various forms of infantile reactions are common during this period until the individual begins to reorient himself and to discover what his new role is. He can then develop his techniques to match his new conception of himself and his environment. During the period before this orientation takes place, his old techniques seem inadequate when applied to the changing situation that develops for him, and he is confused and uncomfortable for a time. It is natural that he would fall back on some of the old sources of satisfaction. Nothing about such behavior is dangerous until the symptoms become so intense and pervasive that they take charge of his whole life and become substitutes for any constructive effort.

Infantile reactions that are relied on to the exclusion of constructive efforts to solve problems are dangerous for the same reasons as compensatory reactions.

4. The *psychoneuroses* constitute a fourth type of maladjustment. The forms of deviant behavior discussed up to this point may often be handled by any intelligent teacher who makes an effort to become acquainted with them. Psychoneuroses are almost exclusively the domain of the psychiatrist. The teacher must become able to recognize indications of psychoneurosis and should report suspicious cases to the proper agencies. With that as a premise, one should be familiar with the symptoms listed in Figure 12, but under no condition should one undertake the treatment of psychoneurotic behavior except as directed by a skilled technician.

5. Some undesirable behavior is due to *immaturity* rather than to conflict. The characteristic feature of such behavior is that it would be more appropriate to an earlier stage of life than the one in which it appears. It differs from infantile behavior in that the individual has never progressed to a more mature form of behavior. Hence he does not *revert,* he simply *remains* immature. A child is not expected to have a well-developed philosophy of life, but when an adult is confused about his basic values he may be said to be immature in that area. Immaturity is usually due to lack of experience, with resultant lack of development. Competent self-direction is not possible until the individual has gone through a period of trial and error in deciding his own problems. When parents or teachers refuse to let children govern themselves, some degree of immaturity is likely to result. The principal identification of immature behavior is that it is inappropriate to the person and the situation. Its dangers are obvious. If the individual has reached a stage in life where

he would be seriously embarrassed if he were to engage in the first tentative efforts to function in some previously denied manner, it is often difficult to overcome the condition.

This is the problem that was discussed in Chapters XII to XIV. It is introduced here because it is a significant source of poor adjustment. It is not accompanied by the psychiatric symptoms of the kind outlined in Figure 12 unless one's immaturity provokes additional conflicts and gives rise to other forms of maladjustment also.

2204. *Indicators of maladjustment.* There is always danger in making out lists of symptoms or signs of any given condition or set of conditions. Nevertheless, there is, in the case of maladjustment, an even greater danger in failing to offer teachers some sort of guide for the discovery of undesirable behavior tendencies. Accordingly, a list of common indications of adjustmental difficulty is presented in Table 6.

TABLE 6. COMMON INDICATORS OF MALADJUSTMENT IN
YOUNG PEOPLE

I. SYMPTOMS INDICATIVE OF UNSOLVED PROBLEMS

A. *Casual overt behavior:* Frowning; blinking; nailbiting; running hands through hair; adjusting clothing; biting lips, habitual wiggling of feet or other parts of body; constant moving around; restlessness; frequent minor complaints; muscle twitching; stammering; sudden changes in emotional tone, as in blushing.
B. *Intensive or explosive reactions:* Sudden frights; obsessions; tics; compulsions; anxieties; obvious fears; hysterical giggling, laughing, or crying; violence in argument; rigidity in ideas; inability to give attention to on-going tasks; hurt reaction to criticisms; explosive behavior when excited; apprehension; free-floating fears; emotional depressions; loss of contact with reality.
C. *Exhibitionism:*
  1. *Aggression:* Teasing; bullying; pushing others; picking on younger children; surly behavior in class; threatening others; assuming a tough attitude; ordering others around; efforts to belittle or embarrass others; blaming others for troubles.

2. *Self-display:* Seeking prominent roles; showing off; attempts to be center of activity; acting funny; bragging; bluffing; effusive efforts to be courteous or act in grandiose manner; lavishness; resistance to criticism; over-agreeableness; exaggeration.

D. *Preoccupation:* Use of excessive detail; worry over failures; daydreaming; absent-mindedness; marked inattention; insensitiveness to social situations.

E. *Withdrawal:* Excessive reading, especially for vicarious excitement and adventure; avoiding others; being as inconspicuous as possible; keeping out of social activities; inability to take praise; confusion at social advances of others.

F. *Minor physical disfunction:* Fatigue; shifting aches and pains; frequent headaches; motor retardation; loss of appetite; insomnia; digestive disorders.

II. SYMPTOMS OF IMMATURITY

A. *Poor motivational health:* Inability to work alone; constant seeking for advice; shifting responsibility to others; lack of curiosity; dependence on opinions of others; poor judgment due to lack of clear ideas of value; inconsistent or vague ideals; difficulty in making choices; constant seeking for assistance.

B. *Fixations or delays in normal progress:* Crushes on older persons, or age-mates of same sex, if they occur beyond adolescence; inability to make friends; efforts to win sympathy of teachers or others in charge; lack of interest in opposite sex during adolescence; dependence on parental authority in place of recognizing other authorities and facts; tomboy behavior; maintenance of any mode of behavior clearly typical of an earlier age.

A word of caution in the use of this table is appropriate. Since it is true that maladjustment is not a clearly separable category of human behavior apart from normality, it is also true that many, if not most, of the symptoms of maladjustment can be found in perfectly normal individuals. Hence, the mere presence of one or two of the characteristics described in Table 6 does not constitute a clear case for maladjustment. If the characteristics are present in any quantity, and they show up in an intensive manner, and pervade many areas of the person's activity, they justify the suspicion that the individual needs help. As a matter of fact, because normality means having the quality of the average, it allows for the presence in normal individuals of minor difficulties of all sorts. It is probably because of these minor difficulties that many of the characteristics in Table 6 are present in normal individuals; thus, although they are not maladjusted in the usual sense, neither are they perfectly adjusted. It is doubtful if there is such a thing as a perfectly adjusted person. Skillful use of any list of behavioral characteristics depends on an awareness and allowance for the *relativity* of any standard of judgment.

The *casual overt symptoms* are usually present in every person's behavior when he meets current problems, and in temporary conflicts that are not resolved quite soon. All they indicate is the presence of more energy than is needed, and therefore the presence of some inner disturbance. Since this is frequently a normal state, it is to be expected that these symptoms will be found in the behavior of many people who are not really maladjusted. If the symptoms disappear regularly, and recur later, it is probably because the individual keeps meeting new problems and solving old ones.

Intensive or explosive types of symptoms may indicate more serious disturbances, which are probably also of longer duration. They usually infer need for some adjustmental help in the form of improved circumstances, or re-education in one's ways of meeting issues.

Exhibitionism is usually compensatory in nature. It is a very common method of trying to establish one's importance, competence, or adequacy in the eyes of himself and others. That means it is probably a reaction to a feeling of inferiority and frustration. The person needs ways of getting acceptance, which are within his capabilities and socially approved. Among young children this is almost always an educational problem, but it can easily become a psychiatric problem.

Sections D, E, and F of Table 6 indicate deep-seated disturbances and serious dangers. *Preoccupation* and *withdrawal* produce quiet people who never disturb, and who are easily overlooked in a classroom. They need help as much or more than those who are active and aggressive. Their reactions mean that they are starting to sever contact with the world, and they need cultivation of their abilities so that they can cope with their problems in a realistic way and get satisfaction from so doing. The *psychosomatic symptoms* in section F almost always require clinical help and should not be excused as minor physical ailments that will soon wear themselves out. Where there is the slightest suspicion that a student is showing these symptoms because of emotional disturbance, there should be an investigation.

It is not the presence of one of these symptoms now and then that indicates maladjustment. It is a persistent cluster of them that is to be regarded as serious. Watch for pervasiveness, because symptoms that come and go now and then do not indicate continuous underlying disturbances. Watch also for concentration, because when real tensions are present the individual will display several, not just one or two, of the symptoms in any category. These are two fairly useful guides in deciding whether the symptoms are serious.

2205. *Delinquency is not personal maladjustment.* The symptoms of maladjustment are almost all outward signs of inward or mental distress. It is usually true that such mental distress is suffered because the individual will not resort to antisocial or illegal forms of behavior knowingly. The delinquent is usually different, that is, if he has no other personal conflicts with his delinquency. When that is the case, and he has no scruples against violating law or social custom, he is able to make a satisfactory adjustment in almost any situation. By so doing he avoids the mental distress that leads to psychological trouble. The problem in his case is not one of solving a complex psychiatric problem, it is one of re-education and redetermination of goals and values. The notable exception to this statement is found in the case of those psychoneurotics who steal or perform other antisocial acts compulsively. For them the psychiatric treatment is a prerequisite to curing the delinquency.

Without doubt, most of the student behavior to which teachers object is of the delinquent type. Dealing with it is not as simple as the mere enforcing of school rules and class procedures. On the other hand, a great deal of student behavior that is not objectionable to many teachers is very objectionable from the psychiatric point of view. It escapes the notice of many teachers because it does not disturb the work of the class. It is because of the two complicating factors, its psychological seriousness and the difficulty of discovering it, that teachers must become familiar with some sort of guide to its identification.

Illustrations of some of these sets of symptoms, and conditions of maladjustment, are available in cases cited throughout the book. Exhibitionist behavior is nicely illustrated in Case 12 in Chapter XVIII. A combination of exhibitionism and symptoms of immaturity are shown in the case of Dan in Chapter XXIII. Following is the case of a boy who has been withdrawing from normal social contacts. See how his values and process concepts have become patterned through past experience, and the manner in which he is trying to make his adjustment. Although he has been performing antisocial acts, it will be seen that they have been done in a manner intended to keep him out of contact with people. His behavior in the institution is quiet and unobtrusive, just as it would be were he in school. He could easily escape notice in a large classroom. The case history presented here is the one furnished by the institution to which he was committed. The analysis of his values and process concepts is furnished by DiVesta,[2] who assembled the case in his doctoral research.

Case 20

A Withdrawn Adolescent

Background of the Case

The boy was committed on the charges of larceny, unlawful entry and malicious mischief.

His father is 60 years old and was born in Scandinavia. The father has had a grammar school education and is a contractor. He lost a job paying ten thousand dollars a year and now works

[2] Francis J. DiVesta, *The role of personal values and process concepts in the personal and social adjustment of adolescents*, Ph.D. thesis (Ithaca, N. Y.: Cornell University, 1948).

at odd jobs. His interests are centered in the home and not in outside contacts. He is not warm or affectionate and has no plans for the boy. He is self centered and is not sympathetic toward the boy's interest or affection.

The mother is 57 and went through grammar school. She had one child who died and later she adopted the present boy. She is very domineering and rigid in her standards. She has no understanding or sympathy with the boy and is disinterested in his hobbies. There is anxiety about the boy's behavior.

The boy has had a gland operation for wire neck. He had glasses at the age of seven. His I.Q. on the revised beta examination is 119 and on the Otis S.A. is 129.

The following is copied from the clinical case record.

The boy likes to read and has electrical interests. The parents complain about this because he refuses to help with the housework. He took small amounts of money and items which he used for radio experimentation. He returned everything but the money. The boy feels bitter about commitment. Feels he got a "lousey" deal and doesn't belong here. Hates mother. Close relationship between boy and new foster parents. Boy placed in foster home at six years of age. Now has difficulty with public school teachers. Parents can't control him. A year ago he began getting involved in burglaries. He was placed in a private school by the mental hygienist. He was rejected because of misbehavior. He entered another public school. He was not considered a behavior problem there. Mother said he never engaged in the usual sports with other boys. He was excused from gym class in school. Unable to adjust to other boys. The same situation exists in present institution. He was given musical lessons at an early age. Took little interest in them at that time. Later developed an enthusiasm and tried to learn by himself and to compose musical compositions. At fourteen years of age parents requested that the boy be placed in an institution because he was ungovernable and incorrigible. A month after this request he stole and was placed immediately thereafter. Boy claims to be frail. Very introspective. Hypochondriacal. Facial mannerisms. He claims, "No one likes me, everyone acts queer to me." Self-pity. Feels that he is not accepted. Is ill at ease. Isolated. No close friends. Indulges in isolated activities. Little skill in anything due to no experience. Got to taking things because of his unhappiness, he claims. Ambivalent attitude toward mother. Denies hostility in second interview. Feels rejected. Never acquired skills in group. Requires long handling and group therapy.

VALUE PATTERN AND PROCESS CONCEPT PATTERN OF CASE 20

Privacy (group privacy and solitude)
Recognition
Friends (conformist and non-conformist)
Formal social activity
Freedom (intellectual and physical)
Home life (family and home setting)
Acclaim
Informal social activity
Power (leadership and control)
Religion (living and organization)
Excitement (pure and work)

	Excitement	Freedom	Friendship	Prestige	Religion	Privacy	Leadership	Soc. Activity	Home Life	Attitude Score
Belonging to a club	2		1	1	1	5	5	1	1	2
Playing sports	1	1	1	1	1	5	5	1	1	2
Attending school	3	1	1	4	1	5	5	1	1	
Going to western and crime movies	4		2		1	1	5	1	1	1
Going to parties	5		1	2	1	5	5	1	1	4
Living in the city	5	5	5		5	5	5	1	5	5
Skipping school	5	5	5	1	5	1	5	5	5	5
Playing pool	1		2	1	1	1	5	5	1	1
Belonging to the boy scouts	5	1	1	3	1	5	5	1	1	4
Hitchhiking	2	5	5	4	5	5	5		5	5
Raising cain in school	3		1	1	5		1	5	5	5
Being able to win a fight	5		1	1	3	5	1		1	5
Obeying the policeman	2	1	1	4	1	1	5	1	1	1
Getting away with something	5	5	5	1	4		1		5	2
Being a class officer	4	1	1	1	1	5	1	1	1	2
Staying at home	1	1	5		1	1	5	5	5	1
Doing something daring	1		1	1	1		1	1	5	1
Living in the country	1	1	3		1	1	5	1	1	1
Smoking and swearing		5	5	1	1	5	1		5	1
Obeying the teacher		1	1	4	1	1	1		1	2
Making others do what you want	5	5	4	3	5	1	5	5		5
Being tough	5	5	1	5	5	1	5	5		5

Aggression score = 43
Average = 3.3

Explanations and interpretations. Before interpretation of the patterns is made, one caution must be presented to the reader. This case, as in other cases used in the present study, is selected as an ideal example of the type for which it was chosen. This caution is made lest the reader conclude that every case is as clear cut or as clearly defined as the one presented. As in the use of any other test a certain degree of judgment must be made on "border-line" cases. Another caution must be observed in that a small sample has been used to represent the withdrawn cases. The data presented here are for purposes of further investigation.

The value pattern of this individual shows a marked consistency between parts. Social activity and prestige were the only two values which ranked differently in each part of the test in which they appeared. This is an indication that he was not sensitive to the differences in meaning between the representations of the other values in each part. For example, privacy is highly valued by him regardless of the situation with which he is confronted. Excitement is unimportant to him, if not a circumstance to be shunned, in any situation.

Ranking privacy or solitude at the top of the pattern is characteristic of individuals studied in the withdrawn classification. The need for recognition is second only to privacy. Excitement, which is the antithesis of privacy is placed last. Power and religious activity rank among the unimportant values for this individual. A possible explanation of this is that power, as a circumstance of living, would place him in a position he would expect to cause him to feel more ill at ease and unaccepted than he is now. The value pattern of this individual corroborates the description of, and the symptom syndrome for, individuals in this group to a high degree.

The concept pattern indicates that being tough, making others do what you want, being a class officer, being able to win a fight, and attending school are some of the processes which are detrimental to the achievement of privacy. On the other hand, going to movies, skipping school, playing pool and staying at home are some of the processes beneficial to the achievement of privacy. An examination of the responses on the process concept test reveals a predominance of 1 and 5 responses. These responses reflect the caution with which he behaves in a situation and his general highly positive or negative beliefs about the processes as means of achieving values. The aggression score of 43 indicates that the boy dislikes aggressive means of doing things.

The value pattern and process concept pattern may be taken as a framework around which to structure the personality pattern from the case material. The role he has assumed in his adjustment is partly influenced by his self centered father who has taken little interest in other matters. Since the boy believes he is disliked and unaccepted, privacy has emerged as an important value. In privacy he has no one bothering him and he is able to continue in his interests which he is unable to do otherwise. His mother being domineering and rigid in her standards is detrimental to the furtherance of the boy's needs. In the investigator's opinion the boy's interests and intelligence are indicative of a high level capacity. He would be capable of making a good adjustment were these capacities allowed development. The social skills he needs can only be acquired through an understanding of the way he evaluates the situations he is in. This is provided to some extent in the value and process concept patterns.

2206. *How the teacher can help.* The process of discovering maladjustment is treated in Chapter XXV. At this point it is appropriate to direct the teacher's attention to a few facts concerning the treatment of undesirable behavior:

1. If the problem is in its incipient stage, a teacher may be able to find the conflict or frustration and correct it. This is especially true if it is a problem created by the educational work of the school.

2. If the problem does not respond fairly soon to whatever treatment the teacher has selected, or if the cause is not clearly ascertainable, it should be referred to a capable psychologist or psychiatrist as soon as possible.

3. Problems that show symptoms of the psychoneuroses are clearly beyond the teacher's reach. Help should be obtained without delay.

4. Problems that obviously stem from troubles outside the school or classroom are probably beyond the reach of a single teacher. The cooperation of other teachers, administrators, or parents may be needed.

5. When there is any question of whether the matter is amenable to educational treatment, skilled help should be secured in the diagnosis. If the teacher can then carry out the indicated treatment, the technician will tell him so.

6. Teachers must not be *afraid* to refer pupils to special personnel for study. Doing so involves no loss of prestige; rather, it signifies a degree of judgment and sensitivity that is very commendable. It is far better to refer too many than too few.

7. When the problem has an educational origin and is subject to educational treatment, two lines of effort are involved: (a) changing the point of view of the person toward the matters involved in the problem, and (b) changing his situation or setting to meet his needs.

(a) *Changing the person's point of view.* Prejudice is a form of blindness. It arises, not from a desire to be arbitrary, but from an unfortunate interpretation of one's personal experiences. If, over a period of time, a student has unpleasant relations with schoolteachers, and suceeds in laying the blame on the teachers by means of rationalization, he will have a prejudice against teachers. His prejudice will make it very difficult, if not impossible, for him to view impartially any measure a teacher may take in dealing with him. Therefore, a plan of action devised by the teacher and offered to the student will probably be viewed with suspicion or worse. The fact that the plan was genuinely beneficial to the student would not change his point of view. His past experiences have led him to believe that anything a teacher does is bad for the student.

This is an extreme example of the effect of a point of view on a student's adjustment in school, but it differs from the true situation of most students only in degree. At the other end of the scale, there are students so sure that teachers would do nothing to hurt them that they would accept any teacher-made suggestion uncritically and without an effort to understand its purpose.

These attitudes or prejudices are of tremendous importance in determining whether any given situation is helpful or harmful to a student. A disillusioned, soured, rebellious student can be in a psychologically damaging situation even when he is surrounded by the kindest teachers in the world, if all he sees around him is a threat to his well-being. The power to help a student depends on the ability to win his confidence and respect. There are times when to do that requires a demonstration of good intent so convincing and so far-reaching that many school administrators balk at the proposal. It is unwise, of course, to upset the normal program of a school to any greater extent than is necessary in meeting the problems of individual students. On the other hand, there is no adequate substitute for the necessary pupil-teacher rapport. Unless this can be developed, there is little the school can do to help the students. Changing a student's point of view may involve various lines of attack:

(1) An unfavorable attitude toward a given subject may be due to a deficiency in that area. The deficiency may take the form of a missing technique or an inadequate concept. Diagnostic procedures may help the teacher find and correct the deficiency, and change the student's disinterest into interest.

(2) Unfavorable attitudes toward school are often due to lack of understanding of the value of education in general, or of any specific subject in the school program. A change in point of view in such cases depends on a reinterpretation of the place of education and schoolwork in life, its relationship to success and happiness.

(3) Unfavorable attitudes toward the regulations and procedures in school may stem from failure to comprehend the value of cooperative activity and sharing of responsibility and privilege. A change in point of view in such cases hinges around discovery that there are values in such procedures.

(b) *Changing the situation.* The process of adjustment of pupil and school requires that *each* learn to give and take to some extent. Changing a student's situation in school may involve a number of approaches. A partial list is given here:

(1) Modification of requirements in a class. This can take the form of a change in the amount of work required, or a change in the nature of the work required. Students' special interests can be used effectively in almost every class in school.

(2) Change in registration. A student's situation may be materially improved by shifting him to a different teacher, another grade, another section of the same grade or subject,

or a new subject. Shifts should be made in harmony with the student's point of view if he is to regard them as helpful.

(3) Change from one curriculum to another. Individuals differ in their adaptability to any given line of work. College preparatory courses are unsuited to some. They should be able to study materials that will be profitable to them.

(4) Provision of special facilities and arrangements to meet unusual physical, emotional, or mental conditions. This may require a fundamental alteration of such routine procedures as attendance requirements, registration requirements, graduation plans, or the definition of what constitutes a course of study. It is common practice to make such provision for mentally retarded students. It is exceedingly uncommon to find such provisions for those who are emotionally upset, but their need is just as great. When it is believed that a student might be helped by allowing him to work along some line such as shopwork under the informal man-to-man influence of a teacher who is respected, such a program may be greatly superior to an effort to enforce regular attendance at classes in which the student is moving toward sure failure. The development of confidence under such an arrangement might lead to the gradual reconstruction of the student's point of view concerning school and life.

School administrators are properly cautious about allowing innovations where the need is not apparent. Needs, not whims, should be the basis of special modifications of a school program. Guesswork is not an adequate basis for deciding which is which. Each case should be studied objectively and carefully.

QUESTIONS FOR REVIEW

1. What is a good, short definition of normal?
2. Is a person with an IQ of 140 abnormal? Why?
3. Is it often desirable to be abnormal? Why?
4. What is deviant behavior?
5. Define adjustment. Define maladjustment.
6. What can you infer about cause from the symptoms of maladjustment?
7. Define a non-adjustive reaction and give an illustration or example.

8. Define compensatory behavior and give an example.
9. Does compensatory behavior have any value? How can you decide?
10. Define infantile reaction and give an example.
11. Define psychoneurosis.
12. What are four types of psychoneurosis?
13. List the common symptoms of the types of psychoneurosis.
14. Why is immaturity a cause of maladjustment?
15. What is the characteristic feature of behavior due to immaturity?
16. Define delinquency so as to differentiate it from personal maladjustment.
17. How would you proceed to change a student's faulty point of view?
18. How would you decide when a case should be referred to special personnel?
19. In what ways can the school attempt to change a student's situation?
20. What is the difference between compensatory behavior and substitution?
21. In what form of psychoneurosis will you find:
    a. Phobias, compulsions, etc?
    b. Fatigue, inferiority feelings, emotional depression?
    c. Uncontrolled laughing or crying, or dissociation?
    d. Apprehension, or free-floating fears?
22. What are some of the general clusters of behavior characteristics that indicate maladjustment?

SELECTED REFERENCES

Theodora M. Abel and Elaine F. Kinder, *The subnormal adolescent girl* (New York: Columbia University Press, 1942), Chapters 6, 7, and 8.

Luella Cole, *Psychology of adolescence* (3rd ed.; New York: Rinehart and Co., Inc., 1948), Chapter VI.

Arthur I. Gates, Arthur T. Jersild, T. R. McConnell, and Robert C. Challman, *Elucational psychology* (New York: The Macmillan Co., 1948), Chapter XX.

Walter C. Langer, *Psychology and human living* (New York: Appleton-Century-Crofts, Inc., 1943), Chapter 12.

E. D. Partridge, *Social psychology of adolescence* (New York: Prentice-Hall, Inc., 1939), Chapter XIII.

CORRECTION OF MALADJUSTMENT 459

E. K. Wickman, *Teachers and behavior problems* (New York: The Commonwealth Fund, 1938).

CLASS EXERCISES ON DEALING WITH MALADJUSTMENT

Things To Do outside Class

1. Using cases 12, 13, 15, 16, 20, 21, or 26, have each student carry out the following steps:

    a) Check the behavior against Table 6. Does the student display in concentration any of these sets of symptoms? If so, which?

    b) Check the behavior against Figure 11. Which kinds of symptoms are present, and which kinds of barriers seem to be involved?

    c) Check the behavior against Figure 12. Is the student in one of these four categories? If so, which?

    d) Sketch out copies of Tables 13, 14, 15, and 16. Fill them in as fully as possible for each case.

    e) In the light of the preceding analyses, and if this student were in your class, what would your diagnosis be? What would you do *next?* Would you need the help of any other specialized personnel? If so what kind? Can you now suggest any remedial plans for some of the cases, and if so what would they be?

    The instructor might, if he wishes, furnish the students with a set of specific diagnostic questions for each case used. The students working on each case could confer or act as a panel for a class discussion after they have made their preparations.

2. Discuss the students' replies to the questions in Case 21, after they have worked on them outside of class. In this discussion see that the students learn how to go back to the data and make a careful evaluation of them before making decisions concerning the questions.

Case 21

The Case of Dan, an Exercise for the Students

The case of Dan illustrates the gradual development of maladjustment over a period of several grades.

A. How can the school help Dan?

B. After reading the case carefully, discuss the following questions:

1. Indicate YES, NO, or NO DATA for the following:
   _____ a. Dan had speech difficulties in early years.
   _____ b. Dan is tall for his age.
   _____ c. Dan is physically weak.
   _____ d. Dan's whooping cough affected his eyes.
   _____ e. Dan's first four teeth were slow in coming.
   _____ f. Dan needs special help in reading.
   _____ g. If Dan transferred to a public school he should go back one grade in arithmetic.
   _____ h. Same as g, with relation to spelling.
   _____ i. Same as g, with relation to reading.
   _____ j. Dan has been consistently ill-mannered.
   _____ k. Dan lacks poise and becomes confused easily.
   _____ l. Dan bullies younger children.
   _____ m. Dan developed signs of nervousness in grade 3.
   _____ n. Dan is in poor physical form.
   _____ o. There are good indications of overprotection at home.
   _____ p. Dan is not happy at home.
   _____ q. Dan's stuttering is clearly due to his shift from left- to right-handedness.
   _____ r. Dan's heterosexual adjustment is satisfactory.
   _____ s. Dan seems to be trying to evade reality.
   _____ t. Dan is physiologically still a child.

2. Indicate whether the following procedures would probably (1) help, (2) hurt, or (3) not affect Dan's development. Answer by writing numbers.
   _____ a. Transfer him to a public school.
   _____ b. Demote him one grade.
   _____ c. Put him in a new group of children.
   _____ d. Have him rest one hour each day.
   _____ e. Control his diet.
   _____ f. Make him realize he is doing inferior work.
   _____ g. Stimulate him more strongly to compete with others.
   _____ h. Send him to a boys' camp in summer.
   _____ i. Find him a task involving some responsibility and leadership.
   _____ j. Educate him at home with private tutors.
   _____ k. Keep him out of group sports.

3. Tell as briefly as possible how Dan has attempted to gain status.

4. Which of Dan's adolescent tasks are progressing satisfactorily?
5. Which of Dan's adolescent tasks are giving him trouble?
6. Justify each item listed in question 5.

SCHOOL RECORD OF DAN

Birth Date: December 28, 1926.

Status on February 28, 1941: Age—14 years 2 months; 8th grade.

Attendance: Entered elementary school October 29, 1934, in Grade 2. Withdrew June, 1935, and re-entered in November, 1935. Regular since then.

Home Background: Father and mother both Jewish, with Austro-Hungarian background. Father was 36 years 8 months old, mother was 32 years 10 months old when Dan was born. Father completed elementary school, and mother completed high school. Dan was a full-term baby, and birth was normal. He has a brother born September, 1916. The family occupies a 9-room apartment with one servant. Father is in a manufacturing business in a large midwestern city.

Physical Growth: Dan had the following childhood diseases:

Whooping cough	1927	Mumps	1931
Chicken pox	1930	Measles	1934
German measles	1931	Scarlet fever	1934

Naturally left-handed, but forced to switch to right-handedness as a very young child. Has been from 38 per cent to 64 per cent overweight continuously since entering school. Abdominal protrusion since 1937. Posture poor.

Sexual development normal except delayed descent of right testis at age of 9.

Knock-kneed 3° and flatfooted since December 19, 1934.

Mother reported him to be sensitive, and to have a vivid imagination, when he entered the school. Myopic vision since December 19, 1934; eye muscle effect since October 7, 1936; has worn glasses since December 19, 1935.

Mental Tests:

Date	Test	C.A.	M.A.	I.Q.	P
1/11/35	Binet	97	106	110	
1/29/36	K-A	109	98	90	
1/5/37	Binet	120	130	108	
2/2/37	K-A	121	138	106	22
11/15/37	K-A	131	132	101	11

Mental Tests: (continued)

Date	Test	C.A.	M.A.	I.Q.	P
11/3/38	K-A	142	137½	97	7
10/19/39	K-A	154	146	95	10
10/19/40	K-A	166	176	106	17

The percentiles for the Kuhlmann-Anderson tests are based in independent school populations similar to that of Dan's school.

High School Marks:

Grade 7, 1939-40			Grade 8, 1940-41	
English I	C	C	Eng. II	Cond.
Shop I	C	D	Soc. Sci.	C
Typing	C	Dropped	Math. II	Cond.
Math. I	D	D	Science II	D
Soc. Sci. I	C	C	Shop II	Cond.
Music		C	Remedial Math.	
Band		C	Phys. Ed. II	D
Phys. Ed.	C	C	Band 3	
Science I		D		

Some Achievement Test Data:

Date	Test	Score	Grade Place-ment	Grade Equiv.	Age Educ.	Chron. Age	P
			General Achievement Battery				
4/6/37	Metro.	323	4	5.6	133	132	
4/27/38	Metro.	369	5	6.1	140	136	24
5/9/39	Metro.	519	6	7.8	160	148	25
4/3/40	Metro.	567	7	8.3	165	159	19
			Reading Achievement				
4/6/37	Metro.	44½	4	6.4½	145	123	
11/1/37	New.St.	81	5	6.8	151	130	
3/16/38	N.S.	82	5	7.0	152	135	
4/27/38	Metro.	47	5	6.8	148	136	35
11/2/38	N.S.	87	6	7.6	161	142	
11/9/38	Iowa Sil.	114	6	7.7	161	142	
5/9/39	Metro.	62	6	8.2	164	148	33
10/10/35	Iowa S.	66¾	7	8.0	154	153	
4/30/40	Metro.	72	7	9.3	176	159	52
10/16/40	Iowa S.	68	8	8.7	161	166	

Arithmetic Achievement

4/6/37	Metro.	28	4	4.8½	124	123	
11/8/37	N.S.	67.5	5	5.4	135	130	
4/27/38	Metro.	35	5	5.5	132	136	23
11/4/38	N.S.	77	6	6.3	146	142	
5/9/39	Metro.	48	6	6.8	148	148	10
4/3/40	Metro.	55	7	7.6	157	159	10

Descriptive Comments Recorded by Teachers:

Grade II

Behavior good, application good; very polite and well-behaved. No emotional difficulties. Careful of his own and others' property. Does not disturb others. Has no nervous habits. "Fairly high" in posture when walking and sitting, and "average" when standing. Muscular coordination average or below. No speech difficulties. Always right-handed.

"Dan has been in the lowest reading ability group but his progress has been very satisfactory. . . He read in a very affected manner. . . Now he is one of the most fluent readers in the small group and he reads in a very pleasing and interesting expression."

Second semester: "Dan went to Florida for two weeks before our spring vacation. Then shortly after his return he contracted scarlet fever and was absent five weeks. These absences have had a marked effect on his progress. In arithmetic, especially, he will need help in third grade. He was a slow learner and careless. He had a good start in learning the addition combinations but has not learned the larger subtraction facts. Dan should not need special help in reading if he continues some practice during the summer. . . Tests show he is ready for the third grade."

Grade III

"Dan does not work to the best of his ability, and his progress has not been as marked as it would have been had he not been lazy and absent so much. . . Spelling and arithmetic are his most difficult subjects. . . He will probably not be a strong fourth-grade pupil unless he mends his ways. He does have the ability to work."

"Dan's emotions are not especially strong. He is a jolly, good-natured boy. He lacks poise and is easily thrown off balance

and confused. He evades the issue when faced with any difficulties or failures. He lacks a feeling of adequacy to meet
situations and does not appear to feel secure. . . Dan's long and
many absences from school have been a handicap. He is honest
and truthful. He does not fight but he likes to tease. He is never
irritable and seldom daydreams. He bites his nails occasionally."

"He entered late in the year and has been absent frequently
for days at a time. He went to Florida for several weeks so there
are gaps in his learning."

"He works with little energy. He usually is cooperative—to
the best of his ability."

"This year he is a little less well-behaved about fighting in
line and talking excessively. Not so careful of his own and
others' property. He argues at times, and quarrels with others,
and is occasionally overstimulated by competition. He bites his
nails, and eats paste. Ordinarily well-behaved. No speech defects."

"I fear Dan does not always work to the best of his ability.
He learns arithmetic quite readily but is careless and unwilling
to check his work unless urged to do so. Dan is very friendly
and sociable and the children like him. I hope that his attendance
will be more regular and uninterrupted."

"Dan seems to be much more sluggish in his movements than
he was earlier in the year. He appears to try to spare himself
any exertion. . . Lately he has been having rather silly streaks
of behavior. . . I do not believe that his lower rating is due to
lack of cooperation, but probably there is some physical cause
back of it. He is extremely heavy for his age . . . Dan is an
unusually polite boy . . . Perhaps the silliness previously spoken
of may be a defense mechanism to cover embarrassment for his
size . . . Dan has a very wholesome personality. He is a most
desirable member of the group. Dan shows fine home training,
based on much that is inherently fine. In spite of his great
handicap of overweight, Dan enters wholeheartedly into every
form of activity whether it be rhythm, apparatus work or
games. . . (in June) Dan has several physical handicaps: his
vision is poor; his feet are flat and pronated and he is much overweight . . . I think he needs more training in facing reality, as
there seems to be a growing tendency to make excuses for himself. Dan is quite an outstandingly courteous child, not in a
superficial way but due to really nice feelings."

Grade IV

"Dan has perhaps the most serious emotional problem which has come to my notice in the elementary school. He feels very insecure. His disturbed condition colors his behavior in all situations.

"His size, his enormous appetite which is greatly overindulged, his loquaciousness, his grandiose manner, his lavish spending of money, all make him conspicuous in an undesirable way.

"He does not face reality but evades situations which do not look easy. He bluffs—pretending to read a book in half an hour. He volunteers frantically and is laughed at for his ridiculous responses. His mind continually goes off at a tangent. Also he stutters."

"If there ever was a case in school in need of the services of a good psychiatrist, in my opinion, this is one."

"I feel that Dan faces the problem of weaning himself from kindly but oversolicitous parents. He could readily be one of the most popular boys in his group if he continues to show the other boys that he can fight his own battles. I feel that Dan's scholastic success will, in part, depend upon his emancipation from home influence (within reason). He has apparently conquered many of his fears of others. He has gained the respect of many boys who used to laugh at him. His disposition helps him to refrain from taking unfair advantage of others whom he has intimidated. He needs further guidance and encouragement in this adjustment."

Dan has a tendency to telephone his parents as soon as there is anything wrong, such as a loose tooth, bent glasses or an imagined ache. He is inclined to complain of little aches and pains so he can go home. He seems to be afraid of work.

"Dan began the habit of stuttering soon after the beginning of the school year. It developed quite suddenly from some emotional state of mind through events in the home. When one checks him, he ceases to stutter. He has partially overcome this temporary speech defect."

"Dan is handicapped by emotional instability. He feels insecure, I am sure. His work was fairly good at first, but through absence and more particularly from a disturbed mental outlook his work has gradually decreased in amount and in quality. I think Dan's case is serious. We have conferred with both parents and it is obvious what the difficulty is. In an attempt to make life as ideal as possible for Dan, he has been indulged and sheltered from all unpleasantness and from difficult situations, with the result that he is afraid of the world and more specifically the fourth grade.

"In reality, Dan could, and has established a place in the group that many boys might envy. What he needs most is intelligent letting alone. He should not be sheltered and pampered by his parents. He needs broader social contacts in play situations. Apparently Dan has successfully learned to play on the imagination of his parents and is thus able to magnify imagined situations which are apparently only a subterfuge he employs to evade reality. Lately he has shown improvement and it seems like an ideal time for him to gain a real feeling of adequacy and independence."

ABSTRACT OF GROWTH DATA FOR DAN

Weight and Height					Arithmetic			
Date	C.A.	Weight	W.A.	Height	H.A.	Date	C.A.	Test	A.A.
12/19/34	96	84.6	152	52.1	113	4/6/37	123	Metro.	124
12/19/35	108	97.5	167	53.97	123	11/37	130	N.S.	135
10/7/36	118	105.0	189	55.78	136	4/38	136	Metro.	132
9/17/37	129	121.0	202	57.28	145	11/38	142	N.S.	146
10/26/38	142	143.25		59.68	156	5/39	148	Metro.	148
11/1/39	154	157.75		62.00	169	4/40	159	Metro.	157
11/6/40	166	191.75		64.76	182				

Hand Squeeze					Dentition			
Date	C.A.	Lbs.	Kgms.	G.A.	Date	C.A.	No. Perm. Teeth	D.A.
12/19/34	96	31	14.1	92	12/34	96	11	101
12/19/35	108	31	14.1	92	12/35	108	12	107
10/7/36	118	36	16.4	103	10/36	118	12	107
9/17/37	129	40	18.2	110	9/37	129	19	134
10/26/38	142	50	22.7	136	10/38	142	24	143
11/1/39	154	72	32.7	180	11/39	154	28	159
11/6/40	166	73	33.2	183	11/40	166	28	159

Mental Age			Reading Age				
C.A.	M.A.		Date	C.A.	Test	Score	R.A.
97	106		4/37	123	Metro.	44.5	145
109	98		11/37	130	N.S.	81.0	151
120	130		3/38	135	N.S.	82.0	152
121	128		4/38	136	Metro.	47.0	148
131	132		11/38	142	N.S.	87.0	161

Mental Age				Reading Age			
C.A.	M.A.		Date	C.A.	Test	Score	R.A.
142	137.5		11/38	142	Iowa	114.0	161
154	146		5/39	148	Metro.	62.0	164
166	176		10/39	153	Iowa	63.75	154
			4/10	159	Metro.	72.0	176

Educational Age

Date	C.A.	Test	Score	E.A.
4/37	123	Metro.	323	133
4/38	136	Metro.	369	140
5/39	148	Metro.	519	160
4/40	159	Metro.	567	165

CHAPTER XXIII

MALADJUSTMENT AND THE SCHOOL

2301. *Introduction.* The two preceding chapters discussed maladjustment without reference particularly to how
it is related to the school. Its development was considered
first, and its recognition and correction after that. While
it is a matter of concern everywhere, it has special importance to the school where the circumstances are such that
it can very seriously impair the whole program. There is
such close contact between the teacher and all the members
of a class, maintained over such a large part of each day,
that unless relationships are of the best the work must suffer.
Because of those close relationships it is also very easy for
tensions to develop, and grow into maladjustment. Hence it
is a factor that affects the work of the school, and it is
an effect produced by the work of the school. It may exist
in the student and upset the teacher and the student, and
it may also exist in the teacher, and upset both him and
the students. In such close-working relationships it is especially important for the school staff to be conscious of the
problem, and to have some insight into its relationship to
schoolwork.

The human being is a remarkably resilient creature. He
can absorb an enormous amount of disturbance, disappointment, frustration, and strain, and continue to push it behind
and come back for more. The wonder is not that so many
hospital beds are now occupied with mental cases, but that
there is not a much larger number so occupied, in view of
the tension of modern life. Perhaps because of this, we have
somehow come to feel that the school has done a good
job if it only keeps from making students neurotic. Actually, little credit can go to any social institution on that
score. It is the individual who absorbs the shocks and gets

over them. There is a great deal of room for improvement in the hygiene of the school atmosphere, both for the students and the teachers. We should be less satisfied with the escape from neuroticism, and become interested in the promotion of optimal development. This is not difficult to do, provided we become seriously interested in it, and take the trouble to study the problem. To combat maladjustment, and move toward higher goals, one must know quite thoroughly how it is produced, how it affects us when it is present, its symptoms and most prolific sources in schoolwork, and how to eliminate the points of origin. Surely teachers should be able to see that their own lives could be made inestimably more enjoyable if this were done.

2302. *Student maladjustment as a product of the school.* Most maladjusted people owe their conditions to a long-continued succession of disturbing experiences. A child may acquire from his family during the preschool years a well-established set of social techniques, habits, and process concepts, which begin to embroil him in difficulties from the moment he enters school. After a few months or years of such difficulty it is not surprising if he becomes maladjusted in his school relationships. Such predisposing problem tendencies may have been acquired outside the home, through a gang, and again over a period of some time. Another child may come into school with typical past experiences, and encounter a series of frustrations, rebuffs, and struggles with his own ideas of right and wrong, which in time throw him off balance and into the use of deviant behaviors.

Sometimes a reasonably well-adjusted individual can be thrown off balance by one very serious and far-reaching difficulty. A transferred student may, for example, unwittingly become the victim of an unfortunate introduction to his new schoolmates, and thereby acquire a place in the eyes of his new teachers and associates that prejudices his adjustment from the beginning. Some of the incidents reported in this chapter illustrate this, as well as several other disturbing situations. The possible sources of disturbance may, in other words, range from little episodes that in themselves are of minor significance except as they accumulate, to major dramatic experiences that are sufficient in themselves to upset adjustment and set the stage for further conflict. They may also be found in every aspect of the school's program and in all the relationships between students and teachers. There is no possibility of making up a complete list of trouble spots in school, and it is not necessary to do so. If a teacher is really interested in preventing maladjustment, he cannot hope to do it by memorizing a list of troublesome situations to avoid. He must understand the psychological factors that make conflicts possible, and be prepared to recognize the essential elements of a conflict wherever and whenever they appear, and in whosoever case. He must be able to read the symbols of trouble for himself, as a child learns to read the symbols of words, so that he can find the meaning as easily in new pages of life as in those he has memorized in the past.

In a suggestive vein, then, some of the most common sources of friction for students will be cited here, as illustrations of general types of situations. There are many others, and they appear in constantly changing form.

1. *The teacher's personality and manner.* As indicated in Chapter XXI this factor seems to be the most common offender in creating stress for students. There are unfortunately quite a few embittered, short-tempered teachers in the schools, who do not hesitate to use sarcasm, angry epithets, insulting criticism or other equally dangerous ways of venting their own inner sourness on students who for any reason fail to comply with their orders and wishes. Outside of school this would be bad enough even when the aggrieved party can defend himself or turn and walk away. In school it is intolerable. The student is in no position to defend himself, nor can he walk away. Such abuse of a student by one who is in a dominant position is cowardly and uncivilized. See Case 5.

Not all of the personality clashes come from embittered or angry teachers, however, because even those who think they are being jovial and kindly sometimes create real disturbances. Attempts to be funny, especially at the expense of another person, are dangerous at any time. Some of the episodes reported in this chapter and elsewhere show that to be the case. Any effort on the part of the teacher to make himself appear clever or admirable is not only in poor taste but is frequently due to his own disturbed feeling, and runs the danger of being clumsy and irritating to others. Some students are easily embarrassed, by such seemingly innocuous events as the one reported in Case 28, later in the chapter, or by Cases 22 and 23, which follow immediately. Perhaps the most dangerous fault a teacher can have is lack of social sensitivity, by which is meant the ability to sense what others feel, and to influence a situation so that it helps others adjust and feel secure. Regardless of the particular act, then, for there are countless ways in which a teacher can put a student into a disturbing situation, the best approach to the elimination of such difficulties is in the cultivation of social sensitivity. This is possible, and not particularly difficult, if the teacher will learn to *see* and *hear* what is going on around him. He can't do this and do very much talking at the same time. Those who have really learned how to listen are in the minority, and the same is probably true for the ability to observe what is really happening within others around us. Observation can be cultivated by frequently allowing the group to carry on its activities as if the teacher were not there, while he just watches and listens. There is a wealth of insight into human nature to be gained in this manner.

Cases 22 and 23 are typical instances of disturbance due to a clumsy act on the part of a teacher.

Case 22

"Funny" Teacher Frightens a Child

I had finished the eighth grade having had one term of Algebra during that year. On entering high school in the fall, I was admitted to the second term Algebra class. About the second or third day of class, I was called on for something, and I used terminology which I had learned in the eighth grade. I don't remember what the term was. The teacher spoke to me and called me (jokingly, I know, but it was scathing to me then) "A little one-term freshman." It was one of the most embarrassing moments of my life.

Much is behind this incident which made it embarrassing for me. I had always been timid, often walking around a city block to avoid meeting someone, especially if it was a girl. My grade school work was in a rural school, and considerable adjustment was necessary when I entered the city high school of 1,200 students. I was overwhelmed those first few weeks, and to have a teacher address me in such fashion was almost too much.

Case 23

Crude Gesture of Teacher Embarrasses a Child

This situation sounds silly, but I remember it made a deep impression when it happened. When I was in first grade we were expected to study our reading lesson before coming to class. One day I had not done it and consequently was unable to recite. I can remember the teacher leaning over and tweaking my nose. I was humiliated and near to tears. The incident did not leave my mind for a long time afterward. The teacher thought it a joke and laughed to my mother about it. It was not funny to me.

2. *Poor methods of teaching.* One could profitably run down all the steps in teaching from the introductory moments in a new course, through the presentation of specific lessons and assignments, discussion of new ideas and concepts, use of illustrations and practice material, evaluation of the progress of students, use of textual material, class discussions, and all the rest. In every possible phase of instruction there are pitfalls that catch students because the teacher failed to keep things articulated, or to make his instructions understandable, or to provide enough instruction to make new ideas clear, or in some other way failed to meet the needs of his students. The lack of clear objectives in classwork, inability to diagnose the difficulties students have with the work, expecting too rapid progress or moving so slowly that interest is lost, may all contribute to frustrations of all degrees of seriousness among students. Since this is not a text in methods of teaching, there is no point in going into each of these steps in detail. The psycho-

logical basis for them has already been laid down in the chapters on learning, where there are clear implications for teaching methods. Here it is enough to point out that these are potentially dangerous spots in school, unless the teacher is doing a nearly perfect job in conducting the work of the class. Cases 24, 25, and 26 illustrate some of the possibilities.

Case 24

Poor Teaching and a Bad Temper Hinder Learning

For elementary algebra in high school I had a young male teacher with an awful temper. The first semester of the course was very easy for me and I got very good marks in all homework and tests. Nevertheless I was aware of the way he scolded the students, often to tears, when they were unable to answer his questions correctly. When we started on mixture problems I found that for the first time I was unable to understand the work. A few days passed before I was called upon to put my problem on the board. The many students who had gone to the board before me had received angry reprimands for not being able to do their work. After putting my problem—which I was certain was wrong—on the board, I sat down waiting for him to start on his scolding. When he found I was unable to explain how to work the problem he was very much provoked and he lectured angrily about our stupidness. If I was afraid before to ask for special help in that part of the work I was doubly terrified by that time. The tests on that part of the work that followed were complete failures. I knew I didn't know the work, and his attitude was not helping me any. On my report card for this period I received a D which was quite a drop from the Bs I had received for the first semester. With a great deal of time and effort my family and I finally discovered how to do these mixture problems, but there were many in the class who never passed over the obstacle of mixture problems.

Case 25

Inadequate Explanations Hinder Learning

Not that I wish to condemn any part of my high school "alma mater" but the mathematics department almost caused me to become maladjusted. All of us know that a firm foundation is necessary to build on—well, the seventh and eighth grade math teacher and I somehow didn't accomplish this. She was none too patient with those of us who didn't readily grasp her point. Mathematics was always my most difficult and least liked subject and to have a teacher I didn't feel free to ask questions of made a rather bad situation. However, at that early stage in the game I didn't realize the disastrous consequences which were to befall me in advanced high school math courses. Knowing but the barest essentials I attempted taking Intermediate Algebra, etc., and what a time I and my family had. I knew I needed these subjects for a college entrance diploma which made things seem all the more tragic. Before exams and finals I would be a nervous wreck! All of this would have been so needless if I had learned the first, underlying principles. Sometimes when I was struggling the hardest I would say, "Oh, heck, I didn't want to go to college anyway." My family would smile to themselves and gently steer me back to the matter at hand.

Well, what did I do about the situation, or rather I should say what did my parents do about it? First of all, they hired me a tutor and secondly, they used a little psychology on me. This was the nearest I ever came to being maladjusted and to me at the time it was a pretty serious barrier. There were physical and mental effects from the whole affair. From the tutor and extra books I gained needed knowledge. I made repeated attempts to solve the problem and finally won.

Case 26

Severe Criticism Versus Wise Correction

In our school, which was a private church school, it was the custom for each member of the freshman class to take turns reading the lesson from the Bible in chapel every morning. As there were sixteen girls in the class my turn would come every sixteen days. On one occasion I was reading from the New Testament and I came to a section where Christ was going to Calvary. When I came to the word "Calvary" I pronounced it "cavalry" and the entire school went into a burst of laughter. I was so embarrassed I ended the class abruptly. The minister, who was our religious teacher and conducted the chapel service, rose and told the assembly that they had little to do to laugh at my stupid unforgivable mistake. This made me even more chagrined than before. When I got to religion class that day he bawled me out again for my negligence, emphasizing the fact that a class officer should be able to assume a small responsibility.

He was intensely sarcastic and caustic. I said nothing and the tension increased to a point where I felt hysterical. I then and there made up my mind never to read again in chapel. Therefore, every sixteenth day I would be ill, and if I had any other announcements to make I always prevailed on someone else to make them. Every time I met my religious teacher I got more and more furious at him. I ignored assignments and laughed at him in class. In general I became obnoxious as the tension grew. Finally, I was reported to the headmaster. He knew where the root of my trouble lay and forced me to read in chapel for one week straight. At first I was hysterical the night before I was to read and I practically memorized the passages. On the last day I was given a passage with the word "Calvary" in it again. I begged the headmaster to let me out of it because I thought I would not be able to say the word. I choked every time I came across it. Before chapel on that last day he talked to me and made me realize I must overcome my fear or I was defeated. He knew that I would never admit defeat, consequently I read the passage without any outward signs of embarrassment, although within my mind I was terribly upset. After I finished, the minister made the remark that the lesson was read well. Immediately the tension was relieved and I even began to like him. I feel that although the method was painful, forcing me to overcome my obstacle was the only way. From time to time since then people have laughed at my various pronunciations, but it does not bother me. Had I been allowed to use my escape method. I probably would have had a remnant of maladjustment that I would not have been able to throw off as I grew older.

3. *Irrational rules and discipline.* The progressive movement in education was in many respects a revolt against irrational discipline and formality in school. Fundamentally, a growing person is opposed to control, and develops most advantageously when he is allowed to express his capacities freely. The effect of restricting the self-management of children is so clearly known to be damaging to their later competency in such matters that no one can argue for it. The hideous destruction of personality through "thought control," as exemplified in the case of Cardinal Mindszenty, represents the extreme, to be sure, but any extreme is made up simply of more and more of that which makes up a milder illustration.

Now, on the other hand, any form of social life requires that individuals adjust their individual urges in such a manner that they can live with others with the least possible mutual annoyance, and the greatest possible mutual advantage. Out of this necessity rules usually develop in every social structure. Everyone must at various times abide by rules. However, there is no reason whatsoever why anyone should abide by rules that are not thoroughly based on *mutual* advantage, and one of the few ways of insuring mutuality in the advantages is through joint participation in the making of the rules, *without coercion.*

Where this is the practice in school, the atmosphere is healthy, and where it is not the practice, there is always trouble for those who do not easily give in, and some form of stunted development for those who do give in. If this seems harsh, it is because we have become so accustomed to laying down rules for students that we have long since lost the power to see how inconsistent it is with our major democratic objectives. This is not an argument for the so-called progressive movement. It is simply a statement of fact about human development, and social contact. Rules serve an excellent function in keeping opportunities open to everyone, but the rules must be confined to necessities. When they become devices for furthering the comfort and convenience of a teacher or principal they have gone a long way from their legitimate purpose.

Insistence on certain ways of raising the hand, prohibition of any talking in a schoolroom that is supposedly designed for active work, unnecessary restrictions on the use of books and other equipment, arbitrary seating arrangements that violate social ease, reduction of marks for absences or other misdemeanors that have nothing to do with what the marks are said to represent, insistence on dragging students through certain courses that they have no possible business being enrolled in, and the use of several kinds of punishment in a punitive fashion completely divorced from any natural relationship to the act for which it was administered, these and others like them constitute arbitrary controls imposed on defenseless children by those in power.

Students who are forced to carry out some arbitrary rule when it has no apparent value to them are annoyed by it with good reason. This is especially true when the rule interferes with some activity that is clearly of interest to them. Even a good rule is no good unless the students see the need for it. By way of contrast, Case 27 illustrates the positive side of this matter, wherein a teacher is shown directing the classroom situation in such a manner that freedom is given for every kind of expression of need that does not produce interference with the development of others. Arbitrariness is a prolific source of conflict and maladjustment.

Case 27

An Understanding Teacher Solves a Problem

I had a crush on Billy who sat over by the windows. I also had a stiff competitor who sat by me on the opposite side of the room. Competition grew greater and greater, often interfering with our classwork. I decided to do something about it, asked the girl behind Billy to change seats with me, and then obtained permission from the teacher to trade seats, telling her that I wanted to sit where the light was better because of my eyes. (I thought I was fooling her!) She consented, I traded seats, and the problem was immediately adjusted, with things going smoothly the rest of the year. (Incidentally, competition soon ceased.) Now I realize the teacher knew what was going on, accepted it, and let us do what we wanted to, since it didn't interefere with schoolwork at all and settled the whole problem.

4. *Competitive marks and artificial pressures.* A discussion of the use of marks in the various levels of school is presented in Chapter XXV, where it is pointed out that there is no justification for the use of competitive marks in the elementary school. There is little if any justification for them in the high school. They have a function farther up the educational ladder, where it is imperative that comparative ratings be made for very real social reasons. In the public schools there are several serious indictments against the use of competition as the chief incentive for study. In the first place, it is based on the use of distinctions and status, for its effectiveness. Those who receive the low marks are quite

clearly stigmatized, all rationalization to the contrary. In the second place, it is not important that any student demonstrate that he is better than another in the things that are taught in public schools. What is important is that he get all the development he can get. The contrast that is important is the one between what he can become, and what he is. Marks given on this basis do not carry the threat of competitive marks, nor the stigma. Hence they do not create the conflicts either.

Furthermore, competition is stimulating only to those who can win. It is discouraging to others. In fact, if a person will become intimately acquainted with what actually goes on among students, he will find a quiet undercover truce has been arranged in many student groups, as a protection against the pressures of competitive marks. Once the group has discovered the approximate "pecking order" of its members, from an academic point of view, there is a tendency for the competition to fade out by mutual consent. The group then settles down to a comfortable pace of its own choosing, a nice easy level of mediocrity, as long as each person stays about in his accepted relative position. In the end competition has turned out to constitute a ceiling on effort, imposed by the group to protect itself against the strain.

The opprobrium that has thus come to be attached by college students to "the brain," the student who works for high marks, is such that it is often considered much more socially acceptable to receive C's and a few B's than to flaunt the A's of superiority. There could be no more convincing evidence of the potential maladjustment contained in the competitive system than the manner in which its victims have contrived to render it harmless. Such safety measures would scarcely be taken against circumstances that hold no threat to adjustment.

Note in Table 5 the prominence of "extraneous pressures to do well," "too high scholastic standards," "too much competition," and others with smaller frequencies down through the list, all of which have the same element of pressure.

5. *Ignorance of the general characteristics of youth.* The amount and kind of mental activity that can be expected at

each grade level, the personal interests of children at each age level, the important objectives and non-academic tasks of children and adolescents, and their individual ways of evaluating the school and its contribution to their lives are very important items of knowledge in a teacher's work. To be without them means a high probability that the facts involved in them will be violated in some manner by the teacher.

Preparation of this kind is to be had from a study of the psychology of childhood and of adolescence, and of educational psychology. There is a background of information about young people of each age level in general, which forms a foundation for the development of specific knowledge about each individual student. Mastery of the general background information is a distinctly profitable achievement, since it provides the teacher with most of the understanding needed in the school. After such preparation it is not a difficult or burdensome thing to learn to understand an individual student.

Not to know what can be expected of students at a given grade level means that a number of errors will be made in supervising their learning, and the errors will tend to affect all of the students, not just a few. This is a general proposition that produces its strains in groups rather than in single cases, although some students will be more sensitive to such hindering circumstances than will others. Illustrations are much more clearly seen in connection with the individual aspect, which follows.

6. *Failure to meet individual needs.* Cases 28, 29, and 30 show poor sensitivity to individual problems in social adjustment, level of conceptual development, and personality difficulties, respectively.

Case 28

Teacher Threatens Student's Social Adjustment

One day when I was in the sixth grade I had some red grapes in my desk, which I had for recess time. During the forenoon I just couldn't resist eating one so I put one in my mouth. Soon the teacher noticed I had something in my mouth and asked me what I had in my mouth. I told her, "A grape." She made some remark about it and then said, "I guess we'll have to call her grapes from now on." When recess time came I was "Grapes" to everyone. I am an only child and up to the year before I had gone to a small country school. The year previous I had ridden the thirteen miles each way to school with my mother. We had moved to the town where mother had a position just that fall. For these reasons and the fact that I do not make friends very quickly and had not become a part of the group as yet, I was deeply hurt. I had been doing my best to get into the group and with this I was ready to quit. This "Grapes" kept up for quite a while and I avoided the kids and the teacher as much as possible and spoke only when necessary. After quite a while they forgot it or something, but I was left high and dry and practically had to start over. I still had the strong urge to be a part of the group and I think that that is the only thing that brought me back to the group gradually.

Case 29

Child Failing in Too-advanced Class

My schooling was begun in the traditional one-room country school with the traditionally poorly trained teacher. At the age of six and a half I started the second grade. Somehow or other the teacher got the mistaken idea that I was in some ways more advanced than the other second-grade pupils. Consequently she had me do certain things with the second grade, others with the third grade, and in geography she put me to doing fourth-grade work. The meaning of maps, the concepts of time and distances, why the world was round yet the Chinese didn't fall off, was all beyond my comprehension. I don't remember that I realized that there was anything unusual in my being placed as I was. I didn't tell my parents what was going on at first and later when I couldn't do the work I was afraid to tell them since I thought that I was supposed to do whatever the teacher demanded. I remained with this group for the first four weeks of the term without the teacher's offering to put me in a different group. I never understood much of what was discussed and I only knew that eventually I would be exposed as the school dunce. Gradually, I worked up to the point where I cried all the way to school, when I went to bed at night, and whenever I could go off by myself and be unobserved. On several occasions I told the teacher I was sick and was thus excused from school.

I would then go toward home and stay in a woodlot until the other children went past at the close of school. After doing this several times I was one day discovered by a neighbor who found me wandering around the woodlot crying. I was taken home and after considerable effort my parents found out the cause of my troubles. I was then placed in the proper group in school and conditions returned to normal. However, it was some time before I could be made to realize that my parents were not condemning me for the complete fool which I thought myself to be.

Case 30

Poor Student Expelled instead of Helped

This boy definitely did not have the intelligence to get really high grades. However, he was not stupid by any means. He was the "smarty" type who was always in trouble. This was his way, perhaps, of getting recognition. Anyway, he kept getting worse and worse—all the kids hated him and so did the teachers. He disturbed every class he was in. Several times he was threatened with expulsion.

There was just one teacher with whom this boy got along—the science teacher. This man recognized his trouble. He used to try to reason with him—he was the only one that Ed trusted at all. Thus his first step was to get the boy's confidence. Then he had him come into the lab and help him with experiments. As far as this teacher was concerned Ed was O.K. but he still persisted with his deviltry in other classes and with other teachers. Finally he was expelled.

The science teacher used good technique but he did not have the cooperation of the principal who had a particular dislike for the boy. If they had let the science teacher handle him I think he would have turned out O.K. Just the presence of the principal was a barrier to this problem. The principal should have recognized this but to complicate matters the science teacher and the principal didn't get along—consequently the boy suffered.

These are only three of the kinds of individual needs that are often overlooked. Here are other ways in which equally disturbing situations are created. (a) The student may be in the wrong curriculum for him. There is no motivation when the whole curriculum is meaningless. (b) When a uniform amount of pressure is used on a whole class there is almost surely someone in the class being pushed too hard, and someone who is being allowed to become a loafer. (c) Overlooking a physical handicap is inexcusable, even when the handicap is not apparent on first inspection. (d) Failure to provide adequately for the student with sensory handicaps is a possible cause of his frustration. Poor hearing and vision are the most common of these. (e) A maladjusted student whose condition is ignored by his teacher will either become a source of irritation to the class or withdraw from life. In either event the school will be doing him considerable harm. (f) The student who is not socially secure needs individual attention to help him correct his difficulty. (g) A student in poor health is in a poor condition to profit by schooling. When the poor health interferes with attendance to a serious extent students are often either allowed to fail or are hounded at home while sick with lesson assignments to be completed. There is no good reason why a modification of requirements cannot be made when conditions justify it. (h) Children often have responsibilities outside the school. In some cases they are so heavy that it is impossible to study outside the regular school hours. There have been many instances where the outside burdens were so heavy that students could not keep wide awake when they were at school. If such outside burdens must be carried, the school must adjust that student's schoolwork on the basis of his weekly and twenty-four hour program.

This list is not exhaustive. Numerous other situations arise in which students are frustrated. The safest approach for the teacher is not in memorizing a list of things to do or not to do, but in becoming sensitive to student frustrations and situations that may cause them. All frustration cannot be removed from any social situation. Most of the objectionable sorts can be eliminated, however, if everyone in the school is aware of the problem and making an effort to do something about it.

2303. *Essay on teachers.* It is refreshing and healthful to look for periodic reminders of what students think about teachers. Dr. Dorothy M. Howard secured the written reactions of students in the seventh grade. From their responses the following essay was compiled.

Once upon a time I liked teachers but now, sometimes I like them and sometimes I do not. When I was little I loved my teacher so much I cannot tell.

Some teachers are good. Some teachers are bad and some are about half one way and half the other. Some teachers are nice and some are not nice. Somtimes the nice ones get grouchy but I guess they can't help that. If a teacher is grouchy all the time, the children will not think of her any more than they can help. They might not think to do their home work for her. She should be calm. Then the children will think about her and then they will think to do their home work.

I like teachers who are jolly and serious at different times. A teacher should be both strict and sociable. A teacher should like jokes and also tell some once in a while. The room will not get too noisy.

Some teachers don't like to answer questions. I like a teacher who explains things and takes time. Teachers should help children. They should not scold children for nothing. I think a teacher has a right to scold and get mad when the children act like little devils. A good teacher understands the children and knows when to get mad. Although she should scold and get mad, she should not get excited about it. She should be calm about it.

A nice teacher is one all the children like. A teacher should be easy to work with and helpful. Some teachers just like the children who have the best clothes. They do not like children who do not have good clothes. A teacher should like everybody in the class. I like teachers who have an interest in me.

A good teacher is kind. A good teacher does not insult you in front of the class and all your friends. A good teacher does not talk too much. A good teacher is patient. A good teacher will not give work that is too hard and not explain because she says you should know how already. A good teacher does not holler a lot at children who are not doing anything to be hollered at about. A good teacher minds her own business. If a pupil acts like a silly, a good teacher will not jump up and scold him. She will tell him the right way to act and teach him to speak nicely to everybody.

I think a teacher should know how to teach every subject. It is not good for a teacher to know only one thing.

Teachers should speak the truth. We need to know more about the history of our country, and about our president and about the laws of the state. We need to know about Congress. We need to know these things so when we are big, we can understand the laws and make better ones. We want to know how to vote. Teachers should allow children responsibilities. They should teach us respect for our elders and how to get along with everybody. They should teach us how to get acquainted, how to hold a conversation and also how to be polite in front of all people.

Teachers should teach useful things. Maybe I will get a job in a grocery store and I will need to know arithmetic and spelling. If I am in a club, I will need to know how to be the president or some other officer. Teachers should teach children to take care of their money and other things and to be thrifty, because when I get out of school and get married, I will have to support my wife and children, if any, and if I spend all my money, my wife and children, if any, will starve. Teachers should teach children to repair things about the house. They should also teach them about airplanes, engines, and trucks.

I don't care what kind of clothes teachers wear, but I do think they should wear something. Teachers should keep up with the styles and they should change off and not wear the same old thing every day. They should wear clothes that look right on them. Everybody is different.

I like to see women teachers wear sports skirts and blouses or sweaters—and sports shoes. Their clothes should be gay but not flashy. A teacher shouldn't come to school with herself all full of perfume. She should put on just enough to give her a nice little smell. She should not be too fancy but she should wear little jewels like a pin or ear rings. Her hair should be combed the latest style and should be neat and never messy. Her hats should be the latest styles, too. Her stockings should be light color. She should not wear too much make up but a little face powder and other things to take off the plainness.

A man teacher should look neat. His suit should be pressed, his shoes clean and bright, and his hair combed and his face clean looking. His clothes should not have wrinkles. When the men sit down, they all get wrinkles and of course they cannot help that. But they should have nice pressed pleats. Men should change off too and should not wear the same old thing every day. It is all right for a man to wear a V neck sweater if he wants to. Sometimes for a change, he can wear a coat that is a different color from his pants. That makes a nice difference. His pants should not be too long. He should not smoke and get a bad breath. Children do not like that.

Some teachers are queer.

2304. *Teacher maladjustment as a product of the school.* A number of conditions that are common to most American schools are potential sources of frustration for teachers:

1. Most teachers are overloaded both with students and with classes. When the class load consists of six consecutive classes with five or ten minutes intermission, a problem in preparation is created. The teacher may do all the extra classroom work such as reading papers, preparing lesson materials, searching for new materials, and reading for self-improvement during the afternoon and evening hours after school. If such work is done with the proper thoroughness, it leaves little time for personal interests or relaxation. A common alternative to evening work is doing such chores during class periods by giving the students time for study. In that case an inferior type of classroom contribution is the inevitable result. Supervised study is so called because it is supervised; if the teacher withdraws from the process it is something else. Another alternative is to meet each class on a catch-as-catch-can basis, relying on native wit rather than on planning to take care of contingencies that may arise. In this case the quality of the teaching is usually poor and the teacher often becomes uneasy. Whatever scheme is adopted to meet the problem of an overloaded schedule, it is almost sure to have a serious weakness that will have an adverse effect on the students or the teacher or both.

2. Salary ranges are usually lower for teachers than for many other workers of lesser training. It is difficult for teachers to develop a truly professional *esprit de corps* when they are asked to be content with a standard of living that is lower than most of them could maintain in some other line of work.

3. Insecurity due to the use by school officials of various ways of dodging the tenure issue is a source of concern to teachers in many, but not all, school systems.

4. The typical community accords a relatively obscure social status to schoolteachers. Participation is rarely avail-

able in the higher social classes. It is not uncommon to find business people who regard teachers as ne'er-do-wells who have drifted into teaching for want of ambition and ability worthy of something better.

5. It is easy for teachers to lose touch with recreation. This is especially true when the teacher's contract forbids attendance at public dances, or having dates with a member of the opposite sex, or in other ways proscribes his non-school life in such a way that little freedom is left. While such practices are diminishing, they are still fairly common, especially in small towns where recreational activities are already much too limited without such proscription.

6. Numerous teachers may be found who are dissatisfied with their work because they are not suited to the life of a teacher. Their values, interests, aptitudes, or temperaments may be such as to find disappointment or irritation in teaching. Lacking the courage or the resources to make a change, many of them remain in the profession at the expense of their own happiness and the well-being of their students.

7. Failure to keep up with developments in one's field may result in becoming out-of-date to such an extent that one is unable to fit into the work as new generations come along with different problems. Contention within faculties is common when progressive and reactionary elements clash over what is considered the thing to do.

8. Lack of understanding of the administrator and his problems prevents many teachers from working cooperatively and smoothly with the administration. True, the fault may lie on both sides, but the teacher who makes a point of knowing how to deal with an administrator can avoid most of the friction and misunderstanding that otherwise may arise.

9. Until recently, it was impossible for a woman to teach while married. When that is the case the woman teacher must decide between marriage and her job. If both are quite important to her, the choice is a difficult one. If she remains in teaching and fails to marry because the conditions of her work make it difficult or impossible for her to meet eligible men and go through the normal process of

courtship, she may feel bitter and frustrated the rest of her life.

There are other factors that involve teachers in frustration of one sort or another. In the worst teaching situations, many of these factors operate simultaneously. In the best situations they may be nearly or completely absent. The teacher can do much to avoid such difficulties by holding to a platform of practices that are basic to mental health. They are discussed later.

2305. *Maladjustment as a factor in education.* When the flywheel of a motor is perfectly balanced the motor runs without vibration. The speed is limited only by the source of power. Suppose, however, the flywheel were moved out of balance so that there was greater weight on one side of the motor than on the other. The resulting vibration would cut down the speed, reduce the power, and, if uncorrected, destroy the motor in time. So it is with maladjustment. The progress of a normal student is limited only by his source of power—intelligence and motivation. Maladjustment is like being out of balance. It can be produced only when important needs are seriously thwarted. Consequently, any serious form of maladjustment becomes a matter of great importance to the individual. It tends to monopolize attention to the detriment of such competing stimuli as classwork, lessons, books, tests, marks, etc. It destroys the speed and the power of the individual, and, if its outcome is left to chance, it may eventually wreck the individual. In pupils, it tends to do at least the following things: (1) distract attention, (2) retard learning, (3) produce failure in studies and involve the student in clashes with school requirements, (4) warp social outlook and estrange the individual from his schoolmates, (5) concentrate attention on various devious ways of dealing with the fundamental problem, so that behavior is apt to irritate or annoy others. In teachers it tends to (1) destroy initiative and enthusiasm for work, (2) sensitize the teacher to minor sources of irritation in daily problems, (3) discount teaching ability, and (4) operate adversely on the personalities of students. It is vicious in its effect, in that it feeds upon itself unless corrective measures are taken.

2306. *How the school can prevent maladjustment.* This heading is optimistic. All maladjustment cannot be eliminated. Even so, it is better to be optimistic than to become resigned to conflict and do nothing to reduce it. Therefore, four general lines of attack on maladjustment are outlined here. They are essentially preventive in nature, but they incorporate a number of corrective values. The details involved in putting the general approaches into actual programs cannot be anticipated in advance for any particular school with its unique characteristics, but such details always manage to take care of themselves when people address themselves seriously to these approaches.

1. *Methods of control.* In an earlier section of this chapter it was stated that controls must be mutually advantageous or they create conflicts and tensions. As long as the view persists that a school is composed of two disparate groups, faculty and students, there is a schism present that makes mutually advantageous planning difficult. There are no more real lines between students and teachers in a school than there are between children and adults in a community, or in the home. The school is a community of people, some of whom are younger than others, but all of whom have a vested interest in the management of the community. The students are just as obligated to be there as the teachers, neither of them own the school, it is not created in order to give advantage to either one over the other, and their well-being is contingent on exactly the same basic factors. If this incontrovertible fact is frankly faced, it leads to abandonment of such fallacies as student government, teacher government, or any composite made of elements of the two. What is clearly implied is community government, with proper representation from all parts of the community. Obviously, the adult portion of the community should be able to take care of its interests in such a government, or it is scarcely capable of furnishing leadership to the students in intellectual matters. It is not necessary to hold control within the staff to keep things safe.

Business matters are always handled by administrative personnel, but even there they do not all have to be members of the staff. Beyond business matters, the general community spirit of the school, its whole social philosophy and mode of operation, should grow up from representative councils and committees composed of both teachers and students. For example, disciplinary matters are traditionally thought of as the prerogatives of the staff. When a departure is attempted, it is usually a complete swing to student courts and laws. Neither is realistic or democratically sound. The student court is not safe, for it is stampeded into undue harshness by immature judgment. Better judgments could be made in almost all cases if the points of view of older and younger members of the school community were brought together in all policymaking or administrative bodies. Furthermore, such procedures would be highly educational for students, who could learn to work with adults in handling their affairs. It would be educational for the adults, too, who would learn much more about the capacities of youth for responsibility, and how to develop such responsibility in them. At no time should the older group draw back and leave the work to the younger ones. All through American political and social life there is a mixture of older and younger people of both sexes sharing in the determination of the patterns of mutual activity.

If community government were practiced, many of the arbitrary and unsound regulations that create conflicts would disappear. There would be a much better chance that regulations would be functional and acceptable to all. Suppose students and teachers composed the curriculum-planning committee of the school. Such responsibility is not at all beyond the capacity of children around nine or ten years of age, or perhaps even younger, who are full of serious and worthwhile ideas about what is worth doing. Would it not be much more possible with such a committee to keep in touch with the points at which the curriculum puts a strain on the students? It should be easier to obtain close integration with life needs. There would be greater acceptance of the curriculum by students, and a general feeling that there is a channel through which suggestions, complaints, and questions could go on up to the planning group and be heard with consideration.

As the children become older, this sort of control system will multiply in its advantages, particularly if it is practiced at all levels so that the children will take it more and more seriously, and rise to their rights and possibilities in it. Student meetings would have some tendency to deal with school policies, and such requirements as regular attendance, required courses, rules of personal conduct, methods of dealing with infractions and the like would become the will of the whole community, as contrasted with an imposed set of controls to be avoided if possible. The whole atmosphere would be conducive to better adjustment for everyone, through development of a sense of membership and belongingness and common interests.

2. *Breadth of school experience.* The term "general education" has taken on such controversial and emotional coloring that it is losing its usability. It stands for an important type of preparation for good adjustment. A great many difficulties develop for people because they do not see broadly enough into the several ramifications of life to keep from stirring up unnecessary controversies and obstacles, or from getting themselves into contradictory and disappointing situations. "If I had just known what I know now." Every time someone says this he is testifying to the value of a more general education. Such a program is not only academic. It is also recreational, spiritual, social, political, and more. The type of control system suggested above would provide several general education values in political and social living. Its values would be real, for it would be real government, which is almost never the case with student government.

General education in a recreational sense should result in learning some forms of recreation that could be carried right over into adult life. Such is not the case in school now.

General education should incorporate a deliberate and defensible approach to the job of selling education to students, teachers, and the community. Particularly to the students. Therein it would yield its greatest contribution to the prevention of maladjustment. It should never be taken for granted that the students know why they are in school, and especially why they are in a particular course, or working on a particular lesson. As a matter of fact, some teachers don't know why. It would be good mental hygiene for everyone to find out why, and, if there is no good reason after the analysis is made, to make a change in the program.

One of the truly sad facts about education is that those who are out of school make the discovery too late that the school program was a very good program, and they should have taken advantage of it. This discovery can be moved up quite a bit, if the reasons behind it are made real to the students themselves, and it can result in a wholesome change in motivation and adjustment.

3. *Quality of the academic curriculum.* A considerable portion of any educational psychology text is devoted to the facts that make for an effective curriculum. They need not be reiterated here. Those facts should be put to work, however, in the planning of every curriculum, course, and unit of instruction. Beginning with clarity in the objectives, both for the teachcer and the students, every academic step should be psychologically sound. The subjects that constitute progressions from course to course should be articulated so that there are not gaps between them, no matter who the teachers are. Every lesson plan should have a genuine relationship to the whole course, and that relationship should be clear to all concerned. Each class activity and outside assignment should be properly related to the objective and to the psychology of learning. Every evaluative procedure should fit its purpose, and students should be doing most of the evaluating themselves.

A great many conflicts could be eliminated if these precautions were taken by teachers.

4. *Provision of guidance.* Three particular aspects of this approach might be mentioned here, although there are others that could also be discussed with profit.

Many students with conflicts are capable of solving their problems themselves because they have learned how to go about such solutions. What they have learned can be taught to others, and it is difficult to think of a more valuable thing to teach people. If an individual has sufficient breadth of vision to find profitable paths to his needs when those he has been using are blocked, all he needs in addition is a little insight into such processes as substitution, arriving at compromises, getting around barriers, or fighting it out with the opposition in ways that achieve success. These things are sometimes discussed in courses in mental hygiene or personal psychology for young people. They have a legitimate place in the curriculum, although the materials of instruction for them are not as available as might be desired. Table 7 contains a suggestive list of ways of meeting problems.

TABLE 7. WHOLESOME WAYS OF RESOLVING CONFLICTS AND OVERCOMING BARRIERS

I. Direct attack on the barrier
   a. Acquiring needed knowledge
   b. Developing needed skill
   c. Making repeated attempts to solve a poblem

II. Seeking the original goal by evading the barrier
   a. Trying new tactics
   b. Enlisting the help of others

III. Resolving a conflict in goals
   a. Deciding the relative merits of each goal
   b. Renouncing one goal when the two are incompatible
   c. Compromising the two conflicting goals

IV. Substituting for unattainable goals
   a. Recognizing the need to be met by the unattainable goal
   b. Finding another activity that fills the same need

Here is a case in which both the teacher and the parent were helping the student learn how to handle a difficult situation. It is clear that the lesson was recognized.

Case 31

Alert Teacher Saves a Student from Embarrassment

In the fifth grade I had an experience which threatened to hinder my "getting along" socially in school. The strong motivation present in this goal made the incident serious.

The teacher was checking the records for the school files on each child's family, birthplace, etc. She asked who in the class were born out of the country. I raised my hand and standing up told her I was. The teacher was very surprised and looked at the records in front of her. Then she told me I was born in New York (this took place in New Jersey). I said, "Yes," and a few in the class started to laugh. I persisted that I was born out of the country, though, having confused the meanings of country and state. The teacher realized this, as the whole class started to laugh. She tried a direct attack to avoid the social barrier of ridicule by saying, "New York may be thought of as another country because it is so big, but it is one of the forty-eight states so it is in this country." This statement straightened me in my meaning and gave the class an excuse for me which was easy to accept because the teacher made it sound so plausible. The laughter stopped and I sat down very ashamed for mixing my meanings. Trying to overcome the barrier of shame I was frustrated as classmates referred to it. I learned to laugh when it was referred to, as my mother said my classmates would forget it quicker, and she told me embarrassing incidents that had occurred to her so I wouldn't feel alone in overcoming my barriers, and would feel that they were surmountable.

These procedures could stand discussion among students, to show how they are used in real situations, and how one might decide which is the most appropriate procedure in a given situation.

Table 8 contains some safeguards of mental health, the practice of which tends to ward off many conflicts and to provide the individual with resistance and resources for managing other conflicts successfully when they develop.

Several of these safeguards would be more fully turned into realities under the type of school program outlined in the preceding three approaches than they are under conditions in many schools now. Items in a list like this mean little to a young person who reads them, but they will come to life if a class will discuss a case in which one of them is illustrated and point out how the practice contributed to the good adjustment of the individual. Almost every biography in the library contains such illustrative material, either in positive

TABLE 8. FOUNDATIONS OF MENTAL HEALTH

1. Physical health.
2. Ability to see one's self realistically and objectively.
3. Ability to use problem-solving approach to difficult problems.
4. Adequate social participation and belongingness—security and recreation.
5. Realistic goals in life, within possibilities of individual, and offering adequate creative experience.
6. Ability to work with others, balancing freedom with self-discipline and responsibility.
7. A growing philosophy of life based on wide acquaintance with the world and an acceptance of change as a part of life.
8. A sense of humor.
9. A few close friends in whom vital problems may be confided.

examples, or in cases of failure due to the lack of such qualities.

A second general approach to the guidance factor is through individual counseling. The system should be set up so that there is direct carry-over from the counselor to the student's school program. It is not particularly important who does the counseling, as long as it is someone who is adequately prepared for the function. It could be a homeroom teacher, or any other teacher who finds a need for it in one of his students. It could also be the person whose sole responsibility is in the field of counseling. At any rate whatever the needs of the individual are found to be, there should be an adjustment in the school program of the student to take care of them. In most instances these adjustments are very minor, as illustrated in Case 32.

Case 32

Diagnosing and Correcting a Student's Fear of Reciting

In my early grade-school years, I had a great dislike for the recitation, before an audience of any kind, of certain poems or speeches that had been previously memorized. Every time the teacher called me for recitation in class, I virtually "froze in my tracks," as a strong emotional reaction would seize me. I would stutter, my heart and my stomach would pound away with increasing intensity, and my brain would work double time thinking of all the things that might possibly happen to me if I didn't recite the poem. In this emotional condition, I was usually unable to recite the poem.

One day, after I had experienced one of these emotional situations, the teacher called me aside and told me that she would like to see me after class. When I reported to her after the class, she talked with me for several minutes, possibly to make me feel at ease, and then she asked me to recite the poem that I had memorized. At this time I was able to recite the poem, whereupon she asked me the reason why I couldn't have done it in class. In as few words as possible, she explained that there was no reason that I couldn't have done it in class. She talked to me gently for quite a while trying to help me get it in my mind that I could have recited the poem in class without any difficulty. Several times after our little "confab" together, the teacher called upon me in class for recitation, and although, for the first few times, I did not feel at ease, I was able to recite the poem with a maximum of difficulty. However, I noticed that after a period of time, I was able to recite poems or speeches with a minimum of difficulty whenever I was called upon.

In this instance the teacher carried out the needed actions herself. In other cases the cooperation of other teachers and school personnel might be required, and the final line of help might fall to someone other than the one who picked up the case. The principles of counseling cannot be presented in this text, but it is fast coming to be recognized that every teacher needs to become familiar with them, and to be prepared to practice them frequently.

The other approach is particularly concerned with those few students who find it almost impossible to fit into the regular program of the school. Ralph Richards was such a student (see Case 16) and Case 30 in this chapter was another. When a student finds nothing in the school program that seems to him to contribute to his own personal goals, there is no reason, logical or otherwise, for him to support administrative requirements that are entirely unrelated to his well-being. In fact, the case often involves more than a mere lack of interest. Since the student's goals are not being met in any way by the school program, he will inevitably seek satisfaction for them in another direction. Hence, the attendance requirement becomes a barrier to his progress toward his own goals, and something to resist or elude at every opportunity. In such cases a rigid application of the usual methods of keeping a student in attendance will enhance the conflict already going on within him and result in dangerous psychological tension. Surliness, outbursts of temper, deliberate disturbance of classwork, or any of a number of other forms of rebellion or escape may be expected to appear.

There is no single way of handling such cases, except to squash them by pure force. Nothing is quite so likely to make a public enemy as that procedure. Each case may be different. Each will need to have a modification of the usual program made to his own specifications. Although it is administratively uncomfortable, there is no escape from the necessity of flexibility. Ultimately, the choice must be made between helping such people at the cost of extra effort and a loss in administrative convenience, or avoiding the effort and not helping the needy student. Any middle ground is inadequate. As conditions now stand throughout the country, however, there are students in almost every school who, far from being helped to success, are being systematically pushed into progressive maladjustment, which may be personal, social, or both.

2307. *Mental health guides for teachers.* The conditions described for students contain most of the elements of a healthful school environment for teachers, but there are some things of a personal nature that every teacher should do consistently. They are mentioned here quite briefly, but they need no elaboration. They are just ways of keeping fresh and alive so that there will be zest for the daily requirements. (1) Read the professional literature pertinent to the current tasks. A minimum might well consist of one journal in the subject-matter field and one in the field of teaching activities. (2) Make a regular effort to establish and maintain effective relationships with other educators, particularly those on the same faculty. Sharing of problems and ideas is valuable in many ways. (3) Participate in the development of improvements in the educative process. Take part in research projects. Work on committees set up to study and improve conditions and practices. Use imagination and initiative in developing better ways of doing regular work. (4) Reduce as much of the day's work as possible to routine and put it on an efficient basis. Subdivide responsibilities and tasks to responsible students for the good of all concerned. Good management of one's time and abilities can do much to overcome the handicaps of a heavy schedule and crowded classes. (5) Maintain adequate social relations. The teacher has a life to live as well as a contribution to make to others. The life is important in its own right, and the contribution will be richer if the life is full. (6) Have some form of recreational activity regularly. To be truly recreational, activity must have the effect of rebuilding the participant. Shop around until such activity is found and then use it.

There are some people who cannot make a good adjustment to the life of a teacher under any circumstances. Such people should stay away from teaching for the sake of the students as well as themselves. There are some who enjoy teaching under certain conditions, but not under others. Such people may become very good teachers if they are employed by the right school. Conditions of life vary with communities. Under no circumstance should a teacher accept a position in a school or community in which he cannot make a good adjustment. When the school and community make demands on his personal life to which the teacher cannot agree, it becomes his duty to say so frankly, find a position that is more to his liking, and leave the former community free to find a teacher who is more to its liking.

Teachers and students are living people. Most of what they do is done for the sake of developing the good life. Therefore, it is a perversion of logic to undertake such a search under any conditions except those of the good life itself. The educative process should be a most enjoyable experience.

Whether it is or not depends on the care with which the basic conditions of good adjustment are maintained by all parties concerned.

QUESTIONS FOR REVIEW

1. If a school succeeds in creating no neurotic symptoms in students, how well has it carried out its responsibility for development?
2. What type of preparation does the teacher need, if he is to help students with their adjustmental problems?
3. What effect does a poor teacher personality have on various students? For example, on an aggressive, delinquent boy, or on a submissive, insecure boy.
4. What is wrong with attempts to be humorous in class?
5. Of what value is social sensitivity in a teacher? How does it help student adjustment?
6. What are some common faults in methods of teaching?
7. What is the cause of the trouble in Case 24?
8. What need is being threatened in Case 26?
9. When is a disciplinary procedure irrational?
10. Under what conditions are rules psychologically safe?
11. What are the weaknesses of competition as an incentive?
12. How should a marking system be set up to make it as healthful as possible?
13. What are some very important things a teacher should know about students?
14. In what ways do teachers often fail to meet students' individual needs?
15. What is the best way in which a teacher can prepare to deal with the problem of maladjustment?
16. What are the common sources of maladjustment for teachers?
17. In what way does maladjustment interfere with a student's work? A teacher's work?
18. What are the best safeguards to adjustment for students? For teachers?
19. What is meant by the term "community government" and what arguments can you offer for it?
20. Define general education. What does it have to do with adjustment?

SELECTED REFERENCES

Luella Cole, *Psychology of adolescence* (3rd ed.; New York: Rinehart and Co., 1948), Chapter V.

Arthur I. Gates, Arthur T. Jersild, T. R. McConnell, and Robert C. Challman, *Educational psychology* (New York: The Macmillan Co., 1948), Chapters XX and XXII.

Walter C. Langer, *Psychology and human living* (New York: Appleton-Century-Crofts, Inc., 1943), Chapters 13 and 14.

Daniel A. Prescott, *Emotion and the educative process* (Washington, D.C.: The American Council on Education, 1938), Chapter XI.

W. Carson Ryan, *Mental health through education* (New York: The Commonwealth Fund, 1938), Chapter IV.

CLASS EXERCISES ON ADJUSTMENT AND MALADJUSTMENT

Things To Do in Class

1. Select one of the anecdotes in Chapter XXIII and discuss it in these ways:
   a. Using section 2302 of the text, identify the cause of the difficulty.
   b. Refer to Chapter VII and tell what needs were being thwarted.
   c. Refer to Table 7 and analyze the process by which the difficulty was eventually overcome.
   Repeat for other cases, until all types of difficulties have been examined.

2. From a study of the problems of 254 schoolteachers, the following table [1] was made up to show what per cent of the group was genuinely concerned with each problem. Those problems that caused concern for over 20 per cent of the teachers are included in the table. Make an analysis of the kinds of psychological help the teachers need in order to handle such problems comfortably. In how many cases is the problem due in whole or in part to deficiencies in the teacher?

[1] Asahel D. Woodruff, "An exploratory evaluation of teacher education," *Educational administration and supervision*, 32 (January, 1946), 1-18. Reproduced by permission.

TABLE 9.—PROBLEMS RANKED ACCORDING TO THE PERCENTAGE OF REPLIES THAT INDICATE SERIOUS CONCERN

	All 254 Teachers Ungrouped		
Question Number	N	Per Cent Replies Showing Concern	Question
30	231	66.67	My students have trouble knowing how to study.
27	216	60.65	My students have trouble getting the deeper meanings and ideas in the reading assignments.
24	236	54.23	My students have trouble using their own judgment in problems.
28	233	50.21	My students have trouble thinking independently in my course.
39	217	45.16	I don't know how to deal with students who read poorly.
48	208	41.83	I can't get students to keep working on hard problems until they solve them.
3	229	41.48	It is difficult to discover what students value in life.
25	235	39.58	My students have trouble understanding simple straightforward instruction.
7	219	39.27	I don't know how to deal with students who are all-round misfits in school.
46	215	39.07	I am concerned over the great variation in quality and quantity of work done by the students in a single class.
1	212	36.34	I feel that there are many extraneous factors that influence learning in a classroom which I have not recognized yet.
53	213	34.27	I don't know how rigidly to mark students whose work is near failing.

Question Number	N	Per Cent Replies Showing Concern	Question
45	209	33.49	I am concerned over the familiarity between boys and girls.
29	207	32.85	My students have trouble using notes.
35	227	31.72	I don't know how to deal with students who are so busy they can't get their studies.
23	230	30.43	My students have trouble with the reasoning involved in the course.
2	230	30.00	Students have little consideration for each other or for teachers.
58	198	29.80	I don't know how to help those who can't study effectively.
10	224	27.68	I don't know how to deal with students who don't care what you do to them.
31	186	27.42	I can't get students to do effective studying in a study hall.
49	184	25.54	Pre-instructional tests are of little value to me.
32	201	25.37	I can't get students to respond to my efforts to develop appreciations for such things as beauty, music, art, etc.
41	187	24.07	I don't know how my pupils' study requirements affect their non-academic activities.
51	208	24.04	The use of marks is a source of annoyance to me.
4	223	23.77	I don't know how to deal with students who are generally "bewildered," "lost in the shuffle."
9	221	22.62	I don't know how to deal with students who persistently fail to conform to customary school procedures.

Question Number	N	Per Cent Replies Showing Concern	Question
44	200	22.50	I have difficulty knowing a pupil's basic capacity to learn.
50	210	22.38	Pupils ask lots of silly questions.
59	218	22.02	I don't feel that I am accomplishing much as a teacher.
19	206	20.88	Pupil participation in class management is not successful.
8	221	20.81	I don't know how to deal with ,students who are usually irritable and quarrelsome.
34	207	20.77	I don't know how to deal with student cliques at school.
56	193	20.73	I don't know how to help those who never know their reading materials.

CHAPTER XXIV

PERSONALITY, MOTIVATIONAL HEALTH, AND SOCIAL RELATIONSHIPS

2401. *Introduction.* It may be disturbing to some that this section of the book began with maladjustment rather than adjustment, in some ways a negative rather than a positive approach. The much-expressed feeling that one should always use a positive approach seems to partake a little too much of devotion to a system as contrasted with the organization of attention around functioning realities. The positive and significantly hopeful aspects of personality cannot be adequately discussed without a solid background of processes that produce both desirable and undesirable results. It is often *only* through the observation of a personality breaking down or moving in the direction of maladjustment that a complete understanding of the processes which can produce a healthy personality is possible. This, therefore, seems a more appropriate place to talk about the positive side of adjustment than in the beginning when the underlying processes and factors have not been recognized.

Today's desperate social situation places a demand on education, and therefore first of all on educational psychology, to indicate how people might be brought to a state of better relationships before they destroy each other. This problem is certainly related to the question of personality, and to the motivational factors that are said to control behavior. It might well be called, then, a problem in motivational health. If there is no actual relationship between the nature of human behavior as outlined in this book and the behavior through which people are now threatening their own and others' existence, then our psychology is either very wrong, or woefully incomplete in its most significant area.

Here is a problem that cannot be ignored. From the beginning of human history until 1940 men have been able to play with war in seeming safety. The loss in potentiality was never noticed. The numbers killed were never much greater than were losses through disease or traffic accidents. There was no power to hurt people on a significant scale. As long as war was not *really dangerous* there was no serious effort to explain it, or to prevent it through an all-out drive on its causes. Hence, no one paid much attention to realistic and critical analysis of the human motives that seem at one time to show people up as idealists, and at another time as calculating murderers. It was convenient to think of wars as caused by leaders, and of individual participants as impressed victims fighting against their wills. The facts are otherwise. Individual soldiers, imbued with some systematic ideology, will fight fanatically whether they are under the eyes of others, or by themselves. Nor is their fighting all in self-defense. If it were, there would be much less vigor on the part of an aggressive force, as compared with the countless incidents of individual aggression reported in every battle.

Since 1940 a sinister turn in events has changed the picture. Annihilation is not only possible, it is feared to be probable. All of a sudden, war has become really grim. With the awful discovery that there is no defense for the new weapons, and that they are practically unlimited in the territory they can desolate, there is a sudden desire to know how to persuade people not to fight. When the only preventive for annihilation is to be found in the motives of people, attention turns compulsively to motivation. It finds very little in the way of real help in the educational programs of the schools, or in the available psychological material on factors that account for social conflict and ways of overcoming it. Inasmuch as this is now a problem of first importance to everyone, it should be treated in a book of this kind. Although it may not be possible to defend every point in a suggested approach by means of experimental evidence, there is an impressive amount of observational backing for some ideas, which can be tentatively offered. There is *no* contradiction to any of these ideas in psychological studies, and there is a great deal of oblique support.

In keeping with the foregoing position, an effort will be made in this chapter to present a way of thinking about personality in general, then a discussion of what constitutes health in one's motivational elements, followed by the extension of these ideas into the broader area of social relationships, social conflict, and the kinds of traps that have kept us from a constructive approach to peace. If some of the thoughts offered seem objectionable because they upset our good opinions of ourselves, or because they seem to contradict certain time-honored maxims, it is suggested they be "entertained" a while before being cast out. During the entertainment, they should be checked by observation of the behavior of people, and of oneself, with all the objectivity and honesty one can muster.

2402. *Personality.* This is one of the catch-all terms in the field. It has as many definitions as the term "attitude," but for some reason there is a little more interrelationship in them. Through most of the definitions runs a core of reference to the behavioral tendencies of the individual, and especially to those patterns in which the individual is consistent.[1] It also tends to include one's adjustment and the characteristic modes of achieving it. Thus it refers back also to motives, which lie behind a choice of action. All of these and other elements usually included refer to the *whole organism* and how it impresses others, as shown in the definition of personality as one's *social stimulus value.* Personality rarely refers to any single aspect of the individual, or to any single area of his participation with others, such as business, religion, or recreation. It is his over-all rating or description, with particular reference to the characteristics that continually repeat until they come to be the stable cues by which he is known.

Within this broad concept are certain less-inclusive concepts, which are usually known by certain familiar names. *Character,* for example, refers usually to those parts of one's

[1] Peter Blos, *The adolescent personality* (New York: Appleton-Century-Crofts, Inc., 1941), Part 1, Chapter 1.

behavioral patterns that involve the major ethical ideals of the culture. A good character is one that approximates the cultural ideal. A strong character is one that puts force behind the ideals, and refuses to compromise on them.[2] A person is known for how vigorously he stands for whatever he stands for.

Morality refers ordinarily to one's conformity to the most highly protected mores of a group. It carries the connotation of goodness or badness, with reference to a particular set of norms. From an anthropological point of view, there is no single standard of morality because every group has its own set of protected values, as a consequence of its own unique experiences. From a religious point of view, it is assumed that such variations are due to the incompleteness and atypicality of the experiences of individual groups, and that in the long run experience will stabilize and support a set of moral principles that will be increasingly verified with subsequent experience.

There is a certain amount of independence in these three terms. One may have a very attractive personality, with certain weaknesses in character, and without morals. One may have a powerful character, but no personality so to speak, meaning that the personality is not attractive. One may be of the highest moral quality and have either an attractive or an unattractive personality. One may be considered by a given group to be immoral to the extreme, but to have a strong character and a very engaging personality.

The three elements are not always kept in mind when reference is made to personality. Personality tends to be the over-all term, and to be made up of whatever combination of parts there may be present. This results again in an organismic way of looking at the individual, his impressions to others being made up of a composite of all that he does, and everything about him.[3]

---

[2] Vernon Jones, "Character development in children—an objective approach," in L. Carmichael, ed., *Manual of child psychology* (New York: John Wiley and Sons, 1946), Chapter 14.

[3] The biosocial approach to this problem is rather well handled by Gardner Murphy in *Personality* (New York: Harper and Bros., 1947). See especially

Although one tends to take in a whole organismic impression in meeting people in daily relationships, such impressions scarcely furnish the basis for an analysis of personality and for the development of an instructional program or guidance program designed to help in personality improvement. Consequently, one possible way of approaching the analysis of personality is suggested here. It does not indicate what will be found in any particular person, nor does it give any samples of personality structure. Its chief purpose is to act as an indicator of the details a person might look for if he cares to examine the underlying components that add up to an organismic whole.

A natural starting point is found in the *consistencies in the organismic behavior of the individual.* If a checklist were being developed on which to enter specific details, it might be constructed on the basis of the outline in Table 10.

TABLE 10—CONSISTENCIES IN ORGANISMIC BEHAVIOR THAT
CONSTITUTE PERSONALITY

I. Physical qualities and behavior
    A. Bodily form and physical features
    B. Posture and bearing
    C. Grooming
II. Personal qualities and behavior
    A. Concept of self as revealed in actions
    B. Aspirations and goals shown in behavioral trends
    C. Type of adjustment and control of reactions
    D. Quality of thinking and speech, e.g.,
        Clarity
        Decisiveness
        Initiative
    E. Traits of a personal nature
        Introversion or extraversion
        Persistence
        Originality

Chapters 26, 27, 30, 31. The Freudian approach is offered by Walter L. Langer, in *Psychology and human living* (New York: Appleton-Century-Crofts, Inc., 1943) , Chapter 9.

III. Social qualities and behavior
    A. Manners, e.g.,
        Precision
        Tact
        Courtesy
        Consideration
        Cheerfulness
        Loyalty
        Responsibility
        Friendliness
        Sympathy
    B. Traits of a social nature, e.g.,
        Dominance or submission
        Gentleness or sadistic tendencies
        Aggression or reciprocity
IV. Character
    A. Morality, or conformity to social norms
    B. Cherished values, as shown in behavioral trends
    C. Religious practices
V. Intellectual qualities
    A. Brightness
    B. Persistence
    C. Originality
    D. Economy
    E. Objectivity

This does not constitute a complete list of the elements of behavior that tend to take on consistency. A class might very profitably undertake the task of revising or extending this list, and discussing the basis of its actions. It could be set up in rating-scale form with a normal description in the center and positive and negative variations going each way, as in the Simplified Student Inventory in Chapter XXV. Carrying out such a project would result, more effectively than almost any other type of study, in the development of familiarity with the nature of each of the items included.

These are the kinds of "output," so to speak, by which a person affects others around him. They constitute his social stimulus value. In this list, we are dealing with developed behavior, which has come about through learning and is built up on the underlying structural properties of the individual. What has emerged in the behavior of any person is the joint product of the biosocial factors discussed briefly in Chapter XI. One of these factors, the *experiential* one, is unique to each person, and can be studied only by going back over the experiences of the individual. The other factor, the *structural* one, can be described in generalized terms, just as the preceding outline has suggested an approximate description of the points of *consistency* in behavior. When any effort is made to foster the improvement of personality, it should certainly be realistic enough to take into consideration the basic structural properties with which the person has to work. Personality is firmly anchored to these properties and cannot become something for which there is no foundation or capacity. That suggests the need for another outline, one which will make explicit what some items of that structural foundation are. Here is a suggested outline, Table 11, which again might profitably be subjected to revision and completion as a project of the class.

TABLE 11. STRUCTURAL FOUNDATIONS OF PERSONALITY

I. Protoplasm, the most basic property, with its characteristics
    A. Irritability
    B. Chemical homeostasis
    C. Tropismic reactions
    D. Organ behavior, in more specialized stages
II. Nervous system
    A. Brain and spinal cord, responsible for
        Total capacity for behavior
        Intelligence and aptitudes
        Individual differences in capacities
    B. Sensory nerves and receptors
        Vision
        Touch
        Hearing
        Smell
        Taste
        Heat and cold
        Pressure

    C. Motor nerves and effectors
        Muscular action ⎫
        Glandular action ⎬ Joint effects on behavior
    D. Autonomic system
        Involuntary activity
        Feelings and emotions
        Available energic output

III. Learning and adjusting mechanisms
    A. Response to new situations, by sequential steps
    B. Modification of response by all properties in this list
    C. Non-selective nature of learning
        Healthful or harmful
        Moral or immoral
        Realistic or unrealistic

IV. Recollection and thought
    A. Sensation
        Stimuli and their qualities and attributes
        Thresholds
        Sensitivity and efficiency
    B. Perception
        Attention
        Grouping
        Contour
        Constancy
        Fluctuation
        Space
        Time
    C. Language
        Symbol perception
        Symbol-concept relations and configurations
    D. Meaning and concepts
        Beliefs
        Concepts
        Impressions
        Preferences
        Values
        Ideals
    E. Imagery and recollection
    F. Imagination

V. Drives and needs
    A. Physiological
        Organic activity

        Appetites, fatigue, etc.
        Homeostatic principle in organismic reactions
B. Social
        Contact
        Dependence
        Absorption of custom
        Acquired preferences
C. Ego or personal
        Self-discovery
        Self-evaluation
        Self-assertion
        Self-realization, etc.

These are concepts that play important parts in a course in general psychology. They were introduced early in the book, to some extent, in connection with the discussion of the four aspects of behavior, since their operation is the basis of all the data of psychology. In the same sense, they constitute the first foundation of all forms of behavior, so that whatever personality may be, it is established on these basic elements or properties. As suggested in connection with the first list, these characteristics of an organism can only mean something significant when they have been studied with a little concentrated attention. They contain, among them, all of the processes that give each personality its peculiar nature. A clinical psychologist could not carry out his responsibilities without understanding them and their effects on personality. It follows without argument, then, that teachers and parents who work with personality problems in their children or students may easily be misled in their efforts, overlook a significant factor, or be victimized by some of the catchy formulas for becoming the life of the party in six easy lessons, unless they understand the basic psychological processes that influence the development of personality.

Discussion of these items in detail would be out of place here, but is available in any of the texts in general psychology.[4]

One of the significant aspects of personality is the manner

[4] See footnote 3 in Chapter II.

in which the individual responds to stimulation; that is, the amount of drive that seems to lie behind his behavior, the variety of stimuli that seem to be able to catch his attention and hold it, and the presence or absence of a tendency to inquire into a situation as contrasted with placidly accepting the first structure of impressions that registers. These seem to be the aspects of personality with which American educational philosophy is most concerned. They are certainly vital to the success of democracy, which requires initiative in all members of the group for its operation. As suggested in the introductory comments, this is a matter of such vital importance to society today that further discussion of personality in this chapter will be turned in that direction.

2403. *Motivational health.* Along with most other human characteristics, motivation has lately been discussed as if it were something that could be healthy or sickly. Such an approach is particularly appropriate in a democratic school system, where the major objectives are concerned with the development of a free-thinking, self-governing, and confident citizenry. Such objectives imply that students should become conscious of their basic directive values, that they should be continually challenged in their school life without being discouraged, and that they should be provided with wholesome outlets for their emotions and made to feel that they are achieving real well-being rather than failure. It is perfectly clear that dictatorial social organization depends on the very opposite mental habits in the citizenry to those on which democratic processes are founded. Unless initiative is to be found in the minds of most individuals, democracy will be an empty form.

Many factors enter into making a person subservient and unable to think. Very low intelligence is marked by inability to engage in abstract or original thinking. Persistent failure and discouragement may destroy the creative mental activity of an individual. Narrowness of outlook through limited experience denies to the individual the tools with which he can think broadly and soundly, and results in prejudice, superstition, fear, and other such unwholesome mental states. The forces that destroy motivational health are so thoroughly scattered through American life on the whole, including school life, as to cause serious concern to conscientious teachers. They are to be found in the use of artificial incentives, inconsistency on the part of teachers and parents, domination of children by adults, and similar unsound techniques.

It is the inescapable responsibility of the school to make every possible effort to counteract those factors that tend to destroy initiative and to see that the whole school program is woven around a framework of circumstances and activities that encourage and develop in the pupils those mental powers that will make democracy effective. For that reason it is essential that teachers understand motivational processes, and how they are modified by the experiences of the individual and the group.

The nature of motivational health. Motivational health may be thought of as a condition in which the individual is interested in much of what is around him, curious about things he contacts, eager to explore new areas and to explore old areas of experience more fully, aware of the value-implications for himself and his group of the things that happen to him and others, generally alive to the whole of life, and able to make intelligent choices.

Sickly motives are characterized by passivity, a feeling of being at a loss in situations, being bored without knowing what to do about it, having no ideas to contribute to the activity of oneself or the group, a preference for the role of follower rather than leader or cooperator, and inability to think or choose for oneself.

Since all development and learning are built from within the individual through his own self-effort, and since it is a psychological fact that each person's actions are determined by his own motivational machinery, it is difficult to avoid the conclusion that good motivational health is the most important single factor in development. It is almost the one factor without which learning and development cannot go on. It is practically impossible to prevent a person with good motivational health from learning and developing. The child who is active, alert, and curious will find out for himself what makes the world go around. He is likely to do it in spite of poor teachers, dull books, reactionary curricula, or the complete lack of any formal schooling at all. Every alert teacher soon comes to know that such students keep him on his toes to avoid losing his place of leadership. He also soon comes to know that the other sort of pupil cannot be dragged into a state of education by any device now known, except those devices that first arouse him to a state of active curiosity.

It is further true that motivational health may be cultivated by means of a democratically sound environment. Democracy is said to be a way of living. It feeds upon itself. What a person does he is able to learn to do. Motivational health is therefore not a detached possession of the individual, but a way of behaving. Whether it grows or declines depends on the extent to which it is used, and the circumstances under which it is used. If the teacher is to set up a healthful school atmosphere, it will be necessary to know what sorts of experience contribute to or detract from motivational health.

The cultivation of motivational health. Beneficial experience may be said to consist of at least the three following phases. (1) The individual must be *aroused from within.* Arousal is ordinarily associated with an inadequacy that becomes to some degree intolerable. All of this must be genuinely felt by the individual; it cannot be effective if imposed upon him from without. A student does not find it intolerable to be ignorant of certain academic facts or skills simply because a teacher tells him he must learn them. It is a mistake to assume that students who force themselves through a required routine of homework from fear of poor marks, scoldings, or failure have been aroused. They are being dragged through school. They go unwillingly. For the great majority of high-school graduates there has been so little arousal that graduation has meant the final escape from all fields of study, rather than a true commencement. Franklin was aroused when curiosity over the nature of lightning made him play with his kite. Watt was aroused when his mind probed into the action of the teakettle. When students are aroused they forget the limitations of mere requirements and dig into things with zest, read widely on topics, talk about them with others, keep at the teacher for help and ideas, and do these things in a realistic manner. When it is remembered that the essence of arousal is an intolerable inadequacy, it is not surprising that aroused individuals become active.

(2) As already suggested, the second phase of beneficial behavior is one of *exploratory and consummatory activity* leading to a satisfactory achievement of some sort. The intolerable lack must be taken care of. The boy who must talk about bombers and who does not know their names has an intolerable lack that he must overcome. How he overcomes it depends on the materials and experiences he is able to get hold of, but until he acquires the knowledge he needs to converse about bombers with his friends, his learning activity will continue. It is obvious that this active phase of experience must follow the direction indicated by the arousal. It is fatal for teachers to try to lead students through a process in which they are not interested when they are aroused by another problem leading in a different direction.

Skillful teachers know how to arouse pupils over issues that are inherently useful in the educative process. The teacher cannot be content to supply books and study materials. He must see to it that the students' activating problems are the sort that lead into profitable activity. Then, to the extent of their ability, students must be allowed to master their problems by their own efforts. The teacher guides this activity at times, but never takes it out of the learner's hands. Teachers often supply information to students, but this must be done in such a way that it fits into the student's search for something, rather than by trying to tack on some irrelevant package of facts.

(3) The third phase of beneficial experience is one of *consolidation of gains and their orientation into the person's whole being.* It is like adding the new achievement to what was already possessed, so that one can stand up on a higher level and take another look at things from a better point of view. It involves a reorientation of the self within an enlarged world. Because the learner is changed, his power of observation is also changed. To the extent that he has changed

himself in his achievement, he will see something new in his subsequent observation of his world. Because of his new vantage point he is likely to find another condition that needs changing, thus plunging him again into the cycle of beneficial experience.

The factors in beneficial experience correspond to these three phases, *arousal, achievement,* and *consolidation.* The most crucial phase is the first. Because of the relative difficulty of arousing pupils, desperate but unwise educators have developed a host of artificial incentives upon which the typical school hobbles painfully along. Such incentives include final exams, marks, promotions, honors, punishments, sarcasm, and the like. They have little if any logical relationship to the major objectives of education in America. It is no idle remark to say that such incentives have done untold damage to the motivational health of American youth. It is not a mere coincidence that the schools most rigidly controlled by such artificial devices are in countries whose people are most easily led into dictatorial forms of government and rigid class lines. When American schools are able to replace such techniques with *natural incentives, creative activity, realistic problems, freedom of choice, free play of cause and effect, allowance for mistakes and their inevitable results,* and *dependence of reward on what is accomplished,* American youth will be forever free from intellectual domination by dictators. What is more, they will be free to live and act fully in their own world, and will have the skills necessary to do so.

One thing more needs to be stressed concerning the phases of experience just described, and that is the need for submitting the individual to *contact with reality* all the way through. Autocratic controls in the home and the school quite often set aside the natural consequences of behavior, and impose artificial consequences that will occur only as long as the one in charge can carry out his controls. This is done by removing or preventing naturally unpleasant consequences from following an act, and replacing them with harmless or pleasant consequences, or by preventing pleasant consequences and replacing them with unnaturally unpleasant consequences. For example, if a child goes out and gets.

his last clean suit muddy, the mother will probably stay up into the night getting it ready for church the next morning. The natural penalty is not allowed to operate, for it is a rare mother who will tell the child that inasmuch as he has dirtied his only wearable suit, he will either have to wear it to church or stay home. Conversely, two students who collaborate in the preparation of a term paper that is better than either one could have done alone are punished when their collaboration is discovered by being marked "F" for their effort. In the first case, the child was protected from the embarrassment or disappointment that his act should have brought, and in the second case, the students were punished for an act that would normally have brought each of them a sense of achievement, and some valuable training in teamwork.

In the process of arousing students, helping them make achievements and then integrate what they have gained into their existing structure, it is important to their ultimate motivational health that they get in touch with realism early and become accustomed to working out their adjustments in a realistic way. This is important, first, in *cause and effect relationships.* An individual should be on his own at the earliest possible time in this connection so that he will master the world in which he lives and avoid getting himself into frustrating situations when his artificial protections or controls are lifted. It is important, secondly, in connection with *the demands of situations,* where the individual must learn what has to be done under various circumstances, and prepare himself to do the things he must do throughout life. For example, the child is often allowed to disrupt life in the home to the extent that others in the family must set aside their own activities for him. If he is raised in this manner, he is being prepared for rude bumps when he tries to carry on the same disregard of others outside the family, or he may be getting ready to abuse others who cannot defend themselves. Social situations make certain very important demands on people, which must be met if social life is to proceed satisfactorily for all. Realism in this matter during the early years of childhood, and in all learning experiences, would vastly improve the motivational health of the individual and make him a safer member of society.

Third, a form of realism is involved in *getting the child exposed to all of life* instead of a narrow segment of it. Every time a person is aroused and in the process of going through the cycle of beneficial experience the teacher or parent has an opportunity to turn him toward new discoveries in wider and wider views of life, or to turn him back into the same narrow and restricted paths he has already used. Since one does not escape from the breadth of the world simply by refusing to look at it, it is not realistic to confine one's conceptual structure to any smaller segment of the world than necessary. Once more, social life is made safer for everyone, and more satisfactory to the individual, when he knows what all of the possibilities are and can make his adjustment without leaving out of consideration some factors that may upset him without his knowledge.

Motivational health and methods of teaching. Specific ways of incorporating these factors into school experience are determined for each class and each course as the circumstances warrant. Detailed studies of such procedures are generally handled through courses in methods of teaching. Problem-centered units of study, contract plans, activity programs, and all other innovations whose chief purpose is to stimulate purposeful student activity are based in theory on the psychological facts discussed in this chapter. That they sometimes go astray and become mired down in disorderly and confused bedlam is not the fault of the psychological facts upon which they are based. It is due to failure to keep the procedures closely geared to the psychological facts. As suggested earlier, any method of teaching that is detached from the psychological considerations upon which it was originally based is a wholly unreliable tool in the hands of the average teacher. A method that is appropriate under one set of conditions may be quite inadequate when the conditions are changed in some subtle but important way. In addition to this difficulty, it is a common experience of teachers to set a class in motion by sound motivational procedures, only to see the class drift into disorganized busywork because the lesson plan was incomplete or unsound in the later phases of the learning cycle. Such trouble is especially prominent when the goal in learning is the development of concepts. This is because it is not possible to provide complete or meaningful experience with a referent without considerable careful planning of procedures and materials, not to mention the difficulty encountered when the teacher fails to evaluate the students' present status as a starting point. Since psychology is supposed to be the root of all good methods, this discussion can most profitably end with a list of questions which the method-maker would do well to keep in mind at this point.

1. *On making children conscious of their basic directive values.* What experiences bring values to a state of recognition and analysis? How can experience be made to yield socially proven values? What would be revealed by analysis of one's classroom practice to see what values are actually produced for the child? Do school experiences on the whole yield a consistent meaning to students, or are they unstable and contradictory? How can one's work be planned to yield consistent meaning to the student?

2. *On development of motivational health.* What opportunities can be given for realistic and unhampered use of one's free-agency? What motivational artifacts are used in school? How do they affect various kinds of students? How would you replace them in practical situations, thinking in terms of a specific subject area?

3. *On experiencing success instead of failure.* How can school tasks be tied to the important goals of students? How can success be insured and failure eliminated for all students? When has a student failed?

4. *On challenging students without discouraging them.* What constitutes a challenge? What does one have to know about a person to know what will challenge him? When does a challenge become discouraging? How does this apply to reading assignments, mathematics problems, literature lessons, dressmaking or agricultural projects or jobs?

5. *On the emotional aspects of school.* How can a pleasant emotional atmosphere be provided without getting into

strong emotional experiences? What school experiences carry unpleasant emotional tone? Can they be replaced? How? What can be done to allow expression of those emotions that are inevitably aroused in schools regardless of the nature of the program? Is school experience an asset to a student when it is marked by emotional disturbance? How can emotionally upset students be handled for their own good in the light of the present attitudes of school authorities toward school attendance law, discipline, and administrative regularity?

School administrators and teachers have not discharged their basic responsibilities to students until they have satisfactorily taken care of these questions. The psychologist is primarily concerned with discovering and analyzing the problems. The administrator and teacher have the primary responsibility of carrying the matter to its logical conclusion. Unless both groups work together throughout the process, however, it will never be adequately done.

Summary. The development of motivational health depends on the presence in school experience of opportunities to think and choose realistically. People think and choose when they are aroused through the force of circumstances that demand change. To keep aroused students from moving in meaningless directions it is essential for the teacher to see clearly what experiences the students must have in order to reach their goals and how those experiences can be made to yield their greatest possible value to the learner. This requires a thorough knowledge of the psychological facts about learning and motives, and much careful planning of activities and materials appropriate to the problems involved.

2404. *Motivational health and social survival.* Of all the aspects of personality, that which has to do with social interaction has been singled out for emphasis because of the critical problems that face society today. Throughout section 2403 an effort was made to describe the problems involved in getting people ready to act constructively through their own controls, and in harmony with factual realities that control life. Now attention is to be directed to an application of those ideas to the problem of human relationships, in the light of modern social conditions. No apology is offered for the fact that it is not yet possible to document this approach with experimental evidence for its soundness. The reader is advised to read it with as much reserve as he needs to make him feel safe, but the claim is immodestly set up, now, that all the documentary evidence needed for this approach is to be found in human history, and in observation of people anywhere in the world today.

Sources of social conflict. If there were enough of all the things that satisfy need to give everyone what he needs when he needs it without threatening the supply of anyone else, and to give it in such a way that he would not limit the need-fulfilling activity of anyone else, there would be no conflicts between people. Such a condition may have existed at one time in human history, but it does not exist now. Whenever the demand begins to equal the supply of such things as jobs, homes, food, cars, and other specific means for filling needs, and whenever a society becomes class conscious and develops a system for honoring certain individuals above others, and attaches privileges to the honors, the elements of competition are present. Regardless of the techniques by which people finally come to seek their satisfiers, there will be an inverse relationship between the number of individuals in a group and the amount of satisfaction each individual can have. This can only be changed when the group develops methods of production that increase the supply beyond what individuals can supply for themselves.

The first state of competition is usually laissez faire, since there is no need of controls as long as there is no competition. Controls come along as a device for softening the competition. When people begin to tire of competition, some sort of control begins to appear. Its nature depends on who does the planning, and how many people are involved in it. It may go in one of two general directions. There can be a contest to determine who is strongest, the winner determining the rules of procedure from then on. This can be a malevolent or benevolent rule. It depends on the philosophy and general development of the one in power. Or, there can be an effort to get all parties together for the purpose of agreeing on rules of procedure, and for delegating authority from the group to those representatives who are charged with regulating the competitive activities in harmony with the adopted rules. In practical situations there is usually some mixture of these two types of control.

In any situation in which there is domination by one person or group, there is inevitable and continued conflict because of the persistent tendency of the healthy human being to act as a free agent. Trends in government throughout the world are evidence of this tendency. Men work and plan to get out from under domination one way or another and, in spite of setbacks, continue to move toward democratic forms of control in the long run. It is primarily when the physiological needs of a nation are not being met that authoritarian forms of government are best able to take control and maintain it. This is in harmony with Maslow's theory of the hierarchy of motives,[5] for under such conditions the social and personal needs of people fall into unimportance and they sell their souls for bread and security. Freedom is a contributing condition to the fulfillment of personal needs, for upon it depend some very important elements of self-respect, but it is not necessary for the satisfaction of physiological needs, and sometimes it is a hindrance. In America now, individual and group life is motivated almost entirely in its significant aspects by social and personal needs. Physiological needs are so automatically cared for in most cases that they rarely rise to a prominent level in the control of group behavior. Relatively few people in America know what it means to miss a meal, or to live constantly in weariness or pain. Sexual needs are fulfilled through marriage or through surreptitious patterns for adults, and adolescents are not embroiled in such matters much of the time. Hence the fight for freedom and for belongingness and recognition and affection stands high in the priorities of modern man, as a rule.

In modern American society there is a distinct and power-

[5] A. H. Maslow, "A theory of human motivation," *Psychological review,* 50 (1943), 370-96.

ful class structure. Personal and social satisfactions are not equally available to all people. Physical things, such as money, cars, and homes, have become to a serious extent the symbols of prestige. That means that we have an authoritarian form of control over the competition for need satisfiers, no matter what the form of the state or federal government. Furthermore, since there are never enough satisfiers to meet the needs of everyone at the same time, there is an intense struggle for the symbols of status, which shows up in all parts of the industrial structure of the world.

Democracy offers a way in which processes that are socially safe might be developed if it were not for the unofficial domination of life that stems from caste, class, and wealth status. The problem of resolving serious social conflicts in our culture will not be solved until the unofficial but very real restraints are faced frankly and recognized for what they are, and for their role in the creation of conflicts.

It is not enough to say that the new generation must be taught socially safe processes for satisfying its needs. The new generation cannot be taught anything that is not in operation around it. The older generation holds the control in our social machine, and the younger generation will ride whithersoever the older generation drives it. Therefore, the educational problem cannot be solved by working only with children in school. It requires attack at all age levels, and in all status groups in life. Since learning never takes place apart from a conflict in which there is a barrier preventing achievement of some desired adjustment, the older generation will never change its manner of dominating, and preserving its privileges, until it finds itself in a real conflict that threatens its survival unless it gives up its methods of control. Actually, such a conflict exists today, but no one will be moved to learn anything from it until he senses his own jeopardy. That does not seem to be happening to any extent at present. People do not generally see that their privilege system is stimulating the threat to their survival. How such a realization is to be brought about is an interesting question, which might well absorb the serious attention of students of human life.

Verbal teaching will not help. The most serious danger facing any program of social alteration is the temptation to proceed on the assumption that people can be talked into a new point of view. Talk has its place in the program, but it is a subordinate place. Conceptual learning is essentially pragmatic. It takes place quietly. It happens in spite of or without any discussion. It takes a direction that has no necessary relationship to verbalizations going on concurrently. While a person is memorizing a code of ethics and nodding verbalized agreement with it, his behaviorally significant learning may be supplying him with a technique for knocking out his opposition. The thing that counts is the thing that happens to him in the realm of his important needs. If this fact is overlooked, it will continue to cause the downfall of any educational program, and particularly one that attempts to alter well-established cultural patterns. Before any process concept begins to exert influence on behavior, it must have served its apprenticeship and delivered the goods in reality. This means we learn to do that which works, whether we recognize it or not, and whether we or anyone else believe it is a good thing or not.

If propaganda or any other verbalized approach is capable of giving individuals significant experiences with controlled and made-to-order meanings, then it may accomplish its purpose. That, however, is the test it must pass before it becomes helpful.

In the following section it is suggested that a certain series of concepts must somehow become part of the functional pattern of meaning of an individual before he will act in a socially desirable and productive manner. With all the modern emphasis on the activity curriculum, the problem-centered curriculum, and the use of creative experience in the educational process, it is not an easy task to guide people into just those experiences that will yield desirable meanings. Nevertheless, something of that sort must be done, for there is no other way in which the pattern of meaning can be guided in its development.

Some essentials in developing socially desirable behavior. A proper beginning must include acceptance of the fact that *self-interest lies at the heart of all behavior.* It doesn't matter whether the individual has broadened his concept of himself to include one or a worldful of his contemporaries, his behavior will still abide by this principle. He will seek the well-being of himself and those whom he has identified with himself and made a part of his concept of self-realization. Although it is not at all flattering, it would appear to be safe to suggest that most people have not broadened out very far in this manner, and that any reconstruction program must cope with individuals who have a rather narrow self-concept within which most of those with whom they do business are not included. For some reason, perhaps a rationalized sense of pride in the assumed nobility of ourselves, it is difficult to get people to recognize this self-centered quality in behavior. So the unpleasant fact must be faced, unless we are willing to go on wandering down fruitless roads.

Recognizing the search for personal well-being, the next step must be toward the establishment of *a concept of enlightened self-interest.* Again this is resisted by those who feel that it is a cheap answer to the problem. It appears to be an unsatisfactory answer because it is often presented as if it were the final step in social development, and thus put into false contrast with the doctrine of love of neighbor. This is an error, the truth being that it is only a stage in the development of the latter doctrine. It has the advantages for an immediate improvement in human affairs of being the first step away from a blind policy of isolationism (which is really unenlightened self-interest) and of operating firmly on the basis of the principle of self-interest. Therefore, it is essential in social development that each individual somehow become progressively aware of the fact that the welfare of others is essential to his own welfare. Some suggestions about the steps in this conceptual development are offered soon.

The third major step in the full socialization process consists of continued participation with others in such a way that the individual may discover in them some of the characteristics he recognizes as the good or admired parts of his own self-concept. In this process lies the key to *develop-*

ment of affectional relationships, which grow into close bonds of brotherly love and hold people together. Under this condition the individual will begin to identify others with himself and to draw them into his own concept of self. He will never give up the principle of self-realization, but with these new additions to himself he will alter his processes of behavior so as to preserve and favor all those who make up his broadened self. This is not the crafty calculating thing that is involved in enlightened self-interest, the using of others as one would use a good cow. It becomes a labor of love in which each included person becomes part of the life that is being lived.

Of course this devotion will not be extended to those who have not been included in the concept of self. There are thousands of people whose personal worlds have somehow broadened out to include a mate and some children, or perhaps an additional friend or relative or two, but no more. These people would give their lives, and they often do, for those so included, but can act with the coldest disregard for the feelings of others not included. That is the typical situation throughout the world, and it accounts for the lack of solidarity and mutual consideration that are so obvious a charact ristic of social and community life.

Except for those closest to the typical individual, it has never been standard practice to love one's neighbor as oneself. Scattered throughout history, there are those who have come to do so. Their lives have been devoted as fully to the well-being of those who came to be included in their self-concepts as they could ever have been to themselves as individuals. Beyond those limits of inclusion they have been as heartless as the next fellow. The measure of expansion of the self-concept has always been the number and variety of people for whom one would give his life and all his talents. The fact that so few in world history have grown to worldwide scope in their identifications indicates something of the difficulty of such growth, and offers an explanation of the inertia within people which counteracts all that such individuals can do to promote a world brotherhood. Gandhi is one of the latest examples.

The only possible hope for social solidarity lies in this concept of universal love. It does not require or imply loss of the self, or sacrifice of the self in the least. Its strength lies in the realness of its self-realization. Jesus did not show any symptoms indicating that he felt he was losing anything through his devotion to others. Lincoln never at any time gave evidence that he felt he was destroying himself in his fight for a better national life. None of the great martyrs has shown such an attitude. On the contrary, they have given evidence that their actions were satisfying to themselves, and that what they did for others was done with all the solicitude and concern that could possibly accompany any self-ministrations. They seemed to be happy and satisfied with their own status. Any sorrow they exhibited was over the misfortunes of others.

From where the world stands today it is a long climb to the sort of inclusive identification that would make each individual seek the well-being of all others. In fact it is so long a climb that the chances of completing it within human history seem to be almost nil. The best that can be hoped for is a somewhat more realistic and compelling enlightened self-interest, in which the masses may begin to see somewhat realistically that their welfare is contingent on the elimination of serious conflicts over need satisfiers throughout the world. Such a point of view is not beyond possibility, given a proper educational program aimed at young and old alike. Along with that, some education in the rudiments of human motivation should become part of the diet of all people, so that no one will act in ignorance of what people everywhere are trying to do, or overlook the fact that the other fellow is in serious competition with him for the goods of the earth. It should also become clear that most people the world over have somewhat similar values, and that their serious differences are in *processes,* which might very well be brought up for examination and criticism. They could be changed without destroying the values we cherish.

Enlightened leadership and control of disturbers. In addition to this work with people in general, it is essential to develop some leaders with certain qualities. They must be people who have broadened within their concepts of self until they are characterized by a real brotherly love. This is not enough, however, under present conditions. They must also have a very solid knowledge of economic, social, and political principles. Furthermore, they must know that until others reach the same basis of enlightened self-interest or its succeeding condition there will always be danger from unenlightened self-seekers, and that whatever is required to keep them under control must be done.

With such dependable planners in positions of leadership, where they may determine policies, it might be possible to get the partially enlightened masses to participate in programs that will make world peace a practical possibility. At the best, it is an extremely difficult thing to achieve. It may not be possible at this point to say in detail how it can be done. Some of the essential steps involved in getting the individual up to a desirable conceptual level can certainly be indicated, however.

Concepts that will produce enlightened self-interest. At this point it is necessary to talk about things the individual must come to believe if his behavior is to become socially productive. Again it must be emphasized that verbalized expression of a so-called belief is not what is needed. These beliefs must be functional elements of the pattern of meaning, gleaned from actual experience. It isn't even necessary for the person to hear one of them mentioned verbally, but he certainly must learn them from experience somehow. Here they are.

1. The individual must *discover* that he can get what he wants in life *only* when there is *a supporting society that operates as a line of supply.* Unless someone operates the power plant he can't have light. Unless the factory operates he can't have shoes. There is nothing he can have if people do not produce it for him and deliver it to him. This should not be a particularly difficult concept to develop. We tend to learn about it sometimes when a strike stops production. Some direct attention must be given to it, however, for it must be more than a casual type of education. It must be highlighted as one of the significant facts of modern life.

Nearly everyone agrees verbally that it is so, but then nearly everyone *acts as if* he did not believe it. What he does is the only safe indication of his functional beliefs.

2. The second discovery that is essential is that *members of society will not continue to produce for others unless they get what they want also*. This is not so easily achieved. The direct connection is not so apparent. Because we buy shoes in a store, we do not learn how the worker feels about making them, or of his demands for living wages and decent working conditions. If the miners walk out of the mines today, it will still be possible to buy coal a month or more from now, and if coal can't be bought we can turn to oil or gas and let the miners starve if they wish. It is not readily apparent to the average person that in such a course lie the seeds of eventual dissolution of the whole supply system. There is too much lag in a society between the producer and the consumer for the consumer to be able to find out that the produer has to be satisfied, too.

People do not work because of their love for me. They work for pay, in the form of money, affection, and belongingness, and the status that permits self-approval. When this pay gets too low they will leave their jobs and seek something else. Notice the effect of this pressure on boys, who aspire to jobs they can't possibly hold, because of the prestige attached to them. Revolutions occur because of underpayment in prestige and social recognition. Production goes up in factories where the pay in prestige is increased. A strike is an expression of unwillingness to be underpaid, and it is not always because of the money part of the pay. People will not work unless they are paid to their satisfaction. It is not immoral, it is just a fact. Underpayment always results in an inefficient, disgruntled, unstable, production line, which never delivers enough. People subscribe to this fact verbally, but they continue to *act as if* they do not believe it. Part of the educational problem is to help them *discover this fact in a functional way*.

3. The third discovery the individual must make is that *if society can get what it wants without his help, it will begin to squeeze him out*, but that if he makes a significant con-

tribution he will be more and more secure in his social status. No economy will go on indefinitely supporting a non-contributor, unless he happens to be the dictator, with an army to maintain his domination. Few of us are in that position. Unless we produce, we have no share in the products.

We are worth to others no more than we can give them of what they want. Here are some ways in which we squeeze people out: The hobo is rushed out of town. The young delinquent is shunned, punished, and banished. The poor worker is demoted, fired, blacklisted, or sometimes just cursed and belittled. The poor entertainer is booed, shunned, and forgotten. Here are some ways in which we cut people in for a larger share of society's products: The hero is fêted and honored. The capable man is promoted and paid well, and bowed to by others. The funny man, the entertainer, is made rich, and given prestige. It all depends on how much we feel he is worth to us, for any reason at all that matters to us.

The weak point in the establishment of this concept lies in the fact that children rarely acquire a sense of obligation or of contribution toward their own maintenance until their wants begin to exceed the ready opulence of the family purse. By that time it is a little late to tell the child that no one gets anything unless he makes a contribution. Nevertheless, that is the case in most adult lives, and we must find some way of bringing this realization to the front in all those who are supported by others, at whatever age. The fact that exceptions seem to contradict the idea does not invalidate it for society as a whole.

4. The fourth concept that must be discovered by the individual is that *no one can really help society, or make a true contribution to the work of anyone else, unless he understands the one he is helping.* The most devastating blunders performed in the name of charity are those in which someone imbued with a desire to help, but completely immersed in the infallibility of his own idea of what is needed, proceeds to inflict upon others, circumstances that are worse than those from which they are being "saved." Nothing is

really a help unless it furthers what the individual is already trying to do with himself, and a knowledge of what that goal is cannot be possessed without understanding the individual.

It is fatal to be a do-gooder. Don't do to others what you want done to you. What you want may be quite distasteful to them. Do to others what *they* want done to *them,* if you would make a contribution. Jobs are lost because the worker' knows better than the boss. It makes no difference if the worker was really right. Good employees are lost because the boss knows better than the worker. It makes no difference if the boss was right. Candidates are defeated because they know better than the people, and again it makes no difference if the candidate is right. Wives divorce husbands because husbands ignore what the wives want from the marriage. Do-goodism is a very rampant disease.

What has just been said is psychologically true, even though it seems to oppose any efforts to change people. Continued effort to change people through education is not a violation of this idea, provided it is carried out in harmony with the principles stated in section 2403. Even in educational programs, however, people will resist efforts to get them to do things that are contrary to their wishes, and in which they see no value. Those who attempt to force them into such actions are always regarded as annoyers, at least with reference to those acts.

Here again, as in the former instance, it is difficult to realize what our blunders do to others, and why they get angry, because such comprehension requires almost the same understanding as is needed to make the help really helpful in the first place. Nevertheless, it would not be difficult to bring this principle to dramatic and conscious attention through many episodes in human life, in such ways that those being taught could *feel* the experiences of those whose stories were being told.

5. The fifth concept that is required in this chain is the discovery that *it is impossible to understand an individual without listening to him sympathetically and with an open mind.* Most conversation is not interchange, but two one-way activities in which each is just talking, not listening.

It is hard to learn to listen, but it opens the door to the world of human beings around us. This concept can be dramatized through human episodes and made real through bringing to life the past experiences of almost anyone, for all of us have been embarrassed in the past through failure to listen, with consequent misunderstanding and blunder. Listening is helped greatly when one learns how to probe for real understanding. There are many ways of getting people to make their feelings clear, if one will quit talking and develop ways of getting people to repeat themselves until their meaning is clearly understood. This is a concept, like the others, that must be *discovered*. It can't be imparted verbally. People *act as if* they see no value in listening.

These five concepts, if built upon each other and well established in the experience of the individual, will put him into a frame of mind in which he is ready to try to operate on a policy of enlightened self-interest. It does not take him all the way into expansion of the self, and love of neighbors, but it sets the stage for such development. Affectional ties can scarcely be kept from developing when one begins to listen to others and to search their lives sympathetically. It is one of the clichés of friendship that it is difficult to dislike those whom we come to know well. If this sort of exploration produces results in real neighborliness, it has provided the dynamics for group solidarity.

Traps that keep us from learning these things about life. In closing this discussion, here are three rather intriguing facts that explain why we do not learn to live together in the manner just described. When they are seen, they will probably help us avoid the difficulties we now face. We need be victims of them no longer, if we will adjust educational programs appropriately. They are fundamentally psychological facts about human perception, the interference that set furnishes to learning, and the screen that verbal ability puts in front of empirical and subliminal learning.

Most of the social, economic, and political laws that operate so relentlessly throughout society to bring us to the verge of world annihilation are very slow and deliberate laws. They do not run their courses in seconds, as some chemical laws do, or in minutes, weeks, or even a few years. They operate over a cycle that requires many years, and sometimes whole historical epochs. Man is not constituted so that he can perceive things on that time scale. He can sense time in small units, such as seconds, hours, days, or perhaps weeks. From there on up he would be completely helpless without timers and calendars. With such a sensory handicap he is unable to experience the effects of these leisurely laws. They would never be discovered were it not for the techniques by which social scientists gather up a record of what has happened, telescope it, and play it back in condensed form so that they can see all of the forces at work in connection with each other. That is essentially what history consists of.

What they have done for themselves, we must do for everyone, so that the basic laws of human living can be discovered by every individual. Then he can readjust his patterns of behavior so that he can profit by them, instead of being destroyed by them.

Man is the only creature who has the marvelous capacity for symbolic and verbal behavior, but he is the victim of his unique capacity. It is so noisy, so attractive, that it obscures the non-verbal forms of learning which go on empirically through experience. The latter control behavior, but the verbal facility is used to rationalize and to lead its possessors into self-deceit. The whole school system is built on verbal activities. It has left out almost completely any functional approaches to learning. Lessons are learned verbally and recited back verbally, and no one pays any attention to what people are learning empirically from experience. Hence we do not know what we are really doing, because we are so enamored with the power of speech. Our verbal patterns are quite distinct from our functional patterns, as mentioned in the discussion of values. Education is in desperate need of a shift from verbal teaching to experience teaching, and to a way of finding out what is being learned at the functional level. That which is being learned at the verbal level is so harmless and insignificant that we could afford to ignore it.

The last trap is the hallucination that we can learn to love others by self-denial. Somehow this has become the sole interpretation of the doctrine of love, and it is completely impossible. Through this trap, we have been trying for centuries to force people down a path which, by virtue of all the basic laws of individual psychology, they must not take. Through this preoccupation with a false path, we have failed to discover the only real path to brotherly love; consequently, we have done literally nothing in the only fruitful direction that is available. Self-interest is so basic in human life that survival is impossible without it. Self-interest, however, hasn't a chance until we learn how interdependent we are in modern society. We need a definite shift in our attack on this problem.

2405. *Conclusion.* Throughout this chapter, beginning with the discussion of personality, there has been an attempt to build up the case for a revision in our ways of preparing people for adjustment and social life. A number of rather compelling socio-psychological concepts have been presented, even though some of them must for the present stand on their own logic and their verifications from personal observation. There is a way to bring about a wholesome world, and to prepare wholesome people to live in it, but in certain ways we have been moving at right angles with reality in our educational programs both in school and in other agencies. Perhaps the pressure of a threat to civilization will make us susceptible to new ideas, so that we can take our accustomed patterns apart and rebuild them on more solid lines.

QUESTIONS FOR REVIEW

1. What is the basic element in definitions of personality?
2. What is meant by social stimulus value?
3. What is the relationship between personality and character?
4. What has morality to do with personality and character.
5. What are the organic and fundamental properties on which personality rests?
6. What consistencies are important in describing personality?
7. How would you proceed in trying to change one's personality?
8. Why are the social manners not a good starting point?
9. Define motivational health.
10. What is there about democracy and what is there about motivational health that makes them so essential to each other?

11. What are some of the common enemies of motivational health?
12. What forces in a typical school program give rise to the kinds of experience that may destroy motivational health?
13. What is there about growth and development that makes it dependent on motivational health?
14. Make up a brief description in your own words of each of the essential phases of an experience that is motivationally beneficial.
15. Certain types of realism should be present in all phases of a learning experience. What are they?
16. How would you answer the questions in the chapter on school atmosphere?
17. What causes social competition? When will it develop in noticeable form?
18. What do democratic forms of control imply for the production of need-satisfiers?
19. What restraints exist in all democratic societies that thwart the purpose of democratic principles?
20. Why has education failed to overcome social competition and strife?
21. Where does the principle of self-interest fit into social survival?
22. What are the steps involved in developing enlightened self-interest?
23. Why must there be police power in democratic societies?
24. Explain the way in which time perception has prevented learning about causes of social disintegration.

SELECTED REFERENCES

John E. Anderson, "Freedom and constraint or potentiality and environment," *Psychological bulletin*, 41 (January, 1944), 1-29.
Peter Blos, *The adolescent personality* (New York: Appleton-Century-Crofts, Inc., 1941), Part, Chapter 1.
Henry E. Garrett, *Great experiments in psychology* (New York: Appleton-Century-Crofts, Inc., 1941), Chapter IV.
Walter C. Langer, *Psychology and human living* (New York: Appleton-Century-Crofts, Inc., 1943), Chapters 1, 2, and 9.
Gardner Murphy, *Personality* (New York: Harper and Bros. 1947), Chapters 26, 27, 30, and 31.
Daniel A. Prescott, *Emotion and the educative process* (Wash-

ington, D. C.: The American Council on Education, 1938), Chapters IX, X, and XII.
Donald Snygg and Arthur W. Combs, *Individual psychology*, (New York: Harper and Bros., 1949), Chapter IX.

Class Exercises on Social and Motivational Health

Things To Do outside School

1. List all incentives you can think of as used in school. Divide the list into those that are motivationally healthful and those that are motivationally harmful. Discuss the items in class to justify your allocation of them.

2. Divide the class into five groups, appoint a chairman for each group, and assign to each group one of the sets of questions contained in section 2403 under the heading *Motivational health and methods of teaching*. Each group is to meet and prepare to discuss the questions in any manner it chooses, for a specified length of time, in one of the ensuing class periods. Discussions might take the form of panels, or the members of each group might pool their efforts and appoint a spokesman. Class discussion should follow the presentation.

3. Select two or three personality tests for analysis. Assign each one to a small group of students. They are to go through the test, examining its contents, to see how they are related to the outlines of personality in section 2402, and how they are divided among the four aspects of behavior in Chapters II to V. Findings of each committee can be reported and compared.

4. Set up committees, each of which is to work on one of the five concepts presented in section 2404. The assignment is to show how such a concept could be taught at some level in school, in an experiential way, not a verbal way. Special attention should be given to the traps that keep people from learning these things about life. Class discussion may follow presentation of the recommendations.

PART VI

EVALUATION AND COUNSELING

CHAPTER XXV

EVALUATION IN EDUCATION

2501. *The role of evaluation.* Every enterprise requires some system for keeping track of its business. Where survival depends on keeping informed, and upon changing procedures to fit the demands, as in economic competitive business, evaluation reached an effective level much earlier than in non-competitive enterprises. Educational institutions have had a monopoly in their line. They have not had to demonstrate their success, or account for their failures. Consequently, evaluation has not reached the level of efficiency found in business. Furthermore, the evaluation of human development is the most difficult problem in the whole field. Its complexity plus the fact that the only spur behind its development is the curiosity and discontent of the educator who wonders about the results of his work are responsible for a long period of rather slow development and a still unfinished task that will require much more time and ingenuity.

Business long ago developed accounting, with cost analysis, sales graphs, records of business cycles, and methods of gauging demand and competition, as its evaluative system. Medicine uses the thermometer, measures of pulse rate, chemical, analyses, X-rays, blood tests, and many other evaluative devices for keeping track of conditions. Art has its criteria of composition, form, design, esthetic effect, and other qualities, much less precise than the two fields previously named, but quite effective in the hands of skilled individuals. Political circles use the poll, the ballot, extensive personal contact, letters and other communications from constituents, and endless varieties of reports on conditions throughout the domain, for evaluating trends in thinking, and for planning activities both in governing and in seeking re-election. In guidance, the counselor uses interviews, records of activities, and tests, to obtain a clear understanding of the counselee's capacities and other resources for adjustment, from which he lays out an attack on the problem at hand. All of this is *evaluation,* which might be defined as *a systematic way of determining the state of affairs in any enterprise, with particular reference to the principal objective of the enterprise.*

Evaluation is especially important in educational programs. Students are expected to move smoothly through a very close schedule of graded tasks, each of which depends to some extent on the mastery of the preceding one. Failure to achieve, when it is discovered at the end of a course, creates a major disruption in the program, and results in an unnecessary and serious loss to the student. Retardation and friction introduced into the educational process by maladjustment take a toll that could be minimized by early and efficient evaluative procedures. General improvement in the whole educative system waits largely on proper evaluation of procedures and results obtained with individuals and with large groups. Without the spur of competition, and with no demand from society for an accounting, evaluation has grown only on its own dynamics, from the beginning given it by oral examinations reported in Biblical stories, written examinations in early Chinese history from 2200 B.C., and the more formal rise of regular school tests around A.D. 1700 in England.[1]

The testing movement, which should not be mistaken for the more recent development of the idea of evaluation, has had a vigorous history since 1900. Tests are fascinating devices. They permit themselves to be handled by exact statistical methods, and can be subjected to correlations, tests of difference, and factor analysis without limit. Furthermore, they supply the teacher with precise scores, which can be recorded, added, translated into final marks, and used to rate

[1] Harry A. Greene, A. N. Jorgensen, and J. Raymond Gerberich, *Measurement and evaluation in the secondary school* (New York: Longmans, Green and Co., 1943), Chapter III.

students without the need of laborious personal study and thoughtful judgment. They have a deceptive absolutism about them which leads to fine cutting lines between, let us say, a 59 and a 60, which marks the point of passing in a course. These conveniences and securities were sure to be welcomed by overloaded teachers who dreaded the personal responsibility involved in making personal judgments of students' performances. In general, the teachers did not think to inquire about whether the tests were measuring the important outcomes of a course, or were accurate in their measurement. Such problems have gradually come up for recognition as research has dug in here and there, questioning assumptions, and demonstrating weaknesses.

In recent years the first absorption with the "gadget" aspect of testing has worn off to some extent, and tests have been recognized as techniques whose utility depends entirely on purposes that lie outside the instruments themselves. With this wholesome turn in thinking, teachers are beginning to realize that all tests are not alike, that each type of test has its own peculiar use and is appropriate only when the purpose requires that kind of device; that no test may be assumed to give valid scores until it has been validated, and that even valid scores do not provide the full answer to a student's achievements. Attention is moving back to purposes, and evaluation is a movement designed to appraise the accomplishment of purposes. Measuring instruments have taken a decidedly secondary place, a subordinate place, their use being determined by their ability to contribute in some way to the final appraisal, which is a composite thing.

The central function of evaluation lies in its application to the student. Here it consists of all procedures by which we determine how near to a given objective are the student and the class, and what aspects of the task still remain to be accomplished. It has some subsidiary aspects that, as far as the school is concerned, are important because they contribute to the efficiency of the educational program. One of them consists of evaluating the educational program itself to determine how good it is, whether and how it can be improved, including the evaluation of the measuring instru-

TABLE 12—SUGGESTIVE TYPES OF EVALUATIVE AND ADVISORY CONTACT BETWEEN STUDENTS AND STAFF MEMBERS

GENERAL TYPE OF CONTACT	STAFF MEMBERS		
	Teacher	School Psychologist	Vocational Counselor
Educational Counseling	Diagnostic testing in school subjects, identifying deficiencies, remedial teaching. Analysis of study methods, and their improvement. Evaluation of progress in courses, or of readiness for a course or new experience.	Appraisal and recommendations in cases of extraordinary retardation or acceleration. Analysis of sensory and neurological difficulties, as in reading disability, with help of medical staff as needed. Assignment to special classes, as for sight saving, or other disabilities.	
Personal Counseling	First contact with disturbed students. Refer questionable cases to psychologist. Sociometric testing for class structure, with help for isolates. Personal conferences in cases of non-psychiatric personal problems, visits with parents and other staff members, alterations in program at school or home as needed and agreed.	All cases involving repression, with psychiatric help as needed. Complex personal problems, serious clashes with staff or school requirements. Delinquency, or transitional cases, causing disturbances in school, neighborhood, or home.	
Vocational Counseling	Provide information about world's work. Exploration of many areas through readings, trips, visitors. Instruction in need for work, value of all constructive work, dignity of all labor, sharing of responsibilities, privileges and rewards by all parts of nation's productive team.		Provision of literature on vocational information. Group guidance, keeping choices open at early ages. Exploratory tests and interviews with high-school students. Guidance in tentative and final choices of fields, and information on sources of training.

ments themselves. Another consists of an evaluation of the student's personal objectives, and the use he makes of his resources, for the purpose of helping him work in the most profitable directions and at his highest level of efficiency. This function is what we call counseling and guidance, as contrasted with teaching where the emphasis is placed on how much progress the student is making through his educational program. These three functions of evaluation make up the content of this chapter and the ones that follow. To some extent the teacher participates in all three, although special phases of the last two are ordinarily better handled by people who are trained especially for such functions. This is particularly true of the last of the three.

In anticipation of the following discussion, Table 12 is intended to suggest a way of looking at the division of responsibility for evaluation and advisory work between the school staff and the students. There is no suggestion that any given individual is necessarily limited to the functions in one of the columns, provided he is *prepared* to do the sorts of things indicated in the other columns. The divisions are functional, rather than personal. Some few teachers are capable of discharging many of the functions of a school psychologist, or of a vocational counselor, but as a rule one's preparation is more specific than that, and the individual should not attempt to perform functions for which he has no background.

2502. *Evaluation in teaching and educational counseling.* The school presumably is trying to accomplish something definite through its program. It is not just a system for keeping children off the streets, such as the child-care centers that were established during World War II. No constructive educational program can be established without a description of the end product, nor can an evaluative program be set up until it is known what is to be measured and what is to be used as the standard of comparison. The rise of evaluation has driven attention sharply to the matter of objectives. As long as no quantitative appraisal of progress was attempted, it was not apparent that there was any particular difference between educating children and "keeping school."

It is permissible to talk about educational objectives in terms of good citizenship, worthy home membership, or wholesome adjustment as long as no one presses for measurement of them. It doesn't need to be clear whether they are measured in inches, pounds, quarts, or ohms as long as no one challenges the assumption that they are being accomplished.

The moment someone asks how near a given student is to the attainment of these objectives, the inadequacy of their generalized nature begins to become apparent. Someone asks how you tell a worthy home member from an unworthy home member, or a good citizen from a bad citizen, and the answers begin to come in the nature of the things he does. Since you can't measure what you haven't yet described quite thoroughly, this analysis is pushed further and further, until it is apparent that there are no objectives in education except those that can be stated in the form of behaviors of rather specific kinds.

By way of contrast, education is not working to achieve a given level of cost in production, or of quantity of output of a commodity, or a particular number of votes or a certain chemical balance. These are objectives of some programs, outside the field of education. They are not human behaviors, nor are they necessarily objectives that consist of the operation of a whole system as such. Some of them are minute atomistic processes, some of them are matters of size, and others are matters of rate or speed in a mechanical process. As a matter of fact, some of them could be processes going on within the human body, such as biochemical changes during digestion. The objectives of education differ from these and many other objectives, however, in the highly significant fact that education deals with the organismic behavior of the whole organism, and that only. Behavior below that level, or of a non-human type, doesn't mean very much to us in school. The neurologist, the physiologist, and the doctor must work at the sub-organismic level, but not the teacher. It is what the whole person does that has significance in the educative process.

The whole educative program and the evaluative program within it must be kept tied closely to clearly stated objectives, in the form of specific kinds of behavior to be produced. In Chapter XVI six different types of behavior were recognized, and studied within the learning process. All the objectives of education could be distributed throughout those six types. They include sensory-motor skills such as walking, perceptual-motor skills such as painting, conceptual reactions illustrated in perceiving situations and making choices of behavioral responses to them, verbal repetition of memorized symbolic material, the expression of tastes and preferences, and the ability to solve problems by developing new conclusions from factual data.

When objectives are stated in the foregoing terms it becomes possible to devise instruments to measure the behavior of an individual, and see how much of a desired level of behavior he has acquired. Sometimes objectives are stated in other forms, but invariably they prove under analysis to lead nowhere from an educational point of view, and to be incapable of measurement. When a teacher's objective is said to be to have the class spend the hour working in the library, we are left wondering for what purpose, in what sort of activity, or on what sorts of problems. When the hour is gone how is one to know whether a goal was reached? Similarly, the objective "to read three chapters in the text" leads nowhere. It implies that the sole purpose was to read the chapters. It was not expected that anyone would glean an idea from the reading. It is impossible to evaluate anything in either of these cases, because no change in human behavior was visualized. As far as teaching procedures are concerned, such objectives are equally useless. There can be no choice of method as long as there is no particular direction of effort. Such a thing as a psychologically sound lesson plan is an impossibility because there are no psychological principles involved in the passing of one hour. "Yes," says the teacher, "but we were spending the time in the library in order to learn how to use the reference room." Here, then, is a hidden objective that is guiding the teacher's actions to some extent, but that certainly does not enlighten the students until it is made clear nor permit evaluation until it is made precise.

A number of important considerations have been touched in these pages. Let us gather them up systematically. First, since all educational efforts are directed toward making changes in behavior at the organismic level, all objectives should be stated in terms of the specific behavior to be developed. Second, evaluation consists of measuring the amount of progress in the attainment of an objective, and the determination of what is left to be accomplished. Third, even when no objective is stated, or when an objective is stated in some other form than a change in human behavior, investigation will show that there is some behavioral objective behind it, although it may not be clear to the teacher or the class. There are a few other basic considerations about objectives, which must now be added to these.

2503. *Begin with objectives.* Evaluation gets its direction from the goal of teaching. Hence it is well to see what an objective should be and how it should be stated.

Make the objective specific. There are two aspects to this problem. One is getting all of the objective into its formulation. The other is delimiting it to what it is supposed to include. With regard to the first, it is often true that there is more than one objective in a given course or lesson. Some of them may be unrecognized by the teacher himself, but may be involved in his work.

For example, when assigned reading material goes beyond the stated objective of the course, the unstated objectives can be inferred from the reading materials. Students find themselves wondering how much of what they are reading they are expected to master. To avoid taking chances they may try to absorb all of it, and are usually safer in doing so than they would be to pass it by. Another source of hidden objectives may be the course examinations. Very often they include requirements that were not stated in the publicized objective of the lesson. This does not necessarily constitute trickery by the instructor, for he may himself have been unaware of the discrepancy between his stated objectives and the actual requirements of his readings and examinations. This is unsound practice, because it confuses students, and permits the instructor to be haphazard in planning his attack on the objectives. It is much better to go through all the requirements one expects to make of a class, and draw out of it all the objectives that are implied in them, so that they can be made explicit at the outset. Then the evaluative procedures can be aligned with the full objective right from the beginning.

The other side of this problem is the delimitation of the objective. It is just as important to a class to know what is *not* included as to know what *is* included. Assignments may be made to readings that go considerably beyond the objective of a lesson. If the delimitation is clear, then the student is able to select his study activities discriminately and spend his time on the thing that is important at the time. At the same time the evaluative instruments can be restricted to those behaviors that are included in the objective.

Confine objectives to measurable behavior. There is little to be gained by setting up objectives that cannot be evaluated. It is easy to get lost in high-sounding hopes, but experiments have shown in many fields that there is no improvement in any function without knowledge of progress. When an objective cannot be evaluated there is no way of knowing whether the behavior of students is moving toward, or away from, the objective. One is as likely as the other. Time spent on such objectives is time taken away from other valuable objectives that *can* be evaluated, for there is far more to accomplish in the school years than is humanly possible.

Make objectives single and simple, not compound. A complicated objective, which involves several expected changes in behavior, imposes a most difficult problem in lesson planning, and a rather heavy burden of evaluation. Sometimes a lesson plan begins with as many as eight or ten objectives stated one after the other. Each one is enough to keep the class occupied for some time. To work on all of them at the same time is as impossible as taking several forks in the road at once. As a result the activity tends to follow one objective and leave the others out, or it dissipates itself in a futile attempt to do everything and gets nothing done well.

Arrange objectives logically for a unit or course. Every

course contains several levels of generalization and specificity in its structure. Its large areas may be set up as units, each of which has a set of smaller subdivisions of more specific nature. If a course is described at the most general level by a statement of the type of behavior it is intended to produce, then each progressively more specific area can also be described by more specific behaviors, which together make up the generalized description. The same is true of each part of a unit. As the over-all behavior pattern is broken down into its smaller component parts, the plan of teaching is indicated at once by the type of behavior involved, and the evaluative procedure is indicated in the same way. When this relationship between the general and specific levels of a course is clear, it becomes possible to plan the evaluation at any level desired. It may not be necessary to measure the performance of students on every sub-process involved in a more comprehensive act. In the case of mathematics, for example, it is assumed that the student who can furnish the correct solutions to several problems that incorporate a number of mathematical functions may safely be assumed to know the sub-processes involved in the problems. Therefore an evaluation at a complex level sometimes obviates the need for a battery of tests to measure the more detailed functions. If the student cannot produce the correct answer at the complex level, it may then be necessary to make the tests more diagnostic, by putting into them problems that involve only single sub-processes, so that the source of the student's difficulty can be found.

This is a relative matter, however, since what constitutes a sub-process in one grade is likely to be the whole subject matter in an earlier grade. Using the mathematical illustration again, solutions to problems in buying food may be required in the sixth grade, assuming the students can do the simple processes of addition, subtraction, multiplication, and division. At the fourth-grade level, however, each of these is a goal or objective in itself and has still simpler sub-processes that may have been mastered earlier.

2504. *Make objectives and evaluative programs agree.* Two of the important requirements here are making sure that any final evaluation of a student's work is based on some kind of measurement or credit for his progress in *every aspect* of the objective rather than in just the easily measured aspects, and the use of measuring instruments which are so constructed that they permit the student to display the behavior required by the objective.

In the first instance, experience shows that students tend to concentrate their efforts on those parts of a course that are consistently evaluated, and slight the rest of it.[2] In practice it is not uncommon to find teachers who limit their evaluation to factual tests, and sometimes to one kind of test such as the true-false. Their students will follow the lead, even without being aware of it, and concentrate on facts to the neglect of integration of the facts into anything systematic or applicable to practical situations. The reverse is also true, so that unless the teaching procedures correspond to the evaluation procedures learning will tend to follow the evaluation procedures rather than the teaching plans.

This should be taken into consideration in the planning of the course, at which time it is possible to arrange a parallel teaching and evaluation program. Where evaluation is an afterthought, and tests are produced on the spur of the need, there is too much chance for faulty articulation. A satisfactory teaching-evaluation plan for a given unit may not be developed in full when a teacher first plans and executes a unit, but it can be matured as repeated use of good units permits their constant improvement. It is in this respect that a systematic method of organizing and filing instructional and evaluational materials makes its greatest contribution to the work of a teacher, and ultimately results in conserving a tremendous amount of time and effort while it produces superior results. This, by the way, does *not* refer to the repeated use of *unimproved* outlines and tests that are never changed after they are first made up. There are few practices better calculated to lower the quality of teaching and testing than that.

In the second matter, that of matching the test to the

2 C. C. Ross, *Measurement in today's schools* (New York: Prentice-Hall, Inc., 1941), Chapter XI.

behavior implied in the objective, it will help to reiterate the types of behavior mentioned earlier, and go from that into the kinds of tests available. The two types of learning most prominent in school are conceptual and associational, those that involve development of meanings and understanding, and the partial or complete remembering of symbolic material related to the conceptual meanings, or, in other words, memorization of vocabularly, formulas, lists of characteristics, literature, or any other similar material. Within this cluster of objectives there are three stages that may or may not be recognized by the teacher and students, but are nevertheless present. One is assimilation of the body of facts and ideas that constitute the basic subject matter of the area being studied. The second is the organization of this raw material into larger meaningful comprehensions within which one sees real relationships throughout the whole structure. This is what is ordinarily meant by integration, or the development of insight and real meaning. The third is the development of the ability to use this understanding in new situations so that one can meet practical problems with it. Beyond the conceptual and associational types are the motor or skill objectives that require neuromuscular coordination raised to a high level of skill, the development of tastes and preferences, and the mastery of problem-solving procedures.

In the early stages of *conceptual and associational objectives,* the concepts are relatively simple and concrete, rather easily understood as individual ideas, but still lacking integration. There is also a great deal of memorization involved in learning the names of the objects, functions, and qualities of the new experiences. The concepts can be tested by free response, questions asking for descriptions, or by objective tests of several kinds, or through oral interview or recitation. Definition tests are simple ways of evaluating the student's conceptual learning. The symbolic learning can be tested in the same way. Symbols are expressed through verbalization, which can be either oral or written. Concepts are expressed through descriptions. These behavioral characteristics indicate what sorts of tests will permit the individual to make such a response.

In the secondary stage, where *integration* is involved, the behavior is again explanatory for the concepts, but at a more complex and abstract level. A simple test of definitions, of the type that makes up a dictionary for example, does not necessarily show that the individual has an integrated view of the concepts. A test requiring illustrations, or furnishing illustrations to be matched to the names of the concepts, may be better. For example, at the simpler level, a matching test might ask the student to identify the correct response for the phrase, "cephalo-caudal sequence," and the response might be "shift in rate of growth from head to tail." This answer can be identified without requiring a very well-developed understanding of the idea. A more difficult form of the question, which tends to require its integration with other facts about growth, would be to put the answers in the form of illustrations, which either illustrate *only* the concept involved, or illustrate it in connection with a somewhat complex situation. Such an answer to the same phrase might be "The brain is 90% full grown when a child is 6 years old." This item has been used repeatedly in psychology classes and has proved to require much better comprehension for the second response than for the first.

The third stage, *application to problems,* requires performance-reactions of the student, both in teaching and in evaluating. The usual objective tests are not as easily adapted to this as they are to the earlier stages of a course, but they can be made to offer functional tests of ability. Reference was made earlier in the book to the case studies of Horrocks and Troyer, which permit a student to try his hand at evaluating and diagnosing a student's difficulties. Connie Casey [3] is a girl whose social adjustment is poor because her home does not give her a setting in which she can make social contacts with security. The case-study instrument presents data to

[3] John E. Horrocks and Maurice E. Troyer. *A study of Connie Casey* (Syracuse, N. Y.: Syracuse University Press, 1946), Case booklet, answer sheet, and key.

the reader in a sequence approximately like that in which the teacher or counselor would gather it. With the data are questions on the diagnosis of the case, and questions on corrective procedures. Sam Smith [4] is a boy with colossal indifference to school and scholastic difficulties. He comes from a highly respected family in which the father's influence on the boy is unwholesome in spite of his own unquestioned success in life. Barry Black [5] is an aggressive boy, poorly adjusted socially, and doing a mixed quality of work in school. He gets little encouragement at home. In these instruments there is an opportunity for the student to apply his knowledge of individual psychology to the diagnosis of human problems, including description of the behavior, analysis of the background influences, and determination of the needs for further investigation or for remedial treatment. Sometimes this sort of evaluation is helped by furnishing additional diagnostic devices, such as the forms for analysis of behavioral symptoms, analysis of developmental status and adjustment, and analysis of sources of influence, shown in Tables 13, 14, 15, and 16. The first three forms are marked by putting a heavy cross in the center of the space under the appropriate column heading for each numbered item on the left side of the chart. The judgment of what is the appropriate square to mark depends on the student's ability to read the data in each case, and to interpret them in the light of his knowledge of the psychology of adjustment. The instructor should be able to mark the forms with the correct responses if he wishes to use the instrument as a test, but otherwise it can be used as a teaching device through discussion of the questions in class.

In the case-study instruments themselves, the questions are so arranged that they can be used as objective test items if desired. For example, in the diagnostic part of the instrument appears the following:

[4] John E. Horrocks and Maurice E. Troyer, *A study of Sam Smith* (Syracuse, N. Y.: Syracuse University Press, 1946), Case booklet, answer sheet, and key.
[5] John E. Horrocks and Maurice E. Troyer, *A study of Barry Black* (Syracuse, N. Y.: Syracuse University Press, 1946), Case booklet, answer sheet, and key.

Part I

DIAGNOSIS

DO NOT TURN TO PART II until you have recorded your appraisal of the following statements on the answer sheet.

Directions: On the answer sheet under *Diagnosis, Part I*, appraise each of the statements below in the light of your knowledge of human growth and development. Each column in the answer sheet is headed T, PT, N, PF, or F. Indicate your appraisal of each statement with an X in the appropriate column according to the following code:

T—*True.* On the basis of the evidence supplied, this statement is definitely warranted.

PT—*Possibly True.* On the basis of the evidence supplied, this statement is possibly true, although more complete information is needed.

N—*No Evidence.* The evidence as presented gives no information that would indicate that this statement is either true or false.

PF—*Possibly False.* On the basis of the evidence given, this statement is possibly false, although more complete information is needed.

F—*False.* This statement is fully contradicted by the evidence given.

1. Connie lacks sufficient vitality to have many social relationships.

2. Connie's chief problem centers around emotional instability.

3. Connie is the kind of person who seeks self-justification through blaming others or untoward circumstances.

14. Connie is laboring under excessive feelings of guilt.

22. Connie is losing ground in intellectual ability as she grows older.

25. Connie's truancy was due to fatigue and overwork which made school unbearable for the time being.[6]

In Part I, *remedial analysis,* the student is asked to "strongly agree," "agree with reservations," "remain "undecided", "disagree with reservations," or "strongly dis-

[6] Reproduced by permission of Dr. Horrocks, from *The case of Connie Casey.*

agree," with each of the questions. Samples are reproduced here.

1. Enough is known about Connie at this point to enable the school to institute a comparatively complete remedial program where Connie is concerned.

2. If Connie's truancy and absence from gym are symptoms of difficulties, the school will not gain satisfactory results by trying to eliminate them.

7. An investigation should be made as to why Connie's meals disagree with her.

13. Since this was her first truancy, nothing further should be done or said about it unless the truancy reoccurs.

Part II of the instrument furnishes more information, and then provides further opportunities for diagnosis and prescription, as does Part III also.

This is a good illustration of the use of case material for teaching and for evaluation, and of the possibility of putting a functional test into objective form. Another illustration is furnished in Chapter XXVI, in connection with the Case of Dan.[7]

Much less elaborate, but still of high value are the familiar student reports, themes, outlines, recitations, discussions, individual conferences, and interviews. When classes are small enough, these are still among the best evaluative devices for finding out how well a student knows his field.

In the field of *motor skills*, including the *esthetic performances*, there is no adequate substitute for actual performance. The products of one's performance represent the most general level of the skill, as in the case of problem solutions in mathematics, and it may be assumed that a perfect product indicates adequate skills in all the processes involved. Where diagnostic evaluation of the individual skills that make up a complex ability is desired, however, check lists permit quick scoring of the various acts that constitute the sub-processes. Check lists may also be used in rating the finished product.

[7] See discussion of the uses of objective tests in the social studies, the sciences, and industrial and practical arts, in Greene, Jorgensen, and Gerberich, *op. cit.*

TABLE 13—ANALYSIS OF BEHAVIORAL SYMPTOMS

		Normal	Indication of Difficulty	Indication of Maladjustment
Casual Overt Behavior	1			
Intensive or Explosive Reactions	2			
Aggression	3			
Display	4			
Preoccupation	5			
Withdrawal	6			
Motivational Trouble	7			
Fixations or Delays in Development	8			

Refer to Table 6 for descriptions of behavior under each of the numbered items. After becoming familiar with a case, indicate how you interpret the subject's behavior, by putting a cross in the center of the space under the appropriate column heading. Responses to this sort of rating form can be scored by using a cut-out stencil to be laid over the form, showing the weighted value of any entry the student may have made.

In a piano solo, for example, the performer can be rated on technique, interpretation, stage presence, attack, and level of difficulty in the selection. These items can be divided into still further analytical ratings if desired. In shop work the student can be rated on the use of the several tools, with different media such as hard or soft woods, and on ability to plan and carry out a project. Ratings can be prearranged numerically, with whatever discrimination in judgment is deemed possible.

In the area of *tastes and preferences* there is little available except interest tests. Nevertheless, the paired-comparison technique that is used in several interest and value tests

TABLE 14—ANALYSIS OF DEVELOPMENTAL STATUS AND ADJUSTMENT

	Normal	Immature	Suggests Developing Problem	Suggests Maladjustment
1. Mental Development				
2. Interests				
3. Philosophy of Life				
4. Motivational Health				
5. Physiological Development				
6. Relations with Parents				
7. Relations with Other Adults				
8. Relations with Girls				
9. Relations with Boys				
10. Economic Independence				
11. Use of Leisure				

After becoming familiar with a case, indicate how you interpret the subject's status and adjustment by putting a cross in the appropriate space opposite each numbered item. Help on some of the items might be had from Figure 3 in Chapter XII.

is not difficult to handle in the making of tests for local situations. It consists of matching every item in a list of items to be rated, against every other item in the list, and having the subject make a choice in the case of every pair of items so matched. The number of times each item is selected is counted, and preference is said to be established by the frequency of choice. Sources of available interest

TABLE 15—ANALYSIS OF SOURCES OF INFLUENCE

		Major Healthful	Minor Healthful	Neutral	No Data	Minor Harmful	Major Harmful
Home	1. Emotional Security						
	2. Instruction in Socially Approved Ways of Living						
	3. Consistent Supervision						
	4. Encouragement of Self-sufficiency						
	5. Provision of Life Necessities						
School	6. Teacher-relationships						
	7. Boy-relationships						
	8. Girl-relationships						
	9. Academic Pressures						
	10. Nature of Curriculum						
	11. Co-curricular Program						
	12. Guidance Program						
Community	13. Ideals and Codes of Ethics						
	14. Provision for Youth Activities						
	15. Caste and Class Lines						

After becoming familiar with a case, analyze the background factors by placing a cross opposite each numbered item, under the appropriate column heading.

tests are listed in the *Cornell University Test List* discussed in Chapter XVIII.

Problem-solving skill cannot be successfully measured at present by any test now available. Approaches to the display of good judgment are possible by supplying the student with all the necessary data to make a solution to a problem, and requiring him to decide on a course of action. The case-study instruments previously mentioned offer this kind of situation, as does the Case of Dan, but it is difficult to be sure of the validity of the instruments. One of the most extensive discussions of the problem is that which developed from the eight-year study of The Progressive Education Association, on the relation of school and college.[8]

In view of the scarcity of tests in this field, the teacher should explore the development of tests of his own adapted to the particular problems involved in his courses. At first it may be easiest to give the students problems to discuss in free-response form, or projects to be completed and turned in. It is also valuable to use some class discussion in this area, as an instructional device, to enable members of the class to observe the activities of those who have ability in analyzing problems and arriving at conclusions.

2505. *The construction of tests.*[9] Ways of making and scoring some of the most useful achievement tests are suggested here,[10] for the teacher who would like to begin constructing a file of good test items. See Section 2605.

The principal objectives of any test are to evaluate the progress of a given student in a course and to determine the relative status of each student. A second consideration is to

---

[8] E. R. Smith and R. W. Tyler, *Appraising and recording student progress* (New York: Harper and Bros., 1942), Chapter II.

[9] The following texts are devoted primarily to the construction and use of tests: Greene, Jorgensen, and Gerberich, *op. cit.;* H. E. Hawkes, E. F. Lindquist, and C. R. Mann, *The construction and use of achievement examinations* (Boston: Houghton Mifflin Co., 1936); H. H. Remmers, and N. L. Gage, *Educational measurement and evaluation* (New York: Harper and Bros., 1943) ; C. C. Ross, *op. cit.*

[10] The following material on test construction is adapted with little alteration from bulletins of the Cornell University Testing Service, prepared and issued by the writer and research assistants Robert L. Egbert and Glenn Hawkes, during the year 1949.

provide a teaching device for the student and the instructor. In order to accomplish these ends best and most efficiently certain considerations must be kept in mind.

1. The subject matter must be adequately sampled.

2. The test should measure the general objectives of the course, such as terminology, principles, application, and ability of the student to organize.

3. The test items must be balanced with easy, medium, and difficult questions so as to discriminate clearly between good and bad students.

4. Scoring methods should be such that should two people score the test they will arrive at approximately the same grade.

5. Test items should be so made that they keep at a minimum the effects of guessing and bluffing.

6. By use of the proper technique it is possible to save time and energy in both construction and scoring.

7. There is no good reason for having the maximum possible score on a test equal 100, or for reporting or recording test scores in percentages. A system in which raw scores are used (that is, scores that consist of the number of actual points earned on an exercise) is more in keeping with the facts about student performance and student comparisons. See the discussion later on Translating Raw Scores into Marks.

The essay-type test.[11] This form is best suited to indicating the organizational ability of the student. It is also well adapted to discovering knowledge of principles and skill in application of principles. It is easy to construct and can be made sufficiently difficult for purposes of discrimination. Its chief weaknesses are that agreement between readers on quality of response is difficult to obtain; it is difficult for the reader to rate the paper the same in two situations—e.g., read when rested or tired; reading requires great concentration to penetrate clumsy expression and to tell if the student is dodging the issue; the time consumed reaches great proportions when large numbers are considered.

[11] More extensive treatments are available in Ross, *op. cit.*, Chapter VI, and Greene, *et al.*, *op. cit.*, Chapter VII.

Hints for construction:

1. The question must give directions on what phase of the topic is to be treated in the answer.
   a. (poor) Discuss the Civil War.
   b. (good) Discuss the relationship between Lincoln's platform and the outbreak of the Civil War.

2. An effort should be made to keep possibilities within the time period. There should be no more questions than the students can handle reasonably well. Time pressure is not advisable in situations where the essay test is appropriate.

3. There may be choice among questions only when the alternate questions are of equal difficulty. Such equality is difficult to obtain or to recognize.

4. An attempt should be made to indicate what sort of knowledge the student is expected to display, e.g., vocabulary, application, principles, enumeration of facts, etc.

5. Observe the rules of rhetoric, grammar, and punctuation. Avoid ambiguous items. As a check on ambiguity have someone else read the questions to see if he agrees with you about what the question calls for. On an essay test there are so few questions that one which is misunderstood by the student has undue influence on the total score.

6. The student will be helped in preparing his answer by such information as:
   a. Relative credit to be given for each question.
   b. Desirable length of answer—that is, if it is desirable to limit the quantity of writing to any given number of words, etc.
   c. Suggestions to the student not to start writing until he has organized his answer.
   d. The type of exposition desired, e.g., full description, topical outline, cryptic listing of ideas, etc.

Helps for scoring:

1. Make a list of criteria of good answers for each question. Assign appropriate number of points to each criterion, e.g., grammar, organization, quality of ideas, number of items mentioned, conciseness, skill in use of words, literary quality, etc.

2. Avoid reading when fatigued. If necessary to read while fatigued, spot check papers later to be sure you are satisfied with results.

3. Do not read each paper all through, but go through all the papers reading only one question. It is helpful to sort the papers

into from three to seven piles based on relative quality, putting on marks after all are read and any necessary readjustments made.

4. If the student's name appears only on the back the instructor is not likely to be biased by knowing whose paper he is reading.

Types of questions that may be used to advantage for various purposes: [12]

1. Specific comparison.
   E.g.: Compare James and Thorndike on the validity of their basic teachings.
   Compare the pioneers who went to the Northwest and those who went to California during the days of '49 on their basic motives.
2. General comparison.
   E.g.: Compare education in seventeenth-century New England with that of the same time in England.
3. Declaration and support of position.
   E.g.: Whom do you admire more, Washington or Lincoln? Why?
4. Causes, effects, or relationships.
   E.g.: Why do we have three independent departments in American Federal Government?
   What forces seem to threaten continuation of their mutual independence?
5. Precise description of the nature of some process, object, phrase, or statement.
   E.g.: Explain how a siphon works.
   What does "equal" mean in the statement, "All men are created equal."
6. Summary of some assigned reading.
   E.g.: Reduce the chapter on "American Foreign Policy" to four or five fundamental ideas.
7. Analysis.
   E.g.: What are the common elements in the careers of Washington and Lincoln?
8. Application of principles to practical situations.
   E.g.: Give two examples of the use of pure carbon in industrial work.

[12] These suggestions are patterned in general after Walter S. Monroe and Ralph Carter, *The use of different types of thought questions in secondary schools and their relative difficulty for students.* Bureau of Educational Research Bulletin, No. 14 (Urbana, Ill.: University of Illinois, 1923), 26 pp.

The true-false test.[13] This form is good in that the course material can be well sampled; knowledge of terminology, knowledge of principles and ability to apply principles can be tested; two people scoring the test will get approximately the same results; the test is very easy to score by hand or by machine, and it is easier to construct than any other except the essay. The true-false is especially useful for short quizzes. It is weak in these areas: Organizational ability cannot be measured satisfactorily; and it is difficult to make a true-false test hard enough to discriminate good from poor students. Care must be taken to avoid ambiguity in statement or cues in the manner of the statement concerning the right answer. Guessing is easier on the true-false than on any other test.

Hints for constructing:

1. Keep these things out of true-false statements: double negatives, hidden catch words, and alterations of a single word in a quotation to be identified or judged on correctness.

2. Analyses have shown that a majority of questions containing such words as "only," "alone," "all," "none," "never" are usually false. At the same time questions containing "some," "should," "may," "generally" are most often found to be true. Students become aware of these "specific determiners."

3. Use as precise statements as the nature of the question permits. If the statement becomes clumsy, it is best to abandon it and start over again.

4. Attempt to have a balance between true and false questions. Random distribution should be attempted in the arrangement. Questions, whether true or false, should be of nearly the same length. True statements are usually longer because of the number of qualifiers used and this gives the answer away.

5. Avoid involved, complex sentence structure. Any question that can't be read and comprehended quickly interferes with good response.

6. The student should be informed whether there will be a penalty for guessing, i.e., what scoring formula will be used.

7. Ambiguity and double propositions should be avoided. There should be one idea only in each question.

[13] For more detailed discussions see Ross, *op. cit.,* pp. 146-151; Greene *et al., op. cit.,* pp. 174-77.

EVALUATION IN EDUCATION   561

The multiple-choice test.[14] The strong points of the multiple-choice test are that enough questions can be put in a test so that the subject matter can be adequately sampled, they can be so constructed as to measure knowledge of terminology, principles, and application of principles and, in a more limited degree, the ability of the student to organize and integrate his material. Multiple-choice questions can be rapidly scored by hand or by machine. Two people scoring the same test paper will arrive at the same score. The weaker features of the test are that the construction of good questions is time-consuming and the multiple-choice test is not ordinarily as satisfactory a measure of organizational ability as is the essay test.

The multiple-choice test item consists of an introductory part and several alternative answers that may be divided into the true answer, or answers, and the incorrect alternatives. The number of true answers need not be constant for all questions, but if not students should be so informed.

Hints for constructing:

1. The introductory part may be in the form of a direct question or it may be in the form of an incomplete statement. If the latter form is used, the introductory statement should have meaning in itself and should infer a direct statement rather than a series of true-false items. The sentence structure should be as simple as possible, and free from unnecessary clauses and parenthetical phrases that make it difficult to read.

E.g.: (poor) New York State
  (1) touches four of the Great Lakes.
  (2) leads the United States in the production of copper.
  (3) has the largest population of any of the United States.
  (4) leads the nation in the production of wheat.
(better) The population of the State of New York is larger than:
  (1) the population of Italy.

[14] For additional discussion see Ross, *op. cit.*, pp. 151-58; Greene *et al.*, *op. cit.*, pp. 177-82.

(2) the combined population of the states west of the Mississippi.
(3) the population of any other one state.
(4) 25,000,000.

2. The incorrect choices should be so plausible that the uninformed student will be as likely to choose any one of them as the correct answer. This insures discrimination between good and poor students.

3. It is possible to increase the discriminatory power of a question by increasing the homogeneity of the alternatives. This is particularly important with advanced students who may be expected to know more about a given subject. In this example the second question requires greater knowledge than the first.

a. (less homogeneous): Carbon has a greater atomic weight than (1) radium, (2) helium, (3) gold, (4) lead.
b. (more homogeneous): Iron has a greater atomic weight than (1) zinc, (2) silver, (3) lead, (4) magnesium.

4. The length of the alternatives should not vary systematically with the correctness of the alternative. Otherwise the students come to realize that the long alternatives are usually the correct ones, or vice versa.

5. If possible there should be at least four or five alternatives with each question. This reduces the factor of guessing. If this is not possible, without using obviously false choices, it should not be adhered to.

6. It should be possible to form a grammatically correct sentence by attaching any of the alternatives to the introductory incomplete statement. Otherwise incorrect alternatives may be identified through a knowledge of grammar.

7. Multiple-choice questions can be made more thought-provoking and discriminating by having more than one correct choice, especially when the student is not told in advance how many are correct for a specific question. One successful plan is to have from one to three correct answers for each question, where the number is not uniform for each question. Where this is the case, fewer questions are needed to obtain a good distribution of the students.

8. The number of questions that can be handled successfully in an hour depends on how discriminating they are, how many correct alternatives they contain, and how clear and readable are the statements. It may vary from twenty to one hundred or more.

The matching test.[15] This form allows a good sampling of material. It will measure knowledge of terminology, principles, and application of principles. It can be made discriminating enough to separate the good from the poor students. Two people scoring the test will arrive at the same mark. It is relatively easy to construct, and, with special care, can be made for machine scoring. It does not ordinarily measure well the ability of the student to organize, and, through a process of elimination, guessing can frequently be fairly accurate unless careful checks are observed in the construction of the test.

Hints for construction:

1. The chances of the student's guessing the correct response may be reduced:

    A. By increasing the number of response alternatives beyond the number of items.

    Example: (In hand-scoring form)

    Directions: After each age listed in B, write the numbers of the emotional patterns in A that can be identified at that age according to Bridges. Use the most specific patterns that are correct for each age.

A	*B*
1. Elation	
2. Distress	1. Birth .... _____
3. Fear	
4. Affection	2. 3 Months .... _____
5. Delight	
6. Excitement	3. 1 Year .... _____
7. Anger	
8. Disgust	
9. Rage	
10. Deceit	
11. Love	

    B. By permitting some of the response alternatives to be used more than once in the same matching set.

    Example: (In machine-scoring form)

    Directions: For each of the following items, *blacken* answer space

[15] For more extended discussion see Ross, *op. cit.,* pp. 158-64; Greene *et al., op. cit.,* pp. 182-87, 194-96.

1 if it is a native of *New York*
2 if it is a native of *California*
3 if it is a native of *Alabama*
4 if it is native to *two or more* of the above
5 if it is native to *none* of the above

1. The Whippoorwill   5. The Albatross
2. The Mockingbird   6. The Killdeer
3. The Robin   7. The Falcon
4. The Egret   8. The Parakeet

C. By requiring more than one answer for some of the test items. If this is done, it is necessary to score rights minus wrongs in order to keep students from filling in an abnormally large number of responses.

D. By keeping the answers within a delimited field of subject matter. The more narrowly one delimits the scope within which answers are given, the more discrimination is required to select the right answer.

2. The basis upon which the matching is to be made should always be clearly indicated. E.g., are you asking the student to match definitions, examples, items of similar content, etc.?

3. The following will help the student find quickly the answer he thinks to be correct.

A. One of the lists of items to be matched should be made up of single words, short phrases, numbers or other quickly examined types of material.

B. The list of response alternatives should be arranged in some sort of logical order. E.g., dates may be arranged chronologically and terms alphabetically.

4. The number of response alternatives in one set of matched items, while preferably greater than the number of questions, should never be more than ten or twelve. (For machine scoring five is a better number.) Refer to example 2. Where as many as twenty or more questions are needed, they should be arranged in two or more sets of matched items. Otherwise the student loses too much time hunting through long and cumbersome lists.

5. All of the matching alternatives for one set of questions should be contained on a single page.

The problem-solving test. This type is ordinarily most useful for such subjects as mathematics, physics, and chemistry. It can be made to sample the course material. It will cover knowledge of principles, application of principles, and ability to organize, and in some instances knowledge of terminology. The problem test can distinguish the good from the poor students. As a rule, two people scoring the same paper will give the same grade. This type of test will practically eliminate bluffing and guessing. Depending on the material, it may be fairly easy or very difficult to construct. It can be made into a multiple-choice test and be machine scored. Its great weakness lies in the fact that it is applicable to only a few kinds of courses.

Hints for construction:

1. The statement of the problem should be clear and concise. It should embody all needed information for the full solution. If it is intended that the student provide some factual material, he should fully understand what is expected of him.

2. The desired form of the answer should be clearly indicated. E.g., 100 lbs. poultry at .25 per lb. totaling $25.00; or 100 lbs.; or $25.00.

3. If method is stressed more than the correct answer, the student should fully understand so, in order that he can properly organize his time and also know where to lay emphasis.

4. The student should have at hand all needed material for the solution, such as scratch paper, slide rule, protractor, tables, etc. He should know in advance what will be furnished and what he is expected to bring with him.

5. It is possible to construct problem-solving examinations in the form of multiple-choice questions. If this is to be done, the methods described in connection with the multiple-choice test will apply. Plausible alternates should be provided, together with a work sheet for the calculations required. Again, if method is important it is possible to collect the work sheets for examination by the instructor. In this case it is well to have students designate which calculations are related to a given problem. This can be helped by mimeographing a work sheet with areas designated for each problem.

6. When the answers in a multiple-choice question consist of symbols (numbers, letters, etc.), it is necessary to have the obviously involved symbols in each of the alternative answers, although not in the same combination. Otherwise, an alert student can identify the right answer by eliminating those that do not contain the right numbers or letters, without carrying out the solution. E.g.,

(poor)   Simplify $\dfrac{10^9 \times 10^6}{10^3}$ (1) 5^6; (2) 15^5; (3) 10^{18}; (4) 10^{12}

(better) Simplify $\dfrac{10^9 \times 10^6}{10^3}$ (1) 10^6; (2) 10^5; (3) 10^{18}; (4) 10^{12}

> In this case only items 3 and 4 can possibly be correct in the first case, because the number 10 must appear in the answer.

Hints for scoring:

1. Decide in advance on the amount of credit to be given for such things as are described in points 1, 2, 3 of hints for construction.

2. If a margin of error is to be allowed in final answers, this should be determined so that all papers can be graded alike.

3. Unless you wish to stress such things, and have done so in class, avoid penalizing for failure to round off numbers, to use certain symbols such as dollar signs, to conform to certain abbreviations, or to maintain a given level of penmanship, spelling, or punctuation.

4. Since it is often desired to look for facility in a particular process that is involved in a problem, it may be advisable to score all papers for one problem at a time so that the particular functions may be easily kept in mind from paper to paper.

2506. *Preparing tests for machine scoring.* The International Business Machines Corporation, at Endicott, New York, has machines on which tests may be scored by electrical impulse. The machines count the right or wrong answers on a test, and give a score that consists of any combination of those items for which the machine is set. Any test that can be answered objectively, through merely marking one of two or more alternative answers, can be scored on this machine. It employs special answer sheets that fit into the machine and that may be purchased in a variety of styles. The sheets must be marked with electrographic pencils, which may also be obtained from IBM.

Tests to be scored on such machines must be arranged so that the answers can be recorded on the printed forms. Figure 13 shows how the recording is done. The directions appear on almost all regular IBM answer forms.

DIRECTIONS: Read each question and its numbered answers. When you have decided which answer is correct, blacken the corresponding space on this sheet with the special pencil. Make your mark as long as the pair of lines, and move the pencil point up and down firmly to make a heavy black line. If you change your mind, erase your first mark completely. Make no stray marks; they may count against you.

SAMPLE: I—I a country
1. Chicago is I—2 a mountain   1   2   3   4   5
            I—3 an island   1 ∷   ∷   ∷   **I**   ∷
            I—4 a city
            I—5 a state

FIG. 13. DIRECTIONS FROM AN IBM ANSWER SHEET

Scores are recorded by good operators at rates as high as fifteen tests per minute for tests with as many as a hundred and fifty questions. For large classes and long tests this offers significant help to teachers. True-false questions are easily arranged. The student marks in column 1 for true, and column 2 for false. Multiple-choice questions use more of the columns, the answers being numbered to match the columns. Matching tests are easily put on such forms. In a test that has ten items that are to be matched up with fifteen alternative selections, each of the ten items will need to have fifteen possible answer spaces. This is provided by using the first three answer rows on the sheet, each of which has five spaces. Those on the first row are for possibilities number 1 to 5. On the second row for possibilities 6 to 10. The third row is for possibilities 11 to 15. That means that the second of the ten items to be matched will have to use the next three answer rows, or rows number 4, 5, and 6. This sort of flexibility permits any combination of matching items to be used. In the example used here, the second of the ten items to be matched should be numbered 4 instead of 2, to avoid confusing the students in their search for the appropriate place to mark the answer sheet. In the same way the third item would be marked 7, and so on.

Information concerning the machines and the places where scoring service is available throughout the country may be had by writing to IBM, Endicott, N. Y. An Education Department is maintained for services to schools.

Operators of such services must be given an answer sheet correctly completed. From this a stencil is made for use in the machine. Any scoring formula can be used, but it must be specified which is wanted. It could be all rights, or all wrongs, or rights minus any part of the wrongs, or rights weighted in any desired manner. Weighting scores may involve difficulties in scoring unless the operator is consulted in advance of setting up the test.

Machine scoring is much more economical than hand scoring for large classes or large tests. The machine will handle a test of a hundred and fifty questions at the rate of about fifteen tests per minute. An even greater advantage, however, lies in the ability of the machine to furnish an item analysis of the test. This permits the test items to be improved through correcting their weaknesses. The procedure is indicated later.

2507. *Published tests.* The vast number of standardized tests now on the market make it possible for teachers to meet many of their measurement needs without making their own instruments. The tests cover a grade range equivalent to the whole educational ladder, but not uniformly in all subjects. For the elementary grades there are some good batteries of tests with graded difficulty, for which age-equivalent and grade-equivalent scores are available. Beyond the elementary grades the tests tend to deal with single subjects more than with the whole curriculum. In the table of contents of the *Cornell University Test List* are such subjects as aeronautics, automobile driving, Bible, commerce, engineering, geography, handwriting, health, history, home economics, human growth and development, journalism, languages of all kinds including English, grammar, vocabulary, library information, mathematics, arithmetic, algebra, calculus, geometry, industrial mathematics, trigonometry, psychology, reading, science for all grades, agriculture, astronomy, biology, botany, chemistry, geology, social studies, and spelling. The list includes over eleven hundred tests of all sorts, among which are about seven hundred standardized achievement tests and four hundred other psychological tests. In the latter are aptitudes, attitudes, concepts, critical thinking, intelligence, interests, personality and adjustment, personnel selection, preschool readiness, rating scales, status information, study skills, and values.

Selection of a test from those available should be made on the basis of how closely the test fits the need in a class, and how well the test will serve the evaluative needs. Specimen sets of most of the tests may be purchased for nominal prices. They usually include a copy of the test, an answer form, a key, and the instructions for administering and scoring. A test should have the coefficients of reliability and validity indicated, but this is not always the case. Critical reviews of most of the published tests are available in Buros' *Mental measurements yearbook*,[16] which is kept up to date and constitutes the best single source of information on the results obtained from using the tests. The Cornell list shows the publisher for each test in the list and constitutes the best available comprehensive list of all tests at present. It is printed in mimeographed form by the University Testing Service.

2508. *Tests as aids in teaching.* Although tests have been regarded primarily as aids in evaluating progress, and hence for marking students on progress, they serve one of their best and least objectionable functions as diagnostic devices. Knowledge of progress is one of the best aids to learning. Students find the frequent use of short tests desirable and helpful, when the making of marks is not the aim. Such tests may be scored by the students themselves. There is no need for recording scores. A class may well discuss the results of a quiz, where the questions serve as stimuli for penetrating analysis of an idea. Students also find stimulation in preparing questions for quizzes. A test that is not to be used for marking presents a totally different aspect to the learner from one in which competitive pressures are present. Evaluation

16 Oscar Buros, *Mental measurements yearbook*, (New Brunswick, N. J.: Rutgers University Press, 1948).

of progress toward an objective is often more easily carried out in this manner than when a test must yield scores that can be turned into marks.

2509. *Marks in elementary and secondary schools.* Education prior to college is generally not vocational, and noncompetitive. The purpose is preparation for good adjustment and the general ability to participate in modern social life. The only source from which competitive demands are forced into the secondary school is the college-entrance problem. Until colleges can find their own ways of selecting students, without depending on high-school marks, there will always be a certain amount of pressure of that sort to mark high-school students on a competitive basis.

If marks were relieved of such pressures, they should then become a means of telling how well a student has used his resources in getting himself ready for responsible social life. His achievement on tests is an important part of such marks, but not the whole matter. Far more important to social solidarity and good human relationships is the way in which a student comes to conceive his society and his own situation in it. If he can learn to see in the school, the home, and the community, satisfying ways of meeting his needs, which are also desirable from the standpoint of others, he has made one of his most significant achievements. This is far more worth recognizing in a rating scale than his mastery of any number of specific facts in science or any other subject-matter field. Even within a course such things as effort, contribution to the wholesomeness of the class atmosphere, and improvement in interest in the field are important qualities to recognize in the final evaluation. Even though achievement in the subject is still used as the basic element in making marks, it should be modified by the other consideration.

In the elementary school final reports on progress should never be competitively arranged. It is far more helpful to parents and children to know to what extent the child has done his best work, and the areas in which he needs help. Numerical or letter marks have no value in this type of evaluation.

Systems of translating scores into marks can become complicated, but a simple system is all that is needed for the amount of precision in marking needed in secondary school. When the final scores of students are distributed on a scale of some sort, it is usually possible to detect by inspection where the dividing points can be set to separate the A, B, C, and other grades. It should be a relative method, letting the scores themselves set their own average, rather than having an absolute scale of expected scores against which to judge the students.

Final scores can be made up of simple totals of all the raw scores earned by the students throughout a term. It is not necessary to translate any quiz score into a percentage mark. It is quite as informative to know the number right and the number wrong as to know what percentage they constitute of something. The improvement of learning is not going to proceed from a percentage figure but from a knowledge of what was missed and what has been learned. A test might have any conceivable possible maximum score, for there is no particular virtue in possible total scores such as 100, or 10, or any such figure. If 67 is the highest score that can be earned on a test, and a student gets a score of 42, then he knows what he has accomplished fully as well as if he were told he had made a mark of 63 per cent. The raw score of 42 can be recorded, added to other scores, and put through any desired manipulation without difficulty. Percentages may not be added or averaged without causing distortion.

When the final scores are ready to be translated into marks, the teacher should bring all the other objectives of the course besides subject-matter mastery into consideration, using whatever evaluative information he has accumulated, to decide what the final mark will be. It should be a fairly accurate indication of the extent to which the student has attained *all* the objectives said to be involved in the course.

Make the test discriminative. Since test scores are to have some weight in final marks, the tests should be made discriminative enough to yield valid differences between students. There is rarely a class in school that does not approximate a normal distribution of ability, as long as the class has not been deliberately sectioned on the basis of ability.

Therefore, it should be assumed that a valid test will distribute achievement scores in roughly symmetrical form. Tests that fail to do this might well be suspected of being faulty in one of the three ways suggested here. If it is too easy for the class, the scores will pile up in the upper end of the distribution, and there will be a tendency to think the class is made up of superior students. If the whole test is too difficult, the scores will pile up at the bottom, and the class will look inferior. These effects can be produced in any class quite easily, because the difficulty of a test is easily altered. If there are not enough possible scores in a test, so that it is inevitable that many students will get the same scores, then it is not possible to discriminate between them in achievement. A test with a maximum of ten points, for a class of fifty students, cannot do a very good job of discriminating between individual students. Over a period of time, a great many such tests might eventually give total scores running up beyond 100, and thus provide some discrimination. If the test does not sample all the material in a unit or lesson, it may automatically handicap some students whose best achievement was in that part of the lesson which was not included in the test. Others would be somewhat luckier, but not necessarily better students.

These three considerations should be kept in mind in making up any test. Keep it difficult enough so that there is an ample ceiling for the best students, but include enough items of less difficulty so that everyone can get some of it. Have a large enough possible range of scores to provide room for spreading out in the class. Sample all of the objectives involved in the work of the class. Marks made up on the basis of such tests are much more fair than those made up on poor tests which discriminate unfairly and on the basis of chance.

2510. *Interpretation of tests.* Tests are given to find out what the status of the student is, and what he has left to accomplish to reach his objective. The scores are incidental to this more serious purpose.

For a class as a whole, the test may be analyzed by counting the number of times each possible answer was used by the students. A survey of such an analysis will show the teacher the areas in which the class is strong or weak, and give him a fresh point of departure from which to continue his work. It will also show him, if he studies the questions on the test in the same way, where the questions need improvement, and how to make the improvement.

On an individual basis, it is quite helpful to a student who is having difficulty to go over his test item by item with the teacher, discussing why he selected certain wrong answers, why he did not select the correct answers, and seeing whether he can explain why the correct answers are correct and the incorrect answers incorrect. In a large percentage of cases this procedure will reveal specific difficulties which keep the student from mastering the material.

Evaluation was described earlier as the appraisal of progress toward an objective. In the light of that concept, interpretation of test results is a very important part of evaluation. Where it is not practiced, the usefulness of the test stops with its role as a device for making marks. Where it is practiced, the test serves as a transition from a temporary checking point to the next phase of the course, and gives direction to further work. This is by far the best educational use of measurement.

QUESTIONS FOR REVIEW

1. Explain the role of evaluation in non-academic enterprises. How is it like the academic use of evaluation?
2. Define evaluation. What is it intended to do?
3. What is the difference between testing and evaluating?
4. What is the difference between teaching and counseling?
5. Explain what is contained in Table 9.
6. Describe three phases of evaluation, and then combine them into a single definition.
7. Define an objective so that the term is useful in evaluation.
8. What do objectives have to do with evaluation?
9. What is peculiar about educational objectives compared to other enterprises?
10. Give some guides in making objectives usable.
11. In what ways do hidden objectives show up in courses?
12. What happens to objectives that are not evaluated?
13. What are some different levels of objectives with which evaluation may be concerned?

14. Show how evaluative techniques vary with the type of learning involved.
15. What are some general guides in test construction?
16. What are the safeguards in making and scoring essay tests? Other forms?
17. How would you determine the type of marks to use?
18. On what would you base your marks?
19. What sort of marks would be appropriate in elementary school? Secondary school? Graduate school? Why the differences?

SELECTED REFERENCES

Arthur I. Gates, Arthur T. Jersild, T. R. McConnell, and Robert C. Challman, *Educational psychology* (New York: The Macmillan Co., 1948), Chapter XVI.

Harry A. Greene, Albert N. Jorgensen, and Raymond J. Gerberich, *Measurement and evaluation in the secondary school* (New York: Longmans, Green and Co., 1946), *passim*. See footnotes in this chapter for specific references.

H. H. Remmers and N. L. Gage, *Educational measurement and evaluation* (New York: Harper and Bros., 1943), *passim*.

Charles C. Ross, *Measurement in today's schools* (New York: Prentice-Hall, Inc., 1945), Part I, Chapter I, and Part V, Chapter XVII, and others that follow.

CLASS EXERCISES ON EVALUATION

Things To Do in Class

1. A definition test consisting of the following words was given to a ninth-grade class in cooking. The listings below show the number out of six who were wrong and right. What can you learn from these data? Try several kinds of analysis of the results, such as grouping together the terms missed most and least.

Words	Right	Wrong	Words	Right	Wrong
Provision	6	0	Roughage	2	4
Essential	6	0	Comparison	6	0
Braising	1	5	Neutralize	1	5
Cellulose	0	6	Procedure	3	3
Environment	2	4	Griddle	6	0
Classification	5	1	Garnish	2	4

Established	5	1		Sub-standard	3	3	
Requirement	6	0		Proportions	3	3	
Au Gratin	2	4		Scalloped	5	1	
Responsibility	6	0		Poach	4	2	

2. The following scores were obtained by administering two forms of a concept test, and two forms of a true-false test to the same group of students. Both forms of each test were administered at the same time so that no learning would occur between the times each form was used. All scores on one line are for one student.

True-False		Concepts		True-False		Concepts		True-False		Concepts	
A	B	I	II	A	B	I	II	A	B	I	II
30	26	9	7	30	36	8	8	33	32	9	7
35	17	5	8	23	30	8	7	21	19	9	7
26	25	5	5	13	24	10	8	27	21	8	7
32	33	6	9	37	31	10	7	28	31	7	6
49	29	7	6	29	23	7	8	22	35	9	9
20	24	5	4	31	25	8	8	33	35	11	10
44	46	12	11	27	26	8	9	19	11	6	7
31	30	4	9	31	35	9	6	37	30	9	10
22	18	8	7	30	25	5	7	41	26	8	11
24	28	5	6	29	34	8	7	28	23	6	8
15	27	3	6	24	27	7	8	20	38	6	7
24	26	8	8	30	30	4	7	16	30	10	7
38	35	11	7	28	28	9	9	29	18	6	7
34	21	9	8	29	25	10	6	26	17	5	6
34	31	7	10	30	24	7	6				
22	30	7	6	26	14	6	6				

Think about the following problems:

A. How reliable are these tests? Are the forms of each test equivalent? To what extent? Can you use them as preinstructional and postinstructional tests for individuals? For the class?

B. Supposing the four tests were administered at equal intervals throughout the school year, what can you tell about the nature of performance of various students? Which students are doing the most detailed study?

C. In what ways could these scores be converted into marks?

3. Evaluate the short stories in the exercises at the end of Chapter XVIII of the text, assuming the objective was to produce

something with imagination, grammatical quality, and attractive ideas.

Things To Do outside Class

1. Resume work on the lesson plan that was begun earlier and was further developed during the course. Each student is to prepare tests for the lesson in a well-organized evaluation plan. He is to show how his whole objective is cared for in the evaluation and that the evaluation plan does not attempt to measure results not involved in the objective. A few of the plans should be discussed before the class, illustrating evaluation in different types of learning and different subject fields.

2. Have each student prepare some tests for use in this course, on material already covered. One test should be prepared on each mode of measurement in section 2505, and the tests should be set up in machine-scoring form, except for the essay test. When the reports are ready, let them be exchanged within the class, for review and criticism, with discussion of a few after that.

3. Give to the class a mimeographed copy of a test used earlier in this course, on which is shown the item analysis count for every possible answer to each question. The students are to do these things:

   A. Reconstruct the test questions that seem to need changing to improve their discrimination power or to overcome weaknesses.

   B. From the item count, prepare a guide sheet for subsequent discussion with the class on ideas that did not show up well on the test. This should avoid discussion of questions and turn attention to ideas.

   C. Discuss the instructor's method of teaching for that particular test's content, in the light of the analysis.

CHAPTER XXVI

EVALUATION OF THE INSTRUCTIONAL PROGRAM

2601. *Introduction.* There is an inescapable relationship between the quality of the teaching program and the success of the students. To lay the blame for failure on the laziness, indifference, or deliberate uncooperativeness of the students, or to explain failure by decrying the mental capacity of the group is mere rationalization. There is a very high stability in the mental capacity of all groups of public-school students, and the chances of finding a particularly stupid or brilliant concentration in any one class are practically zero. No one impugns the integrity or designs of the teacher whose class does not achieve well, unless the performance is regularly repeated. In either case the only acceptable reaction is to undertake an analysis of the situation, and to find out what parts of the instructional plan need changing. Even in the case of a teacher whose efforts seem to be successful, self-evaluation will lead to improvement and to increased enjoyment in the work. This type of evaluation may in large part be a secondary product of the academic evaluation program, through use of the tests beyond the help they furnish for individual students.

2602. *Evaluation of course and lesson objectives.* The measurements used to appraise student progress do their work by showing how well the students have attained the objectives. Therefore, they offer a way of appraising the objectives themselves. Objectives that are rarely attained by anyone, or that are scarcely approached by anyone, should be examined critically to determine why this is so. They may be too difficult, or involve too much for the time available, or be beyond the possibilities of students at the level of maturity in the class. There may be too little relationship between the objective and the course plan of activities, or it is possible that the larger objectives may never be attained because there is poor interrelationship between them and the more specific parts of the course which should furnish the foundation for the large objectives.

Objectives may also be too modest for a class, and too easily attained. They may not furnish sufficient scope for a busy group of students. Such a condition could go unnoticed if measurement of progress were deferred too long, but it would be indicated in a class in which there is a sense of lost motion or of forced activities to use up a designated length of time.

If a person has difficulty comparing the results of his evaluation with the objectives, it may be because the objectives are too vague to have any clear relationship to the kinds of things that can be measured in the group. Where this is so, and it is not an unusual situation, the vagueness will no doubt create difficulty in setting up measuring instruments in the first place, since there is no description of identifiable behavior around which to construct an instrument. That should be the point at which to do something about the vagueness of the objectives. Nevertheless, a teacher can overlook this problem, and go ahead with the development of some tests, or the selection of some published tests, along lines that are felt to be related to the course. It can scarcely be necessary to point out the lack of logicality in such a procedure, but if it is not detected when the tests are prepared, it should be noticed when the teacher attempts to appraise his progress in the light of what he thinks he is trying to accomplish.

Almost every teacher will discover some part of his objectives that is not being achieved satisfactorily. A good evaluation program enables him to engage in a systematic and continuing reconstruction of his objectives and of his methods of moving toward them.

2603. *Evaluation of teaching and learning activities.* As in the case of objectives, the progress of the students is an index to the effectiveness of the procedures. Where progress is not materializing satisfactorily, the teacher is often able to detect a faulty relationship between the type of behavior involved in an objective and the nature of the teaching plan for that part of the course. Arrangement of lessons, introduction plans for units, types of learning experience provided, instructional materials, and method of using class time should be subjected to scrutiny when progress is shown to be less than it should be.

Student reactions apart from their performance on tests is also valuable in developing a live course. Unidentified papers collected from students now and then on which appear evaluative responses along lines requested by the teacher may be expected to be serious and constructive on the whole. The few who take advantage of such situations to show off or exaggerate will be covered by the total response of the group, particularly if there is fair rapport between the teacher and the students.

Questions put to students in such evaluations may deal with several aspects of the course. As to content, they may be asked whether there is not enough, too much, or about the right quantity. The course can be evaluated on its difficulty, complexity, interestingness, and usefulness. The pace of the class can be evaluated, whether it is too fast, too leisurely, or about right. The method of conducting class can be tested regarding its clarity, interestingness, or effect on the students' feelings of security in the class. The reading materials and all other parts of the course may be similarly submitted to appraisal. This sort of evaluation should be conducted by the teacher himself, if he makes arrangements so that he cannot identify the response of any student; or by someone invited to do so by the teacher, from whom the results will be given to the teacher himself. It is successful at all levels of education in getting ideas that contribute to the improvement of a course.

2604. *Evaluation of out-of-class activities.* The whole program of the school is educational under modern points of view and may well be submitted to the evaluation suggested for the classroom activities. Students could comment on extent of participation, enjoyment of activities, reasons for participating or not participating, ways of improving the whole program or any part of it, and the values that should be cultivated in some way in the school program.

2605. *Evaluation and improvement of tests.* Good tests are hard to make and deserve preservation, but not simply through being saved and used time after time. With systematic effort, an evaluation system can be built up over a period of months and years that will give rich returns for the time and effort spent on it.

The first step in such a program is the establishment of a file for test questions. A convenient arrangement is a four by six file box in which cards may be filed according to subject matter or whatever is being tested. When a test is to be made up, and its form has been decided, each question prepared for it should be written on a separate card somewhat according to Figure 14.

Source: text, p. 2-5   Topic: population, N. Y.

The population of the State of New York is larger than:

(1) the population of Italy.

(2) the combined population of the states west of the Mississippi River.

*(3) the population of any other one state.

(4) 25,000,000.

*(5) all of the New England states combined.

FIG. 14. A SAMPLE FILE CARD FOR A TEST QUESTION

Room is left on the card in which to enter the item count after the question has been used in a test. The card is kept handy until the test has been analyzed, and the item counts written on each card, together with the ratios which show the discrimination power of each possible answer in the question. Then if the question seems to need alteration along lines suggested below, the alterations are made and the card filed under its subject matter. When alterations are made, the item counts are marked so that the tester will know later that the alteration has not yet been tried out in the class.

In time, a surprisingly large file of such items will be accumulated. It is then possible to go through the file while preparing an examination for a given part of the course and select questions from among those available. A few new questions may be produced for each test, which keeps up an inflow of new ideas, and gradually enlarges the supply of available items. These questions come in time to be improved to the point where they are truly discriminative, and their level of difficulty is known before the test is given. It is not hard, then, to make up a test that contains a few rather hard items, a few easy items, and many medium items, because the item counts on the card will reveal the level of difficulty.

Use of item count for test improvement. A machine-scored test can be analyzed by the same machine that scores it. A graphic record of the number of times each answer was chosen can be made by the machine. This is the item count recorded on the card. Before the item count is made, it is a good idea to sort the test papers according to score, so that the upper one-third of the scores are in one pile, and the lower one-third in another pile. The item count is then made separately for each of the two piles. It is assumed that a good test question will be answered correctly by the better students more often than it will be by the poorer students. If the question were capable of separating all the better students from all the poorer students, it should theoretically be answered correctly by all of the better, and none of the poorer. An index of its discriminative power may be obtained in this manner. For correct answers, divide the count for the better students by the count for the poorer students. For incorrect answers, reverse the division. If the quotient obtained is 1.00, the item is being correctly marked by as many good as poor students. As it goes higher, the item shows increasing power to separate the two groups. If it goes below 1.00, the item is being missed by the good students and correctly marked by the poor students.

These fractions or their quotients, preferably both, should

be entered on the cards and used in determining how difficult the question is, and whether it needs alteration. Any item that falls below 1.00 should certainly be changed. A quotient around 1.00 or a little higher means that the item has no real value, because it does not discriminate to a useful degree.

The ratio will not tell how difficult the item is on the whole. That is revealed by the actual counts. If the ratio is favorable, and only a few students have answered the question, the difficulty is high. If most of the students answered it correctly, the difficulty is low. From this analysis, the teacher can tell whether he has enough items of moderate difficulty, and if not can begin to cut down the difficulty of some of the hard items, build up the difficulty of some of the easy items, or make some new items to fill the need, depending on whether he has more hard or easy items than he wants.

This procedure applies alike to any objective test question, whether of the true-false, multiple-choice, or matching type.

The most forbidding aspect of a good evaluation program is the expected heavy demands in time and effort. This turns out in practice to be largely an illusion. Systematic planning accomplishes surprising results with little if any more time than is used in the rather haphazard test construction practiced by some teachers. There is a progressive saving of time under such a system, along with a decided improvement in the quality of evaluation, and the subsequent satisfaction derived from the work. Machine scoring is a labor-saver of significant degree, although hand scoring of an objective test, by means of a cut-out stencil, is almost as fast unless the tests are very long and the classes large.

IBM machines are located in all states, and are generally available for scoring by arrangement with the institutions that rent them. Sometimes renting institutions make a practice of scoring tests for schoolteachers on the basis of a small charge. Answer sheets are shipped by mail. The service is quite satisfactory on the whole, if the distances are not very great. Item analyses may be made by hand where machines are not available, by laying the answer sheets on a table, one sheet overlapping the next, with the questions lined up in straight rows. Each question's count can then be tallied quickly.

Good units of study, which can be repeated in subsequent classes, may sometimes be improved over a period of time. If a good test is used at a given point in the unit, the scores may be filed for reference later, as a basis for comparing the performance of students in the two classes. Although this does not produce data upon which generalizations may be based, it does offer the teacher a way of experimenting with various ways of securing progress in a particular section of a course. It may not be kept up for more than one or two retrials, because the test should be varied and improved too, and this will make the scores incomparable.

2606. *Conclusion.* The suggestions made in this chapter touch on only part of the ways in which evaluative procedures can be made to contribute to the improvement of teaching. The movement is contagious. Each attempt to evaluate part of the program furnishes some sort of satisfaction and discovery, which whets the appetite for more. If learning can be improved by knowledge of progress, then why not apply the same principle to the task of learning to teach, so that it, also, may be improved. Any move that has such widespread advantages and so few disadvantages can scarcely be overlooked. The benefits extend to student and teacher alike. There is no other method of making any significant improvements in our educational system.

QUESTIONS FOR REVIEW

1. What aspects of the school program may be evaluated from analysis of achievement test results?
2. How would you evaluate your objectives? Name several aspects of this.
3. What evaluation of teaching procedures is possible through test scores?
4. How can teaching procedures be evaluated other than by test scores?
5. Describe a good filing system for test items.
6. What should be shown on a file card for a test item?

7. How should a test item be changed?
8. How can you keep students from anticipating the same test all the time, and still use items that have been improved through past use?
9. What is a graphic item count? Describe two ways of obtaining one.
10. Show how it facilitates improvement of a test item.

SELECTED REFERENCE

Arthur I. Gates, Arthur T. Jersild, T. R. McConnell, and Robert C. Challman, *Educational psychology* (New York: The Macmillan Co., 1948), Chapter XVII.

CLASS EXERCISES ON EVALUATION

Things To Do outside Class

1. Have each student prepare a test item file box and put into it cards on which are entered the test items used in his lesson plan evaluation scheme. This file can be taken with him directly into his teaching activities.

CHAPTER XXVII

EVALUATING AND COUNSELING THE INDIVIDUAL

2701. *The nature of counseling.* There is so much talk about personal counseling, vocational counseling, educational counseling, teaching, and advisory programs that it is easy to get the impression that there are certain well-defined areas which can be separated and kept apart. There is antipathy between psychiatrists and psychologists about who should be permitted to do this or that type of work with disturbed individuals. All of this departmentalization infers that the student consists of a set of functional areas, each of which may be handled alone, like the inventory of a department store. This is misleading, for the student has no such areas as suggested by educational, vocational, or personal counseling. He is just a person with problems that pay no attention to such lines of demarcation. What upsets him in his social relationships may also upset his classwork and interfere with his feeling of personal well-being. The problem may be very simple and temporary or very complex and lasting, or it may have elements of both kinds. It will have to be met by *all* those with whom he works or plays, each carrying a role in its solution or further development according to his ability and understanding in the continued relationship.

Counseling has been variously thought to consist of:

Telling a person what is good for him.

Telling a person what is right and wrong.

Telling a person what vocation to select.

Making a person conform to the rules of a school.

Solving a person's problem.

It is none of these things. It is *an effort to help the individual adjust effectively, orient himself wisely, and develop optimally.*[1] Counseling is not of unique concern to any one aspect of life, such as education, vocation, or socialization. It is an approach to complete and balanced living.

Counseling is an aid to problem-solving; it is not telling. The counselor does not approach his work by asking, "What do *I* want this person to do?" He begins by asking, "What does this person want to do with himself?" Furthermore, the problem-solving is not to be done by the counselor. It is to be done by the student with the counselor's help. There are wide variations in the amount of initiative a young person is able to take in solving his own problems, but the procedure most valuable to him is that which puts the greatest possible initiative in his own hands. This is true at every age level, and in every situation—home, school, or elsewhere.

Counseling is not limited to solving problems as they arise. It serves most constructively when it helps students become aware of matters that will concern them in the future and prepare to meet such matters. Evidence of failure to do this in one important field is the almost universal reluctance of students to register for required courses during the early years of college. Not sensing the tremendous value of a broad background, freshmen customarily fail to see why they should take a broad array of courses which seem to have no relation to their chosen field of specialization. Failure in early vocational counseling is evident in the demonstrated fact that the vocational choices of college students tend to be unrealisic and often turn out to be unsatisfactory.

In the broader sense the child himself defines the functions that should be provided for his help when he needs help. He has imperious needs that continue to drive him to effort aimed at their satisfaction. The process leads him progressively farther and farther into a complex life which is marked by increasingly involved ways of meeting needs, both in the present and in the future. More and more attention goes to providing for the meeting of future needs, which means that the chances of running into conflicts and barriers increase at the same time. Every conceivable kind of problem

[1] Robert H. Mathewson, *Guidance policy and practice* (New York: Harper and Bros., 1949), Chapter 7.

that might require the help of a counselor, or a guide of any sort, is apt to appear any day throughout his life. The solving of personal problems is a lifetime occupation, and as long as there is a chance that the individual may hit a problem in which he needs help of some kind, he is a candidate for some kind of counseling.

In this chapter an attempt is made to sketch four kinds of problems which continue with the individual through most of his life in one way or another, and for which counseling service of some kind would be helpful. No one of these problems "belongs" to a psychiatrist, a psychologist, a teacher, a parent, a religious adviser, or a friend. Since in each type of problem there is a possibility that every known kind of specialization might be needed, each of those who counsel can serve as his talents, insights, and abilities permit.[2] *The one limiting factor, however, must be ability and training of sufficient scope to enable the counselor to do what is required in a particular case with genuine benefit to the counselee.* There is no room in any human life for someone to "practice" in. There are no expendable personalities that can be used as guinea pigs for the would-be counselor who feels endowed by nature with a gift for helping others and who has not had adequate preparation for what he is trying to do. What is thought of as "common sense" does not constitute preparation for counseling in involved cases. A counselor who touches on vocational problems should have had enough training in a recognized university to be competent in all aspects of such work before he attempts to influence the whole life career of a human being. Similarly, anyone who proposes to work with an individual in a conflict of any complexity should have had the equivalent of the training provided for clinical psychologists and as much more as possible. As long as each person who serves as a consultant to any individual at any time refrains from trying to handle problems that are beyond his preparation, there need be no other artificially imposed restrictions on the service rendered to students and young people by those who work with them.

[2] *Ibid.*, Chapters 8, 10.

There is one troublesome circumstance in the schools, however, that must be frankly recognized. It is the exceptional school even today that has at its service the kind and amount of help needed for dealing with complicated cases of maladjustment. As a result, classroom teachers find themselves practically alone in many situations with one or more individuals whose condition is such that they need psychological help. What is the teacher to do? Principals are not prepared to help such cases. By tradition they handle the severe discipline cases that teachers cannot handle in the classroom. Of itself that is a poor way of meeting such issues, and in the case of maladjusted disturbers it is even worse. There is nothing in administrative procedures to make a person a good counselor. It is usually unwise for a teacher to attempt to penetrate a severe personality disturbance, even when a psychologist or psychiatrist is not available. Every effort should be made to bring attention to such cases. The students should be handled as patiently and understandingly as possible in school, since in most cases they have been there for some time already when their difficulties are discovered, and they can continue under a teacher who will try to help them with their work. There is no easy way to escape the difficulties imposed by their troublesome symptoms, but they should be treated as people in need of understanding and help, and given every possible encouragement to work with the others in the educational activities.

2702. *A teacher's approach to his students.* The teacher has the responsibility of becoming acquainted with each new class as rapidly as possible. In this process he should identify students in three categories which will have considerable influence on the work of the class.

One type is the student who is so superior in capacity, adjustment, achievement, alertness, and so on that he will require a distinctly higher type of classroom challenge than the others. These people can be serious disturbers, or loafers who waste their valuable possibilities, if they are not taught at their own level of operation.

Another type is the student who is so poorly equipped in

capacity, adjustment, or preparation that he needs individual attention to help him work back toward the center of the group. This type of student may need less pressure. He may do best when requirements are adjusted down to his possibilities, and when his situation in the class is so arranged as to help him meet his problems, even though it may sometimes require special dispensations and effort to do so.

The third type is the student who is reasonably well adjusted, somewhere in the normal group with reference to achievement and ability to work out his own academic and personal problems.

Rarely does a teacher find himself with more than a very few of the unusually advanced or unusually handicapped students. The great majority will fit into the typical middle group, and often a class will have no more than one student who stands out on either side. This means that a little early attention to the deviates will enable the teacher to cast his approach to the class early in the course and to make his plans so as to meet the problems he knows are awaiting him. The typical group is capable of going along well with a minimum of personal attention. What is done for the group will suffice for all those in it most of the time. Knowing about that group and the students who constitute it will save much time and confusion for the teacher. Some of that time can be given to those whose needs require more attention. When these facts are known early, a much better year's program can be planned than when the classroom personality distribution is never clearly discovered at all throughout the year.

As an aid in making such an analysis of a class, many kinds of personnel records have been devised, and the customary system of office files for every student has grown up. The typical system is capable of giving a great deal of useful information if it is kept up, but it is difficult to maintain because it is too complex and time-consuming for the teacher. Table 16 presents a Simplified Student Inventory, which is an attempt to compromise between the extensive detail of a full record and the need for ease of handling in a minimum of time. The various parts of the inventory will be discussed in the next four sections of this chapter. After that its over-all significance will be discussed from the point of view of its value to the teacher.

Since this discussion is directed primarily to schoolteachers, it seems appropriate to present these four continuing types of problems from the standpoint of the teacher's contact with them, and the teacher's contact with a new class.

2703. *Continuing problems in personal adjustment.* The whole course of life consists of activities that move toward the fulfillment of needs.[3] This means that the individual must continually find new paths over which to move to his adjustments. The paths must be safe for him, in that they do not upset any other needs, particularly of a personal type. There are always conflicts of some sort involved in this ad-justment process. Most of the time the individual can resolve them himself in a variety of ways, many of which were dis-cussed in Chapter XXIII. Sometimes he cannot do this on his own resources, but finds himself pushed toward acts that violate his own personal standards, or paths that seem to him to be destructive of his highly cherished values. Either of these experiences will disturb him deeply, leaving either a feeling of guilt, or a feeling that his very self is being threat-ened. In their less severe form these states of maladjustment produce such symptoms as are listed in section I, A of Table 6 on page 446. In more severe forms they may give rise to some of the more explosive symptoms, or to some of the deeper but less noticeable symptoms as indicated in sections B to F of the same table.

When the individual's conflicts become a little too much for him to handle with his own immature abilities, a teacher, parent, or other available adult may be able to help him appraise his situation and find a solution to it. As it be-comes progressively more involved, and moves toward repres-sion, it will require the help of more and more adequately trained counselors.

The teacher is in an ideal position to detect the presence of problems that require any of these different levels of help. Unless he uses a systematic approach, however, he is almost

---

[3] This point of view is well stated by Mathewson, *op. cit.,* Chapter 2.

sure to overlook many of the symptoms that reveal such problems. In Table 16, section III on emotional status contains five rating scales that pertain to some of the most helpful indicators of personal maladjustment. Item A, Nervousness, is similar to the Casual overt behavior symptoms in Table 6 on page 446. Item B, Dependence on others, is similar to the Poor motivational health indicated in section II, A of Table 6. Item C, Breadth of contact, is similar to Preoccupation, and Withdrawal, in Table 6. Item D, Display, is similar to Exhibitionism in Table 6. Item E, Self-control, is related to the Intensive or explosive reactions, in Table 6.

TABLE 16.—SIMPLIFIED STUDENT INVENTORY

Directions: Indicate with a check the approximate position on each of the scales below of the individual you are studying. Use the three descriptions on each scale as general guides in determining that position. Some of the scales require the collection of objective data, and some can be marked from observation.

I. SOCIAL STATUS

| A. Friends | Isolated, lonely | Enough friends for good adjustment | Well-liked, many friends |
| B. Social techniques | Drives people away, irritates or antagonizes | Easily liked but makes few advances | Seeks and makes many friends |

II. MENTAL STATUS

A. Capacity	Dull, very low capacity	Average ability	Brilliant, does everything easily
B. Mental alertness and interest	No curiosity, very narrow interests	Has a few interests that challenge, and a little variety	Lively interest, curious, likes many things
C. Drive	Easily discouraged, no push or vigor	Gives up occasionally, usually does what is required	Unlimited confidence, tasks rarely hard enough to challenge

III. EMOTIONAL STATUS

A. Nervous-ness	Fidgety, jumpy, obviously nervous	Ordinarily calm and easy, fidgets a little, but not habitually	Always calm, self-controlled, at ease
	|_____|_____|	|_____|	|_____|_____|
B. Depend-ence on others	Can't act alone, or without much advice. Depends on others' opinions	Partially dependent on others, often makes own decisions	Makes all own decisions, stands alone with ease
	|_____|_____|	|_____|	|_____|_____|
C. Breadth of contact	Withdrawn, pre-occupied, lost in own thoughts	Daydreams some, not regularly, usually alert	Alert, aware of and in touch with all that happens
	|_____|_____|	|_____|	|_____|_____|
D. Display	Clearly a show-off, bluffer, bully, etc.	Enjoys attention, makes little effort to get it	Able to lead or follow without fuss
	|_____|_____|	|_____|	|_____|_____|
E. Self-control	Unpredictable, hysterical, anxious, or fearful, etc.	Emotionally balanced, but not afraid to show feelings	Never upset or caught off balance
	|_____|_____|	|_____|	|_____|_____|

IV. PHYSICAL STATUS

A. Health	Dull, inspid, tired	Plenty of energy	Robust, vibrant, tireless
	|_____|_____|	|_____|	|_____|_____|
B. Sensory appa-ratus	Very poor, misses much that goes on	Good, no difficulties	Keen, catches everything
	|_____|_____|	|_____|	|_____|_____|
C. Gross physical state	Serious handi-cap, limits ability	No serious deficiency	Perfect physical condition and coordination
	|_____|_____|	|_____|	|_____|_____|
D. Develop-mental status	Very retarded	Average for age	Very advanced
	|_____|_____|	|_____|	|_____|_____|

V. SUMMARY OF DIFFICULTIES (IF ANY)

A. Specific social difficulties_____

_____

B. Nature of physical handicap_____

_____

C. Specific needs not being satisfied_____

_____

Such symptoms as exhibitionism, nervousness, and explosive reactions can scarcely escape notice by the teacher, but can easily obtain an annoyed and irritated reaction, rather than a recognition of what they signify about the student's adjustment. The other symptoms, dependence on others, withdrawal, and preoccupation, are so easily overlooked in a classroom as to require deliberate and planned methods for their detection.

In a new class, the teacher should arrange two or more opportunities at the earliest dates to observe his students systematically. This can be done while supervised study is in progress, or while someone else is leading the class, or even in piecemeal fashion, while the teacher is conducting a discussion or learning activity of any kind. What it requires in any case is a systematic check on every student. When the class is quiet, and the teacher is free for a brief period, a satisfactory technique is the time-sample observation. This consists of giving direct attention to each student, or to a pair of students, for a short period of time, at periodic intervals through an hour or a day. If the behavior of a given student were watched for fifteen seconds, at five different times within an hour, a significant beginning would have been made in getting a record of what he may be expected to be found doing in class. Only in this pointed manner will the teacher discover the student who is quietly removing himself from contact with others, and sometimes it is only through this technique that a student is discovered to be plagued with a constant pattern of minor symptoms of tension. Unnecessary trips to the pencil sharpener, the fountain, the window, the book shelf, or the wastebasket; frequent trips to the desk for unimportant questions, shifting in the seat, fiddling with objects; these and many other little things can become so customary as to escape significant attention.

Dependence on others is sometimes mistaken for diligence and industriousness. The student who is always trying to do things the way the teacher wants them done may be unable to get away from dependence on others and do his own thinking. All of these five rating scales are significant in personal adjustment. If a student must be marked somewhere on the extreme left side after being observed for a while, it should be assumed that he has some unsolved problems, and is probably in need of some kind of help. That sort of person should be singled out for much more observation, after it is found that the others can get along quite well on their own resources.

This sort of systematic evaluation is not time-consuming, because it can be done within the framework of the class period. Although it takes longer to get around, the teacher can even do it while presenting a lesson, by making a point of being conscious of the behavior of three or four particular students during a given period, and recording his observations after the period is over. When the time-sample is used, a coded entry should be made on an observation sheet each time the behavior is observed, or it will be impossible to recall what was observed earlier for each individual student.

When counseling begins, it should by all means be kept within the point of view presented in the opening of this chapter, whether the teacher or a clinical psychologist is doing it. It will be an attempt to help the individual get to the root of his problem and to find a solution to it. The process may require some additional evaluation. If so, this may include any or all of such techniques as intelligence testing and diagnosis, measurement of traits, discovery of process concepts and the conflicting elements in them, discovery of the frustrations, unmet needs, preoccupations, and self-concepts of the individual, records of past experience, personality tests, value tests, and measurements of interests. None of these forms of evaluation can furnish an answer to anyone's problem, but they can help the counselor and the individual bring the available resources to bear on the problem, in a joint effort to work out a solution. Such a relationship must be marked by confidence, mutual respect, intimacy in sharing, breaking down of protective reserves, sometimes cathartic opportunities to drain off tensions, and the arrival at productive lines of effort that lead toward rebuilding one's ways of meeting problems.

At the lesser levels of complexity the teacher may do a great deal of this type of counseling, but at the deepest levels it is a psychiatric problem. The teacher should, above all, try to cultivate a sensitivity to such problems, and the ability to detect those that must be referred to someone else for help. Contrary to the old notion that a teacher who has to send students to others is incapable, that teacher who is able to send maladjusted students to the attention of those who can give them the help they need is greatly to be praised. It is far better to err on the side of referring too many than too few.

2704. *Continuing problems in social adjustment.* Here, as in personal adjustments, the individual is constantly in pursuit of social satisfactions. He must find paths to his needs, which not only provide the other necessities, but also help him attain belongingness, affection, approval, and a comfortable working relationship with others. Again, because of the increasing complexity of social life as one grows older, there are inevitable conflicts in the problems of every day. While the normal student can solve most of them himself, he will strike one now and then beyond his own powers, and the individual who is not normally adjusted will be bothered by many of them. Unfortunately, even the highly superior student finds himself frequently at a loss in social relationships, because of the stress created by his superiority in behavioral skill. Even if he avoids attempts to dominate others, his higher powers are often resented by others, or make others feel uneasy.

Social conflicts may arise in one's general adjustment to the community or the whole school, they may arise within a class, or within a smaller group of associates. The teacher is in the logical position to make the first discoveries of social maladjustment, if he is conscious of the problem and watching for its indicators.

In the student inventory in Table 16, section I is devoted to social adjustment. Two ratings are suggested, one on relationships, and one on social techniques. If there is any social maladjustment, it will show up on one or both of these items. There are several ways of getting at one's circle of friendships. Observation is fairly informative, but again it must be systematic so that no one is overlooked. A much quicker method is to be found in some of the approaches to sociometry, or the measurement of social relationships.

For practical purposes it is not necessary to make a sociogram of the relationships in a class, but such diagrams do present a vivid picture of the whole class structure. They also require time and some interest in the making of graphs, which constitutes one of their chief difficulties for a busy teacher.

A much simpler approach, which is practical and effective, is the tallying of the number of people who indicate a preference for a particular person. The class can be asked to write on individual slips of paper the names of one, two, or more students with whom the writer prefers to work, or play, or serve on a committee, or sit near in class, or do anything of that sort with. The teacher may then simply tally opposite the name of each student in the class the number of times he was mentioned by someone else.

If it is desired to know in addition which of those listed the individual feels himself to be intimate with, the students can be asked to indicate that by a check mark opposite the name. It is possible that some of those who are poorly adjusted socially can tell with whom they would like to associate, but have no feeling of intimacy with anyone in a room. Such tallies quickly reveal the students who are socially isolated and in need of better relationships. The results of this technique may furnish enough evaluative data to permit checking item A on the profile, for all the students.

Item B, Social techniques, requires some observation. Having completed item A first, however, the teacher can limit this observation to the social isolates if pressure demands, and begin finding out *why* they are isolated. They may be shy, clumsy, unattractive for a variety of reasons, or in other ways deficient in the qualities that make friendship easily cultivated. This further evaluation gives the teacher insight that enables him to take up a helpful counseling relationship with the isolate, and to pass on his insight to other teachers who are also trying to help the student.

Social maladjustment can be due to personality defects in an individual whose social process concepts are perfectly safe and accepted. This requires some work with the personality structure, and therefore may range all the way from fairly simple readjustments to complex psychiatric problems. Obviously, this is a task at which almost every level of skill in counseling may be directed, as long as the skill is kept appropriately related to the complexity of the problem.

Such maladjustment may also be due to atypical process concepts in an individual who has a perfectly attractive personality structure. This presents a problem in re-education. Such problems are usually resistant, slow in responding, demanding on patience and persistence, and worthy of all the ingenuity and persuasiveness one can muster. Of course not all atypicality is so stubborn, but the typical delinquent fits this description. On the other hand, there are others who are not committed to antagonism in their unapproved acts, and who are re-educated without great difficulty. All they need is an opportunity to learn, which they will do quite willingly and happily for the social rewards at stake.

Social problems are not ordinarily psychiatric in nature. Even the antisocial aggressive delinquent is not in need of psychotherapy; what he needs is a learning situation in which his existing perceptual set can be penetrated by new insights, and the discovery that there is considerable value in some processes or paths that he had thought to be useless or worse. If the delinquent is also suffering from *personal* maladjustment, there is a significant difference in what is required to help him, for his delinquency is not apt to be improved, nor his inability to make friendly contacts, until his personal problems are settled. This is well illustrated in Case 20 on page 450.

The counselor or teacher must have the insight that comes from a knowledge of the nature of personal and social maladjustment, and how they differ, and must have enough patience and objectivity to be able to see things over a long period of time from the point of view of the difficult student. With this stipulation, the teacher is certainly in the best position to do the kind of social counseling that is needed in the bulk of such cases in school, particularly if he has the backing and advice of a competent psychologist to whom he can go for help as it is needed.

2705. *Continuing problems in determination of goals.* The first shadows of decisions that will be made throughout life are often cast in childhood play in the roles children assume. Girls play at being mother, nurse, teacher, stenographer, and many other responsible adult roles. Boys are railroad engineers, cowboys, robbers or cops, pilots, soldiers, and explorers. Through many years of maturation and experience there will be tentative goals established and changed. Even in adult life there is a vast amount of altering of vocational goals, educational goals, goals in personality development and adjustment to various social groups.

In all these determinations there are frequent possibilities of need for counseling. Sometimes it is easier to see what is happening by looking at the end of the process, and by regarding each earlier phase as a contributing stream toward a stable pattern of work and life in maturity. The teacher does not see it from that end in school, however, but is faced with the student's struggles to set up his own aspirations in class relationships, in mastery of his lessons, in selection of courses and curricula, and in the long and exploratory process of selecting a vocational goal.

Not knowing in advance what the end of it will be or should be means there can be no system of street signs for any young person, telling him what course or curriculum to take, what job to seek, what college to go to, or what social relationships to cultivate. Most of those decisions must be kept open as long as possible, to permit the accumulation of all possible information and understanding upon which to base the final choice, and this must be done without wasting time in false moves through the growing years. It is a difficult problem at best and requires the help of counselors who can keep their own biases and preferences out of sight. They must direct the individual toward educational experiences and helpful information, and leave completely uncorrupted his own freedom of choice.

During the earlier years the principal need is for information. Teachers, parents, and adult friends can serve this need very well. As the student moves into the higher grades and secondary schools, he needs more and more specific vocational information. At first it should be about the kinds of work going on in the world, what it accomplishes, the conditions under which it takes place, and its importance to the whole social production team. Later it should include information about comparative levels of remuneration, requirements in ability and training, and all the concomitant facts about the kind of life required or possible in the various fields.

Evaluation becomes important when the individual begins to match his own resources to his tentative goals. The vocational counselor offers a type of help that is sometimes indispensable for a good adjustment.

When a serious evaluative program begins, it must proceed along certain lines that represent the ways in which one's vocation affects one's entire life. One such line involves the person's values. Any vocation tends to determine in large measure the type of living conditions that are possible. It affects the attainment of wealth, the kind of home one can have, the pattern of friendships, the amount of continued personal development, the excitement in one's life, and almost every other major value concept. Hence, the value pattern must be known, and the job must be examined in the light of the values of the individual. Jobs that deny the power to attain one's values become intolerable.

Another line of influence is that exerted by the type of activity involved in the job, and the pattern of interests of the individual. The job requires one to spend a large part of most days engaged in whatever activities it includes. Those activities should be in harmony with the person's interests, or he will find himself annoyed and frustrated by the requirements the job makes of him during his working hours. Since interests are known to change with age, this is something that cannot be determined much in advance of any final adjustment, and certainly cannot be determined in secondary school. Final vocational choices made at that level constitute serious and dangerous gambles with good adjustment. The task of the counselor is to keep up the accumulation of experience without permitting choices to harden prematurely.

One other line of influence concerns the individual's capacities to do what the job requires. When the demands are too much for the potentialities of the individual, there is no escape from failure and frustration. Evaluation in this connection must take into account general intelligence, aptitudes, and skills, and should pay attention to personality traits that make the person well or poorly adapted to the interrelationship demands of various kinds of work.

Aside from these three types of fit, which must be good within the job itself, the vocational counselor must help the individual match his financial and time resources to the requirements in preparation for the various kinds of work that are otherwise attractive to him.

In its final and more technical aspects, this type of counseling requires considerable preparation as a vocational counselor. The technical nature of the knowledge involved makes it inadvisable for anyone not so trained—a teacher, parent, clinical psychologist, or psychiatrist—to engage in a serious attempt to help an individual make his final selection of a vocational goal. It is better to allow an individual complete freedom without advice than to push upon him the personal preferences of the adult. This is what usually happens when vocational "advice" is handed down to young people.

2706. *Continuing problems in optimal use of resources.* Health is one of the fundamental resources. Along with good adjustment, broad interests, and adequate study skills, it furnishes the basis for optimal development and progress. Evaluation of this area, and counseling for the purpose of keeping development at a high level, fall largely upon the teacher in school, but require the help of the doctor, the nurse, sometimes the psychologist, and not infrequently special teachers for remedial work.

Two sections of the student inventory in Table 16 are useful in this general area. Section II on mental status contains three rating scales. Capacity can be rated best for schoolwork through the use of intelligence tests. It is impossible to guess intelligence safely. Ordinarily an IQ or the MA and CA scores for a test are available in the cumulative records of each student. If the central position on the inventory is equated to an IQ of 100 and the two outside positions to 50 and 150 for the grades, a reasonably accurate comparative picture can be obtained on a profile basis. In high school it is probably advisable to equate the central position to an IQ of 110, and move each of the outside positions up accordingly. An even higher set of figures would be appropriate in some schools, since the significant comparison is that between the individual and the average intelligence of the group with which he is associated. In college, as indicated in Chapter XVIII, the range might well run from 75 on the left, through 100, 125, and 150 to 175 on the extreme right. It is doubtful if anyone could be found in college who could be placed at the extreme left even on that scale.

Item B, Mental alertness and interest, must be checked from observation of the sort suggested earlier in the chapter. Item C, Drive, should be checked in the same way, but it is helped greatly by paying attention to the manner in which each student tackles his more difficult assignment and reacts to the more demanding challenges in the course. A student who is rated at the extreme left on any of these items, or at the extreme right, will require some special attention for obvious reasons, and the rest of the students will get along very well with the academic requirements and provisions made for the class as a whole.

In section IV, Physical status, there are four scales. Item A on health requires ordinary observation, but should be supplemented by reference to the reports of the doctor and nurse in the office files. Item B, Sensory apparatus, refers principally to eyes and ears, which can be·checked for practical efficiency in class. Printing of graduated size can be placed on the blackboard, and the students asked to copy it. Any student who cannot copy what is copied accurately by most of the others needs some attention in the nature of a change in position, or an eye examination. For hearing, a similar procedure is used by reading a few short sentences, in a gradually diminishing volume, with the back turned to prevent lip reading. A check with the office files is also helpful in this evaluation.

Item C, Gross physical state, can be observed, but the doctor's reports should always be checked for special conditions in the heart or a similar defect that may require special consideration in school activities.

Item D, Developmental status, can be reported by the nurse or doctor upon examination, but it can also be determined satisfactorily for school purposes by the teacher during regular class periods. For the boys, changes in the voice, appearance of hair on the face, rapid growth in the long bones, and an awakened interest in girls are good indications of the rate at which maturation is approaching. Before that period the principal difference of any importance is size. Boys who are far ahead or behind their group are likely to be worried in some way about it. For girls, signs of developing maturity are found in the long bone growth, changes in breast pattern, and in the general contour of the body, and in the transition from what might be called a typically girlish face to a more womanly appearance. These signs are ordinarily obvious enough to detect significant deviations among students, and they do not require laborious measurements and the use of conversion tables.

Study skills constitute an area in which the teacher must evaluate and counsel constantly. They include reading ability, outlining and organizational ability, selection of significant ideas, expression, ability to memorize, library skills, the mechanics of written expression, and any other tools that are basic to study in course. Such evaluation is often helped by diagnostic tests, many of which are available in several subjects. They are easily given, easily scored, and exceedingly helpful in locating trouble.

When special disabilities are found, particularly in such a skill as reading, the student may need to participate in a remedial class. Some types of disability cannot be diagnosed, however, without the help of a psychologist who is familiar with the possible forms of interference. Reading sometimes involves more than failure to learn to read. Writing sometimes holds back because of a tendency to write in mirror form or with some other peculiarity. Spelling difficulties may be due to some kinds of visual deficiency. The teacher does most of the evaluating and counseling in the general area discussed here, but in such cases as those just mentioned he needs the help of a specialist who is ready to push the diagnosis into technical lines of analysis.

The problems in this area are never settled permanently as long as the individual is growing and learning. They are just as operative in adult education as in the elementary school, and the extent to which they are present in graduate education is appalling.

2707. *Real problems are usually combinations.* Poor study skills are usually present in cases of personal maladjustment, because the maladjustment interferes with the acquisition of new skills and even with those skills that are possessed. Social maladjustment tends to be accompanied by poor study skills, and often by problems in vocational selection. Many other combinations are possible, in both degree and nature. Because of the manner in which various kinds of problems tend to weave together, a clinical axiom has developed to the effect that the problem that is brought to the counselor by an individual is seldom the real problem that is causing the fundamental disturbance, although it can be used as an entry through which to dig into the real problem.

This characteristic of maladjustment must be watched by the teacher or counselor with only a moderate amount of insight into the deeper problems. It is easy to be deceived in such cases. A student complaining of inability to study may successfully hide from an inexperienced counselor the signs that reveal a personal maladjustment, but he is not likely to hide them from an experienced clinical psychologist who can recognize them. The teacher may labor in vain to help the student correct his study faults, without knowing why it is impossible to achieve any progress. Any suspicion of such an involvement furnishes grounds for a request for help in diagnosis.

2708. *Counseling and the school program.* There are a number of effective barriers to the establishment of a sound counseling system in most public schools. The most important is the lack of adequate preparation of teachers. The isolation of educational psychology courses from the period in which the student-teacher is getting practical experience tends to prevent those facts that are discussed from carrying over into schoolwork. As a corollary of that isolation, there is not enough emphasis on counseling and its related psychological problems in the courses taken by most prospective teachers. The other outstanding barrier is the lack of provision in the typical secondary or elementary school for a sound counseling program. The teacher's load is set as high as possible without consideration for any activity other than class teaching. The facilities needed in the way of records, tests, and special personnel are seldom or scantily provided. No provision is made in most schools for meetings in which teachers confer on counseling problems and arrive at cooperatively won goals. Faculty meetings, which could often serve this purpose, tend by and large to gravitate to the level of announcement periods.

In spite of the barriers to a complete counseling program, each new class of teachers carries with it into the schools the responsibility of working toward an improvement in practice.

Counseling in its best form is broader than, and includes, teaching, evaluation, school administration in many of its aspects, parent-child relationships, and all such situations which have as their principal feature the furtherance of child growth and development. Its inclusive nature and its intimate relationship with everything the student does makes it a difficult task to do well when it is separated from the daily work of the student. Shared by a faculty, it becomes more effective and much easier than when left to a principal or to any other single school officer.

Ideally, the school should be so organized that the teacher has time for attention to individual students during the school day. In addition to this very important possibility, there should be some personnel available, especially in high schools and colleges, to advise students on their registration problems. There should be a vocational counselor to whom individuals could go, and who could engage in group guidance and instruction. There should be a school psychologist with sufficient advanced training, preferably a doctorate, to enable him to diagnose and prescribe for most of the maladjustments that are present. He in turn should have access to the services of a physician and a psychiatrist as situations may require. This psychologist, if he is properly acquainted with the whole school program, should hold such a relationship to the administration of the school that he can prescribe any necessary changes in program, either for one student, or for the whole school. Only through this close liaison is it possible for the counseling services to accomplish their purposes.

These are the fundamental necessities. In addition there are other important functions, such as the visiting of homes by teachers, close relationship with the community and vocational area surrounding to permit the use of all the available resources in helping students arrive at the best kind of adjustment in every way. It is impossible to be dogmatic about any particular organization scheme for the counseling services. Some schools have extensive clinical facilities and some do not. Some ideas of what might be done are contained in a chapter on the Psychoeducational Clinic, by Brian Tomlinson.[4] There is one best point of view, however, which is that counseling is a rounded effort to promote a person's optimal growth, development, and adjustment to life as a whole, and that this is best accomplished when the person is able to make wise choices as he meets the problems of his daily life.

---

[4] Charles E. Skinner, and Philip L. Harriman, *Child psychology* (New York: The Macmillan Co., 1941), Chapter 17.

1. What *natural* divisions of counseling can be shown to exist? Defend your answer.
2. What are some of the erroneous definitions of counseling? Why are they bad?
3. Give a good definition of counseling, one that is good for the individual.
4. What are four continuing problems in everyone's life that may give rise to a need for counseling?
5. What should a teacher do with maladjusted students when no psychological help is available?
6. What is a preliminary approach to a class, which helps direct counseling to those who need it?
7. What causes difficulty in personal adjustment? In what cases can the teacher help?
8. Explain the use of the Simplified Student Inventory.
9. What kinds of social stresses may operate in a classroom? How can they be managed by the teacher?
10. What are some of the evaluative techniques for discovering social problems?
11. What kinds of goal-determining problems arise at each of the major levels of school?
12. How does the vocational counselor help in elementary school, and in secondary school? Compare this with his task in college?
13. What sorts of evaluation are involved in keeping personal resources up to their maximal usage?
14. What are the barriers that keep teachers from doing the right amount and kind of counseling in school? Can you suggest ways of overcoming them?

SELECTED REFERENCES

Gertrude Driscoll, *How to study the behavior of children* (New York: Bureau of Publications, Teachers College, Columbia University, 1941).

Arthur I. Gates, Arthur T. Jersild, T. R. McConnell, and Robert C. Challman, *Educational psychology* (New York: The Macmillan Co., 1948), Chapter XXI.

Robert H. Mathewson, *Guidance policy and practice* (New York: Harper and Bros., 1949), Chapters 2, 8, 10, 16, 17, and 18. The others if possible.

E. D. Partridge, *Social psychology of adolescence* (New York: Prentice-Hall Inc., 1939), Chapter XIV.
Charles E. Skinner and Philip L. Harriman, *Child psychology* (New York: The Macmillan Co., 1941), Chapter XVII.
Donald Snygg and Arthur W. Combs, *Individual psychology* New York: Harper and Bros., 1949), Chapters XII, XIII, and XIV.

Things To Do outside Class

1. Using the case of Dan in Chapter XXII of the text, or a case selected from an outside source,[2] make the following evaluation:

   A. Identify the significant symptoms in the behavior of the person. Use Table 6 and summarize it on the "Analysis of Behavioral Symptoms" form, Table 13 in Chapter XXV. After becoming familiar with the case, indicate how you interpret the subject's behavior. Rate each of the numbered items in the chart by putting a heavy cross in the center of the space under the appropriate column heading.

   B. Find the needs not being met, and any immaturity indicated. Refer to section 1805, and indicate your conception of the subject's developmental status and adjustment in the form for "Analysis of Developmental Status and Adjustment," Table 14, Chapter XXV.

   C. Find the weak spot in the effort to meet those needs or to develop maturity. The "Analysis of Sources of Influence" form in Table 15, Chapter XXV, will be of some help in this task. Rate each numbered item by placing a heavy cross in the center of the proper space.

   D. Discuss how the problem might be handled.

2. This exercise is for students who are engaged in observation of teaching or are participating in teaching. It involves

2 Allison Davis and John Dollard, *Children of bondage* (Washington, D. C.: American Council on Education, 1940). Harold E. Jones, *Development in adolescence* (New York: D. Appleton-Century Co., 1943). Austin L. Porterfield, *Youth in trouble* (Fort Worth, Texas: The Leo Potishman Foundation, 1946). Peter Blos, *The adolescent personality* (New York: D. Appleton-Century Co., 1941). John Horrocks and Maurice E. Troyer, *Tests of human growth and development* (Syracuse, N. Y.: Syracuse University Press, 1946), Case studies.

the use of school records and various techniques discussed in Chapters XXV and XXVII.

A. Make up a brief but fairly complete statement of the psychological characteristics of the age group represented by the class in which you are participating. Reference to a text in the psychology of childhood or adolescence may help.

   1. Common normal characteristics.
   2. Common interests and activities.
   3. Common sources of difficulty and common problems.

B. Obtain specific data about members of the class. Techniques mentioned in Chapters XXV and XXVII will be of value in this task.

   1. Learn their names.
   2. Make some friendly contact with each one if possible.
   3. Find the important ambitions of each.
   4. Determine the social relationships in the group.
   5. Complete the "Simplified Student Inventory" for each one, and on the basis of the profiles and your other information select the few who are most in need of individual attention. These may be different in either direction from the center of the group. Discuss each such case with the teacher in charge as a check on your evaluation, and to determine what can be done for the student..

INDEX OF NAMES

INDEX OF SUBJECTS